NOVEL RELA

In *Novel Relations*, Ruth Perry describes the transformation of the English family as a function of several major social changes taking place in the eighteenth century, including the development of a market economy and waged labor, enclosure and the redistribution of land, urbanization, the "rise" of the middle class, and the development of print culture. In particular Perry traces the shift from a kinship orientation based on blood relations to a kinship axis constituted by conjugal ties as it is revealed in popular literature of the second half of the eighteenth century. Perry focuses particularly on the effect these changes had on women's position in families. She uses social history, literary analysis, and anthropological kinship theory to examine texts by Samuel Richardson, Charlotte Lennox, Henry Mackenzie, Frances Burney, Jane Austen, and many others. This important study by a leading eighteenth-century scholar will be of interest to social and literary historians.

NOVEL RELATIONS

*The Transformation of Kinship in English Literature
and Culture, 1748–1818*

RUTH PERRY

CAMBRIDGE
UNIVERSITY PRESS

CAMBRIDGE UNIVERSITY PRESS
Cambridge, New York, Melbourne, Madrid, Cape Town, Singapore, São Paulo

Cambridge University Press
The Edinburgh Building, Cambridge CB2 2RU, UK

Published in the United States of America by Cambridge University Press, New York

www.cambridge.org
Information on this title: www.cambridge.org/9780521687904

First published 2004
Reprinted 2005 (twice)
First paperback edition 2006

Printed in the United Kingdom at the University Press, Cambridge

A catalogue record for this publication is available from the British Library

Library of Congress Cataloguing in Publication data

Perry, Ruth, 1943–
Novel relations: the transformation of kinship in English literature and culture / Ruth Perry.
p.   cm.
Includes bibliographical references and index.
ISBN 0 521 83694 8
1. English fiction – 18th century – History and criticism.   2. Family in literature.   3. Women and
literature – Great Britain – History – 18th century   4. Domestic fiction, English – History and
criticism.   5. Family – Great Britain – History – 18th century.   6. Marriage in literature.
7. Kinship in literature.   8. Women in literature.   1. Title.
PR 858.F29P47   2004
823′.6093552 – dc22   2003064022

ISBN-13 978-0-521-83694-4 hardback
ISBN-10 0-521-83694-8 hardback
ISBN-13 978-0-521-68790-4 paperback
ISBN-10 0-521-68790-x paperback

This book is dedicated to my father, Marvin K. Opler (1914–81),
who taught me to think cross-culturally,
and to my mother, Charlotte Fox Opler Sagoff (1914–),
who taught me to love to read,
and to my grandchildren, Vikram and Roshan Charena,
who carry it on.

Contents

Acknowledgments

This project has taken so long that I no longer remember all the people who gave me aid and comfort along the way. Some colleagues I have been able to thank directly in footnotes for references or ideas; for those not specified let me thank you all here. I could not have written this book without the many friends and colleagues who heard and discussed papers from this work over the years and encouraged me by their interest.

In particular, Susan Staves has been an inspiration, a generous source of information, and a sustaining friend. Janice Thaddeus read sections of the manuscript, supplied many references, and gave her loving support to this and other efforts; she is deeply missed. Mandy Nash supplied references and information early on. Betty Rizzo read every word, caught many errors, and rekindled my confidence with her enthusiasm. Jan Fergus read the MS more times than even the claims of kinship warrant. Donald A. Duncan literally soldered an electrical connection in my laptop, discussed many of these chapters with me, solved all my computer problems, and helped me through the hardest times. My mother, Charlotte Sagoff, critic and proofreader *par excellence*, helped me in many different ways. Tilly Shaw read most of the MS and cheered me on. Special thanks to Leo Marx who intervened with excellent advice at a critical moment. Bob Ferrara tendered invaluable computer help which guaranteed that the bibliography was finished on time. I am also grateful to Phyllis Mack for talking over many aspects of this book and offering wise, savvy, and humane suggestions, to Olwyn Hufton for historiographical suggestions and references, to David Sabean for his enthusiasm and counsel, to Amanda Vickery for her intelligent critique, to Naomi Tadmor for her searching questions, to Anne Janowitz for sending me her copy of John Clare when she did, to Maxine Berg for her suggestions despite our disagreements, to Barbara Taylor, whose "Feminism and Enlightenment" seminars created the arena for trying out several of these ideas, to the MIT Women's Studies Reading Group (Lora Wildenthal, Diana Henderson, Sally Haslanger, Elizabeth Wood, Anne

McCants, Marlene Manoff) for their shaping suggestions about Chapter 5, to Christine Gailey and the students of the Graduate Consortium class on "Narratives of Kinship" where some of these ideas were hatched, to Jean Jackson for anthropological references and conversations over the years, to Menju Mehta for discussions of bride price, to Allen Grove, a memorable research assistant in the early stages of this work, to Ellen Pollak for stimulating conversations about kinship and incest, to Michael McKeon and John Richetti for their letters of support, to Wini, Marcia, and Susan for helping me to laugh, to Susan Lanser for her intellectual friendship, to Lawrence Hallahan and Soraya Lima for helping me with life's tasks, to Sarah Wall and especially Tamar Gonen Brown for their invaluable aid at the end.

Librarians at Harvard's Houghton Library and the British Library have been invariably helpful and courteous; support from the Guggenheim Foundation, the American Council of Learned Societies, and the Rockefeller Foundation at Bellagio provided me time and space for serious work. Briony Keith and Julie Saunders in MIT's Literature office performed innumerable acts of helpfulness over the years.

Part of Chapter 1 ("The Great Disinheritance") appeared in Vivien Jones (ed.), *Women and Literature in Britain 1700–1800* (Cambridge: Cambridge University Press, 2000); part of Chapter 4 ("Brotherly Love in Life and Literature") appeared as "Suis-je le gardien de ma soeur?" in Guyonne Leduc (ed.), *L'Education des femmes en Europe et en Amérique du Nord de la Renaissance à 1848* (Paris: L'Harmattan, 1997), pp. 279–96; part of Chapter 6 ("Sexualized Marriage and Property in the Person") appeared as "Good Girls and Fallen Women," in Roberto de Romanis and Rosamaria Loretelli (eds.), *Narrating Transgression: Representations of the Criminal in Early Modern England* (Frankfurt am Main: Peter Lang, 1999), pp. 91–101; another section of Chapter 6 appeared in "Sleeping with Mr. Collins," in Suzanne R. Pucci and James Thompson (eds.), *Jane Austen and Co.* (Albany: State University of New York Press, 2003), pp. 213–28; and part of Chapter 9 ("Family Feeling") appeared as "Incest as the Meaning of the Gothic," *The Eighteenth-Century: Theory and Interpretation* 39, 3 (Fall 1998), 261–78. I am grateful to the editors of these publications for allowing me to retain the rights to these sections of this book.

Introduction

What Goddess, or what Muse must I invoke to guide me through these vast, unexplored regions of fancy? – regions inhabited by wisdom and folly, – by wit and stupidity, – by religion and profaneness, – by morality and licentiousness.

Clara Reeve, *The Progress of Romance*, p. 109.

If you think about it, the wreckage of families in the novels of Jane Austen is unnerving. In the novels of her sister authors it is appalling. These women – Charlotte Smith, Mary Wollstonecraft, Fanny Burney, Maria Edgeworth, among the less obscure ones – describe what was to them a terrifying shift in their society's concept of the family, a profound change that marks the difference between the world of *Grandison*, the world they had lost, and the world in which unhappily they found themselves adrift.

Edward Copeland, "The Burden of *Grandison*," pp. 98–9.

. . . the family will be studied less for its own sake, as an isolated phenomenon of historical social structure – a statistical mean household size – but rather as an important and still poorly fathomed intermediary between economic change and its qualitatively experienced effects, as for example on social relations.

K. D. M. Snell, *Annals of the Labouring Poor*, p. 332.

This book is about how family relationships were represented in eighteenth-century English fiction and what those representations tell us about changes in actual families in that period. My argument moves between literature and history: literary texts provide the insights about how the conception of "family" changed in eighteenth-century England and the strain that put on existing relationships. History provides the causal or correlative explanations for the social and psychological phenomena that literature reveals. It also corroborates these changes from the perspective of another discipline. Eighteenth-century novels taught me that the meaning of "family" in eighteenth-century England was undergoing a seismic shift; economic

1

and social historians helped me to understand why it happened at that particular time and how it was connected to other more evident material changes in the society.

I will be arguing that the significant shift in the basis of kinship disclosed by the fiction of the period was a change in the definition of what constituted the primary kin group. It involved a movement from an axis of kinship based on consanguineal ties or blood lineage to an axis based on conjugal and affinal ties of the married couple. That is, the biologically given family into which one was born was gradually becoming secondary to the chosen family constructed by marriage. For the individual caught in this cultural shift, the conflict was between belonging to a family with intergenerational blood lines that ran through both parents, or belonging to a nuclear family with responsibility only to one's spouse and immature offspring. In a kinship system based on the conjugal bond, the obligations of spouses to each other are stressed above and against their ties of filiation. In a consanguineal kinship system, bonds of filiation and siblinghood are stressed above and against the conjugal tie.

The fiction that eighteenth-century writers wrote and that the public bought and read tells this story from many different angles: it is in the plots and characters of the novels of the period, in the tyrannical fathers, absent mothers, and long-suffering children. From the evidence of these novels I believe that this shift from a consanguineal to a conjugal system had very different consequences for women than for men, some of which will become clearer in the chapters that follow. Suffice it to say here that it was a mixed blessing for women to exchange whatever power and status they had in their families of origin for the power and status of women in conjugal families. Novels dramatized confusions about the reciprocal duties and responsibilities of individuals to their families, communities, and society. Much of the suffering represented in these novels derives from contradictions between the two systems of kinship as one gained ground on the other and slowly replaced it. In what follows I have tried to gather and summarize the psychological effects of what I see as an overall restructuring of kinship ties and how it affected what it meant to be a daughter, a sister, an aunt, an uncle, a son, or a brother.

Family historians, recognizing that crucial changes occurred in the eighteenth century, have argued about the meaning of demographic drifts, the changing size of households, alterations in the position of women, and new attitudes towards children. The central thesis of this book – that loyalty to the new conjugal family undermined the claims of the consanguineal family – sheds light on all these issues although I have not derived it from demographic sources or public records but from the novels that people were writing and reading. The paradigm shift described in this book is not visible in the family reconstitution studies made possible by the computer, because it is not reflected in the number of births, deaths, and marriages recorded in the parish registers. These statistics do not reveal the transformation in the psychological meaning of kin relations that I believe had taken effect by the later eighteenth century. What interests me is how this shift from a dominantly consanguineal kinship system to a dominantly conjugal kinship system restructured the experience of family life if not always the actual make-up of households. I have tried to synthesize the findings of family historians in relation to my own discoveries to clarify the contribution of this literary evidence. I also sketch in some of the other major economic and political features of the eighteenth-century landscape in order to understand how and why this kinship shift took place when it did. I have focused on women's situations within families because I think the psychological effects of this kinship shift show up most clearly in women's altered positions. If this movement from a consanguineal axis to a conjugal axis seems self-evident to students of the period, I hope to show how wide-ranging were the implications of this change.

I was led to this formulation by the texts themselves, by the obsessive concern with defining family membership in the novels of the period.[1] When I began to read this fiction, for what I first conceived of as a purely literary exploration of uncharted literary terrain of the novel from 1748 to 1818, the *terra incognita* between Samuel Richardson and Jane Austen, I was struck by the way that novel after novel asked similar questions about the meaning of family ties and obligations. To whom did one belong – to one's family of origin or to one's conjugal or contractual family? To whom did one owe allegiance? Who had claims on one's love and obedience? With whom should one share one's resources? These questions constituted the cruxes of the fiction of the later eighteenth century, and I came to feel that the themes and narrative structures of the novel in this period could not be understood without reference to tensions in the structure and meaning of kinship. The dilemmas staged in these novels again and again lined up competing ideological systems. Should a heroine marry a man chosen by her parents, a

---

[1] Christopher Flint writes brilliantly about the family portrait in Goldsmith's *Vicar of Wakefield*, a figure that displays the "literary anxiety in the eighteenth century about the family's conception of itself." Although commissioned by the family, the portrait is too expensive and too large to hang "on any wall in the house or even to be moved out of the room where it had been stretched and painted." See "The Family Piece: Oliver Goldsmith and the Politics of the Everyday in Eighteenth-Century Domestic Portraiture," *Eighteenth-Century Studies* 29, 2 (Winter 1995–6), 127–52; quotations 128, 131. For Flint's understanding of the meaning of family change in the period, see n. 19.

man whom she does not love, or should she marry a suitor whom she loves or thinks she could love – but whom her parents will not accept? What are the ethical dimensions of choosing between romantic love and parental approbation? What is the nature of female sexuality? Can a woman learn to love her husband if she begins without feeling attraction to his person? Should a chaste woman ever have sexual feelings? Does love build slowly out of shared domestic circumstances or is true love involuntary, absolute, and without restraint? Can men, can women, fall in love more than once?

Kinship arrangements in a society determine who should marry whom and how money or other resources are to be distributed; these are also the standard cruxes of fictional plots. In traditional societies the rules of kinship determine both the obligations of the individual to his/her kin group or family in the broadest sense, and, reciprocally, the claims of an individual on the resources of the kin group. These resources include absolute property rights and use rights, productive labor and care-giving (raising children and caring for the ill, indigent, and elderly), political power, and the social position, rank, or reputation of one descent group vis-à-vis other descent groups. The arrangements of kinship govern the way a culture handles marriage and procreation, the way young adults find their own livelihoods and household space, the timing of childbearing and childrearing, and the transmission of property. In the period under consideration, 1748–1818, in modernizing England, these complex relationships and expectations were disrupted owing to myriad political, social, and economic factors. Families in all classes were transformed, although families in different classes changed in different ways.

In the chapters that follow, I try to make sense of the psychological effects of the restructuring of English kinship as these effects were thematized in the popular fiction of the period. Although I have already stated my conclusion – that the principle of consanguinity came to be replaced by conjugality as the primary principle of kinship – my evidence unfolds in the chapters that follow, relationship by relationship. The story is in the details of which family connections were reinforced and which were eroded as major social and economic changes transformed late eighteenth-century English society: commercialization of agriculture and the restriction of common land rights, rural-urban migration and other forms of geographical and social mobility, the rise of an industrial workforce, state regulation of marriage, the intensification and complication of the laws protecting private property and determining inheritance and legitimacy. It is a story about how capitalism affected the family structure that existed in England at the time of the Restoration. In the details accumulated over many novels, a pattern emerges which emphasizes strains and fissures in the family of origin between aging parents and their newly adult children, between siblings, between uncles and aunts and their nieces and nephews or other collateral cousins. Individuals' loyalties are divided between the families they were born to and their newer loves. In novel after novel, parents and children are parted, brothers and sisters estranged, uncles and aunts misinformed about beloved nieces and nephews, casting a shadow on the lives of the heroes and heroines. When these tragic separations are resolved by the plot, and the members of the consanguineal family reunited at the end, the happy denouements are structured as the triumph of nature over the forces of chance or evil.

I am not arguing that these literary examples represent lifelike situations, hold up a mirror to nature, or are "realistic." But I do think they represent the foci – the obsessions – of the culture, and that in their issues one can see the working out of the particular problems facing this society at that time. For literature is one way to think about life, to cope with problems that have no solution. Narrative is a universal human response to dilemmas about the metaphysics of existence. Both readers and writers of fiction – then and now – use stories to face the exigencies of their lives. In the structure and verbal qualities of a work of art, in the anxieties and pleasures pictured there, one can trace the configuration of forces operating on people. The fiction that a society produces and consumes offers the literary critic an opportunity to interpret which public versions of reality are satisfying to the popular imagination.

Literary critics often claim to see evidence of cultural change in the texts they read – but they do not always compare what they see to the current state of historical knowledge. From the other side, historians often find literary examples that seem to embody their theses – but they usually do not know the full range of literary production for that period, whether their examples are typical of the genre or idiosyncratic, or how to interpret the details. Because this is not simply a work of literary criticism or history or anthropology, some remarks about my methods and assumptions are in order. This interdisciplinary project, combining literary analysis and social history, is an attempt to understand symbolic economies from a period with a radically different historical consciousness from our own. In addition to describing what happened to the family in England in the eighteenth century, I have tried to be self-conscious about how I reconstruct cultural history from the patterns and emphases in literary texts – and thus connect literature to lived experience. In the following sections of this Introduction, I offer the reader some basic historical information about the period, about later eighteenth-century fiction and families, and about some of the present relevant debates in social history.

FICTION

If the English novel "rose" out of that yeasty mixture of romance, journalistic reportage, and personal letters in the late seventeenth and early eighteenth centuries,[2] it was shaped into the form familiar to us all in the period between Richardson and Austen. That was when multiple characters with complex interrelationships began to appear on the pages of fiction, when dialogue was perfected and free indirect discourse invented, and when the epistolary format gave way to a third-person narrator who knew everything that was going on and passed judgment on it. The invention of characters with interior lives and psychologized human relations began to replace two-dimensional protagonists who existed for the sake of their improbable adventures. By the 1750s, fiction was competing with religious works and political tracts for a significant share of the reading market. The success of the genre and the development of an infrastructure to support it (the establishment of circulating and subscription libraries and review sections in journals such as the *Monthly Review*, the *Critical Review*, and the *Gentleman's Magazine*) helped to produce a consciousness in the population susceptible to new forms of literary power. The novel was part of the explosion of printed materials for sale – an exponentially expanding reservoir of translated and original writings to instruct and entertain an increasingly literate population alienated from communal sources of information about how to maneuver materially and morally in the world.

In addition to all the other crucial purposes that literary critics have ascribed to the eighteenth-century novel in recent years, I believe it functioned to explore and work through the changing kinship arrangements which regulated domestic life and intergenerational relationships in a world rapidly being transformed by market forces, urban anonymity, and the spread of literacy.[3] The particular narrative conventions and thematics of this new

---

[2] In the years following Ian Watt's *The Rise of the Novel* (Berkeley and Los Angeles: University of California Press, 1957), a number of books have tackled the question of the origins of English fiction. See Ruth Perry, *Women, Letters, and the Novel* (New York: AMS Press, 1980); Lennard J. Davis, *Factual Fictions: The Origins of the English Novel* (New York: Columbia University Press, 1983); Jane Spencer, *The Rise of the Woman Novelist: From Aphra Behn to Jane Austen* (Oxford: Basil Blackwell, 1986); Michael McKeon, *The Origins of the English Novel 1600–1740* (Baltimore: Johns Hopkins University Press, 1987); Ros Ballaster, *Seductive Forms: Women's Amatory Fiction from 1684 to 1740* (Oxford: Clarendon Press, 1992).

[3] Paul Hunter, in *Before Novels: The Cultural Contexts of Eighteenth-Century English Fiction* (New York: Norton, 1990), his study of the origin of eighteenth-century fiction, rejects the thesis that "sometime

genre were suited to exploring concerns about family membership and individual obligation in this society in transition. The more than 2,500 or so British novels written in this period are, no doubt, about a great number of things.[4] But reading them as a response to eighteenth-century confusions about the claims of family on the individual brings into sharper focus the issues that they obsessively rehearse. When the "master narrative" of this fiction is understood to be a reconsideration of the basis of membership in a family, it changes how we read the standard plots. The courtship plot begins to look more like the story of women scrambling to find new homes and to negotiate new families, their rights within the consanguineal family having been undercut by a shift in kinship priorities. The relations between siblings become a moral index more sensitive than any other rather than just a plot device. The convention of the absent mother together with the compensatory presence of an intelligent, independent, older woman who guides and comforts the heroine tells a story about disappearing maternal power and the suppression of maternal inheritance in this changing world.

I have always been interested in the refracted relation between literary texts and the historical conditions of their production.[5] Stories, insofar as they rehearse, predict, embellish, validate, and even deny human experience, always reveal something about the culture from which they come. But using fiction as a source for writing the history of the family is a tricky business. Very little theoretical work has been done on the question of *how* literary texts distill, distort, fabricate, and represent reality. Fictional representation can be compensatory, imagining perfection rather than loss. Fiction usually highlights irony, sharpens contrasts, and overstates

---

between 1719 and 1750, the English reading public developed specific new needs that the novel quickly identified and immediately came to address" (68). Despite Hunter's informed skepticism, I am arguing that this is precisely what happened. The "new" needs that the novel developed to address from the 1740s onwards included the need to understand one's moral, psychological, social, and economic obligations to a range of relatives.

[4] This estimate of the number of novels written in this period comes from James Raven's Introduction to the first volume of James Raven and Antonia Forster, *The English Novel 1770–1829: A Bibliographical Survey of Prose Fiction Published in the British Isles*, 2 vols. (Oxford and New York: Oxford University Press, 2000), vol. I, pp. 15–123, and from James Raven, *British Fiction, 1750–1770: A Chronological Check-List of Prose Fiction Printed in Britain and Ireland* (London: Associated University Presses, and Newark: University of Delaware Press, 1987). See also James Raven's discussion of the publishing industry in Great Britain in the eighteenth century in *Judging New Wealth: Popular Publishing and Responses to Commerce in England, 1750–1800* (Oxford: Clarendon Press, 1992), especially Chapter 2, "Publishing Profiles," pp. 19–41.

[5] In my first book, *Women, Letters, and the Novel*, I tried to understand the cultural function of an imaginative form based on heightening individual consciousness of privatized thought and desire. That monograph, written in almost complete isolation, was completed in 1977. It is astonishing to remember what it was like to work without mentors or colleagues – ordinary conditions for a woman with a feminist project when I entered the academy.

paradox, making the humdrum more dramatic and conferring meaning on
the mundane. Thus, the representation of life in fiction is never transparently mimetic, although the problematics of any text are derived from the
culture. As Pierre Macherey puts it: "The writer, as the producer of the
text, does not manufacture the materials with which he works."[6] Although
literary representations are caricatures, symbolic images and not "realistic"
renditions, they give us a feel for the psychology of another period that
demographic statistics or public legal documents cannot match. Raymond
Williams considered that literature recorded "structures of feeling," residues
of lived experience which are condensed and stored as forms in dialogue
with other forms.[7] Thus social consciousness – and the formal tropes of
popular art that embody it – can be said to be derived from lived experience
although they are not reducible to it. A critic trying to extrapolate the "real"
from fictional texts must be able to recognize the literary conventions of
a text and to distinguish its secondary elaboration and ornament from its
emotional center.

My method has been to read what I think of as the unconscious of the
literary texts I use – the anxieties that propel them. The fiction I examine
in this book was written largely in the 1750s, 1760s, and 1770s, although
I draw on some examples from earlier and later decades. Sometimes the
narratives of families lost and families found are tragic; sometimes they are
pure, triumphant wish-fulfillment. Some imagine powerful bonds between
the protagonist and his or her rediscovered consanguineal family, while others portray the relationship between the protagonist and his or her newly
constructed conjugal family. What is common to these fantasies, whether
consoling or disturbing, is intense anxiety about family membership, represented variously as extreme loneliness, longing, or long-deferred but finally
perfect happiness. Belonging to a family is never taken for granted or quietly
subsumed as background for other adventures; being cast out of a family
or taken into a family *is* the adventure in eighteenth-century novels.

In much of what follows I assume that sentimental literature is compensatory – evidence of persistent nostalgia for what had been lost in a
changing society rather than a glorification of what existed in that present.
I am less interested in the way literature constructed or naturalized the new
conjugal family that most critics take for granted than in the way it sentimentalized the consanguineal basis for obligation that was being phased
out in the new dispensation. All cultures retain trace elements of previous

---

[6] Pierre Macherey, *A Theory of Literary Production*, trans. Geoffrey Wall (London: Routledge and Kegan
Paul, 1978), p. 41.
[7] Raymond Williams, *Marxism and Literature* (Oxford: Oxford University Press, 1977), pp. 128–35.

formations which coexist with those attitudes that have come to replace them; temporally successive ideological positions can be held simultaneously in the same society at the same time. Raymond Williams called these "residual" elements – elements left over from "some previous social and cultural institution or formation" but still present as an aesthetic or moral force, "still active in the cultural process, not only and often not at all as an element of the past, but as an effective element of the present." In defining the cultural residual, Williams emphasized that such elements often had "an alternative or even oppositional relation to the dominant culture," but that they survived alongside of it, often for a long time, before dwindling into the "archaic."[8] In reading eighteenth-century fiction, I have been struck by these residual elements, traces of family loyalties that could no longer be taken for granted, represented with a sentimental fervor whose excess suggests that they were no longer commonplace. Most of the chapters that follow are preoccupied with the cultural residual of consanguineal kin formations: paternal responsibility for daughters, fraternal responsibility for sisters, the importance of maternal relatives, marriage to maintain or consolidate property or lineage despite the protestations of individuals.

From the publication of Richardson's *Clarissa* to that of Austen's *Persuasion*, 1748 to 1818, the literary production of the novel took off, both in sheer numbers and in terms of cultural prestige. Mrs. Barbauld's canonizing collection of fifty English novels was published in 1810. This period also witnessed the transformation of England into a modern industrial society. While men and increasing numbers of women writers experimented with this new genre (writing novels was, among other things, a new way to earn a living in the evolving national economy), the country changed from a rural to a predominantly urban society. At mid-century, 79% of the people in England still lived in the countryside; 58% of the rural population engaged in commercial agricultural production and 42% supported themselves with various forms of manufacture and service activities.[9] By the end of the eighteenth century there were at least 50 cities in England with populations of more than 10,000 inhabitants (London had 950,000 inhabitants); only the Netherlands in all of Europe had a more urbanized population.[10] An enormous amount of land was enclosed in the second

---

[8] *Ibid.*, p. 122.

[9] E. A. Wrigley, *People, Cities and Wealth: The Transformation of a Traditional Society* (Oxford: Basil Blackwell, 1987), pp. 168–71.

[10] M. J. Daunton, "Towns and Economic Growth in Eighteenth-Century England," in Philip Abrams and E. A. Wrigley (eds.), *Towns in Societies: Essays in Economic History and Historical Sociology* (London and New York: Cambridge University Press, 1978), pp. 245–77, especially p. 248.

half of the century, nearly 7 million acres claimed for private ownership, amounting to more than a fifth of all the arable land in England.[11] It was taken out of common fields and intercommoned pasture, from reclaimed "waste" lands and forests, and from bought-out smallholdings of cottagers in an unprecedented geometrically escalating number of parliamentary acts of enclosure. Forty thousand small farms disappeared in the course of this enclosure sweep, creating a large population of wage laborers not tied to the land.[12] This process changed the proportion of landless workers from 25% of the population at the beginning of the century to something more like 60% by the end of the century. In addition to this proletarianization of agricultural labor, the restructuring of class in this period involved an increase in the proportion of the population with incomes between £50 and £400 per annum from about 15% to 25% of England's total population.[13] This is the growth of the middle class that has fascinated so many cultural historians, a phenomenon simultaneous with the pauperization of the laboring class.

During the period covered in this book, England stopped exporting grain and began importing it – in part to maintain its standing army through a stunning series of colonial wars, and in part to feed a national population in the process of doubling itself. The growth of a bureaucratized system of taxation and the development of the legal means to subdivide the profits of landed property (into ultimate ownership, transferable management or use rights, and current credit or the right to mortgage) created the legal infrastructure of a modern state designed to serve monied interests. This legal bureaucracy reorganized inheritance law and liability so as to permit the risky capitalizing of agricultural and manufacturing production and to protect the economic security of the relatives of those who took the economic risks. The development of suburbs outside the large urban centers constructed a new kind of split between public and private – different in association and meaning from that of ancient Greece or Renaissance

---

[11] Michael Turner, *Enclosures in Britain 1750–1830* (London: Macmillan, 1984), p. 21.

[12] According to A. L. Morton, *A People's History of England* (New York: Random House, 1938), p. 327, between 1740 and 1788 the number of separate farms declined by 40,000. In a series of lectures delivered in 1881–2, Arnold Toynbee Sr. quotes Sir Frederic Morton Eden in 1795 as remarking that there were only two farms in a Dorsetshire village where twenty years before there had been thirty farms. Toynbee also notes that under Elizabeth I an act had been passed providing that every cottage should have four acres of land attached to it. This act was repealed in 1775. *Lectures on the Industrial Revolution of the Eighteenth Century*, 6th edn. (London: Longmans Green, 1920), pp. 68, 47.

[13] Neil McKendrick, John Brewer, and J. H. Plumb (eds.), *The Birth of a Consumer Society: The Commercialization of Eighteenth-Century England* (London: Europa, 1982), p. 24.

Italy – and one that spatially reinforced newly evolving ideologies of gender for men and women.[14]

Because I want to trace the long-term cultural effects of the industrializing economy and centralizing state on the form and meaning of the family through the fiction that helped to name, shape, and interpret the social changes that were taking place in England, my treatment of literary texts before 1790 is more thorough than my treatment of the productions of that revolutionary decade. The anomalous nature of those novels and the various ways in which they responded to the French Revolution have been handled thoroughly and expertly by other critics.[15] Rather than treating them in their 1790s political context, I handle novels published in that last decade of the eighteenth century and the first decade of the nineteenth century in this study insofar as they continue the themes and motifs traced through the second half of the eighteenth century. Drawing a straight line from Richardson to Austen, I examine those texts that grapple with the complex and changing relation among love, sex, generations, and money. I read novels for the light they shed on the new economic pressures on kinship and for the way evolving cultural attitudes about families affected economic arrangements.

Whether or not novels affected rates of marriage – or the other way around – both phenomena seem to have peaked in 1771 and thereafter to have declined at the time of the American Revolution, recovering in the 1780s and then multiplying steadily, with a few dips, from about 1783 on.[16] Graphed together in the second half of the eighteenth century, they have a similar curve. It seems likely that novel production affected the cultural context of matrimony just as the increasing numbers of people marrying gave substance to the ideology of romantic love promulgated in fiction. Mindful that human expression affects history – that the formulation and framing of issues always affects how people perceive them and therefore act on them – I also posit the inverse relation here: that powerful forces of capitalism and new forms of agricultural and industrial production pulled

---

[14] Leonore Davidoff and Catherine Hall, *Family Fortunes: Men and Women of the English Middle Class, 1780–1850* (Chicago: University of Chicago Press, 1987), pp. 57, 58, 232, 251.

[15] There are already a number of excellent treatments of English fiction of the 1790s. See below n. 18 for references to some of them.

[16] See James Raven and Antonia Forster, *The English Novel 1770–1829: A Bibliographical Survey of Prose Fiction Published in the British Isles*, vol. 1, pp. 26–7. James Raven also graphs the production of novels between 1700 and 1790 in *Judging New Wealth*, p. 34. For a chart of marriage in England between 1671 and 1821, see E. A. Wrigley and R. S. Schofield, *The Population History of England, 1541–1871*, fig. 10.11, reproduced in E. A. Wrigley, "Marriage, Fertility and Population Growth in Eighteenth-Century England," in R. B. Outhwaite (ed.), *Marriage and Society: Studies in the Social History of Marriage* (London: Europa, 1981), p. 154.

people in new directions and that the fiction of the era expressed these pressures and offered a rationale for new behaviors. Marrying for love rather than in the economic interests of one's family is an example of a cultural attitude circulating in fiction that looks at first as if it is subverting the dynamic of accumulation and the crudest commodification of kin relations.[17] On the other hand, the attitude that "love is more important than money" reinforced the uni-directional flow of resources from the older to the younger generation and absolved the young of any responsibility for their elders' welfare. Thus, the material disinterestedness that was an essential ingredient of fictional heroism – that made the triumphal gathering in of love *and* money by the good characters in fictional climaxes all the sweeter – expressed an individualistic drive for economic independence as much as the paramount importance of love in marriage. This plot thus expresses anxiety about money as a source of value at the same time as it celebrates the capitalist virtue of independence.

Although I am making an historical argument about changing kin relations reflected in novels, my sampling of fiction has been necessarily selective; nevertheless I have surveyed enough of this fiction to feel that I can identify its patterns with some specificity. The second-rate novels as well as the canonical examples have been helpful in this process. Although some of the novels I have read for this study have been crude or awkward, reading them clarified the formulas that could not be seen in such bold relief in novels of greater sophistication and literary interest. Second-rate novels sometimes give one the terms, the critical vocabulary, and the insight with which to read the better literary works. One is a better reader of *Clarissa* or *The Vicar of Wakefield* because one has encountered before certain scenes or characters drawn more crudely in the anonymous *The Life of Patty Saunders* (1752) or Elizabeth Justice's *Amelia; or, the Distress'd Wife* (1751). I hope that the framework I develop here for seeing the problematics of fiction in terms of kinship conflicts will provide a fruitful way to read for other scholars of this literature.

The standard way to discuss novels of this period has been to classify them – as an eighteenth-century intellectual would have done – as sentimental (Elizabeth Griffith or Henry Mackenzie), gothic (Horace Walpole or Ann Radcliffe), picaresque (Tobias Smollett or Richard Graves), comic prose epic (Henry Fielding), or the novel of manners (Frances Burney, Maria Edgeworth, Jane Austen). The novels of the 1790s have been categorized by

---

[17] Erica Harth, for example, argues that love was perceived as an anarchic force that threatened prudential reasons for marriage and had to be controlled by the Hardwicke Marriage Act. Erica Harth, "The Virtue of Love: Lord Hardwicke's Marriage Act," *Cultural Critique* 9 (Spring 1988), 123–54.

their relation to individualism, democracy, and other radical ideas in the air at the time of the French Revolution.[18] The eighteenth-century novel has been treated in conjunction with prisons, with law, with imperialism, and with monetary credit as a crucial fact and metaphor in the creation of the modern subject. It has been written about as a spiritual force, an aesthetic object, and as a subversive instrument. Feminist treatments of fiction have dealt with (among other things), courtship, seduction, repression, the public and private spheres, women's friendships, the interchangeability of female fictional subjects, and moral alternatives offered by women writers. In this study I read eighteenth-century fiction as a series of problem-solving scenarios and rhetorical responses to a disorienting change in the axis of kinship. Understanding the changing basis of kinship clarifies the other meanings of this fiction, too, the extent to which it is concerned with subjectivity, friendship, moral choices, and the like. For family membership is the ground on which everything in these novels happens; characters' responses to their kin place them in a moral continuum.

FAMILIES

The family is the intermediate term between the individual and society. Tracing its vicissitudes would seem to be essential to any examination of changing cultural constructions of the self. Yet cultural critics assessing the social construction of gender or any other dimension of individual identity often leave out the family, and place the individual directly in the field of immense national forces, such as imperialist ideology or new class formations, without acknowledging the intermediate shaping influence of the family. Conversely, family historians (such as Lawrence Stone or Edward

[18] Marilyn Butler invented the terms "jacobin" and "anti-jacobin" novels in *Jane Austen and the War of Ideas* (Oxford: Clarendon Press, 1975) to distinguish between "radical" novels which depicted the upright individual opposed to a corrupt society and "conservative" novels which showed the disastrous consequences of individualism and the cult of self. See also Nicola Watson, *Revolution and the Form of the British Novel 1790–1825: Intercepted Letters, Interrupted Seductions* (Oxford: Clarendon Press, 1994); Gary Kelly, *The English Jacobin Novel 1780–1805* (Oxford: Clarendon Press, 1976) and *English Fiction of the Romantic Period 1789–1830* (London and New York: Longman, 1989); Mitzi Myers, "'Reform or Ruin': A Revolution in Female Manners," *Studies in Eighteenth-Century Culture* 11 (1982), 199–216; and "Sensibility and the 'Walk of Reason': Mary Wollstonecraft's Literary Reviews as Cultural Critique," in Syndy McMillan Conger (ed.), *Sensibility in Transformation: Creative Resistance to Sentiment from the Augustans to the Romantics* (London and Toronto: Associated University Presses, and Rutherford, NJ: Fairleigh Dickinson University Press, 1990), pp. 120–44; Claudia L. Johnson, *Equivocal Beings: Politics, Gender, and Sentimentality in the 1790s: Wollstonecraft, Radcliffe, Burney, Austen* (Chicago: University of Chicago Press, 1995). See also the essays in Linda Lang-Peralta (ed.), *Women, Revolution, and the Novels of the 1790s* (East Lansing: Michigan State University Press, 1999).

Shorter) have been oddly ahistorical, tracing connections simply between family structures and the personalities they foster, but failing to place this functional unit in the context of larger political or economic forces – such as the relations of production or state formation.

In arguing that in the period under consideration a kinship system favoring conjugal ties replaced an earlier kinship system based on consanguineal or blood connections (as in a lineage, tribe, or clan), let it be understood at the outset that I am not simply rehashing the discredited thesis that the multi-generational, extended family gave way sometime in the seventeenth or eighteenth century to a nuclear family form consisting of a single couple and their immature children.[19] Consanguineal and conjugal families can both be "nuclear" in structure, although they derive from very different principles and, as I hope to show, have very different implications for men and women of alternating generations. John Hajnal and Peter Laslett long ago established, albeit for very different intellectual ends, that the nuclear family form was dominant in England long before proto-industrialization, migration to the cities, or even the final wave of enclosures.[20] Both Alan Macfarlane and Jack Goody, from the comparatist perspective of social anthropologists (or historical sociologists as they are sometimes called), make the point that the nuclear family is not a consequence of the industrial revolution, but instead a function of a system of direct inheritance involving the ownership and transmission of absolute property – an inheritance system that existed in England long before the 1750s.[21] According to Peter Laslett,

---

[19] This is the argument of Christopher Flint's *Family Fictions: Narrative and Domestic Relations in Britain 1688–1798* (Stanford: Stanford University Press, 1998) which builds on Lawrence Stone's thesis: that an "emphasis on 'individualism' and 'affective' relations caused a shift in family structure from a relatively porous one that stressed kinship, lineage, and economic concerns (while repressing affection, marital choice, sexual pleasure, and children's needs) to a more limited one that encouraged individual gratification and intense loyalty among the 'elementary' members of the family (husband, wife, and children)" (4–5). Flint assumes the conjugal family as the only real family form. As will become clear, I believe that economic concerns in marriage intensified rather than diminished in the period under examination (see Chapter 5). Flint also advances a different view of the relationship of fiction to family change. He theorizes that fiction modified existing notions of family and naturalized the new version of the family. I am arguing, conversely, that fiction was often nostalgic and compensatory in dealing with social change.

[20] John Hajnal, "European Marriage Patterns in Perspective," in D. V. Glass and D. E. C. Eversley (eds.), *Population in History: Essays in Historical Demography* (London: Edward Arnold, 1965) and "Two Kinds of Pre-Industrial Household Formation Systems," *Population and Development Review* 8, 3 (1982), 449–94; Peter Laslett, "Introduction: The History of the Family" and "Mean Household Size in England since the Sixteenth Century," in Peter Laslett and Richard Wall (eds.), *Household and Family in Past Time* (Cambridge: Cambridge University Press, 1972), 1–89; 125–58.

[21] Alan Macfarlane, *Marriage and Love in England 1300–1840* (Oxford: Basil Blackwell, 1986), and Jack Goody, *The Development of the Family and Marriage in Europe* (Cambridge: Cambridge University Press, 1983).

the relatively small household of 4.75 persons had long been standard in England.[22]

But household residence – people who share the same living space – is only one definition of family, although, as Naomi Tadmor reminds us, "family" in seventeenth- and eighteenth-century common parlance often meant just that: "a household, including its diverse dependents, such as servants, apprentices and co-resident relatives."[23] The word did not come to signify the unit of spouses and immature children until later in the eighteenth century. According to one historian, the Quaker listings of households in London drawn up in 1737, and again in 1762, include "children, servants, and apprentices . . . as constituting the family unit, but in 1782 the servants and apprentices were omitted."[24] Discussing the different meanings of the terms "friend" and "family," Tadmor points out that, while "unrelated persons may constitute a 'family'" (and she offers evidence from diaries, letters, and novels that one's household was often called one's "family"), relatives as an entire body of interested parties were often referred to as one's "friends." She makes the interesting observation that the many kinds of relationship designated by just these two words – "family" and "friend" – seem evidence of a "highly variegated social world, possibly in the throes of a process of transformation not yet incorporated in specific linguistic terms."[25]

Nevertheless, household residence is not necessarily the same thing as the kin group to which an individual feels allegiance. Moreover, it seems that the household that Laslett pegged in England at 4.75 persons from the sixteenth century to the twentieth century was not a strictly nuclear family as he assumed, but a fairly fluid entity with a changing cast of characters as late as the eighteenth century. It may be that the household was only the

[22] See n. 20 above.

[23] Naomi Tadmor, "The Concept of the Household-Family in Eighteenth-Century England," *Past and Present* 151 (1995), 111–40, quote 112. For this point and those that follow in this paragraph, I am also indebted to Tadmor's fascinating book *Family and Friends in Eighteenth-Century England: Household, Kinship, and Patronage* (Cambridge: Cambridge University Press, 2001).

[24] Beatrice Gottlieb quotes this from J. William Frost, *The Quaker Family in Colonial America* (New York: St. Martin's Press, 1973), p. 140, in *The Family in the Western World from the Black Death to the Industrial Age* (Oxford and New York: Oxford University Press, 1993), p. 12.

[25] Naomi Tadmor, "'Family' and 'Friend' in *Pamela*: A Case-Study in the History of the Family in Eighteenth-Century England," *Social History* 14 (1989), 289–306, quote 301. Tadmor concludes her discussion of the multiple meanings of "friend" and "family" with an observation that corroborates my own sense of the timing of a shift in the meanings of kinship: "The findings of the semantic analysis indicate that the metamorphosis of these familial and social configurations was much slower and more complex than is sometimes supposed in the periodization of the history of the family: as late as the mid-eighteenth-century, 'traditional' and even 'ancient' patterns – patterns of speech and thought, if not actual social patterns – were forceful and influential" (303).

lower limit of a larger extended kin group with which individuals identified
and to which they felt they owed obligation. Hans Medick remarks that
although the pre-industrial family in England was not "the classic three-
generation stem family, consisting of grandparents, parents and children," it
still included kin members who were beyond the immediate conjugal configuration. This suggests that the nuclear family was still porous, and that
the psychological idea of "family" still included a larger circle of extended
kin. "Nuclear family households which contained widows, unmarried sisters or brothers, nieces and nephews of the married couple occurred fairly
frequently," he adds.[26]

When Michael Anderson summarized the work on family history in
1980, he referred to the "life-cycles" of families, stating that the make-up of
an English household might change over a lifetime. That is, virtually every
nuclear family had other kin residing within it for part of its cycle, but
this fluidity only affected 20 percent of the population at any one time.[27]
Lutz K. Berkner, reconstructing peasant households in Austria in 1763,
observed that in that society a household structure changed several times
over the course of its existence. A son might grow up in a nuclear family
of origin but then dwell in a two-generation household when he married
and his parents retired. When his parents died he might live again in a
one-generation conjugal family. Meanwhile, servants, apprentices, board-
ers, lodgers, and extended kin might come and go. According to one family
historian: "Households expanded and contracted in accordance with the
family's needs."[28] Thus, nuclear families were embedded in relationships of
mutual aid and cooperation with an extended kin network even when they
did not reside with them in the same household. Analyzing the eighteenth-
century use of terms such as "relations," "friends," "kindred," and "con-
nexions" for their social meaning, Naomi Tadmor concludes that "not only

[26] Hans Medick, "The Proto-Industrial Family Economy," in Peter Kriedte, Hans Medick, and Jurgen
Schlumbohm (eds.), *Industrialization before Industrialization: Rural Industry in the Genesis of Capitalism* (Cambridge: Cambridge University Press, 1981), pp. 38–73, especially p. 59. Naomi Tadmor
uses the term "extended-nuclear" to refer to kin ties that were maintained over time and across generations. She concludes that the nuclear family of the eighteenth century was probably less isolated
structurally than has been assumed by some historians. *Family and Friends in Eighteenth-Century
England*, p. 166.

[27] Michael Anderson, *Approaches to the History of the Western Family 1500–1914* (London and
Basingstoke: Macmillan, 1980), pp. 30–1.

[28] Lutz K. Berkner, "The Stem Family and the Development Cycle of the Peasant Household: An
Eighteenth-Century Austrian Example," *American Historical Review* 77 (April 1972), 398–418; Tamara
K. Hareven, "The History of the Family and the Complexity of Social Change," *American Historical
Review* 96 (February 1991), 95–124; quote 105.

was the nuclear family not isolated by these usages, but they actually served to submerge the nuclear family in broader kinship relationships."[29]

Miranda Chaytor demonstrated in her family reconstitution study of Ryton in the late sixteenth and early seventeenth centuries that the nuclear family may have been the ideal family form in early modern England, but it was more observed in the breach than in the practice. Many households consisted of "hybrid" families owing to geographical mobility and high mortality rates. Remarriage, adoption of foster children as well as stepchildren, the presence of servants who were relatives, and the frequent deaths of spouses created families very different from that implied by Laslett's figure for an average household of 4.75 persons. Given the fluidity of relatives coming and going, obligations to one's consanguineal family could very well coexist with an ever-changing household averaging 4.75 persons. Household size does not necessarily tell us either who was in the household nor to whom the members of that household felt their deepest obligations.[30]

Indeed, the emphasis on statistical regularity made possible in the last twenty years by computer processing of parish records obscures significant changes in the psychological and social meaning of family life in the period under examination. The size of a residential group hardly establishes the psychological meaning of belonging to it; it tells you nothing about how chores and authority are distributed or about the sharing of resources. The way a family makes its living and apportions inheritance in the next generation constitutes its meaning as much as the number of members who live under the same roof. Moreover, the social or psychological meaning of membership in a family can change even when its numerical size remains the same. One could even argue that the demographic data on the household in the eighteenth century are an artifact of the records kept by the church and the state, the household being a unit established for purposes of taxation

---

[29] Naomi Tadmor, *Family and Friends in Eighteenth-Century England*, p. 132. She also remarks that "kinship ties in seventeenth- and eighteenth-century England may have been richer, more complex, and altogether more significant than sometimes estimated" (113).

[30] Miranda Chaytor, "Household and Kinship: Ryton in the Late 16th and Early 17th Centuries," *History Workshop Journal* 10 (Autumn 1980), 25–60. A critique of Chaytor's article, entitled "Critique: Household and Kinship in Sixteenth-Century England," was published by Keith Wrightson in a subsequent issue, *History Workshop Journal*, 12 (1981), 151–8. Articles by Cicely Howell ("Peasant Inheritance Customs in the Midlands, 1280–1700") and Margaret Spufford ("Peasant Inheritance Customs and Land Distribution in Cambridgeshire from the Sixteenth to the Eighteenth Centuries") in Jack Goody, Joan Thirsk, and E. P. Thompson (eds.), *Family and Inheritance: Rural Society in Western Europe, 1200–1800* (Cambridge: Cambridge University Press, 1976) offer many local examples of additional family members residing in households with those of the nuclear unit. See especially pp. 145, 154, 175.

or military recruitment. It is not necessarily the same thing as the social unit that supported its members, determined inheritance of property or use rights, or arranged the reproductive activities of its descent group. In a trenchant critique of Laslett's assumption that the residential household was a "family" in the modern sense of the word, Lutz Berkner observes that "a parish priest trying to increase his allotment of poor relief would have been well advised to represent widows and lodgers as separate households, even if they lived with another family, while a military recruiter whose quota was based on the number of households could make his job easier by grouping as many families as possible together."[31] In other words, until proper censuses were taken in the nineteenth century, the evidence used to determine the size of households is suspect. Berkner goes on to point out that it is a very different thing to claim, as Laslett does, that structurally the nuclear family has been the dominant familial formation in most societies, rather than the more neutral finding that his data do support – that "at any given point in time the majority of basic residential units in any society will be composed of nuclear families."[32]

Anthropological kinship theory has provided some of the explanatory constructs – not the least of which is the distinction between consanguineal and conjugal kin formations – that have helped me to refine the historian's notion of the "nuclear family" and to interpret the family tensions symbolized in fiction. For example, the assertion that the placing of a high value on father-son and brother-brother relations occurs in cultures "at the expense of the relationship between husband and wife" corroborated my sense that consanguineal and conjugal loyalties might be experienced as mutually exclusive.[33] Descriptions of kinship systems from other parts of the world (Asia or Africa, for example) remind one of the non-universality of the western family and the culture-specific nature of English kin arrangements. When one learns that a society's marriage patterns are related to its principles of descent, it focuses one's attention on the possible connections between conflicted marriages and contested inheritance in the fiction of eighteenth-century England. When one learns that strong and indissoluble marital bonds are incompatible with matrilineal descent principles and that

---

[31] Lutz K. Berkner, "The Use and Misuse of Census Data for the Historical Analysis of Family Structure," *Journal of Interdisciplinary History* 5, 4 (Spring 1975), 721–38, quote 725. David Levine includes a cautionary appendix about the reliability of parish records for family reconstitution and about the representativeness of the results in *Family Formation in an Age of Nascent Capitalism* (New York: Academic Press, 1977), pp. 153–74.

[32] Berkner, "The Use and Misuse of Census Data," 738.

[33] Robert Wheaton, "Family and Kinship in Western Europe: The Problem of the Joint Family Household," *Journal of Interdisciplinary History* 5, 4 (Spring 1975), 601–28, quote 625.

"strong bonds of solidarity between husband and wife, and stable marriage, are possible with patrilineal descent groups in proportion to the degree to which the tie of the wife to her own unit is relaxed," it sensitizes one to a dynamic in England that downplayed maternal inheritance over time while strengthening patrilineal ties.[34] When one reads that "in cases where the brother-sister tie is strong, the husband-wife tie is weak,"[35] it directs one's attention to the representation of relations between sisters and brothers in fiction at this time of rising rates of marriage. In other words, the formulations of anthropology teach one to look at patterns – sometimes carried in secondary plots – that might be overlooked in uninformed textual analysis.

In thinking about changes in the patterns of women's inheritance and dowry in eighteenth-century England, the distinction that anthropologists make between bride-price and dowry societies is instructive. When the financial transaction at marriage is bride-price (given by the groom's family to the bride's family "in payment" for their daughter), rather than dowry (given by the bride's family to the new couple – understood as her inheritance and controlled by the groom), it suggests a greater respect for the contributions of women's productive and reproductive labor. The function of dowry, on the other hand, seems to be to concentrate capital. Although these practices have been known to coexist in different strata of the same family, there are also class differences between families that pay bride-price and families that expect dowry. Bride-price cultures often have few real differences in wealth; these societies tend to respect women's sexuality for energizing men and creating social ties. Dowry cultures, on the other hand, are marked by greater disparities in wealth and are more preoccupied with women's reproductive capacities and motherhood than with their sexual natures. The adoption of a dowry practice may signal the devaluation of the productive labor of the woman herself.[36] Thus changes in dowry practices in eighteenth-century England are probably related to capital accumulation, class disparity, and changing attitudes towards women's labor and reproduction and sexuality. Becoming aware of the internal dynamics of different

[34] David M. Schneider's Introduction to David M. Schneider and Kathleen Gough (eds.), *Matrilineal Kinship* (Berkeley and Los Angeles: University of California Press, 1961), pp. 1–33, quote p. 17.

[35] Annette B. Weiner, "Reassessing Reproduction in Social Theory," in Faye D. Ginsburg and Rayna Rapp (eds.), *Conceiving the New World Order: The Global Politics of Reproduction* (Berkeley: University of California Press, 1995), pp. 407–24, quote p. 416.

[36] Prem Chowdhry cites the case of a middle-class agriculturist in India who paid the bride-price for his son to marry a woman from a poorer family, while at the same time giving a dowry with his daughter to marry into a better class ("pride-price"). *The Veiled Woman: Shifting Gender Equations in Rural Haryana 1880–1990* (Delhi: Oxford University Press, 1994), p. 70; see pp. 63–74 for a discussion of dowry and bride-price in India. Jack Goody and S. J. Tambiah, *Bridewealth and Dowry* (Cambridge: Cambridge University Press, 1973) examine the practice of bride-price in Africa.

kinship systems helps one to understand how capitalizing production in agriculture and manufacturing might have affected changing generational and gender roles in the family in eighteenth-century England.[37]

HISTORICAL DEBATES

The debate about household size and what it implies about family structure is only one of several contested issues in the social history of eighteenth-century England. Historians also argue about why the industrial revolution occurred in England earlier than in other European countries. Was the cultural ethos of England unusually individualistic rather than collectivist from early on – and how was this ethos related to family form? How did English marriage customs and inheritance law facilitate the amassing of larger and larger estates in the late seventeenth and eighteenth centuries? Did the land enclosures of the eighteenth century really dispossess the poor? Did the standard of living of laborers improve or deteriorate in the course of the eighteenth century – and did that change the shape of the family? What were the characteristics of the proto-industrial family? Did the English begin to love their children more when child mortality rates dropped? Were marriages more affectionate and egalitarian in the later eighteenth century than at any time before? Was a sexual revolution responsible for a rise in illegitimate births in the course of the eighteenth century? And most important of all: what accounts for the tremendous reproductive rise in the eighteenth century, an exponentially expanding birthrate that almost doubled the population – and what did it have to do with the industrial revolution, land enclosure, commercial agriculture, or any of the other changes in the modes of production? My argument touches on all of these questions, although not decisively. Nevertheless, the formulation that a consanguineal family formation was giving way to a conjugal family formation ties many of these issues together and fills in another piece of the historical puzzle.

Family historians have not reached consensus about any of these issues – nor about where to look to find the answers. Michael Anderson divided historians of the eighteenth-century family into those who used the "demographic" approach, those who used the "sentiments" approach, and those who used the "household economics" approach.[38] Peter Laslett,

[37] For a study of the effects of state formation on kinship in Tonga, see Christine Gailey, *From Kinship to Kingship: Gender Hierarchy and State Formation in the Tongan Islands* (Austin: University of Texas Press, 1987).

[38] Michael Anderson, *Approaches to the History of the Western Family 1500–1914*, p. 15 and *passim*.

E. A. Wrigley, and the Cambridge Group for the History of Population and Social Structure (established in 1964) represented the demographic approach, looking at population changes and using a family reconstitution technique based on information from parish registers (tracing surnames) to extrapolate what they saw as an unvarying family structure. The "sentiments" approach, represented in Anderson's schema by Philippe Ariès' *Centuries of Childhood* (1962), Edward Shorter's *The Making of the Modern Family* (1976), Lawrence Stone's *The Family, Sex, and Marriage in England 1500–1800* (1977), and Randolph Trumbach's *The Rise of the Egalitarian Family: Aristocratic Kinship and Domestic Relations in Eighteenth-Century England* (1978), attempted to reconstruct the emotional reality of family relationships, in particular parents' feelings about their children and about each other.[39] As I will argue later, this emphasis on spousal and parental love by Shorter, Stone, and Trumbach is anachronistic, reading twentieth-century concerns back into a culture that may not have privileged these relationships as much as ours does. Furthermore, the "sentiments" approach relies on documents (memoirs and letters) produced for the most part by the middling and upper classes and hence tends to privilege the literate classes. David Levine, Jack Goody, and Wally Seccombe represent the "household economics" approach – investigating how the family functioned as an economic unit, how labor was deployed, resources distributed, and reproduction arranged – in England as well as other countries. These historians and anthropologists posit a relationship between family form and the way families support themselves.[40] As Wally Seccombe puts it, "Modes of production facilitate and foster the reproduction of certain family forms and preclude or hamper the development of others." Of course it works the other way around too: "Family forms are active elements in the constitution and development of modes of production," continues Seccombe, "because they are central in the production of people and their capacities for work, compliance and resistance."[41]

Historians who posit a relation between economic arrangements and family structure seem closer to what is expressed in the fiction of the period,

---

[39] Linda Pollock's intelligent overview and critical analysis of these and other books dealing with parental attitudes towards children in this period is an important corrective to all these works. See *Forgotten Children: Parent-Child Relations from 1500 to 1900* (Cambridge and New York: Cambridge University Press, 1983).

[40] David Levine, *Family Formation in an Age of Nascent Capitalism*; Jack Goody, *Production and Reproduction: A Comparative Study of the Domestic Domain* (Cambridge and New York: Cambridge University Press, 1976); Wally Seccombe, *A Millennium of Family Change: Feudalism to Capitalism in Northwestern Europe* (London and New York: Verso, 1992).

[41] Wally Seccombe, *A Millennium of Family Change*, p. 9.

which is always concerned with economic matters. Peter Laslett's assertion that household size remained stable for three centuries – a position taken even further by Alan Macfarlane, who believes that the essential features of the English family can be traced to the thirteenth century[42] – assumes that family form was impervious to economic change despite radically new modes of production. Laslett's claim that English families were essentially nuclear in form, that there was no age difference between spouses, and that marriage and reproduction were relatively late, built on a thesis first articulated by John Hajnal about the distinctive characteristics of European marriage that might account for European industrial precedence. Hajnal argued that the late age of marriage, the high proportion of those who never married at all, and the concentration of property owing to these factors as well as to the practice of impartible inheritance, probably accounted for the capital accumulation necessary for the industrial revolution.[43] But Hajnal was not arguing that the passage from feudalism to capitalism and the industrial revolution made no difference to the fundamental structure of the family.

Despite Laslett's assertion of the irrelevance of economic factors to family form, the population increase in England in the decades leading up to full industrialization suggests some kind of influence between production and reproduction.[44] The fluctuating relation between mortality and birthrates in England that had eventuated in steady growth 1541–1656, population decline 1656–86, and stagnation or a low increase until 1730, ended abruptly in the second half of the eighteenth century. Rather suddenly, people began to marry younger, fewer people than ever remained unmarried, and reproductive rates skyrocketed. Until then, fertility had always been regulated organically by life expectancy and economic opportunity in England's land-based agricultural economy; young adults had always waited to marry until their parents died or retired so that they could inherit the family holdings or workshop or otherwise receive aid from the older generation.[45]

Delayed marriage had been made possible by the custom of service-in-husbandry: adolescents hired out to work in households more or less like their own to be trained in life's tasks, develop skills, meet a wider range of possible marriage partners, and earn a modest nest egg towards their own

---

[42] Alan Macfarlane, *Marriage and Love in England 1300–1840* (Oxford: Basil Blackwell, 1986).

[43] John Hajnal, "European Marriage Patterns in Perspective," pp. 101–43.

[44] David Levine's *Family Formation in an Age of Nascent Capitalism* is the *locus classicus* of this thesis. Wally Seccombe synthesizes much of the research supporting this position in *A Millennium of Family Change*.

[45] E. A. Wrigley and R. S. Schofield, *The Population History of England, 1541–1871* (Cambridge, MA: Harvard University Press, 1981), pp. 176, 179, 373, 403.

marriages, would then come back and marry late.[46] This custom had been practiced for many centuries in England; even aristocrats sent their sons to court as pages. An Italian text from the fifteenth century describes how the English kept their children at home until the age of seven or nine, and then

they put them out, both males and females, to hard service in the houses of other people, binding them generally for another seven or nine years . . . few are born who are exempted from this fate, for everyone, however rich he may be, sends away his children into the houses of others, whilst he, in return, receives those of strangers into his own.[47]

The heroine of Richardson's *Pamela* is in just such a phase of her life story when we first meet her. Sending children out to service was still a fairly common practice in all but the wealthiest classes at the beginning of the eighteenth century. This practice enabled grown children to maintain an independent existence away from their families of origin for a while, and then to return, marry late, and take over the land holdings and often the literal dwelling place of one or another of their sets of parents. Grown children, marrying late after a separate adult existence, might also have been less rebelliously in conflict with their parents than the romantic children depicted in fiction at the end of the eighteenth century.

The discontinuance of service-in-husbandry in the course of the eighteenth century, together with changes in land use, the disappearance of smallholdings, and the consolidation of large estates, began to alter the traditional norms of marriage and reproduction in English society. Although marriage had historically kept pace with mortality rates, now, for the first time, "the nuptial valve *failed to tighten* in response to falling mortality and a massive increase in rural landlessness, as it had in the past."[48] Proto-industrialization, that is, small-scale manufacturing on a putting-out system, gave full-time waged labor to people who had previously earned their subsistence from the land and had only worked for money seasonally. It put cash in the pockets of young men and women and made them independent of their parents at younger ages than had previously been the case. Emigration from the countryside to urban centers disrupted the hold families had on their younger members. In the upper classes, too, the meaning

[46] More than 60 percent of the youth between the ages of 15 and 24 in England were in service between 1700 and 1750. Ann Kussmaul, *Servants in Husbandry in Early Modern England* (Cambridge: Cambridge University Press, 1981), p. 3.

[47] Quoted in Philippe Ariès, *Centuries of Childhood: A Social History of Family Life*, trans. Robert Baldick (New York: Random House, 1962), p. 365.

[48] Wally Seccombe, "The Western European Marriage Pattern in Historical Perspective: A Response to David Levine," *Journal of Historical Sociology* 3 (March 1990), 50–74, quote 67.

and practice of marriage changed as the laws regulating inheritance increasingly facilitated the accumulation of wealth for the eldest son, from whose estate settlements on daughters and younger sons began to be resented as a drain.

In a fascinating study comparing the age of marriage – and by extension the number of children – of those who engaged in waged proto-industrial work with those who continued to live in an agrarian subsistence economy in eighteenth-century England, David Levine compared the age of marriage of people living in the proto-industrial village of Shepshed, where the inhabitants engaged in cottage industry, with that in the agrarian village of Bottsford, fifteen miles away. Bottsford was dominated by the dukes of Rutland who assiduously kept out industry of any kind on the theory that it would raise the poor rates. They assumed that the introduction of manufacturing would impoverish their agrarian laborers and render their tenants unable to pay their rents. Comparing the two populations, Levine found that the framework knitters of Shepshed "were more likely to be married, married earlier, and had more children living at home, and, in addition, more frequently shared their households with other families" than the agrarian laborers of Bottsford.[49] Levine attributes the lower marriage age in proto-industrial households to the fact that young adults attained their prime earning capacity earlier than in agrarian areas. He also points out that large families were functional in these independent production units in which tasks could be shared out among the children: yarn had to be carded, spun, and threaded as well as knitted.[50]

Contrary to Peter Laslett's postulated steady state household size, Levine argued that major changes in the system of production had significant effects on marital and reproductive behavior. One could also argue that cultural innovations in print changed the marital and reproductive behavior that led to this demographic effect. The proliferation of novels with their evolving ideology of highly self-conscious, privatized, heterosexual relationships may have contributed to these changes in the dynamic of fertility.[51] But however this change is understood to have happened, however overdetermined by both economic and cultural factors, the effect on individuals in families was profound in the way it divided their loyalties. It

---

[49] David Levine, *Family Formation in an Age of Nascent Capitalism*, p. 51.

[50] Rab Houston and K. D. M. Snell review this and other work on proto-industrial families and criticize and refine the thesis in "Proto-Industrialization? Cottage Industry, Social Change, and Industrial Revolution," *Historical Journal* 27, 1–2 (1984), 473–92.

[51] Henry Abelove, "Some Speculations on the History of Sexual Intercourse during the Long Eighteenth Century in England," *Genders* 6 (November 1989), 125–30, and Tim Hitchcock, "Redefining Sex in Eighteenth-Century England," *History Workshop Journal* 41 (1996), 73–90.

became less and less clear how much one owed to one's family of origin – to siblings and parents and even parents' siblings – and how much to the new family one made for oneself with a stranger. Was a man responsible for his sister or his wife? How should he choose when there was a conflict between these obligations? Should a woman obey her father or the promptings of her own heart? These dilemmas were served up in the novels that as much as 80 percent of the population was reading by the late eighteenth century.[52] An anonymous farce about novels from 1789, "Half an Hour after Supper," shows a novel being passed around a gentry household, a quadruple-decker about Lord X and Harriet. Everyone both upstairs and downstairs reads it avidly – including the stable boy, the maids, the middle-class daughters, and their maiden aunts. Indeed, the book gets dirty from being passed around so much. Such novels defined and investigated issues of relationship and obligation – and offered readers of all classes moral guidance through the labyrinths of newly conflicting kin claims.

Another debate about eighteenth-century English society that I will be addressing in this book turns on the effects of enclosure on the rural laboring poor. Some argue that the capitalizing of agriculture stimulated the economy and made more work for landless workers.[53] Others claim that

---

[52] Literacy – which is to say the ability to sign one's name – has been calculated as high as 80% in the late eighteenth century. In 1815 in Bethnal Green, a working-class neighborhood of London, 92.5% of the men and 83% of the women who married could sign their names in the marriage register. R. K. Webb, *The British Working-Class Reader 1790–1848: Literacy and Social Tension* (London: George Allen and Unwin, 1955; 1971), p. 25. James Lackington, a successful bookseller, states in his autobiography of 1791 that "four times the number of books are sold now than were sold twenty years since. The poorer sort of farmers, and even the poor country people in general, who before that period spent their winter evenings in relating stories of witches, ghosts, hobgoblins, &c. now shorten the winter nights by hearing their sons and daughters read tales, romances &c. and on entering their houses, you may see Tom Jones, Roderic (sic) Random, and other entertaining books, stuck up on their bacon-racks, &c." *Memoirs of the Forty-Five First Years of the Life of James Lackington*, 13th edn. (London, 1794), p. 257.

For studies of literacy in this period, see David Cressy, *Literacy and the Social Order: Reading and Writing in Tudor and Stuart England* (Cambridge: Cambridge University Press, 1980), Geoffrey Holmes and Daniel Szechi, *The Age of Oligarchy: Pre-Industrial Britain, 1722–1783* (London: Longman, 1993), and W. B. Stephens, "Literacy in England, Scotland, and Wales, 1500–1900," *History of Education Quarterly* 30, 4 (Winter 1990), 545–71.

Jan Fergus has shown that servants read in the eighteenth century – and that their book orders ran mostly to self-improving books, reference works, and religious texts. Among this class, there was an increasing demand for entertaining fiction after the 1770s. See her "Provincial Servants' Reading in the Late Eighteenth Century," in James Raven, Helen Small, and Naomi Tadmor (eds.), *The Practice and Representation of Reading in England* (Cambridge: Cambridge University Press, 1996), pp. 202–25.

[53] This is the argument in G. E. Mingay, *Enclosure and the Small Farmer in the Age of the Industrial Revolution* (London: Macmillan, 1968). An earlier statement by J. D. Chambers, calling for a reappraisal of the work by the Hammonds, also argued that enclosure improved rather than impoverished the lot of the agrarian laboring population. J. D. Chambers, "Enclosure and Labour Supply in the

cottagers and smallholders were impoverished by the loss of use rights with
the enclosure of wastes and commons. No longer able to keep animals because there was no place to graze them, without access to woods or streams
or even a little garden plot, the rural laborer became entirely dependent on
wages to buy food and fuel. Whereas in the late sixteenth century two out of
three laborers owned at least one cow, by the beginning of the eighteenth
century only one in five did, or 20%, and by the end of the eighteenth
century only 1% owned cows, 15% pigs, and 33% had gardens.[54] Pasture
rights, fishing rights, the right to cut turves for fuel or wood for housing,
fencing, implements and so on – all these rights disappeared as the wastes
and commons were absorbed into the large estates.[55] Subsistence could no
longer be coaxed from the land; cottagers now needed cash to buy their
food. The disappearance of use rights and the need for capital to fence,
irrigate, and fertilize land also put new pressure on the small landowner
in the second half of the eighteenth century. Many of these smallholders
sold up to men consolidating large estates, men with the necessary capital to enclose and improve their holdings.[56] These changes inevitably had
an effect on the families of the several classes involved and were reflected
in the fiction about farming as well as the sentimental fiction about the
vicissitudes of the deserving poor and the charity of the philanthropically
inclined well-to-do.

Historians also disagree about whether or not the increasing production
of goods and grain in the later eighteenth century, the first stages of the
industrial revolution, brought with it a higher standard of living. The so-
called pessimists in this debate argue that real wages dropped between
1750 and 1810, precipitously in 1795, 1800, 1812, 1816, etc.; that the cost
of housing – rent – rose relative to other consumer goods throughout the
industrial revolution because so many laborers had been displaced from
the land; and that the misery of these years did not begin to let up until the
1820s. The so-called optimists argue that the hardships of the late eighteenth

Industrial Revolution," *Economic History Review* 2nd Series, 5, 3 (1953), 319–43 and reprinted in D. V.
Glass and D. E. C. Eversley (eds.), *Population in History: Essays in Historical Demography* (London:
Edward Arnold, 1965), pp. 308–27.

[54] Carole Shamas, "The Eighteenth-Century Diet and Economic Change," *Explorations in Economic
History* 21 (1984), 254–69, especially 256, 264, quoted in Wally Seccombe, *A Millennium of Family
Change*, p. 176.

[55] K. D. M. Snell, *Annals of the Labouring Poor: Social Change and Agrarian England 1660–1900*
(Cambridge: Cambridge University Press, 1985), p. 180. See also J. M. Neeson, *Commoners: Common
Right, Enclosure and Social Change in England, 1700–1820* (Cambridge: Cambridge University Press,
1993). The social and economic effects of enclosure will be further discussed in Chapter 7.

[56] Arthur H. Johnson, *The Disappearance of the Small Landowner*, Ford Lectures, 1909, Introduction
by Joan Thirsk (London: Merlin Press, 1963).

century were just the growing pains of industrialism but that ultimately the lot of workers was improved by the burgeoning economic system, that real wages rose in relation to prices at the end of the Napoleonic wars, and that the increase was substantial after 1820.[57] Both sides agree, however, that life was more difficult for most workers in the second half of the eighteenth century, that it was harder to earn a living with soaring food prices and increased dependence on wages.

One way agrarian workers made ends meet in these difficult years was by working at various cottage industries in the home. These proto-industrial families, like the Shepshed framework knitters that David Levine wrote about, worked as teams, women and children too, making cloth, gloves, glass, and leather, plaiting straw into baskets, making metal into nails and the like.[58] They produced these goods for middlemen who provided the materials and distributed the goods nationally at a better margin of profit. Although there is disagreement among historians about the meaning of this family form of production, it has been claimed by some as an essential stage in the development of capitalism. Whereas the economy of the small farmer or cottager families had been based on owning land and occasionally working for wages, this new family form evolved as a source of labor for capitalist production. A transitional form often identified as the economic missing link in the changeover to the scale of production known as the industrial revolution, this family, as Hans Medick has argued, "functioned *objectively* as an internal engine of growth in the process of proto-industrial expansion precisely because *subjectively* it remained tied to the norms and rules of behaviour of the traditional familial subsistence economy."[59] That is, the family worked without stint to support itself, increasing its labor output when the cost of material rose, working not for a profit but only to make ends meet.

Meanwhile, the advantage of accumulating more land had been changing the marriage and inheritance practices of the affluent. Widow's dower was being replaced in most marriage settlements by jointure (the annual income

---

[57] The modern round of this debate seems to have been begun by M. W. Flinn, "Trends in Real Wages, 1750–1850," *Economic History Review* 2nd series, 27, 3 (August 1974), 395–413. Responses came from T. R. Gourvish, "Flinn and Real Wage Trends in Britain, 1750–1850: A Comment," *Economic History Review* 2nd series, 29, 1 (February 1976), 136–42; and G. N. Von Tunzelmann, "Trends in Real Wages, 1750–1859, Revisited," *Economic Review* 2nd series, 32, 1 (February 1979), 33–49. For additional information about cost-of-living and wage levels, see Peter H. Lindert and Jeffrey G. Williamson, "English Workers' Living Standards during the Industrial Revolution: A New Look," *Economic History Review* 2nd series, 36, 1 (February 1983), 1–25.

[58] See, for example, Rab Houston and K. D. M. Snell, "Proto-Industrialization? Cottage Industry, Social Change, and Industrial Revolution," 473–92.

[59] Hans Medick, "The Proto-Industrial Family Economy," p. 52.

settled on a widow if her husband predeceased her) which was always less than dower;[60] and the amount of dowry that a woman brought to her marriage was rising in relation to the amount of jointure settled on her in the marriage contract. In other words, the price of husbands was going up. The strict settlement – a legal mechanism that insured the passing on of estates whole – was invented to prevent spendthrift heirs from mortgaging or selling what their forebears had gone to such lengths to amass.[61] The strict settlement also stipulated what, out of the estate, would be left to daughters and younger sons, an arrangement that some historians have understood as a limitation on what younger or female children could inherit and others have seen as a positive guarantee of their portions.[62]

The emotional quality of relations between marriage partners and between parents and their children began to change according to some historians, although there is disagreement as to which class should be credited first with this change. Lawrence Stone described what he saw as a "closed domesticated nuclear family" evolve in the late seventeenth century and "predominate" in the eighteenth century, a family in which "husbands and wives personally selected each other rather than obeying parental wishes," motivated by love rather than economic factors, and in which parents loved their children as never before. Stone describes this sentimental, egalitarian family as predominating among the lesser nobility, the squirarchy and gentry, and the professional and upper middle classes. As he looks down the social scale, however, the family forms he sees in the lower orders all display more male domination in marriage and more neglect of children.[63] Edward Shorter, on the other hand, traces the eighteenth-century belief in individualism and romantic love to the capitalist marketplace, which he believed effected a sexual revolution among the laboring class first and foremost. Randolph Trumbach's study of the aristocratic family in

[60] Susan Staves, *Married Women's Separate Property in England, 1660–1833* (Cambridge, MA: Harvard University Press, 1990), pp. 56–130. For further clarification of these terms, see Chapter 5, "Privatized Marriage and Property Relations."

[61] This thesis was first stated by H. J. Habakkuk, "Marriage Settlements in the Eighteenth Century," *Transactions of the Royal Historical Society* 4th series, 32 (1950), 15–30. Lloyd Bonfield demonstrated, however, that only about 48 percent of fathers survived to their eldest son's marriages – which is to say long enough to entail the estate to their future grandson and hence prevent their own son from directly inheriting the estate with full powers of disposition. See Lloyd Bonfield, "Marriage Settlements and the 'Rise of Great Estates': The Demographic Aspect," *Economic History Review* 2nd series, 32, 4 (1979), 483–93.

[62] The opinions of Habakkuk, Stone, and Clay, among others, on the meaning of the strict settlement can be found in Eileen Spring, "The Family, Strict Settlement, and Historians," *Canadian Journal of History/ Annales Canadiennes d'Histoire 18* (December 1983), 379–98.

[63] Lawrence Stone, *The Family, Sex, and Marriage in England 1500–1800* (New York: Harper and Row, 1977), pp. 7–8, 361–5, 451–6.

the eighteenth century makes a case for the first appearance of these same qualities (a growing belief in egalitarian marriage and affection for one's children) among the English aristocracy of the eighteenth century.[64]

A CHANGING SOCIETY

The restructuring of kinship from a consanguineal to a conjugal basis for family identity was part of the transformation of England in the eighteenth century from a status-based society to a class-based society and from a land-based agrarian economy to a cash-based market economy.[65] As the old socio-economic relations of production and consumption began to be disrupted, new economic motives developed for limiting what once may have seemed to be the natural claims of relatives. The volatile expanding economy was creating wide disparities between the fortunes of members of a single kin group – disparities that put new pressures on those ties. Margaret Hunt gives a vivid sense of this pressure when she explains that, because entrepreneurs were personally liable for business debts, before the invention of limited liability whole families could be dragged to financial ruin by the failures of one member. Restricting kin responsibilities may have been a defense against increasing risks of business in early capitalism.[66]

The shape of the English family was also affected by mobility, by migration to areas with proto-industrial production, by the general dissociation of families from communities in urban centers, and by the steadily dropping age of first marriages. On a national level, the birthrate climbed – both for illegitimate and legitimate births. After a century of stability in which the population of England hovered around the 5 million mark, it nearly doubled in the course of the eighteenth century. By the beginning of the nineteenth century the population of England was about 9 million. The reasons for this stunning increase are complex and include a declining mortality rate; but by now most historians accept as the main reason for

[64] Edward Shorter, *The Making of the Modern Family* (New York: Basic Books, 1975); Randolph Trumbach, *The Rise of the Egalitarian Family: Aristocratic Kinship and Domestic Relations in Eighteenth-Century England* (New York and London: Academic Press, 1978).

[65] For a discussion of the changing social order, see Keith Wrightson, "The Social Order of Early Modern England: Three Approaches," in Lloyd Bonfield, Richard M. Smith, and Keith Wrightson (eds.), *The World We Have Gained: Histories of Population and Social Structures* (Oxford: Basil Blackwell, 1986), pp. 177–202.

[66] Margaret Hunt, "Time Management, Writing, and Accounting in the Eighteenth-Century English Trading Family: A Bourgeois Enlightenment," *Business and Economic History* 2nd series, 18 (1989), 150–9. See also the history of limited liability in H. A. Shannon, "The Coming of General Limited Liability," in E. M. Carus-Wilson (ed.), *Essays in Economic History*, 3 vols. (London: Arnold, 1954), vol. I, pp. 358–79.

this enormous population jump that the age at which men and women cohabited and married was declining across classes. More people were marrying younger and having more children in those extra years of fertility and heterosexual reproductive contact.

Many are the signs of the cultural dislocation caused by these changing kinship arrangements. Books telling people how to assess their responsibilities and behave towards family members, dependents, or employers found a ready audience with the reading public. There were letter manuals that advised people how to write carefully calibrated letters correcting a wayward son, asking to borrow money, or accepting or declining a proposal of marriage with different gradations of encouragement. The novel of manners, with its preoccupation with standards of behavior, reflects a volatile social context rather than a settled one.[67] Between 1715 and 1727 Daniel Defoe – who always wrote for the market – produced six books dealing with family relations: courtship, marriage, childrearing, and relations with servants.[68] The public was interested in advice on how to manage relationships within the family. Novels circulated about mismanaged kin relations – daughters pressured to marry against their wills, older brothers who gambled away the inheritance of younger children, brothers who lived off the labors and savings of their sisters, mothers who died leaving children ignorant of their paternity. This fiction characteristically included elements of disrupted kinship: orphaned children with complicated relations to their guardians, secret marriages, illicit seduction, sibling rivalry, lost inheritance. The customary isolation of the heroine dramatized the absence of community, of an hospitable, protective neighborhood, or of an extended family network that could provide an individual with subsistence and protection.

In addition to this evidence from print culture of disturbed kin relations, there were signs of institutional attempts to shore up the weakened structure of the traditional family. In London, in 1739, a Foundling Hospital was established to try to save some fraction of the abandoned and exposed infants whose bodies, usually dead but sometimes alive, were to be found along the roads leading out of town and in the dust heaps, waterways, ditches, and parks of London. Unmarried women, raped or seduced with

---

[67] Barbara Zonitch observes that the unstable and ever-changing settings in Frances Burney's novels "bespeaks a contemporary anxiety about the possibility of turbulent and unruly desires erupting at the social surface." *Familiar Violence: Gender and Social Upheaval in the Novels of Frances Burney* (Newark and London: University of Delaware Press and Associated University Presses, 1997), p. 31.

[68] David Blewett makes this point in "Changing Attitudes toward Marriage in the Time of Defoe: The Case of Moll Flanders," *Huntington Library Quarterly* 44, 2 (Spring 1981), 77–88, esp. 82–3.

promises of marriage, unable to support their infants – or indeed themselves while tending a baby – were told that they might bring them to the Foundling Hospital for shelter and care. Crowds of women with children gathered on the steps of the Foundling Hospital the evening it opened, and "the Expressions of Grief of the Women whose Children could not be admitted" as well as those "of the Women who parted with their Children" made an extraordinarily moving scene.[69] In 1753, Parliament passed the Hardwicke Marriage Act regulating marriage, making it illegal for under-age young adults to marry without the permission of their parents and stipulating a number of formalities for a fully legal marriage. These were institutional attempts to control what was happening to the English family.

The novel relations that I describe in this book, the new expectations for kinfolk, were not radically discontinuous with the system that had existed in England for hundreds of years but rather involved a perceptual shift about relational priorities: which obligations mattered more and which mattered less. English society had always had propensities in the direction of a one-generational nuclear family rather than the extended stem family, as evidenced by the English doctrine that husband and wife became one flesh at marriage and that a woman's separate legal identity disappeared at marriage.[70] To the English way of thinking, the relationship between a parent and a child is a closer kin connection than that between siblings, although according to the canon law of the Roman Catholic church, the sibling bond was ranked as equal to the parent-child bond.[71] But the movement from canon law to civil reckoning privileged the limited nuclear family of spouses with their immature children over the laterally defined kin group including the siblings of spouses (uncles and aunts) and the offspring of those siblings (cousins).

Sybil Wolfram makes the point that although in other kin systems marriage creates an alliance between two groups, in English society it simply

---

[69] R. H. Nichols and F. A. Wray, *The History of the Foundling Hospital* (London: Oxford University Press, 1935), p. 39. A more recent history is Ruth McClure, *Coram's Children: The London Foundling Hospital in the Eighteenth Century* (New Haven and London: Yale University Press, 1981). The Foundling Hospital only accepted infants of two months or less if they had no signs of disease. Randolph Trumbach gives the case histories of many raped and seduced women and explains that "a servant lost her employment once she became pregnant, and after she had used up her savings and sold her clothes, she was obliged to turn to the parish for relief or to give up her child to the Foundling Hospital." *Sex and the Gender Revolution: Heterosexuality and the Third Gender in Enlightenment London* (Chicago: University of Chicago Press, 1998), p. 16.

[70] Jack Goody, "A Comparative Approach to Incest and Adultery," *British Journal of Sociology* 7 (December 1956), 286–305, esp. 291.

[71] Sybil Wolfram, *In-Laws and Outlaws: Kinship and Marriage in England* (London and Sydney: Croom Helm, 1987), p. 15.

amalgamates the two individuals getting married but creates no further relationship between these spouses' kin. "The blood relations of a husband and wife are in no way related," Wolfram explains. "Relationship exists only between the married couple and the kin on each side."[72] In other words, the in-laws of one spouse do not become kin to the in-laws of the other spouse in English marriage. Thus, in Jane Austen's *Emma*, when Emma's sister, Isabella Woodhouse, married John Knightley before the opening of the book, his older brother George became her brother-in-law. If John Knightley were to die, Isabella could not marry George because marriage to a brother-in-law would have been considered incestuous. But George Knightley does not stand in the relation of a brother to Isabella's sister Emma. "Brother and sister! – no, indeed," he says emphatically.[73]

Nevertheless, despite the evidence for an unusually early form of the nuclear conjugal family in England, I am going to argue that what changed in the eighteenth century was the extent to which each member of the spousal pair continued to belong separately to his or her natal family. An advice book called *The Relative Duties of Parents and Children, Husbands and Wives, Masters and Servants* (1705), from the beginning of the century, was still privileging consanguineal obligations – loyalty to a man's female kin – over his conjugal obligations or loyalty to his wife. In order to learn their duty to wives, readers were encouraged to perform a thought experiment in which they summoned their deeper care for their mothers or daughters. A man not inclined to fidelity need only "consider it in the case of his Mother or his own Daughter, whether he would not think them injur'd in the highest manner, if either of their Husbands should prove false and wander from their Beds ... And if the sense of their injurious grievous treatment, move him either to rage or pity, it may sufficiently instruct him, what deep Wounds his own vile Perjuries are dealing daily to his Partner."[74] Thus the moralist relied on the power of consanguineal ties to inculcate the new obligations of the conjugal.

In trying to find explanations for the concerns I find obsessively re-peated in fiction, my argument cuts across the grain of several disciplines, ignoring some of the insoluble controversies in those fields. I avoid being sidetracked by most of the debates about childrearing practices, patriarchal domination, or women's domestic power that have hitherto concerned such historians of the family as Lawrence Stone, Randolph Trumbach, and Linda

---

[72] *Ibid.*, p. 17.

[73] Jane Austen, *Emma* (1816), ed. Ronald Blythe (Harmondsworth: Penguin, 1966), p. 328.

[74] Willam Fleetwood, *The Relative Duties of Parents and Children, Husbands and Wives, Masters and Servants* (London, 1705), pp. 320–1.

Pollock. Although I am fascinated by Paula Marantz Cohen's observation that daughters are the family's safety valve – that it is the daughter whom the family tacitly agrees to sacrifice in order to maintain its emotional economy – I find the family systems theory framework of her study less useful to my understanding of wider kin functions.[75] Claude Levi-Strauss' formulation that kinship is created by the exchange of women, that the incest taboo is foundational in determining kinship by defining which women are available to reproduce with and which are not, is too limited to explain the cultural anxiety about kin relations that pervades the fiction of late eighteenth-century England.[76] It does not explain the meaning of kinship for the women represented blankly as the objects of exchange, nor for those who are (in this fiction) occasionally the agents of exchange. Moreover, it assumes that marriage creates kinship rather than, say, siblinghood.[77] As Annette Weiner observes, "his synthesis never departs from the traditional biogenetic assumption that defines kinship and society as the exchange of women's biologically ordained procreative roles."[78]

I rely chiefly upon these economic and social "facts": that in the period under consideration the population almost doubled, the available arable land for subsistence economies decreased, food prices rose, men and, to some extent, women entered the waged labor market, the age of first marriages dropped for both men and women, there was a rise in illegitimacy rates, and with the notable exception of a quarter of the daughters of the peerage, celibacy rates across classes fell drastically.[79]

The psychological and social dislocations that I am going to be exploring all ramify from the redefinition of kin relations from a consanguineal to a conjugal basis in the second half of the eighteenth century. This redefinition meant that families could be conceived of as constructed, even earned, rather than simply given by birth. The democratizing implications of this reconceptualization for men across classes (and in the peerage especially

[75] Paula Marantz Cohen, "Stabilizing the Family System at *Mansfield Park*," *ELH* 54, 3 (1987), 669–93.

[76] Gayle Rubin elaborated this formulation in a classic feminist article "The Traffic in Women: Notes on the 'Political Economy of Sex,'" in Rayna R. Reiter (ed.), *Towards an Anthropology of Women* (New York: Monthly Review Press, 1975), pp. 157–210.

[77] Defoe assumes this formulation in *Moll Flanders*, according to Ellen Pollak, representing Moll in an incestuous relationship that signifies her *refusal* to be an object of exchange. See her "*Moll Flanders*, Incest, and the Structure of Exchange," *The Eighteenth Century: Theory and Interpretation* 30, 1 (1989), 3–21. The anthropological theories regarding the exchange of women and the subject position of women in such systems of exchange are explored by J. Van Baal in *Reciprocity and the Position of Women* (Amsterdam: Van Gorcum, Assen, 1975), pp. 70–96.

[78] Annette B. Weiner, "Reassessing Reproduction in Social Theory," in Faye D. Ginsburg and Rayna Rapp (eds.), *Conceiving the New World Order* (Berkeley: University of California Press, 1995), pp. 407–24, quote p. 413.

[79] Susan Staves, *Married Women's Separate Property*, pp. 210–17.

for younger sons) were profound. Cut loose from rigid responsibilities to lineage descent groups, men began to make their own way economically. The state provided many avenues for them to make their fortunes, such as the East India Company, the clergy, the navy, or the army. Law and business also provided lucrative opportunities. Increasingly their gendered roles were assimilated to ideas about production, including making the children that would constitute their kin. More men in this period began to exercise domestic power as husbands and fathers of immature children than as members of lineage descent groups sharing responsibility for more extended kin groups.[80]

For women, the shift was somewhat more complex. The transfer at marriage of their subordination from fathers to husbands, the movement from father patriarchy to husband patriarchy, the weakening of their ties with their brothers, and the increasingly child-centered nature of the family, probably resulted in a net loss of social power for women. Women lost power as sisters and daughters and gained it as wives and mothers. The strengthening of conjugal bonds and the weakening of ties of filiation – in combination with enhanced emphasis on primogeniture in inheritance – reduced the responsibility of parents for their daughters (and feminized younger sons). The relative significance of maternal kin dwindled as wealth was concentrated in the male line; their claims on the resources of the larger kin group became seriously attenuated. Politicians and pop sociologists who glorify "family values" ought to take notice that the ideological system they admire so single-mindedly is a relatively recent – new in the eighteenth century – corruption of the earlier bilateral cognatic kinship system which had traced lineage through both the mother and the father, distorted towards patrilineal inheritance in the interest of accumulating property, overlaid with a healthy dose of individualistic profit motive.[81]

The development of an increasingly centralized national state is also key to the changed forms and emphases of kinship during this period – not least because state policies tended to reinforce testamentary law over common law, recognizing alienable property rights before use rights and the rights

---

[80] For an excellent study of literary evidence for the sentimental construction of masculinity in these roles, see Shawn Lisa Maurer, *Proposing Men: Dialectics of Gender and Class in the Eighteenth-Century English Periodical* (Stanford: Stanford University Press, 1998).

[81] Edmund Leach, "Complementary Filiation and Bilateral Kinship," in Jack Goody (ed.), *The Character of Kinship* (Cambridge: Cambridge University Press, 1973), pp. 53–8. Leach writes that the practice of marriage and the rules of inheritance among the property-owning sector in eighteenth-century England were "so contrived as to create notionally permanent property owning corporations which [were] conceived of as patrilineal descent groups even though, in detail, they [were] nothing of the sort" (53).

of marital kin before natal kin. State intervention in the regulation and validation of marriage, which created more stringent requirements for a legal marriage and hence inheritance, encouraged some forms of kin connections by creating the legal structure to protect them and undermined others by not protecting them. As Nancy Cott points out, marriage regulations "sculpt the body politic" by providing incentives for some kinds of marriage while discouraging others.[82] As the gap widened between those who controlled the means of production and those who worked for wages, critics of the Hardwicke Marriage Act complained that the policing of sexuality by the state, the regulation of marriage and legitimate reproduction, was being done to protect the rich and disadvantage the poor. The state also played a central role, as we will see, in centralizing ownership of land in the late eighteenth century, authorizing some 226 enclosure acts under George II and 3,554 enclosure acts under George III, permitting the enclosure of 5,686,400 acres.[83]

In many areas of life, the state replaced family functioning and appeared to insert itself in matters once handled by kin, such as poor relief. The nation state's extraction of surplus in the form of taxes to pay for colonial wars was at the expense of family incomes. Similarly, taking male kin from their families as soldiers for these wars, and exchanging nationalism for family loyalty, created a substitute family in the militarized state. In many ways, national identity became a male identity, reinforcing patrilineal rather than bilateral lineage identifications. State formation, in short, proceeded apace at the expense of family and extended (especially matrilineal) kin networks.

The legal restrictions on property ownership and the general assumption that it was a male right – together with an increasing dependence on waged labor which was also highly differentiated by gender – had the effect of defining women not by their class but by their gender. As women's (lower) earning power and their inability to own property and to control capital became more salient, they were increasingly defined by their capacity for sexual service and reproduction. As Keith Thomas noted long ago, "the value set on female chastity varied directly according to the extent to which it was considered that women's function was a purely sexual one."[84] In

---

[82] Nancy Cott, *Public Vows: A History of Marriage and the Nation* (Cambridge, MA: Harvard University Press, 2000), p. 5.

[83] W. Hasbach, *A History of the English Agricultural Labourer*, trans. Ruth Kenyon (London: P. S. King & Son, 1908), pp. 57–8.

[84] Keith Thomas, "The Double Standard," *Journal of the History of Ideas* 20, 2 (1959), 195–216; quote 213.

other words, an insistence on virginity is linked to women's specialization as sexual beings. The separation of sexuality from reproduction – the construing of women as private sexual partners rather than as co-producers of lineage – was another aspect of the shift from consanguinity to conjugality as a basis for kinship. With the cultural ideal of love-in-marriage and the ever-increasing commodification of sexuality, women lost power in their natal families although potentially they could regain it in their conjugal families. Finally, the strengthening of marriage as the foundational tie for kin relations meant that persons who remained outside marriage, especially widows or spinsters, experienced new levels of social isolation and impoverishment.[85] Because of my work on women and gender ideology in eighteenth-century culture, I am clearer about the meaning to women of the kinship shift I am trying to document here; the emphasis of this book falls on women's positions within the family.

The elaboration of print culture generally and the phenomenal spread of the novel in particular – a genre, as Michael McKeon has argued, that developed as an intervention at a time of epistemological and social crisis – also changed the nature of family relations.[86] As I hope to show, the new emphasis on the affective meaning of conjugality – as opposed to consanguinity – was fed by the narrative structure of the novel. One consequence of this emphasis was the sexualization of conjugal family ties – the married couple and their immature children – and the neutralizing of consanguineal ties. When Foucault observed that "since the eighteenth century the family has become an obligatory locus of affects, feelings, love," he meant the conjugal family, in which the sexuality of immature children was forged. For this reason, he concludes, "sexuality is 'incestuous' from the start."[87] These complicated emotional chords reverberate in the fiction of the period, particularly in sentimental and gothic novels.

Each of the chapters that follow describes a symptom of the kinship shift I propose here. I examine in turn the effects of that shift on fathers and daughters, brothers and sisters, the reconception of marriage, maternal power, household economics, and the interplay between highly emotional fictional forms, such as the gothic novel, and this new dispensation in family life. I have also devoted one chapter to the representation in fiction

---

[85] For a discussion of the treatment of single women in England in the eighteenth century, see Susan Lanser, "Singular Politics: The Rise of the British Nation and the Production of the Old Maid," in Judith M. Bennett and Amy M. Froide (eds.), *Singlewomen in the European Past, 1250–1800* (Philadelphia: University of Pennsylvania Press, 1999), pp. 297–323.

[86] Michael McKeon, *The Origins of the English Novel 1600–1740*, pp. 20–2.

[87] Michel Foucault, *The History of Sexuality*, trans. Robert Hurley, vol. 1: *An Introduction* (New York: Random House, 1978), p. 108.

of a major economic change – land division – both to show its effect on families in literature and to ask how historians have assessed its impact on family structure in the "real" world. Separately, each chapter is a little case study of a particular set of relationships as represented in eighteenth-century English fiction and, occasionally, life. Each of these relationships is part of a larger whole; none alone defines the shift I see occurring in family structure in eighteenth-century England. But together, I hope, they constitute compelling evidence of a significant overall transformation in English kinship.

I

The great disinheritance

From the beginning to end, then, landowner's legal history is much to be seen as the effort to overcome the common law rights of daughters.
Eileen Spring, *Law, Land, and Family*, p. 35.

The basic kinship structure both in England and in Kandyan Ceylon is unquestionably bilateral but, in both cases, in the property owning sections of society, devices were introduced which greatly restricted the possibility of a female heir who had male siblings from inheriting property in land. These devices were of various kinds and patterned in different ways: they included primogeniture, entailment, and dowry payments in cash and jewellery (rather than land).
Edmund Leach, "Complementary Filiation and Bilateral Kinship," p. 54.

Kinship societies are the only truly democratic societies on this planet; for women to share social power again, we must learn from them.
Christine Gailey, "Evolutionary Perspectives on Gender Hierarchy," p. 62.

The disinheritance in the title of this chapter refers to the psychological not to say legal disinheritance of daughters that I believe occurred in the eighteenth century as a result of the kinship shift I have been describing. Fictional treatments of the phenomenon vary widely. Clara Reeve's *The Old English Baron* (1777), like Frances Burney's *Evelina* (1778), is the wish-fulfillment story of initial disinheritance followed by legitimation and adoption. Samuel Richardson's *Clarissa* (1747–8), on the other hand, is more purely tragic about the psychological meaning of disinheritance. The relevant historical facts to read with this fiction are about changes in women's work and women's inheritance patterns. To my mind the historical account and the literary record reinforce each other as explanation and description of the meaning for unmarried women of this change in kinship.

Frances Burney's first, celebrated, young heroine, Evelina, denied by her father and raised by her grandfather's old tutor, Arthur Villars, exemplifies that existential state of disinheritedness that I want to examine in this chapter, a disinheritedness that is the condition of so many female protagonists of fiction in the second half of the eighteenth century. As Villars describes her situation to his old friend, Lady Howard, Evelina is the "child of a wealthy baronet, whose person she has never seen, whose character she has reason to abhor, and whose name she is forbidden to claim" (19).[1] This man, her father, long since burned his legal marriage certificate, disavowing his marriage with her mother. Evelina's mother died in childbirth, orphaning her daughter as she brought her into the world. Being without a family leaves Evelina no tenable social location since she has "too much beauty to escape notice" and "too much sensibility to be indifferent to it" but "too little wealth to be sought with propriety" by men of her own class (18). Quintessentially a disinherited daughter, she exists on the printed page as an exemplar of that condition. Nameless, she exclaims in her first letter to Villars from London "I cannot to you sign *Anville* [the name he has arbitraily assigned her], and what other name may I claim?" Her disinheritance defines her – until the very end of the novel – as much as her beauty, her sensibility, her cultivation, or her obedience. That condition creates her special difficulties and opportunities; it underlies at once her mystery and her promise.

All of Frances Burney's heroines, sooner or later, contend with disinheritance, and their plots repeatedly embarrass them with their lack of protection, resources, and family membership. The heroines of *Cecilia* (1782) and *The Wanderer* (1814), as well as *Evelina*, illustrate the excruciating difficulties for a woman without a family name. Other authors used the plot device as well. Charlotte Smith's *Emmeline* (1788), Mary Hays' *The Victim of Prejudice* (1799), Mary Robinson's *The Natural Daughter* (1799), and Elizabeth Helme's *Louisa, or the Cottage on the Moor* (1787) are just a few of the many novels, popular in their own day, featuring disinherited daughters who triumph in the end by proving that their births were legitimate after all. Usually the offspring of a love-match made secretly behind the backs of controlling, prideful, or venal parents and then tragically terminated by the death of one or both of the secretly married couple, the infant daughter is cast adrift in the world. But however the plot is managed and the heroine separated from her rightful name and place, the denouement always

---

[1] This and subsequent page numbers refer to the World's Classics edition. Fanny Burney, *Evelina or the History of a Young Lady's Entrance into the World*, ed. Edward and Lillian Bloom (Oxford: Oxford University Press, 1968).

involves an explanation that absolutely vindicates her rightful claim to title and (usually) property.

These literary formulas represented the probing of a relatively new problem in English society. Unlike many societies of the world, English society had always prized its daughters. Women had never been barred from inheriting even the English throne – as they had been in France, for example. The traditional bilateral cognatic kinship system that had been a hallmark of English society since the earliest times had been relatively symmetrical with respect to gender. Under this system, which traces lineage through both the maternal and paternal lines and makes no distinction between them, daughters inherited as well as sons, and widows had substantial property rights in their deceased husbands' estates. Daughters inherited property before collateral male relatives, and in landed families daughters were sometimes given land as their marriage portion.[2] According to Amy Louise Erickson, "ecclesiastical rules of inheritance in intestacy [i.e. dying without a will] followed Roman civil law, in so far as all children regardless of sex were entitled to equal portions of their parents' moveable goods. Similarly, the goods of unmarried people dying intestate were equally divided among all their siblings."[3]

But the drift of this bilateral, cognatic kin system to a lineage system defined predominantly through the marriage of first-born sons, a change that gathered momentum in the seventeenth century, had the consequence of disinheriting daughters. Visible signs of this consequence are everywhere in the literature of the period, in portraits of younger sisters victimized by the machinations of stepmothers, cousins, evil servants, self-serving siblings; images of educated and respectable women who find themselves, through no fault of their own, alone in the world without "friends" (that is to say, relatives or protectors); stories of orphans who turn out to be well-born after all and who, by the end of the novel, are miraculously reunited with their missing mothers, fathers, sisters, or brothers; stories of illegally diverted fortunes set right by indisputable documents long hidden in inherited caskets and then corroborated in the flesh by the minute testimony of ancient, loyal servants; and most dramatically in tearful tales of daughters long-separated from their fathers but recognized and lovingly claimed in the end because

[2] According to John Habakkuk, before the invention of the strict settlement, estates had often been settled in tail general, so that daughters inherited if there were no male issue of the marriage. He also reports that as late as the early seventeenth century women were still being given land as their marriage portion. *Marriage, Debt, and the Estates System: English Landownership 1650–1950* (Oxford: Clarendon Press, 1994), pp. 32, 117.

[3] Amy Louise Erickson, *Women and Property in Early Modern England* (New York and London: Routledge, 1993), p. 28.

of their uncanny resemblance to their dear departed mothers. These literary formulas, although not necessarily invented in the eighteenth century, took on a new life in the novels of the period and bear witness to a new, tragic displacement of daughters. In all of these familiar plots, daughters are somehow expelled from their families of origin at the beginning of the story but relocated again in time to claim their rightful names and fortunes. Sometimes the displaced heroine was even named "Stuart," the name of the exiled king whom Jacobites and romantics believed displaced from the English throne.[4] Justice invariably prevails in these fictions, and in the end the outcast daughters inherit what is due them and marry the men they love as fully endowed equals.

WOMEN SEPARATED FROM THEIR KIN

These textual enactments, whatever their complications, obsessively recur to the dispossession of daughters as the originating problem: that is the social disruption that needs to be resolved, the disquieting circumstance from which all subsequent adventures flow. Many critics have offered explanations of this focus on the isolated woman. Long ago, Myra Jehlen argued that the embattled heroine of the eighteenth-century novel represented the drama of the suppressed interior self, doomed in the newly alienated materialist public world.[5] My own earlier formulation was that unproductive and isolated women were ideal subjects to illustrate the pleasures and dangers of heightened and privatized consciousness represented by the new domain of novels.[6] Others have claimed that the lone woman best represented the new individualistic, self-made person; only her inner worth, not her family name or property, determined what she would become. Women were the first members of society to be judged on the basis of their own individual qualities of mind and heart rather than on the basis of their inherited class, status, or origins, asserts Nancy Armstrong: "the modern individual was first and foremost a woman."[7] This formulation implies that the ties of filiation that bind people to their families and

---

[4] This was the name of the heroine of Charlotte Lennox's *The Life of Harriot Stuart* (1751); it was also the real patronymic of D'Arcy Beaufoy, the heroine of *D'Arcy*, a novel by "Charlotte Smith" according to the title page (but clearly not written by the same person who wrote *The Old Manor House* or *Emmeline*) and published in Philadelphia in 1796.

[5] Myra Jehlen, "Archimedes and the Paradox of Feminist Criticism," *Signs* 6 (Summer 1981), 575–601.

[6] "Romantic Love and Sexual Fantasy in Epistolary Fiction," in my *Women, Letters, and the Novel* (New York: AMS Press, 1980), pp. 137–67.

[7] Nancy Armstrong, *Desire and Domestic Fiction: A Political History of the Novel* (New York and Oxford: Oxford University Press, 1987), p. 8.

communities were loosened first for women, with the result that women were the first beings conceptualized as atomized, free-standing, isolated individuals in the modern world. Susan Staves argues that the trope of the seduced maiden showed that society no longer considered daughters in terms of their status within families but rather as free-standing individuals.[8] Susan Greenfield argues that orphaned daughters in women's novels "resolve the problem of the mother's victimization and reputation" thus representing "authorship as a maternal preserve."[9] While all of these formulations have great heuristic value and are in some sense "true," I now think that this compulsively repeated plot premise – the dispossession of daughters – is a mythic recording of a banal and literal truth: shifts in the social and economic purposes of kinship over the previous half-century resulted in a reconception of the daughter's place in the family as temporary, partial, and burdensome.

Many novels, especially novels written by women, register this sense of protagonists being unfairly de-legitimated, of rightful inheritors having to make their way in the world without being recognized as such, incognito. One of the most elaborate versions of this narrative of lost identity, discovery, and validation is Clara Reeve's *The Old English Baron* (1777). Written by a woman who lived through the mid-century changes I am positing, the plot of re-legitimation is worked out through a male protagonist. Although set in the feudal past and involving male characters, the situations and forms of expressiveness in this novel are transparently from the female-centered sentimental novel of the day: the hero and his supporters blanch and blush and weep as often as they engage in manly exercise and swordplay. *The Old English Baron* features a virtuous youth whose pedigree is lost but who in the end proves his legitimacy and claims his rightful place in the family lineage.[10] That the displaced protagonist is male should not obscure the similarity of this plot to the dozens of others in which the protagonist must reclaim her rightful place in a family. The author's gender defines the shape of this story more than the gender of the particular character who is its vehicle.

[8] Susan Staves, "British Seduced Maidens," *Eighteenth-Century Studies* 14, 2 (Winter 1980–1), 109–34, esp. 122.

[9] Susan Greenfield, *Mothering Daughters: Novels and the Politics of Family Romance* (Detroit: Wayne State University Press, 2002), pp. 54–6.

[10] Clara Reeve, *The Old English Baron* (1777; Manchester: J. Gleave, 1821). All subsequent page references are to this edition. Ann Radcliffe's first novel, the anonymously published *The Castles of Athlin and Dunbayne: A Highland Story* (1789) is another gothic novel in which the hero (Alleyn) appears to be born to a peasant family but turns out to be highborn royalty and in the end comes into his rightful inheritance.

Edmund, the hero, apparently the son of a peasant but with accomplishments and bearing far above his station, discovers by supernatural means that he is the rightful heir to Castle Lovel. With the help of several father figures (an old servant, a priest, the knight Sir Philip Harclay – just returned from the Holy Land and a friend in his youth to Edmund's real father – and, finally, Baron Fitz-Owen, present occupant of the castle), Edmund proves his legitimacy and claims his inheritance. In the climactic scene in which Baron Fitz-Owen and Sir Philip Harclay acknowledge Edmund as the rightful heir – the two men to whom he most owes filial obedience – he throws himself at their feet and embraces their knees, unable to utter a word. When they raise him up, symbolically as well as literally, he faints in the arms of Sir Philip, "deprived of strength and almost of life" by the emotional strain (225). A hero with the sensibility of a woman, Edmund occupies a feminized position in this novel: patient and enduring when his class position requires it and supplicating rather than demanding, grateful rather than triumphant, when he receives undeniable proof of his real social position.[11]

Published in 1777 as *The Champion of Virtue* and reissued in 1778 under the new title *The Old English Baron*, the novel was announced by Reeve as the "literary offspring" (105) of Walpole's *Castle of Otranto* (1764).[12] But Reeve made very different use of her materials while imitating the gothic trappings and atmosphere of *Otranto*. Although her protagonist is, like Theodore in *Otranto*, a handsome peasant who carries his birthright in his visage and looks just like the noble ancestor's portrait on the wall, Reeve's hero Edmund does not want to destroy the present tenants of his noble family's castle, but to be acknowledged by them. Where Theodore, in *Otranto*, does generational battle to supplant the incestuous father, Edmund

---

[11] The sense that one is adopted, and was originally born to a higher sphere, is such a common fantasy that Freud named it the "family romance." He wrote about it in "Der Familienroman der neurotiker," which was first composed in 1908, published in Otto Rank's *Der Mythus von der Geburt des Helden* (1909), and translated into English in 1913. He believed that this fantasy was a response to a child's disillusionment with the father after some experience of the world, when the earliest belief in parental perfection dissolved. That is when the child begins to daydream about his "real parents," says Freud. It is the child's way of "getting free from parents of whom he now has a low opinion and of replacing them by others, who, as a rule, are of higher social standing. He will make use in this connection of any opportune coincidences from his actual experience, such as his becoming acquainted with the Lord of the Manor or some landed proprietor if he lives in the country or with some member of the aristocracy if he lives in town" (238–9). *The Standard Editions of the Complete Psychological Works of Sigmund Freud*, ed. and trans. James Strachey, 24 vols. (London: Hogarth Press, 1953–74), vol. IX, pp. 237–41. See also Chapter 9, n. 69 below.

[12] *The Old English Baron* was the most popular of Clara Reeve's novels. Published in 1777, it went into a second edition in 1778 and a third in 1780. It went through ten editions by 1800 and was translated into French and German. It was reprinted in the Ballantyne Novels collected by Sir Walter Scott.

above all desires emotional and legal acceptance by the father. The point in Reeve's novel is not to triumph over Baron Fitz-Owen and his sons, but to be acknowledged by them as legitimate; not to overturn established authority but to be welcomed by it. When Edmund returns to take possession of Castle Lovel, all the doors spring open of their own accord (216).

Indeed, the structural oddity of this novel is that the sequence of supernatural discovery is completed before the novel is half over and the entire second half is devoted to working out in legalistic detail the means by which Edmund can claim his place. Each step along the way is shored up in writing, so that he can clinch his case quietly and effectively without disrupting or displacing the rest of the noble family into which he is so unexpectedly inserted. Fathers and sons, real and symbolic, are compulsively reintroduced, recombined, and reunited with much shedding of tears. Pledges of obedience and protestations of eternal loyalty, made by servants to masters, sons to fathers and fathers to sons, brothers to brothers and cousins to cousins, are obsessively repeated, furnishing the emotionally dramatic events that are then guaranteed by the legalistic recording of Edmund's discoveries and reversals. This is no romance world in which revelation instantly changes rank and property ownership. The changes revealed by dreams and ghostly visitation must be bureaucratically registered; the interloper – he who profited from the foul murder – must make over his property to Edmund in writing with witnesses. Commissioners are appointed to investigate and document Edmund's alleged discoveries about his birth and the reader retraces with them the steps to visible proof: bloody armor, the aristocratic tokens found with the infant and mother, testimony of servants and adoptive parents. An account of all the evidence is drawn up, scrutinized, attested, and proclaimed: "There is no appearance of any fraud or collusion . . . if any man thinks he sees any, let him speak" (206). The money that has been collected in the years that Castle Lovel has been unlawfully held must be calculated and reimbursed. The purchase price, the yearly rents, the expenses of Edmund's education – all these are part of the functional solution that gets worked out. In addition to these financial adjustments, the estates and entourages of all the principals are sorted out and reassigned at the end of the novel – who will live where with whom – in an attempt to square worldly accounts with moral and social readjustments. Sir Philip and the baron discuss the best way to establish Edmund's legitimacy and decide to appeal to the king for a parliamentary writ.

Within the world of Reeve's novel, female lineage is portrayed as competing with – and disruptive of – male lineage. For example, the villainous relatives who try to discredit and even kill Edmund are the baron's maternal nephews, his sister's sons. When Sir Philip Harclay, Edmund's protector, introduces him into society as his adopted son while working out his strategy to regain Edmund's proper patrimony, he gives Edmund the temporary name of Seagrave, a name borrowed from Sir Philip's mother's family. Actual female relatives in the novel, on the other hand, have no functional role beyond cementing the entitlements of the male line. Daughters are deployed by their fathers to ratify alliances by marriage. The endogamous first-cousin marriage that integrates Edmund's line with Baron Fitz-Owen's and places him at the head of a strengthened patrilineage is welcomed on the last page of the novel as "the band of love that unites all my children to me, and to each other" (235).

The mixture of conventions in this novel, which begins as gothic romance and ends with the realistic working through of the legal consequences of Edmund's recovered identity, might be read as the narrative of one kind of family dissolving into another. Edmund's champions begin by vowing fealty to him, but by the end of the novel they are calculating damages, witnessing testamentary documents, and appealing to the government for bureaucratic writs. Although bodily evidence is important in the narrative – such as the fact that Edmund looks just like Sir Arthur Lovel's youthful portrait or that a skeleton tied neck to heels is discovered locked in a trunk where the evil Sir Walter Lovel confessed to burying it – such bodily evidence coexists with equally important testamentary evidence, such as statements made separately by two witnesses and then corroboratively compared (this happens no less than five times), or written statements prepared and signed for legal filing.[13] Evidence of the senses must be validated by written documentation if it is to have the weight of truth; it is legal language that makes things real. As Edmund says in another context: "words are all my inheritance" (123).

This preference for written proof, good even at long distance and valuable in any context, more durable than custom or memory, goes with the emphasis in this novel on the equal viability of adoptive families with blood or consanguineal families. All of Edmund's fathers are adoptive fathers, because both his biological parents are dead. The last of his line, Edmund inspires family-like loyalty in others, voluntary bonds of love and obligation that are as powerful as those given by birth. Nonetheless, the cross-cousin marriages that tie up the novel with its final bow at the end ratify these chosen and voluntary relationships with a blood bond and naturalize in

[13] Alexander Welsh emphasizes this dependence on evidence in much eighteenth-century fiction in *Strong Representations: Narrative and Circumstantial Evidence in England* (Baltimore and London: Johns Hopkins University Press, 1992).

biology what had been socially constructed. Thus the created family and
the biologically given family dissolve back and forth into one another in
this novel, each with its own appeal, neither sufficient to the requirements
of narrative, together satisfying a need in the readership to see both kinds
of family configuration in play. The suppressed biological relationship in-
stigates the action, asserting itself with the aid of the supernatural and
offering family revenge and restitution as a primal motive. But this motive
is soon supplemented by connections based on affinity, loyalty to merit, to
character, to intrinsic quality – all of which are made fully equivalent to
blood relationships sooner or later by legal means. Thus the feudal coexists
with the bureaucratic in this oddly mixed tale of birth and merit. Written
by a conservative woman who believed in class and racial determinants
of social status, but who, as a woman, objected to gender prejudice, this
novel simultaneously dramatizes the wish-fulfillment fantasy of the wrong-
fully disinherited child who eventually takes his (her) rightful place while
it reinscribes and naturalizes the entitlements of class.[14]

WOMEN'S PROPERTY RIGHTS

The disinheritance illustrated by this novel of the 1770s did not, of course,
happen overnight. It had been building slowly for several centuries, with
the erosion of provisions for daughters (and wives and widows) in equity,
manorial, and ecclesiastical as well as common law. Amy Louise Erickson
has argued that British historians' emphasis on common law, with its pri-
mogenitary emphasis, to the exclusion of three other forms of law – on
just this one dimension of a triadic legal system – is anachronistic and
often results in a misapprehension of Englishwomen's entitlements in earlier centuries. Women's property rights were often better protected under
equity, chancery, and ecclesiastical law, she claims, than under common

---

[14] This belief in hierarchies of race and class but not gender is visible in Reeve's *Plans of Education*
(London, 1792). There she asserts that the abolition of slavery in the West Indies is quixotic, and
she denies the cruelty of English slaveowners: "Englishmen were never reckoned cruel, though there
may have been some instances of it, as there have of the most exalted virtues in the negro race; but
these do not characterize a whole nation" (81). Later in this epistolary fiction, she ascribes racist
ideas to the more or less admirable Lord A—, who believes in maintaining hierarchy and "due
subordination of rank," because "in their different degrees and occupations men are most useful to
each other, and that the result is the harmony of the whole" (89). Lord A— opposes miscegenation,
which, he says, is bound to produce "a vile mongrel race of people, such as no friend to Britain can
ever wish to inhabit it," and suggests as a remedy that all "negroes" be banished from Britain (91).
After asserting the inferiority of "negroes," this spokesman (who is nowhere refuted) goes on to say
"If we have known an Ignatius Sancho, and a Phillis Wheatley, they are exceptions to the general
rules of judgment, and may be compared with a Bacon and a Milton, among the most civilized and
refined of the race of Europeans" (92). At the same time, this text defends women's right to live
alone, to improve their (equal) minds, and to support themselves by working (119–23, 138–9, etc.).

law. Common law did not recognize contracts made by a woman before marriage, for example.[15] Hence, familiarity with only this body of case law misrepresents the entitlements that were being chipped away.[16] Under provisions in ecclesiastical law, for example, a family's land descended to daughters in the event that there were no sons even in preference to collateral male relatives; England had always had large landowners who were women. M. K. Ashby notes that in the village of Bledington, Gloucestershire in the early seventeenth century, daughters were "handsomely treated, in both fathers' and mothers' wills; their legacies are usually equal to their brothers' except where one of the latter is going to carry on the farm with his mother."[17] Sheila M. Cooper, reporting on a broad cross-section of wills in late seventeenth-century King's Lynn in Norfolk, observes that daughters inherited as well as sons – but that daughters were more likely to inherit money and household goods than land, unless there were no sons.[18]

By the late seventeenth and early eighteenth centuries, however, provisions in common law began limiting women's inheritance of land, and a series of statutes in ecclesiastical law reduced women's rights to reasonable parts from their husbands' or fathers' moveable goods from as much as two-thirds to one-third or less.[19] Partible inheritance, dividing land and goods among all the children equally, practiced in earlier centuries, was being discontinued.[20] Although the aldermen of London, as late as 1690, enforced this custom in the Court of Orphans despite legal alternatives of wills and prior bequests, and although partible inheritance did survive in

---

[15] John Habakkuk, *Marriage, Debt, and the Estates System*, p. 71.

[16] Amy Louise Erickson, "Common Law versus Common Practice: The Use of Marriage Settlements in Early Modern England," *Economic History Review*, 2nd ser., 43, 1 (1990), 21–39.

[17] M. K. Ashby, *The Changing English Village: A History of Bledington, Gloucestershire in Its Setting 1066–1914* (Kineton: Roundwood Press, 1974), p. 116. Ashby adds, "A Bledington girl of to-day who had to go back to some earlier era would not make a mistake in choosing Elizabeth's reign."

[18] Sheila M. Cooper, "Intergenerational Social Mobility in Late-Seventeenth and Early-Eighteenth-Century England," *Continuity and Change* 7, 3 (1992), 283–301. According to John Habakkuk, this difference in the provision for younger children – land for younger sons and lump sums of money for daughters – can be found in sixteenth-century wills as well. *Marriage, Debt, and the Estates System*, pp. 3–4.

[19] Amy Erickson, *Women and Property in Early Modern England*, pp. 28–9.

[20] In Jane Austen's first edition of *Sense and Sensibility*, in describing the path of inheritance of Norwood in the first chapter, she wrote "but to his son, and his son's son, a child of four years old, it was secured, in such a way as to leave to himself no power of providing for those who were most dear to him, and who most needed a provision, by any division of the estate, or by any sale of its valuable woods." In the second edition she changed "by any division of the estate" to "by any charge on the estate," a change which her brother Henry may have suggested as more legally correct. The implication is that Austen apparently imagined that women could inherit land, and that estates could be divided to provide for them – a misapprehension that Henry, or someone, caught and corrected after this novel was first published in 1811. See Ros Ballaster's notes on the changes between the first and second editions in her edition of *Sense and Sensibility* (London: Penguin, 1995), p. 327.

a few counties according to Richard Grassby, opposition to it "gathered momentum during the seventeenth century."[21]

Eileen Spring argues, following E. A. Wrigley's famous calculations, that the proportion of families who by chance have no heirs at all and only female collateral relatives, combined with those who have only female heirs, adds up to between 25% and 40% of all cases. If the earlier provisions of ecclesiastical and common law had been faithfully followed, these are the cases in which inherited property would have passed to women.[22] But, she argues, property owners who were heads of families had tampered with these rules of inheritance so as to reduce the number of inheritances going directly to women to less than 8%. For example, landowners in Kent and Wales secured legislation, the last of it in 1624, to substitute primogeniture for gavelkind inheritance, or equal division.[23] This was true even before the invention of the strict settlement in the last third of the seventeenth century. Using data collected by Lawrence and Jeanne Stone, and by Peter Laslett, Spring demonstrates how collateral male relatives – such as the brothers of a woman's father or even a nephew – were often placed in the inheritance line before the woman was, if there were no male offspring in a family.[24] This was done, presumably, to keep the property attached to the family name. Nevertheless, many thought that women should never inherit, even when arrangements were made to maintain the family name. Samuel Johnson, for example, affirmed "the dignity and propriety of male succession" when opposing the decision of a friend in 1773 to leave his property to his sisters rather than to a remote male heir. "An ancient estate

---

[21] Richard Grassby, *Kinship and Capitalism: Marriage, Family, and Business in the English-Speaking World, 1580–1740* (Cambridge: Cambridge University Press, and Wishington, DC: Woodrow Wilson Center Press, 2001), pp. 342–4.

[22] For Eileen Spring's discussion see her *Law, Land, and Family: Aristocratic Inheritance in England, 1300 to 1800* (Chapel Hill: University of North Carolina Press, 1993), pp. 10–15. She cites Wrigley to the effect that in a stationary population there is a 40% chance that a man will die without leaving a male heir. E. A. Wrigley, "Fertility Strategy for the Individual and the Group," in *Historical Studies of Changing Fertility*, ed. Charles Tilly (Princeton: Princeton University Press, 1978), pp. 150–1. Brian McCrea's *Impotent Fathers: Patriarchy and Demographic Crisis in the Eighteenth-Century Novel* (Newark: University of Delaware Press, and London: Associated University Presses, 1998) claims that the demographic crisis in the period 1650–1740, during which as many as 52% of English fathers died without male heirs, accounts for the fatherless state of heroines in the fiction of this period. He argues that this crisis is reflected in fiction: "'Failure in the male line' is at the center of eighteenth-century fiction by men and women alike" (18). The data for his assertion comes largely from Lawrence and Jeanne C. Fawtier Stone, *An Open Elite? England 1540–1880* (Oxford: Clarendon Press, 1984), pp. 141–84.

[23] John Habakkuk, *Marriage, Debt, and the Estates System*, pp. 7–8.

[24] Although Lawrence and J. C. F. Stone conclude in *An Open Elite?* that the percentage of English heiresses rose to a high of 17% in 1760–79, Eileen Spring points out that given equal numbers of female and male offspring, 33% of the women should have inherited directly from their fathers in families in which there was no son. She concludes that the Stones' figures "tell a decided story of the reduction of female inheritance." Eileen Spring, *Law, Land, and Family*, pp. 14–15.

should always go to males," Johnson argued. "It is mighty foolish to let a stranger have it because he marries your daughter, and takes your name."[25]

The legal document known as the strict settlement codified these asymmetrical arrangements.[26] Drawn up as part of a marriage contract, the strict settlement designated provisions for the as yet unborn children of the coming union, insuring that the property jointly owned by the new couple would be entailed on any males born to the line.[27] The full value of the property to be entailed on male offspring could be further enhanced by limiting the monetary share set aside from it for possible female children. Estates were thus protected against future owners who might have a change of heart about dynastic aggrandizement and leave the family property instead to an adored daughter. Women's hereditary rights in property were thus inexorably made secondary to the imperative for accumulation – "engrossing" was the eighteenth-century word – in large landowning families.

Aristocratic women's portions, in the literal meaning of that proportion of the parental estate designated for them when their parents died, had been steadily shrinking over the course of the seventeenth century. Although land prices were rising and the real income from land rents increasing, smaller and smaller proportions of the overall estate were assigned to daughters so as to reduce as little as possible the estate designated for the males in the family – including collateral males outside the nuclear unit such as uncles or nephews.[28] As Naomi Tadmor has observed, "In this system females may be said to be more valuable as wives than as daughters, because as wives they

---

[25] James Boswell, *The Life of Samuel Johnson*, 2 vols. (London: Dent, 1973), vol. 1, p. 487. Entry dated May 8, 1773.

[26] Lloyd Bonfield has argued that the strict settlement was not simply a legal device intended to concentrate landed wealth in the hands of the male heir, although it often functioned that way. It was a legal device that conceded alienability of the estate to the next generation and at the same time provided for the portions of female offspring and younger sons to be paid from the estate. Lloyd Bonfield, "Affective Families, Open Elites and Strict Family Settlements in Early Modern England," *Economic History Review*, 2nd ser., 39, 3 (1986), 341–54.

[27] These devices tied up the property for two successive life tenancies (the father's and the eldest son's), until the as yet unborn eldest son of the couple about to marry reached his majority. Habakkuk explains the evolution of this legal device during the Interregnum as a means of preserving royalist family estates from confiscation for unborn generations even if individual landowners were fined or ruined. Although common law had previously favored the free alienability of land (because of the Crown's revenue from transfers and because free alienability promoted "industry, trade, arms and study"), the insecurity of property during the civil war and again in the era leading up to 1688 led many landowners to try to secure their estates for future generations with this legal device. *Marriage, Debt, and the Estates System*, pp. 12–13, 18–19. He also notes that the strict settlement was one of several means the landed classes used to reinforce their privilege after the Interregnum, the Game Law of 1661 and the Poor Law of 1662 being further examples. *Ibid.*, p. 58.

[28] Eileen Spring, *Law, Land, and Family*, pp. 149–59. The absolute size of the lump sums given to aristocratic women as dowry grew in the course of the century although not proportionally to the way estates overall grew. See pp. 53–4 below for an explanation of this dowry inflation and its meaning.

bring property into a family whereas as daughters they have a share in the estate" – however diminished a share – and hence reduce what is passed on to successive generations.[29] Sometimes daughters' portions were omitted entirely from the marriage settlement of an eldest son. Habakkuk notes that "the marriage settlement of the second Lord Gower did not contain powers to provide for younger children or make a jointure in the case of a second marriage, a not uncommon omission in the first half of the century."[30] He also observes that "one of the most interesting of Bonfield's conclusions is that many of the settlements he has examined for the late seventeenth and early eighteenth centuries did not provide for the raising of portions [i.e. from the estate] for daughters."[31] With the shift away from consanguinity, the daughter's significance as the carrier of a particular bloodline became less important than her instrumental value to her new family of destination in aggrandizing their ambition or reproducing their lineage. An autobiographical account (probably fictional) by John Gunning published at the end of the century, listing his affairs with 145 women and cataloguing his progeny – which were "almost as numerous as my conquests" – expressly omits all mention of female progeny as irrelevant to his list of descendants.[32]

In light of this change in the status of daughters, it is probably more accurate to reinterpret the so-called courtship plots of this period as being about homelessness and negotiation for an establishment rather than about disinterested love. Like newly fledged birds forced from their nests, young women in this period had no place in their families of origin but had to seek new homes elsewhere. As Mr. B. explains in *Pamela*, "A man ennobles the woman he takes, be she *who* she will; and adopts her into his own rank, be it *what* it will."[33] Every woman is intrinsically orphaned, he implies, lacking social identity until she is "adopted" by a husband and brought into his family.[34]

---

[29] Naomi Tadmor, "Dimensions of Inequality among Siblings in Eighteenth-Century English Novels: The Cases of *Clarissa* and *The History of Miss Betsy Thoughtless*," *Continuity and Change* 7, 3 (1992), 303–33; esp. 311.

[30] John Habakkuk, *Marriage, Debt, and the Estates System*, p. 17.

[31] Habakkuk contines: "Moreover, those that did provide for the raising of portions most commonly 'postponed them to the estates limited in remainder to the sons of the marriage'. The daughters received nothing unless the male issue failed. Moreover, the amounts they were to receive were often not specified." *Ibid.*, p. 15.

[32] *An Apology for the Life of Major General G—* (London, 1792), pp. 30–2.

[33] Samuel Richardson, *Pamela* (1741), ed. Peter Sabor and with an Introduction by Margaret A. Doody (Harmondsworth: Penguin, 1980), p. 441.

[34] This observation is from Maaja Stewart, *Domestic Realities and Imperial Fictions* (Athens: University of Georgia Press, 1993), p. 163.

I have been suggesting that in the movement from a consanguineal to a conjugal kinship system women's power no longer came from their relations as daughters or sisters but from their positions as wives and mothers. Obviously, women have always been all these things, and there have always been exceptional individual cases. But I am claiming that, in the period under examination, women came to have more power in their new conjugal families than in their families of origin, and that their autonomy may have been more limited as wives and mothers than it had been as sisters and daughters. It must also be said that the narratives that I discuss on these pages helped to consolidate the shift I am describing, by lamenting it. By showing what was lost, or imagining the loss retrieved, these narratives confirmed the new conjugal paradigm of kinship.

It is important to remember that there is nothing universal about basing a woman's identity on her conjugal family unit. In some cultures, age mates – across families – confer social identity. In others, the relative importance of one's lineage – the age and permanence of one's family name and the honor attached to it – far outweighs whatever family one marries into. In certain African tribes, for instance, daughters of important men carry that distinction with them throughout their lives; no accident, however disastrous, can erase that honor. Although in England the importance of daughters as carriers of the blood lineage of a great family could not be denied, and a woman's class position was remembered whenever she was in danger of making an unsuitable marriage, her sexual definition was becoming more significant to her identity than her membership in any particular family. Gender had overtaken class as a determinant of personal identity for women.[35] As Johnson so clearly understood, willing property to a daughter meant letting it go out of the family.

Jack Goody has argued that a daughter's dowry is comparable to a son's inheritance, given at the time of her marriage rather than at her father's death. Taken together they illustrate what he calls "diverging devolution" or the transmission of property from parents to male and female offspring.[36] But kinship theorists, notably Wally Seccombe and Diana Hughes, have pointed out that when viewed from the perspective of several centuries, "far from being a daughter's simple or natural inheritance claim in a system

[35] I make this claim in *The Celebrated Mary Astell: An Early English Feminist* (Chicago: University of Chicago Press, 1986), pp. 104–5. The history of the word "spinster" reveals the chronology of these changes: originally the term for professional women spinners, with no derogatory connotations, by the late seventeenth century it meant an unmarried woman of whatever class.

[36] Jack Goody, *The Development of the Family and Marriage in Europe* (Cambridge and New York: Cambridge University Press, 1983), appendix 2: "From Brideprice to Dowry?" pp. 240–61.

of bilateral descent, as Goody has suggested, the medieval Mediterranean dowry rose to prominence as a form of disinheritance within a social group whose organization had become significantly *less* bilateral."[37] Hughes argues that the German *morgengabe*, or morning gift, the husband's gift to his bride, is a vestigial remnant of indirect dowry, a custom associated with the earlier practice of true bilateral descent, in which the landed bride was welcomed by gifts from the groom's family. Indirect dowry, that is, property from the husband's family given to the bride at marriage, included dower, which was a wife's clear right to one-third of her husband's property if he should predecease her. Direct dowry, or the payment given by the bride's father to the groom or groom's family, with its attendant substitution of jointure for dower (see Introduction, pp. 19, 27–8), was a late development that undercut the earlier concept of purchase by the groom's family of a bride with all her assets, and substituted instead a kind of quitclaim payment by the bride's family. As Hughes explains it, "Dowry flourished to drive out other marital assigns where men used their rights over women of their lineage, particularly their daughters, as a way of asserting status or competing for it."[38] Rather than being a premature form of inheritance, as Goody claimed, dowry became the mechanism by which a woman relinquished all further claims to her family's resources. It signaled a severing of the connection to her family of origin, not a reconfirmation of it.

The truth of this formulation is attested to by the extent to which a woman's dowry was actually hers to enjoy whether or not she married at all. In some cases – both in life and in fiction – daughters did inherit their portions when they reached twenty-one and not merely when they married. But, as Susan Staves has demonstrated, this portion was increasingly left to daughters in the form of trusts – that is, they did not have direct access to the capital themselves – and was often not paid at all if the estate's income was heavily burdened by the expenditures of sons or fathers.[39] This was frequently true in novels as well. More often a woman's portion was paid when she married, and in effect given to her husband. The psychological effect of this was a perception that the daughter was being endowed in order to get her off her parents' hands, rather than that she was inheriting her due share of the family estate. After the early part of the century, courts

---

[37] Diana Owen Hughes, "From Brideprice to Dowry," *Journal of Family History* 3 (Fall 1978), 262–96, quote 290; see also Wally Seccombe, *A Millennium of Family Change: Feudalism to Capitalism in Northwestern Europe* (London and New York: Verso, 1992), pp. 62–5.

[38] Diana Owen Hughes, "From Brideprice to Dowry," 290.

[39] Susan Staves, *Married Women's Separate Property in England, 1660–1833* (Cambridge, MA: Harvard University Press, 1990), pp. 27–55, esp. pp. 42–3.

often even deferred the necessity for raising daughters' portions during the
lifetime of the father so as not to compel the sale or mortgage of any part of
the estate. According to Habakkuk, the last legal judgment clearly "on the
side of children and the early payment of their portions" was in 1710. After
that, fathers were rarely compelled legally to sell or mortgage reversions so as
to raise portions – ostensibly to prevent the disobedience or rash marriages
of daughters that could result from too much early independence.[40] In the
fiction of the period, hard-hearted and selfish relatives welcomed suitors
who were willing to take a woman without her dowry.[41]

The substitution of jointure for dower and the steady diminution in the
ratio of jointure granted relative to dowry is another material manifestation
of the disinheritance of daughters. Jointure provisions, however generous,
were generally less than the third of the estate which was a widow's dower
right by common law. (Although variable, jointure usually ran to about
20 percent of the gross income of an estate.[42]) Jointure terms had to be
written into a marriage settlement if they were to bar a woman's right to
dower, and the general acquiescence to jointure provisions can be seen as
the abridgment of the daughter's invariable right in law by a private contract
signed by her own father.[43] The ratio of jointure to dowry dropped from
about one to six in 1600 to one to ten in 1700. In other words, heiresses had
to bring ten times as much property to their new conjugal estates by the
beginning of the eighteenth century as they would receive as annual income
should their husbands die before them. H. J. Habakkuk, who first observed
this change in 1950, interpreted it as meaning that the growth of large estates brought with it competition among heiresses for husbands.[44] He has
since argued that a fall in the rate of interest over the course of the seventeenth century meant that more capital outlay was necessary to guarantee
a certain income.[45] These explanations are not mutually excluding: the
effect of dowry inflation would be to increase the financial competition
among heiresses for husbands. Moreover, to argue that heiresses needed

[40] John Habakkuk, *Marriage, Debt, and the Estates System*, p. 123.
[41] Solmes in Samuel Richardson's *Clarissa* (1747–8) and Mr. Foxchace in Anne Dawe's *The Younger Sister* (1770) are examples of crude suitors encouraged by greedy relatives. "The Cruel Father," in volume IV of Eliza Haywood's *The Female Spectator* (London, 1744–6), also tells of a parsimonious father who insists that his daughter marry a suitor who requires no dowry with her hand. Book 10, pp. 98–112.
[42] John Habakkuk, *Marriage, Debt, and the Estates System*, pp. 84–6.
[43] Susan Staves, "Equitable Jointure," in her *Married Women's Separate Property in England, 1660–1833*, pp. 95–130.
[44] H. J. Habakkuk, "Marriage Settlements in the Eighteenth Century," *Transactions of the Royal Historical Society*, 4th ser., 32 (1950), 15–30.
[45] John Habakkuk, *Marriage, Debt, and the Estates System*, pp. 128, 232.

larger dowries to guarantee the same jointure income implies that their maintenance in their husband's households, if widowed, depended on the property they brought with them rather than on their husbands' wealth.

Lawrence Stone also observed that the size of dowries rose in the seventeenth century, but rather than interpreting it relative to jointure size as a decline in women's bargaining power, he reads it as a sign of greater equality within the family and warmer affective feelings on the part of fathers for all their children, including daughters.[46] Neither historian notes that jointure substituted for the much more substantial right of dower and neither compares the size of the dowry contribution to what the groom contributed to the conjugal estate. Husbands, of course, under the doctrine of "feme covert," had immediate access upon marriage to the whole of a woman's dowry property, and many a villainous husband in fiction, having run through that, tried to "kiss or kick" his wife into signing over her jointure property as well. Despite Habakkuk's thesis about heiress-hunting aristocrats forcing up the size of dowries, the heroes of novels never married women wealthier than they (unless her disapproving parents disinherited her), but always managed to inherit fortunes themselves in the nick of time to marry the woman of their dreams while preserving their gendered superiority as to net worth.

If proportions of familial property designated for the use or control of female offspring declined in the nobility and their inheritance of title postponed (as the legal phrase goes), middle-class daughters were also deployed in the service of their families – either to enrich or to ennoble them.[47] The novels of the second half of the eighteenth century abound with examples of young women thus used by their families. Indeed, it is difficult to think of a single novel in which no woman is pressured to marry against her will – or not to marry where she wishes to – because of some family exigency that creates an unresolvable dilemma between duty and desire. Even if this standard fictional situation did not reflect a social reality, it

---

[46] Lawrence Stone, *The Crisis of the Aristocracy, 1558–1641* (Oxford: Clarendon Press, 1965), pp. 643–5; *The Family, Sex, and Marriage in England 1500–1800* (New York: Harper and Row, 1977), pp. 243–4; "Family History in the 1980s: Past Achievements and Future Trends," *Journal of Interdisciplinary History* 12, 1 (Summer 1981), 51–87.

[47] Applying family systems theory to familial arrangements in nineteenth-century novels, Paula Marantz Cohen argues that the daughter functioned as the homeostatic mechanism regulating, stabilizing, and perpetuating the family in nineteenth-century society. "It is my contention that this cross-sexual, cross-generational relationship of father and daughter functioned as the core of the nuclear family," she writes. She argues that this alliance gave daughters power, however, whereas I am arguing that it was the daughter's powerlessness that forced her to be whatever the family required her to be. Paula Marantz Cohen, *The Daughter's Dilemma: Family Process and the Nineteenth-Century Domestic Novel* (Ann Arbor: University of Michigan Press, 1991), p. 22.

conditioned the oppositional terms in which marriage choice and inheritance were commonly considered: daughters were not expected to share equally in the resources of their families of origin despite the legal foundation for them to do so. These novel plots tested love (with the sacrifice of inheritance) and obedience (with the sacrifice of love) rather than the legal rights of daughters in their families of origin.

Margaret Hunt has observed that a number of charities developed in the eighteenth century for middle-class widows who would otherwise have been destitute when their husbands died. Provision for widows in the form of jointures was less common in this merchant or petty business class than among the gentry, because they could not afford to tie up their capital in land. Dower rights were also irrelevant in this class "because so many men left estates heavily encumbered by debt."[48] But because a man *was* his wife's family, if he predeceased her, no one was responsible for her; she was in some sense "orphaned" by his death. No support could be counted on from her extended family – whether her family of origin or her husband's family. Some collective solutions therefore evolved for such familyless women: life insurance policies, pensions, funds collected for the purpose by certain occupational groups – such as the Corporation of the Sons of the Clergy (chartered 1678), a charity for widows and orphans of clergy of the Church of England. These corporate and impersonal means supplied what a woman's own consanguineal kin might have supplied in earlier times.[49]

THE VALUE OF WOMEN'S WORK

Although there was less material wealth involved, the disinheritance of daughters can be seen in the lower classes as well as in the middle and upper strata. In the rural laboring class or servant class, the position of daughters altered too, so far as I can determine, although chronologically it happened a little later. The parliamentary enclosure acts of the second half of the eighteenth century, the transformation of agriculture, the mechanization of spinning, and the reorganization (and masculinization) of the dairy industry decreased the economic value of young women to their

---

[48] Margaret R. Hunt, *The Middling Sort: Commerce, Gender, and the Family in England, 1680–1780* (Berkeley: University of California Press, 1996), p. 165. Habakkuk makes this point as well: that merchants and professionals made wills that distributed their goods, money, and paper assets rather than settlements arranging for the inheritance of land. *Marriage, Debt, and the Estates System*, p. 4.

[49] Margaret Hunt, "The Bonds of Matrimony and the Spirit of Capitalism," in her *The Middling Sort*, especially pp. 164–6.

families.[50] By the 1770s, the subsistence peasant economy in England was pretty well at an end.[51] Feudal tenures had been put on a cash rent basis, and few laboring-class people could avoid the cash nexus, whether to sell their labor, their surplus produce, or their cottage manufactures. Such families were increasingly dependent on the money economy for their livelihood, and the women's sheer lack of possibilities for earning, not to mention the level of wages set for women in this new cash economy, reduced their economic value to their families and probably their psychological value as well. The centuries-old system of service-in-husbandry was falling into disuse, even in the laboring classes, further reducing the options for unmarried daughters (see Introduction). Service-in-husbandry had been an important part of the growing-up process. The young person in service boarding with his or her new patron family had received a small stipend for services in addition to room and board, and these arrangements offered young adult women a respectable although temporary alternative to marriage.[52] The discontinuance of this practice, a function of the rise in food prices and other subsistence costs which made it cheaper to hire seasonal day labor than to board so many servants, bore heavily on the daughters of cottagers, farmers, yeomen, and laboring-class families. It made them more of an economic burden on their families of origin and put a premium on getting married as a way of leaving their parents' establishment.

Debates about women's employment opportunities, and whether industrialism – or proto-industrialism – helped or hindered the status of women in the long run, are part of this story about the place of daughters in the family. So long as women could earn their own keep, whether living with their parents or on their own, there was less pressure on them to find husbands or for their parents to maintain them. There is evidence that the female labor market in the early part of the eighteenth century was varied and active both in urban centers and in the countryside. Peter Earle, analyzing the data on occupation for 2,000 women who appeared as witnesses in the London court records between 1695 and 1725, reports that 72 percent of these women worked for pay: as domestic servants, in the needle or cloth

---

[50] Deborah Valenze, *The First Industrial Woman* (New York and Oxford: Oxford University Press, 1995), Chapters 2, 3, 4, and 6.

[51] J. M. Neeson summarizes the arguments about the vestigial existence of an English peasantry in *Commoners: Common Right, Enclosure and Social Change in England, 1700–1820* (Cambridge: Cambridge University Press, 1993), pp. 4–14.

[52] Ann Kussmaul estimated that half the youth of England had the experience of service-in-husbandry. *Servants in Husbandry in Early Modern England* (Cambridge: Cambridge University Press, 1981), pp. 3–5; see also R. Schofield, "Age-Specific Mobility in an Eighteenth-Century Rural English Parish," *Annales de Demographie Historique* (1970), 261–74.

trades, in petty sales, in victualling – the preparation and sale of food and drink – and in personal services such as laundering, nursing, or midwifery.[53] They were silk-winders and linen and woolen drapers, mantua-makers or dressmakers, staymakers, cap-makers, glovers, periwig-makers, milliners, innkeepers, and grocers. Girls were apprenticed to a wide variety of trades in the early part of the century, many in the same trades as their fathers, with premiums the same as those of boys.

But in the course of the century these possibilities contracted. At least half the trades in which women worked became closed to girls and women and the number of female apprenticeships seriously diminished.[54] There was a shift towards apprenticing women exclusively in the lesser trades as time went on, in victualling or the service industries. In a study of five counties between 1710 and 1731, only 5 percent of the apprentices were women.[55] Only as daughters and widows, inheriting shops from deceased husbands or fathers, did women operate as independent entrepreneurs in the toy trades, as makers of buttons or buckles or watches, as brass manufacturers and braziers, and the like.[56] Women retailing corn, livestock, poultry, vegetables, and fruit in local markets were becoming a thing of the past.[57] In 1739, "a Lady" complained in the *Gentleman's Magazine* about the lack of employment opportunities for women without fortunes. In "a new Method for making Women as useful and as capable of maintaining themselves, as the Men are; and consequently preventing their becoming old Maids, or taking ill Courses," she recommended that Gentlemen and Tradesmen with several daughters apprentice them in the "genteel and easy Trades, such as Linnen or Woollen Drapers, Haberdashers of small Wares, Mercers, Glovers, Perfumers, Grocers, Confectioners, Retailers of Gold and Silver Lace, Buttons, &c" – especially if their dowries were so small as

---

[53] Peter Earle, "The Female Labour Market in London in the Late Seventeenth and Early Eighteenth Centuries," *Economic History Review*, 2nd ser., 42, 3 (1989), 328–53.

[54] K. D. M. Snell, *Annals of the Labouring Poor: Social Change and Agrarian England, 1660–1900* (Cambridge: Cambridge University Press, 1985), p. 331; Maxine Berg, "Women's Work, Mechanisation and the Early Phases of Industrialisation in England," in Patrick Joyce (ed.), *The Historical Meanings of Work* (Cambridge: Cambridge University Press, 1987), pp. 64–98.

[55] Richard Grassby, *Kinship and Capitalism*, pp. 313–35, esp. p. 316. Grassby notes that in addition to victualling and lodging, the textile trades and publishing, women could also be found occasionally in the metal trades. There were forty female working goldsmiths in London in 1697. He also notes that women held stock and voted in the Hudson's Bay Company, the Bank of England, and the East India Company; they were also sometimes silent partners in business. Still, when it was added up, women – mostly widows – only controlled 9 percent of the investment capital in England.

[56] Maxine Berg, "Women's work, Mechanisation and the Early Phases of Industrialisation in England," pp. 73, 86–7.

[57] Anthony Fletcher, *Gender, Sex and Subordination in England 1500–1800* (New Haven and London: Yale University Press, 1995), p. 246.

£200 or £300, the interest of which was inadequate to support a woman "genteelly."[58]

Where women worked in new industrialized trades, such as nail manufacture or glass-making, they made substantially lower wages than did men. Even as spinners, in which labor women predominated, they could earn merely one-third of a male day laborer's wage.[59] At mid-century, the mechanization of spinning – Lewis Paul's invention for making cotton thread and Richard Hargreaves' spinning jenny – began to supply the needed thread for weavers and ended even this low-paid form of women's labor.[60] A study of women's employment in Colyton, Devon, shows women as independent wage earners doing lacemaking, wool spinning, dairying, and fruit gathering in the seventeenth century, but notes that these opportunities declined in the course of the eighteenth century.[61]

Nevertheless, Maxine Berg argues that in the new industrial towns such as Birmingham and Sheffield a higher proportion of women owned real property and had substantial amounts of cash to bequeath to their children. In those metal-working centers, 22.8 percent (Birmingham) and 18.1 percent (Sheffield) of the women, nearly all of them spinsters or widows, left wills over the course of the eighteenth century. Men in these cities were also more likely to leave parcels of land and shops to their wives and daughters than in other parts of the country, presumably because there was a higher level of female participation in the metal trades than elsewhere. Women were also appointed executors in these towns more frequently than women in other areas of the country, a practice that was being discontinued elsewhere.[62]

In London, too, as Margaret Hunt has shown, there was significant evidence of middle-class women's independent economic activity in the number of women shopkeepers in London (more than 15,000 women shopkeepers operating between 1775 and 1785), the naturalization in the

---

[58] *Gentleman's Magazine*, vol. 9 (1739), 525–6.

[59] Eric Richards, "Women in the British Economy since about 1700: An Interpretation," *History* 59, 147 (October 1974), 337–57.

[60] Deborah Valenze reports that "In 1740, a Manchester merchant employing 5,000 spinners engaged the inventor Lewis Paul to develop a machine that would ease the inconvenience and expense of employing so many women." *The First Industrial Woman*, p. 72.

[61] Pamela Sharpe, "Literally Spinsters: A New Interpretation of Local Economy and Demography in Colyton in the Seventeenth and Eighteenth Centuries," *Economic History Review*, 2nd ser., 44, 1 (1991), 46–65. This article also makes the point that the decline in lacemaking corresponded to a decline in age of marriage for women, which contradicts Levine's theory that thriving cottage industry lowered the age of marriage. Sharpe suggests that when women were earning good money independently, they put off marriage. She also indicates that poor single women in the mid-eighteenth century often lived together.

[62] Maxine Berg, "Women's Property and the Industrial Revolution," *Journal of Interdisciplinary History* 24, 2 (Autumn 1993), 233–50.

course of the century of women's separate estate (property that was hers apart from her husband's), and in the number of women holding life insurance policies who lived on their own or with other women. "One sees here evidence of the first substantial body of independent, literate, and self-supporting women in English society," writes Hunt.[63] The opening up of authorship for women is another example of new economic opportunities for women in eighteenth-century England. Women's work tended to be labor intensive rather than capital intensive, Hunt observes.[64]

But the trend in the trade guilds was to exclude women and the growing prejudice against women in them deterred their activity. Maxine Berg reports that, although substantial numbers of women belonged to trade organizations earlier in the eighteenth century, they were increasingly pushed out of them over the course of the century. "In 1769 the Spitalfields silk weavers excluded women from higher paid work, and in 1779 journeymen bookbinders excluded women from their union. The Stockport Hatmakers' society in 1808 declared strikes against women in the trade, and the Cotton Spinners' Union in 1829 excluded women."[65] Widows were limited in the numbers of apprentices or journeymen they were allowed to take, and women were increasingly persecuted for trading without permission. Richard Grassby makes the point that the "ancient practice" of appointing wives as sole executors was increasingly discontinued as women were defined out of the world of business. More and more they were appointed executrix only until the heir came of age or were appointed co-executors with male relatives. He also notes that women rarely served as legal witnesses of wills.[66]

In the rural south and east, too, there was an unprecedented division of labor by sex between 1751–92, with new patterns of seasonal unemployment emerging for women. Women no longer worked at harvesting grain, as they had earlier in the century, or ploughing, threshing, following the harrow, or sheep-shearing.[67] They were hired instead at springtime, to pick stones, weed, plant, and glean, at wages that were significantly lower than men's money wages. One historian has argued that the introduction of the more efficient scythe for harvesting grain, a tool that required more upper-back strength than the sickle, accounts for the increasing exclusion of women

[63] Margaret Hunt, *The Middling Sort*, pp. 133, 158, 134.   [64] *Ibid.*, pp. 136–7.

[65] Maxine Berg, "Women's Work, Mechanisation and the Early Phases of Industrialisation in England," p. 73.

[66] Grassby shows that the percentage of surviving widows appointed sole executrix decreased between 1580 and 1740. *Kinship and Capitalism*, pp. 127–31.

[67] K. D. M. Snell, "Agricultural Seasonal Unemployment, the Standard of Living, and Women's Work in the South and East, 1690–1860," *Economic History Review*, 2nd ser., 34, 3 (1981), 407–37; 427.

from higher-paying harvest work.[68] But since this women-excluding employment pattern has historical parallels in this period in other trades and other kinds of work, this argument is probably only part of the story. Only in the west, where the growing specialization in pastoral agriculture entailed a large dairy industry, were women employed with the frequency and at the real wage rates that they had enjoyed in the early part of the century.[69]

The commercialization of the English economy, the growing proportion of the population dependent on waged labor for a livelihood, the rise in men's wages for day labor, and the decline in women's employment opportunities along with their lower wage rates – and the disappearance of a land base to support a non-waged subsistence – were factors that were accompanied by a sudden spurt of proto-industrial cottage industry among cottagers and small landowners in order to make their rent and pay their expenses. Proto-industrial manufacturing offered a temporary respite from the structural dependence of daughters on the resources of their laboring-class families. This kind of small, rural manufacture – weaving, spinning, gloving, straw-plaiting, lacemaking, leather-working, calico-printing, hand or framework knitting – thrived in many of the still unenclosed villages supported by arable agriculture.[70] These goods were being produced for non-local markets in domestic settings, by a range of family members, to supplement the family income. As E. J. Hobsbawm has observed, "the *obvious* way of industrial expansion in the eighteenth century was not to construct factories, but to extend the so-called domestic system."[71]

Women's labor within their families was key to this process of proto-industrialization. They created the subsistence on which this small-time manufacturing depended, tending a few animals such as chickens or cows that added protein to the family's diet, making butter and cheese for home consumption, spinning and weaving the family's linen, growing vegetables for home consumption in a kitchen garden, gathering fuel, cooking, washing, and the like. They also participated in the production itself, whether combing wool, dressing and spinning flax, weaving silk, or seaming and finishing the stocking or other garment produced by framework

---

[68] M. Roberts, "Sickles and Scythes: Women's Work and Men's Work at Harvest Time," *History Workshop Journal* 7 (1979), 3–28.

[69] K. D. M. Snell, "Agricultural Seasonal Unemployment," 421–2.

[70] Rab Houston and K. D. M. Snell, "Proto-Industrialization? Cottage Industry, Social Change, and Industrial Revolution," *Historical Journal* 27, 1–2 (1984), 473–92.

[71] E. J. Hobsbawm, *The Age of Revolution, 1789–1848* (New York: New American Library, 1964), p. 55, quoted in Eric Richards, "Women in the British Economy since about 1700," 345.

knitting.[72] Until the invention of the spinning jenny, it took several spinners' labor to supply the thread for a single weaver. Spinners were also hired directly by merchants or putters-out who provided the raw wool or cotton and delivered the finished thread to the clothier.[73] Handicrafts such as lacemaking and straw-plaiting were almost exclusively women's work. The labor of unmarried children was valuable at home, and daughters must have been welcome under the parental roof. The households of rural cottage workers at mid-century were significantly larger than farm workers' households, probably because grown children or collateral kin were useful to the older generation during this phase of mixed economies, sharing their subsistence base and contributing labor to the tasks of rural manufacture.[74]

When women left domestic manufacture and joined the waged workforce, their economic leverage within their families declined significantly. There was an enormous difference between income that supplemented a basic subsistence and income that was expected to buy all necessities, including housing. The mechanization of the textile industry, and the introduction of power looms and spinning jennies, did not at first force women out of these handicraft trades, but rather "set women against women, especially young women working in the shops or mills against older married women working at home."[75] During the brief period of proto-industrialization, when women combined subsistence agricultural labor with the tasks of cottage industry, their contribution to family income was varied and substantial. As Eric Richards stated, "the participation of women in the economy (though not necessarily as wage-labour *per se*) was substantially *greater* before the Industrial Revolution than during that process itself."[76]

It could even be argued that by providing the subsistence base for proto-industrialization, women's labor made possible the surplus – in the sense of capital accumulation and technological innovation – for the industrial

---

[72] Maxine Berg, "Women's Work, Mechanisation and the Early Phases of Industrialisation in England," pp. 71, 80.

[73] For an excellent overview of the vicissitudes of spinning for wages, see Deborah Valenze, "The Quarrel with Women's Work: Spinning and the Displacement of Female Labor," in her *The First Industrial Woman*, pp. 68–84.

[74] Richard Wall, "Mean Household-Size in England from Printed Sources," in P. Laslett and R. Wall (eds.), *Household and Family in Past Time* (Cambridge: Cambridge University Press, 1972), pp. 159–203 and Hans Medick, "The Proto-Industrial Family Economy: The Structural Function of Household and Family during the Transition from Peasant Society to Industrial Capitalism," *Social History* 1, 3 (October 1976), 291–315.

[75] Maxine Berg, "Women's Work, Mechanisation and the Early Phases of Industrialisation in England," p. 82.

[76] Eric Richards, "Women in the British Economy since about 1700," 342.

revolution. But as manufacturing was moved to workshops and factories, and labor increasingly timed and waged, women's work was paid at lower rates than men's work. The movement, for women, from piece work in a domestic setting combined with subsistence tasks such as milking the cow or tending the garden, to waged labor in shops and factories, was a movement from centrality in the family fortunes to marginality, pauperization, and dependence.[77] As Maxine Berg summarizes the sequence, "it was the mixed character of women's household, waged and community work whose purpose above all others was to ensure the subsistence of their families, which made women workers so vulnerable to exploitation, and their labour such a lucrative source of profit to capitalists."[78]

The contribution that laboring-class women made to the subsistence of their households, which supplemented the wages brought in by male farm workers and family income from handicrafts, depended upon access to the resources of commons – meaning marshes, fens, woods, meadows, and open fields. The parliamentary enclosures of the second half of the eighteenth century, in depriving women of these resources, simultaneously ended this phase of proto-industrialization, forcing a sizeable proportion of rural people off the land and into cities, and entirely reconfiguring the economic power of women's labor in society. Contrary to Engels' assumption, women's entry into waged labor was anything but equitable and triumphant: women's wages were only a half to two-thirds of what men could earn, and as real wages went down in relation to necessities in the final decades of the century it became increasingly difficult for a woman to survive without being part of a family unit. The pathetic story of Jemima in Mary Wollstonecraft's *Maria, or the Wrongs of Woman* (1798), trying to keep herself alive by fair means or foul, is a melodramatic version of the difficulty for a woman alone to earn her own subsistence. Juliet, the aristocratic heroine of Frances Burney's *The Wanderer* (1814), despite her education and accomplishments, equally showed how impossible it was for a woman of her class to support herself. Fiction is full of heroines who make desperate attempts to find employment as paid companions, governesses, schoolteachers, sempstresses, actresses, musicians, painters, or writers – but who, in the end, can only establish themselves by marrying well.[79]

---

[77] Bridget Hill makes this point in "The Undermining of the family Economy," in her *Women, Work, and Sexual Politics in Eighteenth-Century England* (Oxford: Basil Blackwell, 1989), pp. 47–68.

[78] Maxine Berg, "Women's Work, Mechanisation and the Early Phases of Industrialisation in England," p. 96.

[79] For fictional accounts of women looking for work, "fictions of employment," see Edward Copeland, *Women Writing about Money* (Cambridge: Cambridge University Press, 1995), pp. 159–212. Betty

The contribution rural women had made to family economies had varied with the natural resources of the local environment. In Surrey they gathered blueberries and whortleberries and made besom brooms from long heath for which they netted as much as 3s a week. Along the Lancashire coast, women gathered cockles and mussels; they grew hemp as a cash crop on common lands in Dorset. In Norfolk there was "watercress from running streams, rabbits, pigeons, wild raspberries, wild plums and blackberries, crabapples, hazel nuts, chestnuts, walnuts."[80] Women kept poultry and pigs, cows and sheep, for meat and eggs and milk as well as wool. They gleaned grain fields after harvest, collected fuel from fields and forests, and scavenged wild food to supplement their family's diet.

These expedients were worth a good deal to a family in real money – especially in comparison to what a woman could earn in wages. Ten sheep could be grazed for a year for sixpence in Westmoreland, and a cow was worth more than a man's annual half wages. Milk and butter or suckling calves produced as much as £9 2s for the year; the dung manured the kitchen garden or could be sold to a farmer for 15s a wagon load, and skim milk could be fed to pigs. So valuable were cows in providing subsistence when they had free commonage to pasture in that it was not uncommon for parish overseers to bestow a cow upon a single, poor woman as a way of maintaining her, like a kind of social security pension. Jane Humphries speculates, "The widow and her cow were probably as common in reality as they are in fairy tales."[81] Fuel, too, for both cooking and heating could be gathered from unenclosed waste lands and the ashes sold to neighboring farmers for fertilizer. The fuel for a town cottager with four rooms to heat and no access to waste lands cost more than £4 a year. With access to common and waste lands, rural workers burned wood or peat, pinecones, heather, broom, gorse, and dung, instead of having to earn that £4. Finally, gleaning – usually women's work – was worth as much as £3 or £4 in grain for a family's use. A woman's unwaged contribution to household subsistence was substantial, and compared favorably with what men's wages could buy. Especially in combination with cottage industry, women's subsistence

Rizzo's *Companions without Vows: Relationships among Eighteenth-Century British Women* (Athens: University of Georgia Press, 1994) is a wonderful account of the life and circumstances of female paid companions in life and literature in the eighteenth century.

80 Jane Humphries, "Enclosures, Common Rights, and Women: The Proletarianization of Families in the Late Eighteenth and Early Nineteenth Centuries," *Journal of Economic History* 50, 1 (March 1990), 17–142, quote 40.

81 Jane Humphries, "Enclosures, Common Rights, and Women," 38–9. The preceding information about the market value of the subsistence economies practiced by women in the eighteenth century also comes from this valuable article.

contributions made the difference between dependence on waged labor and independence. During the debates about enclosure, labor-hiring farmers grumbled that access to the commons made their laborers unreliable and complained that foraging promoted indolence and undermined work discipline. Laborers with livestock and gardens and the right to gather fuel and wild food were more independent of waged labor than laborers without access to land.[82] Not surprisingly, the greatest opposition to enclosure came from areas "where open fields and rural industry coincided," and women often played a leading role in these protests. In 1791 Arthur Young claimed that "the advantages of inclosing to every class of the people are now so well understood and combated at present but by a few old women."[83] Ten years later he changed his mind about the beneficial effects of enclosure on the rural poor, but by that time it was too late. Enclosure had proceeded very far by then, bringing in its train the decline of cottage industry.[84]

Thus one broad effect of the eighteenth-century enclosure movement was to curtail women's measurable contribution to the family economy, depriving laboring women of their traditional means of support and income, and making them more dependent upon the wages of men.[85] While the drive to consolidate large estates among aristocrats and the upper gentry promoted the development of strict settlement, dowry-jointure exchanges, and trusts for women – thus reducing wealthy women's independent access to their inherited estates – among the cottager class enclosure undercut laboring women's access to rural subsistence.[86] For different but interrelated reasons, then, women of both the landowning and working classes lost economic power within the family and status in society in the course of the eighteenth century. Only in the middle class could it be argued that women gained ground in society, and a new domestic ideology evolved to naturalize their reconceived roles.[87]

[82] Jane Humphries, "Enclosures, Common Rights, and Women," 28–9.

[83] Maxine Berg, "Women's Work, Mechanisation and the Early Phases of Industrialisation in England," p. 89; Arthur Young, *Annals of Agriculture and other Useful Arts*, 16 (1791), 502, quoted in Jane Humphries, "Enclosures, Common Rights, and Women," 38.

[84] Maxine Berg, "Women's Work, Mechanisation and the Early Phases of Industrialisation in England," pp. 89–90.

[85] This consequence is spelled out in Bridget Hill, *Women, Work, and Sexual Politics in Eighteenth-Century England*, pp. 9–23. See also Jane Humphries, "Enclosures, Common Rights, and Women," *passim*.

[86] There was a decline in the number of heiresses from the mid-eighteenth century onwards "because of demographic changes." John Habakkuk, *Marriage, Debt, and the Estates System*, p. 220.

[87] See Nancy Armstrong, "The Rise of the Domestic Woman," in her *Desire and Domestic Fiction*, pp. 59–95.

CLARISSA

Many different factors thus contributed to the psychological and material disinheritance of daughters represented in fiction by Burney, Reeve, and others. The virtual familylessness of a number of Jane Austen's prominent women characters – Fanny Price, Jane Fairfax, Harriet Smith, Anne Elliot – can be read both as a literary convention inherited from these earlier writers and as corroboration of its symbolic truth. Curiously, Clara Reeve dedicated *The Old English Baron*, which symbolically enacts the longed-for restitution of the disinherited daughter, to the daughter of Samuel Richardson, author of one of the greatest novels about this tragedy of disinheritance. *Clarissa* (1748) enacts this disinheritance drama with the clarity of dumbshow, for all the heroine's highly wrought verbal acuity. Like an economic morality play, the action of this novel demonstrates the combined effects of primogeniture and capital accumulation for female offspring in landowning families, of class mobility and "family aggrandizement" (82) – as Clarissa herself puts it – on the position of middle-class daughters, and even the effects of diminished subsistence economies on laboring-class women.[88] Clarissa's isolation proceeds inexorably despite her moral perfection and her powerful intelligence.

The family, as it is represented in this novel at mid-century, is hardly a nuclear family. Besides parents and children, the "Harlowes" consist of Clarissa's parents' siblings on both sides, cousins, and servants. As Clarissa remarks, "never was there a family more united in its different branches than ours. Our uncles consider us as their own children, and declare that it is for our sakes they live single" (56). In this delicately balanced power structure, her paternal uncles – her father's brothers – have significant authority, certainly more than her maternal aunt – her mother's half sister. These male relatives, together with her father, line up their interests behind the inheriting son, James Harlowe Jr. Although Clarissa's uncles have always loved her, they are not willing to sacrifice their relationship to the heir of what promises to be a great estate for the sake of a younger sister refusing to play her part in the family's aggrandizing fortune.

As early as her fourth letter to Anna Howe, Clarissa observes her brother's power in the family hierarchy. When he returns from inspecting his estates in Scotland and Yorkshire (property left him by a generous godmother), Clarissa notes that he thanks his father for waiting to consult him about Lovelace's suit "in such a manner, I thought, as a superior would do when he

---

[88] In this discussion, all page numbers refer to the Penguin edition of *Clarissa* edited by Angus Ross in 1985, which is based on the first edition of Richardson's text.

commended an inferior for having well performed his duty in his absence" (48). This distortion of intergenerational relations as well as cross-gender relations is caused by the combined effects of primogeniture and strict settlement, whose result was to entail the family wealth upon the first-born son when he reached his majority and reduce the father's claims to a life tenancy in the estate. As Clarissa explains her brother to Anna Howe, "Possessing everything, he has the vice of age mingled with the ambition of youth" (55). She reports his frequent remark "That his grandfather and uncles were his stewards; that no man ever had better" (77). She observes resentfully to Anna Howe that "previous to every resolution taken by his superiors, whose will ought to be his," they ask: "How will my *son*, how will my *nephew*, take this or that measure?" (54). Clarissa tries repeatedly to return family relations to what they were before distorted by acquisitiveness and her brother's will to power. She reminds her parents of their moral authority over their first-born son and insists to her brother that he is her sibling and peer and not her superior. He has "no more right to control me than I have to control him" (307), she writes to Anna. "[Y]ou are *only* my brother" she keeps telling him (57).

Clarissa's story illustrates how women could be deprived of their rightful inheritance and psychologically blackmailed as well as threatened legally if they resisted their dispossession. The "real life" truth of this situation for women is attested to by the readers who recognized Clarissa's story and wrote to Richardson indignant that he had exposed their family secrets.[89] Lady Mary Wortley Montagu said the book made her sob "in a most scandalous manner" and "touch'd me as being very ressembling [sic] to my Maiden Days." The cultivated Mrs. Delany, whose "maiden days" also resembled the first two volumes of *Clarissa*, observed when she had finished the book:

I never had so great a Mixture of Pain and Pleasure in the Reading of any Book in my Life. I was almost broken-hearted at some Passages, and raised above this World in others . . . it is impossible to think it a Fiction.

Catherine Talbot wrote to Elizabeth Carter about reading the novel in her household. "One can scarce persuade oneself that they are not real characters, and living people," she said, attesting to its verisimilitude. Lady Bradshaigh wrote to Richardson that the book affected her so powerfully

---

[89] See T. C. Duncan Eaves and Ben D. Kimpel, *Samuel Richardson: A Biography* (Oxford: Clarendon Press, 1971), pp. 287–8.

that she woke in the middle of the night "in a passion of crying; so I did at breakfast this morning, and just now again."[90]

The novel shows how owning property confers power, even within the family, and how the disinheritance of their rightful access to property renders women totally dependent on their male relatives. Clarissa declares to her mother that "although I am to be treated by my brother and, through his instigations, by my papa, as a slave in this point, and not as a daughter, yet my mind is not that of a slave" (111). "It is hard . . . to be forbid to enter into the cause of all," she pleads when refused the right to defend herself against her brother, to expose his venal motives for misconstruing her attitude, "because I must not speak disrespectfully of one who supposes me in the way of his ambition and treats me like a slave" (95).[91]

To her brother, Clarissa is a financial liability. Her inheritance from her grandfather, as she explains, "lopped off one branch of my brother's expectation" (77). The dowry inflation of the early eighteenth century, noted by Habakkuk in his famous article on the growing use of marriage alliances to amass great estates, drove a wedge between inheriting brothers and their portioned sisters; inheritance law and the drive to accumulate larger and larger estates constructed their material interests increasingly at odds with one another.[92] James Harlowe Jr. wants to marry Clarissa to Solmes because his promised terms, as her mother explains, "will very probably prevent your grandfather's estate going out of the family and may be a means to bring a still greater into it" (98). She resists his violent attempt to dispose of her hand, literally enacted when her brother grabs, crushes, and violently tosses her hand and arm, making her weep with pain (304). In addition to thus embodying the economic allegory precisely, Richardson's genius in splitting patriarchal authority between Clarissa's father and her brother permits him to criticize the misuse of male power while preserving and reinscribing it. This doubled attitude is what feminists weigh in their debates about Richardson's treatment of women. He simultaneously represents his heroine as obedient and independent, respectful of her father but

---

[90] These reactions of Lady Mary Wortley Montagu, Mrs. Delany, Catherine Talbot, and Lady Bradshaigh are given with more detail in my essay "Clarissa's Daughters, or the History of Innocence Betrayed: How Women Writers Rewrote Richardson," *Women's Writing* 1, 1 (1994), pp. 5–24, esp. pp. 6–7. This article also appears in *Clarissa and Her Readers: New Essays for the Clarissa Project*, ed. and intro. Carol Houlihan Flynn and Edward Copeland (New York: AMS Press, 1999), pp. 119–41, esp. pp. 120–1.

[91] Anna Howe sounds this note again in lamenting women's fate in marriage: "to be courted as princesses for a few weeks, in order to be treated as slaves for the rest of our lives" (133).

[92] H. J. Habakkuk, "Marriage Settlements in the Eighteenth Century," 15–30.

scornful of her brother, fully aware of the illegitimacy of male power but never unnaturally – ungenteely, unfemininely – disrespectful of patriarchal authority.

In traditional societies, the purpose of exchanging women was not to accumulate property and capital, but rather, according to Levi-Strauss among others, to forestall violence, create alliances between clans, cement peace treaties, and the like. Giving one's daughter in marriage was a political pledge of good faith; she was a hostage to one's peaceful intentions. It was precisely because she carried the clan's blood in her veins that a daughter could function as a kind of voucher for good intentions in such exchanges between clans. Examined in this context, the social meaning of the Harlowes' change of heart about Clarissa in the months before she finally flees her father's house recapitulates the changing position of daughters within a family structure undergoing the transition to capitalistic modes of accumulation. When Mrs. Harlowe asks Clarissa to maintain her correspondence with Lovelace for the sake of family peace – to pacify him and to prevent him from responding with physical force to James Harlowe Jr.'s provocative gestures – Clarissa's letters function as a kind of propitiatory offering, maintaining the balance of power between the two families, ensuring that their individual male representatives will not fight a duel and spill blood. But what begins as a collective tribal offering ends up as the sacrifice of an individual on the altar of Mammon, as the meaning and functioning of the Harlowe family changes before our eyes. Although Clarissa begins her correspondence with Lovelace "with general approbation" (47) and continues it to keep the peace (and it is important to remember that Mrs. Harlowe reads these letters rather late in the game and approves Clarissa's replies to Lovelace's letters even though she hides the fact of the correspondence from Mr. Harlowe), it becomes an increasingly desperate last resort in her retreat from a family that refuses to recognize her rights within it.

Clarissa's skill in managing the Harlowe establishment – relieving her mother of her "household cares" – illustrates the contribution of domestic labor among women of several classes. Early in the process of her subjugation, her brother proposes that she go to Scotland to put his house there in order; but her mother needs her skills at home and Clarissa has no mind to be her brother's housekeeper where she is sure to be "treated rather as a servant than as a sister," demonstrating the ambiguous difference between the labors of women of one class and another. As things worsen, "the keys of everything are taken from [her]" (116) and Clarissa is forbidden to continue her responsibilities in the Harlowe household. Disgraced, her employment taken from her, she is at once deprived of her mobility (she is no longer allowed to go to church), her power (her own servant, Hannah, is dismissed), and her usefulness within the household.

Clarissa can be read as a kind of everywoman, standing for womankind under siege. Her fate not only records the historical trajectory of genteel and middle-class women, but also – in its trace elements, in its details – inscribes the dissolution of the subsistence economies and the impoverishment of rural women who depended on these economies, during a period of rapid and thoroughgoing parliamentary enclosure of common lands.

Throughout her struggles with her family while still in her father's house, Clarissa's autonomy is best protected in those places associated with the subsistence economies that had customarily been controlled by women. "I dare not ask to go to my dairy-house," she writes to Anna Howe, "for I am now afraid of being thought to have a wish to enjoy that independence to which [my grandfather's] will has entitled me" (56). The "dairy-house," an estate originally called The Grove by her grandfather, had been renamed synecdochically for the dairy-house that he erected and fitted up on the premises for Clarissa's use and pastime. The estate itself he left free and clear to Clarissa for her own use. Her grandfather's bequest gave Clarissa economic independence from her family, as everyone understood, for it is remarked upon textually by her relatives – her father, her Uncle Antony, her brother, and her sister. Dairying was one of the most important subsistence economies traditionally managed by women's labor and made possible their customary access to common or "waste" land for pasturage and fodder. Indeed, when their family allotments permitted them to keep cows, women could pursue the practice professionally – for a healthy profit. Although very labor intensive,[93] there was enough profit margin in keeping cows – especially if pasturage was free – to enable an enterprising woman to earn enough from selling her butter and cheese to make the rent on the family farm. Arthur Young recorded that with eight cows on a Shropshire farm in 1776, the dairy earned £1 15s a week, producing five cheeses of 45 lb each and 20 lb of butter.[94] In the same period, a small farm renting for £90 a year more than paid for itself out of the £140 made on butter and cheese, and a larger farm renting for £185 made a return of £306 8s a year on 121 firkins of butter (a "firkin" was 56 lb) and 65 weys of cheese (each

---

[93] Ivy Pinchbeck, *Women Workers and the Industrial Revolution 1750–1850* (1930; rpt. London: Virago Press, 1981), p. 13. See also Mary Collier, *The Woman's Labour: An Epistle to Mr. Stephen Duck; In Answer to His Late Poem, Called The Threasher's Labour* (London, 1739).

[94] *Annals of Agriculture*, 4, 171–2, cited in Ivy Pinchbeck, *Women Workers and the Industrial Revolution*, p. 15, n. 2. Young estimated that an average dairymaid in the 1770s would have handled three cows.

"wey" was between 2 and 3 cwt).[95] For women with children, a cow or a
few cows provided an important dietary supplement of milk and cheese
for the family. In fact, after the period of the heaviest land enclosures, rural
children no longer drank milk as a matter of course and the majority of
rural laborers could no longer eat cheese every day.

In the period when *Clarissa* was being read, dairying was being contested
as a system of kin-based production, a locus of women's expertise and skill.
Men had begun to show an interest in this relatively lucrative business and
to write treatises about the practice of dairying, often decrying women's ignorance about the matter and offering up-to-the-moment scientific advice
for better dairy processing. Middlemen, buying up the produce of small-
time dairywomen to ship to urban centers or to supply the army, ignoring
local networks, were transforming dairying into a system of capitalized production involving transportation and distant markets.[96] The dairy was no
longer indisputably women's space, the "unchallenged preserve of female
authority and labor,"[97] and the site of women's economic independence.
As more and more common land was enclosed, so that pasturage had to be
rented, housewives could no longer pursue dairying as a profitable endeavor.

In *Clarissa* the dairy-house is still a potential site of women's economic
independence although, historically speaking, the struggle over capitalization and larger scales of operation had already begun. That dairying was
disappearing as an economic safety net for women makes the discussion in
Clarissa about the heroine's inheritance still more poignant. Anna Howe
is convinced that the "dairy-house" is Clarissa's best possible hope for a
satisfactory life. But Clarissa is afraid to claim it as a refuge because she
knows her male relatives will litigate if she does. It will then appear to the
world that she is claiming property not legally hers, and she is not willing
to survive on those terms, at the cost of losing her family and reputation.

The other important site for Clarissa during her struggles with her family was, of course, the poultry-yard where she left her letters for Anna
Howe and picked up the replies. Keeping chickens was, in and of itself,
another kin-based subsistence economy grounded on access to common
or "waste" lands. Milk and eggs – symbolic female substances – thus also
carried resonances of gender-specific labors and domains from another era.
Clarissa's poultry-yard is also an extension of her inherited estate insofar as

[95] Arthur Young, *Annals of Agriculture* 5, 206–7, cited in Ivy Pinchbeck, *Women Workers and the Industrial Revolution*, p. 15, n. 8.
[96] Deborah Valenze, "The Art of Women and the Business of Men: Women's Work and the Dairy Industry," in her *The First Industrial Woman*, pp. 48–67, especially pp. 54–64.
[97] *Ibid.*, p. 49.

her favorite birds – the bantams, pheasants, and peahens – came from her grandfather, who recommended them to her care (66). Evocative of pastoral scenes and wholesome country life, the poultry-yard is on Green Lane, which, as Clarissa writes to Anna Howe, runs past two or three farmhouses. Anna was to send her servant Robert there to exchange the letters of these two disobedient daughters, tokens of their defiance and individualism. It is in the empowering poultry-yard, hidden by a high hedge, that Clarissa overhears her brother and sister laughing and talking with Solmes about how to subdue her (225), information that helps her to better understand what she is up against.

Besides running her dairy-house and tending her poultry-yard, Clarissa is involved in another vestigial kind of economic transaction – giving alms to the deserving poor. In this practice, which harkens back to feudal obligation rather than the more modern urge to accumulate capital, she is contrasted to Bella, who hoards her money and cares about interest. As Donna T. Andrew has noted, an historic change in attitudes towards charity occurred in this period, in which the notion that charity was a responsibility that came with luck and surplus – "the rent on property payable to the only absolute proprietor" – was disappearing. No longer did people believe in redistributing God's wealth; there was an overall decrease in the number of charitable bequests to the needy in wills – despite the fact that greater and greater amounts of wealth were being left behind. "Charity derived from superfluities" came to be considered as special mercy rather than justice.[98] As another historian puts it, "private philanthropy was increasingly regarded as an act of beneficence and virtue toward carefully chosen causes rather than a community-based obligation."[99] In the matter of charity as in so much else, Clarissa is a traditionalist.

Thus elements of the historical processes that attenuated the position of daughters within their families are present in Richardson's novel, the processes that positioned them, as James Harlowe Jr. so pungently puts it, as "chickens brought up for the tables of other men" (77). Eroded by family strategies for capital accumulation and by the disruption of customary use relations, women's rights within families lost definition – as seen in Clarissa's deteriorating relations with the larger Harlowe family. Clarissa's brother is simply giving voice to a commonplace sentiment when he declares that "daughters were but encumbrances and drawbacks upon a family" (77). One sees how strict settlement identified the interests of families with the

[98] Donna T. Andrew, *Philanthropy and Police: London Charity in the Eighteenth Century* (Princeton: Princeton University Press, 1989), pp. 41–2.
[99] Richard Grassby, *Kinship and Capitalism*, p. 262.

interests of firstborn sons and how the growing potential for industry and commerce (or military employment) created further economic opportunities for non-inheriting younger sons. The Harlowes' fortune has been improved by all these modern means: Clarissa's uncle Harlowe enlarged his fortune by wisely investing it in industrial enterprises; his father's will mentions the "unexpected benefits he reaps from his new-found mines" (53). Uncle Antony, the youngest Harlowe son, without the advantage of the firstborn, made a fortune in East India traffic, that is, in commercial ventures based on colonial exploitation. But these two means of increase – industry and commerce – are sterile, and neither men have offspring. Clarissa's father, on the other hand, a second son, made his fortune by marrying well. Clarissa's mother, the daughter of a viscount, brought an enormous fortune into the family by way of a dowry supplemented by inheritances from the unexpected deaths of several relations. With the important exception of the "dairy-house" estate left to Clarissa by her grandfather, all the inherited wealth in the Harlowe family flows from women to men, including the two estates left to Clarissa's brother James Harlowe Jr. by his godmother Lovell.

The growing obsession with capital accumulation in the eighteenth century, well represented in the Harlowe acquisitiveness, meant that dowries and jointures – which were the dominant forms of women's property – were increasingly seen as unnecessary clogs on family estates rather than as the rightful shares of equal family members. Different legal systems governed men's and women's inheritance. Women's property descended in fee simple, according to common law, and was expected to maintain a woman rather than provide the basis of an independent fortune to be invested and improved. When men's property descended in tail according to equity law, it did not matter how uneven the distribution was with regard to other heirs, for descent in tail superseded descent in fee simple.[100] Thus, daughters could expect to receive allowances from the family wealth but they could not expect to share in an equal division of it. This change was one of the hallmarks of the late seventeenth-century emphasis on capital accumulation. It coincided with the conversion of communally held use rights-in-property (in which women participated) to fully alienable absolute rights-in-property (usually held by male heads of families); thus, property ownership came to be understood increasingly as a male prerogative.

[100] J. Johnson, *The Laws Respecting Women* (London, 1777; facsimile reprint, Dobbs Ferry, NY: Oceana, 1974, with a foreword by Shirley Raissi Bysiewicz), p. 122.

It is certainly true that Clarissa's troubles begin with the reading of her grandfather's will. As James Thompson observes, inheritance usually precipitates a crisis for female characters in eighteenth-century fiction: "inheritance is enabling or authorizing for male protagonists and disabling for female protagonists; inheritance works as resolution for males and dissolution for females."[101] The bequest that made Clarissa financially independent of her father and brother, that put her needs before theirs, infuriated them. Even before she was tricked by Lovelace to leave her father's house, her grandfather's untimely gift had isolated her and marked her fate. Her generous grandfather comments on the anomaly of his act within the will itself, insisting that he means no offense. Her father calls it an "unjust bequest" and threatens to go to court to have it set aside if Clarissa dares to claim it. Arabella comments on the peculiarity of what their grandfather has done. "To leave the acquired part of his estate from the next heirs, his own sons" (194) – that is, to have improved or added to a fortune but not to leave it all together to the next in line – was contrary to the spirit of the age. And then to leave it "to his *youngest* grandchild! A *daughter* too!" only added insult to injury.

The weakened position of mothers and maternal relatives was another effect of the concentration of wealth in the male line and the growing sense that women were the agents of accumulation but never its beneficiaries. As the Harlowe family demonstrates its real basis in capital accumulation, Clarissa's maternal line – her mother and her mother's kin, the relatives traditionally most responsible for protecting female offspring – are visibly weakened. It is no coincidence that Cousin Morden, Clarissa's ultimate defender and trustee of her grandfather's will, is a maternal relative and is sojourning in Italy, a country coded female in eighteenth-century English fiction. Everyone expects Cousin Morden to save Clarissa from the greed of her paternal relatives upon his return. Indeed, their pressure is geared to his imminent arrival. As she tells Anna, her brother is "continually buzzing in my father's ears that my cousin Morden would soon arrive, and then would insist upon giving me possession of my grandfather's estate, in pursuance of the will, which would render me independent of my father" (167–8).

Richardson explains the diminished power of Clarissa's maternal relatives (despite their higher class status) by inventing a financial obligation owed by Mr. Hervey, her mother's sister's husband, although the diminished rights of mothers and of maternal relatives over the persons and property

---

[101] James Thompson, *Models of Value: Eighteenth-Century Political Economy and the Novel* (Durham, NC: Duke University Press, 1996), p. 174.

of children is a fact of legal history that needs no objective correlative. In Richardson's plot, Clarissa's brutal older brother, James Harlowe Jr., has paid off a mortgage on part of Mr. Hervey's estate and taken the debt upon himself. It is, according to Anna Howe, "a small favour . . . from kindred to kindred: but such a one, it is plain, as has laid the whole family of the Herveys under obligation to the ungenerous lender, who has treated him, and his aunt too (as Miss Dolly Hervey has privately complained) with the less ceremony ever since" (212). This indebtedness is used to explain Mrs. Hervey's uneasy silence in the face of Clarissa's mistreatment by her paternal relatives. Clarissa's mother's passivity in the face of the tyranny of the Harlowe men is explained by her husband's increasingly irascible temper due to pain from his gout. These plot expedients explain the inability of Clarissa's maternal relatives to protect her; but, as we shall see in Chapter 8, "The Importance of Aunts," this inability has historical resonance.

If, in Clarissa's case, Richardson represents the suppression of maternal power, Anna Howe's case shows the other side of the coin. Anna is an only child, without male siblings, and her mother is a wealthy widow with full testamentary guardianship of her daughter and no competition for the family assets from any patrilineal family. In this situation – with her husband dead and with legal control of her property and her child – a mother could fully protect her daughter's interests.[102] That Mrs. Howe chooses Mr. Hickman for Anna, a man who enjoys her daughter's spirit and promises to respect her autonomy and her desires, structurally confirms this important principle: only a mother or a maternal relative could be counted on to defend the rights of daughters.

I have been arguing that *Clarissa* is a novel about the dissolution of "family values" – at least with respect to daughters. "Our family has been strangely discomposed" (41) writes Clarissa to Anna at the outset. "You are all too rich to be happy," replies her friend (68). Competitive and individualistic rather than cooperative and communal, members of this family are at odds with one another and they appear to be afraid and suspicious of one another. The novel is a masterpiece of indirect commmunication, of intelligence gathered by snooping, spying, overhearing: everyone secretly monitors everyone else's conversations. These tendencies are only

---

[102] Cheryl Nixon shows how the novel "signifies its anxiety concerning maternal power" in the representation of Mrs. Howe's economic power in combination with her failure as a feminine nurturer. She further explains how this representation indicates conflict in the culture about maternal power in her excellent article, "Maternal Guardianship by 'Nature' and 'Nurture': Eighteenth-Century Chancery Court Records and *Clarissa*," *Intertexts* 5, 2 (2001), 128–55.

exaggerated, not basically changed, when Clarissa and Lovelace begin to share the same household. "We are both great watchers of each other's eyes," writes Clarissa, and "more than half afraid of each other" (460). Thus, the family of consanguinity is represented as unstable, its ties of affection and obligation all but effaced by material considerations.[103]

Nevertheless, despite being mercilessly persecuted by them, Clarissa remains loyal to her family – it is part of her traditionalism – much to Lovelace's irritation. "Sordid ties!" he exclaims. "Mere cradle-prejudices!" (145). She would prefer never to marry at all but to remain living at home, as she explains to her "second papa," her uncle Harlowe:

> Marriage is a very solemn engagement, enough to make a young creature's heart ache, with the *best* prospects, when she thinks seriously of it! – To be given up to a strange man; to be engrafted into a strange family; to give up her very name as a mark of her becoming his absolute and dependent property; to be obliged to prefer this strange man to father, mother – to everybody. (148)

Her pain at being forced out of the family is continually before us, both because of Lovelace's perfidy and because of her incessant longing to be reinstated in *some* family – even *his* family. She leaves with Lovelace originally hoping for protection from his maternal aunts. Indeed, the only thing he ever offers her that really tempts her is family. Every time she is pushed to desperate measures, the one thing that reconciles her to patience is the possibility of kin. "Father-sick" and "family-proud" (521) he calls her, playing to this one unabashed desire of hers with all his skill. First he delays their marriage with the hope that his uncle, Lord M., can be present as a kind of surrogate father. More than the marriage itself, what draws Clarissa into his scheme is the possibility of a "paternal wing." "Father had a sweet and venerable sound with it" (599) she says.

Later, when he creates the impersonated Colonel Tomlinson as a supposed friend and agent of her uncle Harlowe, again holding out the hope of reconciliation with her family, she cries out with an emotion that moves even Lovelace:

> How happy shall I be, when my heart is lightened from the all-sinking weight of a father's curse! When my dear mamma . . . shall once more fold me to her indulgent bosom! When I shall again have uncles and aunts and a brother and sister. (695)

---

[103] For a "real life" example of a woman who, like Clarissa, incurred the enmity of her consanguineal family because of an inheritance, see *The Life of Mary Anne Schimmelpenninck: Author "Select Memoirs of Port Royal" and Other Works*, 2nd edn., 2 vols., ed. Christiana C. Hankin (London: Longman, Brown, Green, Longmans, and Roberts, 1858). Thanks to Phyllis Mack for this reference.

Her later outburst similarly affects him:

Oh Mr. Lovelace . . . what a happiness, if my dear uncle could be prevailed upon to be personally a father on this occasion to *the poor fatherless girl*! (709)

These scenes move Lovelace to tears for all his sneering that she is "mother-spoilt" and "father-fond," for there is great cultural power in the invocation of consanguineal connection. What *Clarissa* enacts – besides the power of language to recreate emotion and reinterpret events – is the dispossession of daughters in the new capitalist dispensation, and the daughters' difficulty in finding a place in the world to belong to once this dispossession has taken effect. All the orphaned women in eighteenth-century fiction are witness to this cutting loose, this great disinheritance, a function of changing legal, political, and economic systems. Discharged from their consanguineal families and forced to bargain for terms with their potential families by marriage, caught between one system and another, daughters were an early casualty of the effects of capitalism on social relations. It is this devolution that is diagnostically represented in the tragedy of Clarissa.

2

Fathers and daughters

The particular fatality that regulates a woman's lot in fiction is always bound up with fathers.

Nancy K. Miller, *Subject to Change*, p. 175.

What the novels helped to reinforce was the sense that [marriage] was the most important decision, really the *only* decision of any significance, that a daughter would ever have the chance to take; and that the success or failure of that decision was intimately bound up with the relationship which she had with her father.

Caroline Gonda, *Reading Daughters' Fictions*, p. 37.

He . . . went straight to his desk, whence, taking out and untying the parcel, he opened the first volume [of *Evelina*] upon the little ode to himself, – "O author of my being! far more dear," &c. He ejaculated a "Good God!" and his eyes were suffused with tears.

Frances Burney, *Memoirs of Doctor Burney*, vol. II, p. 137.

The relationship between fathers and daughters was perhaps the relationship most deeply affected by the disinheritance of daughters, judging from the intense preoccupation with it in this period. Indeed, if the literature a society produces can be said to reflect its obsessions, eighteenth-century England was obsessed with fathers and daughters. Margaret Doody notes that "close relations between fathers and daughters were insisted on as never before" in eighteenth-century fiction and drama. If the Restoration drama had been largely interested in relations between fathers and sons, eighteenth-century serious drama was much occupied with relations between fathers and daughters – "even to the point where we can question the emotional health of the culture whose literature gave rise to such elaborate representations of those feelings." Speaking of the "cultural investment" in the "beautiful purity" of father-daughter relations, she speculates that the reason for the enormous cultural stake in this relation was that it reinforced patriarchal authority: "filial duty from the female . . . does not

remind the father of his brute physicality but vindicates his authority under the guise of tenderness."[1] The theme was equally prevalent in narrative
fiction. "The father-daughter bond was, throughout the century, a staple of
fiction," writes Caroline Gonda in her study of the trope.[2] The representation of this consanguineal relation seemed to pull at the heartstrings of the
eighteenth-century English public like no other: sentimental treatments of
the father-daughter connection could be counted on to move audiences.

THE VIRGIN WIFE

As we have seen, the daughter's role was changing in the reconfigured family. As her importance to the family's lineage waned, paradoxically, her
centrality to its psychodynamics increased. Redefined as a stranger in the
house, her emotional availability to all members of the family – which
may have been a function of her decreasing economic role – shored up the
stability of the whole unit. A virgin wife/mother, her presence multiplied
the female resources of the family. Indeed, she usually looks exactly like
her mother's younger self in late eighteenth-century fiction. According to
Paula Marantz Cohen's analysis of the daughter's role, the "cross-sexual,
cross-generational relationship of father and daughter functioned as the
core of the nuclear family, because, unlike the husband-wife relationship,
where complementarity was purely a matter of convention (aided by the
imaginative projection produced by romantic love)," the father-daughter
relationship was genuinely complementary. Age and gender reinforced gender hierarchy while, at the same time, the father had a stake to some extent
in the happiness of these offspring of his loins, his dependent daughters.[3]
Following Doody, one can see how the ideological power in the father-
daughter relationship came from imagining tenderness where authority
indisputably ruled. It reinforced a sentimental belief in filial obedience
by emotional blackmail rather than naked force, in a society in which
feudal patriarchal prerogative was losing ground to newer, subtler forms
of male authority. The tender father was a new invention in fiction at
mid-century, according to Caroline Gonda, "the openly tyrannical rule of
Mr. Harlowe or Sir Thomas Grandison" giving way "to the suffocating

---

[1] Margaret Doody, *Frances Burney: The Life in the Works* (New Brunswick: Rutgers University Press,
   1988), pp. 24–5, 184.
[2] Caroline Gonda, *Reading Daughters' Fictions 1709–1834: Novels and Society from Manley to Edgeworth*
   (Cambridge: Cambridge University Press, 1996), p. 9.
[3] Paula Marantz Cohen, *The Daughter's Dilemma: Family Process and the Nineteenth-Century Domestic
   Novel* (Ann Arbor: University of Michigan Press, 1991), pp. 22–3.

moral and pedagogical care of Mr. Tyrold" in Frances Burney's *Camilla* (1796) at the end of the century. Far from showing a diminution in fathers' domination of their daughters, this change in the representation of paternal power shows the daughter internalizing her "willing submission" to her father and romanticizing her filial love.[4]

Part of the concentration and intensification of all intimate, affective relations in family life, sentimental relations between fathers and daughters created the terms for a daughter's future heterosexual marital and maternal roles. The wellspring of women's sense of familial duty, father-daughter relations socialized girls to their heterosexual identifications while providing stability and emotional power in the new conjugal family. But since *her* adoration and *his* protection inevitably ceased – or altered – at the time of her marriage, this perfect complementarity had but a brief duration. Indeed, as Lynda Boose has suggested, one can look at marriage as "primarily a father-daughter separation rite" in a culture that had no other effective mechanism for dissolving this powerful tie.[5] This social reality is reflected in the conflict that characterized a daughter's marriage in novels of the mid-to-late eighteenth century. The power of a woman's attachment to her natal home and to her father, according to Caroline Gonda, is represented in the wrenching dramas in which she leaves his jurisdiction, in scenes that developed their "own repertoire of actions and gestures: tears, kneeling, swooning, speechlessness, fits, threats, doors slammed, letters torn up."[6]

Remodelling the daughter as a kind of virgin surrogate for the mother helped to solve "the inherent contradiction between idealized feminine purity and the sexual realities of childbearing which was at the core of motherhood" in the latter half of the century, according to Davidoff and Hall.[7] That this psychological configuration was evolving in conjunction with a new focus on the conjugal unit and the abridgment of daughters' rights to family resources made it all the more poignant. The emotional power of the father-daughter relationship thus coexisted with the more absolute termination of fathers' responsibility for daughters when those daughters married, and with the fathers' growing sense of daughters as property to be deployed in the family interest rather than as lifetime kin. These contradictions created complicated human situations recycled again and again in

---

4 Caroline Gonda, *Reading Daughters' Fictions*, p. xvi; see also p. 140.
5 Lynda E. Boose, "The Father's House and the Daughter in It: The Structures of Western Culture's Daughter-Father Relationship," in Lynda E. Boose and Betty S. Flowers (eds.), *Daughters and Fathers* (Baltimore: Johns Hopkins University Press, 1989), pp. 19–74, quote p. 46.
6 Caroline Gonda, *Reading Daughters' Fictions*, p. 4.
7 Leonore Davidoff and Catherine Hall, *Family Fortunes: Men and Women of the English Middle Class, 1780–1850* (Chicago: University of Chicago Press, 1987), p. 346.

numerous fictions, which tested the relative strength of daughterly loyalty against exogamous romantic love and fatherly devotion against the force of family ambition. The love between fathers and daughters, in fiction, was thus pitted against the most powerful emotional and economic motivations of the day.

WRITING DAUGHTERS

In "real" life the publication of several memoirs by daughters, whose most excessive sentimentality is triggered by reflections about their fathers, attests to the special intensity of this relationship. Charlotte Charke's *Narrative* (1755), written to propitiate her alienated father – as well as to expose and coerce him – funnels her extravagant and daring adventures into a daughterly plea for forgiveness.[8] If only she could "move his heart to pity and forgiveness," she wrote, she would "with pride and unutterable transport throw myself at his feet to implore the only benefit I desire or expect – his blessing and pardon." She structures her narrative to show that her father's reactions to her always made the deepest impression and to indicate that it is her mistakes in relation to him that she most regrets. Publicly, she pleads with him to reinstate her, printing a recent letter she has sent him confessing those "unhappy miscarriages which have for many years justly deprived me of a father's fondness" and assuring him that "the hours of anguish I have felt bitterly repaid me for the commission of every indiscretion."[9] Blacklisted by the only two patented theaters in London, destitute from too many years in marginal provincial acting companies, notorious for her independence, cross-dressing, and "mad pranks," Charke attempts to rehabilitate herself in her *Narrative* as a penitent, supplicating daughter, positioning herself as a "sentimental heroine, that dependent, vulnerable, and victimized woman struggling to do the morally right thing, struggling to please the father."[10] She confides to her audience that her letter has been returned unopened, which preys upon her heart "with the slow and

---

[8] See Philip E. Baruth's excellent "Who Is Charlotte Charke?" in Baruth (ed.), *Introducing Charlotte Charke* (Urbana and Chicago: University of Illinois Press, 1998), pp. 9–62. For an interesting exploration of Charlotte Charke's cross-dressing in relation to her theatrical career, see Jones DeRitter, "'Not the Person She Conceived Me': The Public Identities of Charlotte Charke," in *Genders* 19: *Sexual Artifice: Persons, Images, Politics*, ed. Ann Kibbey, Kayann Short, and Abouali Farmanfarmaian (1994), 3–25.

[9] Fidelis Morgan with Charlotte Charke, *The Well-Known Trouble Maker: A Life of Charlotte Charke* (London and Boston: Faber and Faber, 1988), pp. 4, 81.

[10] Sidonie Smith, "The Transgressive Daughter and the Masquerade of Self-Representation," in Philip E. Baruth (ed.), *Introducing Charlotte Charke*, pp. 83–106, quote p. 86.

eating fire of distraction and despair till it ended in a fever, which now remains upon my spirits."[11] Whether this was simply the most certain way to appeal to her audience, or whether her relationship with her father really did dominate her life – beginning with her earliest recollection of dressing up in his periwig and clothes – she parades the drama of her unhappy estrangement from him before her readers, testimony to the contemporary psychological significance of the father-daughter relationship.

Frances Burney and Maria Edgeworth, both successful writers who were devoted to their respective fathers, edited the memoirs of those fathers when they died, confirming in their eulogies the overwhelming importance of paternal support to their lives. To be sure, these fathers – Charles Burney and Richard Lovell Edgeworth – were notoriously seductive both within their large families and towards a wide and devoted circle of friends. Moreover, both women had lost their mothers young, and Frances Burney married late while Maria Edgeworth never married at all. However overdetermined their father fixations, the culture reinforced and rewarded them and encouraged expression of their father-love.

Maria Edgeworth's *Memoirs of Richard Lovell Edgeworth, Esq.* (1820), "begun by himself and concluded by his daughter,"[12] prefaces the second volume by testifying to her father's importance to her career as a writer, both as a shield and as an editor. Overstating his role in her work,[13] she writes:

Till now, I have never on any occasion addressed myself to the public alone and speaking in the first person. This egotism is not only repugnant to my habits, but most painful and melancholy. Formerly I had always a friend and father, who spoke for me and wrote for me: one who exerted for me all the powers of his strong mind, even to the very last.[14]

She recounts how close they were, how he even discussed with her his fourth and last marriage choice, of which she did not appprove. She reports that

[11] Fidelis Morgan with Charlotte Charke, *The Well-Known Trouble Maker*, p. 82.
[12] *Memoirs of Richard Lovell Edgeworth, Esq. Begun by Himself and Concluded by His Daugher, Maria Edgeworth*, 2 vols. (Boston: Wells and Lily, 1820).
[13] Caroline Gonda points out that despite Maria Edgeworth's public stance that she was merely her father's instrument, she did not work on a collection of his plays when he was dying as he wanted her to do, but rather followed the dictates of her own artistic conscience and worked on her novel *Ormond*. *Reading Daughters' Fictions*, pp. 224–5, 237.
[14] Maria Edgeworth, *Memoirs of Richard Lovell Edgeworth*, vol. II, p. 6. For an overview of the way Edgeworth has been "embalmed" as her father's partner rather than a pathbreaking writer, as "daddy's girl" rather than her own woman, see Mitzi Myers, "Shot from Canons; Or, Maria Edgeworth and the Cultural Production and Consumption of the Later Eighteenth-Century Woman Writer," in Ann Bermingham and John Brewer (eds.), *The Consumption of Culture 1600–1800* (New York: Routledge, 1995), pp. 193–214, esp. pp. 202–5.

he once told her that he thought "no human creature ever saw the heart of another more completely without disguise, than you have seen mine."[15] His final days were cheered by reading and correcting her novel *Ormond*, the pages of which she wrote all day and handed him in the evening.[16] While not so sentimental as Burney's treatment of her daughterly relation, Edgeworth's memoir nevertheless depicts an intense connection with her father involving her in a large family with many children and sheltering and encouraging her writing.[17]

Frances Burney's *Memoirs of Doctor Burney* is even more lavish and intense in depicting her histrionic father in relation to herself and his other children. The overwrought tone of this work may be attributable to the fact that she used these volumes to tell her own story as well, a fact which has infuriated Dr. Burney's modern biographers.[18] Respectable women of Burney's generation did not publish their own memoirs (Charke was not respectable), and Burney had to weave her own story into her father's memoir if she was to tell it at all.[19] Her intense need to write the story of her writing self, together with her psychological distress at setting aside conventional female modesty to do so, is evident in the stagey tone in which she speaks about herself in the third person – as the "Memorialist" – and in her hyperbolic descriptions of her emotional interactions with her father. "Whenever Burney begins to discuss her father," Jan Thaddeus writes, "she chooses her most exalted and periphrastic style, muffling Dr. Burney in trailing clauses of glory."[20] Her fervid descriptions emphasize his approval of her career. The episode in which he tells her that he has read *Evelina*, which was published anonymously, and that he thought it had "merit – it is, really, – extraordinary!", reads like a scene from a sentimental novel. "She fell upon his neck with heart-throbbing emotion; and he folded her in his arms so tenderly, that she sobbed upon his shoulder; so moved was she

---

[15] Maria Edgeworth, *Memoirs of Richard Lovell Edgeworth*, vol. ii, p. 110.

[16] *Ibid.*, vol. ii, p. 248.

[17] Edgeworth's novels contain several father-daughter dramas. In a subtext of *Belinda* (London, 1801), Virginia St. Pierre is reunited with Mr. Hartley, who turns out to be her father. Jewish Mr. Montenero and his daughter Beatrice are extremely close in *Harrington* (London, 1817). Caroline Percy, in *Patronage* (London, 1814), marries but does not leave her family home. Indeed, Caroline Gonda observes that "Edgeworth repeatedly avoids depicting that moment of separation which comes when the father gives his daughter away in marriage." *Reading Daughters' Fictions*, p. 220.

[18] Roger Lonsdale, for example, refers to "Fanny's senile egotism" in his section on the *Memoirs*. Roger Lonsdale, *Dr. Charles Burney: A Literary Biography* (Oxford: Clarendon Press, 1965), pp. 433–55, esp. p. 451.

[19] Janice Farrar Thaddeus, *Frances Burney: A Literary Life* (London: Macmillan, and New York: St. Martin's Press, 2000), pp. 189–94, and Margaret Doody, *Frances Burney*, p. 10.

[20] Janice Farrar Thaddeus, *Frances Burney*, p. 195.

by his precious approbation."[21] Although not published until 1832, these memoirs reflect an eighteenth-century sentimental excess about fathers and daughters.

The sanctity of the father-daughter relation in the eighteenth century can also be gauged by the horror with which the public responded to the Mary Blandy case, a case of parricide. London was mesmerized by the story of this attractive, well-bred woman who fed her father poisonous "powders" procured by her lover, presumably to get her inheritance sooner. Pamphlets on the case poured from the press, including Blandy's own account.[22] So notorious was the case that 5,000 people came to see Mary Blandy hang. Although the Blandy case was not in his jurisdiction, Henry Fielding scrutinized its details fruitlessly for a motive that he could recognize. She "had the education of a Gentlewoman," he wrote, puzzled, and "Ladies of great Rank and Fashion were fond and desirous of her Acquaintance."[23] In her account, she relates how her parents "took all imaginable Care [to instill in her] moral and religious Principles"; in this way, her story contrasts with that of Elizabeth Jeffryes, another notorious parricide to whom she compares herself, who had the "Unhappiness to be debauched when very young" by an uncle "who had taken her under his Protection and Patronage."[24] Most of those who wrote about the case, including Fielding, assumed that Mary Blandy had been led astray by her unprincipled lover – that hers was an extreme case of romantic love. She had been smitten with a bad sort. It all went to show that romantic love, if extreme enough, could undermine even the most sacred of consanguineal ties.[25]

Although the fiction of the earlier eighteenth century does not concern itself with the father-daughter relation – it is not emphasized in Manley, Haywood, or Defoe – its growing emotional weight can be felt by 1744 in

[21] *Memoirs of Doctor Burney Arranged from His Own Manuscripts, from Family Papers, and from Personal Recollections. By His Daughter, Madame D'Arblay*, 3 vols. (London: Edward Moxon, 1832), vol. II, pp. 144–5.

[22] Caroline Gonda points out that stories of "female cruelty" got more attention from the press than stories of male violence. She gives the case of a man who murdered "his own daughter by repeated acts of torture," a case contemporary with the Blandy case but given much less publicity than Blandy's slow and relatively painless poisoning. *Reading Daughters' Fiction*, pp. 7–8.

[23] Henry Fielding, *The Covent-Garden Journal and A Plan of the University Register-Office*, ed. Bertrand A. Goldgar (Oxford: Clarendon Press, 1988), p. 135. For this reference and all others referring to this case, I am indebted to Kristina Straub's unpublished article "Feminine Sexuality, Class Identity, and Narrative Form in the Newgate Calendars."

[24] *Miss Mary Blandy's Own Account of the Affair between Her and Mr. Cranstoun. From the Commencement of Their Acquaintance, in the Year, 1746. To the Death of Her Father, in August 1751, with All the Circumstances Leading to That Unhappy Event* (London: A. Millar, 1752), pp. 25–6.

[25] I rely here on Kristina Straub's reading of the literature about this case in "Feminine Sexuality, Class Identity, and Narrative Form in the Newgate Calendars."

Mary Collyer's *Felicia to Charlotte*. The first volume of this novel contains
all the twists and turns of the fate of a pair of lovers, Lucius and Felicia;
by the second volume they are married. Felicia's father provides most of
the obstacles to their union in the first volume. Misinformed about their
relationship at first by an anonymous letter, he orders his daughter to
break it off with Lucius. When it turns out that the anonymous letter had
been written by a jealous rival, Prudilla, whose machinations are uncovered,
father and daughter embrace with relief. But there are several more contests
of will before them – each with its own resolution – as if the point of the
novel is the repetition of the cycle of estrangement and reconciliation,
the spotlight on the father and daughter, rather than on the couple whose
consummation is repeatedly deferred. There seems to be a textual reluctance
to pass on to that predictable climax and to leave behind the delicious
possibility of father and daughter scenes.

FATHER-DAUGHTER SEPARATION

Everywhere in the fiction of the second half of the eighteenth century,
fathers and daughters are separated, whether literally or figuratively, with
intense and wrenching emotion. Lost or estranged by any number of plot
devices, they come together joyfully and tearfully in reunion scenes that appear to be all but inevitable. The reunion of parents and children had been a
plot feature of the earlier romances, but the disrupted families of romances
were usually royalty or aristocrats and the retrieval of an heir or a long-lost
daughter had public significance and was not simply a fact of private life as
in these fictions.[26] Caroline Gonda interprets all the father-daughter separations in these eighteenth-century novels as a sign that "paternal authority"
is "in a state of collapse," and that fathers are "no longer willing or able to
exercise their protective powers over their daughters." She sees these many
fictional separations as addressing "the plight of daughters left to fend for
themselves in a world where paternal authority seems to be collapsing or in
decline" – or, as I will suggest, where that authority has been withdrawn.[27]
In a somewhat different context, Brian McCrea has read this absence of
fathers literally, attributing it to a demographic crisis in the English aristocracy.[28] But what strikes me about this pattern is not so much that fictional
daughters lose their fathers as that they find them again. Again and again,

---

[26] .Susan Staves reminded me of this continuity.
[27] Caroline Gonda, *Reading Daughters' Fictions*, pp. 13, xvi.
[28] Brian McCrea, *Impotent Fathers: Patriarchy and Demographic Crisis in the Eighteenth-Century Novel*
(Newark: University of Delaware Press, and London: Associated University Presses, 1998).

the father embraces his long-lost daughter with mutual exclamations of joy and delight. He then solemnly blesses her, and she who has suffered thoughout the narrative for want of a name and lack of money or friends is gladly given his name, his protection, and in most cases his wealth. Whatever the ostensible plot of a particular novel, sooner or later it makes its way to this moment, staged variously as a scene of recognition, reconciliation, legitimation, forgiveness, or some other form of mutual validation. Fathers and daughters throw themselves at one another's feet, burst into tears, and/or clasp the lost or estranged other to their bosoms with calculable regularity. From about 1745 on, in novels by men and by women, this culturally overdetermined scene provided the emotional climax and catharsis of many a sentimental novel.

Many years ago Susan Staves read this scene of tearful reunion between a father and his seduced and ruined daughter as a lamentation for the passing patriarchal social order and the idealized older family form – the father's loss represented by his ruined daughter.[29] But in the more generic version of this plot, the separation between father and daughter can happen for many reasons other than her seduction and ruin. Sometimes the father is captured by pirates or misinformed of her whereabouts. Sometimes he is in another country. Indeed, rather than being a figure for the father's loss of his daughter, it seems to me that this sequence of separation and reunion represents the daughter's loss – and recovery – of her father. Moreover, the reconciliation with the father is usually prelude to the conventional tying up of threads with marriage, transmission of property, continuation of bloodlines, and so on. Thus, the scene of legitimation or acceptance by the father precedes and prefigures the heroine's marrying. Indeed, finding her father is usually a necessary precondition for a heroine's marrying, the reunion plot often preempting and displacing the romance plot. For social reasons, psychological reasons, and financial reasons, a woman needed a father's recognition before she could enter into marriage.

The anonymous *Leonora* (1745) is one of the earliest prototypes of this rule of eighteenth-century fiction that the heroine must find or be recognized by her father – must, in short, be claimed by him – before she can marry.[30] Camilla and Hippolytus have many chaste adventures together as friends before they fall in love with each other. But no sooner do they recognize that they *have* fallen in love than her father reappears. In other words, once Leonora discovers whom she loves, she recovers her father, demonstrating

---

[29] Susan Staves, "British Seduced Maidens," *Eighteenth-Century Studies* 14, 2 (Winter 1980–1), 109–34.
[30] *Leonora: Or, Characters Drawn from Real Life*, 2 vols. (London: Thomas Davies, 1745). The tearful father-daughter reunion takes place in vol. 1, pp. 287–99.

the interrelation between these two attachments. The reunion with the father legitimates the woman and readies her for marriage. It also reminds the daughter of her subordinate status and is prelude to her renewed pledge "to honor and obey." For the waning of the patriarchal order did not mean greater freedom for women, but only that women traded authorities. The daughter's recovery of her father is thus doubly poignant for she finds her father only to lose him again. In the movement from father patriarchy to husband patriarchy in these novels, the daughter is separated a second time from her father, as she becomes the responsibility of her husband in the new conjugal family.

The daughter's loss of her father is often represented as an extreme form of orphanhood. Heroines alone in the world, cut off from their consanguineal families, feel most keenly of all the absence of their fathers. Frances Burney's *Evelina, or The History of a Young Lady's Entrance into the World* (1778) conforms to this pattern. Raised in the simplicity and purity of "Berry Hill" by Mr. Villars, the surrogate patriarch who was guardian to her unfortunate mother before her, Miss "Anville" enters London's fashionable society to learn its ways and to find her own place in it. Since degrees of birth, family, and social position are key to her reception in that corrupt world, her biological father's refusal to recognize her as his daughter is a profound problem. For those with discernment, however, she carries her pedigree within her – her birth certificate in her countenance as Mr. Villars says – for she has been educated in a manner befitting her station. Her intelligence, native refinement, and extraordinary beauty prove dowry enough, and worthy Lord Orville falls in love with her and asks her to marry him before she confronts her father. But like many another heroine, Evelina insists on her father's blessing before she bestows her hand. It equalizes the power between them to have her father on her side. Two complex and ambivalent recognition scenes between father and daughter thus precede the marital denouement, whose immediate effect is to catapult Evelina into another (surrogate) father-daughter embrace. In the last words of the novel, Evelina writes that "the chaise now waits which is to conduct me to dear Berry Hill, and to the arms of the best of men."[31]

Although in the case of Frances Burney, as Margaret Doody's biography makes clear, one could argue that these scenes project the novelist's longing for and resentment of her own father,[32] the phenomenon I am speaking

[31] Frances Burney, *Evelina or the History of a Young Lady's Entrance into the World*, ed. Edward and Lillian Bloom (Oxford and New York: Oxford University Press, 1982), p. 406. All subsequent page references are to this edition.

[32] Margaret Doody, *Frances Burney*, pp. 30–3.

of is not biographically determined or psychological in a narrow personal sense. Freud, of course, believed that a woman's desire for her father was a necessary step in her turn towards heterosexuality. Without it, she would be "trapped" in an intense, pre-Oedipal relation with her mother. Mary Poovey, updating this model to analyze both Burney's *Evelina* and Mary Shelley's *Falkner*, suggests that the idealization of fathers in these texts substitutes for the longed-for missing mothers. The unrealistic idealization then reverses itself to show its resentful side when the daughters fall in love. That is, when the daughter has another love object, she is able to confront the negative aspects of the man whose wilful and passionate nature destroyed her mother before her, the "mother whose self-denying love was powerless before him." The daughter then civilizes and socializes the man whose desire killed the mother she reincarnates. Her own power vis-à-vis the father is released when she makes her "own" heterosexual choice – when she is backed by another man.[33]

Another Freudian interpretation of this plot places the daughter at the center of a more standard male Oedipal conflict. She is the disputed object in the rivalry between men, the goods to be exchanged or the symbolic site on which agreements between men are ratified. Thus Janice Haney-Peritz argues that Clarissa is trapped in an Oedipal script, caught in the crossfire between Lovelace and her male kin.[34] The father-daughter relationship has also been read as a displacement of Oedipal mother-son incest. As grown and grizzled sons still longing for their own mothers, fathers confuse their daughters with these mourned and missing women. Reciprocally, daughters, disillusioned by their mothers' lack of power, accede to their fathers' needs.[35]

These psychoanalytically inflected explanations are attempts to account for the cultural power and deep psychological ambivalence of father-daughter relations in eighteenth-century fiction and later. But they do not explain the unexpected intensity and the narrative weight given to the *daughter's* desire for paternal benediction in the novels of the later eighteenth century. These longings boil up in the fictions with an immediacy that belies more complicated projections. Although paternal power was

[33] Mary Poovey, "Fathers and Daughters: The Trauma of Growing Up Female," in Janet Todd (ed.), *Men by Women* (New York: Holmes and Meier, 1982), pp. 39–58, quote p. 56.

[34] Janice Haney-Peritz, "Engendering the Exemplary Daughter: The Deployment of Sexuality in Richardson's *Clarissa*," in Lynda E. Boose and Betty S. Flowers (eds.), *Daughters and Fathers*, pp. 181–207.

[35] Sandra M. Gilbert, "Life's Empty Pack: Notes toward a Literary Daughteronomy," *Critical Inquiry* 11 (1985), 355–84; reprinted in Lynda E. Boose and Betty S. Flowers (eds.), *Daughters and Fathers*, pp. 256–77.

often depicted as claustrophobic and arbitrary, it was also sustaining. To be without it was to go naked into the world. Readers understood without being told why the heroine needed to find her father before she could get on with her life. The emotional urgency of the father-quest – and the way it superseded the marriage plot – was taken for granted. Although regressive and anachronistic, I would argue that the quest for the father can also be read as a quest for legitimacy, signaled by the frequency with which the father's recognition provides the proof required by the plot of the legality of the mother's marriage and hence the literal legitimacy of the daughter. The body of the daughter, who usually looks exactly like her dead mother, is the first text which proves that she is her mother's daughter. This metaphor is made literal in *The Beggar Girl* (1797), in which the heroine actually has her parents' initials inscribed on her left breast.[36] Legitimacy is then corroborated by some form of external documentation. In *The History of Betty Barnes* (1753), for example, the heroine always carries under her stays a folded letter, written by her father to her mother, signed only with initials; it is the only evidence she has of her parents.[37] Because it is signed "your loving husband," it proves to the heroine the legitimacy of her birth, despite continual aspersions to the contrary throughout most of the book. It is this letter that leads to the discovery of her actual father, an old sailor who had lent her money earlier when she was in distress. When he sees the letter and learns why she treasures it, he throws his arms around her "crying in a tone of utmost tenderness, 'You are, you are my child! My long lost child!' "

The extatic delight of being incircled in a father's embraces, rendered her unable for some time to return an answer to this tenderness, and they both enjoyed a speechless rapture too great for words: when the swell of joy . . . would give her leave, she answered his tenderness with the strongest expressions of filial duty, and affectionate reverence. (vol. II, 109)

---

[36] For this example from Agnes Maria Bennett's *The Beggar Girl and Her Benefactors* (1797), I am indebted to Susan Greenfield's *Mothering Daughters: Novels and the Politics of Family Romance Frances Burney to Jane Austen* (Detroit: Wayne State University Press, 2002), pp. 51–6. The novels Greenfield lists with heroines who look exactly like their (dead) mothers include Frances Burney's *Evelina* (1778), Elizabeth Helme's *Louisa; or, the Cottage on the Moor* (1787), Charlotte Smith's *Celestina* (1791), Agnes Maria Bennett's *The Beggar Girl and Her Benefactors* (1797), Regina Maria Roche's *Children of the Abbey* (1796), and *Fatherless Fanny* (1819), written in part by Clara Reeve. See John K. Reeves, "The Mother of *Fatherless Fanny*," *ELH* 9 (December 1942), 224–33.

[37] *The History of Betty Barnes*, 2 vols. (London, 1753); rpt. New York: Garland, 1974. Joyce Grossman argues for Mary Collyer's authorship of this novel, on the basis of the attribution by Ralph Griffiths, editor of the *Monthly Review*, as jotted in the margins of his copy of the book. See her "Social Protest and the Mid-Century Novel: Mary Collyer's *The History of Betty Barnes*," *Eighteenth-Century Women* 1 (2000), 165–84.

After this discovery, our heroine is no longer called "Barnes," which was after all only the name of the place she was born. She has a father, a proper cognomen, and her future happiness is assured.

SHARING HER FATHER'S POWER

Anthropological literature on women in patrilineal societies highlights their double membership in consanguineal and conjugal/affinal groups – in both their families of origin and their families of marriage. Poised on the threshold of their consanguineal kin group, ready for exogamous exchange, daughters inhabit a liminal position between families. Many factors are thought to influence a woman's position in her affinal family of marriage, but none so centrally as the importance and power of her family of origin and the necessity of honoring her membership in that kin group. If a woman's "natal patrilineal group is bound to her husband's by reciprocal ties of exchange, political support, or military alliance . . . she can count to a certain extent on the intervention of her father and brothers to support her in stressful situations."[38] In other words, so long as a woman continues to be defined as the daughter of her father, she has more leverage in her negotiations with her husband. A daughter is the property of her father to "give away" – as Lynda Boose has pointed out – not only in the negative sense of being treated as a commodity, but also as an extension of himself. Boose writes: "She is explicitly a *sexual* property acquired not by economic transaction but from the father's sexual expenditure and his own family bloodline – which makes the father's loss of her a distinctively personal loss of himself."[39] As a member of a patrilineal family or tribe, her power derives from her father's backing. In other words, a daughter's connection to her father enhances her power insofar as she is his representative or the representative of his family.

Karen Sacks has suggested that the transformation from a status society to a class society undermined the power of kin groups, which in turn lessened the overall status of women.[40] That is, because women's power and autonomy generally derive from their consanguineal kin relations, a woman born into a powerful family shared the power of that family. When this basis of power in kin is undercut – as when power comes to be centralized in the state or a ruling class of private owners – it reduces women

[38] Ernestine Friedl, *Women and Men: An Anthropologist's View* (New York: Holt, Rinehart and Winston, 1975), p. 68.
[39] Lynda E. Boose, "The Father's House and the Daughter in it," p. 4–6.
[40] Karen Sacks, *Sisters and Wives* (Urbana and Chicago: University of Illinois Press, 1982), pp. 216–41.

to perpetual subordinates in their affinal groups. Well might the wealthy Miss Mary Warde observe in 1742 that "No Woman of understanding can marry without infinite apprehensions." When she married in 1745, giving up the protection of her male relatives, she wrote: "leaving my Father & Brother is more painfull than I will attempt to express, or perhaps a steadyer mind would feel."[41]

Although existing family histories do not track changes in the father-daughter relationship over time, I believe that by the late eighteenth century the responsibility of fathers for daughters was so far attenuated that the fantasy of paternal responsibility was the subject of nostalgic yearning. Daughters were increasingly at the mercy of husbands in respect to the disposal of their property and income, as well as their liberty and happiness. Law and custom increasingly defined women as wives rather than as daughters. Whose daughter a woman was carried less and less weight in relation to whose wife she was.

I would argue that these scenes of tearful reunion in late eighteenth-century fiction are a backward glance at an outmoded system, a nostalgic and compensatory recreation of a time when a father's word protected his daughter from the vicissitudes of the marriage market or the arbitrary power of the man she married. The feudal dispensation that invested the daughter with her father's power for life had come to an end. I believe that these father-daughter scenes are an enactment and a record of what women lost in the movement from a status to a class society, in capitalist transformations of family relationships. Obsessive father-daughter scenes dramatize the social problem that fathering of a certain sort had become a fiction, a set of empty forms for women, concerned largely with keeping property in the male line, ending for the girl child with her marriage. Paternal interventions in difficult marital or financial situations had become the exception rather than the rule. The tearful urgency of the heroine's quest for a father who would legitimate her before she married, whose name would elevate her to the status of her intended spouse, was an old solution to a new problem. Male authority and natal class would balance out the handicaps of sex; a father's loyalty would weigh against the power a woman lost in marrying.

Although I am claiming that these scenes of fathers and daughters are a compensatory literary response to the sociological facts of women's lives, they might also be understood as expressions of ontological nostalgia for an earlier time in any woman's life, when she was protected by her parents

---

[41] Quoted in Amanda Vickery, *The Gentleman's Daughter: Women's Lives in Georgian England* (New Haven and London: Yale University Press, 1998), p. 32.

as a child. The ending of Jane Austen's *Emma*, for example, has all these resonances. On the brink of growing up, the necessity of marriage revealed to her, Emma is rescued, as it were, by Mr. Woodhouse's inevitable resistance to her ever leaving his hearth and jurisdiction. In what could be construed as a regressive move for Emma, the new couple decide they will remain at Hartfield with her father. Knightley agrees to a matrilocal practice and joins Emma's consanguineal kin group. Mr. Woodhouse's authority will protect Emma, one feels, from the worst excesses of Knightley's exasperating correctness. Her father will weigh in on her side, and help her maintain a proper balance of power.[42]

SENTIMENTAL REUNIONS

Symptoms of a society undergoing change rather than psycho-biographical projections, these father-daughter sequences appear in novels by men as well as by women. Goldsmith's *The Vicar of Wakefield* (1766), that quizzical expression of naive generosity rewarded, builds to its climax in two sentimental scenes between Dr. Primrose and his erring but repentant oldest daughter, Olivia. In the first, he intervenes to save her when she has been ruined and cast off. He happens to be on the spot when a heartless innkeeper's wife evicts Olivia because she cannot pay the reckoning.

I instantly knew the voice of my poor ruined child Olivia. I flew to her rescue, while the woman was dragging her along by her hair, and I caught the dear forlorn wretch in my arms. 'Welcome, any way welcome, my dearest lost one – my treasure – to your poor old father's bosom! . . . though thou hadst ten thousand crimes to answer for, he will forget them all!'

Idealized and sentimental though it may be, this expression of unconditional paternal love is powerful. Few subsequent writers granted their fictional fathers the vicar's all-forgiving love; his paternal authority saves, protects, and redeems his lost daughter, modeling a true Christian charity.[43]

---

[42] For the view that Emma must be reined in, disciplined, and made to submit to male authority by marrying, see my "Interrupted Friendships in Jane Austen's *Emma*," *Tulsa Studies in Women's Literature* 5, 2 (Fall 1986), 185–202.

[43] Oliver Goldsmith, *The Vicar of Wakefield* (1766; London: Dent, and New York: Dutton, 1976, p. 137. Mr. Thomas, the local vicar in Arthur Young's *The Adventures of Miss Lucy Watson* (London, 1768), may have been based on Goldsmith's vicar. He acts as a protective and forgiving father to the "fallen" Lucy Watson. Indeed, he pleads – unsuccessfully – with her biological father to forgive her and let her come home. Samuel Pratt's *Shenstone-Green; or the New Paradise Lost* (1779) similarly contains a scene in which Hackney Oldblade is reunited with his daughter, Fanny, who has become a prostitute because she had no other way to support herself. "[S]he *wanted* to be a good girl but nobody would give her the *means*" (2nd edn., 3 vols. [London, 1780]), vol. II, pp. 176–7). Charles

After several turns of the whimsical wheel of fortune, the kindly vicar is given to understand that he has again lost his daughter – but it is all so that readers can have the pleasure of another sentimental reunion when she reappears.

Henry Mackenzie's *The Man of Feeling* (1771) includes a dramatic scene of father-daughter reconciliation as well. In the course of Harley's rambles he is solicited by a poor and hungry prostitute. Ever gallant, he takes her to a tavern and buys her some wine and some food, for she is starving, and sends her home in a chair promising to wait on her the next morning. The story she tells is the familiar one of seduction by a man without principles who breaks his promises and abandons her "to the common use of the town." While she is telling her sad tale, she hears her father's voice outside the door. She runs to him and falls at his feet. In an iconic sentimental gesture borrowed from the stage, the astonished father looks up to heaven and then back at his long-lost daughter. "He laid his left hand on his heart, the sword dropped from his right, he burst into tears."[44]

A sentimental father-daughter sequence usurps the spotlight in Robert Bage's first novel, *Mount Henneth* (1782). Henry Cheslyn, one of the novel's heroes, rescues the brave American Miss Melton from a house of ill repute where she has been sequestered by a kidnapper and would-be ravisher. Henry wants to marry his liberty-loving beauty, but she pines after her father, from whom she was separated by the vicissitudes of travel and war. The love-and-marriage plot is interrupted – postponed – and transformed into the story of a daughter seeking her father. Twice she is reunited with him: the first time in prison where he has been detained as a spy and again after she has been abducted and saved a second time. The narrator of this second scene of reunion remarks: "It brings to my mind Rousseau's picture of . . . the meeting of St. Preux and Eloisa, after many years absence." He describes how he "saw them rush into each other's arms, and was retiring as quick as possible, when I perceived them sink gently on the floor together." Smelling salts are applied, and Miss Melton revives. We are told that her father "hung over her, enamoured, she threw her arms around his neck and glued her lips to his in speechless ecstasy."[45] Robert Bage, whose own offspring, incidentally, were all sons, features father-daughter dramas in

Johnstone's *Chrysal, or the Adventures of a Guinea* (1760) includes another such father, who forgives his daughter's ruin and implores her "to return to him, and hide her shame from the world in his bosom; but despair made her reject his offer." Ed. E. A. Baker (London: Routledge, 1907), p. 421.

[44] Henry Mackenzie, *The Man of Feeling* [1771] *and The Man of the World* [1773] (London: Routledge, and New York: E. P. Dutton, 1931), pp. 70, 72.

[45] Robert Bage, *Mount Henneth*, Ballantyne's Novelist's Library, vol. 9 (London: Hurst, Robinson, and Co., 1824) quote p. 220.

his other novels as well. In *Hermsprong* (1796), for example, the heroine, Caroline Campinet, obeys her father's unreasonable and tyrannical will and steadfastly refuses to marry the man she loves until she receives his paternal consent. She continues to exhibit daughterly submission until he relents in his prohibition on his deathbed, in a scene in which father and daughter exhibit their mutual tenderness tearfully and clasp hands in forgiveness.

Tony Tanner has argued powerfully for the eroticism of the father-daughter relation in Rousseau's *Julie, ou La Nouvelle Héloise* (1761). He reminds us that all the romantic episodes in this novel have an incestuous cast. With this in mind he examines closely the scene in which Julie's father, irritated by her refusal to marry as he would have her marry, pushes and slaps her and then pulls her to his lap and kisses her. "Nothing remotely comparable in physical contact is ever evoked as occurring between Julie and Saint-Preux," Tanner observes.[46] The ultimate meaning of this confusion of desire and authority marks for Tanner "some kind of imminent crisis in the particular family structure on which Western society was based, [and] carries within it a sense of doom concerning the very emotions and institutions that the book strives to celebrate."[47] I will return to this question of incestuous affect, both in this chapter and at greater length in Chapter 9, but for now I simply want to underscore Tanner's hunch in light of Robert Bage's explicit intertexual reference, that the dramatization of father-daughter conflict and resolution in this ur-text of sentimental family relations registers a crisis in the western family – and to add that the relationship of the father and daughter is diagnostic of this crisis precisely because it is no longer clear to whom the daughter belongs.

Charlotte Smith's *Emmeline, or the Orphan of the Castle* (1788), a novel about a woman torn between her grateful loyalty to a man who loves her and her duty to a guardian who forbids the union, continues this eighteenth-century obsession with fatherless daughters unable to marry until their true fathers are discovered. The subplot repeats the motif of a woman caught between her lover and her family – and driven mad by it, like Ophelia, or like Clementina in *Sir Charles Grandison*. In the same year, de Sade published *Eugenie de Franval*, the libidinous essence and paradigmatic inversion of

---

[46] First published as "Julie and 'La Maison Paternelle': Another Look at Rousseau's *La Nouvelle Héloise*," *Daedalus* 105, 1 (Winter 1976), 23–46, the longest version of this piece by Tony Tanner is a chapter in his *Adultery in the Novel: Contract and Transgression* (Baltimore: Johns Hopkins University Press, 1979), pp. 113–178. I am quoting from the version of the essay published in Jean Bethke Elshtain (ed.), *The Family in Political Thought* (Amherst: University of Massachusetts Press, 1982), pp. 96–124, quote p. 104.

[47] Tanner, "Julie and 'La Maison Paternelle,'" in Elshtain (ed.), *The Family in Political Thought*, p. 96.

this narrative, about a father who raises his daughter to be his most perfect sexual partner and his brutal companion in crime.

Elizabeth Inchbald's *A Simple Story* (1791) is a mix of these motifs of incest and fatherlessness. It tells of an orphan who falls in love with her handsome, ardent guardian – and he with her. She continually tests her power as a beloved mistress against his authority as a father or guardian, a conflict that is exacerbated by their difference of religion. Their contest of wills ceases after they are married; but when, during his prolonged absence in the West Indies, she becomes involved with another man, they become estranged and she dies repentant and broken. At her death she sends their daughter to him, but he refuses to receive the girl or permit her into his presence. He sends this daughter to live in one of his country houses and forbids anyone even to mention her. During the two weeks a year that he visits that remote estate, the girl is ordered to stay out of his sight and hearing or be banished for ever. The ultimate rapproachement between Mathilda and her father resolves so many issues of power, obedience, and love – and atones for so many painful misunderstandings – that the denouement is completely overdetermined.[48]

Clara Reeve's less familiar *The Two Mentors* (1783) contains such a fine example of a daughter's search for her father ending with a dramatic reunion scene, that it is worth describing in detail. The book is set up as a contest between two advisors of Edward Saville, a young gentleman starting out in the world. Richard Munden, his legal guardian, the bad mentor, is a wealthy man of *bon ton* who quotes Lord Chesterfield and ridicules his studious ward for believing every hard-luck story told by the unfortunates who apply to him for assistance. But most of all he mocks the young man because he does not seem to be interested in seducing women.[49] The good mentor is Saville's college tutor, Jarvis Johnson, an impecunious fellow with inflexible moral standards, who encourages Saville to withstand the worldly Munden's temptations. Given the terms of the book, the father-daughter sequence seems to come out of nowhere, dictated not so much by literary considerations – whether the structure of the narrative or the demands of a tradition – as by the psycho-social needs of the larger society beyond the frame of the novel. Saville makes the acquaintance of Sophia

---

[48] When Lord Elmwood rescues Mathilda after having proscribed her company, she "clung round his legs, and bathed his feet with her tears. – These were the happiest moments she had ever known – perhaps the happiest *he* had ever known." Elizabeth Inchbald, *A Simple Story* (1791; Oxford and New York: Oxford University Press, 1988), p. 329.

[49] Randolph Trumbach argues in *Sex and the Gender Revolution: Heterosexuality and the Third Gender in Enlightenment London* (Chicago: University of Chicago Press, 1998) that such heterosexual libertinism was becoming *de rigeur* for masculine identity by the middle of the eighteenth century.

Melcombe, a beautiful and refined young woman with the sorrowful air of a "virgin widow" and an interesting lack of antecedents. At this point the plot rotates on its axis and her story – a daughter's anxious quest for her father's recognition – dominates the last quarter of the book.

Raised by foster parents, Sophia knows that the Earl of D is her biological and legal father, but that he is remarried and does not want to acknowledge her publicly. She goes to Grosvenor Square where he lives, hoping just to catch a glimpse of him or any of her half siblings. "I looked at the outside of the house, till I worked my passions into a fit of tears," she writes to her foster mother.[50] Like Juliet in Frances Burney's *The Wanderer* (1814), she knows that this family is her own family, although none of them except Lord D himself is aware of the connection. She cannot bring herself to leave London although she has no reason for being there, and the reader witnesses her prolonged agony.

I wish, I long to see my father! to see my brothers and sisters; to see any part of the family. My heart beats towards them, and an involuntary tear starts into my eye, whenever I think on them I vainly wish that some accident may throw me in their way, or them into mine. (298)

Fate kindly intervenes when Sophia meets her half brother at a play. She knows that they are related although he does not, which intensifies her yearning. Nonetheless, he is drawn to her in the inevitable, invisible way that blood relations are drawn to one another in eighteenth-century fiction even when they are ignorant of their connection. This trope, the *cri du sang* or the call of blood, signified a fictional instinct whose popularity apparently reassured society that consanguinity was still powerful. Like Juliet's half brother in Burney's *The Wanderer*, Sophia's brother misinterprets his attraction to the beautiful stranger as romantic love, while Sophia struggles to maintain the friendship but discourage the courtship.

Meanwhile, Sophia's dreams about "my father, my brother, and all the family" become increasingly vivid. With the usual prognosticating clarity of dream, she imagines one night being "received into their arms, and acknowledged for their relation" (315). Meanwhile, her brother, still ignorant of their true relation, tells his (their) father that he loves and wants to marry Sophia Melcombe. When her father hears her name from his son, he calls upon her, sternly intending to keep her at bay. But her brother breaks in upon their tête-à-tête, kneels, and asks his father's permission to propose to her. At this point, Lord D breaks down and informs his son that Sophia is

[50] Clara Reeve, *The Two Mentors: A Modern Story* (1783; 3rd edn. London, 1803), p. 299. Subsequent page references are to this edition.

"your sister, and my *legitimate* daughter" (emphasis in the original). When he explains further that he has been trying to keep his first marriage a secret from his present wife, Sophia proves her virtue by renouncing his wealth. She tells him

> I never wished to be a sharer in your rank and fortune; it was only your paternal affection of which I so ardently desired to partake . . . I renounce all pretensions to your rank or fortune, only call me your child in private, and sometimes honour me with your presence. (335–6)

Acknowledging the integrity of her dutiful resignation, Lord D announces that the time for concealment is past. He calls in Mr. Saville – the young man whom this novel is ostensibly about – and gives the young couple his blessing, not to mention the promise of a dowry suitable to an earl's daughter.

Like Frances Burney's Juliet Granville in *The Wanderer* (1814), Sophia Melcome gets not only a father but a whole family at the novel's denoue-ment. The fatherless girl is reinstated in her consanguineal family, and the resources and power she is granted by virtue of that reinstatement are the measure of what was lost when estranged from it.[51] Many tears are shed and the reader has the pleasure of seeing generous feelings and persevering loyalties rewarded. The heroine finds her family and is legitimated in time to marry the man she loves. The novel, which originally seemed to be about the conflict between the diametrically opposed mentors of a young man, has resolved into the usual successful quest of an elegant and deserving young woman for her father.

The History of Charlotte Summers, the Fortunate Parish Girl (London, 1750, 2 vols.) an anonymous novel that Lady Mary Wortley Montagu could not put down,[52] is perhaps the earliest prototype of this story of the lost daughter, and contains two satisfying scenes of orphaned girls returned to the protection and support of their fathers. The first, an interpolated tale, tells of a puny two-year-old girl named Jenny Jenkins rescued from a band of traveling gypsies who were mistreating her by the charitable Dorset farmer Dobson and his less charitable wife Moll. They raise her like a daughter, together with their own son Jack. In his fifteenth year, Jack runs away to sea, and after a few letters was heard of no more. His parents mourn him as one dead. But one night Jenny dreams of his return, dressed "like a young

---

51 In the Burney novel, drafted by 1802 although not published until 1814, the family with which the heroine is reunited is similarly wealthy and aristocratic.

52 *The Complete Letters of Lady Mary Wortley Montagu*, ed. Robert Halsband, 3 vols. (Oxford: Clarendon Press, 1967), vol. III, p. 4.

Gentleman with a Sword and laced Waistcoat, his Hair flowing in pretty Curls about his Shoudlers [sic]," accompanied by "an elderly, grave looking Gentleman, to whom he said, Look you here, Sir, is all the Return I can make you for your Kindness to me, this is your Daughter, you know her by the Mark of a Strawberry on her left Breast, which you have often told me of" (1: 95). With the inevitability of fiction, Jack soon returns from Algiers with the kind and wealthy man who redeemed him from slavery there. When this man beholds Jenny, he is struck motionless, exhibiting "the utmost Marks of Grief and Sorrow in his Countenance," and tells those present that she has "all the Features, the very Look, Voice, and Air of my much lov'd Wife, and the identical Mark of my long and forever lost only Daughter" (1: 102). Jenny, for her part, experiences the *cri du sang*; she is drawn to him and "strongly biased to love and honour him." Kissing his tear-wet cheeks, she announces "methinks I feel all that he feels, and sympathize with him, in a manner I never did with any Body in Distress before . . . as much as if I were his Child" (1: 108–9). Later, when she is told he is indeed her father, she avers "my Heart confirms this Claim of Blood" (1: 110).

This interpolated tale in turn prefigures the story of the orphaned Charlotte Summers, whose own father appears just in time to raise her to her proper station so that she is equal to the man she marries. Once again, the *cri du sang* announces a blood relation. Charlotte Summers finds herself "seized with an unaccountable Fluttering of Spirits, as soon as she set Eyes on Captain *Ainsworth*" (II: 296). At her first sight of him, "she found herself strongly disordered, and thought she saw in his Face, and observed in his Voice something that moved her with the greatest Tenderness" (II: 297). He, in turn, looks on her with great attention and confusion, and announces that he is "more affected with the Sight of her than any thing that had happened to him since he came to *England*; for, added he, with a deep Sigh, that young Creature has so great a Resemblance to a much loved Child, and much deserving Wife, that on the Sight of her every tender Idea of them occurred to my Memory" (II: 296). She is his daughter, of course, and we are soon treated to a dramatic scene in which he acknowledges her and she clings to his neck, bathes his face with tears, kneels to him, and is raised in his arms, and they both make suitable exclamations of happiness and surprise.

These scenes illustrate the emotional capital that eighteenth-century English society invested in father-daughter scenes, as well as how the *cri du sang* trope functioned in fiction of this period. A familiar topos from French classical tragedy, and still used in English heroic drama in the seventeenth century, the *cri du sang* disappeared from the literary landscape in England until the second half of the eighteenth century, when it reappeared in sentimental fiction with new force. The "voice of blood" announced itself in hundreds of novels, including Burney's *Evelina* and Smollett's *Roderick Random*, in the instantaneous attraction and instinctive sympathy experienced by apparent strangers when they met. So common was this fictional device that when the eponymous hero's true identity is discovered in Robert Bage's *James Wallace* (1788), another character remarks wryly on the absence of "the instinctive principle, by which these secret ties have been so often felt (in books) before they were known."[53] Even when separated at birth, parents and children, brothers and sisters always knew when they came into one another's presence that there was a mysterious bond between them, a primal and palpable link that caused them to be interested in one another's welfare even though they had never met before. In a society in which consanguineal ties were increasingly attenuated, the *cri du sang* proved that blood relations still counted, at least in the imaginative realm of fiction.

DANGEROUS INTIMACIES

The novels I have described thus far all feature straightforward separations and joyful reconciliations between fathers who ultimately want the best for their daughters. But fictional father-daughter relations were not always so wholesome. There is another class of novels in which the closeness between a father and a daughter is dangerous and needs to be disrupted – because of the father's incestuous designs, because the sacrifices he requires of his daughter are psychically damaging to her, or because their close relationship causes rivalry with her mother. In these novels, the daughter's own good demands that she be separated from her father, to make her way in the world without the dangerous attentions of this parent.

The malignant forms of this relationship are as absorbing and powerful, and play as central a role in their respective narratives, as the more "ordinary" version of the relationship in which the father at last offers love and protection to the daughter who so richly deserves it. Nor is the harm

---

[53] Robert Bage, *James Wallace* (1788), Ballantyne's Novelist's Library, vol. 9, pp. 377–508, quote p. 486. Another example occurs in Mrs. Woodfin's *The Auction* (1770): a woman who has lost her daughter instantaneously loves a girl who turns out to be her real daughter. For a fuller discussion of the *cri du sang* trope as well as an analysis of examples from Burney and Smollett, see my "De-Familiarizing the Family; Or, Writing Family History from Literary Sources," *Modern Language Quarterly* 55, 4 (December 1994), 415–27. See also Chapter 9 of this volume, "Family Feeling."

that the father offers to his too-obedient daughter in his ill-advised acts of paternalism necessarily intentional. Several of Burney's novels feature this kind of overzealous fatherly intervention, in which fathers inflict terrible pain by instructing their daughters in the repressive rules of femininity. They ask for the most exquisite renunciation, "requiring," as Claudia L. Johnson has said, "that a woman both have and conceal her feeling."[54] Mr. Villars warns Evelina to watch her step, that "nothing is so delicate as the reputation of a woman: it is, at once, the most beautiful and most brittle of all human things" (164). Later, when he sees that she is falling in love with Lord Orville, he warns her that she must quit him and get the better of her feelings for him (308–10). Similarly, the eponymous heroine of *Camilla* is enjoined by both Sir Hugh and Mr. Tyrold, her uncle and her father respectively, to disguise her love for Edgar. "They order me to fly from Edgar Mandlebert – to resist his advice – to take the very measures I have promised to forbear – to disoblige, to slight, to behave to him even offensively!"[55] Meanwhile, Edgar is watching her closely – on the advice of the suspicious Dr. Marchmont – to see if she has the sincerity and sensibility he wants in a wife. Claudia Johnson describes the ensuing double bind: "Enjoined by her father to soldierly self-command over the same somatic signs of sensibility (tears, fainting spells, blushes, starts) that Edgar requires on the grounds that they bypass faculties of artful self-control, Camilla is brought to an impasse towards the end of the novel, and death and madness are her only ways out."[56] Fathers are dangerous bunglers in this novel of Burney's – they physically maim their daughters, or spoil them to the point of heartlessness, or torture them psychologically. Notwithstanding this unnerving record, their daughters obey them and cling to them with a masochistically loving submission that is the proof of feminine virtue within the terms of the novel.

The novels of Sarah Scott also demonstrate what Caroline Gonda calls "the appallingly high cost of such 'loving obedience' for daughters."[57] Forced into unwanted marriages, sold by unfeeling parents, pitted against their fathers, made over to tormenting stepmothers, Scott's heroines hold out as long as they can, trying to accede to the impossible demands of

---

54 Claudia L. Johnson, *Equivocal Beings: Politics, Gender, and Sentimentality in the 1790s* (Chicago: University of Chicago Press, 1995), p. 156.
55 Fanny Burney, *Camilla or A Picture of Youth* (1796), ed. Edward A. Bloom and Lillian D. Bloom (Oxford and New York: Oxford University Press, 1983), p. 177. (Book 3, Chapter 2 in first edition.).
56 Claudia L. Johnson, *Equivocal Beings*, p. 158.
57 Caroline Gonda, *Reading Daughters' Fictions*, p. 105. For a more complete treatment of this pattern in the novels of Sarah Scott, see Caroline Gonda, "Sarah Scott and 'the Sweet Excess of Paternal Love'", *Studies in English Literature 1500–1900* 32, 2 (Summer 1992), 511–35.

their elders. In *The Test of Filial Duty* (1772), for example, Emilia Leonard loves and is loved by the man her father has intended for her half-sister, Sophia. Determined to follow his premeditated plan for his daughters, this misguided father tries to marry off Emilia to one of her rejected lovers in order to clear the way for the other marriage he desires. When he commutes Emilia's sentence to exile in Wales, she is so grateful to him for not forcing her into an unwanted marriage that he is genuinely moved by her self-sacrificing obedience. Emilia's submissive dutifulness is contrasted with the spirit of her best friend and interlocutor, Charlotte Arlington, who at first tries to resist a marriage to Mr. Edmondbury simply because, like a character out of Jane Austen's parodic *Love and Freindship*, she feels obliged to resist her parents' choice. But Emilia is the heroine, and Charlotte her foil, and it is Emilia who shows the lengths to which a daughter will go to comply with her father's wishes.

It could be argued that a plot in which a young woman is required to "both have and conceal her feeling" simply continues the tradition of women's self-suppression in fiction begun by Richardson in *Sir Charles Grandison* (1753–4) and continued in such monuments to women's self-abnegation as Frances Sheridan's *The Memoirs of Miss Sidney Bidulph* (1761) and Elizabeth Griffith's *The History of Lady Barton* (1771). Richardson's Harriet Byron is required to stifle her love and admiration for Sir Charles until he has fully discharged his prior obligation to Clementina; her attempts to get the better of her feelings provide the narrative tension for most of the novel. The same is true of Sidney Bidulph, whose life is a series of painful renunciations, disappointments, and struggles with herself. Elizabeth Griffith's heroine, Lady Barton, pressured by her "friends" into marrying a man she does not love, submits patiently for most of the novel to his cruel treatment of her, while the attractive and gallant Lord Lucan watches in wordless attraction and silent indignation. With plots that make "the perfectly obedient woman an instrument of reiterative disaster,"[58] such novels set the terms for fictional fathers who require their daughters to act against their own best interests.

Sarah Fielding's and Jane Collier's *The Cry* (1754) – that odd compendium of multiply narrated stories, personified public opinion, and digressive observation – contains in one of its narratives a vivid image of the daughter's willingness to sacrifice herself for her father. Nicanor, a widower, comes

---

[58] Patricia Meyer Spacks, *Desire and Truth: Functions of Plot in Eighteenth-Century English Novels* (Chicago: University of Chicago Press, 1990), p. 140. Spacks is here referring to *The Memoirs of Miss Sidney Bidulph* (1761), in which the heroine is forced to become "the agent of harm to all she loves" (140).

under the spell of a fascinating woman on whom he lavishes his fortune. In need of more money to indulge his mistress, he is reluctant at first to take his daughter's small inheritance and "by his extravagance expose a beloved daughter to those many insults, to which youth and beauty in distress of circumstances are liable."[59] He struggles with his conscience, thinking of his daughter Cordelia's "amiable qualities": her "filial duty, her gentleness of mind, and a noble generosity of disposition, which he had ever observed in her from childhood" (1: 224). His love of pleasure gets the better of his judgment, however, and he decides at last to ask for part of her fortune. When he visits Cordelia – with her idealized daughter's name and disposition to match – she sees that he has something on his mind and tries to cheer him up. Having "a genius, and a love to painting," she offers him a watercolor painting she has made, copied from an original by Rosa Alba. The subject of the painting is the "Roman Charity," an old theme with an iconographic tradition, in which a daughter, "visiting her father in prison, where he was condemn'd to be starved to death, gave him from her own breast a daily support" (1: 225). Ironically, Cordelia gives her substance to her weak father not to save his life but to feed his unlawful passion. Although Nicanor bursts into tears at the sight of this iconic emblem of daughterly sacrifice, he masters his better impulses eventually and takes his daughter's money. Like Richardson's selfish fathers, Sir Thomas Grandison and Mr. Harlowe, Nicanor thinks of his daughter as a resource at his disposal; her needs count for little when weighed against his own desires.

The ultimate exploitation of a daughter, of course, is sexual. Occasionally venal fathers in fiction sell their daughters to a man who can afford to pay well;[60] but the more common sexual threat from the father is incest. Fatal to the daughter and criminal in the father, incest or near-incest between a father and daughter (or guardian and ward) inverted the essential responsibility of a father to protect his child and violated the hierarchical and respectful relation between generations. Usually episodes of incest in eighteenth-century fiction are accidental. The father-in-law who drugs and rapes his daughter-in-law in Eliza Haywood's *The Fatal Secret* (1724) is unaware of his kin relation to the woman he goes to such lengths to

---

[59] Sarah Fielding and Jane Collier, *The Cry: A New Dramatic Fable*, 3 vols. (London, 1754), vol. 1, p. 224. All subsequent page references are to this edition.

[60] In Sarah Scott's *The History of Sir George Ellison* (1766), ed. Betty Rizzo (Lexington: University of Kentucky Press, 1996), pp. 156–63, Miss Almon tells her sad tale to Sir George Ellison. Her father was addicted to gambling, and after her mother died he and her new, hard-hearted stepmother tried to raise funds by selling her to a wealthy man who had taken a fancy to her. She runs away in the middle of the night to evade his importunities.

"enjoy." Turpius, in Jane Barker's *Exilius: or, the Banish'd Roman* (1715), tries to woo, seduce, and then to kidnap and rape his daughter Clarinda, but without success. Indeed, the assertion of an actual consanguineal blood tie is often enough to avert criminal intercourse although the intergenerational age difference has been obvious from the start. Caroline Gonda describes a scene in the September 1, 1753 issue of the *Adventurer* in which "a libertine father recognizes his daughter in the inexperienced prostitute undressing to go to bed with him." He literally "reads" her body, "identifying her by the mark of his initials under her left breast (imprinted by her neglected and finally deserted mother . . .)."[61] The discovery that the woman he has hired for sexual service is actually his daughter changes him, and he becomes a properly protective father and reforms his voluptuary habits. In Charles Johnstone's *Chrysal, or the Adventures of a Guinea* (1760), a father discovers his estranged but virtuous daughter in the company of a bawd who hires his services as a surgeon to tend her stable of women. This novel also includes the story of a young woman who has fled her father and begs the protection of a respectable woman in utmost distress. Her father's cruelty, she says, has become unbearable, ever since "she had refused to gratify an impious passion which he had long entertained for her, and which had been the motive of all his care and expense in her education."[62]

Ann Radcliffe's *The Italian* (1797) contains a scene in which murder with incestuous overtones is averted at the last possible minute by recognition of a blood tie. Dagger in hand, in the dead of night, Schedoni glimpses the miniature hanging around the neck of the girl he is about to murder and realizes that she is his own daughter! (She is, in fact, his niece.) He drops his dagger and backs off, psychologically repositioning himself to be her protector rather than her attacker. Similarly, the discovery that Dorilaus makes in Eliza Haywood's *The Fortunate Foundlings* (1744), that the ward he has tried to seduce (whom he found as an infant left in his orchard and raised to maturity) is his own biological child, changes his relation to her. However improper the intergenerational sex that he pressed for earlier, it is the consanguineal blood tie that makes it seem wrong.

Several guardians in novels set out systematically to seduce their wards, without an actual blood tie to rein them in. In Delarivier Manley's *Secret Memoirs and Manners . . . From the New Atalantis* (1709), Charlot's guardian

---

[61] Caroline Gonda, *Reading Daughters' Fictions*, p. 57.
[62] Charles Johnstone, *Chrysal, or the Adventures of a Guinea*, ed. and with Introduction by E. A. Baker, pp. 79–81, 130.

gives her novels and plays about love in order to inflame her imagination and weaken her sense of honor. Leading her to the library, "he took down an Ovid, and opening it just at the love of Myrra for her father, conscious red overspread his face."[63] Count D'Elmont, in Eliza Haywood's *Love in Excess* (1719), tries to seduce his ward Melliora, and then to rape her. He never manages to "possess" her illicitly although there are many attempts; in the end, after many plot complications, he marries her legally, having won the reader's approval. Sarah Scott invents a lascivious guardian in *A Description of Millenium Hall* (1762), although she kills him off abruptly before he can corrupt Louisa Mancel, who goes on to become one of the founders of the all-woman utopian community in that novel.[64]

Incest is, of course, the hallmark of the gothic genre; gothic heroines are usually terrorized by those who should be their protectors. I will return to this point in Chapter 9 ("Family Feeling"). Here I want simply to observe that father-daughter incest is an exaggerated version of the dangerous relationship in which the father asks too much of his daughter, a version with its own dynamic of estrangement and reconciliation, and one with a great deal of emotional power.[65] Whether implicit or explicit – acted out, as in *Secret Memoirs and Manners . . . From the New Atalantis* (1709), *Love in Excess* (1719), *The Fatal Secret* (1724), or, for that matter, *A Simple Story* (1791); inhibited, as in the 1753 story in the *Adventurer* or *The Italian* (1797); or averted, as in *Millenium Hall* (1762) – father-daughter incest is the flip side of the pure, sanitized, asexual father-daughter relationship in the English novel that symbolizes the "purest" family ties – domestic love without sexuality. The daughter-protagonist in Clara Reeve's *The Two Mentors* (1783), described as a "virgin widow," is the prototype: a woman doubly de-sexed, representing the evolving ideal of the nurturing woman without desire of her own.

Another fictional formula representing intense relationships between fathers and daughters involves the competition of heroines with their mothers or stepmothers. This dynamic in a number of eighteenth-century novels explains why and how the heroine loses her father's support and protection. The actual position of the mother within the family and her representation

---

[63] Delarivier Manley, *New Atalantis*, ed. Rosalind Ballaster (London: Pickering and Chatto, 1991), p. 35.

[64] Sarah Scott, *A Description of Millenium Hall*, ed. Gary Kelly (Peterborough, ON: Broadview Press, 1995), pp. 97, 100, 101. Subsequent page numbers are from this edition.

[65] There are (at least) two other ideological tasks accomplished by these narratives of incest. They focus the reader's attention on the all-important moment of penetrative sex rather than on any other sexual moment, and they underscore the belief that men are unable to control their sexual urges and are driven to violent rape by their lust.

in fiction is an entirely different matter, to be taken up in Chapter 8, "The Importance of Aunts." Here, I simply want to offer examples of father-daughter relationships in novels affected by – even replaced by – a rivalrous relationship with a jealous mother. These heroines forfeit their father's love and attention because competitive mothers or stepmothers want them out of the way.

The Histories of Lady Frances S—, and Lady Caroline S— (1763), by Margaret Minifie and Susannah Minifie (later Susannah Gunning), tells of a beautiful young woman whose father is affectionate enough, but whose mother dislikes her. First she is forced out to live with her uncle, and then pressured, Clarissa-like, to marry a brutal and underbred man. Her mother's love of admiration blocks her maternal tenderness – until she is taught by a case of smallpox how ephemeral and specious mere beauty is. Then, after her many adventures, Lady Frances S— is invited home again, her forgiveness sought, by her now-penitent parents. The "Memoir of Mrs. Williams," contained in the anonymous *Letters between an English Lady and Her Friend at Paris* (1770), frames the heroine's experiences in a family dynamic in which she is her father's favorite and is educated by him, while her sister is favored by her mother. "As I rose in the esteem of my father, I fell in that of my mother, whose dislike of me had now almost increased into an aversion," she explains.[66] She begs her father to stop showing his partiality for her since it estranges her mother, to educate her privately, and "not to require my presence so frequently in his library, as I perceived that my depriving my mother of so much of his company ... drew upon me her resentment" (1: 66–7). This psychologically powerful novel is as memorable and affecting in its own way as Mrs. Inchbald's *A Simple Story*. The story of a father's partiality and a mother's jealousy, the sense it offers of the vulnerability and confusion of the daughter in this situation, is acute and realistic.

Sometimes the mother's rivalry is explained by her not being the biological mother. In Anne Dawe's *The Younger Sister: or, The History of Miss Somerset* (1770), the rivalrous older woman is the heroine's older sister, whom their father on his deathbed charged to be like a mother to the heroine. He also stipulates that the heroine's entire fortune would be left to this older sister if she marries without her approbation. Miss Almon's interpolated tale in Sarah Scott's *The History of Sir George Ellison* (1766) tells of her mother's death and her own victimization at the hands of her

---

[66] *Letters between an English Lady and Her Friend at Paris, in Which Are Contained The Memoirs of Mrs. Williams, By a Lady* [Charlotte Williams], 2 vols. (London: Becket and DeHondt, 1770), vol. 1, p. 64.

new stepmother. A coarse and brutal woman, originally her father's kept mistress, the stepmother fills the house with the "lowest and vilest people; sharpers and prostitutes were now to be my constant companions." Worse, her violent temper subdues Miss Almon's father, so that "he never attempted to resist her, but was as implicitly obedient as if he had been a child."[67] Miss Almon runs away when a servant tells her of overhearing her stepmother "bargaining with your lover for your person" (159). She takes a coach to London, where, fortuitously, she lodges in the same house as the hero of the novel, Sir George Ellison. He pays for her passage to Jamaica where he has a plantation, and she sails away to start a new life. Miss Melvyn, in Sarah Scott's *Millenium Hall* (1762), is also separated from her father by a designing stepmother. The new Lady Melvyn convinces her father to send her away to school, in part because she does not wish Miss Melvyn's beauty to eclipse her own. Later, she invents a passion between Miss Melvyn and a farmer's boy so as to force Miss Melvyn to marry the repugnant Mr. Morgan, "whose disposition appeared as ill suited to her's as his age" (124). Another novel in which a daughter's relationship with her father is interrupted by an unfeeling stepmother is Mrs. A. Woodfin's *The Auction* (1770). The narrative centers on the daughter of Sir William Forrester's first wife, Fanny, mistreated by his second wife who favors her own biological daughter. She is forced to flee the protection of her family, which gives rise to many adventures, until her father finally traces her whereabouts, and the third volume culminates in a sentimental father-daughter reunion scene in which all her wrongs are redressed and all her problems solved. Overnight her fortunes are reversed and she is at once wealthy, courted, praised, and loved.

This is the range of father-daughter relationships depicted in eighteenth-century fiction. Whether separated by circumstances beyond their control and trying desperately throughout the narrative to find one another again; overcome by transgressive, erotic feelings; or else pried apart by jealous mothers or stepmothers, these dramas of fathers and daughters signal a change in the meaning or arrangement of families. Their turbulent fortunes betoken a repositioning of daughters in the scheme of things, and a change in their fathers' responsibility for their welfare. This shift, with its attendant feelings of loss, guilt, lamentation, and restitutive wish-fulfillment, is recorded in the plots of novels that communicate to readers the significance of these relationships as well as their jeopardy. I take the sheer *number* of these sequences in the fiction of the period, and their centrality in their

[67] Sarah Scott, *The History of Sir George Ellison*, pp. 156–7.

respective narratives, as proof of disruption in the social relation they are at such pains to describe as repaired in the end. More than any other relation in the family, this between fathers and daughters appears to have a symbolic importance in eighteenth-century fiction that far exceeds its actual significance in economic or social terms. I am positing that this is so because, like the brother and sister relation that I will examine in the following chapters, this relationship was diagnostic of the deep rifts that were beginning to show in the ideology and experience of families in England at this time.

3

Sister-right and the bonds of consanguinity

Unfortunately over the past century, anthropological theory also has been critically influenced by these prevailing assumptions, which conflate women's sexual and reproductive roles as spouses, ignoring the other reproductive roles they play – for example, as sisters.

> Annette B. Weiner, "Reassessing Reproduction in Social Theory," p. 408.

It is far less the father than the brother that modern literature calls to account; less the mother than the sister who must be recognized and given her due as the real rather than the imaginary "other" necessary to found male identity and group life.

> Juliet Flower MacCannell, *The Regime of the Brother*, p. 39.

But the relationship of a brother to a sister has received almost no attention. I believe that this omission has contributed to the one-sided view of women as subordinate in marxist discussions of modes of production.

> Karen Sacks, *Sisters and Wives*, p. 120.

The relationships among siblings, older and younger siblings of the same sex as well as brothers and sisters, is a fascinating flashpoint for understanding the deeper psychological meanings of the kinship shift from an axis of consanguinity to an axis of conjugality. Because the relations between brothers and sisters neither reinforce nor disprove contested hypotheses about warmer relations between spouses or greater affection of parents for their children – hypotheses that interpret kinship of earlier periods through a later sentimental discourse – they have been largely ignored by family historians studying seventeenth- and eighteenth-century English culture. Nevertheless, as some psychologists now recognize, siblings are one's "first real partners in life," the peers from whom one first learns about identity and social relationships.[1] Siblings profoundly influence one another throughout their lives, and often represent one another's longest-lasting consanguineal relationship.[2] Furthermore, attitudes about siblinghood and the reciprocal obligations of brothers and sisters in eighteenth-century England illustrate the complications of a society moving from a system in which the claims of blood were giving way to claims of nuptuality or affinity. The changes in kin priorities that occurred in the course of the century repositioned brothers and sisters in relation to each other and in relation to their parents. Under the earlier social organization, sisters and brothers had been more equal in their subordination to the authority of the father. In South Carolina, where partible inheritance persisted because of a greater availability of land and where primogeniture never superseded it to introduce conflict and resentment in the sibling relationship, this equality was even more conspicuous.[3]

Through their common mother, English siblings were uniquely related to a set of maternal relatives as well as their paternal kin. They were the only link between these sets of maternal and paternal kin because although marriage bound their parents together, it created no recognized connection between the blood relations of the spouses. In English, there are no kin terms for the relationship between spouses' affinal relatives. Only siblings in a bilateral system have identical kin, which accounts for an unusual sibling solidarity in the English system.[4] One linguistic trace of the significance of siblings in the English kinship system is the fact that the terms for nieces and nephews – the children of one's siblings – often meant "grandchild" as well.[5] In other words, the children of one's siblings were as significant intergenerationally as the direct line through one's own progeny. Nieces

[1] Susan Merrell, *The Accidental Bond: The Power of Sibling Relationships* (New York: Random House, 1995), p. 12, quoted in Lorri Glover, *All Our Relations: Blood Ties and Emotional Bonds among the Early South Carolina Gentry* (Baltimore: Johns Hopkins University Press, 2000), p. 25. On sibling relationships, Glover also recommends Stephen Bank and Michael Kahn, *The Sibling Bond* (New York: Basic Books, 1982); Michael Lamb and Brian Sutton-Smith (eds.), *Sibling Relationships: Their Nature and Significance across the Life Span* (Hillsdale, NJ: Lawrence Erlbaum Associates, 1982); and Patricia Goldring Zukow, *Sibling Interaction across Cultures: Theoretical and Methodological Issues* (New York: Springer-Verlag, 1989).

[2] Lorri Glover, *All Our Relations*, pp. 31, 160 n. 8.

[3] Lorri Glover, *All Our Relations*, p. 11. The sister whose familial relationships Glover analyzes here left an extensive correspondence, available in Elise Pinckney (ed.), *The Letterbook of Eliza Lucas Pinckney 1739–1762* (Columbia: University of South Carolina Press, 1997).

[4] Sybil Wolfram, *In-Laws and Outlaws: Kinship and Marriage in England* (London and Sydney: Croom Helm, 1987), p. 67. On sibling solidarity in a cognatic system, see Randolph Trumbach, *The Rise of the Egalitarian Family: Aristocratic Kinship and Domestic Relations in Eighteenth-Century England* (New York and London: Academic Press, 1978), p. 31.

[5] Naomi Tadmor, *Family and Friends in Eighteenth-Century England: Household, Kinship, and Patronage* (Cambridge: Cambridge University Press, 2001), pp. 147–9.

and nephews, the children of sisters and brothers, insured the continuity of family as securely as the offspring of one's own child. Sisters, equally with their brothers, were keepers of the family honor, bearers of the family name, reproducers of the natal family's social identity, traditions, stories, characteristics, lineage. Particularly if they lived nearby, brothers were bound to protect and preserve their sisters to the extent that they valued the blood that ran in their veins. In Charlotte Lennox's novel *The Life of Harriot Stuart* (1751), Mrs. Dormer's admirable father divides his fortune in his will among his two sisters and his daughter, the women for whom he is responsible (II: 79).

THE SAME BLOOD

The civil understanding of Roman kinship, one of the historical and cultural sources for the English system, privileged siblings of whichever sex as *consanguinitas*, the closest of agnatic kin, so long as they were offspring of the same father. *Agnatio*, kinship created through the male, included the concept of civil kinship as well as biological kinship, which was a function of being subject to *patria potestas* or the father's power. Women could only create *cognatio*, or natural kinship, "devoid of the privileges attached to legal kinship"; they could not create *agnatio*, which was the bond of dependence created by a paterfamilias and his children. Although, as a daughter, a woman could herself be *agnata* since she was related by birth to a male citizen, she could not create *agnatio*. In other words, a man's daughters were included in his chain of *agnatio*, but they could not extend it beyond themselves. This limitation in transmission held true even though as *agnatae*, daughters under Roman law had as much right to their father's material property as their brothers. Thus, women were *agnatio* only in their families of origin and not in their conjugal families. Under this kin system, siblinghood of persons with the same father was the closest and most egalitarian of all agnatic relationships. In eighteenth-century English law, this principle of *agnatio* survived in the incongruous stipulation that brothers of the half-blood could not inherit from one another.[6] Although English kinship traced lineage through the mother's as well as the father's

---

[6] Gianna Pomata, "Blood Ties and Semen Ties: Consanguinity and Agnation in Roman Law," in Mary Jo Maynes, Ann Waltner, Brigitte Soland, and Ulrike Strasser (eds.), *Gender, Kinship, Power* (New York: Routledge, 1996), pp. 42–64. In Norman law, the prohibition against half brothers inheriting from one another applied only to inheritance between uterine brothers – brothers who did not have a common father. But English judges, who did not understand the principle although they incorporated it, extended it to consanguineous brothers, or sons of the same father but by different wives. Gianna Pomata quotes Henry Maine on this matter: "In all the literature which enshrines the

line, some of the sibling-privileging of this Roman system was culturally transmitted through the Latin literature that all educated men and some women read and admired. In Sarah Fielding's fiction *The Lives of Octavia and Cleopatra* (1757), for example, Octavia's position as Augustus Caesar's sister gives her significant power within the civil arena. Her special standing with her brother enables her to press him to make a peace treaty with her husband, Mark Antony.

The equality between brothers and sisters that derived from shared lineage and class began to weaken in the second half of the seventeenth century as the material expectations of the individual began to outweigh the importance of blood, honor, social identity, and tradition. Changes in English class structure and the nature of property and inheritance enhanced the privilege of male children. In all classes except the titled aristocracy, male offspring came to embody hopes for advancement or for class mobility, whether that meant amassing larger and larger land holdings, making a fortune in trade, attending university with society's blue bloods, or distinguishing themselves in military or naval battles. By 1797 Thomas Gisborne took this gender difference in social mobility as a fact of life, referring to the disappointment of young women "at not perceiving a way open by which they, like their brothers, may distinguish themselves and rise to eminence."[7]

In the landed classes, as I have explained, the invention of the strict settlement put absolute ownership of the family estate in the eldest brother's hands, if his father died before he married and his parents' marriage articles had never been superseded. Even the simple fact that he *was going to inherit* the family estate, that it was signed and sealed in his parents' marriage articles and put beyond voluntary choice, gave him credit and status in his family – not to mention leverage with his father – beyond what he would have had if all offspring were to share the inheritance. As Sir Heneage Finch expressed the matter when he refused to incorporate this legal device into *his* son's marriage settlement in 1673:

It is against nature to make the father subject to his child ... I have known the son of such a settlement cast himself away in marriage, and then offer to disinherit his father by treating to sell the inheritance for a song while his father lived.[8]

---

pretended philosophy of law, there is nothing more curious than the pages of elaborate sophistry in which Blackstone attempts to explain and justify the exclusion of the half-blood" (61). I am grateful to David Corson for first suggesting to me the cultural importance of Roman kinship patterns in eighteenth-century English families.

[7] Thomas Gisborne, *An Enquiry into the Duties of the Female Sex* (1797), quoted in Christopher Flint, *Family Fictions: Narrative and Domestic Relations in Britain, 1688–1798* (Stanford: Stanford University Press, 1998), p. 69.

[8] Quoted in John Habakkuk, *Marriage, Debt, and the Estates System: English Landownership 1650–1950* (Oxford: Clarendon Press, 1994), p. 22.

As gender superseded class as a determinant of social identity, and as family fortunes came to be thought of as extending into the future rather than as a repository and representation of the past, sons, and especially firstborn sons, came to assume disproportionate importance in kin networks.

The sister-brother relation thus foregrounded the difference that gender made in a person's station and expectations in the world. Family, lineage, class, rank, and originating economic circumstances of brothers and sisters were constant – only gender varied. Siblings started off with the same genetic gift and the same class origins but ended up in very different circumstances owing to their different opportunities for advancement, differences in the economic circumstances of the persons they married, and increasingly asymmetrical legal arrangements in inheritance and succession. The diverging destinies of brothers and sisters in the property-owning classes were marked by different educational expectations too. Although the curriculum for girls had been similar to that for boys in the sixteenth and seventeenth centuries – if needlework is substituted for weapon handling – girls' education became more "circumscribed" after the Restoration, according to Linda Pollock. First classical languages were dropped – no need for rhetorical training in those who would wield no influence – and then modern languages – even French. Not expected to be as educated as their brothers, women of the upper classes "routinely" apologized in letters for their bad spelling and handwriting and their trivial concerns.[9]

As sisters came to be more dependent within families, brothers were increasingly expected to take on the parental functions of protection, advice, regulation, permission, and prohibition – especially for unmarried sisters. Tension between these responsibilities and the demands of the brothers' own lives came to be more and more a staple of eighteenth-century fiction. The shift from lateral to lineal inheritance (from sideways to downward transmission), with its emphasis on the new conjugal unit rather than on established consanguineal ties, introduced an invisible barrier in relationships between brothers and sisters, setting them against one another as competitors within the consanguineal family rather than bringing them together as allies belonging to one kin group among many. The additional requirement that an elder brother was expected to invest and shelter his sisters' (and younger brothers') portion if it had been saved when their father died, or to raise it from the proceeds or mortgage of his own estate if it had not been saved, put a further strain on sibling relations.

[9] Linda Pollock, "'Teach Her to Live under Obedience': The Making of Women in the Upper Ranks of Early Modern England," *Continuity and Change* 4, 2 (1989), 231–58, esp. 249.

Although siblings shared a powerful and indisputable consanguineal bond as childhood companions, as each other's earliest and safest sustained cross-sex friendships, they were often nevertheless destined by life for very different affinal kin groups. Despite their responsibility to their new conjugal families after marriage, brothers and sisters retained something of their earlier significance to one another as keepers of one another's social identities and earliest memories. Their shared intergenerational histories along with their sexual difference made their relationship key to their social reproduction and authentication.[10] Occasionally, as we shall see, they also continued to share property and possessions. These complexities are reflected in the fiction of the day, in the omnipresent interest of sibling relations woven into stories of courtship and marriage.[11]

Some cultures construct the strongest bonds of all between those who are uterine kin, who come from the same maternal womb or who have been suckled at the same breast. In Taiwan and among some polygynous societies of West Africa, such siblings are understood to have a mutual and irrevocable obligation to one another for life.[12] There are traces of such biologically based lateral kin connections in English society, but family historians largely ignore the evidence for it in their overwhelming emphasis on the importance of the conjugal bond for adults. Twentieth-century family historians project backwards onto eighteenth-century society a kinship system that reflects a nineteenth-century ideal as seen from the perspective of either the male child or the father: a tightly knit nuclear family with a wise

---

[10] This is the thesis of Annette B. Weiner's *Inalienable Possessions: The Paradox of Keeping-While-Giving* (Berkeley: University of California Press, 1992). She maintains that sibling intimacy between brother and sister is "key to the cosmological authentication of intergenerational histories while reproducing social difference" (16). She develops the analogy, in the course of the book, between sibling relationships and systems of ritual "keeping-while-giving." Objects that are inalienable possessions, which maintain distinction but not necessarily hierarchy and which stabilize identity in a world of change, are important to cultural reproduction. Inalienable possessions characterize sibling intimacy, she reasons fruitfully, just as reciprocal exchange characterizes conjugal relations. Although sisters and brothers marry other people, something remains separate from their new affinal identities, something unhomogenized, that derives from and reinforces their sibling intimacy. These distinctions have been ignored by social theorists because the role of the sister as cultural reproducer is too often lost in the sexually reproductive role of the wife, and because the commodification of capitalism disguises the cultural significance of inalienable possessions.

[11] Jack Goody refers to the "shift from lateral to lineal" inheritance in *Production and Reproduction: A Comparative Study of the Domestic Domain* (Cambridge and New York: Cambridge University Press, 1976), p. 119, without really accounting for this shift.

[12] The "milk tie" is discussed in Peter Farb and George Armelagos, *Consuming Passions: The Anthropology of Eating* (Boston: Houghton Mifflin, 1980), p. 98. For the powerful connection among uterine kin in Taiwanese society, see Margery Wolf, "The Self of Others, the Others of Self: Gender in Chinese Society," Paper presented at a conference on Perceptions of the Self: China, Japan, India, East-West Center, University of Hawaii, August 1989.

and benevolent male head, obedient self-sacrificing daughters, and ambitious, energetic but devoted sons.[13] Imagined this way, women had little need for the backing of their male kin because of the "benevolence" of their husbands and/or their own putative "equality" within the conjugal unit. Yet the centrality of the brother-sister relationship, for good or evil, in many eighteenth-century novels belies this conception of a succession of nuclear families dissolving one into the next, generation after generation, without any residual identification with the consanguineal family and without any lateral pull in the direction of collateral relatives. From the point of view of a mother or a female child, the backing of male kin from her lineage – brother, uncle, cousin, nephew – was often critical in her life, as was the emotional and financial support of her blood sisters. Eighteenth-century novels are filled with heroines dependent on their siblings or the siblings of their parents. Even when married, such support was significant to a woman, especially if she lived in the vicinity of her consanguineal kin;[14] many a heroine's difficulties stem from her literal physical distance from her brother/uncle/aunt. In other words, the solidarity of uterine or agnatic kin presented a possible counterweight to market forces and conjugal pressures, and the absence of such support affected the relative power of men and women in their adult lives.

In *Clarissa*, for example, Richardson accentuates Mrs. Harlowe's powerlessness within her marriage by giving her only a sister for a sibling, a sister moreover married to a man with financial obligations to Mr. Harlowe to offset any leverage she might have exerted in sisterly sympathy. Mrs. Harlowe's only male relative in the novel, Colonel Morden, is out of the country, completing the picture of Mrs. Harlowe's maternal helplessness. Thus Richardson calibrated precisely the degrees of power and kin-based responsibility felt by the collateral relatives present in his fiction, whether they were on the mother's side or the father's side of the heroine, their social standing and relative wealth, to provide a psychologically realistic configuration of family pressures to his contemporary audience. As Naomi Tadmor has demonstrated, novelists always identify the birth position and

---

[13] The observation that most family history is written from the perspective of the father or the male child is elaborated in the chapter on "Family History" in Nancy Armstrong and Leonard Tennenhouse, *The Imaginary Puritan: Literature, Intellectual Labor, and the Origins of Personal Life* (Berkeley: University of California Press, 1992), pp. 69–88.

[14] Ernestine Friedl, *Women and Men: An Anthropologist's View* (New York: Holt, Rinehart and Winston, 1975), p. 68. See also Kiran Cunningham, "Let's Go to My Place: Residence, Gender and Power in a Mende Community," in Mary Jo Maynes, Ann Waltner, Birgitte Soland, and Ulrike Strasser (eds.), *Gender, Kinship, Power: A Comparative and Interdisciplinary History* (New York: Routledge, 1996), pp. 335–49.

rank of siblings, their expectations for inheritance as well as their gender, to mark their power gradations within the family before describing their interactions.[15]

In this chapter and the next I want to examine the vestiges of the earlier consanguineous kinship system in the legal, psychological, and social significance of sisters in eighteenth-century English fiction, biographical anecdote, and legal case studies. The sisters in these stories, particularly unmarried sisters, represent the claim of blood kin in its purest form, uncomplicated by the seductions of wealth, power, or the right of succession. Orphaned brothers and sisters were often responsible for one another in eighteenth-century fiction and the frequency of brother-sister households – and the way those households are normalized – suggests something of their ordinariness in eighteenth-century life. They did not have to be explained or excused. Unmarried women, at least in fiction, could live respectably with their brothers. Even when faintly ridiculous as women because not young or beautiful or married, they nevertheless commanded respect and position when managing their brothers' households. Martha (Miss Patty) Archer in Robert Bage's *Barham Downs* (1784) – the gullible target of a fortune seeker – and Tabitha Bramble in Smollett's *Humphry Clinker* (1771), both comic spinster sisters who live with their long-suffering brothers, are examples of the fictional type.

However, brothers may not always have been so ready in life as in these texts to take in their unmarried sisters – or so William Hayley suggests in the grim picture he paints of the fate of unmarried sisters in his 1785 *A Philosophical, Historical, and Moral Essay on Old Maids.*

Let us take a survey of the circumstances which usually attend the Old Maid . . . it is probable, that after having passed the sprightly years of youth in the comfortable mansion of an opulent father, she is reduced to the shelter of some contracted lodging in a country town, attended by a single female servant, and with difficulty living on the interest of two or three thousand pounds, reluctantly, and perhaps irregularly, paid to her by an avaricious or extravagant brother, who considers such payment as a heavy incumbrance on his paternal estate. Such is the condition in which the unmarried daughters of English gentlemen are too frequently found.[16]

---

[15] Naomi Tadmor, "Dimensions of Inequality among Siblings in Eighteenth-Century English Novels: The Cases of *Clarissa* and *The History of Miss Betsy Thoughtless*," *Continuity and Change* 7, 3 (1992), 303–33, esp. 304–5.

[16] William Hayley, *A Philosophical, Historical, and Moral Essay on Old Maids. By a Friend to the Sisterhood*, 3 vols. (London: T. Cadell, 1785), vol. I, p. 7.

This fate was presumably more likely if the woman's brother was married, and thus had introduced into his household another woman capable of managing his establishment and competing for his resources. The relationship between sisters and wives was symptomatic of the relative power of consanguineal and conjugal bonds, a point I will return to later in this chapter. Suffice it to say here that the contest between sisters and wives exists in a number of eighteenth-century novels as a critical moral test of character. Thus, when Sir Ambrose Archer in *Barham Downs* – who has been living with his sister as a bachelor – decides to marry Peggy Whitaker, there is the problem of reconciling the two women. "Miss Peggy" diplomatically visits Sir Ambrose's sister to make an alliance with her rather than to exclude her. She solemnly asks her help in reforming Sir Ambrose, "on which they parted the best friends in the world."[17] This disingenuous gesture on Miss Peggy's part establishes her moral superiority; her determination to incorporate his sister into their conjugal household rather than exclude her, to enter into her new husband's prior obligations, shows a laudable sense of family responsibility.

The moral high ground in fiction always belongs to those who care for relatives beyond their limited conjugal units, especially the relatives of their spouses. Sir Edward Newenden's willingness to give financial help to his wife's cousins, the Chestervilles (Ethelinde's brother and his wife), in Charlotte Smith's *Ethelinde, or the Recluse of the Lake* (1790), calls forth this cynical – and probably realistic – response from his father-in-law, the well-named Maltravers:

Sir Edward, I cannot [listen] to all these pretences of disinterested friendship to your wife's family. Don't I know that nobody cares even for their *own* family, and that a man now won't lend his own brother an hundred pounds without some good that may come of it to himself, nor without security; why then should you so lavishly lend a considerable sum, or rather give it, for you'll never get it again . . . to the Chesterville's [sic]? people whom you were only distantly connected with . . . [Y]ou had no right to do it, and it was plain you considered them more than my daughter's children, though they in fact have the only claim to it, or than my daughter herself.[18]

But Sir Edward has been designed to be exemplary and he *is* sincere about helping the Chestervilles. Similarly, Sir Thomas Bertram's willingness to

---

[17] Robert Bage, *Barham Downs* (1784), reprinted in Sir Walter Scott's Ballantyne's Novelist's Library, vol. 9 (London: Hurst, Robinson, 1824), pp. 241–375, quote p. 367.

[18] Charlotte Smith, *Ethelinde, or the Recluse of the Lake*, 2nd edn., 5 vols. (London: printed for T. Cadell, 1790), vol. IV, p. 135.

do what he can for the children of his wife's sister Price, in Jane Austen's
Mansfield Park, affirms his moral stature in fictional terms.

In eighteenth-century novels, the fates of adult brothers and sisters are
intertwined to a greater extent than in any modern representation of family
life. Many a fictional heroine must apply to her brother for a place to stay,
money to live, or permission to marry. Brothers have rights over their
sisters unthinkable today – as well as obligations to take care of them that
are similarly beyond our ken. In these novels, brothers often fight duels
to protect or avenge their sisters' honor and sisters renounce their lovers –
or agree to marry where they do not love – for the sake of their brothers'
happiness or credit. It is Mrs. Harlowe's fear that Lovelace will draw her son,
James, into a duel over Clarissa that leads her to accede initially to Clarissa's
correspondence with Lovelace. Francis Thoughtless in Eliza Haywood's
The History of Betsy Thoughtless (1751) duels the gentleman commoner in
Oxford who made free with his sister, Betsy. The corollary devotion of
sisters to their brothers even when down and out, as represented in the
affecting story of Camilla and Valentine in Sarah Fielding's *The Adventures
of David Simple* (1744), or in Henrietta Belfield's dedication to her brother in
Frances Burney's *Cecilia* (1782), was another well-worn sentimental formula
of the day.

I am suggesting that these representations of sibling intimacy corresponded to a real, if deteriorating, significance in the relationship between
sisters and brothers and their respective children. Examples from other
parts of the world can help us to re-imagine the unique benefits of this
relationship. In Oceania and in the Arab world, for example, the intense
bond between brother and sister provides important experience for gender
socialization when siblings are young and guarantees social identity as well
as maintaining cultural memory into the next generation. In these societies, brother-sister relationships also establish the rights to certain material
possessions for their offspring. In slighting or ignoring sibling intimacy,
anthropologists and historians ignore the role women play as sisters in
social reproduction, conflating and subsuming it in sexual reproduction
and hence marginalizing women's cultural roles other than as wives and
mothers.[19]

---

[19] In her *Inalienable Possessions*, Annette B. Weiner illustrates her argument about sibling intimacy
with examples from Hawaii, Samoa, the Trobriand Islands, and Tonga. For a powerful illustration of
the importance of brother-sister relationships from a culture that idealizes first-cousin marriage, see
Suad Joseph, "Brother/Sister Relationships: Connectivity, Love, and Power in the Reproduction of
Patriarchy in Lebanon," *American Ethnologist* 21, 1 (February 1994), 50–73. Thanks to Carla Maklouf
Obermeyer for this reference.

Readers familiar with the fictional clichés of eighteenth-century England about siblings and their relationships knew to expect oldest brothers to be arrogant, profligate, and spoiled. The best ones, although selfish, could be reformed in relation to their often-responsible younger brothers or their deserving and long-suffering sisters. Married sisters, especially if they married well, retained a special influence over their brothers in many novels, especially when this early tie was augmented by the wealth and power of their husbands. Although identified by a new surname, married sisters in fiction nevertheless retained their identity as siblings, as in "my sister Davers" or "my sister Trueworth."[20] Younger brothers with energy and initiative were often sent out into the world, frequently to the West Indies or to India, disappearing for years at a time while their sisters endured hair-raising adventures at the hands of predatory men and/or hard-hearted landladies. Usually the long-lost brothers reappeared, barely recognizable but wealthy and devoted, just in time to rescue their sisters from the brink of ruin and destitution and to translate them miraculously into a new sphere of comfort and security.

In novel families with several girls, older sisters were generally vain while younger sisters were giddy – although not at the same time, for where sisters came in pairs, only one was morally flawed at a time so as to be a foil for the more perfect heroine. This device was used in scores of novels throughout the century including the anonymous *Cleora: Or, The Fair Inconstant* (1752), William Dodd's *The Sisters* (1754), Sarah Scott's *Agreeable Ugliness* (1754), John Shebbeare's *The Marriage Act* (1754), Charlotte Lennox's *The History of Harriot and Sophia* (1761), Jane West's *The Gossip's Story* (1796), Jane Austen's *Sense and Sensibility* (1811), and Susan Ferrier's *Marriage* (1818). Sisters competed with one another for beaux in some novels whereas in others they were the best of friends and confided their hopes and dreams to one another. In *The Memoirs of Mrs. Williams* (1770), the heroine's relation with her sister is the principal consolation of her life. The idealized correspondents in epistolary novels are often sisters, and in that context, as the genre dictated, they were fully sympathetic, frank, and open with

[20] Naomi Tadmor, "Dimensions of Inequality among Siblings," 308. Tadmor emphasizes the loss entailed in renaming married female siblings: "Marriage thus confers upon the sister a new designation of seniority, but this is achieved through an annulment of her previous status and identity, and is delegated through the use of her husband's name" (310).

This method of naming is an instance of the more general tendency that Naomi Tadmor describes in *Family and Friends in Eighteenth-Century England* by which affinal relatives were designated by consanguineal terms (sister, brother, mother, father), differentiated only by surnames. The "in-law" or "step" terminology, which highlights the difference between consanguineal and affinal relatives, although occasionally used, was less common then than now (143–63).

one another. Elizabeth Griffith's *The History of Lady Barton* (1771) is told
through the letters of two such loving sisters.[21] In Robert Bage's *Barham
Downs* (1784), Peggy and Annabella Whitaker, daughters of a wrongheaded
rich merchant who wants to marry the eldest to a corrupt baronet, support
one another in evading their father's misguided commands.

Jane Austen, whose closest relationship throughout her life was with her
older sister Cassandra, depicted the variations on the theme of friendship
subsisting between older and younger sisters with real genius.[22] Louisa and
Henrietta Musgrove in *Persuasion* and the Bertram sisters in *Mansfield Park*
love each other well enough – except when they are competing for Captain
Wentworth or Henry Crawford. In each case one sister withdraws to break
the deadlock when rivalry threatens to extinguish all sisterly feeling. There
is another set of sisters in *Persuasion*, the daughters of Sir Walter Elliot, the
widowed baronet of Kellynch Hall. Elizabeth, his haughty eldest daughter,
who plays the role in society to which her mother was entitled ("walking
immediately after Lady Russell out of all the drawing-rooms and dining-
rooms in the country" and "opening every ball of credit which a scanty
neighbourhood afforded"), identifies more with her father's interests and
social position than with her sister Anne. Beloved and empowered by her
father, like Emma Woodhouse in another novel, she has little incentive to
marry unless she can find a husband to enhance the prestige she already
has. Their sister Mary, married into a prosperous gentry family, has a separate establishment to which she is always ready to welcome – for selfish
reasons – competent, self-sacrificing, soothing Anne. The Ward sisters of a
previous generation in *Mansfield Park*, Mrs. Norris, Mrs. Price, and Lady
Bertram, although divided by marriage into three different social classes,
act upon their continuing obligations to one another. Thus the living at
Mansfield Park is given to Lady Bertram's sister Norris' husband and Sir
Thomas Bertram takes in first one and then a second daughter (another
set of sisters!) of his wife's sister Price. The entire social fabric of *Pride and
Prejudice* is constructed out of sister relationships, from the five Bennet
sisters and Mr. Bingley's two sisters – Miss Bingley and Mrs. Hurst – to
Mrs. Bennet's sister Mrs. Philips and her sister-in-law Mrs. Gardiner. The
éclaircissement between Darcy and Elizabeth involves her sister, just as the

---

[21] Thanks to Betty Rizzo for reminding me that sisters are often the correspondents in epistolary novels.
[22] In a review of Deirdre Le Faye's edition of Austen letters in the *London Review of Books* on August 3,
1995 (and her subsequent rejoinder to protesting letters), Terry Castle went so far as to suggest that
Jane Austen's intense bond with her sister Cassandra had "its unconscious homoerotic dimension,"
London Review of Books, August 24, 1995, p. 4. In this judgment, Castle does not take into account
the significance of kinship or the importance of sibling ties in the period.

alienation between Wickham and Elizabeth centers on the story of Darcy's sister. The social world of this novel could not exist if it were not for the sister tie. Marianne and Elinor Dashwood in *Sense and Sensibility* share a powerful friendship – as real and deep as the sisterhood among Isabella Thorpe and *her* sisters in *Northanger Abbey* is shallow and opportunistic. Variations on the theme of sororal connection, these very different relationships also share a family resemblance.

CONJUGAL TIES AND SIBLING TIES

Examining the legal status of sibling relationships vis-à-vis marriage prohibition is another way to place their meaning in the culture. Two contested forms of marriage in eighteenth-century English culture illustrate most clearly the cultural shift from consanguineal to conjugal loyalty: the prohibition against marriage with the dead wife's sister and the cultural permissiveness about uncles marrying nieces or marriage between first cousins (the offspring of siblings) or "cousins german" as they were called at the time.[23] These cases hinge on whether or not marriage is understood to sever the consanguineal kin tie and replace it – whether or not marriage creates new families that retroactively suppress and replace the family of origin. In the case of marriage with a dead wife's sister – illegal in England until

---

[23] Five eighteenth-century texts dealing with these questions were reprinted by Garland in 1985 under the general rubric of The Marriage Prohibitions Controversy in a facsimile series edited by Randolph Trumbach. They consist of: Simon Dugard, *The Marriages of Cousin Germans, Vindicated from the Censures of Unlawfullnesse, and Inexpediency* (1673); John Quick, *A Serious Inquiry into That Weighty Case of Conscience, Whether a Man May Lawfully Marry His Deceased Wife's Sister* (1703); James Johnstoun, *A Juridical Dissertation concerning the Scripture Doctrine of Marriage Contracts, and the Marriages of Cousin-Germans* (1734); John Fry, *The Case of Marriages between Near Kindred Particularly Considered, with Respect to the Doctrine of Scripture, the Law of Nature, and the Laws of England* (1756); and John Alleyne, *The Legal Degrees of Marriage Stated and Considered, in a Series of Letters to a Friend* (1775).

A statement of legally prohibited degrees of marriage in eighteenth-century England can be found in the Book of Common Prayer or in Robert Philip Tyrwhitt and Thomas William Tyndale, *Digest of the Public General Statutes, from Magna Carta A.D. 1224–5 to 1 & 2 Geo. 4 A.D. 1821*, 2 vols. (London: A. Strahan, 1822). Under the heading "Marriage," this digest states:

The Prohibited Degrees of Marriage are the Following: No Subject of this realm, or in any H. M.'s dominions, shall marry within the following degrees; and the children of such unlawful marriages are illegitimate: viz, a man may not marry his mother or step-mother; his sister; his son's or daughter's daughter; his father's daughter by his step-mother; his aunt; his uncle's wife; his son's wife; his brother's wife; his wife's daughter; his wife's son's daughter; his wife's daughter's daughter; his wife's sister, *25 H.8. C.22. S.3*; and this provision shall be interpreted of such marriages, where marriages were solemnized and carnal knowledge had, *25 H.8. C.22. S.14.*

For a discussion of these prohibitions see Randolph Trumbach, *The Rise of the Egalitarian Family*, pp. 18–33 and Sybil Wolfram, *In-Laws and Outlaws*, pp. 21–51.

1907 – the first marriage was understood to create affinal kin. Because the western conception of marriage involves making man and wife "one flesh," the blood kin of one spouse become blood kin to the other spouse. The English term "in-laws" signals this fact; his brothers and sisters become her brothers and sisters and vice versa.[24] It is because the wife's sister *becomes* the husband's sister that marriage with this second sister becomes incestuous.[25]

This is hardly a universal prohibition, of course. Indeed, the levirate marriage in which a brother-in-law marries the widow of his dead brother, a custom of the ancient Jews and so-named from the tribe of Levi, is preferred in some cultures because it maintains lineage by substitution rather than introducing a new lineage; the offspring of the first and second marriage are all in the family, so to speak. It is still the preferred mode of widow remarriage in rural parts of Haryana and Punjab in India today.[26] But in the English context, the horrified prohibition against marrying the dead wife's sister is cultural evidence of a belief that marriage *creates* kinship, creating a blood tie where none previously existed.[27] Marriage between a pair of brothers and a pair of sisters was not forbidden, however, because marriage only created kinship between the married person and the relatives of his or her spouse, not between the relatives of the spouses. (The difficulty one has in conceiving, stating, and apprehending these differences is an indication of how limited our Anglo-American conception of kinship has become.)

The extension of kinship terms to relations by marriage (sister Trueworth; brother Smith) is another sign of the blurring of affinal and consanguineal ties (see n. 20). As Naomi Tadmor puts it, it was a way of claiming kinship by "speech act," in which individuals declared their new moral and social expectations of one another by calling each other by the kin terms sister, brother, mother, and father.[28] First and last names encoded more subtle distinctions of relatedness: given names usually signified full blood consanguinity (sister Sarah; brother John) whereas surnames (sister Chesterville; mother Porter) usually designated those who were less than

---

[24] Sybil Wolfram, *In-Laws and Outlaws*, p. 64.

[25] For an alternative explanation of the criteria for incest prohibition – involving the sexual sharing of a member of a kin group rather than degrees of kin closeness to a common ancestor – see Françoise Hertier, "The Symbolics of Incest and Its Prohibition," in Michel Izard and Pierre Smith (eds.), *Between Belief and Transgression: Structuralist Essays in Religion, History, and Myth*, trans. John Leavitt (Chicago: University of Chicago Press, 1982), pp. 152–79.

[26] Prem Chowdhry, *The Veiled Women: Shifting Gender Equations in Rural Haryana 1880–1990* (Delhi: Oxford University Press, 1994), pp. 74–87.

[27] Patriarchal right also dictates the prohibition inasmuch as the dead wife's sister ought not be at the disposal of her brother-in-law but should continue to be at the disposal of her own father for the sake of whatever alliances he chooses to make or debts to repay.

[28] Naomi Tadmor, *Family and Friends*, p. 144.

full consanguineal kin. In time this usage changed and consanguineal terms stopped being applied to affinal relatives. "Step," "half," and "in-law" terminology came to be used more exclusively, isolating and separating the nuclear family from affinal kin. Increasingly, consanguineal kin terms denoted biological facts rather than social expectations.[29]

Generally speaking, the importance of affines or "in-laws" increases relative to consanguineal kin with enhanced notions of individualism, individual rights, and free choice in marriage.[30] Thus, in choosing one's marriage partner one also chooses connections with his or her relatives. Consanguineal claims, on the other hand, are stronger in societies that privilege kin corporations or communities over individuals and in which marriages are arranged for the sake of alliances between groups rather than chosen by individuals on the basis of personal attraction. The prohibition on marriage with a dead wife's sister emphasizes the primacy of affinal ties while the legality of marriage between cousins german demonstrates the concurrent belief in the impermanence of consanguineal connection. To allow first cousins (the children of siblings) to marry, or to allow an uncle to marry his niece (the child of a sibling), is to assume that there is no sibling unity that transcends generations and that the sibling tie is dissolved by adulthood and marriage. On the other hand, marriage between the children of siblings also strengthens consanguineal ties, cementing the connections among members of natal families of origin in the next generation. As Randolph Trumbach observed when putting these two cultural regulations next to each other, "When the prohibition against the wife's sister is put alongside the legitimation of cousin marriage, two opposing systems of marriage emerge, one favoring ties with close affines, the other with consanguines."[31] In other words, prohibiting marriage between what we today call "in-laws" demonstrates the cultural primacy of conjugal ties over consanguineal ties, while cousin-german marriage reaffirms the principle that marriage in some sense neutralizes siblinghood so that sibling incest taboos are not transmitted to the next generation. At the same time, and this is what Trumbach was stressing, cousin-german marriages promote endogamy, knitting consanguineal kin together even more closely. In Iran and elsewhere in the Middle East, for example, "patrilateral parallel-cousin

---

[29] Naomi Tadmor suggests that the earlier, more inclusive usage indicates that "the recognition of kin in the seventeenth and eighteenth centuries may have been a less 'permissive,' 'voluntary,' 'fluid,' or 'individualistic,' matter than it is sometimes said to have been." *Family and Friends*, p. 163.

[30] I owe much of this discussion to conversations with Professor Christine Gailey of the University of California at Riverside.

[31] Randolph Trumbach, *The Rise of the Egalitarian Family*, p. 31.

marriage keeps sisters and their brothers closely related and secures the transmission of land and other property into the next generation."[32]

Biological explanations of the basis of the incest taboo and of exogamous marriage would predict the opposite of these cultural regulations, that is, would predict that marriage between blood kin such as the children of siblings would be prohibited while marriage between affinal kin or in-laws, if there were no consanguineal connection, would be permitted. But these matters are not biologically determined. Until the sixteenth century, marriage in England was forbidden between cousins up to and including third cousins by blood or marriage. But when Henry VIII pressed for legislation which was eventually accepted by the church, permitting marriage between first cousins by blood and by marriage, this stricture was legally removed.[33]

Eighteenth-century fiction corroborates the cultural standing of these legal regulations. There is not the slightest indication of the least impropriety in first-cousin marriage in eighteenth-century novels. Although the eponymous heroine of *The History of Indiana Danby* (1765) does not know the story of her birth at the beginning of the novel, the kindly Mrs. Beverley knows Indiana to be her niece, the daughter of her dead younger sister, and delights in the prospect of a match between Indiana and her son. The paragon Clara Freemore approves this first-cousin marriage without a second thought (117).[34] In Charlotte Smith's sentimental novel *Emmeline; or The Orphan of the Castle* (1788), Lord Montreville opposes the marriage between Emmeline and his son, Delamere, not because they are first cousins – which appears to be irrelevant – but because she has no fortune. Eliza Haywood's *The History of Jemmy and Jenny Jessamy* (1753) begins by explaining that the two protagonists – who are destined to marry each other – had the same surname because they were "descended from two male branches of the same family," although their fathers were cousins rather than brothers.[35]

Jane Austen offers several highly developed instances of the English nonchalance about cousin-german marriage. Although Sir Thomas Bertram in *Mansfield Park* has initial doubts about taking Fanny Price into his

---

[32] Annette B. Weiner, "Reassessing Reproduction in Social Theory," in Faye D. Ginsburg and Rayna Rapp (eds.), *Conceiving the New World Order: The Global Politics of Reproduction* (Berkeley: University of California Press, 1995), pp. 407–24, quote p. 418.

[33] Randolph Trumbach, *The Rise of the Egalitarian Family*, pp. 18–19.

[34] The authorship of *The History of Indiana Danby* (London, 1765) is unknown, but the 1773 Dublin edition of *The History of Miss Pamela Howard* advertises itself as written "By the Author of Indiana Danby."

[35] Eliza Haywood, *The History of Jemmy and Jenny Jessamy*, 3 vols. (London: T. Gardner, 1753), vol. 1, p. 2.

household because of her possible intimacy with his two sons – "cousins in love &c." (43) – Austen's authorial "&c." dismisses such worries as familiar, predictable cant, not worth repeating or taking seriously.[36] As the novel progresses and the match between Edmund and Fanny is increasingly the only one that makes any moral or psychological sense, the class differences between Edmund and Fanny make it feel endogamous rather than incestuous. That Fanny and Edmund are maternal cousins means that no material advantage will accrue from the marriage – such as keeping a title or estate in the family – although the union will strengthen consanguineal bonds and consolidate family feeling. Austen's other fully approved first-cousin marriage is also between maternal cousins – Charles Hayter and Henrietta Musgrove in *Persuasion* – whereas the possible paternal first-cousin matches in the novel (William Elliot with either Elizabeth or Anne) are tainted by social ambition and the venal desire for accumulation of wealth.[37] In other words, maternal and paternal first-cousin marriages had very different social and fiscal implications because of the concentration of wealth and title in the male line. Maternal first-cousin marriage did not profit from this fact of inheritance, however; maternal first cousins were no better off marrying each other than anyone else in the world. Without claiming that Austen consciously weighed these legalistic differences in her narrative choices, it seems evident that paternal and maternal first-cousin marriages must have felt intrinsically different to her: the implications for inheritance meant that they carried very different moral valences.[38]

That Austen's own society was comfortable with first-cousin marriage can also be inferred from the match in her own family between her favorite brother Henry and their cousin Eliza de Feuillide, daughter of their father's sister, Philadelphia Hancock. Henry Fielding's courtship of his early love, Sarah Andrew, was foiled by her uncle, Andrew Tucker, who wanted Sarah to marry *his* son, John, in what would have been a perfectly legal and acceptable first-cousin marriage.[39] One could multiply examples endlessly.

---

[36] This happens in the first chapter of *Mansfield Park*. The page number here refers to Tony Tanner's edition (Harmondsworth and New York: Penguin, 1966).

[37] For a discussion of cousin marriage in Austen's fiction, see Glenda Hudson, "Mansfield Revisited: Incestuous Relationships in Jane Austen's *Mansfield Park,*" *Eighteenth-Century Fiction* 4, 1 (October 1991), 53–68, especially 59–61.

[38] Other first-cousin marriages in Austen's *oeuvre* that are morally suspect because they are based on material rather than moral considerations, i.e. their primary advantage lies in concentrating family wealth and social standing, are the proposed matches between Darcy and Lady Catherine de Bourgh's inheriting daughter in *Pride and Prejudice* or that between Collins and any of the Bennet girls.

[39] Martin C. Battestin with Ruthe R. Battestin, *Henry Fielding: A Life* (London and New York: Routledge, 1989), pp. 49–51.

Contrastively, there is a hint of discomfort about the sexual connection between the siblings of two spouses in the by-play Austen depicts in *Emma* between Knightley and Emma, who are in-laws to each other's siblings since her sister is married to his brother. Asked by Knightley with whom she's going to dance, she hesitates, a pregnant pause that has many possible meanings, including the consideration of their relationship from a number of angles. Then she replies "With you . . . you know we are not really so much brother and sister as to make it at all improper." "Brother and sister!" exclaims Knightley, "no, indeed." The passage raises the issue of their degrees of kinship – dancing being only a metaphor, after all – and then allays the anxiety about it with Knightley's authoritative reply. But unlike the question of "cousins in love &c." the psychological impediment created by the marriage of his brother to her sister is given textual weight by Emma's initial hesitation and because she states the possible prohibition without irony.[40]

A SISTER'S PORTION

The inheritance patterns of female offspring can further establish the status of women within their families of origin and hence the strength of consanguineal claims in English kinship. In situations of partible inheritance, as in Mediterranean countries, where children are co-owners and co-inheritors of the family property, the disposition of a sister/daughter in marriage can be much more important to the family of origin because she and her spouse are being brought into the circle of responsible adults who will tend the property and benefit from it. In South Carolina, as Lorri Glover argues, partly because partible inheritance persisted, women as sisters and kinswomen acted as equal partners in family matters and cooperation and mutuality

---

[40] Jane Austen, *Emma* (1816), ed. Ronald Blythe (Harmondsworth: Penguin, 1966), p. 328. Glenda Hudson has pointed out how favorably Austen depicts heterosexual relationships between adopted siblings, in-laws, and first cousins in "'Precious Remains of the Earliest Attachment': Sibling Love in Jane Austen's *Pride and Prejudice*," *Persuasions* 11 (December 1989), 125–31. Both this article and that cited in n. 37 are reprinted in *Sibling Love and Incest in Jane Austen's Fiction* (New York: St. Martin's Press, 1992). She explains this "sibling loyalty" and these "incestuous unions" as a manifestation of Austen's concern to preserve the sacred inviolability of the home in a time of upheaval and social change (40–2). Hudson interprets this impulse as conservative, much as Marilyn Butler located Austen in an "anti-jacobin" tradition in her groundbreaking *Jane Austen and the War of Ideas* (Oxford: Clarendon Press, 1975). But the political dichotomy between radical and conservative is misleading in reference to Austen's interest in consolidating consanguineal relationships and a kinship system that recognized maternal lineage and gave real weight to female family members. A kinship system that privileges consanguineal rather than affinal connection is conservative with regard to class, mobility, and social change but it advantages women with respect to gender politics and sexual power.

characterized their life-long relations with male relatives.⁴¹ I have urged that
Englishwomen's claims on property were seriously undermined during the
eighteenth century, although signs of sisters' equality in family inheritance
are still visible in the palimpsest of laws governing the disposition of family
property, reminding historians that sisters as well as brothers had a claim
on family resources.⁴² Alan Macfarlane claims that women's property rights
in England were historically more extensive than in the rest of Europe; it
is part of his evidence for a longer history of economic individualism in
England than is generally granted. He notes that in Essex daughters received shares in the estate as co-parceners if there were no sons and cites
a Chancery decree from the early seventeenth century from the barony
of Kendal (Cumbria) to the effect that "'the eldest daughter/sister/cousin
inherits without copartnership in tenancy'... a direct equivalent to the
custom of male primogeniture in the area."⁴³ Nor was the pattern in Essex
unusual; daughters often inherited as co-parceners in the absence of sons.
Although Macfarlane concedes that female inheritors were generally excluded if there were sons, under common law daughters inherited before
collateral male relatives – such as uncles or cousins – where no will specified to the contrary, in contrast to the provisions of Salic law that entirely
excluded women from inheritance.⁴⁴

According to an examination by Keith Wrightson of 192 wills recorded
in Terling, Essex between 1550 and 1700, testators primarily left property to

⁴¹ Lorri Glover, *All Our Relations*, pp. xii, 11.
⁴² J. Johnson's Preface to *The Laws Respecting Women* (1777; rpt. Dobbs Ferry, NY: Oceana, 1974) notes:
"In the Saxon times, the rank and consequence of women appear to have been considerable... The
Norman invasion was fatal to the rights of women. By the introduction of feudal tenures, women
were at first totally excluded from holding lands so granted; and the greatest part of the lands in the
kingdom were possessed on such tenures. After some time, indeed, their right of enjoying lands in
chivalry was admitted" Johnson goes on to note that in modern times (i.e., the eighteenth century)
a husband has the right "to bequeath his substance at his own free-will, to the exclusion of his wife,
if he should be so inclined; but a court of Chancery is ever disposed to exert its authority in relief
of women who have been injuriously treated, and in cases of extreme hardship would cause equity
to supply the defects of natural affection" (x–xii).
    In the German context, a study of medieval epics demonstrates an older matrilineal kinship system
in which the important family connection is between the sister's son and the mother's brother; the
hero obtains crucial guidance from his maternal uncle. C. H. Bell, "The Sister's Son in the Medieval
German Epic. A Study in the Survival of Matriliny," *University of California Publications in Modern
Philology* 10 (1920), 67–182, quoted in David Sabean, "Aspects of Kinship Behavior and Property in
Rural Western Europe before 1800," in Jack Goody, Joan Thirsk, and E. P. Thompson (eds.), *Family
and Inheritance: Rural Society in Western Europe*, 1200–1800 (Cambridge: Cambridge University
Press, 1976), p. 100.
⁴³ Alan Macfarlane, "The Myth of the Peasantry: Family and Economy in a Northern Parish," in
Richard M. Smith (ed.), *Land, Kinship and Life Cycle* (Cambridge: Cambridge University Press,
1984), pp. 333–49, quote p. 340.
⁴⁴ J. Johnson, *The Laws Respecting Women*, p. 369.

their children and spouses and next to "grandchildren, brothers, nephews and nieces, sons-in-law and sisters." That is, after their immediate conjugal families they left property to their consanguineal families of origin and even to affinal relatives. He notes that real estate – land and houses – was usually left to sons whereas cash and goods were divided more equally among all the children.[45]

As remarked earlier, the strict settlement that evolved in the late seventeenth century was based not on the principle of equal shares in inheritance but on the principle that the purpose of inheritance for daughters was to maintain them while they lived, while the purpose of inheritance for sons was to preserve and aggrandize family estates and to permit the accumulation of capital within a family.[46] Nevertheless, brothers could not will away property left by parents in joint tenancy to themselves and their sisters, thus dispossessing their female siblings. That such cases even arose, that female offspring's inheritance rights could be contested by their brothers, shows that attitudes towards women's property rights were changing. It puts one in mind of the strenuous preamble that Clarissa's grandfather wrote to his will (Letter 4), begging his sons and his grandson not to "impugn or contest" his bequests to Clarissa, even if "they should not be strictly conformable to law."[47]

One interesting case which tested the competing property rights of a woman's conjugal claim and another's consanguineal claim, a case in which the common-law rights of blood kin in joint property were pitted against the legally designated provision in Chancery for inheritance by a wife, occurred in 1757. Richard Gilbert, who together with his sister Frances Sophia Gilbert had inherited the family house in Wellclose Square, died without issue, willing his part of the house to his wife Jane Gilbert. His unmarried sister Frances contested this disposition of the property and claimed the premises as heir-at-law while his widow Jane Gilbert claimed her part of the house under the will. Frances Gilbert's lawyer argued that since Richard Gilbert had inherited the property as a joint tenancy with his sister, he was unable to devise the property away from her without having legally partitioned it first, an argument upheld by Lord Mansfield and the court.[48] The rights of an unmarried sister in a joint tenancy previously devised and never partitioned prevailed in this case over the claims of a

[45] Keith Wrightson, "Kinship in an English Village: Terling, Essex 1500–1700," in Richard M. Smith (ed.), *Land, Kinship and Life-Cycle*, pp. 313–32, esp. 324, 328.
[46] J. Johnson, *The Laws Respecting Women*, p. 122.
[47] Samuel Richardson, *Clarissa* (1747–8), ed. Angus Ross (London: Penguin, 1985), p. 53.
[48] This case is reported in J. Johnson, *The Laws Respecting Women*, pp. 119–21.

wife – even under a legal will. Although this case may have been decided on a legal technicality rather than on the relative rights of sisters and wives to men's economic resources, the example is significant insofar as it brings to legal scrutiny the competing claims of blood kin and conjugal kin.

KIN CORPORATIONS, STATE FORMATION, AND CAPITALISM

This issue – the power of sisters relative to wives – is key to understanding the changing push and pull of consanguineal and conjugal kin bonds for men and women. Anthropologists who have theorized this relation in the context of state formation have noted that the claims of blood kin are inevitably attenuated or divided by allegiance to a supra-familial entity such as a ruling class or a "state." Since women's status in a society generally is tied to the authority of individual families relative to state power, when this happens the overall status of women in the society in which this formation is emerging is diminished or worsened. States tend to exclude women from the business of governance at the same time as they extend political voice to men beyond family networks. As Ernestine Friedl summarized the evidence in 1976:

in societies in which men conduct egalitarian redistributions and by so doing gain noninstitutionalized positions of prestige or rank, women are by and large precluded from the entire procedure. In other words, if there are no hereditary political or ritual positions of power . . . women are at a distinct disadvantage, regardless of the extent of their participation in food production.[49]

Crudely speaking, as the power of sisters or female kindred within families wanes – often because power is being more democratically redistributed among men – the general level of women's power within a society wanes (and vice versa).

One reason for the connection between the emergence of the nation state and women's waning power in a society is economic. When resources are distributed as a matter of course to kin-based producers, women are granted a reasonable share as members of those units. But when resources are diverted to those elements within a class-stratified society that reproduce state relations rather than kin relations, such distribution systems usually exclude women. The rise of nation states is always at the expense of those social formations that anthropologists call "kin corporations," otherwise understood as laterally extended families or clans, bands, tribes, or chiefdoms within lineage societies. These kin corporations collectively own the

[49] Ernestine Friedl, *Women and Men*, p. 62.

means of production of food and other necessities. Women who are sisters within these kin corporations are co-owners with their brothers and usually co-decision-makers about production and distribution of resources. When the means of production is land, sisters own and inherit the land and derive their subsistence from it. Their relative authority as wives over the property owned by their husbands' kin corporation is considerably less than their authority as co-owning sisters over the land possessed by their own kin corporation.

Except in the case of ruling-class families, the relationship between the state and kin corporations is competitive and mutually exclusive. That is, it is *from* families or kin corporations that the state exacts its tribute and legalized powers; the nation state is formed at the expense of kin corporations. As the ruling class stratifies out and extracts its subsistence from the production of other kin corporations, the gender equality of co-owners within these kin corporations is often undermined. In other words, women's rights in family property as sisters and as daughters – as kindred – are diminished. In Dahomey, West Africa, for example, it has been shown that increased ruling-class control over the means of production "led to subversion and shrinking of sisterly relations," and the same process has been documented for nineteenth-century Tonga.[50] In England, the state itself undermined women's authority as sisters by giving the conjugal family legal precedence over kindred in matters of inheritance or legal claims to support. As Karen Sacks sums it up: "class societies, to the extent that they developed from patricorporations, transformed women from sister and wife to daughter and wife, making them perennial subordinates."[51]

Another explanation for the reduced importance of women as kindred – beyond their subordination in the process of extracting resources for state formation – has to do with the transformation of production for use to production for exchange within an expanding capitalist framework. The creation of value beyond that of use, and its accumulation independent of kin networks, according to Eleanor Leacock, severs the organic connections among need, wealth, and kin obligations and establishes interest groups outside the traditional web of kin networks. These extra-kin interest groups then undermine rather than perpetuate equitable distribution for use. Members of lineage systems or extended family units begin to

---

[50] Karen Sacks discusses the case of Dahomey in *Sisters and Wives* (Urbana and Chicago: University of Illinois Press, 1982), pp. 216–41; Christine Ward Gailey describes the tensions expressed in the relative authority of sisters and wives that arose with state formation in Tonga in *From Kinship to Kingship: Gender Hierarchy and State Formation in the Tongan Islands* (Austin: University of Texas Press, 1987), pp. 60–2 and 122.

[51] Karen Sacks, *Sisters and Wives*, p. 123.

use their membership in kin networks to compete for control over property and resources within their extra-familial interest groups – rather than using their power to distribute resources equitably within their kin networks. In such economically stratifying societies, women's public authority as members of a kin group begins to modulate into the subordinate status of uncompensated members of individualized conjugal family units. As Eleanor Leacock puts it, women's position "begins to shift from valued people who cement networks of reciprocal relations and who have access to various publicly recognized mechanisms for adjudicating their interests as women, into that of service workers in the households of husbands and their kin groups."[52] Bridewealth (dowry) begins to take on the character of purchasing a woman's children to perpetuate her husband's kin group rather than being a way of enhancing her public value. This attitude towards the exchange of women goes with the transformation of production from use to exchange value, subsistence work to abstract labor, and cooperative production to exploitative, extractive production.

The point is that an emphasis on capital accumulation and the competition for resources for exchange rather than use undermines the reliance on kindred and opposes, rather than consolidates, the interests of siblings to one another. Margaret Hunt has indicated the strain that eighteenth-century capitalism put on families in an era when the need for investment capital and credit could only be met by calling on personal connections, without benefit of insurance or limited liability. Before legal distinctions were generated and tested to distinguish private assets or liabilities from business assets and liabilities, family members had to pool their resources for capital to invest in new businesses and stand surety for one another's credit. When these businesses failed, all of the extended kin who had lent their names to a project could lose their homes and household goods – and even be imprisoned for debt. Margaret Hunt tells one story about how the favorite nephew of William Gray's partner jeopardized his uncle's business "through extravagance and misconduct," involving his uncle – and hence the entire Gray family – in serious debt in the late 1770s or early 1780s. For three or four years the families of the partners teetered on the brink of bankruptcy because of the profligacy of this one nephew, trying to shore up the business accounts from their private savings and working superhuman hours to pay back what he had lost.[53]

[52] Eleanor Leacock, "Interpreting the Origins of Gender Inequality: Conceptual and Historical Problems," *Dialectical Anthropology* 7, 4 (February 1983), 263–84; quote 270.
[53] Margaret Hunt, *The Middling Sort: Commerce, Gender, and the Family in England, 1680–1780* (Berkeley: University of California Press, 1996), p. 167; see also pp. 22–45.

In Jane Austen's family, too, a number of her relatives sustained considerable losses when her brother Henry's bank failed in March 1816. Her brother Edward had put up £20,000 and her uncle James Leigh Perrot £10,000 to guarantee Henry's appointment as receiver of taxes; every penny of these sums was lost when Henry's bank failed. Her other brothers, James and Frank, each lost several hundreds that they had banked with Henry; Austen herself lost the £13 7s that had been in her account in Henry's bank.[54] Although these losses apparently did not embitter Austen family feelings, other families did not so successfully avoid acrimony about business matters. Inevitably, misunderstandings arose about the extent to which family members could be relied upon to bail one another out of fiscal difficulties or the extent of liability that collateral family members were expected to shoulder for one another's enterprises. As Margaret Hunt puts it, two strong value systems were in conflict, "one stressing obligations toward kin, the other concerned with individual profit and loss."[55]

The need for family-generated capital and credit and the psychological estrangement caused within kin groups by conflicting expectations is part of the story of how capitalism undermined the custom of families taking responsibility for constitutive members. But in addition to the problems of shared liability for business failure, inheritance law also set the interests of sibling against sibling as they evolved to favor the accumulation of capital. Older brothers inherited estates encumbered by the annuities of younger brothers and the dowries of sisters. From the point of view of these same younger brothers and sisters, their inheritances for years to come seemed swallowed up by the extravagances of their older brothers. In landed families timber was felled and sold, land and houses were mortgaged, tenants were squeezed – but the siblings of a single generation did not profit equally from these measures. Eighteenth-century novels are made up of problems such as these, with endless variations on the themes of income, land, wealth, inheritance, personal enterprise, business luck, romantic love, and family responsibilities in obsessively repetitive dramatizations of these new sources of cultural conflict.

<hr/>

[54] Jan Fergus, *Jane Austen: A Literary Life* (London: Macmillan, and New York: St. Martin's Press, 1991) pp. 49 and 162–3.

[55] Margaret Hunt, *The Middling Sort*, p. 29. Among the sources that Hunt cites are H. A. Shannon, "The Coming of General Limited Liability," in E. M. Carus-Wilson (ed.), *Essays in Economic History*, 3 vols. (London: Arnold, 1954), vol. I, pp. 358–79; P. G. M. Dickson, *The Financial Revolution in England: A Study in the Development of Public Credit 1688–1756* (London: Macmillan, 1967); and Harold Perkin, *The Origins of Modern English Society 1780–1880* (London: Routledge and Kegan Paul, 1969), esp. pp. 80–3. A contemporary writer who gave moral advice about obligations to render financial aid within a family was William Fleetwood, *The Relative Duties of Parents and Children, Husbands and Wives, Masters and Servants* (London, 1705).

The opposition between the earlier moral system that honored kin obligations and the newer value placed on individualized success in the sweepstakes of capital accumulation – or, to theorize it more abstractly, the opposition between a system equitably distributing resources for use among kin and a system manipulating exchange value for individualized capital accumulation and the maintenance of a nation state – accounts for the increasing complication of the laws concerning property and inheritance and women's diminished right to family property.[56] The fact that Jane Gilbert expected to inherit her husband's share of the house he owned with his sister is one small example of how much weaker sister-right was thought to be compared to conjugal right during this new period of centralizing state power.

I am suggesting that the conflict between one woman's sister-right and another's conjugal right, or the extent to which a person had power in a kin corporation as a sister compared with the power she had as someone's wife, is tied to class and state formation. Karen Sacks observed the back-and-forth counterpoint "between sister and wife in a number of preclass or protoclass African societies with corporate patrilineages" and the concurrent "obliteration of the sister relationship in class societies by the relationship of wife, as in Buganda." In the African context at least, women's power construed as conjugal right and obtained through a husband came to replace sister-right and the bonds of consanguinity as a by-product of new forms of class stratification.[57] A comparison between the social standing of wives and sisters may thus reflect the level of class stratification and the extent to which a centralized state permeates all aspects of a society. As people are imagined as abstract, atomized, politically representable individuals – rather than members of particular kin corporations that negotiate with other kin corporations the distribution of power and resources – adult women take their class identifications and their place in the state from their husbands rather than from their natal families. In most eighteenth-century novels, the roles of sisters in their natal families are more egalitarian,

---

[56] Susan Staves has painstakingly documented this process of erosion of married women's common-law property rights in her landmark book *Married Women's Separate Property in England, 1660–1833* (Cambridge, MA: Harvard University Press, 1990).

[57] Karen Sacks, *Sisters and Wives*, p. 110 and *passim*; Christine Ward Gailey, *From Kinship to Kingship*, pp. 59–74; Eleanor Leacock, "Postscripts: Implications for Organization," in Eleanor Leacock and Helen I. Safa (eds.), *Women's Work: Development and the Division of Labor by Gender* (South Hadley, MA: Bergin and Garvey, 1986), pp. 253–66. A number of good essays theorizing the relation between state formation and kin function can be found in Thomas C. Patterson and Christine W. Gailey (eds.), *Power Relations and State Formation* (Washington, DC: American Anthropological Association, 1987); in particular see Viana Muller, "Kin Reproduction and Elite Accumulation in the Archaic States of Northwest Europe," pp. 81–97 of that volume.

more gender-neutral, than those of wives in married life. Contests between women inhabiting these two social positions in eighteenth-century fiction can thus be read symbolically as contests between different kinds of family formations: the consanguineal family, in which the sister's power and place is analogous to that of her brother, and the conjugal family, in which a woman's sister role is submerged and her relation to her husband – whether subservient, dominant, or egalitarian – comes to define her.

SISTERS AND WIVES

The power of sisters in relation to their brothers' wives is explored in a number of eighteenth-century texts, including one of the earliest novels of the period, Richardson's *Pamela* (1741). Lady Davers' paradigmatic superiority in status and power to her brother's wife, Pamela, in combination with her equality to her brother, Mr. B., is set up by the class relations of the novel. The last of the four volumes opens with Lady Davers dictating the names of Pamela's first six children to her – all of whom are to be sons. Although her command to Pamela to bear half-a-dozen male children in as many years is obviously facetious, Lady Davers nonetheless treats Pamela as the servant of her lineage rather than as her competitor and equal, as so often happened in later novels. Identifying herself with her brother's interests, she writes: "our line is gone so low, that we expect that human security from you in your first seven years, or we shall be disappointed, I can tell you that."[58] Mr. B.'s flirtation with the Countess of –, and Pamela's matrimonial jealousy – a brilliant invention of Richardson to probe the workings of marriage – further develops the contrast between his sister's unalterable relation to him and the more tenuous connection of a wife, without a powerful family behind her, dependent on retaining his sexual interest. In their correspondence about Mr. B.'s straying interest, Lady Davers' power and status is clearly equal to that of her brother while Pamela, a mere wife, is subordinate. Indeed, Pamela omits the term "sister" in signing a letter to Lady Davers after having been so delighted to adopt it earlier ("I – *humble* I – who never had a sister before" [IV: 4]), when she feels that her marriage is fraying and that her title to that "beloved name" is in jeopardy. Pamela is alone in her new conjugal family; Lady Davers appears to be her only confidante in this crisis, so completely has Pamela adopted the family connections of her new husband. Lady Davers feels perfectly comfortable censuring her brother's attentions to the Countess of –, and offering company and support

---

[58] Samuel Richardson, *Pamela or Virtue Rewarded*, with an Introduction by William Lyon Phelps, 4 vols. (New York: Croscup & Sterling, 1901), vol. IV, p. 2. Subsequent page numbers refer to this edition.

to her injured sister-in-law. But her own claims on Mr. B. are inalienable, and no matter what happens her relation to him is secure. As she says at the end, "I must always love and honour my brother, but cannot help speaking my mind" (IV: 173). This is a luxury that Pamela, as a wife, cannot afford.

An interpolated tale in *The History of Betty Barnes* (1753), another early novel, presents a situation in which the wife is literally a servant to her husband's sister. When her father's death impoverishes her, Lydia secretly marries her childhood sweetheart and comes into the house that he shares with his father and sister as a servant to the household. His sister treats Lydia with great insolence and is piqued when her brother does not heed her complaints but seems to take the part of the servant.[59] The tension between the two women, and the way they each claim the favor of husband/brother, is built into the fictional situation. The structure of the plot spells out the competing expectations of sister and wife.

There is also anecdotal evidence from the earlier part of the century of the power of sisters over wives. After Mary Delany's first marriage in 1717, she was forced to live with a sister-in-law who watched and criticized her every move. Married at seventeen to a man nearly forty years her senior, Alexander Pendarves, a fat and physically repellent man who was a friend of her uncle and guardian Lord Lansdowne, the young woman had exacted a promise at the time of her marriage that she would never have to live with his difficult older sister. But after two years of retirement in Cornwall, Pendarves broke his promise and, jealous of his beautiful young wife, moved her into unfashionable lodgings in Soho where she found her sister-in-law already entrenched. Embittered by a brief and unhappy marriage to a fortune hunter, Jane Pendarves acted as a spy for her vigilant brother. As Betty Rizzo describes the situation, "the reluctant wife became the suspected outsider, and the despised sister became the valuable ally." She goes on to describe the probable domestic scene:

the high-handed and easily offended sister demanding deference or reparation for unconferred deference at table at every meal; ensconced with her work in the drawing room and tacitly demanding hours of attendance; questioning engagements; proffering herself as a companion when Delany went out; monitoring, because always present, the calls of friends; poking among Delany's possessions and reading her letters; and presiding over the ring of informers who watched Delany's every move in and out of the house and delivered daily reports on her activities.[60]

[59] *The History of Betty Barnes*, 2 vols. (London, 1753), vol. I, pp. 148–9. Joyce Grossman attributes this anonymous novel to Mary Collyer: see her "Social Protest and the Mid-Century Novel: Mary Collyer's *The History of Betty Barnes*," *Eighteenth-Century Women* I (2000), 165–84.

[60] Betty Rizzo, *Companions without Vows: Relationships among Eighteenth-Century British Women* (Athens: University of Georgia Press, 1994), p. 172.

This ménage is fictionalized in Sarah Scott's *Millenium Hall* (1762) in the story of Miss Melvyn or, as she became, Mrs. Morgan. Married to a man she could not love (a marriage she was forced into by a designing stepmother), she found, when she arrived at her new husband's country seat, a maiden sister of her husband's, Mrs. Susanna Morgan, very much in possession of the premises.[61] This ugly maiden lady, envious of every woman who was either pretty or married, was also ill-tempered: "she despised all that were not as rich as herself, and hated every one who was superior or equal to her in fortune" (133). Pedantic and conceited, she received her husband's new wife "with that air of superiority, to which Mrs. Susanna thought herself intitled by her age and fortune" (134). Although both brother and sister had large fortunes, they were both miserly, and the new Mrs. Morgan found herself continually criticized by both of them for the lenient way she tried to run the household. Her "desire that her servants should enjoy the comforts of plenty, and when sick, receive the indulgence which that condition requires, brought her continual admonitions against extravagance, wherein Mr. Morgan readily joined; for his avarice was so great, that he repined at the most necessary expences" (134). Scott paints a dismal picture of the young bride as "victim to the ill-humour of both her husband and his sister" (135). They form a united front against which she is powerless to protest; their alliance goes back many years and their possession of the house predates her introduction to it. She has no recourse but to suffer their mean way of living until his death sets her free.

One can find examples of brothers upholding their sisters' rights to shared property in the working class as well. When John Fielden died in 1726, married but childless, he made provision in his will to ensure his sister's rights to the house that they had inherited from their parents and presumably grown up in. The Fieldens had been a family that made a living from a combination of handloom weaving and small-scale farming. When John Fielden died, he left his house to his "wife and heirs and assignees for ever"; but he also included the instruction that his sister and her husband were to be given the right to rent the house from his wife for £5 a year.[62] Although this was a hardship on his young widow, it undoubtedly registers his sense that, although the house had been legally left to him as a son, his sister had also grown up in the house and had a moral right to its use.

---

[61] Page numbers cited are from the edition edited by Gary Kelly (Peterborough, ON: Broadview Press, 1995).

[62] *Shore in Stansfield: A Pennine Weaving Community, 1660–1750* (Cornholme: Cornholme Branch of the Worker's Educational Association, 1986), p. 22, quoted in Bridget Hill, *Women, Work, and Sexual Politics in Eighteenth-Century England* (Oxford: Basil Blackwell, 1989), p. 251.

Not all sisters wielded their power *against* wives or wives-to-be, of course. In the anonymous *Sophronia* (1761), a novel that celebrates married love on every page, Mr. Vincent's sister tells the woman he is destined to marry: "I am not . . . like many sisters, for engrossing all the family substance to myself: I would fain see him well married, and to you above any woman in the world."[63] But the most usual pattern was that seen in the story retailed by Mrs. Montgomery about her infancy. When her father, a Scottish nobleman, fell at Culloden, her mother, widowed and friendless, came to London and applied to her rich brother for help. "His wife, by whose means his fortune had been promoted, convinced him that his sister and her child could not be commodiously received into his house," she recounted. They were boarded in the neighborhood, where "the pride and ill-nature of his wife, taught her [the young widow, his sister] to experience in all its bitterness the misery of dependence" (130). Indeed, as the century wore on, tensions between sisters and wives in fiction were more frequently imagined with the power on the side of the wife or stepmother, who, like the wife in this interpolated tale, was often as not depicted as a selfish or conniving outsider who claimed the brother/father and turned him against his deserving sister or daughter.

This situation was sketched in Sarah Scott's *The History of Sir George Ellison* (1766), the sequel to *Millenium Hall* (1762). At the beginning of Book III, Sir George (who rescues damsels, true to his name) elicits the story of a woman who lives at Millenium Hall during one of his visits.[64] Born into a good family, well educated, and bred with a "proper share of housewifery," Mrs. Alton recounts how she found herself orphaned at eighteen and left entirely to her brother's generosity, with the entire estate entailed upon him. The lack of separate provision for her by her father, she recalls, "shocked me extremely, although I loved my brother well enough." However, she endeavored to be "contented to accept as an obligation, a provision to which nature seemed to give me a right" (102). She did not doubt that her brother meant to provide for her adequately, but she worried about her sister-in-law, "a woman of low birth, though tolerable fortune, of whom he was so fond, that I was sensible my dependence must be rather on her than him" (102).

Nor was her worry misplaced, for her frequently pregnant sister-in-law required her to be housekeeper, cook, and nurse to her increasing

[63] *Sophronia; or, Letters to the Ladies* (London: William Johnston, 1761), p. 128. Subsequent page references are to this edition.

[64] All subsequent page numbers refer to Betty Rizzo's excellent edition of this novel (Lexington: University of Kentucky Press, 1996).

family. The speaker describes her arduous days – taking care of the children while cooking, watching them closely to keep them from accidents in the kitchen, trying to dress them and herself for dinner in the brief interval between preparing the meal and sitting down with the family, with no leisure, or indeed money, for herself. To make matters worse, when her brother commends her efforts, her sister-in-law feels jealous and diminished by the praise. From that moment on, the latter continually contradicts and criticizes her. She is then put in the untenable position of being "made a slave, and yet reproached as a burden" (105). Her indignation at her sister-in-law's treatment of her vied with her "concern for the uneasiness my brother visibly suffered, of which I was, though innocently on my part, the cause" (105). Her brother gave her frequent presents, but no regular income, no means of living independently. When she asked him for an independent income, however small, so that she could leave his family, he refused, her sister-in-law being unwilling to allow her a separate income. He maintained that his family could not do without her. In this miserable condition, as a servant to his wife, she lived for seven years until she heard of the establishment of Millenium Hall. She immediately applied for admittance. Her references from people in the neighborhood were canvassed and she was accepted, though her brother felt disgraced because it was a charitable institution. Nevertheless, she went eagerly and had lived there happily ever since, for she found in Millenium Hall everything "that can give pleasure to the mind, or mend the heart" (109).

In Tobias Smollett's *The Adventures of Peregrine Pickle* (1751), the hero's unmarried sister, Mrs. Grizzle, solicitous for the "support and propagation of the family name," instigated and encouraged her brother's attentions to the lady who was to become his wife, and continued to live with the conjugal couple on terms of great intimacy.[65] But no sooner was the marital knot tied than the new Mrs. Pickle stopped deferring to her new sister-in-law. Before long, she even insisted on taking over the management of the household. Mrs. Grizzle began to perceive, says Smollett, that she had not succeeded in choosing a gentle and obedient wife for her brother, one "who would always treat her with that profound respect which she thought due to her superior genius, and be entirely regulated by her advice and direction" (37). In Charlotte Lennox's *Henrietta* (1758), the disinheritance of the heroine's aristocratic father is explained by the machinations of his elder brother's

---

[65] *Works of Tobias Smollett* (New York: Routledge, 188?), p. 35. Subsequent page references to *Peregrine Pickle* are to this edition.

wife, who kept up her husband's resentment against Henrietta's father so far that he was never forgiven during his lifetime.

Fictional examples of the victorious wife triumphing over younger brothers or unmarried sisters call to mind William Hayley's description of the reduced circumstances of the unmarried daughter "of an opulent father," dependent on an avaricious brother. Mary Wollstonecraft also portrays a wife "jealous of the little kindness which her husband shews to his relations," and "displeased at seeing the property of *her* children lavished on an helpless sister." She tries to "undermine the habitual affection" that her husband feels for his sister and "neither tears nor caresses are spared til the spy is worked out of her house."[66] It seems a more realistic portrait of the conflict between sister and wife than the version in Richardson's *Pamela*, in which both sister and wife try together to reclaim the relapsed rake.

In records of genteel families from the north of England, Amanda Vickery finds several examples of the tug-of-war between the women of a man's natal family and his wife, a tug-of-war between the competing claims of consanguinity and conjugality. "When Mrs. Shackleton surrendered the management" of her estate to her daughter-in-law, Vickery reports, "she could not hide her pique and sense of rejection."[67] Similarly, when Josias Stout married, his mother expected to keep directing the housekeeping as she had been doing, "more than the young wife (who had been her father's housekeeper) would allow; which made [his] mother uneasy."[68] Although Arthur Young was devoted all his life to his mother, after bringing his new wife home to live with her for two years, he decided that "a mixture of families was inconsistent with comfortable living" and moved away, with his new family, from his family estate.[69]

Again, seeing how other cultures handle these conflicts can be instructive. In Nepalese culture, when a son marries and brings his wife into the compound household, the newly formed nuclear family is prevented from separating out by muting the connection between husband and wife (they

[66] For William Hayley's *A Philosophical, Historical, and Moral Essay on Old Maids* (1785), see n. 16 above. Wollstonecraft's description of the competition between wife and sister comes from *A Vindication of the Rights of Woman*. See Janet Todd and Marilyn Butler (eds.), *The Works of Mary Wollstonecraft*, 7 vols. (New York: New York University Press, 1989), vol. v, p. 134.

[67] Amanda Vickery, *The Gentleman's Daughter: Women's Lives in Georgian England* (New Haven and London: Yale University Press, 1998), p. 109.

[68] J. D. Marshall (ed.), *The Autobiography of William Stout of Lancaster, 1665–1752* (Manchester: Manchester University Press, and New York: Barnes and Noble, 1967), p. 159. Quoted in Amanda Vickery, *The Gentleman's Daughter*, p. 109.

[69] M. Bentham-Edwards (ed.), *The Autobiography of Arthur Young* (1898; rpt. New York: Augustus M. Kelley, 1967), p. 44.

rarely speak to one another in the presence of others) as well as the connection between the young father and his new children (who call him "elder
brother"). As Lynn Bennett describes it, any bonds that might "split the
joint family into nuclear units are kept publicly at a low level in the interests of agnatic solidarity."[70] These measures, which evolved to encourage
men to retain their consanguineal identities and offset the pressure to split
off into separate nuclear units, tell us something about how these bonds
are constructed. For Nepalese women, of course, consanguineal and affinal identifications remain in tension with each other, and their families of
origin – their brothers in particular – remain the loci of protection and
refuge in difficult times, the court of appeal in the case of mistreatment,
and a source of food and clothes when they are witheld in the new affinal
household.

In eighteenth-century England, the competition between sibling loyalty
and wedding vows took on a more material character where there were children. The letters of Eliza Pierce, an intelligent and educated but orphaned
woman of moderate fortune, offer a glimpse into these kinship dilemmas
for a woman at mid-century.[71] Before her marriage, Eliza Pierce had lived
with her aunt and uncle, tending them in their interminable illnesses. Her
uncle was her guardian and financial adviser, her only "friend" in the contemporary lexicon. Depressed by their constant need and her confinement,
she wrote to her fiancé in 1752, "I really do begin to Lose al Hopes of seeing
my Uncle & Aunt well both together," a condition necessary for her to
leave their house and marry. In time she did escape. Her aging relatives
recovered and were able to do without her long enough for her to marry
her accepted suitor. Even though the marriage was a longed-for love-match,
however, before long Eliza Pierce Taylor began to feel that Thomas Taylor
was mismanaging her money, siphoning off her fortune without taking
adequate care of either her or their new child. Her letters to her husband
reveal the perspective of a wife who sees her husband diverting to his own
blood relations the fortune she brought him rather than saving it up for

---

[70] Lynn Bennett describes the "studied mutual ignoring between husband and wife" as a man returning
from work tells his news and shares his purchases first with his mother and father. "This minimizing
of the husband/wife relation in the joint family has as its corollary the playing down of the dependent
son's fatherhood" and any children are "played with and fondled more by the grandfather as long
as the father is dependent." Lynn Bennett, *Dangerous Wives and Sacred Sisters: Social and Symbolic
Roles of High-Caste Women in Nepal* (New York: Columbia University Press, 1983), p. 173.

[71] Violet M. Macdonald (ed.), *The Letters of Eliza Pierce 1751–1775* (London: Frederick Etchells and
Hugh Macdonald, 1927). Eliza Pierce was a cultivated woman, familiar with the poetry of Young
and Milton, with strong opinions about the relative merits of Sir John Denham's *Sophy* and *Cooper's
Hill* (46) and Henry Fielding's novels (57). These letters cover the period between 1751 and 1775; one
of her correspondents was Catherine Talbot.

their children. She complains about his stalling tactics in buying an estate for their son as they had agreed he would. She urges him to pay off his sister's dowry quickly so that the accruing interest will not further drain their son's inheritance:

my Duty to your Son obliges me to speak sometimes of things I know you don't like to hear and yet in fact your own interest is concern'd as much as his, I mean in regard to the payment of your Sisters Fortune – I never think of it but it leaves a dead weight on my Heart, and I cant help saying that it is a most cruel thing in you to keep runing up the interest as you do – I have heard that your Mother is very fond of her Grandson, therefore wonder she as trustee will suffer such an injury to be done him – (97)

Eliza Pierce complains that her husband is not acting in the interests of his new conjugal family but in the interests of his family of origin, including his mother and sister.[72] Furthermore, she accuses her husband, Thomas, of being stingy with *her* money. "I have so great a regard for my Son," she declares, "that if you would this moment, make the addition of the interest of that Money [i.e., the purchase price of the estate for their son] to my income, (instead of laying it out for his benefitt) I would not accept of it – and yet the heart in spite of Religion & Phylosophy does sometimes rebel at the thoughts of living for ever, on fourscore pd: a Year – I say *for ever* – you best know whether you design it to be so, or not – at least while you live you are master of my fate" (87). Apparently Taylor kept her on a short leash and limited her pin money to £80 a year, despite the fortune she brought into the marriage. All in all she felt the restrictions of a husband after the disinterested guardianship of her uncle: "I am got into the net of Matrimony," she complains, "and the more I flounce, the more bruises & Blows, shall I have" (87).

According to the anthropologist and demographer J. C. Caldwell, the devolution of property and wealth downwards from parents to children defines western kinship arrangements – rather than the converse expectation that children will support their parents or contribute to their support throughout their lives common in many other cultures. He describes the "emotional nucleation of the family whereby parents spend increasingly on their children, while demanding – and receiving – very little in return," as part of a pattern in which conjugal ties become dominant and obligations

---

[72] This opposition calls to mind the subtext of brother-sister love in *The Mill on the Floss* (1860). Maggie Tulliver's father gives money to his sister and her improvident husband, feeling responsible for her with an earlier loyalty, despite his wife's angry remonstrance against his generosity. His fraternal fidelity counterpoints the deteriorating relationship between Maggie and her brother Tom.

to wider kin decrease in importance, a pattern which he sees as developing in the west during the century before Malthus.[73] This inheritance practice – the downward devolution of property – inevitably contributed to the pressure on individuals to favor their offspring over collateral consanguineal relatives, and to turn a deaf ear to demands from their sisters in preference to their own children. This, of course, is what Eliza Pierce had been expecting of her new husband.

Bonham Hayes, a Kent farmer who willed his house and 220 acres of land to his second son when he died in 1720, did not leave the treatment of his wife to chance or even to his son's goodwill. He stipulated "that my loving wife shall have the use and benefit of the little parlour chamber and my little parlour below stairs . . . and all the furniture in the same rooms during her natural life and her board gratis with my said son Richard Hayes."[74] Presumably his widow had a legal right to room and board – widow's free bench – without this stipulation. But as Bridget Hill remarks in quoting this provision, "the fact that Bonham Hayes felt it necessary to include such instruction in his will might suggest that the law was not always regarded, or he might have felt that as Richard was not his eldest son he must spell out exactly the conditions his widow should enjoy."[75]

At the other end of the century, Mary Wollstonecraft, in *A Vindication of the Rights of Woman*, laments the fate of unmarried sisters at the mercy of a brother's unfeeling wife. She imagines a situation such as that described earlier in Sarah Scott's *Sir George Ellison* (1766), in which a young woman, "weakly educated," is left by the death of their parents without provision, dependent on the bounty of a brother. Even when these brothers are a "good sort of men," writes Wollstonecraft, they "give as a favour, what children of the same parents had an equal right to." She adds drily, "[I]n this equivocal humiliating situation, a docile female may remain some time, with a tolerable degree of comfort." But when the day comes that the brother marries, the sister's position changes overnight from being the mistress of the establishment to being viewed as "an intruder, an unnecessary burden on the benevolence of the master of the house, and his new partner."

---

[73] Alan Macfarlane, *Marriage and Love in England 1300–1840* (Oxford: Basil Blackwell, 1986), pp. 38–40, quote p. 40: he is here citing J. C. Caldwell, "Toward a Restatement of Demographic Transition Theory," *Population and Development Review* 2, 3–4 (1976), 352, 356. Macfarlane argues that the downward devolution of property was one of the features of English society that fostered and maintained the early development of individualism.

[74] Ralph Arnold, *A Yeoman of Kent: An Account of Richard Hayes (1725–1790) of the Village of Cobham* (London: Constable, 1949), p. 94, quoted in Bridget Hill, *Women, Work, and Sexual Politics in Eighteenth-Century England*, p. 251.

[75] Bridget Hill, *Women, Work, and Sexual Politics in Eighteenth-Century England*, pp. 251–2.

The wife grudges the money spent on his sister because she feels by rights it should go to *her* children. "These are matters of fact," Wollstonecraft writes, "which have come under my eye again and again."[76]

Jane Austen, who never married and hence was never called upon to reassign her family loyalty from her consanguineal kin to a new conjugal family, saw these tensions very clearly. She created what may be the *locus classicus* of sister–wife conflict in the satiric second chapter of *Sense and Sensibility*. The sequence begins with the land itself, the estate of Norland, destined to bypass the protagonists (Mrs. Dashwood and her daughters Elinor, Marianne, and Margaret will inherit *no land*), inhabited at the outset by a single man and his constant companion and housekeeper, his sister. When this sister dies in the opening chapter, the old gentleman invites his nephew (presumably a sibling's child), Mr. Henry Dashwood, together with his wife and daughters, to live with him. Henry Dashwood's son by a previous marriage, John Dashwood, stands to inherit the estate after the old gentleman dies, although it was Henry Dashwood's second wife (*our* Mrs. Dashwood) and three prattling daughters who enlivened the old gentleman's last decade. Henry Dashwood himself dies a year after his uncle, although not before urging his son, John, to look after the interests of his stepmother and half sisters. Thus Austen sets up an opposition between John Dashwood's obligation to his conjugal family, his wife and children, and his duty to his consanguineal family, his blood kin – already somewhat attenuated by their being only a stepmother and half sisters.

Norland, once the site of a family constructed by siblinghood, is transformed into the private castle of the conjugal family. Mrs. John Dashwood immediately installs herself as the mistress of Norland and makes sure her mother and sisters-in-law know that they have been "degraded to the condition of visitors." As the wife of the heir, Mrs. John Dashwood then proceeds to whittle down her husband's intended largesse to his blood kin, from £1,000 apiece for each of his half sisters to £500 apiece to an annuity of £100 for their mother to an occasional gift of £50 to presents of fish and game in season. To give more, she claims, would be to rob their child, to ruin themselves and "their poor little Harry, by giving away all his money to his half sisters."[77] Punctuated by venal reflections on Mrs. Dashwood's good health and probable extravagant longevity, as well as the unpleasantness of placing any clogs on one's annual income, Mrs. John Dashwood's

---

[76] This description appears in *A Vindication of the Rights of Woman*. Janet Todd and Marilyn Butler (eds.), *The Works of Mary Wollstonecraft*, vol. v, p. 134.

[77] Jane Austen, *Sense and Sensibility* (1811), ed. Ros Ballaster (London: Penguin, 1995), p. 7.

selfish urgings stifle her husband's intended generosity towards his consanguineal kin on the grounds that he owes his child – and future children –
everything he can hoard.

Austen did not invent this situation. It was common enough in fiction
written in the preceding half-century, and, as we have seen, Mary Wollstonecraft claimed that betrayal of the sister was a matter "of fact" that had
"come under my eye again and again." But Austen sets up the situation
unequivocally (Mr. and Mrs. John Dashwood have an income of at least
£5,000 or £6,000 a year and his mother and sisters £500 annually) and
plays it out with her usual incisiveness. Scholars have traced resonances in
Austen's chapter to scenes in several other eighteenth-century novels, such
as Charlotte Smith's *Ethelinde* (1790), in which Harry Chesterfield offers
a self-justifying soliloquy about not sharing his newfound wealth with his
sister or anyone else, and Lady Hawkhurst in the same novel makes disua-
sive arguments to her more generously inclined husband. Austen's moral
slapstick also parodies Sir Charles Grandison's promptings in Richardson's
novel, when he gives advice to Sir Harry Beauchamp and his second wife
(in letter 4 of vol. IV) to be more generous to Sir Harry's son, promptings
which Austen's second chapter of *Sense and Sensibility* play out in reverse.[78]
Like her eighteenth-century predecessors, Austen contrasts conjugal loyalty with loyalty to a wider network of consanguineal kin, and associates
these kinds of family feeling with very different impulses. Accumulation for
one's conjugal unit was simply an extension of one's personal selfishness,
mean and grasping. Taking care of one's blood relatives, on the other hand,
particularly where the law did not require it, was coming to be seen as the
heart and soul of proper feeling.

---

[78] These influences, as well as traces of the scene in Shakespeare's *King Lear* in which Lear is divested
by his daughters of most of his retinue, are identified in Stephen Derry, "Sources of Chapter Two
of *Sense and Sensibility*," *Persuasions* 16 (December 1994), 5–27.

4

Brotherly love in life and literature

The intimate relationship between brother and sister, rather than the incest taboo, is the elementary kinship principle.
Annette B. Weiner, *Inalienable Possessions*, pp. 15–16.

The relation of a brother and a sister, especially if they do not marry, appears to me of a very singular nature. It is a familiar and tender friendship with a female, much about our own age; an affection, perhaps softened by the secret influence of sex, but pure from any mixture of sensual desire, the sole species of Platonic love that can be indulged with truth and without danger.
Edward Gibbon, *The Memoirs of the Life of Edward Gibbon*, p. 2.

It is a common observation, that love between brothers and sisters is rare to be met with.
Anon., *Cleora: or, the Fair Inconstant* (1752), p. 24.

One of the main requisites of an eighteenth-century fictional hero was that he be a good brother: attentive, generous, protective, wise. Henry Tilney in Jane Austen's *Northanger Abbey*, about whom we know precious little except that he is a tease, qualifies as the hero of the novel by showing that he is an affectionate brother. Indeed, all the brothers in *Northanger Abbey* display their truest selves in relation to their sisters, as is appropriate in a novel self-conscious about the conventions and clichés of fiction. John Thorpe's boisterous, swaggering selfishness, his adolescent display, is apparent from his first insolent greeting of his mother and sisters. James Morland is only intermittently attentive to his younger sister, Catherine; but when he does focus on her he is honest and caring. Frederick Tilney, the very pattern of a thoughtless, pleasure-seeking older brother, hardly ever home, offers his sister Eleanor neither company nor protection. The brother-sister connections in this parodic novel define the realistic range of moral possibilities; Austen was drawing on a literary tradition in which brother-sister relationships were an essential part of the story. The heroine's relationship with her brother, or the hero's relationship with his sister, were more significant both in life and literature than we can imagine in today's atomized society. So common was the expectation of the responsibility of a brother for his sister – and so commonly was it shirked – that a brother's generosity towards his sister (or lack thereof) became, in fiction, a fundamental marker of his character.

Clarissa reads Solmes' character accurately from the way he treats his sister – and his maternal relatives – in Richardson's novel.

Does not his own sister live unhappily for want of a little of his superfluities? And suffers he not his aged uncle, the brother of his own mother, to owe to the generosity of strangers the poor subsistence he picks up from half a dozen families?[1]

Selfish with his sister, neglectful of a necessitous relative on his mother's side, Solmes proves his coarse parsimony in his subsequent appearances in the Harlowe household. Clarissa begs not to be confined to his "narrow, selfish circle" (153) where her wider-reaching generosity would be stymied. When the authors of *The Cry* (1754), Sarah Fielding and Jane Collier (both of whom had brothers), want to discredit a rich but contemptible suitor for the faithful Cordelia, they describe his exploitation of his sister. Wealthy Ruffinus, who knows a good thing when he sees it, is willing to take Cordelia without a dowry. Her weak and self-indulgent father, who has a bad conscience because he has plundered her fortune, urges this as a sign of Ruffinus' generosity. But Ruffinus' treatment of his own sister is a truer index of his character. The situation is exaggerated to make sure the reader gets the point: "His only sister, whose outward deformity, poor girl, had prevented her ever hoping for any other protection, lived with him as a house-keeper: and how she lived need not be told" (1: 272). As I noted in the last chapter, many sisters kept house for their brothers; but there was a difference between being a dependent servant and being given an establishment to manage. Brotherly love became a moral litmus test in eighteenth-century fiction, because although not required by law, it had the weight of custom as well as necessity behind it. A family obligation from an earlier era, increasingly honored more in the breach than in the observance, brotherly love came to be a conventional ideal in fiction as it was eroded in life by competing demands of conjugal families and the cash requirements of the new economy.

Felicia to Charlotte (1744), by Mary Collyer, features a complex web of brother-sister relationships that reveals truths about characters later verified

[1] Samuel Richardson, *Clarissa*, ed. Angus Ross (London: Penguin, 1985), p. 153.

by other means. The novel begins when Felicia overhears an unknown youth declaiming on the moral lessons of nature while he is wandering in the woods. A Rousseauian romantic *avant la lettre*, the stranger rhapsodizes about the intrinsic order and harmony of nature and its inspiration of human virtue.[2] Felicia falls in love with Lucius while discussing the philosophical basis of moral reasoning. Is morality inborn or learned? Are the same precepts common to all societies or specific to certain cultures? Is morality gendered differently for men than for women? Early in the narrative Felicia receives proof of Lucius' moral reliability from his sister Marilla, who tells her:

there subsists such a harmony between us, as is very rarely seen in such near relations. It is his chief study to improve my mind; and he has taken inconceivable pains in giving me those just principles of virtue, which I hope will always influence my conduct. I find in him not only a brother, but a sincere and affectionate friend. We have but one common interest. He trusts me with the secrets of his heart, and in short, we are so closely united, that were I unhappy he would feel as much for me, as perhaps I should for myself. (59–60)

Lucius' attentive care of his sister Marilla proves that he is worthy of Felicia's love. A friendship grows up between the two women, like the friendship between Catherine Morland and Eleanor Tilney in Austen's *Northanger Abbey*; the sisters-in-law become as close as blood sisters even before the marriage is sanctified. Thus, in the wish-fulfillment of fiction, conjugal love creates new affinal sibling bonds that do not compete with earlier ties. The villainous Prudilla, maiden sister of a local squire who has long nursed a "criminal passion" for Lucius (and who forges a letter to Felicia's father), represents the potential threat of a sister to disrupt conjugal relations when her desire is not contained.

Historically, sibling loyalty played a more important role in people's lives than it does today, although by the eighteenth century that relationship was already somewhat diluted. Still, in eighteenth-century fiction, only a brother could compete for the love of a woman with her husband; only a brother could arouse as powerful feelings as the hero in the sensible heart of a heroine.[3] Charlotte Lennox's *The Life of Harriot Stuart* (1751) uses a

---

[2] Mary Collyer, *Felicia to Charlotte* (London: Jacob Robinson, 1744); subsequent page numbers refer to this edition. This aspect of the novel – its status as a precursor of Romanticism – is emphasized in an early panegyric by Helen Sard Hughes, "An Early Romantic Novel," *Journal of English and Germanic Philology* 15 (1916), 564–98.

[3] David Sabean suggests that the intensity of this love also reflected their gendered difference in agency. In the case of Fanny and Felix Mendelssohn-Bartholdy, he writes, "Her longing for him was a longing as much for the freedom to do what he could do, as for the reestablishment of a lost intimacy"

lovers' vocabulary to express the "ardent affection" of the heroine for her brother who "instilled an early love for virtue into my soul."[4] When he leaves to make his fortune, she hangs "upon his arms in a speechless agony of grief, and it was with the greatest difficulty he forced himself from me" (1: 10). When they are reunited, her "transports were as unbounded as the affection I had for him" (1: 57), and when he dies of a fever in Jamaica, she has a fit of illness that lasts for two months after which she weeps incessantly, hoping for death (11: 7–8). Jane Austen's most backward-looking novel, *Mansfield Park*, privileges the brother-sister tie above all others. Fanny Price, that most old-fashioned of heroines, adores her brother William, and enjoys her greatest happiness in "unchecked, equal, fearless intercourse" with him. (Even Edmund, whom she eventually marries, has the feel of a brother.) Their shared memories, claims Austen, were "a strengthener of love, *in which even the conjugal tie is beneath the fraternal*" [emphasis added].

Children of the same family, the same blood, with the same first associations and habits, have some means of enjoyment in their power, which no subsequent connections can supply; and it must be by a long and unnatural estrangement, by a divorce which no subsequent connection can justify, if such precious remains of the earliest attachments are ever entirely outlived.[5]

Conversely, as Gerard Barker has pointed out, lovers in eighteenth-century novels often have "a pseudo-sibling relationship that conveniently sublimates the sexual realities of courtship." Thus, Sir Charles Grandison calls Harriet his "third sister," Lord Orville tells Evelina to "think of me as if I were indeed your brother," Charlotte Smith's Emmeline tells Godolphin she thinks of him "as an excellent brother," Henry Clinton in Henry Brooke's *The Fool of Quality; or, The History of Henry Earl of Moreland* (1765–70) is enjoined "to prove a kind brother" to the woman he eventually marries, and Caroline Campinet tells the eponymous hero of *Hermsprong, or Man as He Is Not* (1796) that she will consult and confide in him "as a brother." If a man could play the part of a good brother, it guaranteed that he would be a good husband.[6]

---

(715). "Fanny and Felix Mendelssohn-Bartholdy and the Question of Incest," *Musical Quarterly* 77, 4 (Winter 1993), 709–17.

[4] Charlotte Lennox, *The Life of Harriot Stuart*, 2 vols. (London: J. Payne and J. Bosquet, 1751), vol. 1, p. 9. All subsequent page numbers refer to this edition.

[5] Jane Austen, *Mansfield Park*, ed. Tony Tanner (Harmondsworth and New York: Penguin, 1966), p. 244.

[6] Gerard A. Barker, *Grandison's Heirs: The Paragon's Progress in the Late Eighteenth-Century English Novel* (Newark: University of Delaware Press, 1985), pp. 75–6.

THE GOOD BROTHER

Social historians and literary critics often pass over sibling relationships as irrelevant to the "real story" – which they assume to be the development of the conjugal family with its emphasis on romantic love between husbands and wives and strong emotional bonds between parents and children. They overlook the extent to which a brother's protection of his sister was retained as a moral ideal, a vestige of disintegrating consanguineal loyalty, even when in practice it came to be the exception rather than the rule. The idealized "good brother" (as well as his opposite) appears in scores of eighteenth-century novels in the second half of the century. *The Adventures of David Simple* (1744), Sarah Fielding's first novel, prefaced as it was by her famous brother, contains several good examples. In the Preface, Henry praises his sister's "vast Penetration into human Nature, a deep and profound Discernment of all the Mazes, Windings, and Labyrinths, which perplex the Heart of Man to such a degree, that he is himself often incapable of seeing through them" and the wonderfully natural touches in her satiric portraits – "some Touches, which I will venture to say might have done honour to the Pencil of the immortal Shakespear himself." But he also calls attention several times to her errors in grammar, style, and diction – corrected by his fraternal *noblesse oblige* for the second edition – and remarks on her youth and inexperience, referring to her novel several times as a "little" book, a "little" work. He has written this preface, he tells the reader, to repudiate this fiction as his own work (for it had been attributed to him), and also to disown an entirely different work, a slanderous satire on the legal profession, *The Causidicade*.[7] Thus he both claims and disclaims responsibility for the work – and, indirectly, for his sister.

Sibling relations in *The Adventures of David Simple* are extreme: siblings are either entirely devoted to one another or cruelly competitive.[8] David's evil brother, Daniel Simple, forges their father's will so as to disinherit David, though the hero later recovers some of his fortune with the help of an uncle, the brother of another generation. (*Tom Jones* [1749] and *Amelia* [1751] also turn on the plot device of the theft of inheritance by a sibling.) In another episode, sisters make one another miserable in their contests over

---

[7] Henry Fielding, Preface to Sarah Fielding, *The Adventures of David Simple*, ed. Malcolm Kelsall, Oxford World's Classics (Oxford: Oxford University Press, 1987), pp. 5, 7, 6. Subsequent page references to this novel are to this edition. See Kelsall's Introduction, p. x, for more details on Fielding's desire to disassociate himself from the anonymous *The Causidicade*.

[8] Understood psychoanalytically, the mechanism of splitting enables simultaneous idealization and demonization of its objects, permitting the good and the bad to be separated and exaggerated.

suitors – or carpets. Against this background of sibling rivalry, Valentine and Camilla stand out as an exemplary brother and sister whom David Simple rescues from starvation. Their story opens with a description of Camilla's utter devotion to her brother as he lies ill with a fever. Later, assuring us that Valentine reciprocated his sister's devotion, the narrator remarks that he was not one of

those Brothers who, by their Fathers having more Concern for the keeping up the Grandeur of their Names, than for the Welfare of their Posterity, having got the Possession of all the Estate of the Family, out of meer *Kindness* and *Good-Nature*, allow their Sisters enough out of it to keep them from starving in some Hole in the Country; where their small Subsistence just serves to sustain them the longer in their Misery, and prevents them from appearing in the World to *disgrace their Brother, by their Poverty.* (154)

This stereotype, which we have met before, obviously energizes the author; she relishes these details of the victimized sister. In *David Simple* the only characters without guile or selfishness and with the capacity for compassion are the brother and sister Valentine and Camilla, together with the long-suffering Cynthia, whom David Simple also rescues; these are the only characters in the novel worthy of true friendship.

It is noteworthy that the first thing the exemplary Sir Charles Grandison does upon returning home after his father's death, in the novel by Richardson, is to restore his sisters' rightful portions. It is not simply the impulse to protect innocent sufferers that motivates him (although that sentimental impulse seems to have had an increasing appeal to the reading public as the century wore on), but a clear instinct for justice. When he restores his sisters' rightful portions he is not acting out of charity but out of rectitude. He acts quickly and decisively to make them comfortable and independent, giving them each £10,000 irrevocably free and clear. One assumes from the complex and detailed circumstances – narrated with care at great length – that eighteenth-century readers found much of interest in this example of legally providing for unmarried sisters. Richardson tells the Grandison story from the period in which the profligate father skimped on his daughters' dowries the better to supply his mistresses ("Why should I divide my fortune with novices?")[9] to restitution by the admirable Sir Charles. The narrative emphasizes among other things women's dependence on the goodness of their brothers. As Sir Charles' mother explains on her deathbed to his sisters – and it is a lesson many wise older women

---

[9] Samuel Richardson, *The History of Sir Charles Grandison*, ed. Jocelyn Harris (Oxford and New York: Oxford University Press, 1986), vol. II, letter xiv, p. 326.

in eighteenth-century fiction teach younger women—

I am afraid there will be but a slender provision made for my dear girls. Your papa has the notion riveted in him, which is common to men of antient families, that daughters are but incumbrances, and that the son is to be everything . . . Your brother loves you: He loves me. It will be in *his* power, should he survive your father, to be a good friend to you. — Love your brother.[10]

One need only recall Richardson's other fictional brother, James Harlowe, for the other side to this coin, the potential for harm in a selfish brother.

One of the first lessons given to girls in Sarah Fielding's *The Governess* (1749) is that they are going to be dependent on their brothers and so they had best propitiate them. Jenny Peace, the oldest and most admired girl in the school, tells a story about how her brother "being nimbler and better able to jump than myself," leapt over a stream,

but seeing me uneasy that I could not get over to him, his Good-nature prompted him to come back and to assist me, and, by the Help of his Hand I easily passed over. On this my good Mamma bid me remember how much my Brother's superior Strength might assist me in his being my Protector; and that I ought in return to use my utmost Endeavours to oblige him.[11]

Jenny's mother, a wise widow who has cultivated friendship between her children in order to provide for Jenny's future, adds a little later, "I hope he [i.e., her brother] will be a Father to you, if you deserve his Love and Protection" (33). A fatherless girl needed her brother's care; until she married, he was the only man who could be expected to look out for her in the wider world: to protect her honor, invest her money, escort her in public places, fend off unwanted importunities, and the like. A woman's relationship with her brother helped to even the odds against her in a male-dominated world. It enlisted on her behalf someone who thought like her, shared some of her interests, and occupied a similar social location, but who had the advantage of gender.[12]

---

[10] *Ibid.*, vol. ii, letter xii, p. 315.

[11] Sarah Fielding, *The Governess or, Little Female Academy* (1749; facsimile rpt. Oxford: Oxford University Press, 1968), pp. 29–30.

[12] In "Fanny and Felix Mendelssohn-Bartholdy and the Question of Incest," David Sabean writes about this advantage of gender. Although both brother and sister were musically gifted and composed music, their father wrote to Fanny when she was fourteen: "Music will perhaps become his [Felix's] profession while for you it can and must only be an ornament, never the root of your being and doing . . . and your very joy at the praise he earns proves that you might, in his place, have merited equal approval" (711). Likewise Goethe's sister, Cornelia, "after an early education that was not differentiated by gender, was abruptly made to understand that her destiny was to be radically different from that of her brother" (714). Cornelia fell into a deep depression as, Sabean suggests,

In Sophia Briscoe's *Miss Melmoth; or, The New Clarissa* (1771), a book whose subtitle might as well have been "The New Sir Charles Grandison," Sir George Darnley also gives each of his sisters her own fortune, "with the accumulated interest since his father's death." Such financial details update the fairy tale. "I never wish my sisters to be under the least restraint to me," he confides to the heroine, giving her the best possible evidence of his respect for women.[13] Her letter describing his generous act reports that "he gave up all his power" and "offered his advice whenever they would honour him so far as to consult him: his concurrence, he said, should ever go hand in hand with their choice" (1: 60). His sisters, suitably overcome, find relief in tears. "'O my brother,' sobbed the dear grateful girl, 'take, keep this loved testimony of your brotherly affection. Where can my fortune be so secure as in your hands, my brother?'" In a similar scene in Elizabeth Todd's *The History of Lady Caroline Rivers* (1788), the heroine throws into the fire her father's £50,000 draft on his banker, a draft impulsively written by their parent when her generous brother urged him to put Lady Caroline's fortune at her own disposal. As she commits it to the flames she cries "'twas the death everyone deserved to die who distrusted a tender parent."[14] But in *Miss Melmoth*, the good brother refuses to take back the proffered banknotes from his sisters, and, after kissing each one of them, "folding his affectionate arms round them, he left the room" (1: 60). This mixture of brotherly love, banknotes, and grateful tears – the graceful abdication of absolute power and the free resignation of a great deal of money – amounts to a naive version of sentimentality that could only have been written and read appreciatively in eighteenth-century England.[15]

Idealized fantasies about the effects of love (whether family love or romantic love) on the more tangible motives of power and/or money, staged theatrically and with elegant diction, appear frequently in these novels. Examples of such brotherly perfection are legion, but I will restrict myself to one more to make the point. In negotiating a marriage contract for his

did a number of other women in their twenties from intellectual families in Frankfurt and Darmstadt around 1770.

[13] Sophia Briscoe, *Miss Melmoth; or, The New Clarissa* (London, 1771), vol. 1, pp. 57, 58. Subsequent page references are to this edition.

[14] Elizabeth Todd, *The History of Lady Caroline Rivers* (London, 1788), pp. 26–7.

[15] The critical reception of *Miss Melmoth* assumed a positive readership. The *Critical Review* reported to its audience: "There is much *business* in it, and of an interesting nature; several parts of it are affecting; and it contains, upon the whole, a pleasing mixture of instruction and entertainment." The *Monthly Review* was more acerbic: "The good-natured and benevolent reader will receive more pleasure from the perusal of this work than the critic." James Raven and Antonia Forster, *The English Novel 1770–1829: A Bibliographical Survey of Prose Fiction Published in the British Isles*, 2 vols. (Oxford and New York: Oxford University Press, 2000), vol. 1, pp. 159–60.

sister, the eponymous hero of Anna Meades' *The History of Sir William Harrington* (1771) offers her "some thousands" of his own, "left entirely at my disposal by our late dear father," should her intended think her fortune too small.[16] Such disinterested but protective and unconditional love – authenticated with banknotes – was, next to the love of a father for his daughter, the most exalted sentiment a man could feel. A loving brother was better than a father because closer to the heroine's own interests and more of a friend. "So *feminine* his delicacy, and so amiable his nature!" says Evelina of Lord Orville (emphasis in the original); "As a sister I loved him."[17] Like a stronger self, a brother could identify with his sister but had the agency that she lacked. When alarmed by Lord Merton's drunken advances, Evelina cries out "Would to heaven that I . . . had a brother! – and then I should not be exposed to such treatment!"[18] Elizabeth Bonhote's eponymous Ellen Woodley refers to a man who helps her disinterestedly as a "second brother."[19] When most alone and vulnerable, Charlotte Smith's Emmeline laments "I have *no* father, *no* brother to console and receive me."[20]

The ubiquitous presence and significance of brothers in the lives of fictional heroines (and the difficulties they occasionally posed) is one kind of evidence for the importance of this relationship in eighteenth-century life and for the strains on it. Most of the brothers in novels are generous to a fault, although the exceptions are instructive. Eliza Haywood offers a benign and uncomplicated version of sibling relations in her late novel *The History of Betsy Thoughtless* (1751). The somewhat dissipated older brother and the more responsible younger brother[21] are both unambivalent in their desire to protect their sister from male predators and to direct her to a

---

[16] Anna Meades, *The History of Sir William Harrington* 4 vols. (1771; rpt. New York: Garland, 1974), vol. II, p. 40. Miss Harrington's intended, Lord C., in turn proves his perfection by refusing her brother's money, saying that since he himself possesses "an ample share of it, why should I be covetous for more? . . . had your sister only as many hundreds as she has thousands, such as she is in herself, so deserving a lady, I should esteem the favour of her hand the greatest happiness this life could give me" (II: 42).

[17] Frances Burney, *Evelina; or the History of a Young Lady's Entrance into the World*, ed. Edward A. Bloom and Lillian D. Bloom (Oxford: Oxford University Press, 1968), letter xxviii, p. 261.

[18] Frances Burney, *Evelina*, letter vii, p. 314.

[19] Elizabeth Bonhote, *Ellen Woodley* (London, 1790), vol. I, p. 80. Her brother does act *in loco parentis* in vol. II, p. 40.

[20] Charlotte Smith, *Emmeline: The Orphan of the Castle* (1788; rpt. London: Pandora Books, 1988), p. 164.

[21] This common formula was also used by Jane Austen in *Mansfield Park* to describe Tom and Edmund Bertram. The social disparity between brothers, the effects of primogeniture on the first and second son of a baronet, is evident in the way Mary Crawford distinguishes between them as prizes in the marriage market.

wholesome marriage. Neither is corrupted, as are some fictional brothers, by greed for their sisters' fortune or by the power of having the disposal of her person. Francis Thoughtless, the younger of Betsy's brothers, a second son who must advance himself through the university, duels the gentleman commoner in Oxford who led the innocent Betsy into a house and then attempted to rape her. Francis Thoughtless also introduces Betsy to Mr. Trueworth, the man she does eventually marry, and vouches for his quality. A kindly brother, neither dictatorial nor greedy, Francis Thoughtless turns out to be Betsy's best friend throughout the novel, with her interests truly at heart.[22] His letter to her after the duel is the soul of responsibility. Not only does he not chastise her, but he seeks to allay her anxiety about his own injuries and advises her to stay away from his lodgings until the scandal blows over.

Meanwhile, their older brother, Mr. Thomas Thoughtless, has been abroad for five years in Europe and returns to London. The siblings are all very glad to be reunited; family feeling among them is real. Together, her brothers try to advise her about marrying and they take care of the necessary legal transactions to secure her pin money and jointure. Later, when her faithless first husband, Mr. Munden, decamps with another woman, her older brother takes her in and provides support and affection. He also goes with her to engage a lawyer to help negotiate for a separate settlement – until Mr. Munden conveniently dies.

The brother of the heroine in Frances Sheridan's *The Memoirs of Miss Sidney Bidulph* (1761) similarly introduces her to the love of her life, his friend Orlando Faulkland. He advises Sidney repeatedly to marry him and not to waste her life playing games of heroic sensibility. Throughout the heroine's misfortunes he is sensitive and caring, and tries to direct and advise her for her own real good. On the other hand, the brother of Lavinia Knightley in *The Younger Sister* (1772), by Anne Dawe, "that used to give pleasure wherever he came," is an example of a brother who thinks his sister is his property to deploy for his own purposes.[23] He tries to force her to marry the Chevalier who saved his life in Italy and is angry that she has engaged herself to Sir Thomas Watts. "O! Lavinia," he remonstrates, "why would you think of engaging yourself before my return?" He stamps his

---

[22] For a fine article about the relative position of brothers in *The History of Betsy Thoughtless* and *Clarissa*, see Naomi Tadmor, "Dimensions of Inequality among Siblings in Eighteenth-Century English Novels: The Cases of *Clarissa* and *The History of Miss Betsy Thoughtless*," *Continuity and Change* 7, 3 (1992), 303–33.

[23] Anne Dawe, *The Younger Sister: or, The History of Miss Somerset*, 2 vols. (Dublin: R. Marchbank, 1772), vol. I, p. 81. Subsequent page references are to this edition.

foot. He mutters: "inconsiderate girl." He insists that she at least listen to the Chevalier's addresses and exclaims "if you have the least regard remaining for me, you must abate some part of your punctilio" (1: 98–9). More like James Harlowe, this brother thinks of his sister as a subordinate who ought to be under his direction, a counter to be played for his own advantage in the game of life.

Brothers in eighteenth-century fiction, especially if there were no father, were expected to protect their sisters' chastity. In *Anecdotes of a Convent* (1771), Louisa Boothby's brother notices a strange young man loitering about his sister's convent, secretly communicating with her, and challenges the young man to a duel to defend his sister's honor.[24] In Goldsmith's *The Vicar of Wakefield*, George, the oldest brother in the family, returns to England to avenge his sister Olivia's ruin by challenging the vicious squire who traduced her. Arrested and jailed for this act of honor – duelling was illegal and George has already been roundly chastised by Sir William Thornhill for it – his culpability is mitigated by his mother's letter calling him to avenge his sister. Nor does the reader condemn him for this warm-blooded protective act; on the contrary, it proves his quality so that when he is reunited with his faithful Arabella he seems to deserve his good fortune.

Jane Austen built her plots on sisterly dependence and brotherly love too. *Northanger Abbey*, with its complete line of brothers, shows that good characters looked out for their sisters (Henry Tilney, James Morland) and bad characters did not (John Thorpe, Frederick Tilney). Darcy's care and protection for his sister Georgiana in *Pride and Prejudice*, his delicacy in not blaming her for her folly with Wickham, as well as his acting in *loco fraternis* to Elizabeth Bennet by making respectable Wickham's second elopement, this time with *her* sister, demonstrate his excellent moral fiber. Henry Crawford in *Mansfield Park*, selfish and self-centered, writes perfunctory letters to his sister Mary ("that is a complete brother's letter," she says, showing Fanny Price a brief paragraph); but Fanny's brother William, away at sea, writes *his* sister very long letters, making an effort to keep in touch with her. And as I have said, the reader appreciates Edmund Bertram's capacities as a brother – his protection, guidance, and generosity towards Fanny Price – long before we grant him his place as prince charming in her fairy tale.

In eighteenth-century society, brothers were expected to protect their sisters – both because they were representatives of patriarchal power under

---

[24] The irony here is that the "young man" George Boothby challenges knows no swordplay, having been raised as a woman. In fact, Francis Merton first met Louisa in that same convent where he, too, had been living as a woman. This anonymous novel was written "By the author of Memoirs of Mrs. Williams" (1771).

the older, feudal system, and because they were more obviously participants in the newer capitalist system. Sisters depended upon their brothers for financial support and occasionally an establishment, for legal advice and public negotiation, for mobility and escorted travel, and for social and sexual protection. They had no legal leverage to compel these services because theirs was, after all, a sibling relation and not a child-parent relation. Thus their very forms of dependence brought into sharp relief the effects of being born female, and what might have been permitted if one had been born male. Men moved more easily in the world, they could carry weapons for self-defense, and their economic resources were usually greater than those of sisters of whatever age. In these novels, brothers could – and often did – make their own fortunes: they signed up as clerks in a relative's firm, they trained for the clergy, or they shipped out to the West or East Indies, where they invariably made their fortunes. Women's opportunities were much more limited: as Clara Reeve remarked in *Plans of Education* (London, 1792), "There are very few trades for women; the men have usurped two-thirds of those that used to belong to them; the remainder are over-stocked, and there are few resources for them" (119–20). Many indigent but educated young women were "turned loose upon the world," she observed, "without means to support themselves, and disqualified to earn their living" (119). The daughters of "indigent clergymen, of officers in the army and navy, of placement of all kinds, and, in short, of all whose incomes depend upon their lives, and who generally leave their children unprovided for" (139) – these were the women who especially depended upon their brothers: distressed gentlewomen, the very stuff of fiction.

THE SISTER'S PORTION

Where a woman had brothers, primogeniture guaranteed the lion's share of any inheritance to the firstborn son. As one novel of 1771 parodied this favoritism: "the inhuman partiality which Sir *Jasper* and his Lady had for their son, whom in order to enrich, they were determined never to give a shilling to his sisters during their lives, and, at their death, to leave them a small annuity, which was, at their decease, to devolve to their brother, or his heirs."[25] Where settlements divided up the remainder among younger children, both sons and daughters, the portions of male children, as we have seen, usually exceeded the portions of female children, which were

---

[25] *Anecdotes of a Convent*, by the author of Memoirs of Mrs. Williams, 3 vols. (London, 1771), vol. 1, p. 129.

sometimes even further diminished by the needs of other male family members. That is, even where stipulated sums were set aside to endow younger children, the notorious cash requirements of still-living fathers and/or eldest sons often led them to "borrow" against the expectations of younger children, most often daughters. *The Memoirs of Mrs. Leeson* (1795–7), purporting to be the authentic life story of an Irish courtesan born into a genteel family in 1727, recounts what a disaster it was for her family when her father made over his affairs to his oldest son, "on condition of his securing to his brother and sisters, the provisions that my father's paternal care had provided for each." Her brother, as she tells it, "intoxicated with his newly acquired authority," "grudged them a shilling whilst he squandered pounds" (1: 6). Through his extravagance, he soon spent what should have been set aside as his sisters' portions, leading him to object to every suitor and to oppose every match that might have required him to pay their portions.[26] This situation, common enough in "real life," is certainly a gambit in fiction. Sir Charles Grandison's father, as mentioned earlier, made free use of his daughters' portions. Sir Walter Elliot in Austen's *Persuasion* can give Anne very little of her share of her mother's £10,000 as dowry when she marries Wentworth, because he is already in debt.[27] In *The Cry* (1754), Nicanor "borrows" from his daughter's dowry to pay for his profligate spending on his mistress, as described earlier, memorialized in Cordelia's watercolor of "Roman Charity."

Many are the instances in eighteenth-century life and literature of women who sacrificed their financial expectations to the demands of spendthrift male relatives. Susan Staves has suggested that one reason for the rising rate of celibacy among the daughters of the elite in the late eighteenth-century was this intra-familial theft. Women were chronically underfunded on the marriage market, she observes, "either because their portions were too small to attract suitable husbands or because the assets that were supposed by settlement to be made available for their portions were not, in fact, available when needed."[28] Despite their difficulty in collecting allowances or portions left them by settlements or wills, "moral younger children," she observes, "were supposed to have scruples about suing the heads of their families for portions, especially their fathers, but even elder brothers, who were also owed deference, and on whom siblings would continue to depend for a wide variety of favors." She gives one example, however, of a daughter

---

[26] *The Memoirs of Mrs Leeson*, ed. Mary Lyons, 3 vols. (Dublin: Lilliput Press, 1995), vol. 1, pp. 6–10.

[27] I am grateful to Jan Fergus for this point.

[28] Susan Staves, *Married Women's Separate Property in England, 1660–1833* (Cambridge, MA: Harvard University Press, 1990), p. 217.

who had been denied a portion but kept "quiet about it until she married an ambitious barrister, who seems to have enjoyed litigating."[29]

In Sarah Scott's *The History of Cornelia* (1750), a young gentlewoman named Julia is reduced to selling her clothes to pay for food because her brother will not send her the annuity their father provided for her. "He has known the difficulties it has reduced me to," Julia tells Cornelia," "yet will not give up the smallest of his pleasures to procure me the ease that in justice I ought to have."[30] Maria Venables' brother in Wollstonecraft's *Maria; or the Wrongs of Woman* (1798), whom she could barely persuade to spend a few minutes with their dying mother after she had nursed her day and night for months, nevertheless elicited in those few minutes their mother's "little hoard, which she had been some years accumulating," without any thought of sharing it with his sister. Later, when Maria came into her uncle's fortune, her brother "came to vent his rage on me, for having, as he expressed himself, 'deprived him, my uncle's eldest nephew, of his inheritance.'"[31] Selfish and venal, he assumes that all the money in the family should be funneled straight to him; he is furious with Maria for getting any of it.

Unfortunately, such expectations on the part of an older brother were probably not uncommon. By the end of the century it had become customary, even in poorer families where there was little or no inherited property, to scrape together family funds to educate the brothers, whether older or younger, because their ultimate earning capacity and chances of advancement far exceeded anything available to their sisters.[32] In Frances Burney's *Cecilia* (1782), Belfield's mother and sister scrimp and save so that he can appear to advantage at Eton, at university, and then at the Temple-Bar. "Sums that would distress us for months to save up, would by him be spent in a day, and then thought of no more!" his seventeen-year-old sister, the gentle Henrietta, tells Cecilia.[33] The point was that with his education, Belfield ought to have been able to locate and consolidate patronage and

[29] Susan Staves, "Resentment or Resignation? Dividing the Spoils among Daughters and Younger Sons," in John Brewer and Susan Staves (eds.), *Early Modern Conceptions of Property*, (London and New York: Routledge, 1996), pp. 194–218, quote p. 203.

[30] Sarah Scott, *The History of Cornelia* (London: A. Millar, 1750), p. 116.

[31] Mary Wollstonecraft, *Maria, or the Wrongs of Woman* (1798), ed. Moira Ferguson (New York: Norton, 1975), pp. 87, 130.

[32] See, for example, the diary of Miss Weeton, *Miss Weeton 1807–1811: Journal of a Governess*, ed. Edward Hall (London: Oxford University Press, 1936), in which mother and sister squeeze themselves dry to supply the favored son and brother with funds. I am grateful to Leonore Davidoff for suggesting that this journal reveals an important dimension of the brother-sister economic dynamic. Virginia Woolf, in *Three Guineas*, emphasizes the need to educate "the daughters of educated men" and not just their sons, to allocate family resources equitably to male and female offspring.

[33] Frances Burney, *Cecilia, or Memoirs of an Heiress* (1782), ed. Peter Sabor and Margaret Ann Doody (Oxford and New York: Oxford University Press, 1988), p. 222.

thus achieve advancement not available to his female relatives. The need for capital in all professions, from the military to clerking for the East India Company, increasingly channeled the financial resources of families to brothers in preference to their sisters.

In some human societies, interlocking systems of land use, bride-price, and reciprocal marriage or alliance building create contingent and mutually dependent economic outcomes for brothers and sisters. But in eighteenth-century English families, brothers had little motivation other than conventional humanitarian reasons, or old-fashioned sentiments about family honor, to arrange for their sisters' future comfort – when the money might instead be spent on their own business or pleasure. Moreover, as we have seen, once a man married, he increasingly felt he owed his duty to his conjugal family in preference to his consanguineal family of origin. Despite the convention that brothers, in the absence of fathers, were responsible for their sisters, there was very little economic incentive for them to take this responsibility seriously. Many brothers must have viewed their sisters as responsibilities they never chose, rivals for family resources and a debt to the future, occasion for both resentment and guilt. As Clara Reeve comments in *Plans of Education* (London, 1792): "Brothers generally look on sisters as incumbrances on families" (122).

It was therefore unfortunate that, after her father, there was no one on whom an unmarried woman depended more for her welfare and reputation than her brother. He stood in the place of a parent, but with none of the incentives of a parent for pride or generosity. It may be that the strict settlement created a single one-time obligation out of what had been a continuing duty in earlier centuries – and that it functioned as a quitclaim on what had previously been felt as a lifetime obligation. In families with property, the seeming inflation of dowries created tension between brothers and sisters precisely because it was from his inheritance that her portion was to be subtracted.[34]

A subplot in Eliza Haywood's *The History of Betsy Thoughtless* (1751) illustrates how burdensome paying his sister's dowry could be even to a good man. The demonstrably decent Sir Bazil Loveit is unable to marry Miss Mable, Betsy's equally deserving old friend, because Miss Mable does not have a large enough portion to provide him with the stipulated dowry for his own sister. The estate he inherited from his father is "encumbered" with dowries of £6,000 for each of his sisters, chargeable to the estate, to be paid at the time of their marriages, and if he does not marry money

---

[34] As stated earlier, the absolute amount of dowry was increasing although the percentage of family wealth apportioned in dowries was declining.

he will not be able to fulfill this legal obligation. When Trueworth, on the rebound from Betsy Thoughtless, agrees to wed one of Sir Bazil's sisters without requiring her entire fortune be paid at the time of her marriage, it enables Sir Bazil to marry Miss Mable without a large dowry. Thus in the marriage market round robin, each large portion requires another; paying a sister's dowry requires a fresh infusion to the family's fortune from the heiress of another family.[35]

SEVENTEENTH-CENTURY SIBLINGS

It may be the artifact of a partial record, but the available evidence makes it seem that seventeenth-century brothers were less ambivalent about being their sisters' keepers – their mainstays and protectors – than eighteenth-century brothers. Perhaps there was less competition for family resources, less pressure to accumulate capital, and fewer occasions for conspicuous consumption. As stated earlier, charity in general – sharing resources with the poor – was more common in the seventeenth century, the religious obligation of those with plenty. In the eighteenth century, charity came to be thought of more as voluntary and supererogatory.[36] Analogously, seventeenth-century brothers appear to have had a more positive sense of their obligations to their sisters as blood kin, as well as a stronger sense of shared lineage. Ralph Josselin, the vicar of Earles Colne from 1640 to 1683, observes at the beginning of his diary:

Towards my sisters God gave mee a heart to seeke yr good in some measure, my father living and dead, & especially my sister Anna, in hindring her from marrying a widdow, when my father had cast her of, and in reconciling her unto him agayne & this I did before I was 17 yeares old. When my father was dead, in my poverty, I blesse God I did not forgett to doe for them.[37]

That Josselin was fond of his sisters one can surmise from other entries. But here he obviously also feels that he has behaved as he ought, that he has done his duty as a brother and that, in taking stock of his life, helping

---

[35] This situation was not uncommon in eighteenth-century life. Susan Staves gives several examples of men unable to pay their sisters' portions without a large dowry from their own brides. One of these cases involved a private Act of 1733 allocating £4,600 from the portion of the bride, a daughter of the Earl of Berkeley, to pay the unpaid balances of portions that had been due the groom's sister and younger brother since 1699. Susan Staves, "Resentment or Resignation?," p. 203.

[36] Donna T. Andrew, *Philanthropy and Police: London Charity in the Eighteenth Century* (Princeton: Princeton University Press, 1989) See especially Chapter 1, "Religion, Commerce, and Charity, 1680–1740," pp. 11–43. See also the quotations above, p. 71.

[37] *The Diary of the Rev. Ralph Josselin*, ed. E. Hockliffe, Camden Third Series, vol. xv (London: Offices of the Royal Historical Society, 1908), p. 4.

his sisters can be counted to his credit. In August 1644, two of his sisters applied to him for aid, which he appears to have given without resentment. He notes first that "my sister Mary is come under my roofe as a servant, but my respect is & shall be towards her as a sister" (15); and then several weeks later "my sister Hannah came over to mee, I sent her away in some hopes to helpe her about her house, & with some expressions of love; Lord remember mee & mine & hers in mercy" (16).

Among the aristocracy, brotherly love was less a matter of day-to-day support and advice, or even well-timed financial infusions, than of looking out for sisters' long-term legal interests in matters of portion and inheritance. In the Verney family, for example, Sir Ralph arranged the marriages of his sisters and the legal terms of their settlements. His position as head of the family gave him power to help or hinder his relatives – including his sisters and their families – in a number of ways. He could offer or withold documents in his possession to facilitate or block their business dealings; he could lend them money; he could use his influence for the educational or professional advancement of his in-laws or his nieces and nephews; and he could wield political power for a variety of ends. In other words, Sir Ralph was a brother with considerable influence in the public world and could use it or withold it to advance the interests of members of his family.[38]

Where aristocratic parents were absent – whether dead or away at another estate or in London for the season – an older brother might be an important parental figure for a young girl. According to modern psychologists, children who lose their parents intensify their reliance on siblings and are more fiercely loyal to one another.[39] A charming example of a loving brother-sister relationship from the late seventeenth and early eighteenth century can be seen in the letters of George Hastings, eighth Earl of Huntingdon, to his younger sister, Lady Betty Hastings, later a well-known Yorkshire philanthropist and a patron of Mary Astell.[40] Lady Betty's note about how she came by Ledston Hall, her maternal grandfather Lewys' estate, clarifies the financial details of the relationship sketched in their letters. Ledston Hall apparently descended to her mother and aunt because

---

[38] Miriam Slater, *Family Life in the Seventeenth Century: The Verneys of Claydon House* (London: Routledge and Kegan Paul, 1984) *passim*, but especially pp. 140–3.

[39] Stephen Bank and Michael Kahn, "Intense Sibling Loyalties," in Michael Lamb and Brian Sutton-Smith, (eds.), *Sibling Relationships: Their Nature and Significance across the Life Span* (Hillsdale, NJ: Lawrence Erlbaum Associates, 1982), pp. 251–66, cited in Lorri Glover, *All Our Relations: Blood Ties and Emotional Bonds among the Early South Carolina Gentry* (Baltimore: Johns Hopkins University Press, 2000), p. 24.

[40] *Hastings Wheler Family Letters 1693–1704: Lady Betty Hastings and Her Brother*, Part 1 (London: privately printed at the Chiswick Press, 1929).

of the absence of male children. When her brother came into the estate he "lodged a fine upon the whole cut off the entail and settled it upon me without any further limitation." In return, she explained, she signed away all interest in her father's estate, except the £600 per annum that was hers so long as she continued single. "By my mother's marriage settlement," she observes, "I was to have £10,000 out of my father's estate in case he had no other child and if my father left no son by any other lady I was to have £30,000 out of his estate but by the clause in my brother's will I am cut out from everything on my father's estate" (17). As it happened, her father did have other children, including sons, by his second wife. Meanwhile, her brother had secured for her an estate independent of his pleasure or future heirs – just what the idealized hero of an eighteenth-century novel might have done. Ironically, Lady Betty did not wholly approve of her brother's action for, like the rest of her class, she believed in enlarging and passing on family estates. So strong was this ethic that after her brother died she wrote: "I want to know how far in conscience I may be tied to these settlements? cutting off of entails is what I no ways approve of" (16).

One reason for the affection between Lady Betty and her brother George Hastings was that they were siblings from their father's first marriage and neither had warmed to their new stepmother. That George Hastings adored his little sister can be seen by this letter he wrote to her when she was ten, to reassure her about their Jacobite father's incarceration in the Tower after receiving a summons from King James II in France.

I would not have you concerned at My Lords confinement. There is no danger at all. He is very well, and I hope he will come out of the Tower within this three weeks. I believe my lord's intention is to send for you to London within this week or two, and you will lodge at Kensington with Mrs. Hodges as far as I can guess. My dearest dear Betty and Mary [their other sister]. I love you two above all expression. It is my desir to see you. I hope and do not doubt but to see you improve very much, and as studious and witty as I saw you last, which is your most affectionate brother and faithful friend, Hastings. (20)

His tone changes as she grows up, becoming more suitable for a young teenager, but still that of an affectionate older brother: "Your ladyship is pleased to banter me about the besieging of towns and fighting of battles as you call them," he wrote to her, spinning out an imaginary scenario by which she might earn his ransom if he is taken prisoner in war.

[A]fter having dried your first tears and made some moral reflections upon my present misfortune, with some (I dare swear not a few) ejaculations on my behalf, yet wisely considering that prayers will not restore me to my freedom, you might resolve to leave off stitching, stoning of currants, knotting and darning, and take up with the mortification of playing at cards from sunrising to setting thereof at contrelen or wiste at 3d. a corner to get money to pay my ransom, so at a so reasonable computation if you had a perpetual run of luck about ten years hence or so I might hope to see a play at London. (27)

It is done with a light touch so as not to alarm her about the possible dangers to him in war. He assumes their faithful devotion to one another while mocking it, and teases her gently about her life's homely tasks.

Lady Betty's deep attachment to this attentive older brother and his untimely early death may account for the fact that she never married. On the other hand, her spinsterhood may have been a function of the financial independence Ledston Hall assured her. Affectionate commitment between siblings such as this certainly survived into the eighteenth century, some examples of which I will mention later in this chapter. But there are more counterexamples later in the century to suggest that the responsibility brothers took for their sisters was increasingly viewed as supererogatory rather than commonplace.

At the same time, in one of those paradoxes of history, brotherhood as an abstraction came to be emblematized as the kin position *par excellence* in the eighteenth century, the position within the family privileged ideologically, legally, and metaphorically above all others. The "fraternity of men," the "universal brotherhood," came to be imagined in this period as the basis of society – with enormous political and social implications. In revolutionary France, sibling incest was represented as the political means by which society could be reconstructed as a world of "brothers" and "sisters."[41] In other words, men came to think of themselves at their best as brothers, to imagine that particular relation as the most perfected of all human connections, and to think that excelling in "brotherhood" was the pinnacle of social and political achievement.[42]

EIGHTEENTH-CENTURY SIBLINGS

Less metaphorically, the epigraph from Edward Gibbon at the beginning of this chapter, calling brother-sister love "the sole species of Platonic love that can be indulged with truth and without danger," testifies to the

---

[41] Marc Shell, *The End of Kinship: "Measure for Measure," Incest and the Ideal of Universal Siblinghood* (Stanford: Stanford University Press, 1988), p. 17.

[42] This notion of post-Enlightenment social and sexual arrangements as privileging the brother is explored by Juliet Flower MacCannell in *The Regime of the Brother: After the Patriarchy* (London and New York: Routledge, 1991).

contemporary significance of these relationships. So strong was the potential attachment between siblings in the popular imagination, that when the married Hester Thrale was falling in love with Piozzi in the fall of 1780, she fantasized that he must be her brother. Wrestling with her husband's ill health in Brighton, depressed and lonely, she used to go to Thomas' bookshop to listen to Piozzi play the harpsichord. As she was drawn to him more and more, she explained her attraction by imagining that she had found a half brother – that Piozzi was a by-blow of her own father, whom she thought he resembled, gotten during his rambles on the continent in his youth.[43] Piozzi never appreciated this proof of her infatuation: he did not like to imagine his mother having a casual affair with a libertine Englishman. In *A Sentimental Journey* (1768), Sterne similarly feels his closeness to the "fille de chambre" in the register of family feeling. Her simple confidence when she takes his arm unbidden gives him a sentimental rush: "I felt the conviction of consanguinity so strongly, that I could not help turning half round to look in her face, and see if I could trace out anything in it of a family likeness."[44]

The novelist Elizabeth Hamilton describes her relationship with her older brother, Charles, with these elegaic words on the eleventh anniversary of his death:

In him my affections were from infancy wrapped up: all the love, the admiration, the esteem, which other characters have separately excited, were in him united. Betwixt us, there was a sympathy of soul, a correspondence of sentiment and of feeling, of which few can form any conception. Our minds were cast in the same mould, operated upon by the same circumstances, excited by the same objects. It was by viewing my own character in him, that I acquired confidence in my own powers, respect for my own virtues, and a consciousness of my own infirmities.[45]

---

[43] According to Mary Nash, Mrs. Thrale was also drawn to "the literary theme of the chaste, spontaneous love between brothers and sisters who do not recognize each other. *Cymbeline* was her favorite play – especially the scene in which two of Cymbeline's sons meet a beautiful youth in the forest who is actually their long-lost sister, Imogen. Instantly, their lustful or homicidal impulses are quashed by an emotion compounded of reverence, protectiveness, chivalry, and that odd sensation beloved by the eighteenth century called 'natural virtue.'

"Mrs. Thrale herself dealt with this theme in her farce, 'The Adventurer,' (Rylands MS. No. 650), where a married lady excites fierce gossip because she seems to be spending a suspiciously large amount of time tête-à-tête with a mysterious foreigner, who turns out to be her long lost brother whom she is helping out of his difficulties." Thanks to the eloquent and learned Mary Nash for these remarks! Private communication, October 1994.

[44] Lawrence Sterne, *A Sentimental Journey through France and Italy*, ed. Graham Petrie, with an Introduction by A. Alvarez (Harmondsworth: Penguin, 1967), vol. II, p. 92. My thanks to Susan Lamb for reminding me of this passage.

[45] E. O. Benger, *Memoirs of the Late Mrs. Elizabeth Hamilton*, 2 vols. (London: Longman, 1818), vol. I, pp. 184–5.

He was, in short, a second self, living halfway around the world in India while she remained immured in a cottage in Ingram's Crook in Stirlingshire, Scotland.[46] Although this brother-sister pair were separated for most of their lives – Charles lived in Calcutta for many years working for the East India Company – they were faithful correspondents and their letters recount to one another something of their lives and thoughts. Elizabeth made her home with an elderly aunt and uncle – a common enough and usually satisfactory solution for a single woman – her parents being dead and her sister Katherine married and settled in Ireland. They were very kind to her, but it was a lonely life, and occasionally she grumbled to her brother that she seldom went anywhere

farther than the gravel-walk . . . [I]n some cross moments, I can't help thinking it a little hard, that with all the good will imaginable towards the pleasures of society, I should be condemned to pass the best days of my youth in such a solitude, that I might . . . be as well shut up in a monastery. (1: 87–8)

She missed her brother and implored him to return to Scotland for a visit. She refused to come to India, where, he intimated, she might find a husband, both because she did not want to "throw such a burden on your generosity," and because she feared she was not so "*saleable*" as he supposed (1: 92–3). "What would I not give if I could have you an inmate of our mansion!" she wrote, imagining how perfect life would be if only he were there to share it with her. "Your company, if it did not transform our cottage to an absolute palace, would make it the abode of more happiness than is usually to be found in one. How comfortably, how contentedly might we live together in this sweet little spot!" (1: 79).

In 1788 her wishes were answered and Charles Hamilton returned to England where for four years he engaged in a translation of the Persian Hedaya, or legal code, to the delight of his faithful sister, whom he was able to comfort when her uncle died. He traveled to Ireland to see his older sister, Katherine, and indeed reacquainted and reunited his two sisters who, after his death in 1792, began to live together.[47] Charles taught Elizabeth a great deal about India, which she used in writing *Letters of a Hindoo Rajah*

[46] The exaggerated difference that gender made in their destinies may account, in part, for her adoration of her brother. See n. 3 above.

[47] After their brother died, Elizabeth and her then-widowed sister Katherine Blake lived together in Suffolk, Berkshire, and Bath. In 1802–3 they took an extended trip to Wales, the lakes of Westmoreland, and Scotland. In Wales they visited the celebrated ladies of Llangollen, where they noted the "veneration in which they were held in the neighbourhood." Elizabeth Hamilton's description continues: "They are, indeed, characters of a very superior stamp, with just such a degree of difference in their dispositions, as serves to give mutual support, while in all essentials they are perfectly congenial . . . The cottage is the quintessence of taste, elegance, and comfort; and the

(1796). Eight years after his death, writing a paragraph about him in her diary, she was forced to end it abruptly: "I find this subject is still too much for me."[48]

Hamilton's *Letters of a Hindoo Rajah*, written after her brother's death, was undertaken as a kind of occupational therapy to memorialize him. Dedicating the book to Warren Hastings, her brother's friend, she satirizes the accusations of corruption and exploitation against Hastings. The protagonist, the Hindoo Rajah who is visiting England, is asked in a coffee shop about a newspaper story that describes him as coming to England "on behalf of the Hindoo inhabitants of Bengal, to complain of the horrid cruelties and unexampled oppression, under which, through the maladministration of the British governour of India, we were made to groan." Shocked at how badly the newspaper writer has been imposed upon, the Rajah wonders about his punishment when it is discovered that "he had suffered a falsehood to pollute that pure fountain of publick instruction" (1: 152). Hamilton represents her brother in this novel as a learned Englishman named Percy, wise and pure but, alas! mortally wounded. ("The powers of his mind were deep and extensive as the waves of the mighty Ganges. His heart was the seat of virtue, and truth reposed in his bosom" [1: 10]). So impressive is this man that, when he dies, the Rajah, Zaarmilla, decides to visit England to see at first hand the society that produced this great man and that western phenomenon, his educated sister. Indeed, women are significant as sisters in this novel; all the main players have sisters whom they love. Zaarmilla and Maandaara each marry the other's sisters, marriages by proxy that honor the brother-sister bond. Once in England, the Rajah uncovers the absurdities and hypocrisies of English culture with a suitably fresh eye. He finds Charlotte Percy, the surviving sister of his dead friend, mourning the death of her uncle, weeping at the sight of his cottage, his garden, his pony, and even his gravel walk. Weighed down by her sorrow, a wise neighbor convinces her to write to recover her equilibrium, despite "how female writers are looked down upon. The women fear, and hate; the men ridicule, and dislike them." She is assured that if her "heart receive no alloy from the vanity of scholarship," writing will do her no harm

---

ladies have created a little paradise around them. Twenty-four years have elapsed since the plan was formed, and every day has increased their satisfaction in its accomplishment. The few days we spent with them passed in that sort of enthusiastic delight so seldom experienced when the days of youthful ardour are gone." E. O. Benger, *Memoirs of the Late Mrs. Elizabeth Hamilton*, vol. 1, pp. 153–4.

48 Elizabeth Hamilton, *Translation of the Letters of a Hindoo Rajah*, 2 vols. (London, 1796), vol. 1, p. 124. Subsequent page references are to this edition.

(II: 285). Thus Elizabeth Hamilton conflated her losses in this character, this woman author, who deals with death in her family by writing about it.

Richard Barwell and Mary Barwell are another remarkable eighteenth-century brother-and-sister pair – both also unmarried – whose closest family tie throughout their adult lives was with one another. Like Charles and Elizabeth Hamilton, they lived apart. Richard Barwell, too, worked for the East India Company and, like Elizabeth Hamilton's brother, was a close associate and supporter of Warren Hastings. Also like the Hamiltons, this brother and sister maintained an unconditional friendship while he was overseas; his sister Mary Barwell became his closest confidante and factotum in London. Richard Barwell's letters from Calcutta to his sister in London beteen 1767 and 1774 testify to her importance to him as a source of love and family connection as well as his trusted agent for business and political affairs in England. His letters give detailed instructions for disposing of goods, making investments, and other transactions, relying on her discretion where necessary to keep things secret from the rest of their family. His trust in her ability to handle his political interests and his financial investments is somewhat surprising, considering that he might have chosen one of their other brothers or even their father as his representative. He writes to her on January 20, 1769, for example, asking for her help in maneuvering to get him appointed by the board of directors to a more lucrative post in Dacca. He tells her that he is willing to "spend five thousand pounds" for the "chiefship" of that province, "to supervise the collection of the revenues" there. He does not outline a particular strategy for her to follow in attaining this goal, but leaves it to her to work out.[49] Mary Barwell was apparently successful in her efforts on his behalf in London while he maneuvered in Calcutta, for before long he is writing to her from Dacca. In the months that follow, he tells her which of the newly elected directors are his friends, and confides to her the ambiguity of his official relationship to Warren Hastings and his proposal for reducing the rate of interest on the Company's loans. When the leadership of the Company is attacked and charged with corruption, he counts on her influence in London to explain his side of things and gives her an exact account of his own profits. He tells her on May 17, 1775, for example, that he sold his property in the Dacca salt farms in conformance with the 1774 Act of Parliament prohibiting Europeans from trading in salt, although he did so because "I all along esteemed the right in those farms to be more in the station of

[49] "The Letters of Mr. Richard Barwell," *Bengal Past and Present: Journal of the Calcutta Historical Society* 8–13 (1914–16), quote vol. 10, p. 233, letter 132, January 20, 1869 [sic, i.e. 1769]. My thanks to Susan Staves for sharing with me her discovery of this correspondence and even copying it for me!

the Chief of Dacca than in myself after I left that station."[50] He trusts her
competence and discretion utterly, gives her full power of attorney, sends
her diamonds and gold, and opens his coffers to her "to the last farthing of
my fortune." He puts in her hands all the financial arrangements for the
rest of their siblings, including the power "to present [their sister] on her
marriage with any worthy gentleman the sum of five thousand pounds to
be settled on her self and her children."[51]

There is no way of knowing how unusual Mary Barwell's behind-the-
scenes participation was for her time. Women did hold stock and vote in
the Hudson's Bay Company and the East India Company and sometimes
operated as silent partners in business ventures.[52] There are plenty of
examples of remarkable, level-headed women in the fiction of the day:
Mrs. Stafford in Charlotte Smith's *Emmeline* (1788), Mrs. Selwyn in Frances
Burney's *Evelina* (1778), or Mrs. Mason of Elizabeth Hamilton's *Cottagers
of Glenburnie* (1808) immediately come to mind as examples of capable
women handling complex business matters. And Mary Wollstonecraft's
Letters Written during a Short Residence in Sweden, Norway, and Denmark
(1796) were written, after all, while Wollstonecraft was acting as a business
agent abroad for her unfaithful lover, Gilbert Imlay, straightening out his
financial affairs in Scandinavia. Judging from Richard Barwell's repeated
requests that she use more of his money, Mary Barwell was judicious if not
frugal and entirely devoted to his interests. The closeness of their friendship (given its long-distance nature), their mutual trust and affection, his
designation of her as his agent in London charged to work with his banker,
and the level of detail about business and politics in their letters all show
the continued potential of strong blood ties, of brother-sister alliances, as
one possible avenue for women to participate in the public world.[53]

---

[50] *Ibid.*, vol. 12, p. 284ff., letter 441, May 17, 1775.

[51] *Ibid.*, vol. 11, p. 49, letter 180, September 10, 1773.

[52] Richard Grassby, *Kinship and Capitalism: Marriage, Family, and Business in the English-Speaking
World, 1580–1740* (Cambridge: Cambridge University Press, and Washington, D.C.: Woodrow Wilson Center Press, 2001), pp. 332–3.

[53] For examples of eighteenth-century businesswomen, see R. S. Neale's account of two real-estate
managers for the Duke of Chandos in Bath, Anne Phillips and Jane Degge, who did a large volume of annual business involving dealing with bankers and bills of exchange, keeping detailed
invoices, and handling thousands of pounds every year. R. S. Neale, *Writing Marxist History: British
Society, Economy, and Culture since 1700* (Oxford: Basil Blackwell, 1985), pp. 1–19. See also Margaret
Hunt, "Eighteenth-Century Middling Women and Trade," in her *The Middling Sort: Commerce,
Gender, and the Family in England, 1680–1780* (Berkeley: University of California Press, 1996), pp.
125–46 Maxine Berg, "Women's Work, mechanisation and the Early Phases of Industrialisation in
England," in Patrick Joyce (ed.), *The Historical Meanings of Work* (Cambridge: Cambridge University
Press, 1987), pp. 64–98; Peter Earle, "The Female Labour Market in London in the Late Seven-
teenth and Early Eighteenth Centuries," *Economic History Review*, 2nd ser., 42, 3 (1989), 328–53;

Hester Mulso Chapone, author of *Letters on the Improvement of the Mind* (1773), is another eighteenth-century woman whose closest relationship was supposed to have been with her brother although they never lived together. Widowed early, she lived with her father until his death and then with her maternal uncle Dr. John Thomas, bishop of Winchester, and his wife. The account of her life "drawn up by her own family" and attached to her posthumous works states that she lived "in habits of constant intercourse" with her eldest brother, "whose strength of mind and benevolence of heart supported, while they soothed her." Notwithstanding the judgment that he was "her strongest tie to this world" and "her constant companion, friend, and protector," she apparently never made her home with him, even after her uncle and aunt died.[54] While there are many possible explanations for this, it is conceivable that the account that so privileges their relationship conformed more to convention about the importance of brothers to sisters than to Chapone's reality.

A SISTER'S SERVICE

Although much rarer, there are also examples from the period of sisters helping their brothers – protecting and advising them, helping to set them up in their careers. The nineteenth-century novelist Catherine Hutton, daughter of William Hutton the Birmingham bookseller, recounts the aid given by her remarkable aunt, Catherine Perkins, to her uncles and father. "My Aunt Perkins had a spirit of dominion which drew every human being round her into its vortex," she wrote. "Born with talents to command an empire, she governed every creature that approached her" with material aid and wise advice. Once she had "determined not to live with a husband whom she deemed unworthy of her," she took a house and lodged herself and her two younger brothers whom she maintained by spinning yarn while she set them to weaving stockings. "When my father found the stocking frame too narrow for his talents," Catherine Hutton continues, her aunt encouraged him to go to Birmingham to set up as a bookseller. She staked him to £15, and gave him her own "uniform set of the Spectator, Tatler,

and Margaret George, *Women in the First Capitalist Society* (Urbana: University of Illinois Press, 1988).

   In South Carolina, where sibling relationships were more egalitarian than in England, Eliza Lucas ran three of her family's plantations at sixteen and later made a fortune growing indigo. For more details of her business dealings see Elise Pinckney (ed.), *The Letterbook of Eliza Lucas Pinckney, 1739–1762* (Columbia: University of South Carolina Press, 1997). For more information on her relationships with her siblings, see Lorri Glover, *All Our Relations*.

[54] *The Posthumous Works of Mrs. Chapone*, 4 vols. (London, 1807), vol. II, pp. 2, 18.

and Guardian, which Mr. Radsdale, her former master, had made her a
present of," as the foundation of his stock. This was in 1755. Some time
later she

fitted out her eldest brother for his launching into the world, as she had before
done her second. She furnished him with necessaries, and made him out a bill,
which came to three guineas. Tom, says she, this is what you owe me. If you are
ever able to pay me, I expect you will do it. If not, I forgive you. She then gave him
half a crown and bid him farewell. It is needless to say he paid her, as my father had
done before. This circumstance my uncle told me to-day, while the tears ran down
his cheeks, and his voice was interrupted by his emotion. Her youngest brother,
Samuel, only now remained, and he, who had liked a soldier's life while a bachelor,
grew weary of it, when encumbered with a wife and two children. In 1763 she
bought his discharge, bore his expenses out of Scotland, supported his family, and
set him up in his trade of whip making. Thus did this extraordinary woman throw
the golden ball into the lap of each of her three brothers.[55]

When Catherine Hutton Perkins died in her sixties, her detailed will specified the disbursement of considerable material property in addition to more
than £255 in cash. Although she did not make a fortune spinning, weaving,
and selling linens – women's enterprises – she made enough to support
herself, to help her brothers, and to leave this legacy.

Catherine Hutton Perkins' independence was unusual.[56] More commonly, unmarried women were deployed by their families to help care for
unmarried men and for the very young or very old. Unmarried sisters often lived with their brothers; unmarried nieces, like Elizabeth Hamilton
and Eliza Pierce, frequently lived with their uncles and aunts. Often these
uncles and aunts were maternal relatives, for the mother's kin usually took
responsibility for her daughters. Thus unmarried female relatives – be they
sisters, daughters, or nieces – filled in for absent wives and mothers, doing unpaid woman's labor managing the household for a bachelor brother,
son, or uncle in return for a respectable roof over their heads. Whether the
unmarried woman was directing a servant or a staff of servants, or preparing
meals herself and cleaning, doing laundry and minor baking and brewing,
paying tradesmen, and the like, these arrangements often created a real

---

[55] Hutton MS 4/2 in the public library of Birmingham.
[56] Catherine Hutton's once-married status enabled her independence. Single, never-married women
were at a considerable disadvantage in terms of residence and livelihood compared with women who
had been married. To live alone and enter into trade for themselves, it helped women to be older,
orphaned, and of relatively high social status. See Amy M. Froide, "Marital Status as a Category
of Difference: Singlewomen and Widows in Early Modern England," in Judith M. Bennett and
Amy M. Froide (eds.), *Singlewomen in the European Past 1250–1800* (Philadelphia: University of
Pennsylvania Press, 1999), pp. 236–69.

home and mutual satisfactions. On the other hand, sometimes they just reminded the sister of her dependence on her brother and that she only had a home at his sufferance.

Here again, Catherine Hutton Perkins took the male role and summoned a niece from the next generation to live with her in her declining years. The niece in question was the daughter of William Hutton. She, in turn, in her own adult years, lived a perfectly respectable life as a single woman writer in the nineteenth century.[57] With the notable exception of Sarah Scott's *Millenium Hall*, nothing remotely like this aunt's independence and heroic enterprise is fully represented in eighteenth-century fiction.

From William Stout, a Lancaster merchant, to Sir Joshua Reynolds, London connoisseur and portrait painter, unmarried men commanded the services of their unmarried kinswomen. William Stout, who by dint of hard labor became a man of substantial means, lived with his unmarried sister, Elin Stout, when their mother dissolved her household in 1691 and moved in with their unmarried brother, Josiah. The household of this consanguineal couple also expanded to accommodate nieces and nephews. "We had always two of my brother Leonard's children with us," writes William. "[We] tooke them at two years old, and kept them till they were six years old and capable to goe to Boulton Schoole. And my sister was as carfull to nurs and corect them as if they had been her own children."[58]

When their mother was seventy-six and could no longer keep house for their brother Josiah, she urged him "to marry, he not being willing to keepe house with a servant" (159). So Josiah married a woman of thirty; he was then forty-eight. But his new wife did not take kindly to his mother's direction and in a year's time their mother joined William and Elin Stout, where she lived until her death eight years later. Eight years after that, Elin Stout died suddenly, of a "common distemper of paine in her brest and back, and shortness of breath" (191), at which point their brother Leonard sent his second daughter, Janet, to keep house for William Stout. Some years later he took on his irresponsible namesake nephew William as an apprentice in his business and another female cousin with her daughter, to lodge and board. When Janet Stout married, Leonard's other daughter – William's other niece – Ellin supplied her place as housekeeper to William until she, too, married. Later he hired a servant to keep house for him, and invited his great-niece to live with him and to "improve" herself with learning. When

[57] Catherine Hutton was a friend and correspondent of Robert Bage and Sir Walter Scott. See Mrs. C. H. Beale, *Reminiscences of a Gentlewoman of the Last Century* (Birmingham, 1891).

[58] *The Autobiography of William Stout of Lancaster 1665–1752*, ed. J. D. Marshall (Manchester: Manchester University Press, and New York: Barnes and Noble, 1967), p. 142.

she turned twenty, this great-niece, "having knowledge of my way of living, and having no parents living," succeeded to the post of housekeeper, hiring a servant to help with the washing, brewing, or cleaning when there was occasion for it. Thus did this man, William Stout, support – or exploit – his female consanguineal relatives during his lifetime. But only his nephew did he offer to take into his business.

Jane Austen and her sister Cassandra were recruited to help raise their brother Edward's children when Edward's wife Elizabeth died suddenly in October 1808. Soon after her death, Edward offered his mother – and two sisters – either a house at Wye, near Godmersham in Kent, or a cottage at Chawton in Hampshire, so that they could settle on one of his two estates near his now motherless children. Although they had needed a place to live since at least 1805, moving uncomfortably among rented lodgings and sharing a house with their brother Frank and his wife and child, it was only when his wife died that Edward made the offer to his mother and sisters. Edward's alacrity in providing housing for them as soon as Elizabeth died may be explained by the fact that she had disliked his sisters – especially Jane – as much by his now needing their emotional help in raising his eleven children. When news came of Elizabeth's death, Cassandra immediately went to Godmersham to help Edward's sixteen-year-old daughter Fanny with her new responsibilities: "to be companion to her father, mistress of a large household, and surrogate mother to her younger brothers and sisters." Ten months later the Austen women were securely ensconced in their new home in Chawton.[59]

Sarah Fielding, as we shall see, lived with Henry as his housekeeper when he was between wives, from the time of Charlotte (Cradock's) death in 1744 until he married his servant Mary Daniel, who was six months pregnant, in 1747. At that point, Sarah left his household to re-join her sisters, Catherine, Ursula, and Beatrice, in Duke Street, Westminster. There she worked on her third novel, *The Governess*, which was printed in 1749 by Richardson.

BROTHER TROUBLE

In the dreamscape of Frances Burney's fiction, brothers spell trouble. Whether she was symbolically representing the way brothers claimed a

---

[59] Deirdre LeFaye, *Jane Austen: A Family Record* [by William Austen-Leigh and Richard Arthur Austen-Leigh] (Boston, MA: G. K. Hall, 1989), pp. 150–1.

disproportionate amount of a family's resources and/or the way they expected their sisters to serve their needs, Burney's portrayal of her heroine's
brothers, at least Evelina's and Camilla's brothers (not to mention her own
real-life brothers) illustrates much of what I have been saying about brotherly love in life and literature. In *Evelina*, as Margaret Doody observes in
her psychologically astute study, Macartney is Evelina's male counterpart
in several important respects, enacting another version of her story of filial dispossession and offended sensibility.[60] Psychoanalytically, Macartney
and Evelina might be considered to be two parts of one whole, splitting
along the fault lines of ambivalence. Thus, Macartney acts out in a self-
dramatizing way the frustration that Evelina also feels but contains. On the
other hand, because gender is foregrounded in sibling relationships with
respect to other dimensions of social identity, differences between brothers
and sisters also serve to magnify asymmetries of power, agency, wealth, and
mobility.

In *Evelina*, Burney reinscribes parodically the conventional understanding that a brother is his sister's protector and moral guide. The Branghtons
represent a caricatured example of brotherly concern in the shopkeeping
class, with crude Tom Branghton taunting his sisters Miss Biddy and Miss
Polly for their hypocrisy, airs, and self-centeredness. Lord Orville and his
fashionably bored and shallow sister Lady Louisa Larpent represent the
sibling bond in the upper class: Lord Orville gently remonstrates with his
misguided sister, who ignores his advice, while closely watching her companions and looking out for her best interests. But Burney reverses the
usual gender relations of moral superiority in brother-sister relationships in
the encounter between Evelina and the melancholy Scotsman, who turns
out to be her half brother. Evelina stays Macartney's hand as she thinks
to keep him from committing suicide, protecting and supporting him
with her benevolent purse as well as her admonitions. The sister saves the
brother and even – in their separate appeals to their common father, Sir
John Belmont – supersedes him as the daughter of a legitimate marriage.
"Macartney represents," as Margaret Doody says, "the masculine competitor disqualified and the story is a feminist fantasy in which the masculine,
the male heir, is set aside as illegitimate and the female is legitimated" (62).

Not that Macartney in any way facilitates this denouement. On the contrary – his presence in the plot causes Evelina nothing but trouble: first

[60] Margaret Doody, *Frances Burney: The Life in the Works* (New Brunswick: Rutgers University Press,
1988), p. 62.

he embarrasses her with his public verses and then he compromises her
with the watchful Lord Orville by trying to speak with her privately at
Clifton. The function of this character in terms of plot is to make Evelina's
lot harder, to add further difficulties to her trials. A brother who endan-
gers and exposes her, Macartney also embodies the menace of incest. He
is informed later by his mother that the woman he loves is his sister, but
the sexual connection between siblings is foreshadowed in the narrative
by the secrecy and horror of the sequence in which Macartney is introduced into Evelina's life. Sitting in the shop one day, she observes him
slip and fall on a stair in an agitated moment, and unexpectedly sees "the
end of a pistol which started from his pocket." Alerted to danger, she
is "inexpressibly shocked" by the sight and grows "stiff with horror" –
evocative descriptors considering that his disclosure raises the spectre of
incest.[61]

Camilla, or A Picture of Youth (1796) provides an even richer vein of
brother trouble. Lionel, Camilla's younger brother and the Tyrolds' only
son, is a practical joker without concern for others, who puts his sisters at
risk again and again in his thoughtless way. Burney describes him as

The zealot for every species of sport, the candidate for every order of whim . . . A
stranger to reflection, and incapable of care, laughter seemed not merely the bent
of his humour, but the necessity of his existence: he pursued it at all seasons, he
indulged it upon all occasions. With excellent natural parts, he trifled away all
improvement; without any ill temper, he spared no one's feelings. Yet, though
not radically vicious, nor deliberately malevolent, the egotism which urged him
to make his own amusement his first pursuit, sacrificed his best friends and first
duties, if they stood in its way (79).[62]

---

[61] In Burney's family, some twenty years after the publication of *Evelina*, her older brother James
did cohabit with their half sister, the daughter of their father by a second wife, in an incestuous
five-year-long liaison. There is no way of knowing if anything in the Burney family domestic life
prepared the ground for this scandalous acting out.

There is also evidence of another biographical parallel in some eighteenth-century gossip that
Frances Burney herself discovered her brother Charles preparing to kill himself. Hester Thrale heard
that the story of "Macartney's going to shoot himself actually did happen to her own Brother Charles
Burney," and she taxed Dr. Burney with it. "I gave him a hint that I had heard somebody observe
that the story of Macartney was written with such *feeling*, it must *absolutely* be founded on Fact; at
this Discourse he changed Colour so often, and so apparently that tho' I instantly got quit of the
Conversation – I left it however well perswaded that all Mrs Crewe said – or a great part of it was but
too true." *Thraliana, the Diary of Mrs. Hester Lynch Thrale 1776–1809*, ed. Katherine C. Balderston,
2 vols. (Oxford: Clarendon Press, 1951), vol. 1, p. 360. Margaret Doody refers to this passage in her
Frances Burney, p. 61.

[62] This and all subsequent quotations from *Camilla* are taken from Edward A. and Lillian D. Bloom's
edition (Oxford and New York: Oxford University Press, 1983).

Although Lionel is not out to harm his sisters – this passage describes heedlessness without malice – that seems the inevitable effect of their every interaction. That Camilla endures Lionel's unpleasant tricks with such composure, and naively trusts him again and again to such bad effect, can only be a measure of how destructive this relationship is understood to be.

Lionel importunes the ludicrous Mr. Dubster to claim Camilla as a dance partner at her first ball. He drags his sister down a hill, through a rivulet, soaking her so completely that she finds it difficult to walk (245). He goads a bull into attacking a party that includes several of his sisters in order to terrorize them (133). (The sexual overtones to this scene, unmistakably suggested earlier by the similar scene in Sterne's *Tristram Shandy* (1760–5), have an incestuous resonance.) As a prank, he leads Camilla and Eugenia through some brush, which ruins and tears their clothes (281), and then leaves them stranded in Mr. Dubster's half-finished summer-house with the ridiculous tinker himself (282). Finally, he takes advantage of a mistake by which Camilla borrows money from the designing Sir Sedley Clarendel and is unable to repay it, putting her under pecuniary obligations to an unprincipled man. All of these incidents, represented in violent slapstick, are ominous because Camilla is female; none of Lionel's pranks – ruining her dresses, frightening her with a bull, subjecting her to embarrassing encounters with inappropriate men – would matter if Lionel played them on another man. More than inconvenient and less than fatal, the symbolic value of Lionel's influence is to remind Camilla repeatedly of the limitations imposed by gender. Just as Lionel is understood to be favored as the only son although Camilla is everyone's natural favorite, Lionel always manages to displace and discomfit Camilla.

Edward and Lillian Bloom, the editors of *Camilla*, claim that Lionel's portrait is a "composite of three personalities significant in Frances Burney's life: her half-brother Richard Thomas; her brother Charles, Jr.; and her friend Charles Locke" (934). But whereas there is evidence that Burney's younger brother Charles might have been the model for Macartney (see n. 61 above), her older brother James is the more likely inspiration for Lionel's selfish high jinks. That brother "had a natural genius for hoaxing," according to their father: he used to pretend to teach his eight-year-old sister Frances how to read by handing her the book upside down, a trick which he said "she never found out!"[63]

---

[63] Frances Burney was unusually late in learning how to read. This passage, saved from Dr. Burney's 1808 memorandum book and published by Frances Burney after his death, can be found in *Memoirs of Doctor Burney Arranged from His Own Manuscripts, from Family Papers, and from Personal*

THE FIELDINGS AND THE REYNOLDSES

Fortunately, Frances Burney never had to rely on any of her brothers for anything, and managed a life mercifully free of dependence – except for the irksome position at court that she took for her father's sake.[64] She lived and wrote in her parental home until she married. Her husband admired her writing: he called her "Cecilia" when they first met and was her amanuensis, writing out the fair copy of *Camilla*, after they married. Indeed, she supported them both with her literary labors.[65] But other single women with artistic ambitions in the eighteenth century did not fare so well. Contemporary accounts of the relations of Sir Joshua Reynolds with his sister, Frances, or Henry Fielding with *his* sister, Sarah, suggest that whatever the conventions of ideal relations between siblings, public expectations did not shame these two brothers, at least, into providing adequately for their younger kinswomen. Although the parents of these gifted offspring were dead, and legally speaking these older brothers were responsible for their sisters, neither Henry nor Joshua acted the part of protector or educator to their ambitious sisters.

Mrs. Thrale, commenting on these relationships in the privacy of her diary, speculated that sibling rivalry was at the bottom of both brothers' neglect of their accomplished sisters. She thought Henry Fielding begrudged his sister's progress in classical literature, in which Sarah excelled.[66] (Of Sarah Fielding's ten books, the only one she signed with her own name was her translation of Xenophon's *Memoirs of Socrates*, first published in 1762 and still in print in the Everyman's World's Classics series.) Henry Fielding became so jealous of his sister's eminence in Greek and Latin, according to Mrs. Thrale, that he could no longer "perswade himself to endure her Company with Civility."[67] So long as "she only read English

---

Recollections. By His Daughter, Madame D'Arblay, 3 vols. (London: Edward Moxon, 1832), vol. II, p. 168.

[64] Betty Rizzo, in her wonderful book on dependent relationships among women, *Companions without Vows: Relationships among Eighteenth-Century British Women* (Athens: University of Georgia Press, 1994), notes that Frances Burney was especially careful not to slip into a dependent relationship with Hester Thrale (pp. 91–4).

[65] Janice Farrar Thaddeus, *Frances Burney: A Literary Life* (London: Macmillan, and New York: St. Martin's Press, 2000), pp. 110, 115, 118.

[66] Dr. Collier, their Salisbury neighbor, the man who taught Sarah Latin and Greek, according to Mrs. Thrale, "lived much among the Fieldings, and says they all had Parts above the common Run: one of the Girls – *Bee* Fielding he always called her; had an exquisite hand upon the harpsicord, and was otherwise finely accomplished, but Sally was the Scholar." He is said to have "held the Book while she has repeated a thousand Lines at a time without missing one." *Thraliana*, vol. I, p. 78.

[67] Quoted from an undated letter by Hester Lynch Piozzi in Rylands MS 533, no. 16, in Margaret Doody, *Frances Burney*, p. 241. Also in Martin C. Battestin and Ruthe R. Battestin, *Henry Fielding:*

Books, and made English Verses it seems, he fondled her Fancy, & encourag'd her Genius, but as soon [as] he perceived She once read Virgil, Farewell to Fondness, the Author's Jealousy was become stronger than the Brother's Affection, and he saw her future progress in literature not without pleasure only – but with Pain."[68]

A trace of this attitude can be seen in Henry Fielding's account of Mr. Wilson's appreciation of his wife in *Joseph Andrews*. Although Wilson affirms that his Harriet shows none of "that Inferiority of Understanding" attributed to women and declares that none of his own sex was "capable of making juster observations on life or delivering them more agreeably," when Parson Adams misconstrues his meaning, and replies that he has often wished his own wife understood Greek, Mr. Wilson quickly sets him straight. He assures the gentlemen present that he did not mean to insinuate that his wife "had an understanding above the care of her family" but that, on the contrary, she was a devoted housewife, and that few housekeepers understood cookery or confectionary better.[69] In other words, a woman's superior intellect was best used in managing her household, not in learning Greek.[70]

As for Reynolds, continued Mrs. Thrale, comparing the attitudes of the two artist brothers to their sisters,

he certainly does not love her as one should expect a Man to love a Sister he has so much reason to be proud of; perhaps She paints too well, or has learned too much Latin, and is a better Scholar than her Brother: and upon more Reflection I fancy it must be so, for if he only did not like her as an Inmate why should not he give her a genteel Annuity, & let her live where and how She likes: the poor Lady is always miserable, always fretful . . . He is not a covetous Man in any

---

A *Life* (London and New York: Routledge, 1989), p. 381. In Sarah Fielding's *The Adventures of David Simple* (1744), Cynthia's brother hates to read whereas Cynthia enjoys it and is good at it. In her *Translation of the Letters of a Hindoo Rajah* (1796), Elizabeth Hamilton also created a sister "who inherited from Nature a stronger intellect and quicker perception than her brother" and who "became addicted to reading" (vol. II, pp. 90–1).

68 *Thraliana*, vol. I, p. 79. Martin and Ruthe Battestin, in *Henry Fielding: A Life*, take a different view. Although they concede that Fielding had no use for scholarly females, and that "Sarah took up the study of the learned languages against her brother's wishes," they think it unlikely that "Sarah's mastery of the classics could have spoiled her relationship with her brother to this degree" (381).

69 Henry Fielding, *Joseph Andrews* (1742), ed. Martin C. Battestin (Boston: Houghton Mifflin, 1961), p. 191 (Book II, Chapter 4).

70 This point is made by Gary Gautier in "Marriage and Family in Fielding's Fiction," *Studies in the Novel* 27 (Summer 1995), 111–28. Gautier points out that this complex attitude can also be found in *Amelia*, Book X, Chapters 1 and 4, in the scenes in which Mrs. Bennet-Atkinson and Harrison debate the issue of classical education for women. "Both parties agree that women are quite as intellectually capable as men," he says, but having laid to rest the issue of essential difference, they argue that "the practical needs of social order and domestic felicity justify the maintenance of separate education for women" (114–15).

Sense I believe, but seems proud to give, proud to spend, and even proud to be cheated . . . but then why should he who is niggardly to nobody, who leaves £200 in a Draw'r and forgets it – an unlocked Drawer I mean, who lets his Man Ralph maintain his Wife and Family in the house by Connivance; and does a hundred things of the same sort; why should he refuse his Purse and even his Civilities to a Sister so amiable & so accomplished as Miss Reynolds?[71]

James Northcote, Sir Joshua's student and biographer, who lived with the Reynoldses for several years in the early 1770s, also remarked Reynolds' coldness towards Frances in a letter to his brother in 1771: "He never writes to her, and, between ourselves, I believe but seldom converses as we used to do in our family. I found she knew nothing of his having invited me to be his scholar and live in the house til I told her of it."[72]

Frances and Joshua Reynolds were among the last of the eleven children of the Reverend Samuel Reynolds, master of a grammar school in the small town of Plympton's Earl, Devonshire. Six years younger than her brother, Frances Reynolds was twenty-three when she came to London with Joshua as his housekeeper and dependent in 1753. Both brother and sister were already painting at that time, for their older sisters had been very fond of drawing and all the children had copied prints and engravings in their father's library. Joshua began to paint portraits for a living after his father died in 1746 and he had spent three years in Italy copying Raphael and the old masters. A letter from Samuel Johnson to a mutual friend in 1759 notes the prosperity of their early household: "Mr. Reynolds has within these few days raised his price to twenty guineas a head, and Miss is much employed in miniatures."[73]

Although her brother tried, emblematically, to limit her to miniature painting and watercolors (he told her that her oil paintings "made other people laugh and him cry"), Frances Reynolds painted in oils on the sly when she could.[74] She taught herself how to paint by copying her brother's

---

[71] *Thraliana*, vol. 1, pp. 79–80.

[72] James Northcote, *The Life of Sir Joshua Reynolds* (London: Henry Colbourn, 1818), vol. 1, p. 203, quoted in *Johnsonian Miscellanies*, ed. George Birkbeck Hill, 2 vols. (New York: Harper & Brothers, 1897), vol. 11, p. 455.

[73] James Boswell, *The Life of Samuel Johnson* (London: Dent, amd New York; Dutton, 1973), vol. 1, p. 198.

[74] Frances Reynolds painted fourteen portraits that we know of, with subjects including Samuel Johnson, Charles Burney, Mrs. Montagu, Anna Williams, Hannah More, James Harris, James Beattie and his wife, John Hoole, and a self-portrait with her two sisters. They are listed in Ellen C. Clayton, *English Female Artists*, 2 vols. (London: Tinsley Brothers, 1876), vol. 1, pp. 231–2. See also Richard Wendorf and Charles Ryskamp, "A Blue-Stocking Friendship: The Letters of Elizabeth Montagu and Frances Reynolds in the Princeton Collection," *Princeton University Library Chronicle*, 41, 3 (Spring 1980), 173–207, esp. 185–8.

pictures in secret. James Northcote describes an episode in which Frances was copying one of her brother's paintings in the library when she heard him coming. In her haste to hide the picture, she accidentally dropped it, and "a considerable part of the face and the neck of the portrait" fell from the canvas "to the great surprise and annoyance of them both."[75]

Samuel Johnson always appreciated and encouraged "Renny," as he called her. He sat for her no less than ten times, and let her paint him, although he "thought portrait-painting an improper employment for a woman. 'Publick practice of any art, (he observed,) and staring in men's faces, is very indelicate in a female.' "[76] Nonetheless, Johnson enjoyed Frances Reynolds' conversation and was a good friend to her. He revised her poems, praised her to others, read successive drafts of her treatise *Enquiry concerning the Principles of Taste, and of the Origin of Our Ideas of Beauty* (1789), and advised her to put her name on the work.[77] He commended it as containing "such force of comprehension, and such nicety of observation as Locke or Pascal might be proud of" but advised her that it needed further tightening and clarification.[78] Mrs. Thrale observed in her diary that in contrast to Johnson's friendship with herself, dictated by "mere *Interest*," she was sure he really loved Miss Reynolds.[79] From the mid-1760s until his death in 1784, Johnson maintained close relations with Frances Reynolds, visiting her frequently and addressing her in his letters as "my dearest dear" or "my dear Renny."

Although there is no consensus about her satiric intention, Frances Reynolds was apparently honest to a fault. It must have been her directness and unwillingness to dissemble that Johnson found so attractive. She was "an amiable woman, very simple in her manner," wrote a friend, "possessed of much information and talent, for which I do not think every one did her justice on account of the singular *naivite* which was her characteristic quality, or defect."[80] Mrs. Thrale described her as having "an odd dry Manner,

---

[75] Quoted in Ellen Clayton, *English Female Artists*, vol. 1, p. 196.

[76] James Boswell, *The Life of Samuel Johnson*, vol. 1, p. 556.

[77] For an analysis of Frances Reynolds' ideas about beauty, and the gendering of these ideas, see Robert Jones, *Gender and the Formation of Taste in Eighteenth-Century Britain: The Analysis of Beauty* (Cambridge: Cambridge University Press, 1998), pp. 198–210.

[78] Quoted from Johnson's *Letters* in Isobel Grundy, "Samuel Johnson as Patron of Women," *The Age of Johnson: A Scholarly Annual* 1 (1987), 59–77, quote 72. James Clifford edited an Augustan Reprint of Frances' Reynolds' *Enquiry concerning the Principles of Taste, and of the Origin of Our Ideas of Beauty* in 1951.

[79] *Thraliana*, vol. 1, p. 415.

[80] Ellis Cornelia Knight, *The Autobiography of Miss Knight Lady Companion to Princess Charlotte*, ed. Roger Fulford (London: W. Kimber, 1960), p. 26, quoted, in Richard Wendorf and Charles Ryskamp, "A Blue-Stocking Friendship," 180.

something between Malice and Simplicity, which was entertaining enough"
and tells several stories which suggest a manner of willful naiveté that permitted "Renny" to tell uncomfortable truths in social situations without
anyone knowing whether or not she was being rude.[81] Frances Burney's
anecdote about how Frances Reynolds teased her father, Dr. Burney, about
his hair while she was painting his portrait suggests the same sang-froid –
call it malice, simplicity, naiveté – this time in the service of animating her
subject.[82] Burney tells another story about a long "whispering" conversation she had with Frances Reynolds in which the eccentric woman regaled
her with stories about some recent disasters she had had with company
involving a damp bed-gown and a dirty painting rag – stories that resemble nothing so much as the slapstick humiliations of Burney's own female
characters – which made Burney laugh "immoderately."[83] Johnson's letters
to Frances, with their soothing explanations and repeated expressions of
affection and friendship, would seem to be responses to a woman frank
about her own feelings and unwilling to ignore others' sins of omission.
Once, in discussing a microscope for the mind, Johnson exclaimed that he
never knew anyone's mind that could bear such examination, "except that
of my dear Miss Reynolds, and her's is very near to purity itself."[84]

Frances Reynolds apparently maintained this high standard of honesty
and purity even in the ticklish situation of speaking her mind to the brother
who supported her. She criticized him, for instance, for painting on Sundays
when, as a clergyman's son, he should have set a better example. Mrs. Thrale
admired Frances' integrity in not flattering her brother. "She seems resolved – nobly enough – not to keep her Post by Flattery if She cannot
keep it by Kindness: – this is a Flight so far beyond my power that I respect
her for it," confided Mrs. Thrale to her diary. She continued: "[I] do love
dearly to hear her criticize Sir Joshua's Painting, or indeed his Connoisseur-
ship, which I think She always does with Justice and Judgment – mingled
now & then with a Bitterness that diverts one."[85]

Meanwhile Frances continued painting, which irritated her brother no
end. In 1774 and 1775 she exhibited three paintings at the Royal Academy:
a miniature called "Lace Makers" and two oils, "The Garland, from Prior"

[81] *Thraliana*, vol. 1, p. 268.
[82] Frances spoke of his wearing a wig although he repeatedly assured her it was his own hair. Burney
    tells this anecdote in her *Memoirs of Doctor Burney*, vol. 1, pp. 333–4.
[83] Frances Burney, *The Diary and Letters of Madame D'Arblay*, Edited by Her Niece, 7 vols. (London:
    Henry Colburn, 1842–6), vol. II, pp. 219–21.
[84] James Northcote, *The Life of Sir Joshua Reynolds*, vol. 1, p. 80, quoted in Richard Wendorf and
    Charles Ryskamp, "A Blue-Stocking Friendship," 180.
[85] *Thraliana*, vol. 1, p. 79.

and "Children Going to Bed," the latter especially praised by contemporary critics.[86] Her commonplace book reveals her desire to paint and exhibit professionally, although she knew that it was not suitable for a gentlewoman. Richard Wendorf points out the irony that Reynolds had, by his painting, raised his family to a social level that put his sister's professional career beyond the pale. Only an accomplished amateurism would have been socially acceptable in the circle in which they now moved. But "the mind must have some pursuit," wrote Frances in a letter to a friend,

and I, unhappily, have none that is so satisfactory, or that appears to me so praiseworthy as painting . . . I confess I can't help pleasing myself with the hope that I might arrive at a tolerable degree of perfection in these little pictures [of children and landscapes] could I refresh imagination and improve my ideas by the sight of pictures of that sort, and by the judgement of connoisseurs. But I must beg you to believe that nothing but the greatest necessity should prompt me to make any advantage of them in a manner unsuitable to the character of a gentlewoman, both for my sake as well as for my brother's.[87]

As her brother's neglect became increasingly a matter for common gossip and she was forced to leave his establishment, "Renny" apparently drafted a letter to him about the pain it caused her and showed it to her friend, Samuel Johnson, for his advice. Johnson wrote an alternative version of the letter, to be sent as if it were her own if she wished to use it. "I know that complainers are never welcome yet you must allow me to complain of your unkindness," writes Johnson, ventriloquizing for Frances Reynolds,

because it lies heavy at my heart and because I am not conscious that I ever deserved it. I have not perhaps been always careful enough to please but you can charge me, and I can charge myself, with no offense which a Brother may not forgive.

If you ask me what I suffer from you, I can answer that I suffer too much in the loss of your notice; but to that is added the neglect of the world which is a consequence of yours.

If you ask what will satisfy me, I shall be satisfied with such a degree of attention when I visit you, as may set me above the contempt of your servants, with your calling now and then at my lodgings and with you inviting me from time to time with such parties as I may properly appear in. This is not much for a sister who has at least done you no harm, and this I hope you will promise by your answer

---

[86] See Richard Wendorf and Charles Ryskamp, "A Blue-Stocking Friendship," 173–207, esp. 185–8. Contemporary praise of Frances Reynolds is quoted by Richard Wendorf in *Sir Joshua Reynolds: The Painter in Society* (Cambridge, MA: Harvard University Press, 1996), p. 78.

[87] Quoted in Ellen Clayton, *English Female Artists*, vol. I, pp. 210–11 and Richard Wendorf, *Sir Joshua Reynolds*, p. 73. My thanks to Richard Wendorf for permitting me to see an earlier typescript of this chapter, "Other Voices," with this longer quotation.

to this letter; for a refusal will give me more pain than you can desire or intend to inflict.

Johnson added in a note to her: "This is my letter, which at least I like better than yours. But take your choice, and if you like mine alter any thing that you think not ladylike."[88]

Frances did not use Johnson's letter, which she said would not "pass with Sir Joshua as her own," any more "than Johnson himself would pass for her should he appear before her brother wearing her cap and gown."[89] But she must have pressed Johnson to speak for her in his own voice, for he wrote to her in May, 1784, saying "I have not seen Sir Joshua, and, when I see him, I know not how to serve you. When I spoke upon your affairs to him at Christmas, I received no encouragement to speak again."[90]

After leaving her brother's protection, Frances Reynolds withdrew to Torrington, Devon, where she suffered a deep depression.[91] "I am incapable of painting," she wrote, "my faculties are all becalmed in the dead region of Torrington." Recognizing how essential her London community was to her, she returned to town, living first with John Hoole, the translator, and thereafter in different rented lodgings.[92] She apparently thought she might earn her living by writing during this time, for she published her *Enquiry* (1789) and her book of poems, *A Melancholy Tale* (1790). But it was an unsettled time, and she wrote to Elizabeth Montagu that she was "obliged to quit my Apartments in which I thought myself settled for three years at least and I foresee with a heavy heart the difficulties and distresses my unprotected and forlorn state will again expose me to. My luggage of pictures &c require more room than I shall easily find in any lodgings that I can afford to take."[93]

Ironically, if his life as a painter gave Frances Reynolds access to the art world, her brother's death in 1792 freed her to paint. Although Sir Joshua

---

[88] Johnson's draft and accompanying note are in *Johnsonian Miscellanies*, ed. George Birkbeck Hill, vol. II, pp. 455–6.

[89] Helen Ashmore, Prefatory essay for the Frances Reynolds poem printed as a keepsake to mark the 286th birthday of Samuel Johnson and the Forty-ninth annual dinner of The Johnsonians. The Houghton Library, Harvard University, September 15, 1991, pp. 1–19, quote p. 4.

[90] Ellen Clayton, *English Female Artists*, vol. I, p. 228.

[91] After Frances left her brother's establishment sometime in the late seventies, he brought in a succession of nieces to keep house for him. The last of these, Mary Palmer, lived with him until he died, and inherited the bulk of his fortune. She is supposed to have found it difficult to get money out of him to pay the household bills and was forced to ask him for the necessary funds at breakfast almost daily. Richard Wendorf, *Sir Joshua Reynolds*, p. 66.

[92] From Frances Reynolds' commonplace book and her draft of a letter, quoted in Richard Wendorf and Charles Ryskamp, "A Blue-Stocking Friendship," 182.

[93] Richard Wendorf and Charles Ryskamp, "A Blue-Stocking Friendship," 205.

left most of his fortune to his nieces – more than £10,000 to one and nearly £100,000 to the other – with only a stingy £2,500 for his sister, and that left in trust only, still it was enough for an income of £100 a year for the rest of her life, which was another fifteen years. She took a house on Queen Square in London large enough to hang her collection of pictures, painted as much as she liked, and revised several drafts of her memoir of Samuel Johnson. After his death, her judgment of her brother, separating the person from the painter, was that "she saw nothing in him *as a man* but a *gloomy tyrant.*"[94]

Henry Fielding was neither so rich as Sir Joshua Reynolds, nor so churlish towards his sisters. But his sister Sarah never had to depend on his bounty, aided as she was by a succession of wealthy maternal relatives, her sisters, Samuel Richardson, and then by her own publications and her bluestocking friends.[95] Like many another unmarried sister, she was brought in to serve as her brother's housekeeper between marriages, when he had no wife. But with the exception of those three years, Sarah Fielding supported herself without her brother's help – which was fortunate because he is supposed to have been, like his best characters, improvident.

The only evidence we have of Henry's material support of Sarah is the £10 he gave her on August 29, 1750 and £9 the following March, when – following her three sisters' deaths – she was sued for the recovery of an un- specified debt by the man who had bought their family estate in East Stour,

94 Charles Robert Leslie and Tom Taylor, *Life and Times of Sir Joshua Reynolds* (London, 1865), vol. 1, p. 92n; quotation in Richard Wendorf and Charles Ryskamp, "A Blue-Stocking Friendship," 184. Wendorf and Ryskamp also quote the condemnation of another sister, Elizabeth Johnson, whose daughter "Betsey" was one of the housekeeping nieces. In 1776 Elizabeth Johnson wrote to Sir Joshua: "Thy soul is a shocking spectacle of poverty. When thy outside is, as thy inside now is, as I told thee ten year since I will not shut the door against thee. But it may be, thy soul is past all recovery. If so, I shall never see thee more. Thy vissitation is not yet come: and who knows in what shape it will come: or whether it will come at all. Wo be to thee if it does not come." Wendorf and Ryskamp, "A Blue-Stocking Friendship," 184 n. 14.
95 It may be that women who lived with female relatives were more successful in a worldly way than women who married or lived with their brothers. To begin with – then as now – women without brothers were sometimes raised as "sons," given atypical educations and unusual proportions of family property. If wealthy enough, they even married men who took *their* family names. In poorer families, as Margaret Hunt observes, "girls without brothers would fare better in terms of education, job training, and assistance in setting up in business than would girls with brothers." Margaret Hunt, *The Middling Sort*, pp. 252–3 n. 57. Women could also pool resources with their sisters to raise the necessary capital for business ventures – and protect their investment from husbands' claims. Margaret Hunt gives examples of women in business with other women in *The Middling Sort*, Chapter 5, especially pp. 143–4 and p. 247 n. 47. Sarah Fielding's "sisterhood," her household with Catherine, Beatrice, and Ursula, is an example of this – not to mention the household she grew up in under the direction of her grandmother. Jane Austen, too, began to publish and to write steadily for publication only after her father died, when she and her sister, Cassandra, and their mother settled together at Chawton in 1809.

Dorset. Henry died heavily in debt in 1754. After his death, she moved to Bath where she lived for the next fourteen years, assisted by her blue-stocking friends, including the sisters Sarah Scott and Elizabeth Montagu. Their charity, however, was delicately given. As Elizabeth Montagu wrote to Sarah Scott:

Fielding is too much of a Bel esprit to know a little of ye ordinary affairs of life . . . so we can cheat her as to knowledge of ye expence & let her imagine her present income equal to it . . . it can never be pleasant to one as ill provided with money as Fielding to think about it, & feel a dependence upon another for what humanly speaking, she ought to have of her own.[96]

Despite this evidence of Sarah Fielding's relative poverty and her brother's apparent failure to contribute to her support, and despite Mrs. Thrale's observation that Henry Fielding resented his sister's classical attainments, biographers such as the Battestins ascribe to this brother and sister a warm friendship. Financial assistance is only one kind of support, after all, and Sarah praises her famous brother in many of her published works. Moreover, the theme of brother-sister love – even to the point of incest – is in both their texts.[97] The extraordinary scene in *Amelia* in which Booth leaves his betrothed on the eve of their wedding to attend his dying sister – an act of impetuous compassion that almost loses him his Amelia – is generally interpreted as Fielding's response to the appalling loss of three of his sisters (Catherine, Ursula, and Beatrice all died in the space of eight months) during the year he was writing the novel.

Structurally, this scene feels like an intrusion, bubbling up uncon-trolledly, serving no narrative purpose. The sequence pits the anticipated sexual pleasure of a wedding night against grief for a dying sister, a rather theatrical expression of how a man of Fielding's class might have felt pulled between the claims of sister and wife. But the scene has an oddly blank

---

[96] For this and other information about Sarah Fielding, unless footnoted elsewhere, I am indebted to the wonderful Introduction to *The Correspondence of Henry and Sarah Fielding*, ed. Martin C. Battestin and Clive T. Probyn (Oxford: Clarendon Press, 1993), pp. xv–xliii, quote p. xxxvii. On Elizabeth Montagu's generosity towards Sarah Fielding among others, see Edith Sedgwick Larson, "A Measure of Power: The Personal Charity of Elizabeth Montagu," *Studies in Eighteenth-Century Culture* 16 (1986), 197–210.

[97] Martin C. Battestin and Ruthe R. Battestin list the "complimentary allusions to Fielding's works" in Sarah's published work on p. 630 n. 89 of the biography, *Henry Fielding: A Life*. Martin Battestin discusses the Fieldings' obsession with incest in an early article, "Henry Fielding, Sarah Fielding, and 'the dreadful Sin of Incest," *Novel* 13 (Fall 1979), 6–18. He gives the history of a lawsuit brought by Lady Gould against her son-in-law Edmund (the father of Henry and Sarah) for custody of the children after her daughter died, a suit in which the housekeeper testified that while their father was in London courting his second wife, Henry "was guilty of committing some indecent actions with his Sister Beatrice."

affect; there is nothing in it that would lead one to believe that Henry Fielding's feelings were similarly divided – no erotic energy, no longing, no real sense of suffering. The dying sister is never described. Although the passage in *Amelia* begins with an assertion of brotherly love – "Upon my soul, I cannot yet mention her name without tears. Never brother and sister had, I believe, a higher friendship for one another" – it soon modulates into another testimonial to Booth's irresistible loveableness:

Poor dear girl! whilst I sat by her in her light-head fits, she repeated scarce any other name but mine; and it plainly appeared that, when her dear reason was ravished away from her, it had left my image on her fancy... At last, she seemed for a moment to know me, and cried, "O heavens! my dearest brother!" upon which she fell into immediate convulsions, and died in my arms.[98]

THE ELSTOBS

Henry Fielding never appears to have acted in *loco fraternis*, never took the role of protector with his independent sisters. If he was less cold and condescending than Sir Joshua Reynolds, his sisters were also less needy. He lived his own life to the hilt and let them manage theirs as best they could. It is instructive to compare these cases – the Fieldings and the Reynolds – with another intellectual brother and sister from an earlier period: William and Elizabeth Elstob. Not only did William Elstob tutor his sister in Latin and Anglo-Saxon and encourage her progress in these difficult and archaic languages, but he rescued her from the household of a severe uncle who disapproved of women's education and lived with her in amity and equality.

In her brief autobiographical memoir, Elizabeth Elstob writes that she always loved books, "which being observed by her mother, who was also a great admirer of learning, especially in her own sex, there was nothing wanting for her improvement so long as her mother lived." But her mother died when she was eight, which put a temporary stop to her progress, for her brother being under age at the time, she became a ward of her uncle, "who was no friend to women's learning, so that she was not suffered to proceed, notwithstanding her repeated requests." She tried to educate herself with whatever books she could find, and finally, with much difficulty, obtained permission to teach herself French. Tradition has it that Elizabeth joined her brother at Oxford and was privately tutored by him there. She may have joined him when he reached his majority and became her legal guardian, while still at Queen's College, Oxford, well known as a center

[98] Henry Fielding, *Amelia*, 2 vols. (1751; rpt. London: Dent, 1930), vol. 1, p. 70.

of Saxon learning.[99] In her memoir, Elstob simply notes that her struggles ended when she went to live with her brother, who readily assisted and encouraged her studies.

When she was nineteen, they took a little house together near St. Swithin's Church where William was rector, where they translated rare manuscripts from the Cottonian and Harleian collections. Elizabeth Elstob worked with her brother on a translation of King Alfred's Saxon version of Orosius' history and published her own translations of several Saxon works between 1708 and 1715. To the surprised amusement of many of their friends and visitors, they even taught Latin and Saxon to their serving boy, nine-year-old James Smith. The household was happy and productive, but it caame to an abrupt end when William died suddenly. His salary discontinued, Elizabeth was forced to go underground to avoid being imprisoned for debt when her brief experiment running a girls' boarding school in Chelsea failed. She went into Gloucestershire, where she taught the rudiments of literacy to the children of stocking weavers in a dames' school, until she was discovered and rescued by Sarah Chapone and George Ballard.[100]

There seems to have been no competition between William and Elizabeth Elstob (perhaps because he was so clearly the teacher and leader), no sibling rivalry for scholarly honors, no public displays of rancor or witholding, and no disapproving gossip on the part of their community of friends. The subscription list for Elizabeth's 1709 translation of Aelfric's *An English-Saxon Homily on the Birthday of St. Gregory* includes a number of scholars and antiquarians who were William's associates; the Preface includes a lengthy defense of women's learning against the usual charges that it made women conceited and neglect their household duties. William clearly supported her endeavors both privately and publicly.

I am tempted to attribute the unconflicted nature of the Elstobs' relationship in part to their historical and sociological context – a social context with clearer expectations of brothers for their sisters. There is, of course, no evidence other than chronological order that these differences were historically determined rather than a function of individual differences. The

[99] In 1696, when William was twenty-three (Elizabeth was ten years younger), he was elected fellow of University College. This information is from Mary Elizabeth Green's biographical essay, "Elizabeth Elstob: The Saxon Nymph (English, 1683–1765)," in J. R. Brink (ed.), *Female Scholars: A Tradition of Learned Women before 1800* (Montreal, Canada: Eden Press, 1980), pp. 137–60. For a transcription of Elizabeth Elstob's memoir from the Ballard MSS as well as most of the other primary material that has survived on Elstob, see the invaluable Myra Reynolds, *The Learned Lady in England 1650–1750* (Boston: Houghton Mifflin, 1920), pp. 169–85. The quoted passages appear on p. 170.

[100] See my Introduction to George Ballard's *Memoirs of Several Ladies of Great Britain* (1752; ed. Ruth Perry, Detroit: Wayne State University Press, 1985), pp. 21–3.

fact that William Elstob assumed Elizabeth's guardianship as soon as he legally could – and not just so that she could be of use to him as his house-keeper – is proof of his protective concern for her. It seems that between the end of the seventeenth century and the end of the eighteenth century a change took place with respect to the responsibility that family members as-sumed for one another – particularly siblings. Before that change, William Elstob, whatever his character, could not have treated his sister the way Joshua Reynolds treated his sister. Social disapproval would have weighed too heavily against him. By 1724, Thomas Salmon, scoffing at Thomas Aquinas' explanation for the prohibition of marriage between brothers and sisters – i.e., that if conjugal affection were added to the love of kindred, the "Addition will carry the Husband beyond the Bounds of Reason" – was already skeptical about the love of kindred. "[W]ith *Acquiras's* Leave," he retorted drily, "there seems as little Reason to apprehend that a Man should have a greater Affection for a Wife taken out of his own Family, than out of a Stranger's, as there is to apprehend that a Man should be too fond of his own Wife."[101]

A BROTHER'S PROTECTION

Still, many brothers continued to assume financial responsibility for their unmarried female relatives. Austen's brothers all contributed to support the household at Chawton. Richard Barwell put his East India fortune at his sister's disposal. Sir Joshua Reynolds did leave his sister an annuity when he died, although it was a bare subsistence and a tiny fraction of what he left his nieces. Moreover, sibling relationships continued to be psychologically central when brothers and sisters did not marry. William and Elin Stout, Charles and Elizabeth Hamilton, Mary and Richard Barwell – for each of these pairs of unmarried siblings, their relationship with their brother or sister was the most significant relationship in their lives.

Sarah Robinson Scott only languished in a disastrous marriage for nine months before her lawyer father and brothers intervened and removed her from her unhappy conjugal home. They negotiated for the return of half her fortune, and arranged for her estranged husband to settle an annuity of £100 on her for life. "Neither maid, wife, nor widow" (as Betty Rizzo expresses it), Sarah Scott then returned to her ménage with Lady Barbara Montagu – which only ended with Lady Barbara's death in 1765 – and

---

[101] Thomas Salmon, *A Critical Essay concerning Marriage* (London, 1724; rpt. New York: Garland, 1985), p. 176.

continued her career as a writer.[102] But the intervention of Sarah Scott's father and brothers at mid-century was, according to Betty Rizzo, "an extreme and almost a unique response to marital incompatibility."[103] Few male relatives were willing to intervene in the private affairs of their married sisters to protect them from husbands, who were legally privileged, however violent. Indeed, homosexuality was the only reason deemed extreme enough to warrant interference – and that may have been the explanation for Sarah Scott's relatives' intervention.[104]

As the century wore on, a woman's need for her brother's friendship and protection intensified as other forms of kin support fell away. Brothers' obligation to their sisters was increasingly understood as socially and morally supererogatory, at odds with their self-interest as individuals or their duties to wife and children. There is only one story like Sarah Scott's but there are many stories of women forced to suffer in bad marriages both in life and literature, without relief from their male kin. Elizabeth Shackleton's second husband (they married in 1765) was a brutal man and a drunkard, who used to beat his genteel wife with his fists, feet, and even a horsewhip. Her brother had been scandalized by her Gretna Green elopement with this man seventeen years her junior, and had, for a while, stopped speaking to her. Although they were subsequently reconciled, she never called on her brother to intercede, even when John Shackleton's alcoholic cruelties multiplied. She did, however, ask her son from her first marriage to mediate in their disputes – with no perceptible effect – confirming that it took a woman's male kin to intervene successfully in her marriage.[105]

Ellen Weeton Stock's legal account of her insupportable marriage in the early nineteenth century furnishes another example of a brother who failed to protect his sister from the brutal effects of a bad marriage. After three years of strife, her husband, Aaron Stock, turned her physically out of the house, and she had to take shelter with her brother in a nearby town. "Mr Stock wants me either to remain at home pennyless, as an underling to his own daughter, or to be kept by anyone that will take me," she told her brother.[106] She further explained that Stock rebuffed her affectionate

---

[102] See Betty Rizzo's excellent Introduction to Sarah Scott's *The History of Sir George Ellison* (1766; ed. Betty Rizzo, Lexington: University of Kentucky Press, 1996), esp. pp. xiii–xvi.

[103] *Ibid.*, p. xv.

[104] Betty Rizzo suggested this to me in private correspondence.

[105] A detailed account of Elizabeth Shackleton's complex and interesting life is given by Amanda Vickery, *The Gentleman's Daughter: Women's Lives in Georgian England* (New Haven and London: Yale University Press, 1998) *passim*, esp. pp. 58–62.

[106] Amanda Vickery, *The Gentleman's Daughter*, p. 63.

advances, forced her to eat servants' food, informed the servants rather than herself about household affairs, authorized his daughters (from a previous marriage) rather than her to manage the house, ridiculed her face and figure, and regularly ordered her out of his sight. In the years that followed, he assaulted her, arrested her, and threatened her with a lunatic asylum. Afraid for her life, she signed a deed of separation (after hearing it read aloud once, but never reading it herself) that gave her £70 a year, if she agreed never to live in or even visit their town and to see her own child only three times a year. She wrote these details in her autobiography in hopes that her daughter might read them someday. Throughout these years, her lawyer brother sat on his hands and worse, even advised her husband with whom he had substantial business interests. Ellen Weeton Stock never forgave him for his "unbrotherlike" behavior.[107]

The degree and kind of aid and protection a brother owed his sister as well as the degree of obedience a sister owed her brother must have been a psychological conundrum judging from the number of fictional plots that raise these issues. This is the crux of the final episode of Charlotte Lennox's novel *Henrietta* (1758) and central to its later adaptation as a play, *The Sister* (1769). In the novel, a brother and sister who have not seen each other for some years meet without recognizing each other in their respective jobs – she as a lady's companion and he as a tutor to a young aristocrat traveling incognito on his grand tour. The young lord, smitten with Henrietta, wants to propose to her, and his friend and advisor, out of consideration for the young lord's father, tries to preempt his impetuous marriage by proposing to Henrietta that she be Mr. Melvil's mistress instead. When he learns that Henrietta is his own sister, whom he has not seen for several years, he becomes almost pathologically protective. She is frightened by his sternness, although she has proved herself more than capable of handling all exigencies that arise. He thus projects his predatory attempt on her virtue as her vulnerability and weakness. Contrite, he tells her "I never shall forgive myself for having ignorantly practiced on your virtue." "Consider every virtuous young woman as a sister," Henrietta replies, calling attention to the difference between the way women were treated by kin and the way they were treated by the rest of the world.[108]

But the novel is not over. Although the young incognito marquis presses Charles – Henrietta's brother – to give his consent to the marriage, Charles

---

[107] For the reference to Ellen Weeton's diary, see n. 32 above. This case is also reported in Amanda Vickery, *The Gentleman's Daughter*, pp. 62–6, quote p. 65.

[108] Charlotte Lennox, *Henrietta*, 2 vols. (London: A. Millar, 1758), vol. II, p. 226. Subsequent page references are to this edition.

will not permit his addresses to Henrietta without informing the duke, his father, because otherwise it will look as if he has taken advantage of his position as tutor to inveigle his young charge into marrying his own sister. Feeling that he needs to protect his reputation with the father of the marquis, he orders his sister to have nothing to do with the man who continues, nonetheless, to press his case. In the drama that ensues, Henrietta promises her brother not to marry without his consent. "[D]ispose of me as you please," she tells her brother, "you are in the place of my father, I will obey you as such" (II: 228). Protective of her brother's honor, Henrietta proves her delicacy and refinement by managing to let her lover know that she would marry him if she could, all the while maintaining her respectability.

Thus the brother who should preserve his sister's chastity attempts it, and he who should forward her advantageous marriage, prevents it. This is the episode – one among many in the novel – that Lennox dramatized in her play, *The Sister* (1769). But in the play, once Henrietta and her brother have recognized one another, and Henrietta has been charged to resist the young lord's advances, she must also hide the truth of her relationship with her brother. In other words, the central moral dilemma for the heroine is not, as in the novel, refusing to marry the man she loves out of deference to her brother's reputation – even though her suitor loves her honorably and stands ready to share with her his wealth and title. In the play, the central dilemma becomes instead keeping her relation to her brother a secret as she has promised to do – even though their meetings are misinterpreted and her reputation jeopardized.

We have seen this before: secret meetings with a brother being misconstrued as assignations with a lover. Burney arranged matters between Evelina and Macartney for just this ambiguity in *Evelina*, and Maria Edgeworth later imitated it in *Helen* (1834).[109] The brother, whose presence is longed for through many dangers and privations, and whose appearance promises protection and respite from difficulties, becomes instead another threat to his sister's happiness and reputation. But the reversal consolidates the premise. Brothers were supposed to protect and support their sisters – except when their own interests were involved. Then they acted like men of the world, sacrificing their sisters for their own advantage. Thus the relation of brothers to their sisters became in the fiction

---

[109] According to Mary Nash, this same plot twist appears in an unpublished farce written by Mrs. Thrale called "The Imposter," which can be found in Rylands MS 650.

of the eighteenth century another kind of toll that individualism paid to modernity, another test of love's weight in the scales of self-interest. And the extent to which sisters responded to their brothers' claims on them became less a matter of their strength of purpose and persuasive powers, and more a test of their resignation, obedience, and capacity for feminine self-abnegation.

5

Privatized marriage and property relations

Marriage is a sort of Lottery; nor can all the Precautions in the World insure its certain Happiness.

> Philogamus, *The Present State of Matrimony: or, The Real Causes of Conjugal Infidelity and Unhappy Marriages* (1739), p. 33.

Jointures and Settlements . . . are not only the greatest Impediments towards entring into that State [marriage], but also the frequent Causes of Distrust and Animosity in it after it is consummated . . . I have [long] thought the Coldness of Wives to their Husbands, as well as Disrespect from Children to Parents, to arise from this one Sourse [sic]. This Trade for Minds and Bodies in the Lump, without Regard to either, but as they are accompanied with such Sums of Money, and such Parcels of Land, cannot but produce a Commerce between the Parties concerned suitable to the mean Motives upon which they at first came together.

> *The Tatler*, September 12, 1710, from notes by Edward Wortley.

Marriage was, for all ranks, the main means of transferring property, occupational status, personal contacts, money, tools, livestock, and women across generations and kin groups.

> Margaret Hunt, *The Middling Sort: Commerce, Gender, and the Family in England, 1680–1780*, p. 151.

From a 21st-century vantage point looking back three centuries, marriage would seem to be foundational to the meaning of family. But it is by no means clear that marriage was the most significant kin connection in earlier historical periods, even for women, when compared, for example, to daughterhood or sisterhood. When Jane Austen's mother wrote to her prospective daughter-in-law Mary Lloyd in 1796, she wrote as a neighbor who had known Mary Lloyd and her family for many years. "Had the Election been mine, you, my dear Mary, are the person I should have chosen for *James's Wife, Anna's Mother* and *my Daughter*, being as certain, as I can be of anything in this uncertain world, that you will greatly increase & promote the happiness of each of the three ... I look forward to you as a real comfort to me in my old age" (emphasis hers).[1] As late as 1796, then, marriage was not simply a matter of personal attraction between a man and his chosen bride, as so many anachronistic historical descriptions reconstruct it to be. Mary Lloyd's relations to James' sisters and mother and to his children by a former marriage – to her new affinal family, in short – as well as her abiding importance to her family of origin, still had enormous psychological meaning in eighteenth-century England.

The meaning of marriage has been taken for granted rather than questioned in the histories of the English family that have been written hitherto. The problem, as Olivia Harris describes it, has been extrapolating "the normal" from an abstraction based on statistical frequency.

In the case of historical studies of the English family ... a definition of the typical in terms of statistical frequency often moves beyond the statistics to reinstate the typical household as *the* basic unit of society. The norm is arrived at by a process of abstraction: it is then multiplied to recreate an image of society which is based on the prior abstraction. In the process the exceptions to the norm become more and more marginal to the analysis.[2]

The psychological reality of the conjugal household, in other words, has been reconstructed from a statistical norm and corroborated by prescriptive conduct literature.

The emotional meaning of marriage as well as its standard heterosexual form has been assumed in most analyses of families in eighteenth-century England. The fluidity of sexual identity and the occasional anomaly of same-sex marriage is almost never mentioned in this context. The marriage register of Taxal, Cheshire, for example, records two marriages in 1707 and 1708 in which both partners appear to be women, according to Emma Donoghue.[3] Nor do family historians typically take into account the psychological implications of the life-cycles of families.[4] Few have seriously

---

[1] Deirdre Le Faye, *Jane Austen: A Family Record* (Boston: G. K. Hall, 1989), p. 92.

[2] Olivia Harris, "Households and Their Boundaries," *History Workshop Journal* 13 (1982), 143–52, quote 144.

[3] See Mary Turner, "Two Entries from the Marriage Register of Taxal, Cheshire," *Local Population Studies* 21 (Autumn 1978), 64, cited in Emma Donoghue, *Passions between Women: British Lesbian Culture 1668–1801*, (London: Scarlet Press, 1993), p. 65 n.17. See also Patricia Crawford and Sara Mendelson, "Sexual Identities in Early Modern England: The Marriage of Two Women in 1680," *Gender & History* 7, 3 (November 1995), 362–77.

[4] For a discussion of the life-cycles of families and their multiple, changing configurations, see Lutz K. Berkner, "The Use and Misuse of Census Data for the Historical Analysis of Family Structure," *Journal of Interdisciplinary History* 5, 4 (Spring 1975), 721–38. For another treatment of the changing

asked how central or peripheral marriage was to the relationship between parents and children – or to the sibling solidarity that Randolph Trumbach claims was so central to the cognatic kindreds that formed the basis of English society as late as the Restoration.[5]

How misled have we been in our assessments of the importance of marriage in eighteenth-century England by our own diminished kin configurations and by the conjugal bias intrinsic to twentieth-century concepts of evidence and research methods? The statistical reconstitution studies made possible by the computer have been an exciting and imaginative innovation in the area of demographic history. But demographic data by their very nature perpetuate a conjugal bias in imagining family life, for they are drawn from public records of marriages and offspring, rather than recording the lines of connection among consanguineal siblings or between a woman and her affinal female relatives or any of the other filaments in the web of kinship that located people psychologically in the period. Because we cannot represent these other dimensions of affiliation with "hard data," they drop away in descriptions of family life.[6]

Lawrence Stone's misleading term "companionate marriage," still widely cited (at least by literary critics) despite its having been almost immediately discredited by historians in most of its particulars, has also contributed

---

residential configuration of family members, see Miranda Chaytor, "Household and Kinship: Ryton in the Late 16th and Early 17th centuries," *History Workshop* 10 (Autumn 1980), 25–60.

[5] Randolph Trumbach, *The Rise of the Egalitarian Family: Aristocratic Kinship and Domestic Relations in Eighteenth-Century England* (New York and London: Academic Press, 1978), pp. 19, 23, 31. A system of cognatic kindreds is bilateral insofar as the maternal line is as important as the paternal line in terms of inheritance and rank. As Lorraine Lancaster defines it in an excellent article on kinship in Anglo-Saxon England, "descent from ancestors and affiliation to a set of kinsmen may be traced through both females and males" (232). In such a system, only siblings have identical kin. See her "Kinship in Anglo-Saxon Society," *British Journal of Sociology* 9, 3 and 4 (1958), 230–50; 359–77.

[6] The reliability of information coming from parish records can also be overestimated. Christopher Hill, in his review of Lawrence Stone's *Family, Sex, and Marriage* (1977) and Peter Laslett's *Family Life and Illicit Love in Earlier Generations* (1977), makes the point that parish records can be highly unreliable and that there is no way of verifying them with alternative evidence. His example is Laslett's assertion that illegitimate births decreased suddenly in the 1640s and 1650s because fewer were registered. Although elsewhere in the same chapter Laslett shows that he is well aware that registration of births of all kinds collapsed in those years, he nevertheless draws the probably specious conclusion that the Puritans may have reduced the "amount of irregular intercourse in England during the 1650s . . . enforcing an unwonted chastity," an observation which Stone then repeats together with Laslett's graph of illegitimacy in these years as evidence of "Puritan control." *Economic History Review*, 2nd series, 31, 3 (August 1978), 452–4.

An appendix on "The Reliability of Parochial Registration and the Representativeness of Family Reconstitution" by David Levine at the end of his *Family Formation in an Age of Nascent Capitalism* (New York: Academic Press, 1977) explains some of the complexities of using parish records, including how out-migration is not recorded and the difficulty of identifying particular persons because of the repetition of given names in several branches and generations of the same family.

to this misapprehension.[7] Stone imagined "companionate marriage" as a paradigm shift in marital relations, an improvement in refined interpersonal relations and private emotional life, and an advance in the position of women in society. I do not wish to rehearse here all the anachronistic inaccuracies of his formulation but rather to unpack the concept – for which "privatized marriage" is a better shorthand – in its historical context.[8]

---

[7] Although English historians familiar with Stone's subject matter and the period criticized Stone's *The Family, Sex, and Marriage* severely when it first appeared (see n. 8 below), his Whig history of the family was so comfortingly familiar to his contemporaries that these early critiques did not register in the scholarly community. For a contemporary reading of Stone's late twentieth-century bias, see the chapter "Family History" in Nancy Armstrong and Leonard Tennenhouse, *The Imaginary Puritan: Literature, Intellectual Labor, and the Origins of Personal Life* (Berkeley: University of California Press, 1992), pp. 69–88.

[8] Lawrence Stone's *The Family, Sex, and Marriage in England 1500–1800* (New York: Harper and Row, 1977) is most frequently criticized for assuming that parents did not love their children until, in the phrase of Philippe Ariès, "the invention of childhood" in the seventeenth and eighteenth centuries. See Philippe Ariès, *L'Enfant et la vie familiale sous l'ancien regime* (Paris: Librairie Plon, 1960); as *Centuries of Childhood*, trans. Robert Baldick (London: Jonathan Cape, and New York: Random House, 1962).

Stone was also criticized for representing society generally before the eighteenth century as unduly loveless. He imagined life in Renaissance England as hostile and cold, and claimed that most people "found it difficult to establish close emotional ties to any other person. Children were neglected, brutally treated, and even killed: adults treated each other with suspicion and hostility; affect was low and hard to find" (99). In this nasty and brutish society, "hate seems to have been more prominent an emotion than love" (99), a state of affairs attributed by Stone to wet-nursing among the wealthy, tight swaddling, cruel discipline and punitive childrearing methods, the devastating mortality rate among infants, and the early death of parents. Applying post-Freudian assumptions to pre-Freudian culture, Stone pictures a society so traumatized by difficult physical conditions that its people were unable to bond. No one formed affective ties because death was so frequent, sudden, and inexplicable. The impermanence of attachment created personality types that resulted in non-nucleated families. Among the poorer classes, in Stone's analysis, children were simply more mouths to feed.

E. P. Thompson and Alan Macfarlane, among others, called attention to Stone's unreflective class bias, the notion that the family life of the "plebs" (Stone's word) was brutal, calculating, and animalistic until enlightened by the wisdom and sensibility that "seeped downward" (his metaphor) from the elite classes. In Thompson's review of Stone's book, he compares it to Edward Shorter's *The Making of the Modern Family*, published the previous year, which attributes the "new" affective relations in the modern family to "the liberated sexuality of the lads and lasses set free by the industrial revolution, and thence it works its way upwards to the benighted bourgeoisie." Thompson adds, "Stone's view is paternalist and Shorter's view is populist; we may make our choice according to temperament since neither view is supported by any relevant evidence." Calling the book a "curious, hit-or-miss affair" and a "disaster," Thompson notes Stone's errors: "Unless I have misread him, Stone appears to think that assizes were held four times a year: that the Dissenters had become 'conformist Unitarians' by 1720: that there was no radical feminist movement between the time of Mary Wollstonecraft and the 20th century (and that Hannah More was a feminist); and that the system of sinecures in church and state for the sons of the rich did not come under attack until after 1850; and that in 'the early 19th century' parents in Bethnal Green succeeded in hiring out their children for labour for sums . . . well in excess of the wages of skilled artisans." *New Society*, September 8, 1977, 499–501.

Alan Macfarlane also disputed Stone's association of sentiment with demography – the belief that domestic affection was impossible when mortality rates were high and life insecure – as well as his assertion that romantic love did not exist in England until people learned about it from reading novels. Macfarlane charges Stone with ignoring "one of the finest literary traditions attesting to love and

Stone invented his term to refer to a new requirement for compatibility in those marriages voluntarily entered into by men and women who,
in the eighteenth century, began to choose their mates for their "personal
qualities." According to this formulation, the expectation of "emotional satisfaction" had "its effect in equalizing relationships between husband and
wife" (325). In other words, eighteenth-century spouses, having evolved
into modernity, adjusted their expectations of the marital relationship to
include lifelong friendship. Stone's evidence that eighteenth-century men
married women for their companionability comes, in part, from conduct
books such as those written by John Gregory or Thomas Gisborne, who
encouraged women's self-education by holding out the possibility of intelligent conversation with their husbands as the reward for intellectual
application. "By the end of the eighteenth century," Stone claims,

a consensus was emerging about the ideal education for women from the landed
classes and from the higher ranks of the bourgeoisie. She was neither the frivolous
party-going neglectful mother and possibly adulterous wife of the aristocracy, nor
the middle-class intellectual blue-stocking who challenged and threatened men on
their own ground of the classics. She was a well-informed and motivated woman
with the educational training and internalized desire to devote her life partly to
pleasing her husband and providing him with friendship and intelligent compan-
ionship, partly to the efficient supervision of servants and domestic arrangements;
and partly to educating her children in ways appropriate for their future. (358)

This rather 1950s-ish description of a woman's place in the world – an
image of the upper-middle-class Anglo-American woman before women's

affection that the world has ever produced," including "medieval love poetry and Chaucer, through
the Elizabethan sonnets, Shakespeare, Donne and the metaphysical poets, to Restoration drama and
poetry." *History and Theory*, 18 (1979), 103–26. See also Christopher Hill's review in *Economic History
Review*.

In addition to this class bias, a male point of view dominates Stone's ahistorical Whig celebration
of the late twentieth-century nuclear family. When Stone says "family," he usually means fathers
and their sons. There is little awareness of women as sisters or daughters – as anything other than
wives – and nor are men portrayed as brothers, uncles, or sons with maternal relatives. Stone does not
say anything about women's work and traditional occupations, for instance, nor about how nascent
capitalism changed the range of occupations open to women.

In her review of Stone's book, Lois Schwoerer observes that there were loving marriages in England
long before the eighteenth century, and that Stone's treatment of sexuality omits women's attitudes
and conduct. In claiming a pattern of sexual toleration and even license from 1670 to 1800, he fails to
explain why women's age at marriage rose in the late seventeenth century while family size remained
constant; why illegitimate births rose little until the last third of the eighteenth century; and why the
number of spinsters increased 24 percent in the late seventeenth century and then again at the end
of the eighteenth century. See Lois Schwoerer, "Seventeenth-Century English Women Engraved in
Stone?" *Albion* 16 (Winter 1984), 389–403. Eileen Spring also makes some of these points in "Law
and the Theory of the Affective Family," *Albion* 16 (Spring 1984), 1–20. To this critique I would add
that Stone's account also does not explain the increasing repressive containment in women's attitudes
towards their own sexuality apparent when comparing the writings of Aphra Behn and Delarivier
Manley to most later eighteenth-century women writers.

liberation ruined her attitude – never takes into account what a woman might do, or who she might be, if she did not marry. Nor does it imagine the lives of married people in rural or urban settings where both partners labored. Stone's male-centered fantasy assumes that educating women to be companions for men was the best thing that ever happened to them. As Stone posits the new marriage bargain, women of the landed gentry geared their lives to "being there" as attentive wives and loving mothers for their families in exchange for being less subordinated to patriarchal domination – if you can call that being less subordinated.

There is a truth buried in Stone's misleading description of marriage in this period, but it is a very different truth from the one that Stone asserts and that many of his readers accept. The new idealization of marriage as a relationship based on "a union of hearts, the secret propensity of the soul, which draws you towards the object beloved, that mutual confidence, that certainly there is a person in the world, who would not wish to live but for your sake, and who would do any thing to prevent you from a moment's disquiet," as a novel of 1777 expressed it,[9] evolved at the same time as forces were transforming the nature of English families and the balance of primary loyalties within them. The weakening of consanguineal ties, the dispersion of communities, and the growing power of individualism – manifest in a range of legal, economic, and cultural signs – repositioned women with respect to their families of origin, leaving them more dependent than ever before on the goodwill of their husbands. Women, as I have remarked earlier, lost power as sisters and daughters in this new dispensation, as they gained social importance as mothers and wives.

Capitalism was redrawing the social map of England. The old hierarchies of wealth and power had already given way to new ones during the civil war and had to be renegotiated in 1688. New fortunes were being made in commercial ventures in the East and West Indies. Men without rank or family distinguished themselves in naval skirmishes protecting these ventures on the high seas. Old fortunes were being invested in land and industry or being dissipated in gambling and a sophisticated consumerism made possible by the costly goods imported from all over the world. The productivity of the nation as a whole was proudly touted as once Englishmen had boasted of the wealth of their aristocrats. To be engaged in business was less and less a social disgrace and the civic-minded took pride in the expansion of trade. As Voltaire wrote in 1733,

[9] Lady Mary Hamilton, *Memoirs of the Marchioness de Louvoi*, 3 vols. (London, 1777), vol. 1, p. 45.

Commerce, which has enriched English citizens, has helped to make them free, and this freedom in its turn has extended commerce, and that has made the greatness of the nation. Commerce has gradually established the naval forces thanks to which the English are masters of the sea . . . Posterity will perhaps learn with surprise that a small island which has no resources of its own except a little lead, some tin, some fuller's earth and coarse wool has through its commerce become powerful enough to send, in 1723, at one and the same time, three fleets to three extremities of the world, one before Gibraltar, conquered and held by its forces, another to Porto-Bello to cut off the treasures of the Indies from the King of Spain, and the third into the Baltic to prevent the Northern Powers from fighting.[10]

The citizenry performing these world-changing feats were themselves being changed by the escalating production for new military and colonial markets. It was an age of great social mobility and class instability; wealth was being accumulated on a whole new scale by merchants and tradesmen while cottagers and landless laborers were being impoverished – also on a whole new scale. In this newly fluid context, marriage was the linchpin of a system that transferred the sexual, social, productive, and reproductive services of women – as well as the wealth of their fathers – from their consanguineal families to their new conjugal families; matrimonial bliss was supposed to provide the glue to make that transfer stick.

Romantic love-in-marriage as an ideal developed in English culture as women were increasingly isolated from their consanguineal kin and the communities of their youth. In the fiction of the day characters wailed their dismay at their vulnerability to the absolute authority of the men they married. As Richardson's rational heroine Clarissa recognized, it meant that a woman had:

to give up her very name, as a mark of her becoming his absolute and dependent property: to be obliged to prefer this strange man to father, mother – to everybody: and his humours to all her own . . . to go no-whither: to make acquaintance: to give up acquaintance – to renounce even the strictest friendships perhaps; all at his pleasure, whether she think it reasonable to do so or not.[11]

The invisible bonds of love came increasingly to be substituted for the social expectations of wives in earlier times: a husband's love came to be a woman's only protection and her only law. The newly privatized marriage – privatized in the sense of private ownership as well as seclusion in domestic

---

[10] Letter 10, "On Commerce," from *Letters on the English Nation*, trans. with an Introduction by Leonard Tancock (Harmondsworth: Penguin, 1980), p. 51. Voltaire published these letters in 1733, long after he had returned to Paris from England.

[11] Samuel Richardson, *Clarissa* (1747–8), ed. Angus Ross (London: Penguin, 1985), pp. 148–9. Subsequent page references are to this edition.

space – detached a woman from her family of origin and from her pre-existing friendships and concerns in order to put her at the service of being a companion to her new husband. Dudley Ryder understood that these were the terms of the agreement when he recorded in his diary a "strong inclination" towards marriage "not from any principle of lust or desire to enjoy a woman in bed" but because "it ravishes me to think of a pretty creature concerned in me, being my most intimate friend, constant companion and always ready to soothe me, take care of me and caress me."[12]

The ideology of romantic marriage served to de-legitimate earlier pragmatic motives for marriage such as providing care for orphaned infants, young children, or aging parents; prudent management of households; the addition of new wealth or property; avoiding sin; the production of new progeny. It substituted for these the newer motives of love, physical attraction, and personal compatibility. In America, in Massachusetts, for example, none of the petitions for divorce filed between 1736 and 1765 considered lack of conjugal affection as a sufficient cause for divorce. But later in the century, between 1766 and 1785, one-tenth of the divorce cases in Massachusetts cited loss of conjugal affection as one of the significant grounds for divorce.[13]

Privatized marriage put women increasingly in the power of their husbands as if marriage had the alchemical effect of transforming them into property at the same time as it made over the property that they owned to their new masters. One senses this change when comparing the literary representation of Moll Flanders, the creation of an earlier sensibility, always her own person no matter whom she marries, with that of Pamela – whose last name, symptomatically, we never think to use – and who is valued not only for her beautiful face and shape but for her moral and intellectual agency in reforming Mr. B. Marriage made them dependent on "companionate" affection rather than on their entitlements as members of consanguineal families.[14] Even the community pressure that had traditionally balanced the

---

[12] *The Diary of Dudley Ryder*, ed. William Matthews (London: Methuen, 1939), pp. 309–10, entry dated Thursday, August 30, 1716.

[13] Nancy Cott, "Eighteenth-Century Family and Social Life Revealed in Massachusetts Divorce Records," *Journal of Social History* 10 (1976), 20–43, referred to in Rosemary O'Day, *The Family and Family Relationships, 1500–1900: England, France, and the United States of America* (Basingstoke: Macmillan, 1994), p. 155.

[14] In an article distinguishing between two kinds of love represented by Samuel Richardson's hero in *Sir Charles Grandison*, Wendy Jones retains Stone's phrase while utterly redefining his meaning. In "The Dialectic of Love in *Sir Charles Grandison*," *Eighteenth-Century Fiction* 8, 1 (October 1995), 15–34, Jones classifies Grandison's love for Harriet Byron, the marriageable Englishwoman, as the kind of love required for middle-class "companionate marriage," and different from the kind of love he felt for the aristocratic Clementina, the romantic Italian heroine. According to this writer,

inequalities of husbands' and wives' power within marriage dissipated at the threshold of these new private arrangements. Privatized marriage turned women's expectations of life's customary pleasures into men's *noblesse oblige*.

THE DISCOURSE OF WIVES' SUBSERVIENCE

These trends were underway by the turn of the seventeenth into the eighteenth century, and were made all the more perceptible by a chorus of women's voices in the new printed media of the period. The note of alarm that Mary Astell sounded at the beginning of the century in *Some Reflections upon Marriage* (1700), warning women that marriage limited their autonomy and turned them into subjects of an absolute monarch, was picked up and echoed by other voices in the decades that followed. Astell cautioned that marriage turned free women into slaves – or at least upper servants – and that if they voluntarily gave up their freedom and entered into marriage they would have little recourse against tyrannical husbands. Mary, Lady Chudleigh repeated and embellished this caution in her 1703 poem, "To the Ladies": "Wife and Servant are the same, / But only differ in the Name" she wrote.

> When she the word *obey* has said,
> And man by Law supreme has made,
> Then all that's kind is laid aside,
> And Nothing left but State and Pride:
> Fierce as an Eastern Prince he grows,
> And all his innate Rigor shows:
> Then but to look, to laugh, or speak,
> Will the Nuptial Contract break.
> Like Mutes she Signs alone must make,
> And never any Freedom take:
> But still be govern'd by a Nod,
> And fear her Husband as her God[15]

"companionate love" provided a "rational basis" for marriage, entailing prudence and judgment rather than "blindly impulsive romantic attraction and purely physical desire" (16). This reversal of Stone's thesis dovetails with the view of middle-class marriage offered in Leonore Davidoff and Catherine Hall's *Family Fortunes: Men and Women of the English Middle Class, 1780–1850* (Chicago: University of Chicago Press, 1987), which shows middle-class families functioning as economic units in the new cash economy, facilitating capital accumulation and prudent investment while forging a new gendered identity that opposed the feminized home to the masculinized marketplace.

[15] This poem was included in *Poems on Several Occasions* (London, 1703) and is now available online in the Brown University project on Women Writers in English or in *The Poems and Prose of Mary, Lady Chudleigh*, ed. Margaret J. M. Ezell (New York: Oxford University Press, 1993), pp. 83–4. See also Lady Chudleigh's *The Ladies Defence: or, The Bride-Woman's Counsellor Answer'd* (London,

Class hierarchy, foreign despotism, and religious absolutism are all summoned to express the sense of crushing power husbands had over their "mute" wives, who forbidden "to look, to laugh, or speak" without permission once the nuptial contract was signed. Strong-willed Roxana in Defoe's *Roxana, or The Fortunate Mistress* (1724) similarly resisted marriage on the grounds that it turned women into "upper servants" and "slaves". Astell's feminist sentiments lingered in Defoe's imagination from the first decade of the eighteenth century and his protagonist ventriloquized them. His Roxana added that what made matters even worse was the pretence of affection, which took "from a Woman every thing that can be call'd *herself*; she is to have no Interest; no Aim; no View; but all is the Interest, Aim, and View of the Husband."[16] Thus, although the degree of control a husband exerted over his wife may not actually have been greater in the eighteenth century than during the early seventeenth century or the Restoration, the addition of the woman's point of view on the subject, whether in fiction or expository treatises, imparted to the discourse on marriage a new sense of crisis and individual suffering.

In the real world, of course, Roxana's reasons for resisting matrimony, however appealing on the pages of a novel, were untenable for respectable women who found themselves forced to accept its limitations, *faute de mieux*. By the 1730s, the feminist rhetoric introduced by Astell, Chudleigh, and Defoe's Roxana had begun to modulate into bitter resignation about the inescapable implications of marriage for women. The author of *The Hardships of the English Laws in Relation to Wives* (1735) takes a hard look at the institution and concludes that "Wives have no Property, neither in their *own Persons, Children* or *Fortunes*" and that they "may be made Prisoners for Life at the Discretion of their *Domestick Governors*, whose Power, as we at present apprehend, bears no Manner of Proportion to that Degree of Authority, which is vested in any other Set of Men in *England*" (6–7).[17]

1701), another feminist poem (in four voices) about tyrannical husbands and women's right to an autonomous life of the mind.

[16] Daniel Defoe, *Roxana: The Fortunate Mistress*, ed. David Blewett (Harmondsworth: Penguin, 1982), pp. 187–9, quote p. 189. The Introduction to this edition by David Blewett calls attention to the historical sources of the heroine's feminist sentiments.

[17] *The Hardships of the English Laws in Relation to Wives* (London: Bowyer, 1735). This tract was written by Sarah Chapone, who was a friend of Elizabeth Elstob (who knew Mary Astell), George Ballard, and Samuel Richardson. Anna Hopkins, writing to George Ballard on December 14, 1741, says of Sarah Chapone, who was apparently about to lend her copy of Mary Astell's *A Serious Proposal to the Ladies* (1694) to him: "tho' I knew that she was the Author of Hardships of English Laws &c.: I did not mention it to you because I thought it was a Secret." Ballard MSS 43:106 in the Bodleian Library. I am grateful to the late Janice Thaddeus for this reference. For information on Sarah Chapone, see my Introduction to George Ballard's *Memoirs of Several Ladies of Great Britain* (1752), ed. Ruth Perry (Detroit: Wayne State University Press, 1984), pp. 21, 23, 36–7, 40–3.

This tract retails horrific stories of husbands who beat their wives, confined them to attics or to country houses, who kicked or kissed them out of their money – both inherited fortunes and earned wages – sometimes to spend it on other women. One of the more sensational of these stories is about Mr. Vezey, tried at the Old Bailey,

where it was proved that he confined his Wife for some Years in a Garret, without Fire, proper Cloathing, or any of the Comforts of Life; that he had frequently Horse-wipt her; that her Sufferings were so great and intolerable, that she destroyed her wretched Life by flinging herself out at the Window.

But as there was Bread found in the Room, which, though hard and mouldy, was supposed sufficient to sustain Life; and as it was not thought that he pushed her out of the Window himself, he was acquitted, and that Complaint of her Sufferings served only to instruct Husbands in the full Extent of their despotick Power. (10–11)

The author of *The Hardships of the English Laws in Relation to Wives* believed that married women in England were worse off, legally speaking, than captives in other societies. In Portugal, she asserted, a wife had the power to dispose of half her husband's property by will, even if she brought none of it into the marriage; "whereas a Woman by our Laws alienates all her own Property so entirely by Marriage, that if she brought an hundred thousand Pounds in Money, she cannot bequeath one single Penny, even if she left her own nearest and dearest Relations starving for Want" (31). Another pamphlet, the anonymous *The Present State of Matrimony* (1739), asserted that in England "we pay the greatest Deference to the Ladies of any Place in the World before Marriage, and the least after, of any People who allow Women to be born free, as well as men."[18]

Although, strictly speaking, husbands may have always had this degree of legal power over their wives, its exercise had usually been balanced by the surveillance of a community that had known a woman from her childhood and included relatives from both her mother's and her father's side. In a less anonymous world, a woman retained her identity as a daughter, sister, and cousin; she could call on her male relatives, her father and brothers, to defend her interests with an overbearing spouse. Although such protection was occasionally forthcoming later in the eighteenth century – witness the manner in which Sarah Scott was rescued from her unhappy marriage by

[18] "Philogamus," *The Present State of Matrimony: or, The Real Causes of Conjugal Infidelity and Unhappy Marriage* (London, 1739), pp. 53–4. In addition to the two tracts in the 1730s mentioned here, see Gerald MacLean's discussion of the Sophia pamphlets (1739) in his edition of François Poullain de La Barre, *The Woman as Good as the Man* (Detroit: Wayne State University Press, 1988), pp. 26–30.

her father and brothers[19] – such "interference" became more unusual as the century wore on. More frequent were anecdotes like the cautionary tale in *Hardships of the English Laws in Relation to Wives*, in which a clergyman brother was helpless to protect his abused sister from her implacable husband. Although she sought sanctuary with her brother, her husband insisted that she return to the marital abode even though she had a high fever. She was carried back against her will, where he "treated her with greater Harshness, which gave her, her *Coup de Grace* in less than a Month; when she left her Sufferings to be avenged by Heaven, though they were disregarded by Men, from whom she could find no Redress, her Husband never having beaten her, nor threatened her Life, though he took all other Methods to break her Heart" (9). Margaret Hunt gives similarly violent cases from the London Consistory Court clerk's books for 1711–13 in which husbands beat, kicked, starved, and cursed their wives because, among other things, their wives' families had not paid the portions they expected or because they would not advance money or stand surety for loans. Thus, "the wife stood in real danger of becoming a hostage to her husband's financial expectations."[20] Such stories are the consequence of unbalanced power in privatized marriage, the other side of the coin of a wife's dependence on her husband's love.

PUBLIC MARRIAGE

Marriage – both the ceremony and the institution – had been a more public affair in the seventeenth century (at least from the Restoration until the late 1730s), celebrated by the larger community and not just by the principals and their families. In custom and in lore it was treated less sacramentally and more bawdily than it came to be treated later. A betrothal or a spousal – the exchange of vows between two people with or without witnesses – was commonly understood to constitute a legal marriage, especially if consummated by sexual intercourse. Ecclesiastical courts usually upheld such unions as genuine. Since such an exchange would not have happened between strangers, but would have been marked and understood

---

[19] See my discussion of this in Chapter 4, "Brotherly Love in Life and Literature," pp. 185–6. According to Betty Rizzo's Introduction to Sarah Scott's *The History of Sir George Ellison* (1766), ed. Betty Rizzo (Lexington: University of Kentucky Press, 1996), the involvement of Sarah Scott's father and brother, the Robinson males, in extricating her from her brief, unhappy marriage to George Scott rendered the separation swift, clean, and respectable – and hence almost unique among marriage separations (xv).

[20] Margaret Hunt, *The Middling Sort: Commerce, Gender, and the Family in England, 1680–1780* (Berkeley: University of California Press, 1996), pp. 153–5, quote p. 154.

by peers and relatives every step of the way, this system made sense in its social context. In 1686 the learned juridical writer Henry Swinburne wrote:

there is no difference in Substance betwixt Spousals . . . and Matrimony . . . But in *foro conscientiae* they are as much Man and Wife, as if all Legal Requisites and Solemnities had been performed. Nay, as to some Legal Effects also, a Contract *de praesenti* has the same force that a lawful *Marriage* has; for the Contract is indissoluble so long as the Parties live; and if either Party shall after such Contract attempt to marry elsewhere, that Marriage is null and void.[21]

Thus a promise of marriage could be as good as a marriage ceremony, at least within the laboring class, and recognized as such by canon law. This was especially important to women who gave their sexual favors to men who promised to marry them or who assured them they were married in the eyes of God, for when such a connection proved fruitful the ecclesiastical courts safeguarded a woman's legal rights to the man's support of their child.

Traditionally, couples made their promises to each other and their families and then at some later date ratified their decision with a big public display that involved ritual participation by the larger kin group, age-mates, and neighbors. According to John Gillis, an historian of marriage, "the church service . . . was the least important part" of these big, public weddings.[22] Ritual acts and folk customs were significant in the larger sociological scheme of things because they symbolically recognized and tried to reconcile tensions within kin groups and communities caused by the creation of this new family. Among commoners and laborers, unmarried siblings (whose own chances of marriage were lessened by the drain on family resources from the wedding at hand) danced in their stockinged feet in a hog's trough to signify their loss. Age-mates of the bride and groom were treated with drink and favors, such as ribbons or gloves, to symbolically allay their presumed jealousy. Former lovers were teased and sometimes made to pay ritual fines to exorcise and propitiate their feelings. Parents, giving up their daughters and everything they had provided for them, conveyed their daughters' possessions ceremoniously through the streets in a decorated wagon called a bridewain. Sometimes a groom and

---

[21] Henry Swinburne, *A Treatise of Spousals, or Matrimonial Contracts* (London, 1686; rpt. New York: Garland, 1985), quote from "To the Reader."

[22] John R. Gillis, *For Better, for Worse: British Marriages, 1600 to the Present* (New York: Oxford University Press, 1985), p. 62. I am indebted to Gillis for the account that follows of the folk customs connected to marriage in early modern England. See also his "Peasant, Plebian, and Proletarian Marriage in Britain, 1600–1900," in David Levine (ed.), *Proletarianization and Family History* (New York: Academic Press, 1984), pp. 129–62.

his most trusted companions would "break into" the bride's house and ritually steal the bride, who, in Wales, might be disguised as an old woman. A bride might take up the keys or a broom or fire tongs to symbolize her new responsibilities as well as her privileges. When the ceremony was over, the church door might be barred until the groom paid a ransom to have it opened. Sometimes neighbors pelted the couple as they left the church with shoes or other available missiles. Usually the families of the wedding party provided a feast for the community as part of the celebration; sometimes the wealthy local landed family provided it. Money was frequently collected – it was called a bidding – to provide the new couple with a nest egg. Sometimes neighbors raised a "one night" sod house, a squatter's cottage on the common, for the newlyweds. In other words, all those who had a stake in the event – age-mates, unmarried siblings, neighbors, parents, relatives, family friends – were recognized by ritual acts and gifts and public ceremonies whose social purpose was to dissipate bad feeling and validate the union.

Individual desires were rarely distinguished from the good of the community in seventeenth-century conceptions of marriage. Not until 1705, with the publication of William Fleetwood's *The Relative Duties of Parents and Children, Husbands and Wives, Masters and Servants*, did an established moralist of family life suggest that children had a right to disobey their parents' injunctions to marry where they had an aversion, and even then their resistance was justified only when corroborated by local public opinion. Fleetwood wrote: "[I]f the Parent offer what the Child cannot possibly assent to, and what the Neighborhood, and wise and unconcerned Persons blame, condemn, and reject, upon a competent and reasonable information of the whole Proceedings; if such refusal of the offer be made with decency, and great humility, upon the Childrens part, it will not fall under the head of sinful Disobedience" (56).[23] This was a departure from the conventional wisdom that children, who belonged to their parents, ought to obey them in all things, including marriage. It was assumed that, if they did their duty,

[23] This 1705 tract on domestic responsibility is available in a 1985 Garland facsimile reprint. David Blewett first called my attention to Fleetwood's attitude towards arranged marriages and his importance as one of the first moralists to defend children's right to choose a marriage partner. According to Blewett, Fleetwood, appointed Bishop of Ely later in life, was Anglican and Whig: "a staunch supporter of the Revolution [1688] and later of the Hanoverian succession, and a latitudinarian friend of the dissenters" (81). A moderate politically and religiously, he was "a favorite of Queen Anne, who protected him in spite of his ardent Whiggism," and "frequently appointed [him] to preach on state occasions before both the royal family and the houses of Parliament" (81). David Blewett, "Changing Attitudes toward Marriage in the Time of Defoe: The Case of Moll Flanders," *Huntington Library Quarterly* 44, 2 (Spring 1981), 77–88.

love would follow in due course. After surveying didactic writers of the seventeenth century on the question of disposing of marriageable children, David Blewett asserts that "no seventeenth-century moralist would have maintained that the presence or absence of mutual affection was by itself a reason for marrying or not." Not until the end of the seventeenth century was romantic love thought to be a necessary ingredient of a successful marriage.[24]

In 1712, Lady Mary Wortley Montagu (at that time Pierrepont) wrote a letter to her father asking him to desist from plans to marry her to a man she hated. "I said every thing . . . I thought proper to move him, and proffer'd in attonement [sic] for not marrying whom he would, never to marry at all." Her father, greatly displeased with her resistance, told her that if she did not marry where he wished, he would never entertain another offer for her. He also suggested that she consult her "nearest relations" about the matter – which she did, although with no positive result. "I was surpriz'd at their blameing it to the greatest degree," she continued. "I was told they were sorry I would ruin my self, but if I was so unreasonable they could not blame my F[ather] whatever he inflicted on me." She told these relations – presumably her brother, sister, aunts, and uncles – that she did not love the man intended for her. "They made answer they found no Necessity of Loveing" and added that very few women were in love with their husbands but that many were perfectly happy. "They look'd upon me as a little Romantic," she added; nor could she expect any protection from them.[25] In the end, she eloped with Wortley, in a sequence that she compared, years later, to the family pressure on Clarissa and her subsequent flight in Richardson's novel.[26]

Men and women in Lady Mary's social class met at gatherings in one another's houses, and at plays, operas, and the like. Young persons of the lower orders generally met one another at holiday dances, hiring fairs, festivals, wakes, and so on. After this public beginning, courtship – in all classes – often proceeded through emissaries who were friends of the principals rather than in the persons of the principals themselves. Their families often knew one another; indeed, had sometimes arranged the meeting. By the time a couple decided to marry, the pros and cons of the match including the financial terms had been thoroughly discussed by their friends, family, and neighbors. Marriage thus involved what has been called the "multilateral

---

[24] David Blewett, "Changing Attitudes toward Marriage in the Time of Defoe," 80–1.
[25] *The Complete Letters of Lady Mary Wortley Montagu*, ed. Robert Halsband, 3 vols. (Oxford: Clarendon Press, 1967), vol. I, pp. 133–4.
[26] *Ibid.*, vol. III, p. 90.

consent" of everyone involved rather than being a privatized decision by the two young principals.[27] Social recognition bound the couple together, and the community was licensed to intervene after the wedding as well – as in cases of adultery or wife-beating, for example. The massive change in social context, owing to the staggering population growth, geographical and class mobility, and urbanization, was as important as any changes in marriage law or custom. By the end of the eighteenth century one-third of the population lived in towns and cities with anonymous social relations, rather than in face-to-face communities. As Keith Wrightson concludes in his study of kinship in Terling, Essex 1550–1700: "It is perhaps to changes affecting the quality of neighbourly relations, rather than to the enduring structures of family and kinship, that we must look for the key to social change in this period."[28]

PRIVATIZED MARRIAGE

The tremendous increase in private marriages by license in preference to a public calling of banns in church, and the further commodification of such private marriages by the so-called lawless churches trading in clandestine marriage, is also evidence of the privatization of marriage in England. Baptisms and burials, too, became quieter, smaller, more private family affairs as the century wore on.[29] Marrying privately, with only chosen witnesses present and in a quieter and less public place than one's local parish church, had grown as a practice since the fraying of church authority during the

[27] The phrase "multilateral consent" is from David Levine and Keith Wrightson, *The Making of an Industrial Society: Whickham 1560–1765* (Oxford: Clarendon Press, 1991), p. 309.

[28] Keith Wrightson, "Kinship in an English Village: Terling, Essex 1550–1700," in *Land, Kinship and Life-Cycle*, ed. Richard M. Smith (Cambridge: Cambridge University Press, 1984), pp. 313–32, quote p. 332.

[29] See Richard Grassby, *Kinship and Capitalism: Marriage, Family and Business in the English-Speaking World, 1580–1740* (Cambridge: Cambridge University Press, and Washington, DC: Woodrow Wilson Center Press, 2001), p. 260.

In Keith Wrightson and David Levine's book on Whickham in Northumberland, the authors note some changes in burial customs after 1580 that illustrate the dispersion of community and the privatization of family functions. Sums set aside for distribution to the poor at funerals, although increasing in the 1590s, were being phased out of the ritual by the late seventeenth century. A private family dinner came to substitute for the "forthbringing among neighbors," an open house with food and drink for all comers supplied by the family of the person who died, common in the sixteenth century. By the mid-seventeenth century, Wrightson says, "that ritual of inclusion was dead." And finally, testators in the course of the seventeenth century stopped specifying the manner and place of their funerals in their wills, but left the details of burying to their executors. As Wrightson summarizes: "the apparent insouciance and relative privacy that came to characterize the wills and funerals of the Augustan parishioners would have been scarcely intelligible" to the inhabitants of Whickham of 1580. *The Making of an Industrial Society: Whickham 1560–1765*, pp. 341–3.

Interregnum. But even after the Restoration, private marriage continued to be enormously popular. According to one historian, clandestine marriages "reached epidemic proportions in the post-Restoration period, 1670–95, and again in the first half of the eighteenth century."[30] So many couples were evading public marriage by banns, and doing it even more cheaply than marrying by license (which could cost twice as much as a banns wedding) by choosing to be married in those churches exempt from ecclesiastical jurisdiction, that clandestine marriage became a serious problem, especially in London. Preventive legislation was proposed in 1690, culminating in the Marriage Duty Act of 1694 which penalized those who either conducted or participated in clandestine marriages and thus escaped paying the marriage duty.

There were many good reasons for marrying privately, in addition to the growing distaste for exposing one's private life to the unseemly scrutiny of the neighborhood. Many wished to avoid big public weddings with their traditional built-in public embarrassments. Private weddings saved money on a public wedding feast and permitted the couple to retain control of their wedding plans. Some married privately to evade parental opposition or to shade from the public glare embarrassing truths about premarital pregnancy, second marriages, or great discrepancies in age between the two partners. Clandestine marriage was a way for people who were legally minors to marry; moreover it was charged that the secrecy of clandestine marriage made possible bigamous matches or marriage with prohibited kin. Religious non-conformists, as well as those who wanted to get married during prohibited times such as Advent and Lent, sometimes had recourse to the lawless churches.[31] But private marriage, as opposed to marriage by banns, was also becoming a status symbol, a way of emulating the "quality." Paying the fees in one of the so-called lawless churches was cheaper than buying a marriage license, which was how the wealthier classes avoided the publicity of reading banns aloud in the local parish church and the ribaldry of local wags. As a contemporary commentator wrote in 1697:

To proclaim Bans is a Thing no Body now cares to have done; very few are willing to have their Affairs declar'd to all the World in a publick Place, when for a Guinea

---

[30] Jeremy Boulton, "Clandestine Marriages in London: An Examination of a Neglected Urban Variable," *Urban History* 20, 2 (October 1993), 191–210; esp. 208–9. I am indebted to Boulton for most of what follows about clandestine marriages, both from this article and from his earlier "Itching after Private Marryings? Marriage Customs in Seventeenth-Century London," *London Journal* 16 (1991), 15–34.

[31] R. B. Outhwaite, *Clandestine Marriage in England* (Rio Grande, OH: Hambledon Press, 1995), pp. 54–7.

they may do it *Snug*, and without Noise; and my good Friends the Clergy, who find their Accounts in it, are not very zealous to prevent it. Thus then, they buy what they call a *License*, and are marry'd in their Closets, in Presence of a couple of Friends, that serve for Witnesses; and this ties them forever.[32]

Women's sexuality in the earlier, more public and communal context had been less of a burden, less a precious individual possession to be watched and hoarded than a capacity to be exercised and shared. As we have seen, sexual intercourse had often been a mark of marriage rather than its "reward." According to Gillis, in some places marriage was even the fitting consummation of pregnancy, rather than the other way around: "No Portland [Dorset] man would consider marrying a woman until she had shown signs of pregnancy," he writes, "a precaution common in other parts of Devon and elsewhere."[33] It is not that chastity was not considered a virtue in the centuries before the eighteenth. It is more that female sexuality was taken for granted, expected and accepted; it was not necessarily the most important bodily experience a woman could have. The self-conscious internalization of heterosexual penetration as the most important moment in a woman's life – *the* most significant *rite de passage* that turned a girl into a woman – was a thing of the future. In the late seventeenth and early eighteenth centuries, female adulthood was still being defined by work, property, and motherhood at least as much as by marriage or sex. The timing and sequence of marriage and sexual intercourse mattered less than it came to matter later.

This historical change in cultural attitudes towards sex and marriage was reflected in tonal changes in popular drama. Comedy on the Restoration stage had represented both men and women as maneuvering for their own sexual pleasure, with great lustiness and great irreverence for marriage. But by the early eighteenth century, these plots were being moralized in sentimental comedies where characters reformed at the end and renewed their vows of fidelity and chastity. Robert D. Hume has traced these changing attitudes towards marriage and its discontents in comedies produced on the London stage between 1660 and 1737. He has observed that in those years, the lighthearted endings tying up the threads of adultery and deception in Restoration plays gave way to more sober treatments of marriage which took the institution much more seriously.[34] A contemporary column

---

[32] Henri Misson, *M. Misson's Memoirs and Observations in His Travels over England*, trans. John Ozell (London: D. Browne, 1719), p. 183.

[33] John Gillis, "Peasant, Plebian, and Proletarian Marriage in Britain, 1600–1900," p. 141.

[34] Robert D. Hume, "Marital Discord in English Comedy from Dryden to Fielding," *Modern Philology* 74 (February 1977), 248–72. Several modern scholars, notably Ros Ballaster in *Seductive Forms:*

from the *Tatler* of 1710 makes the same point about the change in attitudes towards adultery and marriage between the Restoration and the early eighteenth century. "The theatre, in some late reigns, owed its chief support to those scenes which were written to put matrimony out of countenance, and render that state terrible," wrote the urbane commentator.

In the same column, the *Tatler* writer notes that a new legalism about the property arrangements of marriage coincided with this growing sentimentality about marriage. Quoting a member of his club who had practiced law for a long time as a conveyancer, he reports that the professional frequently remarked "that the marriage-settlements, which are now used, have grown fashionable even within his memory."[35] Sir William Temple, in the late seventeenth century, complaining that "our marriages are made, just like other common bargains and sales, by the meer consideration of interest or gain, without any of love or esteem," added that "this custom is of no ancient date in England." He said he could personally remember "within less than fifty years, the first noble families that married into the city for downright money."[36] Predictably – if ironically – the plots of popular drama reinforced the moral seriousness of marital commitment in the same historical period that the institution was increasingly being defined by lawyers and contractual arrangements. The greater importance of property – and the

---

Women's Amatory Fiction from 1684 to 1740 (Oxford: Clarendon Press, 1992), have made the point that female lewdness in turn-of-the-century fiction figured Whig corruption, which is to say that the immorality of the "private" or "personal" was used to figure the immorality of the "public." The point I am making here is a different one: by the mid-eighteenth century, the "private" was understood to have "public" ramifications.

[35] No. 199: Tuesday, July 18, 1710. See *The Tatler*, ed. Donald F. Bond, 3 vols. (Oxford: Oxford University Press, 1987), vol. III, p. 66. All subsequent page references to the *Tatler* are to this edition. This column and that of No. 223: Tuesday, September 12, 1710, are based on notes against mercenary marriage provided by Edward Wortley Montagu. He drew up these arguments against the practice of entailing estates on unborn heirs and substituting jointure for customary dower in marriage settlements when his own negotiations with Lord Dorchester, the father of Lady Mary Pierrepont, broke down on these points. As is well documented, the couple eventually eloped and married without benefit of lawyers. For the reference to Edward Wortley's part in these *Tatler* columns, see Robert Halsband, *The Life of Lady Mary Wortley Montagu* (Oxford: Clarendon Press, 1956), p. 15; and Isobel Grundy, *Lady Mary Wortley Montagu* (Oxford: Oxford University Press, 1999), p. 36. See also n. 40 below.

[36] "Of Popular Discontents," in *The Works of Sir William Temple*, 4 vols. (London: J. Clarke et al., 1757), vol. III, p. 61. This essay of Temple's was published posthumously but his biographers suggest that it was written shortly after his retirement in 1684–5. See Homer E. Woodbridge, *Sir William Temple, the Man and His Work* (New York and London: Oxford University Press, 1940), pp. 241, 248. Jonathan Swift's note to the first edition of the *Miscellanies* also observes that this essay was written many years before the author's death, which came in 1699. In response to this observation of Sir William Temple's, John Habakkuk remarks that there were, in fact, examples of marriages between indebted aristocrats and cash-rich daughters of wealthy merchants earlier in the seventeenth century. *Marriage, Debt, and the Estates System: English Landownership, 1650–1950* (Oxford: Clarendon Press, 1994), p. 194.

focus on marriage as a means of accruing and securing it – is undoubtedly part of the explanation for the new soberness in literary treatments of marriage.

One could even argue that literary treatments sentimentalizing marriage amounted to a kind of proof that this way of creating kin relationships was becoming too important to leave to common custom, without the benefit of legal regulation and official oversight. Sentimentalizing, as a literary device, occurs when the culture no longer *really* takes something seriously as a matter of sentiment – in this case marriage – and when the sentiment called for by the reader's response is unearned in the text. Sentimentality makes a spectacle of feeling while simultaneously witholding from the object of that feeling any real choice or agency, or indeed any subjectivity. Whenever something is sentimentalized, in short, it is either of no importance or else of too much importance to be left to irrational feeling. Because sentimentality ultimately debases and cheapens feeling, infusions of this cloying, hyperemotional attitude make one suspect that whatever is being sentimentalized is in actuality governed by rational, calculating motivation that is moving beyond the reach of feeling. In the astute words of one critic: "the rhetoric of sentiment may well become the crucial cover for social relations which are increasingly alienated and drained of emotional content."[37] Robert Markley's analysis of sentimentalism adds that it functioned to ennoble the man of feeling more than to actually change the conditions of the poor about whom the man of feeling felt sentimental and to whom he contributed his mite.[38] The cultural work of sentimentalism thus reaffirms existing relations of power while diffusing "good" feelings. Claudia Johnson, writing of later eighteenth-century sentimentalism, calls attention to the way sentimentalism was attached to an oppressive heterosexuality which celebrated and eroticized the vulnerability of women: "Under sentimentality, women's mental and physical deterioration functions ideologically to naturalize monoandry."[39]

These connections were intuited by the author of the *Tatler* column, who observed that at the same time as treatments of married love on stage sentimentalized the institution, a new emphasis on marriage settlements

---

[37] Gary Gautier, "Fanny Hill's Mapping of Sexuality, Female Identity, and Maternity," *Studies in English Literature* 35, 3 (Summer 1995), 473–91, quote 483.

[38] Robert Markley, "Sentimentality as Performance: Shaftesbury, Sterne, and the Theatrics of Virtue," in Felicity Nussbaum and Laura Brown (eds.), *The New Eighteenth Century: Theory, Politics, English Literature* (New York and London: Methuen, 1987), pp. 210–30.

[39] Claudia L. Johnson, *Equivocal Beings: Politics, Gender, and Sentimentality in the 1790s* (Chicago: University of Chicago Press, 1995), *passim* but particularly pp. 17, 61. Quote p. 61.

signaled that property interests were altering the meaning of marriage. He wrote:

That great Ill which has prevailed among us in these latter Ages, is the making even Beauty and Virtue the Purchase of Money. The Generality of Parents, and some of those of Quality, instead of looking out for introducing Health of Constitution, Frankness of Spirit, or Dignity of Countenance into their Families, lay out all their Thoughts upon finding out Matches for their Estates, and not their Children.[40]

Thus this contemporary commentator links the elements – if only by simple contiguity – that help us chart the change in cultural attitudes towards marriage: literary representations of sexuality in and out of marriage; a formalizing of legal contracts of marriage with the increased necessity for the expertise of lawyers; the central importance of property and its transfer as part of the arrangements of marriage. I have tried to organize this and the next chapter on marriage to examine the place of property and sexuality in marriage because I believe that in the conjunction of these elements can be found the historical explanation for the development of privatized marriage.

A revolution in the meaning of property – as well as in the means for distributing it within families – lies between Henry Swinburne's assertion in 1686 that a simple exchange of vows between unmarried individuals might constitute a valid if irregular marriage and the observation of a later social critic who, in summarizing the arguments of the parliamentary debates concerning the Hardwicke Marriage Act of 1753 – which redefined what constituted a legal marriage – observed that stricter, more legalistic attitudes about marriage already permeated the culture. "[I]f in *England* a Couple were to interchange Promises of perpetual Fidelity, Cohabitation, and good Offices ratified by the like Ceremony [i.e., jumping over a stick], and then going to Bed together, were gravely to expect to be called Husband and Wife by their Acquaintance," he wrote in 1753, referring to customs still practiced half a century before, "they would be looked upon as People out of their Wits."[41]

Marriage was becoming more than a matter of adjusting a new couple to a community and of exorcising the negative feelings of younger siblings, other relatives, former suitors, or neighbors to this new addition to their

---

[40] No. 199: Tuesday, July 18, 1710. See the *Tatler*, ed. Donald F. Bond, 3 vols. (Oxford: Oxford University Press, 1987), vol. III, pp. 65–6. This column was probably written by Richard Steele and Edward Wortley: see n. 35 and pp. 214–15 for the circumstances.

[41] Anon., *A Letter to the Public Containing the Substance of What Hath Been Offered in the Late Debates upon the Subject of the Act of Parliament, for the Better Preventing of Clandestine Marriages* (London, 1753; rpt. New York: Garland, 1985), p. 37.

midst – more, in short, than a matter of multilateral consent. Only in the laboring classes, where legitimacy and inheritance were less of an issue than they were among the propertied classes, did these earlier social functions of marriage persist. But wherever property was at stake, marriage was fast becoming a highly commercial game to be played for financial advantage. It was increasingly a central method for accumulating property – and not simply land or capital but also tools, techniques, social connections, and access to customers or to business partners. An analysis of the discursive conflation of marriage and executorship as social practices which distributed wealth and structured human relationships in Samuel Richardson's last two novels reveals a deep cultural assumption about how central property had become to the meaning of marriage.[42]

A comparison between the tone and treatment of the theme of sex with a wife's sister in Aphra Behn's *Love-Letters between a Nobleman and His Sister* (1684–7) and Eliza Haywood's *The Mercenary Lover: or, The Unfortunate Heiresses* (London, 1726) indicates just how much attitudes about money and marriage changed in that brief, formative period. In Behn's novel, Philander marries a woman he loves and then seduces her younger sister and determines to flee to the continent with her. Sexual love is his motive and the issue of transgressive sexual freedom dominates their letters. In Haywood's *The Mercenary Lover*, by contrast, the handsome Clitander decides to marry the younger of two co-heiresses when he sees that she prefers him to all other suitors. Although he appears a most indulgent husband, in truth he was a man incapable of being charmed by either mind or body.

Beauty, Virtue, or good Humour, he look'd on as Things indifferent, and not at all essential to the Happiness of Life, – Money was the only Darling of his mercenary Wishes. (12)

Next he sets about to seduce the other sister – the as yet unmarried Althea – who is a year older and more reserved. When she becomes pregnant, he makes sure that she wills her half of the estate to him; and then he poisons her. Although, like Behn's hero, he promotes transgressive love in his seduction line – maintaining "that the Ties of Blood or Affinity were but imaginary Bars to Love" (24) – his words are but a ruse disguising his real goal, which is her money. Clitander's cold-blooded facility and his single-minded venality create a villain impossible to imagine in earlier fiction. This shocking little novella seems evidence of a new fixation on money – and the possibility of feigning love as one way to get it.

---

[42] See Leah Price, "*Sir Charles Grandison* and the Executor's Hand," *Eighteenth-Century Fiction* 8, 3 (April 1996), 329–42.

ACCUMULATION (RATHER THAN DISTRIBUTION)
OF FAMILY RESOURCES

One sign and symptom of the growing importance of property to marriage was the complex change in the laws concerning property *within* a marriage as well as the laws that governed the passing of property to the offspring of a marriage, from one generation to another. In these legal changes one can see the family's economic function being redefined from being a redistributor of resources among a wider collateral community of consanguineal kin to being the means of channeling family resources, in a uni-directional flow, into swelling estates to be passed on lineally in the male line. Legal devices invented and new practices forged during the late seventeenth century consolidated the importance of lineal inheritance and undercut distribution. The Anglo-Saxon bilateral cognatic kinship system that marked English society until the Renaissance was not a system that facilitated lineal accumulation; new legal modifications were necessary to meet the new demands of mercantile capitalism.

Societies with unilineal descent patterns, by minimizing association with maternal kin and emphasizing the paternal lineage, develop clearly demarcated kin groups that can persist from generation to generation, collecting lore and stabilizing material wealth. But societies tracing relationships bilaterally do not retain structurally persistent consanguineal kin groups across generations. Each sibling group, both within and between generations, has a unique set of maternal and paternal relatives, like a set of overlapping circles, and hence configures its consanguineal kin group differently. Each set of cousins, whether within a generation or between generations, has affiliations with a different set of relatives. Marked by a dispersal of relationship, this system also disperses wealth and property rather than focusing and accumulating it.

Changes in the meaning and function of property under mercantile capitalism led to a legal restructuring of inheritance laws in the late seventeenth century to counteract the distributive effects of the earlier English bilateral cognatic kin system. One could even argue that marriage was being refigured in the priorities of kinship because the new economic system rewarded the consolidation and transfer of property across generations. That is, lineal configurations were increasingly privileged legally over collateral configurations of kin because the lineal system of inheritance reinforced accumulation of property within families and undercut distribution. Property was coming to be thought of not simply as the means to subsistence – or even maintenance, however grand. Property was fast becoming the primary means for getting ahead since investment capital was needed for most enterprises, from millinery to shipping. Property could now multiply itself, could make more property when concentrated in the hands of an enterprising son or nephew; property could even buy status in the form of a university education, intermarriage with the aristocracy, or titles.[43] Increasingly, a family was expected to get ahead by concentrating and using its property.

As we have seen, the effect of these legal innovations in marriage settlements of the late seventeenth century was to diminish the proportion of a family's resources that went to female offspring and younger sons in order to give at least the eldest son a stake in the new economy. The practice of primogeniture, originally followed only in the higher reaches of the aristocracy, was increasingly imitated by the gentry, merchants, artisans, and small farmers as a means of accumulating the capital now required for economic success. In his study of inheritance and property transmission in Preston between 1562 and 1702, Lloyd Bonfield confirms that this had not been a widespread family strategy in the earlier period, when wealth was distributed in such a way as to maximize "the opportunities of as many children as possible."[44]

This redistribution of family resources left women, in particular, with less access to capital than ever before and at a terrible disadvantage in the new economy. As we have seen, the rising figures for daughters' portions among the wealthier classes was a function of the overall increased size of estates – there was simply more and more money in circulation – although the *proportion* of a family's estate inherited by female offspring relative to their male siblings was actually decreasing. Furthermore, women rarely had direct access to this capital, which was usually left to their fathers or brothers in trust for them.[45] The substitution of jointure for widow's dower in marriage settlements, again frequently misconstrued as an improvement

---

[43] Clarissa remarks that her brother's fortune is potentially large enough to "give him such an interest as might entitle him to hope for a peerage. Nothing less would satisfy his ambition." Samuel Richardson, *Clarissa*, p. 77.

[44] Bonfield is here quoting Keith Wrightson's judgment of testamentary transfers in Essex and agreeing with him. See Lloyd Bonfield, "Normative Rules and Property Transmission: Reflections on the Link between Marriage and Inheritance in Early Modern England," in Lloyd Bonfield, Richard M. Smith, and Keith Wrightson (eds.), *The World We Have Gained: Histories of Population and Social Structure* (Oxford: Basil Blackwell, 1986), pp. 155–76, quote p. 175.

[45] This observation opposes Lawrence Stone's assertion in his *Family, Sex, and Marriage in England 1500–1800* that dowry amounts *increased* in the eighteenth century. Stone's evidence for dowry inflation is Habakkuk's venerable research about the changing ratio of dowry to jointure – which actually established that the price of husbands was going up insofar as heiresses were expected to bring larger and larger dowries into marriage while at the same time smaller and smaller jointures were being settled on them. H. J. Habakkuk, "Marriage Settlements in the Eighteenth Century,"

in married women's access to property, was almost always a diminution of what a married woman stood to gain from her dower rights.[46] The misreading of these economic signs has led to serious misunderstandings about the meaning of property and inheritance patterns for women – and hence the consequences of marriage for women.

The strict settlement, too, as we have seen, contributed to the focus on accumulation rather than distribution of a family's wealth. Although marriage settlements had been used from the sixteenth through the early eighteenth century to protect women's financial interests in marriage, by the early eighteenth century this legal device was being turned to a different use – to concentrate and entail property in the male line.[47] The significance of *her* land and money was that it enlarged *his* estate. According to Margaret Hunt: "In cash terms, marriage primarily benefited the groom or his natal family."[48] Even in the middle class, a man might expect his new in-laws to help out with business loans, job opportunities, introductions, or places to live.[49]

In 1710, Edward Wortley Montagu railed against entailing estates on as yet unborn heirs, a practice which he said was based in pride and folly and made it impossible to reward or punish children according to their deserts.[50] When his negotiations with Lady Mary Wortley Montagu's father

---

Transactions of the Royal Historical Society, 4th ser., 32 (1950), 15–30. Focusing on wives rather than widows or spinsters, Stone noted merely that the size of dowries was increasing, without registering the fact that the size of accumulated estates was increasing and that the *proportion* of those estates inherited by women as dowry was decreasing.

[46] Jointure was invariably less than the third to which a widow had always been entitled by common law. Susan Staves explains and documents this point about jointure and widows' dower rights in her indispensable *Married Women's Separate Property in England, 1660–1833* (Cambridge, MA: Harvard University Press, 1990), pp. 27–55. She also discusses "pin money" in this book, an allowance settled on married women to guarantee minimal maintenance as women's access to the joint assets of the conjugal couple diminished in practice.

[47] Amy Louise Erickson makes this point after examining an historical sequence of conveyancing handbooks as well as probate accounts filed in ecclesiastical courts and Chancery cases. If one looks at evidence from equity and ecclesiastical law rather than common law, she asserts, it is clear that "the wife's interest, and not entailment in the male line, was the primary purpose of a marriage settlement from the sixteenth through the first half of the eighteenth centuries" (27). These settlements were drawn up to protect the money that a woman brought into a marriage if, for example, it was more than the third she was entitled to at his death; they could stipulate that husbands paid the portions of a woman's children from a previous marriage; they could establish a fund for a woman's separate use. "Common Law versus Common Practice: The Use of Marriage Settlements in Early Modern England," *Economic History Review*, 2nd series, 43, 1 (1990), 21–39.

[48] Margaret Hunt, *The Middling Sort*, p. 164.   [49] *Ibid.*, p. 153.

[50] As it happens, it was fortunate – according to his lights – that he did not entail his estate on his ne'er-do-well oldest son, although he was fairly generous in his final bequest to this undeserving scamp. Still, the £1,000 a year that Wortley left Edward Wortley, Jr. was a pittance compared to the huge estate that he left his daughter and *her* son. Robert Halsband, *The Life of Lady Mary Wortley Montagu*, pp. 275–6.

broke down over the question of entail in their marriage settlement, he composed a diatribe on the topic that was subsequently mined for a column of the *Tatler*.[51] There he fulminated that clauses in contemporary marriage settlements entailing property on projected heirs really meant "I give to my First-born, be he perverse, ungrateful, impious, or cruel, the Lump and Bulk of my Estate, and leave one Year's Purchase only to each of my younger Children, whether they shall be brave or beautiful, modest or honourable" (III: 162). Signing a marriage settlement with an entail, he continued, was like agreeing to be thenceforth "dead in Law" – and he refused to do it. Lady Mary agreed with him: "I reckon it among the absurditys of custom that a Man must be oblig'd to settle his whole Estate on an eldest Son, beyond his power to recall, whatever he proves to be, and make himselfe unable to make happy a younger Child that may deserve to be so."[52] More than half a century later, Thomas Erskine was still blaming strict settlements for ruining family relations.

A modern settlement is admirably calculated to make a whole family miserable: the wife secure in her pin money and jointure has no object in pleasing her husband, and the children look up to the trustee instead of to the father . . . and to atone for these mischiefs, the indefeasible inheritance protected by cartloads of indentures, occasions by a destructive anticipation that very poverty it was intended to prevent.[53]

The focus on accumulating and passing on property perverted the emotional bonds within a family: the head of the family lost respect when divested of his right to give or withold family resources, and the eldest, inheriting son notoriously dissipated the family fortune if the estate came into his hands before he proved himself able to manage it prudently.

It is important to note that the psychological effect of inheritance practices that funneled property from both parents into ever-larger estates tended to reinforce loyalty to families constructed by marriage and undermined "investment" in those families one had been born into. In other words, this new material emphasis on lineal inheritance recalculated who counted, canceling obligations to consanguineal relatives – including children's responsibility for their parents and parents' responsibility for their daughters. Putting patrilineal conjugality at the center of kin definition also restricted the economic claims of certain important cognatic kindred – such

---

[51] See n. 35 and n. 40 above.

[52] *Complete Letters of Lady Mary Wortley Montagu*, ed. Robert Halsband, vol. I, p. 135.

[53] Anon. [Thomas Erskine], *Reflections on Gaming*, 2nd edn. (London, 1777), p. 15, quoted in John Habakkuk, *Marriage, Debt, and the Estates System*, p. 74.

as father's sisters or mother's brothers – retaining only those claims that were codified by law. Operating under a strict settlement, an eldest son would be required to pay his siblings' portions and his mother's jointure out of the estate he inherited; but that was the sum total of his legal responsibility. After that, his mother and his sisters were on their own; no one expected the kind of ongoing responsibility for family that had obtained in earlier times.

The examination of wills reinforces this sense of the historical narrowing of who counted as kin when it came to property in families of middling or lower classes. People in later periods designate fewer and fewer heirs, and increasingly limit bequests to their spouses and their children rather than to their consanguineal kin – brothers, sisters, uncles, etc. Analyzing the wills of Elizabethan parishioners in Whickham, Yorkshire, David Levine and Keith Wrightson note that most "were sensible of a somewhat broader set of kinship ties" and left legacies to kinsfolk "beyond their own nuclear families as tokens of affection and regard – to brothers or sisters, nephews or nieces, and very occasionally to more distant kin, or to godchildren, servants, or unrelated neighbors." They left advice and commendations as well as material property in these wills to the inhabitants of a "cluster of households linked by close ties of consanguinity and affinity and geographical proximity; that range of effective kin described in contemporary parlance as 'friends.'"[54] In his examination of inheritance in Terling, Essex, Keith Wrightson also observes after 1600 a decline in bequests to godchildren, to illegitimate children, and to grandchildren – a drawing in and focusing of family wealth.[55] Richard Smith implies that by the late seventeenth century adult children did not even necessarily take responsibility for their elderly parents, for he finds evidence in the parish records that such parents were receiving relief even though their adult children lived nearby.[56]

M. K. Ashby, in her detailed study of Bledington, Gloucestershire, finds a striking difference between the wills of the first and second part of the seventeenth century. "At first," she writes, "one is in a world of wide family connections and affections, a valuation of persons and also of objects, of goods: charitable bequests are frequent." But after 1675, the family designated in wills is "the immediate group of parents and children, charity is

---

[54] David Levine and Keith Wrightson, *The Making of an Industrial Society: Whickham 1560–1765*, pp. 284–90, quote p. 285. See especially p. 285 n. 27 for other studies of the degrees of kinship of those specified for bequests in wills.

[55] See Keith Wrightson, "Kinship in an English Village: Terling, Essex 1550–1700," pp. 313–32, esp. pp. 324–9.

[56] See Richard M. Smith, "Some Issues concerning Families and Their Property in Rural England 1250–1800," in Richard M. Smith (ed.), *Land, Kinship and Life-Cycle*, pp. 1–86, esp. p. 79.

absent and money is prominent and in larger amounts."[57] Donna Andrew, analyzing changes in attitudes towards charity, notes the growing suspicion of the impulse to leave money to good works rather than to one's heirs, a suspicion that eventually found legal expression in the Mortmain Act of 1736.[58] Judging from this patchy picture of seventeenth-century practices with regard to money, property, and inheritance, generational transfers had been effected on a fairly broad level earlier, with wealthier members of a family distributing their wealth at death, however sparsely and symbolically, through a wide web of collateral kin as well as to faithful servants and the worthy poor.

To repeat then: the shift from an economic system that redistributed resources among a kin corporation to one that accumulated property in the patrilineal line was reconfiguring the priorities of kinship. Marriage, as the key to the consolidation and transfer of property across generations, was fast becoming the crux of this new system of accumulation. This formulation opposes that of Lawrence Stone and his followers, who celebrate the shrinking of the family to its nuclear core because they claim that marriage was becoming less mercenary and based more on personal attraction between the marriage partners. I believe, on the contrary, that the privatization of marriage choice coincided with a more calculating attitude towards the economics of marriage.

LOVE-IN-MARRIAGE

How, then, is one to account for the insistent repetition everywhere in the culture – in plays, sermons, newspaper columns, and virtually every novel of the period – that only love could be the basis of a happy marriage? So much did marriages of choice become the standard good of fiction – usually posited in opposition to marriages arranged by parents – that Jane Austen satirized the formula in her juvenile parody of contemporary novels, *Love and Freindship*, written in 1790. In this youthful *jeu d'esprit*, she portrays a

---

[57] M. K. Ashby, *The Changing English Village: A History of Bledington, Gloucestershire, 1066–1914* (Kineton: Roundwood Press, 1974), pp. 163–4.

[58] Donna T. Andrew, *Philanthropy and Police: London Charity in the Eighteenth Century* (Princeton, NJ: Princeton University Press, 1989), pp. 46–7. The Mortmain Act decreed that any benevolent bequest that left land away from the deceased's legal heirs would be invalid if it had been made less than a year before the decease of the bestower. Donna Andrews gives this further evidence of the decline in charity: "[w]hile more than two-thirds of the surviving wills of members of the Court of Aldermen, 1690–1719, have some provisions for posthumous aid to the poor, only one-third of the aldermen serving 1739–1778 left similar bequests." Moreover, an 1819 investigation of endowed charities in London revealed that more than half of those charities (59.4 percent) had originated in the period before 1649.

determinedly heroic youth who refuses a marriage proposed by his father in a parody of contemporary novels: "Lady Dorothea is lovely and Engaging; I prefer no woman to her; but know Sir," he proclaims passionately "that I scorn to marry her in compliance with your wishes. No! Never shall it be said that I obliged my Father."[59] This was the new orthodoxy – that marriage should be the culmination of exclusive and individualized romantic love. Austen's joke is that defying a parent – thanks to literary precedent – was more attractive than a lovely and engaging spouse. But insisting on one's own choice did not necessarily represent the narrowing of the motives for marriage to pure love rather than the desire for property in that person or desire for that person's property.

In my own earlier treatment of the appearance in fiction of love-in-marriage at the end of the seventeenth century, I associated it with the gendered redistribution of work in the period. In England, at least, the cultural belief in love-in-marriage coincided with the limiting of the numbers of women working as members of professional guilds and as trainers of apprentices – examples of which can be found in the proletarianization of the female silk throwsters of Alice Clark's landmark study or the increasing displacement of women's herbal lore and midwifery by a new brand of professional medical men and male midwives.[60] The new expectation that the meaning of a woman's life was to be found in consciousness heightened not so much by religion as by romantic love in a domestic context, I argued, was encouraged by the invention of a new kind of fiction, in which the events were not so much plotted in the material world as located in the ever-more-sensitive interior consciousness of the characters. Women, in this view, were *relegated* to romantic marriages as they were excluded from the socially recognized realms of professional work and financial reward.[61]

---

[59] Letter 6th Laura to Marianne. Jane Austen, "Love and Freindship" (sic, written 1790), in Margaret Anne Doody and Douglas Murray (eds.), *Catharine and Other Writings* (Oxford: Oxford University Press, 1993, pp. 75–106, quote p. 79.

[60] Ruth Perry, *Women, Letters, and the Novel* (New York: AMS Press, 1980), pp. 27–62; Alice Clark, *The Working Life of Women in the Seventeenth Century* (1919; rpt. New York: Augustus M. Kelly, 1968). For an account of the extrusion of women from the profession of midwifery, see Barbara Brandon Schnorrenberg, "Is Childbirth Any Place for a Woman? The Decline of Midwifery in Eighteenth-Century England," *Studies in Eighteenth-Century Culture* 10 (1981), 393–408. An excellent recent account of eighteenth-century attitudes towards midwifery and related matters can be found in Lois A. Chaber, "'This Affecting Subject': An 'Interested' Reading of Childbearing in Two Novels by Samuel Richardson," *Eighteenth-Century Fiction* 8, 2 (January 1996), 193–250.

[61] Women always worked in the victualing trades, in the low end of the cloth-and-needle trades (spinning, sewing), and in petty sales (huckstering) – but these were labor-intensive rather than capital-intensive or professional forms of work and were performed by laboring-class women and not the literate, respectable sort of women that novels were written for and about. On the other hand, there were women "of the middling sort" who worked. Margaret Hunt notes that 6 percent of

Through the eighteenth century, the shortage of respectable work for women continued to be a problem and by the end of the century was remarked by many authors, including Priscilla Wakefield and Mary Ann Radcliffe.[62] Margaret Hunt notes that women "of the middling sort" who did manage to earn their own living in the later part of the century, recognizing how hard it was to get by as a single woman, often contributed heavily to their trades' "maiden daughters' funds" or left subsistence bequests to daughters.[63] Looking at the employment possibilities for women of another class, K. D. M. Snell points to a decline in service opportunities for women as well as "reduced scope for female work in agriculture and the trades" in the rural south after 1760.[64] In her early conduct book, *Thoughts on the Education of Daughters* (1787), Mary Wollstonecraft remarked: "Few are the modes of earning a subsistence, and those very humiliating," referring to the possibility of being a humble companion or toadeater,[65] a governess, or a teacher. She added, "The few trades which are left, are now gradually falling into the hands of the men, and certainly they are not very respectable."[66]

the traders in the *Manchester Directory* of 1772 were women; and that 11.5 percent of the shopkeepers listed in the Royal Exchange Assurance insurance company between 1775 and 1787 were women – that is, more than 15,000 shopkeepers throughout England were women in that period. *The Middling Sort*, pp. 129, 133.

[62] See especially Mary Ann Radcliffe, *The Female Advocate* (Edinburgh, 1810) and Priscilla Wakefield, *Reflections on the Present Condition of the Female Sex* (London: Joseph Johnson, 1798). Deborah Valenze has described how work opportunities narrowed for women in the course of the eighteenth century, particularly in their capacities as dairy workers and spinners, in *The First Industrial Woman* (New York and Oxford: Oxford University Press, 1995). For a good introduction to the historiographical issues involved in examining women's work, see the by now classic essays by K. D. M. Snell, Peter Earle, Maxine Berg, Sarah Horrell, and Jane Humphries anthologized in Pamela Sharpe (ed.), *Women's Work: The English Experience 1650–1914* (London: Arnold, 1998), pp. 71–201.

[63] Margaret Hunt, "Capitalism and the Bonds of Matrimony," in her *The Middling Sort*, pp. 147–71; see also p. 279 n. 65.

[64] K. D. M. Snell, *Annals of the Labouring Poor: Social Change and Agrarian England, 1660–1900* (Cambridge: Cambridge University Press, 1985), p. 349. See also Snell's "Agricultural Seasonal Employment, the Standard of Living, and Women's Work, 1690–1860," (1981), reprinted in Pamela Sharpe (ed.), *Women's Work*, pp. 73–121. For more references to the decline of women's work opportunities in rural England, see Chapter 1, "The Great Disinheritance."

[65] For a fascinating account of the profession of "companion" as it was practiced by educated but impoverished women of the eighteenth century, see Betty Rizzo, *Companions without Vows: Relationships among Eighteenth-Century British Women* (Athens: University of Georgia Press, 1994).

[66] *The Works of Mary Wollstonecraft*, ed. Marilyn Butler and Janet Todd, 7 vols. (New York: New York University Press, 1989), vol. IV, pp. 25–6. As a corrective to this view, see n. 60 and n. 61 above, and in particular Maxine Berg, "Women's Work, Mechanisation and the Early Phases of Industrialisation in England," in Patrick Joyce (ed.), *The Historical Meanings of Work* (Cambridge: Cambridge University Press, 1987), pp. 64–98; Peter Earle, "The Female Labour Market in London in the Late Seventeenth and Early Eighteenth Centuries," *Economic History Review*, 2nd ser., 42, 3 (1989), 328–53 [reprinted in Pamela Sharpe (ed.), *Women's Work*]; and Margaret Hunt, *The Middling Sort*, especially pp. 125–46.

A great deal has been written on the so-called marriage plot and the way it figured female subjectivity, identity, and class membership; the new power of middle-class women with respect to the creation of domestic life and the deployment of leisure time; and the importance of emotional realism together with the transcendence of feeling. Most of these readings take at face value the longing for love that provides the narrative tension. But I want to suggest that the endless variations on the theme register not just the mesmerizing appeal of romantic love and individualism in a society just unleashing the enormous power of these possibilities, but also the urgent need of women to find a safe berth, to land somewhere, to relocate domestic life in an establishment other than their families of origin. As Mrs. Delany wrote to her sister Ann Dewes in 1751, "Why must women be *driven to the necessity* of marrying? a state that should always be a matter of choice! . . . Has not *this* made matrimony an irksome prison to many, and prevents its being that happy union of hearts where mutual choice and mutual obligation make it the most perfect state of friendship?"[67] Courtship novels chart women's maneuvers to find themselves new homes, rather than their frivolously obsessional concern with appearances or degrees of delicacy. Beauty, or a commanding appearance, was essential if there were no relatives to intercede for one. We may laugh at Mrs. Bennet's obsessive concern with marrying her daughters in Jane Austen's *Pride and Prejudice*, but Austen's plot vindicates Mrs. Bennet. By the time the happy denouement comes, we are as pleased as she at the ending which settles the deserving heroines in establishments of their own.

William Temple's complaint about noble families marrying into the city for downright money refers, of course, to cross-class marriages. Yet in all classes, the re-centering of marriage on individual choice must be understood as the social concomitant of an economic system that encouraged people to look out for their own self-interest, and a political system that emphasized the importance of the individual – rather than the family or the community – to the state. As William Goode analyzes it, "the ideology of the conjugal family proclaims the right of the individual to choose his or her own spouse, place to live, and even which kin obligations to accept, as against the acceptance of others' decisions. It asserts the worth of the *individual* as against the inherited elements of wealth or ethnic group."[68]

---

[67] *The Autobiography and Correspondence of Mrs. Delany*, ed. Lady Llanover, 1st series, 3 vols. (London: Richard Bentley, 1861), vol. III, p. 25. I am grateful to Barbara Schnorrenberg for this reference.

[68] William J. Goode, *World Revolution and Family Patterns* (New York: Free Press, 1963; rpt. 1970), p. 19.

"Individualism," of course, meant something different for women than it did for men. For men, the political rhetoric about democratizing power across classes included them. It held out to all men opportunities for advancement in the new capitalist dispensation, the chance to serve the state – if only as a foot soldier – and the right to personal autonomy in domestic life. Individualism promised that every man could be king in the castle of his own home. For women, the force of individualism was more equivocal. It did not expand the sphere of their social or political power. Indeed, to a feminist like Mary Astell – who believed that arbitrary power was "more mischievous in Families than in Kingdoms, by how much *100,000* Tyrants are worse than one" – the individualism of privatized marriage felt like a serious curtailment of women's personal autonomy.[69] As one historian puts it, "men were liberated by market individualism, but women were deprived of community support."[70] Nevertheless, this new ideology licensed women to regard themselves as individuals, to put themselves at the center of their own dramas, to pay self-conscious attention to their fates and feelings, and to imagine themselves as the heroines of their own lives.

The literary formula that opposed parental pressure for financially advantageous matches to their children's impulsive choices to marry for love represents an opposition between the value of the individual and his or her membership in a class, religion, or family. The love-match would seem at first glance to be offered as an antidote to the practice of mercenary marriage. But the cultural emphasis on personal choice was fueled by the same forces that encouraged private gain and individualistic accumulation and in that sense the ideology of the love-match helped to rationalize the reality of the mercenary marriage. Opposition to parental pressure pitted the interests of the family and community into which one had been born against the desires of the deracinated individual.

What changed between the seventeenth and eighteenth centuries, as I have said, was a redefinition of family membership and its obligations, rather than simply the degree and kind of emotion one felt for one's husband or wife. Marriage became more central to the definition of family during the eighteenth century not because people learned how to love their mates from reading novels and attached themselves more deeply to their spouses (although there was undeniably a new idealization of domestic love), but because people came to rely less on the families they were born into and

---

[69] Mary Astell, *Some Reflections upon Marriage*, pp. 10–11. For a longer discussion of this issue, see my "Mary Astell and the Feminist Critique of Possessive Individualism," *Eighteenth-Century Studies* 23, 4 (Summer 1990), 444–57.

[70] Richard Grassby, *Kinship and Capitalism*, p. 264.

more on the families they created voluntarily through marriage. There is plenty of evidence for affectionate unions and social recognition of the luck of love-in-marriage – in all classes – long before the eighteenth century in England.[71]

LIABILITY

The overdetermined emphasis on conjugality in English culture and the shedding of wider kin ties grew out of another economic imperative related to, but distinct from, issues of lineal inheritance or romantic love. The growth of capitalism brought with it the urgent need to limit financial liability to the individual rather than extending possible ruin to the larger kindred – and to pay off risk to the individual rather than to the collateral family as well. In other words, reduced expectations of support for collateral relatives (maternal relatives came to seem especially superfluous) were also rooted in the risks and rewards of investment capitalism. Lending money to relatives or rescuing them from debt was a risky business when such personal generosity could result in impounded household goods or imprisonment for insolvency. For although the pooled resources of family and friends were still the main source of venture capital for most enterprises, liability law did not yet discriminate between personal or private assets and business assets, the "public" and the "private" spheres. Personal involvement could result in public ruin. Even relatives at some remove from those in business felt the insecurity of commercial ups and downs. As Margaret Hunt describes the situation, "If catastrophe struck, the moral onus was on kin to stave off eviction or the seizure of a relative's goods or, at the last resort, to get the family out of debtor's prison."[72] In this world of sudden losses and gains – with its near-incomprehensible operations of paper credit, debt, margins, notes, bonds, and joint stock companies – a tension evolved between the older value system that stressed loyalty to relatives and a newer, more pragmatic attitude about individual profit and risk. A person might choose to invest his surplus cash in public funds more safely than in a brother's business, for example, or in a more lucrative enterprise begun by

---

[71] See John Gillis, *For Better, for Worse*, pp. 37–43 and Alan Macfarlane, *Marriage and Love in England 1300–1840* (Oxford: Basil Blackwell, 1986), pp. 174–208. For evidence of affectionate marriage among the lower orders in the seventeenth century, see J. A. Sharpe, "Plebian Marriage in Stuart England: Some Evidence from Popular Literature," *Transactions of the Royal Historical Society* 36 (1986), 69–90.

[72] This sentence, as well as the ideas for this section, come from Margaret Hunt's "Capital, Credit and the Family," in her *The Middling Sort*, pp. 22–45; quote p. 23. See also her "Time-Management, Writing, and Accounting in the Eighteenth-Century English Trading Family: A Bourgeois Enlightenment," *Business and Economic History*, 2nd series, 18 (1989), 150–9.

non-relatives. But such choices were redefining the unconditional support that had once been the moral underpinnings of kin relations.

The terms of helping one's kin had changed. Lending a hand to needy relatives no longer simply meant helping with the harvest, apprenticing a nephew, or sending gifts of extra food or clothing to help a poorer family get through an especially hard winter. Backing bad debts, standing security, or lending money to a relative in a failing enterprise could mean the ruin of an entire family with business debts not of their own making.[73] As Eliza Haywood makes clear in her treatise on duties within families, *The Husband* (1756), a man's first obligation was to his own wife and dependent children – not to his siblings, parents, collateral relatives, or friends. This relatively new principle defined a new financial responsibility. Haywood cautions husbands against standing surety for the debts of any friends or relatives because, although such generosity is "one of the most noble acts of humanity," a husband's primary loyalty must be to his new conjugal family "than whom *no friend or relation whatever can be half so dear*" (emphasis added). "I am sensible," she writes, that this is "a very nice and tender point; and I may possibly be accus'd by some persons as if guilty of attempting to root out all those few remains of friendship, compassion and good-nature, which, in spite of the depravity of the age, still continue among us."[74] Nonetheless, a man must not hazard what he owes first to his wife and children. When Henry Fielding's protagonist William Booth impulsively gives away or loses money that should be provided rather to his immediate family in *Amelia* (1751), we feel the charm of his generosity but also the imprudence of the conduct of this married man caught in a changing system of values.

Thus the intensified pressure on families to come up with venture capital for the new insatiable economy, together with the indiscriminate rigidities of business liability law, created moral dilemmas for persons who felt the pull of kin loyalty against their own best financial interests. Economically motivated drawing-back from financial commitments to kin, together with the new emphasis on individualized choices and risks, meshed well with the notion of marrying to please oneself rather than one's relatives. It was also

---

[73] Margaret Hunt suggests how widespread this problem was in a society with a specie shortage, forced to run its businesses on credit: "The image of whole families failing owing to the fact that they had imprudently provided money or security for relatives is one of the master narratives of middling culture. It recurs over and over again in letters, diaries and autobiographies of urban non-elites of the period . . . And it is difficult to find *any* good runs of personal records from tradesmen's families between about 1650 and 1800 that do not record failures (often multiple failures) among friends, family acquaintances, or business connections." *The Middling Sort*, p. 34.

[74] Eliza Haywood, *The Husband* (London, 1756), quotes pp. 231, 233, 231.

encouraged by other aspects of Enlightenment culture that reinforced separate individuation: privatized reading, the evolving legal system of contracts, culturally approved introspection, and individualized self-expression about private emotional experience – among other new beliefs and practices.

CHILDREN AND THEIR MOTHERS

The much heralded "invention of childhood," described so brilliantly by Philippe Ariès, also privileged the conjugal family. It involved separating parents and their immature children from larger collections of kin and defining this conjugal unit in contradistinction to an extended family. The invention of childhood, according to Ariès and those historians who followed him, is key to this nuclear reconfiguration of kin. Using mainly French sources, Ariès advanced the suggestive thesis that western European society developed a new awareness of childhood's particularity in this period, apparent in an expanded vocabulary for naming and describing infancy and early childhood and in pictorial representations of childhood that preserved their proportional difference rather than depicting them simply as miniature adults. Children's dress changed; games, toys, and pastimes were devised; and adults felt – and expressed – a new solicitude and fondness for the special qualities and natural dispositions of young children. According to Ariès, this change was accompanied by a special emphasis on the moral and intellectual training of children and on their bodily hygiene and physical health.[75] Lawrence Stone's refinement of this thesis was specifically to date a more permissive childrearing and a more child-centered society in England to the eighteenth century. Affective relations between parents and children warmed up, he claimed, when child mortality declined and parents could "afford" "to invest" themselves emotionally in their children because they could hope that these children would live longer.[76]

---

[75] See Philippe Ariès, *L'Enfant et la vie familiale sous l'ancien regime*. For a thorough exposition of Ariès' thesis and its English and American variations by John Demos, Lloyd de Mause, Edward Shorter, Randolph Trumbach, John Gillis, David Hunt, Ivy Pinchbeck, and Margaret Hewitt, as well as Lawrence Stone, see Linda Pollock's excellent *Forgotten Children: Parent-Child Relations from 1500 to 1900* (Cambridge and New York: Cambridge University Press, 1983).

[76] Lawrence Stone, *The Family, Sex, and Marriage in England 1500–1800*, p. 420. The section headings of the second part of Stone's Chapter 9, "Parent-Child Relations," suggest the class inflections of his model: "The Aristocracy: The Negligent Mode"; "The Upper Bourgeoisie and Squirearchy: The Child-Oriented, Affectionate and Permissive Mode"; "The Upper Bourgeoisie and the Squirearchy: The Child-Oriented but Repressive Mode"; "The Pious Nonconformists: The Egocentric Intrusive Mode"; "The Cottager and Artisan: the Brutal but Careful Mode"; "The Poor: The Indifferent and Exploitative Mode."

Whether Ariès' "invention of childhood" or Stone's "permissive" parenting actually signaled a change in attitudes towards children or whether these human phenomena were an artifact of the spread of literacy – whereby parents could record their feelings about their children and historians could reflect on these records – is difficult to say.[77] It is certainly true that by the middle of the eighteenth century in England children were being defined as a new market. Toys, miniatures, and games were for the first time produced for them. There was a demand for advice manuals on raising children, and for children's books – the didactic, the educational, and the purely entertaining.[78] Whether that meant that parents cared more for their children than ever before and gave more attention to their moral and intellectual upbringing as has been argued by some family historians, or whether these toys and games and books were simply a new permutation of commodity capitalism, seems to me likewise unanswerable.[79]

Literary critics have tried to test Ariès' thesis by judging whether children were a presence or an absence in eighteenth-century literature, and whether parental love or neglect is represented there.[80] Attitudes towards the infant in *Pamela II* are canvassed, as well as the extent of maternal authority and the properties of breastfeeding.[81] The parents in Frances Burney's *Camilla* (1797), who give their children to a rich uncle who famously mismanages them, could be read as an instance of parental neglect. The benevolent Dr. Primrose and his wife in Goldsmith's *Vicar of Wakefield* (1766), on the

[77] After summarizing the evidence from a wide range of historians of childhood, and examining evidence from diaries, letters, and memoirs, Linda Pollock concludes that "experience with the medium of writing as a form of expression" is an important variable in historical change. See her *Forgotten Children*, pp. 140–2, quote p. 141.

[78] J. H. Plumb, "The New World of Children in Eighteenth-Century England," in Neil McKendrick, John Brewer, and J. H. Plumb (eds.), *The Birth of a Consumer Society: The Commercialization of Eighteenth-Century England* (London: Europa, 1982), pp. 286–315.

[79] Mary Joe Hughes, after examining 2,000 family letters of the Colliers of Hastings, Sussex, written by both husband and wife between 1715 and 1740 about their children and their household during John Collier's frequent absences from home, concludes that their mixtures of parental affection and authority appear to be commonplace, expected, and well integrated in the society of their day. "It seems unlikely that affectionate concern by parents for their children was anything new in the eighteenth century," she writes. "What may be genuinely new in the eighteenth century is the degree of material indulgence or 'encouragement' of children which an increasingly wealthy commercial society made available to more parents. Such new capacity in families like the Colliers (in combination with other factors like the relaxation of religious intensity) would surely make affection for children more 'visible' to historians." Mary Joe Hughes, "Child-Rearing and Social Expectations in Eighteenth-Century England: The Case of the Colliers of Hastings," *Studies in Eighteenth-Century Culture* 13 (1984), 79–100, quote 96.

[80] See, for example, T. G. A. Nelson, *Children, Parents, and the Rise of the Novel* (Newark: University of Delaware Press, 1995).

[81] See, for example, Toni Bowers, "'A Point of Conscience': Breastfeeding and Maternal Authority in *Pamela 2*," *Eighteenth-Century Fiction* 7, 3 (April 1995), 259–78.

other hand, are a literary example of parents who educated their children, enjoyed their prattle, and encouraged their wholesome pastimes. But it seems fruitless to ask whether or not eighteenth-century parents "loved" their children in the twentieth-century sense. Eighteenth-century depictions of children are centrally concerned with managing children's moral training. Fondness without discipline is clearly frowned upon, whereas parental guidance and religious training answered by children's gratitude and respect are always the kernel of eighteenth-century idealizations of successful family life. The fathers of fictional heroes and heroines were most often given credit for guiding the reading of children once they attained the age of reason "in the best works of philosophy and divinity." Mothers taught them their first letters and numbers, practical aspects of domestic economy and the stewardship of property, gentility and mannerliness, generosity and thoughtfulness, fairness to subordinates and charity towards the unfortunate – all the necessary moral lessons for living in the world.[82]

Jane Austen satirizes parents who abdicate their responsibility for the serious and difficult task of raising children well; children reflect the moral intelligence and self-knowledge of their parents in her novels and as such signify responsibility to a larger world. Two-year-old Walter Musgrove climbing on the back of his aunt Anne in *Persuasion*, or the misbehavior of the children of Lady Middleton in *Sense and Sensibility*, are admonitory early stages of the flaws that can be seen full-blown in such headstrong male protagonists as Lovelace in Richardson's *Clarissa* (1747–8) or Delamere in Charlotte Smith's *Emmeline* (1788), characters who are said to have had too little discipline when young. Charlotte Lennox's *Sophia* (1762) depicts the fates of two sisters treated differently: loved and indulged Harriot turns out weak and spoiled, while Sophia, the less beautiful one who always had to make her own way, grows up to be hardworking and sensible, with a graceful mind "well-furnished with ideas." Whether such patterns constitute proof of parental love or the recognition of childhood as a separate stage of life could be argued either way. What they do show, however, is that the public discourse about children concerned their moral training.[83]

This new interest in childrearing, construed as mothers' responsibility, had serious implications for adult women. The invention of childhood

---

[82] For the tradition of moral pedagogy in women's writing, see Mitzi Myers' "Impeccable Governesses, Rational Dames, and Moral Mothers: Mary Wollstonecraft and the Female Tradition in Georgian Children's Books," *Children's Literature* 14 (1986), 31–59.

[83] Jan Fergus has remarked in private conversation that a number of male authors of the period – Fielding and Sheridan, for example – appear to believe that character is a function of nature rather than nurture; even though they are given the same training, Tom and Blifil or Joseph and Charles Surface turn out very differently.

meant the invention of a new kind of motherhood for them.[84] It created new duties for women in their conjugal families, essentialized by the end of the century as women's work, which further reinforced the configuration of privatized marriage. These evolving expectations suffused the roles of wife and mother with new meaning – as they drained meaning from women's other kin positions as sisters, daughters, and nieces. Paradoxically, the wife and mother aspects of women's domestic roles were redefined as mutually exclusive as they developed in the course of the century. That is, motherhood was increasingly de-sexualized as it was sentimentalized, and a wife's sexual desire was increasingly seen as incompatible with motherhood.[85] By the time Mrs. James in Henry Fielding's *Amelia* (1751) remarks that childlessness is "the only circumstance which makes matrimony comfortable," readers were conditioned to recognize that Mrs. James was not a good woman, not unselfish like Amelia whose first tender thoughts are always for her children's good rather than for her own pleasure.[86]

A further effect of the "invention" – or redefinition – of "childhood" and "motherhood" is that women and children seem to have traded social positions in their relation to the head of the family in a kind of cultural chiasmus. Where children had always been thought of as their parents' property,[87] women within marriage – wives – had retained their own separate personhood with work identities and membership in a women's local subculture. But the movement from father patriarchy to husband patriarchy, to put the matter in a kind of shorthand, and the shift from kinship defined by consanguinity to kinship defined by conjugality, rearranged the positions of the subordinates in the household. No longer was the household imagined as feudal fiefdom, with the oldest male at the head; now the spousal bond was put at the center and the wife's separate psychological identity submerged in her marriage. Wives were thought of more as property and (male) children more as persons in their own right.[88] If the

---

[84] For the invention of the "tender, full-time mother," see the essays in Susan C. Greenfield and Carol Barash (eds.), *Inventing Maternity: Politics, Science, and Literature 1650–1865* (Lexington: University of Kentucky Press, 1999).

[85] For a discussion of the mutually exclusive nature of maternity and sexuality as historically constructed aspects of women's biological function in eighteenth-century English society, see my "Colonizing the Breast: Sexuality and Maternity in Eighteenth-Century England," *Eighteenth-Century Life* 16, n.s. 1 (February 1992), 185–213.

[86] Henry Fielding, *Amelia*, 2 vols. (1751; rpt. London: Dent, 1930), vol. II, p. 143.

[87] David Blewett makes this point in "Changing Attitudes toward Marriage in the Time of Defoe: The Case of Moll Flanders," 78.

[88] By the late seventeenth and early eighteenth centuries, children's property – especially a son's property – was legally guaranteed in some classes by prior marriage settlements, independent of his parents' wishes. It was considered reprehensible, not to say legally culpable, for a father to dip into

"invention of childhood" has any meaning at all, it means that children were increasingly thought of as individuals under this new dispensation, to be molded and educated. A *Spectator* column of 1711, written by Joseph Addison, shows considerable concern for the deplorable psychological fate of illegitimate offspring – especially sons of well-born men – and for their care and education, with the merest mention of the "unfortunate Females" who bore them and who were presumably defiled and endangered by their illicit intimacies.[89] The phenomenon of "wife selling," unheard of before 1690 and gaining enormous popularity in the eighteenth century as a kind of ritual folk divorce among commoners, testifies linguistically and symbolically to this new understanding of women as their husbands' property.[90]

An odd book marketed as a novel in 1751 and called, like Fielding's novel, *Amelia*, but with the subtitle *The Distress'd Wife: A History Founded on Real Circumstances by a Private Gentlewoman* (London, 1751), illustrates some of these points. Written by an estranged wife as an act of desperation to earn some money to live on and, as she explains in the Preface, to "avoid the Necessity of entering into a Second Law-Suit," the text chronicles the injustices of the marriage system. The author (believed to be Elizabeth Justice) tells of meeting her future husband when she was fourteen and he was twenty. He was a man of unexceptionable background, whose "violent" courtship of her for more than three years wore down her parents' resistance. She recounts, for example, how he swooned one afternoon when she smilingly served a cup of tea to another gentleman visitor before him. Once they were married, however, and "the good Man had got the desir'd Prize . . . he changed from a violent Admirer, into a stupid insensible Husband, to the great Grief of poor *Amelia*" (19). Once they were married, her husband

his son's inheritance before he reached his majority. Women's access to their own property once married, on the other hand, had to be increasingly hedged with legal stipulations or guaranteed by special arrangements, such as "pin money." See Susan Staves' chapter "Pin Money and Other Separate Property," in her *Married Women's Separate Property in England, 1660–1833*, pp. 131–61, for a discussion of the legal and social meaning of the invention of "pin money" in the early eighteenth century.

These conditions reversed earlier arrangements about property in previous periods, when land and goods had been left to women independent of their husbands' right to it and when a child's property was naturally at the disposal of his parents until he had need of it.

[89] *Spectator* 203, October 23, 1711.

[90] John Gillis discusses wife sales in *For Better, for Worse*, pp. 211–19. Gillis quotes Aris' *Birmingham Gazette* to show how widespread the practice was by 1790: "As instances of the sale of wives have of late frequently occurred among the lower classes of people who consider such sale lawful, we think it right to inform that, by determination of the courts of law in a former reign, they were declared illegal and void, and considered (the light in which religion must view them) a mere pretense to sanction the crime of adultery" (212).

Anna Clark also discusses this plebian form of divorce, adding that "the symbolism of women as property is inescapable." *The Struggle for the Breeches: Gender and the Making of the British Working Class* (Berkeley: University of California Press, 1995), p. 86.

ignored her. He came and went without telling her his plans. He would not give her household money but expected her to spend her own money – small gifts from her parents – to furnish his table. A dupe of the booksellers, he spent all his money on prints and old books. He brought company to dinner expecting her to entertain his guests and even prostitute herself, intimating that "nothing she could do would be wrong that she got Money by" (23). Finally he struck her, because she would not follow his bidding with the children, and she returned to her father's house where she sued him for separate maintenance. In the complex proceedings that followed, he took the children – for legally they belonged to the father – and tried to get Amelia's jewelry. Although the ecclesiastical court awarded her the pittance of £25 a year, he never paid it, and when she took him to court five years later and was again awarded "Debt and Cost," he countersued for his legal costs, thus further postponing paying her.

The tale is embellished with accounts of Amelia's efforts to be a cheerful and forgiving wife and an attentive and loving mother. As a social document from the mid-century, it illustrates the dialectical relation between the ideology of marriage as loving friendship and the dangers inherent in privatized marriage. Once married, Amelia, along with everything she owned, belonged to her husband. An upper servant and a cook, a governess for his children, isolated from her friends and family, her small allowance commandeered for his expenses, Amelia was even expected to earn money by dispensing sexual favors to men he brought home. Her children were his property, although she was expected to care for them and raise them; her childrearing skill is her best proof of her own human value.

THE CHANGING MEANING OF MARRIAGE

In the foregoing, I have tried to suggest some of the interconnections among the factors that relocated kinship in marriage and shifted the axis of kinship from consanguinity to conjugality: the increasingly patrilineal laws governing legal property ownership, the invention of childhood and the concurrent invention of motherhood, the new orthodoxy concerning romantic love-in-marriage. In his treatment of changes in the English family, Randolph Trumbach further explains the repositioning of conjugality at the center of kinship by connecting it to the triumph of the upwardly mobile classes. He describes the growing conception of marriage as alliance – improving one's status by allying with someone of a higher class or with more land or money – as a particularly modern and middle-class conception of marriage. He distinguishes it from the earlier conception of marriage as incorporation, in which the purpose of marriage was to consolidate the existing tribe or clan, or to extend it by adding new members. Trumbach associates the strategy of incorporation with the older system of cognatic kindreds in which sisters as well as maternal relatives had an importance that would later be eroded by a more universal practice of primogeniture and patriliny. Marriage as incorporation meant continuing and extending the bloodline whereas marriage as alliance meant creating a bridge between two different kin groups as a means to class mobility and/or the accumulation of property. Again, romantic love provided the rationale for inter-class marriages and facilitated upward mobility. In *Mansfield Park*, Jane Austen stages Fanny Price's return to Portsmouth to dramatize the dissolution of her ties with her family of origin and to establish the class gulf between these two branches of the family, giving the marriage between Fanny and Edmund the feel of alliance rather than incorporation, a way for Fanny to move up the social ladder.

Trumbach deduces a tension between these two systems of marriage from the prohibited degrees of marriage posted in every Anglican church after the Restoration. Based on cognatic principles, "a man was equally forbidden to marry the sisters of his father and of his mother."[91] Affinal relations such as brother's wife or sister's husband "were treated equally with the consanguineal," for a man could not marry his wife's sister nor the widows of his uncles, his brothers, or his sons. But this equivalence of the consanguineal and the affinal had a generational limit, "for a man could marry the widow of his consanguineal great-uncle." The prohibition against the incorporation of affinal relatives was also narrowly defined, for although a man could not marry his wife's sister, he could marry the sister of his brother's wife and he could reach into the next generation to marry the daughter of his wife's sister. For Trumbach, these rules – together with the legitimation of first-cousin marriage and the continuing prohibition against the so-called sororate marriage with a dead wife's sister – were proof that the law discouraged marriage as alliance.

He makes explicit the class dimension to this legal preference. First-cousin marriage was preferred by the aristocracy as a way to accumulate property and to keep both the name and the land in the family. For example, in Burney's *Cecilia* (1782), the hero's aristocratic parents – the Delviles – had been cousins before they married. For them, marriage incorporated new affines as if they were add-on consanguineal relatives. For the middle class, on the other hand, marriage was conceived of as an alliance that cemented

---

[91] The discussion that follows is distilled from Trumbach's *The Rise of the Egalitarian Family*, pp. 18–33.

relations between two groups and made possible upward mobility. According to Trumbach, "[T]here was in force in England from the Restoration
to the early twentieth century, a system of marriage that approved cousin
marriage and discouraged marriage to affines, and throughout the eighteenth and the nineteenth centuries there was an agitation to change this."
The earlier system, upheld by law so long as the aristocracy held sway,
maintained social status and kept family names and family property intact.
But the law that made the levirate marriage (marriage with a dead wife's sister) legal in 1907 signals for Trumbach a middle-class triumph that ratified
marriage as alliance.[92]

To illustrate his argument about the aristocratic preference for first-
cousin marriages, Trumbach cites Lady Mary Wortley Montagu's observation that Richardson could not have understood "the manners of high
life" when he represented the liberties taken between Mr. Lovelace and his
supposed cousins in *Clarissa*. Such familiarities between cousins would not
have been realistic among aristocrats, Trumbach reminds us, where cousin
marriage was frequent and expected, for aristocratic cousins behaved with
as much circumspection in relation to each other as towards any other
potential marriage partner.[93]

The marriage-of-incorporation did not pose the same kind of threat to
the consanguineal family as the marriage-as-alliance because by extending
and adding to the natal family it shored up the principle of consanguinity.
The marriage-as-alliance on the other hand expressly put the interest of the
new unit above the interests of either of the spouses' natal families. Awareness of this tension between kin systems opens up new ways of reading the
conflict between filial obedience and individual desire in so many novels of
the period. Romantic love, for example, frequently imagined as the cutting
loose from other kin ties in a scenario of elopement followed by isolated
bliss, is often opposed to powerful longing for family, place, belonging, and
community. Frances Burney's second novel, *Cecilia* (1782), centers on this
dilemma, posing loyalty to kin (marriage-as-incorporation) against loyalty
to exogamous love (marriage-as-alliance). It is simultaneously about the
right of the younger generation to marry whomever they will – and about
the utter impossibility of such a stance.

Unlike the dislocated, dependent, orphaned, and nameless Evelina of
Burney's first novel, the protagonist of *Cecilia* is (like Jane Austen's Emma
Woodhouse) blessed with wealth as well as youth, beauty, and intelligence.

[92] *Ibid.*, pp. 31–2.
[93] *The Complete Letters of Lady Mary Wortley Montagu*, vol. III, p. 97.

Marriage is the only thing Cecilia Beverley still requires. But this time Burney gives her orphaned heroine too much name rather than too little name[94]; Cecilia's almost insurmountable impediment is that the man who marries her must take her surname Beverley, she being the last of her line, or else she will forfeit her fortune. Although Burney was obsessed by names and namelessness in all of her novels, by productions signed and unsigned as it were, this was not a far-fetched plot device; making an inheritance contingent on a name change was not so unusual in the eighteenth century. Jane Austen's oldest brother, Edward, adopted by the wealthy, childless Knights to continue their line, took their name when he came into their fortune. It was not uncommon for families with a sense of their own history, but without a son, to ask a nephew, a cousin, or a son-in-law to carry on the family name. So determined was Edward Colston to preserve his family name that in 1721 he rescinded his bequest of land to a nephew who died leaving only a daughter, and settled it instead on a grandniece in trust for a male heir who would carry on the name.[95] Other cultures recognize the problem more directly: a west African proverb warns men to beware of marrying a woman without brothers because her father might take the sons produced by the marriage. In Burney's novel, this highly charged stipulation immediately sets up a contest between patrilineal and matrilineal systems of naming and inheritance.

The last third of the book brings these issues of naming, inheritance, and family versus individualistic love to crisis. Delvile's parents stand *in loco parentis* to Cecilia because Delvile's father is Cecilia's legal guardian. In the book's terms, she is required to obey them; besides, she genuinely loves and reveres his mother. Cecilia is torn between her love for Mortimer Delvile and her renunciatory obedience to his cruelly rank-conscious parents. If she obeys his mother she will lose Delvile but retain his mother's love and respect; if she clings to him, she will gain a husband but lose a mother. All the Delviles are family and ancestor-proud – even Mortimer himself. His mother only has to ask him "How will the blood of your wronged ancestors rise into your guilty cheeks, and how will your heart throb with secret shame and reproach, when wished joy upon your marriage by the name of *Mr. Beverley!*" to sting him "to the soul" (677).[96] His letter to

---

[94] Catherine Gallagher makes this observation and cites previous critics who noted it as well in *Nobody's Story: The Vanishing Acts of Women Writers in the Marketplace 1670–1820* (Berkeley: University of California Press, 1994), pp. 231–2.

[95] Richard Grassby, *Kinship and Capitalism*, p. 383.

[96] This and all subsequent page numbers are from the World's Classics edition, edited by Peter Sabor and Margaret Anne Doody, *Cecilia, or, Memoirs of an Heiress* (Oxford and New York: Oxford University Press, 1988).

Cecilia proposing marriage tells her of his "perplexities," and "vain-glory," his internal "conflict between bosom felicity and family pride" (563).[97]

Cecilia's story alternates with the Belfield subplot, about a rather unfocused young man whose entire fortune is in his education and manners; Belfield is like the poor-but-respectable heroines of much eighteenth-century fiction. He tries to earn his living as a tutor, a laborer, and a hack writer – a sequence of attempts usually reserved for struggling single women in such novels as these. Indeed, Belfield's uncomfortable attempts to achieve independence through his own earning power resemble nothing so much as the desperate efforts of the Incognita, the heroine of Burney's last novel *The Wanderer* (1814). Belfield illustrates the fate in store for women who are unable to marry; the Delvile plot depicts the inherent familial conflict for women who do.

Burney, whose capacity for describing ever-increasing gradations of pain and humiliation is unparalleled in the history of fiction, uses her formidable talent to depict her heroine bound tighter and tighter, drawn one way by the pleas of a man she adores – with whom she has already consented to a half-performed clandestine marriage – and pulled in the opposite direction by his august mother, whom she admires as her own maternal monitor as well as Mortimer's progenitor. The tug-of-war between them, couched in terms of love vs duty and individual happiness vs rectitude and higher principles, illustrates the antagonism between a conjugal and a consanguineal principle of marriage. Will Mortimer Delvile make an exogamous alliance outside his immediate blood ties or will he "marry in" as did his parents, who are cousins? "How long do you flatter yourself this independent happiness would endure?" his mother demands of him. "How long could you live contented by mere self-gratification, in defiance of the censure of mankind, the renunciation of your family, and the curses of your father?" (676).

The fine torture of this scene between mother and son, for which Burney claims to have written the whole book, is prolonged by the excruciating back-and-forth of resolve and relenting by the deeply ambivalent characters.[98] Mortimer Delvile proves his love for Cecilia by defying the "vain

---

[97] This ambivalent proposal has been cited as the pattern for Darcy's struggle between his love for Elizabeth Bennet and his offended family pride in Austen's *Pride and Prejudice*. The phrase "PRIDE AND PREJUDICE," repeated three times in capital letters in a single paragraph (vol. III, Chapter 10, "The Termination," p. 930) is also evidence of the influence of Burney's book on Austen's novel.

[98] Burney wrote to Daddy Crisp on March 15, 1782: "The conflict scene for Cecilia, between the mother and son, to which you so warmly object, is the very scene for which I wrote the whole book, and so entirely does my plan hang upon it, that I must abide by its reception in the world, or put the whole behind the fire." Frances Burney, *The Diary and Letters of Madame D'Arblay, Edited by Her Niece* 7 vols. (London: Henry Colburn, 1843–6), vol. II, p. 127.

prejudices of the world," whose scruples seem to him frivolous compared to Cecilia's inestimable worth. Mrs. Delvile upbraids her son and accuses him of forgetting "his friends, family, and connections, the opinions in which he has been educated, the honour of his house, his own former views, and all his primitive sense of duty, both public and private!" (673). Cecilia holds tremulously to her prior promise to Mrs. Delvile not to marry without her consent, declaring "every way I now turn I have rendered myself miserable."

This conflict between romantic love and filial obligation can also be found in Charlotte Smith's *Emmeline* (1788), in which the heroine similarly promises her guardian, the disapproving father of her passionate suitor, not to marry him without his father's consent and to keep his parents informed of his movements. Smith was copying Burney's device[99]; but it is an obvious way of representing the double bind in which a woman finds herself in the conflict between love and family. It must be noted that morally impeccable heroines always cast their lot with the consanguineal rather than the nuptial principle – proving their moral worth by siding with families against upstart lovers, tying themselves voluntarily by promises to the parental generation, ironically, as a prelude to marriage. In fiction, duty for the woman lay with the old-fashioned expectations of the consanguineal family. Conversely, heroes proved *their* worth in these novels by taking the trouble to intercede for their affinal relatives or even the relatives of their prospective wives: Darcy straightening out Lydia's marriage with Wickham or Charlotte Smith's Desmond looking after the brother of his beloved Geraldine Verney. These fictional conventions make sense given the reality that marriage disconnected women from their consanguineal families. Women show that love and marriage will not make them break faith with their families; decent suitors demonstrate that they will not force their wives-to-be to renounce responsibility to their families of origin.

Eliza Haywood devotes an entire section of her treatise *The Husband* (1756) to this matter. "Tho' natural affection to kindred, and even the due reverence and obedience to parents, be pretty much out of doors in these latter ages of the world," she begins, " . . . a husband can seldom find a greater opportunity of endearing himself to his wife, than by treating her kindred with tenderness and respect" (125). She goes on to tell of a young woman persuaded by her guardian to sue a cousin about an uncle's will. Once married, she turned over the prosecution of the suit to her new husband, who stopped the proceedings, telling her he could not bear to

---

[99] For a description of the scene that contains Smith's homage to Burney, see Chapter 8, "The Importance of Aunts," p. 354.

offend "a person whose veins run with the same blood as yours." The suit was settled to everyone's satisfaction, and the young wife was "transported with receiving so uncommon a proof of her husband's affection for her in the complaisance he shew'd her family" (128).

As *Cecilia* works through its knots, Mrs. Delvile is prevailed upon to accede to a private marriage between Cecilia and Mortimer. But even this event is fraught with suspense, because Cecilia and Mortimer Delvile have already stood up together at the altar in an earlier episode, when the ceremony was interrupted unexpectedly. Stopped mysteriously, the ceremony half-finished, this prior experience undermines the romance and potential relief of the actual marriage ceremony the second time around and focuses the proceedings entirely on whether or not it will once again be interrupted – so much so that the marriage itself is anti-climactic when it goes forward uneventfully. Thus Burney manages to orchestrate a sequence that is fixated on marriage, and repeatedly examines it as a solution, but never permits it to blot out ambivalence or tie up loose ends. The consanguineal family vs the individual conjugal couple is the central conflict of this complex sequence, figured as a conflict between names, guardians, ancestors, families, fortunes, and moral choices. The difficult choice is repeatedly conjured by the orphaned heroine's heartfelt longing to make her home with the Delviles, to settle in their family, to finally come to rest as their daughter as well as Mortimer's wife.

Although marriage's infinite meanings reflect as many possibilities as there are combinations of people, the cultural and social meanings of the institution have changed radically in the course of the past three centuries. Changes in social expectations, cultural definition, legal effects, and psychological idealizations – all these have altered how people marry, the reasons for marrying, and individual judgments about the success or failure of any particular marriage. In this chapter I have tried to explain how changed attitudes towards property affected the meaning of marriage in the early eighteenth century. In the next chapter I will unpack some of the psychosexual effects of these new property relations which altered irrevocably the legal and demographic basis of English society. These shifts in psycho-sexual orientation are visible in the plots, characters, and rhetorical strategies of eighteenth-century fiction, in which one can trace the changing assumptions and anxieties of the age about sexuality and about marriage.

6

Sexualized marriage and property in the person

I was ever of opinion that the honest man who married and brought up a large family did more service than he who continued single and only talked of population.

> Oliver Goldsmith, *The Vicar of Wakefield* (1766), p. 1.

There is also a love of Natural Relations, different from the rest, which grows up with us insensibly, from our infancy. And the mutual love of Marriage is distinct from all the rest; and therefore when People are call'd upon *to love*, they are call'd upon to pay that Affection that is peculiar to the Relation they stand in to such a Party.

> William Fleetwood, *The Relative Duties of Parents and Children, Husbands and Wives, Masters and Servants* (1705), pp. 297–8.

It is a stock-jobbing age, every thing has its price; marriage is traffic throughout; as most of us bargain to be husbands, so some of us bargain to be cuckolds; and he would be as much laughed at, who preferred his love to his interest, at this end of the town, as he who preferred his honesty to his interest at the other.

> Henry Fielding, *The Modern Husband* (1731), Act 2 Scene 6
> (*Complete Works*, vol. x, p. 35).

In traditional societies, kinship and sexuality are mutually constitutive. The sexual behavior of young adults determines who will be kin to whom in the next generation. Their sexual choices, in turn, are variously constrained by the rules concerning endogamy and exogamy and degrees of relationship or definitional incest in their society, attitudes towards other families, economic and social hierarchies, and age, not to mention the accidents of contiguity and physical attraction. Once sexuality is detached from kinship, once the kin group no longer controls the marriage choices of its younger members, a society must evolve new rules for sexual behavior. In eighteenth-century England, the connection between kinship and sexuality was attenuated by the mobility of the population, by the anonymity of urban life, by the intensifying of individualistic identity, and by the expanding sphere of privatized experience. The message of print culture, as we have seen, was that marriage choice was not the business of community or kin group however defined but could only be decided by the principals involved. As mentioned earlier, the immense popularity of clandestine or private, paid-for marriage, which permitted couples to marry secretly without the knowledge of community or kin, is a sign of that disconnection. By 1740 nearly three-quarters of London marriages were privately transacted in the chapels around the Fleet prison.[1]

The new place of property in the priorities of marriage dovetailed with these changes and, as we have seen, encouraged the shift from collateral to lineal definitions of kinship. This realignment diminished the number of relatives who counted as kin, shrinking the psychological reach of most members of kin groups. As marriage became an increasingly important mechanism for the accumulation of wealth, the place of marriage in social life and the place of sex in marriage had to be reconceived. A new emotion was identified – a new form of emotional consciousness defined and elicited – to govern these choices: a form of sexualized love suitable for marriage. This new emotional consciousness, about which a public discourse mushroomed in journals and sermons as well as novels and poems, was needed to supply the place of earlier kin controls on sexuality; it had to regulate and direct sexual impulses in a way that sustained the values of the society.

THE PUBLIC DISCOURSE ABOUT SEX

The reading public was offered treatises on regulating family life (including responsibility for servants) and instructing children, and conduct books guiding the behavior of people with members of the opposite sex and advising them on their parents' rights in choosing their marriage partners. Letters were written (and ventriloquized) to Mr. Spectator and other editors about how to handle marital disputes and reclaim recalcitrant spouses. There were stories in the "prints" about elopements, separations, abductions, private marriages, criminal conversation (adultery) cases, large, socially mixed parties and masquerades – and endless discussions of the proper levels of prudery and sociability with anecdotes about flirtation and seduction, broken hearts, lucky matches, rakes, coquettes, fashion, sexual reputation, and

[1] Jeremy Boulton, "Clandestine Marriages in London: An Examination of a Neglected Urban Variable," *Urban History* 20, 2 (October 1993), 191–210, esp. 202. For further discussion of clandestine marriage, see above (Chapter 5, pp. 205–7).

tea-table gossip. These were the subjects of illustrative moral tales and entertaining letters, of sermons, plays, and poems. There was more interest
in other people's sex lives than ever before, although such matters, grist
for the new discursive mill, seemed properly more personal and private
and hence inappropriate for the public gaze – which, needless to say, increased their appeal all the more. No wonder the author of *The Present
State of Matrimony: or, The Real Causes of Conjugal Infidelity and Unhappy
Marriages* (London, 1739) complained, "'Tis a deplorable Truth, that our
young Ladies, a great many of them at least, are wiser, and more knowing
in the Arts of Coquetry, Galantry [sic], and other Matters relating to the
Difference of Sexes &c. before they come to be Twenty, than our Great-
Grandmothers were all their Lives. Thanks to our Plays, Songs, Poems, and
modern Conversation, for that"(25). The new discursive spotlight on these
subjects was creating a new knowledge about love, sex, and marriage.

Pornography as well as more euphemistic and sentimental fictionaliza-
tions of individuals' sexual choices and behaviors began to be produced at
home in eighteenth-century England, rather than imported from abroad
and translated. John Cleland's *Memoirs of a Woman of Pleasure* (1748), pop-
ularly known as *Fanny Hill*, was probably the first piece of homegrown
explicit erotic writing and certainly the first to move away from the format
of a dialogue among whores.[2] Its arousing descriptions of heated feelings
and sexually exciting activities were very different from the brutal pranks
retailed in the sexually explicit texts of the Restoration period such as *The
Wandring Whore* (1660) or the indiscriminate promiscuity of Rochester's
poems.[3] The sexually explicit literature of the seventeenth century had
"excelled at making sex shocking" or disgusting, but it was not yet pornographic, not yet written to "arouse or amuse."[4] Pornography (as opposed

---

[2] David Foxon, *Libertine Literature in England 1660–1745* (New Hyde Park, NY: University Books, 1965), pp. 44–5.

[3] According to Roger Thompson, *The Wandring Whore* is copied from a sixteenth-century source. It consists of a series of dialogues in six parts among a bawd, a pimp, a whore, and a lascivious gallant. It retails such unpleasant stories as burning a candle in a whore's "commodity" until the flame sets fire to her "bush," or pouring wine or placing guineas into that part of her anatomy. These unsavory characters also tell about how they steal from customers and about their painful cures for the pox, tales not written to entice or enflame readers but to entertain and distance them. The title page proclaims the virtue of this work in uncovering these "diabolical practices," "publisht to destroy those poysonous Vermine, which live upon the ruine and destruction of many Families, by a late Convert amongst them." Sometimes attributed to John Garfield, *The Wandring Whore* (London, 1660; rpt. New York: Garland, 1986) is ribald rather than pornographic. Its title and characters are supposed to have come from the sixteenth-century *La Puttana errante*. See Roger Thompson in *Unfit for Modest Ears: A Study of Pornographic, Obscene, and Bawdy Works Written or Published in England in the Second Half of the Seventeenth Century* (Totowa, NJ: Rowman and Littlefield, 1979), p. 5.

[4] Roger Thompson, *Unfit for Modest Ears*, p. 212.

to obscenity), designed to deliver sexual effects as the commodity for an anonymous clientele, was not even possible before the alienated relations of industrial capitalism of eighteenth-century England, according to one theorist of the genre. *Fanny Hill* reconceived sex as an industrial process according to this view, with prolific performers in possession of excellent tools, going about a predictable and rationalized set of acts "accruing to somebody's eventual economic as well as social security," with guaranteed outcomes "for the consumption of an economically passive clientele who were interested in the smoothness of performance and the reliability of the product."[5] Following the appearance of Cleland's innovative pornographic text, a more explicit literature exploring, inducing, and celebrating sexual experience grew up in the second half of the eighteenth century, alongside more polite treatments of sexual encounters.[6] This public discourse about sex was visual and aural as well as literary. By 1756, John Shebbeare observed that "every print-shop has its windows stuck full with indecent prints to inflame desire through the eye, and singers in the streets charm your ears with lascivious songs to waken you to the same employment."[7]

At the same time, a legal literature – both transcripts of actual cases and stories about ongoing legal cases concerning adultery (criminal conversation), elopements, fornication, rape, and impotence that were printed in the newspapers and in pamphlets – satisfied the public's growing curiosity about "real life" cases involving these questions. Susan Staves points out that the *Town and Country Magazine*, begun in 1769, "had a regular feature, a sort of 'affair of the month' column, in which fashionable lovers appeared under romance pseudonyms and were treated with considerable sympathy, even glamorized."[8] By the last quarter of the century, compilations of contested cases about sex and marriage were being published for readers who wanted to peruse the titillating details of lawsuits dealing with fornication, criminal conversation, cruelty, incest, impotency, etc. from the

---

[5] Douglas J. Stewart, "Pornography, Obscenity, and Capitalism," *Antioch Review* 35, 4 (Fall 1977), 389–98, quote 397.

[6] The scandalous memoirs of Teresia Constantia Phillips, Laetitia Pilkington, and Frances Anne, Viscountess Vane, are examples of this more explicit literature. For an analysis of mid-century narratives about these and other immodest women, see Vivien Jones, "Scandalous Femininity: Prostitution and Eighteenth-Century Narrative," in Dario Castiglione and Lesley Sharpe (eds.), *Shifting the Boundaries: Transformation of the Languages of Public and Private in the Eighteenth Century* (Exeter: University of Exeter Press, 1995), pp. 54–70.

[7] Quoted in Lawrence Stone, *The Family, Sex, and Marriage in England 1500–1800* (New York: Harper and Row, 1977), p. 621.

[8] Susan Staves, "Money for Honor: Damages for Criminal Conversation," *Studies in Eighteenth-Century Culture* 11 (1982), 279–97; quote 291.

trial records, complete with all the testimony for each case and even the correspondence of the amorous or acrimonious parties.

One such compendium begins by reinscribing the public demand for such reading material:

The great Desire which Readers of every Description entertain for well-reported Cases of ADULTERY, FORNICATION, SEDUCTION and all Kinds of CRIMINAL CONVER-SATION, and the uncommon Avidity with which former Accounts of the kind have always been received together with the Benefits likely to accrue to the Public, by laying before them authentic Relations of the *heavy Damages*, and other fatal Consequences unavoidable attendant on *illicit Amours*, have induced the Editor hereof to select and procure from the Records of the Courts, the most remarkable Trials of this Nature, from the Year 1780 to the present Time, including genuine Narratives of ILLEGAL ELOPEMENTS, UNEQUAL MARRIAGES, CALEDONIAN EXCURSIONS, PRIVATE INTRIGUES, AMOURS, &c.

Such a collection could be expected to serve a more public good than mere sensationalism, moreover, for individuals needed to understand the legal consequences of their psycho-sexual states of mind. By reading these public court cases, "Wives [might be] Kept in Awe by the just Odium that falls on *Conjugal Infidelity* – Husbands convinced of the Folly and Wickedness of abandoning their Lawful Partners and Children, and making Connections which only terminate in Misery and Expense."[9] Litigation records about sexual escapades and marriage informed readers about the kinds of legal redress available for transgressions of the marriage contract.

Such cases, together with the public discourse about them, contributed to the general confusion of sexual, moral, and economic motives that mark so much of the fiction of the time. The commodification of persons repeatedly embodied by beautiful heroines for whom male characters were willing to pay immense sums and/or to forgo any dowry or portion, in combination with the eroticization of wealth achieved by making all fictional heroes handsome *and* rich – the commercialization, in short, of sexuality – was most transparently manifest in those legal cases in which lawyers had to calculate the exact fiscal value of sexual transgression and the pain of sexual jealousy. The point, after all, of criminal conversation cases was to determine whether the aggrieved husband deserved monetary financial reparation from the man who had enjoyed his wife's sexual services. It was, as Susan Staves has so succinctly stated the matter,

---

[9] *A New and Complete Collection of Trials for Adultery: or A General History of Gallantry and Divorces* "containing all the most remarkable trials heard and determined in the *Courts* of *Doctor's Commons*, the *King's Bench*, &c. &c. for Adultery, Fornication, Cruelty, Incest, and other Criminal Conversation, Impotency, &c. From the Year 1780 to the Middle of the Year 1797" (London: J. Gill, 1796).

trading "money for honor." Criminal conversation cases, new to the eighteenth century (and probably dating back no further than the 1690s), assumed that husbands had property in their wives' bodies and asked, absurdly enough, "how much honor" was lost by any individual plaintiff if and when another took pleasure in that body and how much that honor was worth when one "tried to quantify honor so as to give appropriate damages."[10]

Thus, although there had always been a discourse about sex, honor, chastity, and marriage, the meaning of these terms and the points under debate were being changed by the cash economy and the new fluidity of fortune and class. The church in the Middle Ages had preached mortification of the flesh, but its exhortation to resist fleshly delight had not been specific to sexual pleasure and certainly had not focused on unmarried women. The English discourse about human sexuality that had begun to proliferate in the eighteenth century had an entirely different character. It did not treat sex as one of many human weaknesses in a vast panoply of folly. Sexuality began to come in for special attention as a besetting sin, a cardinal sin, a special weakness requiring special vigilance. As Foucault remarks, illustrating the new self-consciousness that came with this special moralized attention by the late seventeenth century and certainly by the eighteenth century, "no . . . pedagogue would have publicly advised his disciple, as did Erasmus in his *Dialogues*, on the choice of a good prostitute. And the boisterous laughter that had accompanied the precocious sexuality of children for so long – and in all social classes, it seems – was gradually stifled."[11] Nor did this new repressiveness about sexuality and sexual practice drive that behavior or consciousness about it underground, or diminish its importance. On the contrary, as Foucault, among others, has made us all aware, the elaboration of rules governing sexual behavior and greater social scrutiny of it leads to an intensification of interest in it as a locus of consciousness and not merely as an instrument of reproduction. The new centrality accorded sexuality, however anxious and admonitory, shaped a new sexual consciousness. The dimensions and parameters of this new consciousness are what I want to explore in this chapter.

[10] Susan Staves, "Money for Honor: Damages for Criminal Conversation," 279. Staves reports but does not entirely endorse Randolph Trumbach's assertion that the first instance of this kind of litigation occurred in 1692 (294 n. 1).

[11] Michel Foucault, *The History of Sexuality*, vol. 1: *An Introduction*, trans. Robert Hurley (New York: Random House, 1978), p. 27.

SEX AND PROPERTY

The most notable thing about the English discourse concerning sexuality in the eighteenth century, as I have said, was the deep interpenetration of economic and sexual motives. Most treatments of the subject at the time – whether novelistic, legal, or expository – tried to grapple with this confusion and to parse the relation between property and sexual exchange, to establish what could and could not be commodified. At the center of these discussions one could usually find a woman, pushed and pulled in different directions by her family, her lover, and her friends, while beset by sexual threat on every side. Novelists and conduct-book writers alike were deeply concerned with questions of ownership and female sexuality because of the new implications for marriage of the transfer of property. Women provided a focus for cultural anxieties about the alienability of the self at this time, not only because their deployment was central to these social and economic processes, but because the commodification of other human capacities – whether skilled or unskilled labor, professional expertise, productions of the mind, sexual services, or spousal affection along with spousal loyalty – became real and recognizable possibilities in this period for the first time.

Both *Pamela* and *Memoirs of a Woman of Pleasure*, for example, can be understood as exploring the relation between property and sexual exchange. A very interesting comparison of these novels by Ann Kibbie on this dimension points out how similarly they deal with issues of self-ownership and self-alienability. "Pamela uses the word 'virtue' to sum up her belief in the inviolable property she owns in herself, her personal integrity," Kibbie writes.[12] Fanny Hill also owns property in herself, but she chooses to commodify it and profit from it. Yet as Kibbie points out (and as Fielding likewise accuses Richardson in *Shamela*), neither Richardson nor Cleland try to resolve the "tension between the mercenary and the sentimental" in their novels (562). Both rather blur the distinction in their happy endings, sinking the difference between withholding and selling sexual services, between virtue and commodification, in all-encompassing marriage. In *Clarissa*, by comparison, Richardson's later heroine scrupulously avoids being turned into anyone's property. As Laura Rosenthal points out, after the rape, Clarissa is very careful not to take anything she cannot pay for, not even from a friend. She sells everything she has, and when her money runs out she refuses all assistance. With nothing left saleable except her

[12] Ann Louis Kibbie, "Sentimental Properties: *Pamela* and *Memoirs of a Woman of Pleasure*," *ELH* 58, 3 (Fall 1991), 561–77; quote 562.

body, she "obsessively refuses to accept *anything* – even food – that could be read as compensation for sex and thus would transform the rape from an act of violence to an implied contract." Her refusal of all favors once she has been sexually "taken" can thus be read as her absolute resistance to being commodified.[13]

Another line of argument exploring the confusion of sexual and economic motives in contemporary discourses about love and marriage, which I want to gesture to here without thoroughly going into it, concerns the way industrialization influenced sexual life and sexual consciousness. Technology has always provided new metaphors for describing human behavior. Just as in the 1940s and 50s the process of starting up and driving a car afforded a suggestive analogy for the way a man might warm up a woman in order to make love to her (i.e., put in the clutch, open the throttle, turn the key, give it some gas, etc.), and as in our own day computers furnish metaphors for the way we think about human consciousness (what's on our screen, hardwired personality, programmed responses), so hydraulic power and the steam engine provided new metaphors for people to use in thinking about their own sexual activity in eighteenth-century England. It has been observed, for example, that Cleland's entire metaphor system in *Fanny Hill* consists of mechanistic and financial images from mining, manufacturing, and banking, which displace the natural imagery of fire, flowers, wind, water, and bird-and-animal figures that had constituted the erotic vocabulary of the English tradition through the Restoration. Thus, male organs become "engines" or "levers"; female parts become the "hidden mine" or "machine" to be worked; while sexual intercourse becomes "work," "labor," "engineering," and Fanny goes into "trade" with a good "stock" of youth and beauty.[14]

Another historian of the eighteenth century, in order to explain the enormous population boom in this period, has suggested, somewhat outrageously, that productivity became phenomenologically and discursively so central during the period of proto-industrialization that non-productive sexual "behaviors, customs, and usages" – that is, the diverse sexual practices that did not produce offspring – were increasingly understood as preliminary or marginal to the main business of sex, which was heterosexual intercourse.[15] The idea of sex came to be localized, he argues, in that one

<hr>

[13] As Laura Rosenthal argues, "*Clarissa* tells the story of one woman's refusal of sexual alienation, first by her parents and later by the whores." *Infamous Commerce: Prostitution in Eighteenth-Century British Literature and Culture* (Ithaca: Cornell University Press, 2006), Chapter 5.

[14] Douglas J. Stewart, "Pornography, Obscenity, and Capitalism," 390.

[15] Henry Abelove, "Some Speculations on the History of Sexual Intercourse during the Long Eighteenth Century in England," *Genders* 6 (Fall 1989), 125–30, quote 128.

particular act. Sexuality, in other words, became industrialized or at least naturalized to its most instrumentally productive form. Part of England's new infatuation with output, this focus on heterosexual intercourse can be classed with other phenomena of production in the century such as the steadily climbing statistics on cloth manufacture or grain harvests. Without explaining the emphasis on penetrative intercourse as a by-product of the industrial revolution, Tim Hitchcock, another historian of sexuality, has also argued that sex became increasingly phallocentric in the course of the eighteenth century. Printed literature about sex and masturbation, he argues, did not describe or instruct readers in non-penetrative sex such as fondling, kissing, or mutual masturbation, but "emphasised the penis as the all-important organ of generation, and together created and reflected a profound shift in sexual practice."[16]

CONTROLLING WOMEN'S SEXUALITY

One social function of the proliferating discourse on sexual conduct and practice was to regulate sexual behavior, and in particular women's sexual behavior. Women's ambiguous status as the property first of their fathers and then of their husbands was adumbrated in an elaborately developed and psychologized sexual double standard, articulated as a necessary paradox in conduct books, plays, and essays.[17] "Want of care . . . is never to be excus'd; since, as to *this* World, it hath the same effect as want of *Vertue*," wrote Lord Halifax to his daughter in his famous *The Lady's New-Year's Gift* (1688).[18] As Clare Brant has observed, this emphasis on women's chastity "turns male agency into female responsibility."[19] Although Lord Halifax remarks on a number of different aspects of his daughter's education – religion, household economy, friendships, diversions – nothing so focuses his attention as the sexual temptations and threats that he imagines in her path. He warns her about predatory gallants waiting to take advantage of her and bids her to "have a perpetual *Watch* upon your *Eyes*, and to

---

[16] Tim Hitchcock, "Redefining Sex in Eighteenth-Century England," *History Workshop Journal* 41 (1996), 73–90, quote 83.

[17] Keith Thomas suggested many years ago that the meaning of the double standard was that it recognized men's property in women's bodies. Keith Thomas, "The Double Standard," *Journal of the History of Ideas* 20 (1959), 195–216, esp. 210–11.

[18] George Savile, Marquis of Halifax, *The Lady's New-Year's Gift; or, Advice to a Daughter* (London: Matt. Gillyflower, 1688), 3rd edn., p. 3. Subsequent page references are to this edition.

[19] Clare Brant, "Speaking of Women: Scandal and Law in the Mid-Eighteenth Century," in Clare Brant and Diane Purkis (eds.), *Women, Texts and Histories 1575–1760* (London and New York: Routledge, 1992), pp. 242–70, quote p. 247.

remember that one careless *Glance* giveth more advantage than a *hundred Words* not enough considered." She must practice a carefully contrived modulation: "To the *Men* you are to have a *Behavior* which may secure you, without offending them . . . *Looks* that forbid without *Rudeness*, and oblige without *Invitation*" (29). He advises her to ignore any sexual affairs that her husband might engage in, since what is "in the utmost degree *Criminal* in the *Woman*" "passeth under a much *gentler Censure*" in a man. "Next to the danger of *committing* the Fault your self, the greatest is that of *seeing* it in your *Husband*" (10) he tells her, never naming the "fault." "Besides," he continues his instruction by innuendo, "so coarse a Reason . . . will be assign'd for a Lady's too great Warmth upon such an occasion, that Modesty no less than Prudence ought to restrain her" (10).

Although such proto-Victorian prudery seems out of place in the era of Behn and Congreve, Halifax's advice to his daughter, historically prevenient in its circumlocutions, also bears the imprint of its own time. He does not expect her to choose her own husband, for instance, and advises her that "modesty" will make it impossible for her to reject the choice of her friends and relatives. She must try to make the match supportable even if her "inward consent" does not entirely go along with their choice – by good humor, common sense, and some astute psychological manipulation. He mentions the kinds of problems she might have to deal with, depending on the husband she draws in the lottery of life. Her husband-to-be might chase women or support mistresses; he might drink too much or be stingy; he might be morose or bad-tempered. But her possible sexual repugnance or disgust for his unwanted marital embraces is never mentioned. Her desire is irrelevant; her possible sexual revulsion is never even thought of. The notion that she might have fallen in love with anyone else and would therefore resist her parents' choice to preserve her love or maintain her sexual integrity – one of the favorite scenarios of eighteenth-century fiction and called, fittingly, prepossession – never appears at all in this or any other advice book of the seventeenth century.[20]

Falling in love, disgust, sexual integrity, prepossession – these issues begin to emerge in the course of the eighteenth century, in plots and essays focused on the nature and duration of women's "love." Treatments of these questions were calibrated to define the new complexities of use and exchange value in human property insofar as women – in all their interesting

[20] David Blewett, "Changing Attitudes toward Marriage in the Time of Defoe: The Case of Moll Flanders," *Huntington Library Quarterly* 44, 2 (Spring 1981), 77–88, esp. 80.

subjectivity – were still changing hands as they did in Lord Halifax's day but in a culture that was more and more sensitive to the commodification of all human services, including sexual services. As the century wore on, novels, plays, treatises, essays, and letters increasingly showed concern with the issue of a woman's sexual agency and the alienability of her love and/or sexual services. Could a woman give her hand (meaning body) where she could not give her heart? Was a woman justified in disobeying her parents if they commanded her to marry where she could not love? Among the literate classes, sexual intercourse was beginning to be construed as so powerful an experience that, as many novels testified, a woman could die if she had sex where she did not love or was not married.[21]

As a woman's sexual experience came to be interrogated as the key to successful (or unsuccessful) social reproduction, new questions came to be asked in story and song. Could a woman love – *really* love – more than once? Was a woman spoiled if she had been married before or had been in love before? Was "love" voluntary and could a woman re-direct her love wherever she was commanded to? Was true love instantaneous, involuntary, ecstatic – love at first sight? Or did true love build up slowly with shared domestic experience? To what extent was sexual attraction important for a woman? Could a woman learn to love her husband if she began without an attraction to his person? Should a chaste woman ever have sexual feelings? Was prepossession the only acceptable excuse for refusing to marry where one's family directed one to marry? Did women experience sexual desire? What, indeed, was the relation between the "love" of women and the sexual desire of men? What was to be the new relation between sexualized romantic love and domestic life?

These questions defined women's sexuality in terms that emphasized their obedience and chastity but also their agency, volition, and genuine passion. A woman was only truly moral if she made her own choices about love, and felt them deeply. This is the issue debated in Sarah Fielding's *Remarks on Clarissa* (1749), which imagines an entire drawing room full of readers discussing whether or not Clarissa acted out of blind obedience to her parents and whether she was capable of womanly passion and torn

---

[21] An early example of this occurs in the anonymous *The History of the Human Heart* (London: J. Freeman, 1749), in which the young Quaker woman, Saphira, having experienced illicit intercourse with Camillo without the benefit of any formal matrimonial blessing, after having been cursed and then forgiven by her mother, expires in his arms (220). This novel is an interesting precursor of *Tristram Shandy* in its playful experiments with form. At the outset, for instance, we watch the protagonist's homunculus "nimbly skipped into the *Ovaria* of his Mother" during his parents' coupling where "for two or three Days he was tossed too and fro in his new Habitation" (16–17).

by opposing allegiances.[22] Some of the readers complain that she is an undutiful daughter, whereas to others she was overly "strict in her Principles of Obedience to such Parents." She is criticized as being "too fond of a Rake and a Libertine," while to others "her Heart was as inpenitrable [sic] and unsusceptible of Affection, as the hardest Marble" (13). There seems to have been genuine confusion about how a woman should feel in these circumstances, as well as about what Clarissa should have done.

Bellario asserts that Clarissa's chief fault was that she lacked affection, and that a "Woman whose Mind was incapable of Love, could not be amiable, nor have any of those gentle Qualities which chiefly adorn the female Character." Although Richardson's defender, Miss Gibson, points out that Lovelace's treachery justifies her suspicious and withholding behavior, she agrees with him that "being Void of all Affection" is "the heaviest Charge a Woman can be accused of" (17–18). Bellario refers to Prior's poem *Henry and Emma* as the very pattern of the unconditional love and acceptance that a woman should give the man of her choice. An imitation of the old ballad "The Nut-Brown Maid," Prior's poem adds a distinctively masochistic, self-abasing streak to the old ballad about the plucky maiden who leaves her father's house and lands to put on men's attire and roam with her outlaw lover through the forests of old England. Bellario compares Clarissa's prudence unfavorably with Emma's unconditional loyalty to Henry, her willingness to follow him anywhere – even if he has killed someone and threatens to leave her for another woman. Bellario condemns Richardson's heroine because she will not throw caution to the winds and give herself entirely to her admirer. Miss Gibson replies by admonishing him that he would not want his own daughter to be pressured to act this way against her own self-interest.

Bellario honestly owned he would not. "Why then, Sir, (replyed she) . . . you will see the Injustice of wishing another Man's Daughter should act so." Bellario ingen-uously confessed, that when he read the Poem of Henry and Emma, the Picture of his Mistress, and not that of his Daughter, was before his Eyes, and he would have his Mistress of all Mankind love but him alone. (21)

Bellario's reply shows, among other things, how incompatible the roles of daughter and mistress were becoming as the consanguineal family grew ever more detached from the conjugal family.

---

[22] *Remarks on Clarissa* was reprinted by the Augustan Reprint Society, edited and with an introduction by Peter Sabor, as nos. 231–2 (Los Angeles: William Andrews Clark Memorial Library, 1985). Subsequent page references are to this edition.

When Bellario charges Clarissa with "being Void of all Affection," he is giving voice to the (relatively new) belief that the capacity for love and self-sacrifice was the most significant indicator of a woman's femininity. That, undoubtedly, explains why *Henry and Emma* is quoted so frequently and approvingly in the fiction of the latter part of the eighteenth century. It was expected increasingly that no woman worthy of the name would marry without love, although the extent to which a woman could will herself to love a husband chosen by her parents was undetermined. The dimension of Clarissa's character that Sarah Fielding created Bellario to misread, to misunderstand, and finally to appreciate, was just this complex mixture of her "woman's capacity" to love wholeheartedly and without reserve in combination with her highly developed moral faculty. Bellario's confusion reflects the culture's mixed signals about women's nature as English society evolved new requirements for its women.

One sort of fictional plot of the later eighteenth century designed to examine the nature of women's love tested the duration of a woman's first attachment. Novels asked implicitly whether or not a woman could love more than once – could give total allegiance to more than one master. What did it mean to love completely and utterly if that love could be recalled and bestowed on another? Plots interrogating the integrity of a woman's first and second love began to proliferate in novels of the second half of the century such as Elizabeth Griffith's *The History of Lady Barton* (1771) or Henry Mackenzie's *Julia de Roubigné* (1777). Mrs. Bonhote's *Darnley Vale; or, Emelia Fitzroy* (1789) and Mrs. Keir's *History of Miss Greville* (1787) were similarly, according to J. M. S. Tompkins, "written to prove that a woman can withdraw her affections from their first object and become perfectly happy in a second attachment, even though she may afterwards discover that she was separated from her first lover by treachery."[23] The heroine of Elizabeth Helme's *Clara and Emmeline; or, The Maternal Benediction* (1788) renounces the man she loves and obediently marries the man whom her tyrannical father commands her to marry, in order to preserve her mother from his wrath. Her sexual loyalty is thus pitted against her deep love for her mother. The reader then witnesses the delicacy with which she performs her conjugal duty despite her contempt for her profligate husband while she struggles to stifle her love for the paragon whom she has renounced. Her ability to walk this tightrope of duty without sacrificing her capacity for feeling is the achievement of Helme's portrait.

[23] J. M. S. Tompkins, *The Popular Novel in England* (London: Constable, 1932), p. 163 n. 2.

One of the earliest examinations of this question of women's loyalty in love occurs in *The Cry* (1754), Sarah Fielding and Jane Collier's experimental collaboration, in a debate between Portia and Serina. Serina pleads the cause of constant love no matter what the consequences before an assembly of other women who represent public opinion and are designated "the Cry." Portia argues that extravagant passion for an improper object – when the man is worthless, cowardly, or vicious – is foolish and could have tragic consequences. Serina, "not yet twenty years old, her heart filled with the image of her own meritorious constancy, pleaded long in defence of the merit of thus resolutely fixing the affections, and concluded with an high admiration of the character and behaviour of *Prior's Emma*."[24] "The Cry" agrees with Serina and declares that Portia "had no heart, no soul, no feeling of tender passions, and was more like an insensible stock than a woman" (II: 91). One can see the cliché taking shape; a true woman gave herself completely, unstintingly, without self-protection or reason – like patient Griselda (even before marriage) or like Henry's Emma. But the question was whether she could give herself with this exaggerated selflessness more than once. This was a serious question if a woman's sexual connection was to regulate society's transfers of money and property, if her capacity for love and loyalty authorized new alliances and the redistribution of wealth among men.

In Georgiana Spencer's *Emma: or, The Unfortunate Attachment* (1773), Emma Egerton gives up her first love, Augustus Sidney, in obedience to her dying father and ambivalently marries a richer man. The results are tragic: her new husband believes that no woman of delicacy and purity can love more than one man in a lifetime; her existence is poisoned by the fear that he will find out about her childhood attachment. Henry Mackenzie's heroine in *Julia de Roubigné* (1777) also marries a man she does not love in obedience to her father's wishes, only to learn later that her first love, Savillon, is *not* married to another but is looking for her. Her husband, in a fit of jealousy, poisons her. In Maria Edgeworth's *Helen* (1834), a late example of the phenomenon, Lady Cecilia Clarendon is afraid to let her husband know that while still single she received love letters from Colonel D'Aubigny. Her husband is one of those men who has vowed never to marry anyone who has ever loved before. This is why, though Lady Cecilia had no physical affair with D'Aubigny, she is afraid of her husband's finding out about this previous connection. To protect herself, she convinces her friend

[24] Sarah Fielding and Jane Collier, *The Cry: A New Dramatic Fable*, 3 vols. (London: 1754), vol. II, p. 91.

Helen to appear to be the recipient of D'Aubigny's letters, with disastrous consequences.

Elizabeth Griffith's *The History of Lady Barton* (1771) is pervaded by anxiety about the virtue of a woman who marries without love a man urged by her "friends." Her husband treats her without consideration and rebuffs her open-hearted and affectionate nature. Louisa, Lady Barton, feels Sir William Barton's harshness the more keenly because of the assiduous attentions of the honorable Lord Lucan who silently adores the neglected and ill-treated lady, and because of the more dangerous attentions of the watchful, unscrupulous Colonel Walter. *The History of Lady Barton* raises the question of whether or not a woman ought to marry where her friends and family direct her to marry if she has no prepossession in favor of another suitor – where she does not love, but, at least at the start, where she has no aversion. The novel asks: should a decent woman require love with marriage? Is she coldhearted or a prude if she does not? Is she a silly romantic if she does? Does marital neglect justify adulterous longing?

The History of Betty Barnes (1753) ridicules the unrealistic expectation that a woman love only once in her life when telling about the "tender sentiments" the unfortunate Mrs. Evans felt for her benefactor, Mr. Gibbons.

> But methinks I hear my reader cry out; what! a woman of virtue capable of loving any other than her husband, after having been married for love too! an excellent proof of delicacy truly! Dear young lady, for such I will suppose you to be, by the vivacity of the remark, I beseech you remember, that you are not now reading the memoirs of some romantic heroine, but a character taken from real life; and that, as an historian, I am obliged to represent circumstances as they are.[25]

In this teasing send-up of the formula "one love for life," the author mocks novel-readers who think they know about virtue without knowing anything about life; she also claims truth status for her fiction. The reader who faults Mrs. Evans for her lack of "delicacy," for falling in love again after her husband betrayed and abandoned her, has read too many bad novels and deserves to be patronized.

Among the better-known texts dealing with this question, *Sir Charles Grandison*, with its hero's tolerant pronouncement on his sister Charlotte's youthful infatuation (and his subsequent desire to marry her to a respectable and devoted man who will protect and care for her even if he does not thrill her), represents Richardson's resistance to the ideology crystallizing in his day about once-and-only ecstatic love, eternal loyalty, and the ineradicability of a man's imprimatur on a woman's impressionable sexual

---

[25] [Mary Collyer,] *The History of Betty Barnes*, 2 vols. (1753; rpt. New York: Garland, 1974), vol. I, p. 42.

consciousness. Marianne Dashwood's ardent belief in a first and only love in Jane Austen's *Sense and Sensibility*, a judgment she revises later in the novel after a little experience of life, was one of the many ways Austen mocked the widely debated question of prepossession, sexual ownership, and men's property in women's consciousness. Anne Elliot's impassioned defense of women's fidelity in *Persuasion*, her *cri de coeur* that women love the "longest, when existence or when hope is gone," must also be read in the context of this late eighteenth-century debate about the alienability of women's love.[26]

These moral debates in fiction were part of the process of reconceiving Englishwomen as the sexual property of their husbands rather than as partners and co-owners of the marital household. The commodification of women as sexual objects can be seen in the reinvigorated fetishization of virginity – visible in the so-called "defloration mania" of the eighteenth and nineteenth centuries as well as in stories of faked virginity and medical instructions for reconstituting or simulating lost maidenheads. Tassie Gwilliam has argued compellingly that a more thorough commodification of women in the marketplaces of the eighteenth century (whether the marriage market, the brothel, or texts describing these cultural sites) accounts for this fascination with narratives of counterfeit virginity. Attempts to simulate virginity were usually undertaken to enhance the market value of a woman's sexual services because the eighteenth-century preoccupation with reified virginity inflated the value of intercourse with a virgin. The narratives Tassie Gwilliam cites, beginning with *Fanny Hill*, demonstrate that a maidenhead was worth more in sexual commerce than any other kind of sexual service, and more than any subsequent experience with the same woman.[27]

This fixation on newness was also fed by contemporary quack superstitions about the healing effects of sex with a young girl. Sexual intercourse with a virgin was supposed by some to cure impotence as well as venereal disease. According to Anthony E. Simpson, widespread belief in this remedy accounts for many cases of child molestation and child rape in eighteenth-century London.[28] Like a commodity whose status is changed

---

[26] Jane Austen, *Persuasion* (1818), ed. D. W. Harding (Harmondsworth: Penguin, 1965), p. 238.

[27] Tassie Gwilliam, "Female Fraud: Counterfeit Maidenheads in the Eighteenth Century," *Journal of the History of Sexuality* 6, 4 (April 1996), 518–48.

[28] Susan Staves has remarked to me in conversation that she thinks this "belief" sometimes operated as a cover for adult/child incest with fathers, stepfathers, or uncles. That is, a child's venereal disease was explained as the result of a "stranger" trying to cure himself.

Simpson also reports that changes in the law in this period *lowered* the age of consensual sex to ten, noting that this legal change meant that there was less rather than more protection for

as soon as the wrapper is torn and it is converted from exchange value to use value (think of the price difference between a new car and one that has been driven for a few months), an eighteenth-century woman who had engaged in heterosexual intercourse – even once – was devalued, particularly if her only property was in her person. Newness constituted her moral capital, and was the most significant form of capital she possessed. Since sexual consciousness, and hence sexual memory, was fast becoming a significant aspect of a woman's marketable femininity, the imprinting of that first sexual experience in a woman's consciousness was thought by some to be of the utmost importance in terms of sexual ownership.[29]

This overvaluation of virginity, this preference for newness, for females who were sexual *tabulae rasae*, was, relatively speaking, a new thing in eighteenth-century England. It would have made no sense in earlier periods when both men and women married later and a third of all marriages were second marriages. In mid-sixteenth-century England 30% of all marriages were remarriages according to Wrigley and Schofield's statistics, calculated by the numbers of widows and widowers recorded as marrying in the parish registers. Given this social reality, the notion of constructing women as the property of one man and one man only, with a value that diminished with more practical experience, would have been absurd. Even in the period under consideration, although the number of second marriages was diminishing, there was still a substantial proportion of widows and widowers marrying – presumably with previous sexual experience. In such a system, men's property in women was contingent, transient, partial, and (as I have already suggested) shared with women's families of origin who retained a stake in their welfare. The parish register of Beccles, Suffolk shows that between 1701 and 1754 21.2% of all marriages were still second marriages but

female children in this period. He points out that this runs counter to received wisdom about the "invention of childhood." In his own words: "The failure of the courts of this time to preserve the ancient common-law rights of female children does not indicate much concern for childhood or its protection. This fact stands strongly against opinion which views this period as one in which childhood became defined as a status demanding care and protection." It seems to me that this legal development is further evidence of the devaluation and "disinheritance" of daughters in this period. Antony E. Simpson, "Vulnerability and the Age of Female Consent: Legal Innovation and Its Effect on Prosecutions for Rape in Eighteenth-Century London," in G. S. Rousseau and Roy Porter (eds.), *Sexual Underworlds of the Enlightenment* (Chapel Hill, NC: University of North Carolina Press, 1988), pp. 181–205, quote p. 200.

[29] This point is made by Freud in his paper "The Taboo of Virginity" (1918): "The demand that the girl [sic] shall bring with her into marriage with one man no memory of sexual relations with another is after all nothing but a logical consequence of the exclusive right of possession over a woman which is the essence of monogamy – it is but an extension of this monopoly on to the past." First published in *Sammlung*, Vierte Folge, 1918; the translation here is by Joan Rivière, in *Collected Papers*, 5 vols. (New York: Basic Books, 1959), vol. IV, pp. 217–35, quote p. 217.

between 1754 and 1780 this figure dropped to 17.8%. By the mid nineteenth century, the percentage of second marriages across England had dropped further to 11.27%.[30] Samuel Johnson, who in 1735 married Elizabeth Porter, a widow of forty with children, remarked to Boswell in 1769 that one of their mutual friends had "done a very foolish thing, Sir; he has married a widow, when he might have had a maid." Boswell also reports that Johnson once almost asked his "Tetty" not to marry again if he died before her, observing that in Johnson's "fond persevering appropriation of his *Tetty*, even after her decease, he seems totally to have overlooked the prior claim of the honest Birmingham trader," "the husband of her youth and the father of her children."[31] Johnson vehemently opposed the second marriage of his good and loyal friend Mrs. Thrale in 1784, even though it promised her real happiness in contrast to her first marriage. Despite Johnson's disapproval – he broke off relations with her when it became clear she was going to marry Piozzi – it proved a happy marriage and Hester Thrale Piozzi lived with her second husband for fifteen years before he died. Such opposition to the second marriage of a respectable woman had hardly existed when Mrs. Mary Pendarves Delany chose to remarry forty years earlier, but the climate had changed. The libidinous desire of older women was becoming less socially tolerable; it confused property relations, including the property a woman had in herself.

Given the frequency of remarriage in the seventeenth century, one can see why "prepossession" was not yet mentioned in conduct books of that century as grounds for refusing a match – and why husbands and suitors in fiction or drama were rarely represented as worrying about whether the objects of their affection had ever loved anyone before them. But by the time that Richardson wrote *Clarissa* (1747–8), he was able to invent the venal and authoritarian Harlowe family who, with the exception of Clarissa's mother, seemed to be unable to imagine any *other* motive than prepossession for Clarissa's rejection of Solmes. Although some critics read perfect Clarissa as more highly evolved in terms of female delicacy and sexual revulsion, able to reject Solmes without loving Lovelace, the Harlowes clearly believed that a women's sexuality could only be given away once. It was not a capacity to be exercised but a possession to be sold and purchased – once. A woman's body was never her own to deploy: only if she was already claimed did her refusal make sense.

---

[30] E. A. Wrigley and R. S. Schofield, *The Population History of England, 1541–1871: A Reconstruction* (Cambridge, MA: Harvard University Press, 1981), p. 258.

[31] James Boswell, *The Life of Samuel Johnson*, 2 vols. (1906; rpt. London: Dent, 1973), vol. 1, p. 360.

Richardson's *Clarissa*, Frances Sheridan's *The Memoirs of Miss Sidney Bidulph* (1761), Elizabeth Griffith's *The History of Lady Barton* (1771), Georgiana Spencer's *Emma: or, The Unfortunate Attachment* (1773), Henry Mackenzie's *Julia de Roubigné* (1777) – these novels and dozens more like them were part of a discourse building up a new complex, introjected attitude towards sexual experience that would construct women as the right kind of sexual property: neither prude nor coquette but trustworthy and warmblooded. Women had to learn to make distinctions between the right kind of sex and the wrong kind of sex. They had to learn a new kind of physical revulsion for sexual experience when not accompanied by a highly wrought and even mystified romantic love that was supposed to infuse ordinary sexual and domestic relations. This refinement was necessary to develop an inner consciousness of the double standard. If women were to stay put as the sexual property of one man and one man only, they had to be trained to feel repugnance for physical relations with anyone else. The emphasis on a woman's sexual allegiance to a mate, rather than her obedience to a father, also signaled the realignment of kinship along a conjugal rather than consanguineal axis.

THE INVENTION OF SEXUAL DISGUST

The invention of sexual disgust in the mid eighteenth century was part of this construction of a new sexual identity for women which answered these cultural purposes. A somatized reaction compelling enough to regulate women's sexual preferences and habits, sexual disgust can hardly be found in the repertoire of earlier English written experience. Even rape is recorded more as pain at physical force than psychological horror at unwanted intercourse understood as invasion of the self.[32] The ribald escapades of such Restoration texts as *The Wandring Whore*, with their gross physical acts, hardly left any place for sexual disgust or sexual delicacy. It is hard to imagine an early eighteenth-century heroine like Moll Flanders or a character from one of Delarivier Manley's fictions feeling sexual disgust. Only when the experience of sexual intercourse began to be invested with meaning greater than other bodily experience – only then could its mishandling horrify and shock.

---

[32] Susan Staves quotes the testimony of a woman who has been raped in her examination of scenes of attempted rape in the fiction of Henry Fielding. The statement she reproduces from the trial testimony of 1768 is powerful in its flat, unemotional description of force. Susan Staves, "Fielding and the Comedy of Attempted Rape," in Beth Fowkes Tobin (ed.), *History, Gender & Eighteenth-Century Literature* (Athens: University of Georgia Press, 1994), pp. 86–112.

Even as late as Jane Austen's *Pride and Prejudice*, originally drafted as *First Impressions* in 1796–7, Charlotte Lucas – who is neither insensible nor crude – makes a cheerful adjustment to her insufferable new husband, Mr. Collins. When Elizabeth Bennet visits her friends and appraises their marital situation after several months, she is pleased to see her old friend taking satisfaction in her pleasant establishment while wisely encouraging Mr. Collins to work in his garden. Although the reader is told that Charlotte deliberately chooses not to hear Mr. Collins' irritating sycophancies, there is no hint whatsoever that she feels sexual disgust in having to sleep with that repugnant man.[33] One is surprised by Austen's acquittal of Charlotte in this matter because by the nineteenth century novel readers could expect their heroines to refuse to have sex with men who were not heroes. But Charlotte Lucas Collins is a vestigial character, left over from an era of pragmatic rather than romantic matches, before the discourse of the second half of the eighteenth century created unbridgeable moral conflict over arranged marriages. The new popular wisdom set up expectations of disgust for sexual acts without love, and even for lustful feelings that had no admixture of moral admiration or mutual social respect.[34]

Although the beginnings of this discourse of sexual disgust can be seen in many places – the *Athenian Mercury*, the *Tatler*, the *Spectator*, sentimental comedies, and finally novels after about 1740 – the classical statement of this repugnance for pure physicality, with or without marriage, was probably Daniel Defoe's *Conjugal Lewdness or, Matrimonial Whoredom: A Treatise concerning the Use and Abuse of the Marriage Bed* (1727). Begun in the 1690s although not published until 1727, Defoe's treatise even-handedly warns men and women alike that sexual enjoyment without mutual affection and regard is morally reprehensible and physically devastating.[35] He deplores the degeneracy of the modern age which makes marriage, that "divine Institution," "a Stalking-horse to the brutal Appetite" (33).

---

[33] In discussing this and other loveless marriages, J. M. S. Tompkins compares Mrs. Strictland in Clara Reeve's *School for Widows* (1791) to Charlotte Lucas Collins, who, she says, is never quite condemned for her practical choice. Reeve's Mrs. Strictland, says Tompkins, "painfully learns enough patience and tact to live not uncomfortably beside her boorish spouse . . . Miss Reeve finds her heroine exemplary and not ill-rewarded. She holds to her bargain, takes comfort in her children, and, after the first revolts, finds even in her confined circumstances opportunities for charity and mental growth. The picture is done in sober tones, without satire and almost without humour, but there is a quality of unassuming realism about it, a simple attention to important things, that commands respect." J. M. S. Tompkins, *The Popular Novel in England*, p. 164. As one can see from this description, sex was not considered one of the "important things."

[34] For a longer historical discussion of the invention of sexual disgust, see my "Sleeping with Mr. Collins," *Persuasions* 22 (2000), 119–35.

[35] Maximillian Novak edited and introduced the reprint of this work issued by Scholars' Facsimiles & Reprints in Gainesville, Florida, 1967.

Defoe's attention to the psychological dimension of sexuality is fairly novel in this period. The seventeenth-century sex manuals and works of anatomy and advice, such as *Culpepper's Midwife* or *Aristotle's Master-Piece: or, The Secrets of Generation Displayed*, did not moralize about attitudes, practices, or legalities. They simply gave the facts of physiological excitation and reproduction as they understood them. Defoe's treatise, subtitled "The Use and Abuse of the Marriage Bed," argues first and foremost that one must take seriously the business of marriage which is "all that can be called happy in the Life of Man," and "the Center to which all lesser Delights of Life tend, as a Point in the Circle" (96). Defoe grants that moderate sexual pleasure is appropriate in marriage where there is mutual affection and especially where there is the desire for children. But the point which he repeats again and again – and the point for which he apparently wrote the book – is that married couples must restrain excessive sexual desire, even for each other, and they must temper their lust with *politesse* in the bedroom: "Married persons must keep such modesty and decency of treating each other, that they never force themselves into high and violent lusts, with arts and devices: always remembring that those Mixtures are most innocent which are *most simple* and *most natural, most orderly* and *most safe*" (55). Married persons must not make use of each other as sexual objects; they must try to retain their sense of their whole relation to one another at all times. "It is a duty of matrimonial Chastity to be restrained and temperate in the use of their lawful Pleasures," he wrote (55). These ideas did not originate with Defoe – religious Protestants had preached sexual restraint for a long time – but he was writing not for a specialized, sectarian audience but for a broad, popular readership. He condemned the expedients that human invention might dream up to fan the flames of desire – some of which have been updated and recycled in our own day in magazines sold in supermarkets offering advice on "how to keep your marriage alive." His concern historicizes the place of sexuality in marriage – indeed, in human life – and reminds us how much attitudes have changed in 300 years.

Defoe warned that criminally immoderate sexual appetite, whether inside or outside of marriage, would enfeeble the body and take its toll on the health of one's offspring. "Palsies and Epilepsies, Falling-Sickness, trembling of the Joints, pale dejected Aspects, Leanness, and at last Rottenness and other filthy and loathsome Distempers" could be expected in later years of those who overdid sexual activity in youth. Defoe's metaphors are mechanical and hydraulic: sex uses up the body's vitality; ill health will result "if the Fountain is drawn dry, if the Vitals are exhausted, the Engines of Nature worked with unreasonable Violence" (91). As for the progeny of unions too self-indulgent about wanton sex: "Nature speaks plainer in her Reproofs of that Crime than I dare do," Defoe claimed, and the revolting effects were visible for several generations: "The Product of those impure and unlawful, however matrimonial Liberties, carry the indelible Marks of their Parents unhappy Excesses and Intemperances in their Faces," where "scrophulous Humours break out, in Scabs and Blisters" and in the "blotch'd and bladdred Skin of their Posterity" (61–3).

Such titillating detail combined with physical revulsion was a new combination in 1727 and both reflected and contributed to changing popular attitudes towards sex. Defoe fulminated against contemporary licentiousness masquerading as marriage. Too many modern couples were willing "to gratify their vitious Part in the formality of a legal Appointment," he wrote, without "one Ounce of Affection, not a Grain of original, chast, and rivetted Love, the Glory of a Christian Matrimony, and the essential Happiness of Life" (105–6). He describes the delicious freedoms of marriage – how "she freely strips off her Cloths in the Room with him; and whereas she would not have shew'd him her Foot before, without her Shoe and Stockings on, she now, without the least Breach of Modesty, goes into what we call the naked Bed to him, and with him; lies in his Arms, and in his Bosom, and sleeps safely, *and with security in her Virtue* with him, all the Night" (58). Initially describing this openness as peaceful and innocent – a wife sleeping in her husband's arms was like a child on its mother's bosom – he soon warms to his message that, however sanctified, these freedoms are fraught with dangers and one must beware "wanton excesses" and "criminal indulgence," excesses and indulgences that he suggests with pornographic effect. Thus he enlists the aroused energy of his readers in the service of disapproval, mingling descriptions of physical desire with moral disapprobation and physical disgust until a whirlpool of feeling is set up around the marriage bed.

Human sexuality – especially female sexuality – was no longer to be unselfconsciously accepted as part of physical life, but needed to be scrutinized, judged, and regulated. As I observed earlier, Richardson's *Clarissa* was one of the earliest texts to naturalize a certain female delicacy regarding these matters. When Clarissa describes to Anna Howe the way Solmes drew his chair so close to hers that "squatting in it with his ugly weight . . . he pressed upon my hoop," the reader feels the threat of sexual violation. Solmes' weight trespassing on Clarissa's hoop also suggests his bodily impatience to force himself on a more private circumference. His physical proximity so panics Clarissa that she loses her self-control and moves involuntarily to another chair. Somewhat later, Clarissa's brother, James Harlowe Jr., deliberately

insults the finely tuned heroine by insinuating that she has sexual feeling
like the rest of the animal creation – in this case, for Lovelace. He sneers
a line at her from Virgil's *Georgics* which, in its original context, refers to
the use of animal mating cycles for agricultural advantage: *amor omnibus
idem* (All feel the same love).[36] If it were not for his cruelty and greed, one
could argue that he was simply teasing Clarissa, as Anna Howe has already
teased her, about her "throbs" and "glows" for the virile villain. But styling
such attraction not as sentiment and feeling but as brute animal instinct
appalls her and makes her squeamish, and the reader shares her shock and
enters into her way of thinking. Clarissa then reinscribes her squeamishness about being placed in Nature's animal continuum when she writes to
Anna about her brother's "infamous hint" (219). Coming as it does from
her crude brother, accompanied by the threat of being carried off to uncle Antony's moated castle and forced to endure visits from the repulsive
Mr. Solmes, the notion that all "love" stems from the same primal instinct
of species survival – that gradations of feeling are ultimately traceable to
this one great reproductive imperative – places the sex drive in a context
that naturalizes squeamishness and makes it the only reasonable response
to an untenable situation.

Defoe's *Conjugal Lewdness* helped to create the climate for Clarissa's
response by arguing that without the right kind of consciousness sexual
intercourse was bestial. A secular version of an older Christian idea, Defoe's
argument for the all-distinguishing importance of separating lust from love
stipulated that sex had to be accompanied by love or else it brutalized the
sensibility. Although he castigated spouses who used the marriage bed for
wanton pleasure, he reserved his worst opprobrium for those who married
with only "slight and superficial Affection." Such persons "are to me little
more than legal Prostitutes" (102), he wrote, insofar as they provide sexual
service without engaging their affections. Twenty years before Richardson
dramatized the matter in *Clarissa*, Defoe charged parents who forced their
children to marry without love as guilty of rape, and gives as an example
a dialogue between a knight and his lady in which she testifies "'twas no
Marriage, 'twas all *Forced*, a *Rape* upon Innocence and Virtue... I was
dragged to Church, I did not go; I tell you, 'twas no Matrimony, tho' 'twas
a Marriage; I was ravished and nothing else" (175). He points out that when
a woman is violated sexually by a man who is not her husband, she can
bring him to court.

[36] Letter 16, 50.1 and 50.2 in Samuel Richardson, *Clarissa*, ed. Angus Ross (London: Penguin, 1985),
pp. 87, 218–19. The quotation from Virgil is from the *Georgics*, book III, l. 244.

If Violence is offered to the Chastity of a Woman, she has her recourse to the Law, and she will be redress'd as far as redress can be obtained. Where the Fact is irretrievable, the Man should be punished, and the Woman is protected by the Law from any farther Force upon her for the future. But here the Woman is put to Bed to the Man by a kind of forced Authority of Friends; 'tis a Rape upon her Mind; her Soul, her brightest Faculties, her Will, her Affections are ravished, and she is left without redress, she is left in the Possession of the Ravisher, or of him, who, by their Order, she was delivered up to, and she is bound in the Chains of the same Violence for her whole life. HORRID abuse! (198)

Defoe's language both sensationalizes and heightens the horror of sex without love. What appears to have been felt as an irritant or annoyance a bare forty years earlier at the end of the Restoration – sex was certainly never a pleasure where unwanted – here is constructed as a violation of a woman's deepest self. What was probably regarded as an unpleasant duty among other unpleasant duties is here written of as a primal affront to her fundamental being. Defoe regards sex as both more important to an individual's identity than it had ever been thought before, and less socially significant in constituting a proper marriage within a community. Thus, marrying where there was no affection and mutual regard – however obediently it might reproduce the family – was not properly marriage according to Defoe's treatise but matrimonial whoredom. And, likewise, marrying to satisfy lust without the urge to create a family and share domestic life was not marriage but conjugal lewdness. In either case, marriage was defined apart from sexual practice. Although a social relation that constructed women as sexual property, marriage now derived its validity from legal or ecclesiastical sanctions rather than from the procreative facts that had heretofore created kin connections. If the sexual practices of individuals could construct kin relations in the seventeenth century, by the end of the eighteenth century only the state could construct and validate such kin connections.

SEX BEFORE MARRIAGE

Defoe's exposition marks the transitional period during which marriage came to be defined less by actual sexual practice and more by a combination of legal arrangements and sentimental attitudes. Sexual activity no longer *constituted* marriage but needed to be rethought and reworked to fit the new conception of marriage. These understandings were fairly new in Defoe's time. First drafted in the 1690s, although not published (anonymously) until 1727, *Conjugal Lewdness* shows Defoe changing his

mind as one ideological system gave way to another.[37] "I have heard some
serious and learned Divines say, that it is a worse Crime, and deserves a
severer Censure," he wrote, "for a Man and Woman under promises of
Marriage to lie together before the Marriage is compleated, than a simple
or single Fornication between two who have no design of Matrimony." In
other words, some learned clergy were beginning to argue that sex with
one's intended was worse than casual sex with someone else. "I confess,
though at first I hesitated a little at it, I am fully satisfied it is so," he added
(65). Thus, when he began his treatise at the end of the seventeenth century, he still had to be convinced that it was worse for a person to fornicate
with their betrothed before marriage, no matter how serious their love or
how long they had known one another, than to fornicate with someone
with whom there was no intention of marriage whatsoever. But he became
convinced:

For a Man to make a Whore of the very Woman who he intends and really designs
to make his Wife, or, in plain *English*, to make a Whore of his Wife; he defiles his
own Bed, pollutes his own Seed, spreads Bastardy in his own Race, and shews a
most wicked vitiated Appetite. (65)

This about-face represents a remarkable change in customary attitudes
towards sex and marriage. Fifty years before, sexual intercourse between
two people who considered themselves married – with or without benefit
of clergy – would have been sufficient by itself to validate their union,
especially if their sexual congress proved fruitful. In other words, sex and
the intention of marriage could have constituted marriage. Now it was
considered the worst kind of fornication if engaged in before the proper
legal and ecclesiastical steps had been taken. Thus, for all the protestations
in Defoe's tract and the popular press that love was all that really mattered in marriage, what in fact mattered most was that sex not take place
outside of marriage. Now that property had become such a critical consideration, too much was at stake to leave the creation of kin up to individual
sexual practice. Women, it seems, had to learn to watch their step, since

---

[37] One fascinating piece of internal evidence corroborating Defoe's prefatory assertion that he began
this treatise thirty years before is his reference to women's immodest talk about the "Secrets of the
Bed-Chamber" and in particular "the diverting Complaint of Madam Arab.— with that of the
new-married Alderman —'s Lady" (122), probably a reference to the marriage of Arabella Hunt to
cross-dressing Amy Poulter, widow of Arthur Poulter, Esq., the scandal of which was widely discussed
and written about in the mid-1680s. For more about this case, see Patricia Crawford and Sara
Mendelson, "Sexual Identities in Early Modern England: The Marriage of Two Women in 1680,"
Gender & History 7, 3 (November 1995), 362–77.

lineage – and therefore inheritance – was in their keeping. Love, it seems, was less important than legal contracts after all.

Many fictional situations were spun out of the complications of this new understanding. In *The History of the Human Heart* (1749), for example, when the hero confesses to his tutor that he has engaged in sex play with his cousin Maria – whom he has always intended to marry when they came of age – he is shocked to learn "that he had been guilty of the most heinous Crime, both in the Sight of God and Man" and "allowed himself to be carried away by the instigation of a wicked Lust to defile himself, and Ruin his dear *Maria* for ever; that now he had made a Whore of her, she could neither be his Wife, nor fit for any other Gentleman"(51). Although from a twentieth-century vantage point this outcome hardly seems inevitable, in this eighteenth-century fable the hero, Camillo, "thunder-struck at this Representation of the Case," renounces his obliging cousin forever. The rest of this picaresque novel retails the sexual adventures and machinations of the now-initiated Camillo, including his seduction of a beautiful sixteen-year-old Quaker named Saphira, who expires in his arms when her mother discovers, condemns, and finally pardons their affair. Although this time Camillo is ready to make restitution by marrying Saphira, the narrative thwarts his good intentions and reinscribes the lesson that sex before marriage can lead to no good.

A character in Sarah Scott's *Millenium Hall* (1762), Lady Emilia Roberts, refuses to marry the man to whom she is betrothed, after permitting the final intimacies on the eve of his departure to join his regiment in Ireland. When she reflects on her own misconduct the next day, she resolves never to marry at all. "What confidence, what esteem could I hope from an husband, who so well knew my weakness . . . I could scarcely bear to see myself; and I was determined not to depend on any one who was equally conscious of my guilt" (213).[38] Despite the frantic attempts of her lover to convince her of his esteem and despite her extreme youth – she was seventeen – and her pregnancy, Lady Emilia remained adamant. She lives single to the end of her days, sharing with her ex-suitor the "tenderest friendship," but never repeating the sexual experience that "fixed a degree of melancholy on my mind, which no time has been able to conquer" (216).

Hugh Kelly's *Memoirs of a Magdalen: or, The History of Louisa Mildmay* (1767) is another novel whose fictional situation put to the test the new code that sex without legal marriage was dangerous for women. Like dozens

---

[38] Page numbers cited are from the edition edited by Gary Kelly (Peterborough, ON: Broadview Press, 1995).

of other novels of the sixties and seventies, this one is heavily indebted to Richardson and extremely literary, with many references to texts and to reading, comparing at every turn the characters in books with "real life" figures in this novel.[39] Studded with intertextual references to *Clarissa* and narrated by a double correspondence between the hero and his Belford-like friend on the one hand and the heroine and her faithful confidante on the other, this novel tells of a woman who is nearly undone by acceding to the "last intimacy" with her fiancé a week before their marriage. Cast out by her father, subject to the dangers and indignities of an unprotected woman, she is only restored to love, family, and respectability after her virtue is subsequently tested, Clarissa-like, by violent abduction and extended psychological pressure.

The novel begins when the handsome and rich hero, Sir Robert Harold, in Bath for the season, attends a party given by his married sister, Lady Haversham. There he meets Louisa Mildmay, "the celebrated toast, who, though no more than twenty-one, has made the whole county a thousand times drunk; and occasioned four duels, in which two hot-headed block-heads were actually killed, and a third so disabled, by a wound in his hip, as to be doomed for life to crutches and repentance" (1: 5). Something of a rake, Sir Robert determines to pay his court to every woman in the room *but* Miss Mildmay in order to pique her pride. He is even tempted to se-duce one of the other women, who flirts shamelessly with him, but resists because of the regard he feels for her brother. The sibling tie between Sir Robert and his sister Lady Haversham is a powerful force in this novel, mitigating to some extent the ruthlessness of the battle between the sexes.

Beautiful Miss Mildmay, whose lineage can be traced on one side to Sir Philip Sidney and on the other to "the immortal Hampden, who so reso-lutely opposed the infamous oppressions of that rapacious tyrant Charles the First" (1: 9–10), also has a brother – universally esteemed a fine gen-tleman with a company in the guard – and a father worth £4,000 a year. Perfectly accomplished, she "speaks French and Italian – plays on the harp-sicord and the guittar [sic]; and sings with an exquisite share of taste, though she has less body to her voice, than you would imagine from the melody and fulness of her tones in common conversation" (1: 10) – this bodilessness a function, no doubt, of her female delicacy with regard to

---

[39] Hugh Kelly, *Memoirs of a Magdalen: or, The History of Louisa Mildmay*, 2 vols. (Dublin, 1767): subsequent page references are to this edition. For an analysis of a dozen novels by women modeled explicitly on *Clarissa*, published in the late 1760s and early 1770s, see my "Clarissa's Daughters, or the History of Innocence Betrayed: How Women Writers Rewrote Richardson," *Women's Writing* 1, 1 (1994), 5–24.

performing and a foreshadowing of her problems with too much body later in the narrative. Louisa Mildmay is an especial favorite of Sir Robert's sister, Lady Haversham, whom he adores because she protected him from disinheritance some years before, sacrificing her own inclinations to save his fortune. "Her marriage with lord Haversham, a man three times older than herself, was the price of my pardon" (1: 102–3) writes Sir Robert to his friend Melmoth.

In Louisa Mildmay's eyes, Sir Robert is as handsome as a prince from a seventeenth-century romance: "he appeared . . . an Oroondates to my fancy" (1: 21), she writes to her friend. "[H]is education is finished; his fortune is extremely large, his courage approved, and his understanding unquestionable. – He has indeed taken some extraordinary liberties among the women; but where a man possesses so many attractions, he must frequently meet with extraordinary encouragement – and if women will be fools, it is but reasonable they should be sufferers" (1: 23–4) she continues, heedlessly portending her own fate. Sir Robert is also a charitable landlord, an essential trait in any hero: "he always makes it a rule to live considerably within his fortune, and to distribute many sums towards the advancement of his poor tenants, which the most of our modern fine gentlemen injudiciously expend in horse-racing, or in some other fashionable amusement equally inhuman and ridiculous" (1: 24).

These two are, in short, made for each other. Their conversation, as reported in their letters, shows that they are well matched intellectually. Their relatives are delighted with the match and they are betrothed. All the parties agree; wedding clothes are ordered; everything is in train. Only Louisa's confidante, Harriot, worries about the outcome and warns her to be on her guard when alone with this man: "Of all the stages in a woman's life, none is so dangerous as the period between her acknowledgement of a passion for a man, and the day set apart for her nuptials" (1: 37). Sure enough, a week before the wedding, by p. 39 of the first volume, the deed is done. Sir Robert tells his friend Melmoth that one night, when Louisa's parents were asleep, she looked so ravishing that "I proceeded from liberty to liberty till she was actually undone" (1: 43). His "guilty triumph" and "mortification," and their mutual "shame and regret" at their indiscretion is instantaneous (1: 43–4). Sir Robert, who feels that it will be impossible to recover his confidence in her self-control and chastity after what has passed, takes steps to break off the engagement. Poor Louisa confesses everything to her parents; her father, in an extravagant rage, sends her away.

This, then, is the novel's frame: an idealized couple indulge in sexual activity a week before their actual wedding, a union which is most dearly wished for by their closest friends. The rest of the novel, 235 pages of it, works out the consequences of this major mistake: Louisa's misery, her outcast status, the importunities of Sir Robert's sister and his friend Melmoth (whose sympathy for Louisa is explicitly compared to Belford's for Clarissa in Richardson's novel), her forced abduction one night while she sits up late reading *Clarissa*, and the further test of her virtue by the libertine who holds her prisoner in his house in Hampstead but does not rape her. On one occasion she holds him at bay by threatening to stab herself with her penknife; they exchange long speeches about morality and what is and is not inevitable; and when he introduces into the room "a most bold looking man, in a clergyman's habit" (II: 101) she passes out in hysterics and is unconscious for six weeks. After seven months of such Richardsonian trials, Louisa escapes one night during the confusion caused by a fire resulting from Sir Henry Hastings' falling asleep while reading *Tristram Shandy*. She is rescued and protected by a kindly working woman and her female relatives. Restored to liberty, despite the protestations of her new friends, she resolves to enter the Magdalen Hospital for Penitent Prostitutes, where she is "received, tho' with some essential deviations from the customary mode of accepting Penitents, the good apothecary managing matters with as much delicacy as could be wished" (II: 112). After three months, she writes to her friend Harriot to tell her what has happened to her, demanding "how am I better than the unhappy poor creatures whom the pinching hand of necessity, or the poignant stings of remorse, have brought to the same salutary, yet humiliating habitation?" (II: 114).

The happy denouement follows in due course. Sir Robert, who learns of Louisa's indefatigable resistance to Sir Harry Hastings from the villain himself, regains his confidence in the unfortunate lady's willpower and kills Hastings in a duel. Noble Lady Haversham, Sir Robert's long-suffering sister (widowed at last but not remarried for she does not believe in second marriages!), reclaims Louisa from the Magdalen Hospital, an institution of which she has long been a benefactress. A touching family scene follows involving Louisa's avenging brother and her parents with a great deal of weeping, her father kneeling to Louisa and Louisa kneeling to her father. After being reunited with her family, she is restored to the arms and good graces of Sir Robert; they marry and live happily ever after.

The unmistakable message of this novel is that terrible things happen to a woman who does not hold out for marriage before sex. One week – and a legal ceremony – make all the difference in the world between happy respectability or misery, isolation, and infamy. A woman who engaged in intercourse before marriage was, at best, a penitent prostitute; only a marriage license could redeem a woman from the whoredom of sex. Since the line between these categories – wife and whore – was a permeable one, a virtuous woman had better stay on the right side of the dividing line.[40] Hugh Kelly's hero, Sir Robert, understands how closely allied fashionable women are to prostitutes when he compares the respectable women with whom he flirts to those "mercenary poor creatures, whom I can purchase for a couple of guineas and a trifling treat at the tavern" (1: 32). The novel thus literalizes the binary opposition between the categories of "good girls" and "fallen women" as well as showing how permeable and open to reversal those opposing categories were.

GOOD GIRLS AND FALLEN WOMEN

This juxtaposition of marriageable virgins with prostitutes, staged with increasing frequency in the fiction of the period, begs for analysis. Beginning with Clarissa, tricked by designing Lovelace into taking refuge in a brothel, paying her respects inappropriately to two high-class whores passed off as Lovelace's aunt and cousin, the reading public was repeatedly treated to the spectacle of fictional heroines side by side with women who sold their sexual services. Historically specific, these scenes begin to appear mid-century. Tonally and figurally they differ from the interviews with prostitutes reported earlier in the century by John Dunton's "nightwalker" or Richard Steele's "spectator," scenes displaying the disinterested forbearance of benevolent male observers, whose curiosity about these women's lives and sympathy for their discomforts (hunger, dirt, and cold) did not include the later sentimental impulse to relieve that suffering.[41] Nor are

---

[40] Another example of a woman discarded for not holding out against the sexual importunities of an intended husband is reported by John Gunning as an unfortunate conquest. Gunning, a notorious libertine who published an account of his adventures in *An Apology for the Life of Major General G—* (London, 1792), describes how he apprenticed himself to Richardson's hero in the art of seduction: "the spirit of Lovelace took possession of my bosom; a congeniality of sentiment and coincidence of desires made me in love with his character," he writes. "*Alexander the Great* could not esteem the *Iliad* more than I did these precious volumes. They were my study by day, and my pillow by night" (8). He succeeded only too well, he tells us, for he could not resist trying his skill on a beautiful and wealthy woman whom he wished to marry. "I pressed for a premature enjoyment, and she had not the resolution to oppose me. In short, she admitted me to her bed the night before we were to have been married, and my *honor* would not permit me to unite myself to her after such a *faux pas*. This was the dearest pleasure I ever enjoyed. – Her fortune was at least thirty thousand pounds" (62–3).

[41] Steele describes in *Spectator* 266, January 4, 1712, being solicited near Covent Garden by "a slim young Girl of about Seventeen, who with a pert Air asked me if I was for a Pint of Wine." He then describes her as having "as exact Features as I had ever seen, the most agreeable Shape, the finest Neck and Bosom, in a Word, the whole Person of a Woman exquisitely beautiful. She affected to allure me with a forced Wantonness in her Look and Air; but I saw it checked with Hunger and Cold: Her Eyes were wan and eager, her Dress thin and tawdry, her Meen genteel and childish."

these scenes to be found in the narratives of Moll Flanders or Fanny Hill, whose rapidly changing fortunes and eventual rehabilitation showed that sexual experience did not alter a woman's nature, and that the thoughts and feelings of good girls and fallen women might coexist in the same bosom.

Scenes from later eighteenth-century fiction, on the contrary, emphasize the gulf between the two sorts of women and the terror felt by good girls when they realize in whose company they have been, how it compromises them, and for whom they might be mistaken. Indeed, they wish the difference between themselves and fallen women were more obvious and visible, because simple contiguity is so frightening and their mistake is so dangerous. Now the degradations of poverty have become menacing – alarming – rather than simply pitiable.

These scenes appear in novels written by both men and women.[42] After Richardson's *Clarissa*, Sarah Scott's *The History of Cornelia* (1750) may be the next earliest instance of this kind of scene in which a beautiful young heroine finds herself in the company of prostitutes. The eponymous heroine of this novel, an accomplished orphan, well-read in the best modern and ancient authors, independently wealthy and living contentedly on her own estate, is forced to flee the detested embraces of her politically powerful guardian uncle. Alone and incognito in the coach to Paris she meets an old woman "very assiduous in her endeavours to amuse her" who offers her lodging at her house "in an obscure part of town." This perfectly suits Cornelia's desire to attract as little attention as possible and she agrees to lodge with the old woman. At the widow's house, they are received by her "three daughters, two nieces, and two that were introduced as lodgers."[43] At first, Cornelia sees nothing amiss although she finds these inmates "too gay to be relished by [her] in her present state of melancholy and fatigue"; innocence never recognizes evil until it is too late. But the reader has begun to suspect what kind of trouble Cornelia has landed herself in. She, of course, is unable to imagine "that any woman was so lost to all virtue, as to live by betraying her own sex" until a strange man is introduced into her room. Cornelia's frantic rejection of his advances soon convinces him of her sincerity: she is not just being coy; there is some mistake. Her beauty, innocence, and dignity "infused an awe into him which the place he had found her in could not overcome" (40). He tells her she

---

[42] Men's texts often represent male agency in luring the heroine into the company of fallen women, whereas women's texts emphasize female agency in luring the heroine into the dangerous setting.

[43] Sarah Scott, *The History of Cornelia* (London: A. Millar, 1750), p. 39. Subsequent page references are to this edition.

is in a place for men "lazy in their pleasures," and helps her to escape. From that moment forward this first client is her devoted servant in all things.

Eliza Haywood's *The History of Betsy Thoughtless* (1751) also includes a sequence in which the heroine has supper all unaware in a brothel and appears later in public with a lady of easy virtue. Miss Forward had been at boarding school with Betsy Thoughtless and enlists her aid and sympathy with a formulaic story: seduced by a handsome aristocrat, betrayed by her lascivious teacher Miss Grenouille (Haywood's morality-play names are hilarious), Miss Forward tells Betsy she has been renounced by her family and appeals for assistance. After hearing her tale, Betsy gives her old friend three guineas and returns home, musing how strange it is "that a woman cannot indulge in the liberty of conversing freely with a man, without being persuaded by him to do every thing he would have her."[44] Later, Betsy again visits Miss Forward who pretends that her improved circumstances are due to the unexpected generosity of a distant maternal relative. This time Betsy is surprised to find her suitor, Mr. Trueworth, in Miss Forward's company – but not half so surprised as he is to find *her* there. He visits her the next day to warn her not to be seen in public with "a woman of her fame" (202). Not believing him, and impatient of correction, Betsy keeps her theater date with Miss Forward (followed and spied upon by her disguised lover), where she is taken for a woman of the town and ends up in a coach wrestling with an importunate client outside a bagnio. Only when she declares "I detest and scorn those wretched creatures of the number of whom you imagine me to be one" and "I would sooner die the worst of deaths, than live with infamy!" does she convince this man-about-town of her virtue. He then kneels to her, assuring her that he reveres truly virtuous women, and warns her that "a young lady more endangered her reputation by an acquaintance of one woman of ill fame, than by receiving the visits of twenty men, though professed libertines" (210–11).

These scenes in *Betsy Thoughtless* are telling because Haywood occupies a liminal position in the representation of female sexuality. Her fiction of the twenties and thirties shows the earlier period's casual acceptance of women's sexual agency and appetite – for which she was burlesqued by Pope – but her tone modulates in her later works to proto-Victorian delicacy and inhibition about sexual matters. Just as Betsy must learn sexual caution in the course of the novel, Haywood's fiction of the late forties and

[44] Eliza Haywood, *The History of Betsy Thoughtless* (1751; rpt. London: Pandora Press, 1986), p. 93. Subsequent page numbers in the text refer to this edition.

early fifties assimilates her society's escalating anxiety about the propriety – and safety – of a woman's unselfconscious movement in the public world.

The historian Anna Clark claims that the elaboration of a public discourse about rape in eighteenth-century England reflected not its increased incidence but an admonitory message to women to stay away from public space. Although actual convictions in rape cases did not increase in the course of the century, prosecutions for rape and publicity about these cases did increase, warning women about the dangers of going out alone. "Magistrates, judges, and journalists dealing with rape cases began to introduce the idea that rape emperilled safety in evening streets; while men could travel freely, 'respectable' women would be safe only at home."[45] Like a Restoration heroine fast-forwarded into a mid-eighteenth-century world, Betsy Thoughtless must be re-educated for life, must learn that it is improper to go anywhere with a gentleman alone. In society of the 1750s, "caution ought to be peculiarly observed in persons of your sex," Mr. Trueworth informs Betsy. "[R]eputation in you, once lost, is never to be retrieved" (203).

In *The History of Betty Barnes* (1753), a pimp meets the wagon on which the ingenue heroine, a simple country girl, has traveled into London. He tells her his sister wants a servant, and gives her a written direction to the place. She goes there the next morning and finds "a jolly elderly woman" at breakfast with three young women "whom she called her nieces."[46]

The first night passed without her having the least suspicion of the house she was in; for tho' the dress and behaviour of the girls, were such as plainly told their profession, yet to our country maid there appeared but little difference between them and those she saw pass the door in coaches, who by their equipages she imagined people of fortune, whom her country innocence taught her to believe must be virtuous, because they were rich; since she had never known any one punished for being wicked, but those whose dress plainly spoke their indigence. (1: 166)

Betty Barnes' education about the deservingness of wealth and the culpability of indigence, about virtuous women and disreputable whores, proceeds the next day when she walks in Vauxhall with one of her new friends. There she is seen by the young gentleman for whom she is destined, and it is his look of contempt and pity that reveals to her what sort of house she has found her way to.

In *The Vicar of Wakefield* (1766), the villainous Squire Thornhill introduces two prostitutes to Dr. Primrose and his family as "women of

45 Anna Clark, *Women's Silence, Men's Violence: Sexual Assault in England 1770–1845* (New York and London: Pandora, 1987), p. 3.
46 *The History of Betty Barnes*, vol. 1, p. 164.

great distinction and fashion from town," Lady Blarney and Miss Carolina Wilelmina Amelia Skeggs.[47] His cast-off mistresses, they will, he hopes, decoy the virtuous Sophia and Olivia into voluptuous practices. The reader knows from their diction that they are only impersonating aristocrats, but, as usual, innocence is oblivious. Once again, the juxtaposition of good girls and fallen women and the potential for contamination – together with the reader's privileged knowledge – was served up for the reader's delectation.

In Sophia Briscoe's *Miss Melmoth; or, The New Clarissa* (1771), Caroline Melmoth is lured to a house of ill repute by a jealous and vindictive female cousin, where, to her horror, she is seen by the hero, Sir George Darnley – much as Betsy Thoughtless is seen by Mr. Trueworth in a brothel or as Betty Barnes is seen by her young gentleman as she is strolling with a whore in Vauxhall. The interpolated tale of Maria Chalmers, threatened by a heartless landlady with being sent to Newgate for her debts if she refuses clients, offers another case of vice and virtue contrasted.

In *Evelina; or, the History of a Young Lady's Entrance into the World* (1778), Evelina goes to the Marylebone Gardens with her shopkeeping relatives, Madame Duval and the Branghtons, et al., to hear a violin concerto played by Mr. Barthelemon and to see fireworks.[48] When the crowds clear, Evelina finds that she has been separated from her party. Accosted by a stranger ("Come along with me, my dear, and I'll take care of you"), she is terrified when she looks around and recognizes no one familiar. "Every other moment," the heroine tells us, "I was spoken to, by some bold and unfeeling man, to whom my distress . . . only furnished a pretence for impertinent witticisms, or free gallantry."

At last, a young officer, marching fiercely up to me, said, "You are a sweet pretty creature, and I enlist you in my service;" and then, with great violence, he seized my hand. I screamed aloud with fear, and, forcibly snatching it away, I ran hastily up to two ladies, and cried, "For Heaven's sake, dear ladies, afford me some protection!" (233)

Predictably, these ladies turn out to be prostitutes, and they mock her fear with bold looks, loud laughs, and impertinent questions. When she realizes who they are she shrinks in terror from them but they only clutch her more tightly until, inevitably, the hero appears on the scene. "[W]hat good

---

[47] Oliver Goldsmith, *The Vicar of Wakefield* (London: Dent, and New York: Dutton, 1976), p. 45.
[48] Fanny Burney, *Evelina; or, The History of a Young Lady's Entrance into the World*, ed. Edward and Lillian Bloom (Oxford: Oxford University Press, 1982), p. 231 ff., letter xxi (superscribed "Holborn, July 1, 5 o'clock in the morn").

Heavens! were my emotions, when, a few moments afterward, I perceived advancing our way, – Lord Orville!" (234).

The same elements thus appear again and again: the fear of exposure and being seen; the widespread perception that a single woman alone is potentially anyone and everyone's property; the promiscuous mingling of classes in urban space; the sexualized danger of public places; the difficulty of telling good women from bad women in such circumstances; and finally, the spectacle of the heroine in the company of prostitutes seen accidentally by the hero. Only a very thin line separated good girls from women of the other sort, and the difference lay in something that was not immediately visible, something entailed in consciousness and memory and not always recognizable in manner.

I want to suggest that this scene of juxtaposition participated in the cultural work that constructed modern notions of femininity – building on the separation of public from private space and the division of paid from unpaid labor. It also elaborated the difference between the respectable reproductive sex and invisible but real non-reproductive sexuality. If sexual disgust and a new emphasis on sexual imprinting were part of the new patterning of women's relations with men, this scene drawing attention to differences and similarities between women whose persons were overtly commodified (prostitutes) and those women whose persons were more subtly commodified on the marriage market also contributed to this new perception.

Roy Porter's exegesis of *Aristotle's Master-Piece*, the most widely read sex manual of the late seventeenth and eighteenth centuries, offers a context for these scenes of juxtaposition by revealing something of the preexisting attitudes in the period towards the body and towards the bodily experiences of sex.[49] This extremely popular book, a redaction of earlier advice literature, first published in English in 1684 and with more than twenty editions in the eighteenth century, is not, according to Porter, simply a "potpourri of remnants of sexual lore," although it has been dismissed as a repository of quaint anachronistic ideas. It was, rather, "an integrated and coherent work whose unifying theme is the subject of reproduction" (5) demonstrating the seventeenth and early eighteenth centuries' straightforward attitude towards sex as the animal means to preserving and perpetuating the species. Emphasizing the "similarities between the sexes rather than the polarities" (15), and assuming that women were no less libidinous than men, this early

---

[49] Roy Porter, "'The Secrets of Generation Display'd': *Aristotle's Master-Piece* in Eighteenth-Century England," in Robert Purks Maccubbin (ed.), *'Tis Nature's Fault: Unauthorized Sexuality during the Enlightenment* (Cambridge: Cambridge University Press, 1987), pp. 1–21.

sex manual offered general advice for promoting conception, "hints on producing a boy or a girl" (9), theories of barrenness and sterility with practical suggestions for remedy, and a functional discussion not of sexual intercourse but of issues involved in childbearing. "Little is said of sexual desire as a source of fear, guilt, or danger (medical, moral or religious)," says Porter, or as "a problem of the self." Most fundamentally, he adds, "sex is not seen as a psychological category; it is not 'in the mind' at all" (5).

The cultural work of the scene juxtaposing good girls and fallen women is precisely to put sex "in the mind." What, after all, is the difference between these two kinds of woman if not something "in the mind" – namely their memories of physical experience and attitudes towards bodily sex? The distinction between the two states cannot be definitively drawn without the comparison implicit in their contiguity, emphasizing this difference and reinforcing its importance. At first it looks as if the opposite is being proved: the visual rhetoric of these scenes would seem to emphasize rather that all cats are grey in the dark; that every woman is a potential prostitute; that all women are vulnerable. That implication must have produced a certain pornographic frisson. But the action of these scenes generally shows that you *can* tell who is who, who is innocent and who is not. Most sequences, for example, feature the dramatic and effective pleading of the heroine to an unwitting "gallant" who thinks he has simply paid for another whore. With the notable exception of Lovelace in *Clarissa*, these clients are always convinced, and transformed instantly from predators to protectors, opposite sides of the same coin.

To put sex "in the mind" is to make it first and foremost a matter of consciousness – whether desire or guilt – rather than a simple, unselfconscious practice. As an anorexic or a bulimic has an obsessive, compulsive, and self-defining relation to food rather than a simple appetite directing her to eat when hungry and not to eat when full, so, I am arguing, putting sex in the mind changed it from being the relatively unmeditated set of practices for pleasure and reproduction that Porter describes from an earlier time to being a central and all-defining subjective state.

The other significant sex manual circulating in England in the eighteenth century was a translation of Nicolas Venette's *Tableau de l'amour conjugal* (1686), a somewhat later and more medicalized text than *Aristotle's Master-Piece*, directed at a more educated class of people.[50] A more expensive book than *Aristotle's Master-Piece*, sprinkled with Greek terms and Latin

---

[50] My discussion of this text relies on "Doctors and the Medicalization of Sex," in Roy Porter and Lesley Hall's *The Facts of Life: The Creation of Sexual Knowledge in Britain 1650–1950* (New Haven: Yale University Press, 1995), pp. 65–90. The earliest English translation of Venette, published

quotations and based more on anatomical drawings and medical explanations than on folk wisdom, *The Mysteries of Conjugal Love Reveal'd* (1712)
nonetheless shares with *Aristotle's Master-Piece* an essentially physical frame
of reference. About the science of the healthy human body in relation to
reproduction, Venette's book offered information about the mechanics of
copulation, pregnancy, and parturition. Rejecting the classical assumption
that female genitals were inverted male genitals, it focused rather on the
parallel nature of the clitoris and the penis, assumed that men and women
both had sexual appetite, and asserted that both men and women produced
"seed" which, intermingling, produced an embryo. But Venette's book concerned sexuality in the context of marriage and the French, at this time, were
worried about depopulation and interested in encouraging reproduction
on a national scale.[51] Accordingly, Venette's text treated marital affection –
"how love and sex would harmonize" as Poster and Hall put it (71) – and in
successive editions increasingly psychologized sexuality "in the mind" rather
than addressing the simple mechanics of reproduction. The tone of these
later editions, according to Roy Porter and Lesley Hall, is "more earnest,
spiritual and elevated"; there is less bawdy humor. Gone are the "raunchy
jokes, double meanings, ironies, innuendoes and sly asides" (85–6).
The spiritual purposes of marriage are emphasized and concupiscence is
frowned upon, whether inside or outside marriage. Women, in particular,
are warned against giving "too great a loose to their desires in conjugal
embraces" or tasting "too freely of the nuptial pleasure" (86). Nature was
no longer a sufficient guide to sexual appetite; by the end of the century
women were advised to rein in sexual desire even in the marriage bed.

REAL-LIFE MAGDALENS

The enormous interest in the founding of the Magdalen Hospital for Penitent Prostitutes in the mid-1750s is another sign of the growing public stake
in regulating female sexuality. Even among other charitable institutions, in
an era known for its great humanitarian projects, the Magdalen Hospital
"raised in the public so great an approbation," according to William Dodd,
chaplain and fundraiser for the Magdalen charity, that more money was

---

anonymously in London in 1712 as *The Mysteries of Conjugal Love Reveal'd*, purported to be the
third English edition of this work (taken from the eighth French edition), although the first and
second editions have not been located.

[51] For an overview of the concern about population in eighteenth-century France, see the forum titled
"Demographic Thought and Reproductive Realities: From Montesquieu to Malthus," introduced
by Carol Blum, *Eighteenth-Century Studies* 32, 4 (Summer 1999).

collected during the initial appeal to the enlightened citizenry than "what almost any other charitable undertaking experienced, in the same compass of time."[52] More than £5,000 in public donations poured in during the first few months and the revenues in succeeding years, between 1759 and 1830, averaged £6,009 annually. The success of the Magdalen Hospital encouraged the establishment of a number of other charitable institutions to rescue fallen women in the years following its opening.[53] The readiness of private citizens to subsidize this institution to rehabilitate fallen women and to reintegrate them into society – as servants – is an interesting cultural phenomenon. An attempt at social engineering, it demonstrates at once a gender-specific thrift about wasting human resources as well as a class-inflected sexual prudery. The possibility of rehabilitating fallen women supposes a permeable boundary between the two types of woman, a boundary that then needs to be policed. Also, if good women might become bad and bad women might become good again, there is a need for scrutiny and regulation to determine to which category a woman belongs. Thus, the rehabilitation of fallen women by those who considered themselves "enlightened" and who could afford to contribute to the enterprise is part of an important cultural progression aligning bourgeois class interests with the regulation of women's sexuality.

Intended as a refuge for fallen women of a better class, the Magdalen Hospital required applicants to petition in writing for admittance (waived for the delicate Louisa Mildmay in Hugh Kelly's novel by the apothecary's intercession). They were fed three substantial meals a day, and assigned to a strict regimen of isolation, prayer, and soul-redeeming work.[54] Three anonymous years behind those walls without identifying surnames, wearing

---

[52] William Dodd, *An Account of the Rise, Progress, and Present State of the Magdalen Hospital . . . Together with Dr. Dodd's Sermons* (London, 1776), p. 215.

[53] According to Donna Andrew, six new institutions were started between 1787 and 1817 "to aid the Magdalen in its attempt to restrain and contain the threat of moral pollution." They were the Lock Asylum, the London Female Penitentiary, the Refuge for the Destitute at Cuper's Bridge, the Refuge for the Destitute at Hackney Road, the Guardian Society, and Robert Young's Refuge for Industry. Donna T. Andrew, *Philanthropy and Police: London Charity in the Eighteenth Century* (Princeton: Princeton University Press, 1989), p. 191 n. 84. For a general discussion of the Magdalen Charity and its context in this "age of benevolence," see pp. 119–22 and 187–94 of this invaluable book. Two earlier sources on the Magdalen Hospital also of interest are W. A. Speck, "The Harlot's Progress in Eighteenth-Century England," *British Journal for Eighteenth-Century Studies* 3, 2 (Summer 1980), 127–39 and Stanley Nash, "Prostitution and Charity: The Magdalen Hospital, a Case Study," *Journal of Social History* 17 (Summer 1984), 617–28.

[54] The suggested daily allotment for each woman of 11 ounces of meat, 3 ounces of cheese, 1 pint of milk etc. was a better diet than most laborers enjoyed, and is another indication of the class of women for whom this charity was intended. These arrangements, as well as those that follow, are taken from Jonas Hanway, *A Plan for Establishing a Charity-House, or Charity-Houses, for the Reception of Repenting Prostitutes to be called the Magdalen Charity* (London, 1758), pp. 25–7.

the neat gray uniform provided, sleeping regular hours in separate beds behind a private curtain, and rising early to prayer and meditation, was the regimen imagined necessary and sufficient to purify the mind and undo the effects of dissolute living. This emphasis on non-punitive discipline – the Societies for the Reformation of Manners had flogged prostitutes until they bled[55] – was geared to reform these women's moral consciousness and to encourage them to introject new codes of behavior.

The social investment in saving these women came at the same time as marriage was being promoted as a national good to reproduce the population decimated in overseas wars and to settle the colonies. Within that framework prostitution was decried as "no less a national than a moral evil" since prostitutes were often barren – whether from disease or design – and it was assumed that "criminal converse alienates the mind from matrimony."[56] One occupation suggested for the penitents at the Magdalen, relevant to these national concerns, was sewing soldier's linen and uniforms. Although disconnected from their own families, these deracinated women were thus recuperated for the state, functioning on a waged basis as unmarried kinswomen for those men also separated from kin groups and appropriated by the state for military service.[57]

Two novels telling the stories of penitent prostitutes from their own point of view, published during this period and said to have been instrumental in eliciting public sympathy – not to say donations – for the Magdalen Hospital, reinforce the sense of a cultural sea change during this period about the social investment in women's sexual restraint. Like reformers urging humanitarian intervention for fallen women, they emphasized simultaneously the delicacy of their undeserving but grateful objects and the redemptive power of the middle-class reader. As Vivien Jones has shrewdly observed, they also positioned their readers with respect to these women, "albeit in moral and financial terms, [in] the sexual power relations of the

---

[55] W. A. Speck suggests that Swift's famous remark in *A Tale of a Tub* refers to this practice. Swift wrote: "Last Week I saw a Woman *flay'd*, and you will hardly believe, how much it altered her Person for the worse." (Quotation taken from *Gulliver's Travels and Other Writings*, by Jonathan Swift [New York: Random House, 1958], p. 343.) See Speck's "The Harlot's Progress in Eighteenth-Century England," 128.

[56] Saunders Welch, *A Proposal to Render Effectual a Plan, to Remove the Nuisance of Common Prostitutes from the Streets of this Metropolis* (1758), rpt. in *Prostitution Reform* (New York: Garland, 1985), quotes pp. 13–14.

[57] Randolph Trumbach states that the new role of the prostitute in eighteenth-century England "arose from a reorganization in male and female gender roles." See his "Modern Prostitution and Gender in *Fanny Hill*: Libertine and Domesticated fantasy," in G. S. Rousseau and Roy Porter (eds.), *Sexual Underworlds of the Enlightenment* (Manchester: Manchester University Press, 1987), pp. 69–85, quote p. 73.

upper-class men who are so often held responsible for the fate of the women in the stories."[58]

William Dodd's *The Sisters* (1754) plays on the sympathies of the benevolent reader, the charitable public-minded citizen, who can see that although Lucy Sanson has forfeited her right to respectability and family – indeed it is best that she dies – she is nevertheless to be pitied for her fatal misstep. A daughter gone astray, more sinned against than sinning, she is continually compared with her sister Caroline, who was saved from degradation and an early death by timely reflection on a cautionary incident. Caroline never forsakes her sister, however, and the spectacle of their pairing – a variation on the theme of juxtaposition – helps the reader compare the trajectories of their lives. Dodd was chaplain of the Magdalen Hospital and preached many fundraising sermons with the same rhetorical and moral tone as this novel, published four years before that charity opened its doors.

The Histories of Some of the Penitents in the Magdalen House as Supposed to be Related by Themselves (1760), probably written by Sarah Fielding, published a few years after the establishment of this new charity, offers a similarly enlightened view of this social problem.[59] All four speakers in this novel are daughters of the middle class, ruined for marriage and

---

[58] Vivien Jones, "Scandalous Femininity: Prostitution and Eighteenth-Century Narrative," pp. 66–7.

[59] If Sarah Fielding wrote these stories – and a letter from Elizabeth Montagu to Elizabeth Carter suggests that she may have been the chief author – they make an interesting contribution to the range of Fielding family opinion and action with regard to the issue of public prostitution.

Elizabeth Montagu's attribution is cited in *The Correspondence of Henry and Sarah Fielding*, ed. Martin C. Battestin and Clive T. Probyn (Oxford: Clarendon Press, 1993), p. 176 n.1 The authors of *Samuel Richardson: A Biography* (Oxford: Clarendon Press, 1971), T. C. Duncan Eaves and Ben D. Kimpel, note that it was Lady Barbara Montagu, daughter of the first Earl of Halifax and life companion of Sarah Scott, who brought this novel to Richardson's attention as written by someone whose fortune was inferior to her birth and education, and urged him to publish it (463). All of these women were friends and patrons of Sarah Fielding: Sarah Scott and her sister Elizabeth Montagu and her companion Lady Barbara Montagu.

Henry Fielding was involved in the so-called Penlez riots of 1749. As chairman of the Westminster quarter sessions at that time, he sent in Saunders Welch, High Constable of the Holborn Division, in July 1749 to quell a riot bent on the destruction of several brothels. He thus extended police protection to brothel-keepers to protect their private property from a mob of outraged citizens seeking revenge for the robbery of a man named Penlez in one of the disorderly houses. Fielding defended his actions in *A True State of the Case of Bosavern Penlez* in November of that year. The Disorderly Houses Act, which passed into law in 1751, was in part a response to the public dissatisfaction with the (mis)handling of the Penlez riots. Intended as a way of deputizing and encouraging citizens to prosecute bawdy-houses, it provided that any "two inhabitants of the parish paying scot and lot" might identify a house of ill repute (in writing) to the police. The Disorderly Houses Act apparently functioned more as a zoning law than anything else. See Martin C. Battestin with Ruthe R. Battestin, *Henry Fielding: A Life* (London and New York: Routledge, 1989), pp. 472–6, 550, 552, as well as Peter Linebaugh, "The Tyburn Riot against the Surgeons," in Douglas Hay et al. (eds.) *Albion's Fatal Tree: Crime and Society in Eighteenth-Century England* (New York: Pantheon Books, 1975), pp. 65–117, esp. pp. 88–102.

motherhood by men who seduced but would not marry them. Without skill enough for plain sewing, strength for laundering, capital for a millinery or haberdashery shop, or personal references for positions as servants, these fallen heroines found themselves unable to earn a living. Their narratives repeat the pairing of good girls and prostitutes that I have already discussed, and they all feature the emblematic sentimental scene in which the innocent woman being prostituted by someone else pleads with the putative client for mercy and deliverance. These scenes were becoming conventions of the genre, emphasizing the all-or-nothing nature of women's sexual conduct, suppressing all mention of her desire or bodily pleasure, and reifying the split between sex and reproduction.

As the four stories unfold, we see each of these fictional daughters of the middling class compelled into a criminal way of life by – to quote a contemporary writer on the subject – "the infernal arts of the keepers of bawdy-houses, who by some means or other contrive to have young women run into their debt for lodging, diet, clothes, &c. and then, by the terror of that debt, and the consequences of it, imprisonment, &c. hanging over them, force them to submit to their hellish designs, to the ruin of their souls and bodies."[60] One could also argue that the focus on prostitution and crime mid-century in treatises and fiction was overdetermined, revealing anxieties presented in sexual terms about a changing social order in which the drive for profit and commodified social relations was replacing older kin and communal obligations.[61] Good girls who succumbed to the pressure stood for all the displaced, kinless, unskilled migrants to the cities, unable to find a place in the anonymous, urban society.

That said, the stories in the *Histories of Some of the Penitents* illustrate that prostitution was no longer imaginable as a temporary expedient as it had

---

[60] Jonas Hanway introduces this letter in the Preface to his *Plan for Establishing a Charity-House, or Charity Houses, for the Reception of Repenting Prostitutes* as "an anonymous letter, from an ingenious and political correspondent, to whom I am much indebted" (xxix). The letter goes on to suggest that just as gambling debts are not recoverable by law, so neither bawds nor prostitutes should be allowed to recover such debts as these.

The figure of the predatory bawd who forces innocent women into prostitution has a longer history. Long before Hogarth's sequence *The Harlot's Progress*, Richard Steele described just such a bawd in *Spectator* 266, January 4, 1712. In a narrative that sounds as if it were already a fictional cliché, Steele describes seeing a beautiful girl just come from the country engaged by "the most artful Procuress in the Town" to be her maid, and given a cheese for her civilities by the girl's "Country Bumkin" of a brother. Unlike the sentimental narrators later in the century, however, this reporter does nothing to save the girl but simply records what he sees.

[61] For an article that treats anxieties about prostitution as a displaced reaction to cultural transition, albeit in a different historical and national setting, see Elizabeth Wood's "Prostitution Unbound," in Jane T. Costlow, Stephanie Sandler, and Judith Vowles (eds.), *Sexuality and the Body in Russian Culture* (Stanford: Stanford University Press, 1993), pp. 124–35.

been, say, for Moll Flanders. These women were not represented with the energy, agency, and cunning of Defoe's heroines or even the brash pluckiness of Haywood's Miss Forward. Abjectly aware of their own wrongdoing, as fully convinced as the most respectable matron of their irremediable ruin, these women defined themselves almost entirely in terms of their sexual experience. Although driven to prostitution by economic circumstances beyond their control, unable to survive on any other terms, their (fictional) self-representations nevertheless project the middle-class judgment that women's sexual history – however necessitous and unwanted – entirely defined them.

One of the penitents, a rich trader's daughter from a country town, tells of being pursued by a gentleman from the university who thought "that a vain girl of my rank was attainable on easy terms by a man of his fortune."[62] She refuses to be his mistress but agrees to a secret marriage. They go to London, are married in the Fleet, and live together for several years. Then one day he tells her that they are not legally married because she was underage at the time of their clandestine ceremony and did not have the permission of her parents. He cites the provisions of the Hardwicke Marriage Act (1753), already passed and in force when they eloped, which he had been counting on to invalidate their marriage.[63] She, who had always believed theirs was a legal marriage, is dumbfounded. He then leaves her, but not before his servant brings her the text of the Hardwicke Act to read to clear up her residual doubts.

As if conjured up by the warnings of opponents during the debates preceding the passage of the Act, this story dramatized how the new requirements for a valid marriage rendered women more vulnerable than ever before to the "solemn and specious Promises and Engagements of those of the other Sex, who either finally design to deceive them, or thro' Fear of some temporal Loss are not willing to enter into a more publick Contract!"[64] As stated earlier, an exchange of vows between unmarried persons – crowned by premarital sex – with the force of custom and community

---

[62] *The Histories of Some of the Penitents in the Magdalen House, as Supposed to be Related by Themselves*, 2nd edn., 2 vols. (Dublin: Wilson and Potts, 1760), vol. 1, pp. 88–9.

[63] The provisions of the Act are as follows: after Lady Day 1754, no ceremony other than one performed by an ordained clergyman of the Church of England, after either the third consecutive publication of the banns in church or the purchase of a license from the bishop, was legally valid; any clergyman performing a marriage in any other manner was punishable by transportation for at least fourteen years; at least one of the parties being married had to be resident in the parish in which the marriage was performed for at least three weeks; parental consent was required for anyone under twenty-one years of age; betrothal was deprived of its legal status.

[64] The victimization of women was a frequently adduced argument against the Hardwicke Marriage Act. The words quoted here are from *A Letter from a Bystander, Containing Remarks on and Objections*

behind it, had been sufficiently binding to reproduce families and socialize offspring at the end of the seventeenth century. Changing the jurisdiction of marriage from the church to the state and secularizing the rules about marriage meant that law, not the unauthorized exchange of vows, created a marriage contract, while sex without benefit of law created a fallen woman. Prostitutes and wives were becoming mutually constitutive categories in this period under the law.

Concerned with legal contracts for the transfer of property rather than social relations between humans, the Hardwicke Marriage Act constructed men's and women's rights as equal despite their biological difference – thus wiping out male responsibility for children which had previously been upheld by ecclesiastical law. Ignoring the very real difference between men and women in social consequences for sexual experience, it put women at risk whenever a contract was challenged. After 1753, if single women pursued traditional sexual practices on the basis of traditional values, they might be abandoned as fallen women, just like the woman in the story here mentioned. As its opponents had predicted, the Hardwicke Act made prostitutes of honest women.[65] One could even say, exaggerating to make the point, that the Hardwicke Act created the need for the Magdalen Hospital for Penitent Prostitutes.

WIVES AND PROSTITUTES

Although the meaning of marriage in England had been changing throughout the first half of the eighteenth century, it was not until the 1750s that it

---

to the Bill Now Depending in Parliament, for the Better Preventing Clandestine Marriages (London, 1753), p. 18.

[65] The debates about the Hardwicke Marriage Act are in vol. xv of William Cobbett's *The Parliamentary History of England from the Earliest Period to the Year 1803* (London: Hansard, for Longman, Hurst, Orme and Brown, 1813). Advocates of the Bill argued that clandestine marriage rendered the succession of all property insecure and doubtful and permitted men and women of infamous character to ruin the sons and daughters of the greatest families by marrying them in the Fleet. They argued that the casual nature of clandestine marriage undermined morality and encouraged polygamy.

Opponents claimed that the Bill protected the interests of the rich and disadvantaged the poor. They argued that it was calculated to engross all the property in the kingdom to a few great and rich families while discouraging marriage among the lesser folk because of the expense and long wait entailed by the Act. They also argued that the Bill would ruin the reputations – and prospects – of women who had succumbed to lovers' vows but who, under the new Bill, would have no leverage to enforce legal marriage. As Robert Nugent put it, such duplicitous men ought to be punishable for rape: "there is the same difference between a man who deflowers a girl under the pretence of a marriage, which he knows to be void in law, and a man who ravishes a girl, that there is between a man who cheats me out of my purse by false dice and a man who robs me of it upon the highway" (*The Parliamentary History of England*, vol. xv, p. 22).

became clear how these changes constrained women in a new set of double binds about love, sexuality, and marriage. The weeks of heated parliamentary debate about the social function of marriage (to procreate citizens for the nation? to consolidate class interests? to discourage promiscuous sexuality?), followed by the passage of the Hardwicke Marriage Act and the opening of the Magdalen Hospital for Penitent Prostitutes five years later in 1758, showed how, by the mid-eighteenth century, women's reproductive capacities and sexual conduct had become a matter of public interest and social regulation more than ever before. The narratives contained in *The Histories of Some of the Penitents in the Magdalen House* (1760) illustrate schematically several ways in which women suffered from this new way of conceptualizing sex and marriage: as single, unprotected women in service far from their families and friends; as dupes of men who purposely violated the Act's legal stipulations so as to invalidate the union later (as in the tale summarized above); as innocent country girls seen as business opportunities by hardened bawds[66]; and as victims of their parents' greed, forced to give up true love for monied matches. In the telling, they also reinscribe the themes of more conventional fiction: the power of virtue to awe and reform men "lazy in their pleasures"; the sexual double standard and how sex without marriage put women beyond the pale; how men not secured by marriage would inevitably lose interest and abandon women who were merely their mistresses; the extreme difficulty women had in earning a living – particularly if they had children to support.

Psychoanalytically, the mechanism of disassociating and splitting qualities that coexist more ambivalently in reality serves to keep a desired quality "pure" or unalloyed and to scapegoat its opposite. Splitting good girls from fallen women discursively in novels reified sexlessness in the one while loading the other with a degraded form of sexuality. It also reflected a new potential for dividing sexual services from reproductive functions in women no longer deployed by their families or communities with these functions unified and intact. The separation of women from their consanguineal kin groups, together with the new paradigm of alienated waged labor, made this division possible. Men have always been able, biologically, to detach sex from kin obligations: the long history of prostitution testifies to that. But

---

[66] According to one contemporary treatise on the subject: "To enumerate all the practises of bawds, the artful means by which innocence is decoyed into dens of lust, and the measures practised to imprison deluded girls; and render their return to industry and virtue impossible, so long as health and beauty render them proper objects of gainful prostitution; would fill volumes." Saunders Welch, *A Proposal to Render Effectual a Plan, to Remove the Nuisance of Common Prostitutes from the Streets of this Metropolis*, p. 11.

because women bear children, they cannot detach sexual service from kin obligations so easily and the splitting of sexual services from reproduction weighs more heavily on them. Narratives about prostitutes in this period emphasize their kinlessness (except the kin produced by their own bodies). As the first penitent in the *Histories* put it, "all ties of kindred were broken by my infamy" (1: 69). The spectacle of a deracinated woman, separated from her family of origin, unable to survive alone by waged labor, is an irony of the age of individualism, a necessary corrective to the myth of the socially mobile individual.

As the century wore on and these ironies deepened, wives and prostitutes came increasingly to be defined by one another, both by their similarities and their differences. In Henry Fielding's words in the epilogue to his *Covent Garden Tragedy* (1732):

> To be a mistress kept the strumpet strives,
> And all the modest virgins to be wives.
> For prudes may cant of virtues and of vices,
> But faith, we only differ in our prices.

It became nearly impossible for anyone thinking about women's condition to mention wives without mentioning prostitutes or prostitutes without mentioning wives. These categories were becoming mutually defining both because women's sexual nature was increasingly a matter of public focus and its social function was being redefined, and also because their structural similarity was so glaring. As those arranging marriages for purely material reasons continued to cant of love, and as the discourse about the sexualized love of married life continued to proliferate, the notion of marriage as legal prostitution came to seem more inevitable. From the publication of Defoe's treatise on "matrimonial whoredom" onwards, the analogy became a cliché.

Lady Mary Wortley Montagu's answer to James Hammond's "Elegy to a Young Lady" (1733) refers to women who are "legal prostitutes for int'rest sake" and who in reality are marrying "titles, deeds, and rentrolls."[67] In his versified sex manual, *The Oeconomy of Love* (1735), John Armstrong cannot resist speaking of prostitutes as soon as he mentions virgins and chaste wives.[68] A character in Hugh Kelly's comedy *False Delicacy* (1768)

---

[67] Thanks to Claude Rawson for sending me references to this phenomenon in Claude Rawson, "The Phrase 'Legal Prostitution' in Fielding, Defoe and Others," *Notes and Queries* (August 1964), 298 as well as in his later note in *Notes and Queries* (January–February 1977), pp. 49–52.

[68] See the critical edition of this poem with commentary by Clive Hart and Kay Gilliland Stevenson in *Eighteenth-Century Life* 19, n. s. 3 (November 1995), 38–69, especially lines 570–98.

pronounces that "a marriage for money" is "at best, but a legal prostitution."[69] Charlotte Smith, referring to the way she was sold into marriage
at fifteen (in 1764) calls herself a "legal prostitute" in a letter to a friend.[70]
John Bennett's *Letters to a Young Lady* (1789), after an inordinate number of
pages extolling Richardson's Harriet Byron as the very pattern of femininity, cannot forbear commenting on the problem of women's alienability –
the problem of giving her hand without her heart. "How wretched must
be a woman, united to a man whom she does not prefer to every other in
the world! What secret preferences must steal into her heart!" he writes.
"And what can men of principle *call* such an act, but *legal prostitution?*" he
concludes triumphantly.[71]

Hannah Cowley makes the point visually in *The Belle's Strategem*, first
produced in 1780. In order to protect Lady Frances Touchwood, a newly
married chaste wife, from the designs of Courtall the rake, her friends
dress up Kitty, a common prostitute, in the same masquerade costume that
Lady Frances wears. Courtall takes the bait and abducts the woman of easy
virtue instead of the virtuous Lady Frances. But these two women become
the focus of Act 4, interchangeable look-alikes, "identical and substitutable
figures" who literalize the ambiguous double requirement that a good girl be
sexually attractive while remaining chaste.[72] Dr. Primrose in Goldsmith's
The Vicar of Wakefield (1766), refusing to acknowledge the marriage of
Squire Thornhill to anyone but his daughter Olivia, makes it clear that she
is either a wife or a prostitute – and that he will never be an accomplice to
the latter designation.

---

[69] Colonel Rivers says this line at the end of Act 1. For an early examination of this play, see Mark
Schorer, "Hugh Kelly: His Place in the Sentimental School," *Philological Quarterly* 12, 4 (October
1933), 389–401.

[70] The letter to Sarah Rose is dated June 15, 1804 and is in the Henry E. Huntington Library, San
Marino, California. It is mentioned by Rufus Turner in his dissertation "Charlotte Smith (1749–
1806): New Light on Her Life and Literary Career," Ph.D. diss., University of Southern California,
1966, and included by Judith Stanton in her edition of Smith's letters.

[71] *Letters to a Young Lady, on a Variety of Useful and Interesting Subjects*, 3rd edn., 2 vols. (London:
T. Cadell, 1803), letter xxxvi, vol. II, p. 175. All of the letters in Bennett's conduct book that deal
with marriage (letters xxxiv–xxxvii) compare chaste women to prostitutes by way of defining proper
conduct. Another conduct book of 1789, *Letters on Love, Marriage, and Adultery; Addressed to the Right
Honourable the Earl of Exeter*, pronounces "But all connections, without that affection, which may
be truly and properly called love; whether effected by the authority of parents, by views of interest,
or by lust, however sanctified by superstitious or legal forms, are PROSTITUTIONS" (75). (London:
J. Ridgeway, 1789; facsimile rpt. New York: Garland, 1984).

[72] I am quoting a paper by Angela Smallwood, "Staging Female Education: Women Playwrights in
Georgian London," presented at a conference on L'education des femmes, Lille, France, March
1996. For a French translation, see Angela Smallwood, "L'Education feminine à la scène: les femmes
dramaturges dans le Londres georgien," in *L'Education des femmes en Europe et en Amérique du Nord
de la Renaissance à 1848*, ed. Guyonne Leduc (Paris: L'Harmattan, 1997), pp. 337–49.

Many texts registered the culture's anxiety about women's status as property and their potential alienability by depicting husbands selling their wives' favors. Henry Fielding's unpleasant little comedy *The Modern Husband* (1731) puts the case with brutal frankness. Remonstrating with Mrs. Modern about her own amours, her husband says: "you shall not drive a separate trade at my expense. Your person is mine: I bought it lawfully in the church; and unless I am to profit by the disposal, I shall keep it all for my own use . . . as I must more than share the dishonour, it is surely reasonable I should share the profit."[73] In *Amelia* (1751), Fielding describes Mr. Trent arranging for the seduction of his own wife in order to black-mail an amorous peer with a well-known weakness for other men's wives (Book IX, Chapter 3). The abusive husband in the anonymous *Amelia* pub-lished the same year also tries to prostitute his wife.[74] In Charlotte Smith's *Desmond* (1792), the heroine's detestable husband tries to sell her first to an English rake, Lord Scarfsdale, and then to a French one, Romagnecourt. George Venables, in Mary Wollstonecraft's *Maria* (1798), invites a creditor to dinner and leaves him alone with his wife encouragingly, declaring "every woman has her price."[75] The heroine, Maria, rebels, announcing to him and his rich friend that by trying to prostitute her he has broken their marriage bond: she removes her wedding ring and abjures his name (Chapter 11). These examples of the slippage between wife and prostitute reveal a new attitude towards women's sexual services coming from a new awareness of – and new possibilities for – commodification. Once women are considered their husband's property, with potential for converting property rights into cash, Fielding's Mr. Modern makes perfect sense.

Angela Smallwood has argued that Fielding's preoccupation with pros-titution was part of his more general anxiety about the corrupting effects of patronage. Concerned as he was with the way power and self-interest polluted human relationships, or the way "protection rackets of the pa-tronage system" and political opinions and services could be bought and traded, Smallwood claims that Fielding represented all these things in the alienability of women's "virtue." "The brutal and corrupt use of power," whether in private or public life, depicted in instrumental relations be-tween men and women, reveal the dishonesty of "relationships between

---

[73] *The Modern Husband* (London, 1731), Act 4 Scene 1. In *The Complete Works of Henry Fielding, Esq.*, ed. William Ernest Henley, 16 vols. (London: Heinemann, 1903), vol. X, pp. 45–6.

[74] See pp. 228–9 in Chapter 5 above for an account of this novel.

[75] *Maria; or, The Wrongs of Woman* (originally published as *The Wrongs of Woman; or, Maria* [1798]), ed. Moira Ferguson (New York: Norton, 1975), p. 110.

the socially strong and the socially weak," she writes.[76] The figure of the prostituted woman, in short, figured the many different kinds of alienation to be found in the new commercial, urban, de-humanized world of the eighteenth century: alienated political service, alienated social relations, capitalized wealth, compromised love, and, as in Swift's Corinna, even alienable parts of the body.[77]

One could also argue that the hard-luck stories of corrupted innocence all have a subtext of class exploitation, sometimes figured as sexual exploitation but not always. Seducers are always rich and highborn – that is what makes them attractive – and the advantage they take of pretty girls is calculated in class terms to have few consequences for themselves. Thus fallen women are represented as the particular victims of the selfishness and greed of newly exploitative social relations. Especially in such novels as Elizabeth Inchbald's *Nature and Art* (1796) or Mary Hays' *The Victim of Prejudice* (1799), in both of which a wealthy man sentences in a court of law the very woman whom he originally seduced and abandoned and set on her downward spiral, sexual seduction simply dramatized the more banal and widespread economic (and gendered) forms of exploitation. You could say that class antagonism contributed to the mythology of women's victimization.

Thus, the focus on prostitution in life and literature was overdetermined and revealed anxieties about a changing social order, presented in sexual terms, in which the drive for profit and commodified social relations were replacing older kin and communal obligations. Certainly the close juxtaposition of vice and virtue also figures class confusion and the blurring of other sociological categories in new urban spaces where rich and poor resorted indiscriminately. In *The Vicar of Wakefield* (1766), for example, anxiety runs through the novel about making proper inferences about others' social class and moral character – in the scenes of the disguised prostitutes, the misidentification of Sir William Thornhill, or the sequence in which the gullible Dr. Primrose does not distinguish the social status of a butler, "who, in his master's absence, made a mind to cut a figure and be for a

---

[76] Angela Smallwood, *Fielding and the Woman Question* (Hemel Hempstead, Hertfordshire: Harvester Wheatsheaf, 1989), p. 101.

[77] This last point comes from Brean Hammond's typescript "Swift's Censorship, Corinna's Dream," which sees the narrator of Swift's "A Beautiful Young Nymph Going to Bed" (1734) as a silent voyeur witnessing the woman's anomie, pain, and de-composition as a "*metaphor* for the alienated plight of the urban victim, a way of experiencing that predicament" (12). James Thompson argues that "Fielding's obsession with prostitution in *Amelia* is connected with capitalization" and with distaste for selling things that should not be for sale. See his "Patterns of Property and Possession in Fielding's Fiction," *Eighteenth-Century Fiction* 3, 1 (October 1990), 21–42, esp. 40 n. 40.

while the gentleman himself; and to say the truth, he talked politics as well as most country gentlemen do" (Chapter 19, pp. 110–11).

Perhaps the point is that, for women, class and sexual conduct were beginning to entail one another. Although historian Randolph Trumbach claims that the actual clients in brothels generally came from the same levels of society as the women themselves – and that, contrary to the fictional stereotype, "gentlemen were no more overrepresented here than they were among the seducers of servant girls"[78] – it seems doubtful that men of position did not abuse their power with women of a lower class as they always had. (Pepys, for example, felt entitled to paw any woman of a lower status within arm's reach.) Eliza Haywood's housewifery-and-conduct-book for maids, *A Present for a Servant-Maid* (1743), makes it clear that unwanted sex with the master was a common occupational hazard of service. Her advice on chastity includes the following: "Being so much under his Command, and obliged to attend him at any Hour, and at any Place he is pleased to call you, will lay you under Difficulties to avoid his Importunities, which it must be confessed are not easy to surmount," she writes. "[Y]our persevering may, perhaps, in Time, oblige him to resist," she concludes weakly. "[R]emonstrate to him the Sin and Shame he would involve you in; and omit nothing to make him sensible how cruel it is to go about to betray a Person whom it is his Duty to Protect." If he is married, Haywood continues, one should try to handle it alone without confiding in the mistress, for "in such Cases the Innocent suffer for the Crimes of the Guilty." If she is afraid of being raped, Haywood advises, her reader should leave the house at once. Ever practical, she predicts: "He will not insist on your forfeiting a Month's Wages for his own Sake, for fear you should declare the Cause of your quitting his Service; and if he should be even so hardened in Vice, as to have no Regard for his Character in this Point, it is much better you should lose a Month's Wages than continue a Moment longer in the Power of such a one" (45–7).

Increasingly, women's sexual behavior became a social marker for class identity; virtue was moral capital and chastity was the signature of class. Just as Richardson's Pamela is rewarded by upward mobility, so careless sexual behavior could reduce any woman to the class position of those poor "women publickly exposing themselves at the windows and doors of bawdy-houses, like beasts in a market for public sale," whose very presence was an insult

---

[78] "Prostitution was pretty much a business between persons of the same class," writes Trumbach. Clients apparently came from the ranks of laborers, artisans, and tradesmen. Randolph Trumbach, "Modern Prostitution and Gender in *Fanny Hill*: Libertine and Domesticated Fantasy," pp. 69–85, especially pp. 81–2.

to respectable women.[79] As Haywood warned her servant-readers: "Every street affords you Instances of poor unhappy Creatures, who once were innocent till seduced by the deceitful Promises of their Undoers . . . they became incapable of getting their Bread in any honest Way, and so by Degrees are abandoned to the lowest Degree of Infamy" (45). The elaboration of an ideology associating women's sexual forbearance with middle-class status (those who had the most to gain or lose from class mobility) displaced onto women's consciousness some of the psychic burden of class restructuring. A girl careless in her behavior deserved to be de-classed; a girl careful of her virtue deserved to move up. Although obviously affected by social and economic conditions, sexual conduct was nonetheless stubbornly conceived as a matter of individual choice and personal morality rather than a function of market forces such as the gendering of waged labor or the changing legal rules regulating marriage and premarital sexual contact. Thus female sexuality was constructed both as a matter of public concern and at the same time as a private matter, an introjected, self-conscious measure of personal worth with its corresponding class location.

The commodification of female sexuality thus functioned to naturalize and reproduce class relations. For despite the fears of those who supported the Hardwicke Marriage Act, personal attraction and sexual power played less of a role in redistributing wealth in the new fluid class structure than the novels of the day would have one believe. Contrary to Erica Harth's claim that the Hardwicke Marriage Act regulated the anarchic forces of sex that threatened existing bases of power and hence "was a victory for patriarchy and capitalism," the ideology of romantic love tended not to disrupt the system but rather to mystify the role of social status and class in mate selection.[80] Mysterious, orphaned heroes and heroines of fiction always turn out to be well-born; no one falls in love with a footman unless he is Peregrine Pickle in disguise. Despite *Pamela*'s being about a servant marrying her master, as Michael McKeon points out, most of the characters in that novel – including Pamela's father – have undecipherable class positions.[81]

[79] Saunders Welch, *A Proposal to Render Effectual a Plan, to Remove the Nuisance of Common Prostitutes from the Streets of this Metropolis*, p. 19.

[80] Erica Harth, "The Virtue of Love: Lord Hardwicke's Marriage Act," *Cultural Critique* 9 (Spring 1988): 123–54, quote 154. Anthony Fletcher makes this point in *Gender, Sex, and Subordination in England 1500–1800* (New Haven and London: Yale University Press, 1995) when he traces to the eighteenth century "the origins of the modern construction of femininity in a set of ideas which allied women's subordination to romantic love and to a high degree of separation from the outside world" (400).

[81] Michael McKeon, *The Origins of the English Novel 1600–1740* (Baltimore: Johns Hopkins University Press, 1987), p. 365.

WOMEN'S SEXUALITY AND CAPITALISM

Whether or not one finds it plausible that women's sexuality was redeployed in this period to regulate social dislocations caused by class fluidity, it is clear that the public discourse about women changed in the course of the eighteenth century. The focus of the debates changed. No longer did people argue about whether or not women had souls or were endowed with reason, or whether or not education made them "mannish" and discontented with their domestic chores. Arguments in the latter half of the eighteenth century revolved, rather, around women's "virtue" – their fidelity, their capacity for attachment, and their passion. Why? What did this obsession with women's sexual nature signify and why was it so satisfying a subject to eighteenth-century audiences that it was scripted and re-scripted? What other social issues did it screen?

As I have tried to suggest in this chapter, the attention in this period to the changing relation of women's sexuality to marriage grew out of a complex set of social and economic conditions. The old social relations of reproduction had been disrupted by urbanization, migration, and class instability, a disruption which the Hardwicke Marriage Act was a weak and misguided attempt to repair. The human bonds that formerly mediated social reproduction were stretched and distorted, and women's sexual love came to stand for that loss and to be thought of as a hedge against it. I have suggested that stories about women not only figured the alienability of human affection and trust but also the corruption of the public trust and exploitative relations of class. These were new problems in eighteenth-century England, or at least old problems in a new form. The fiction written about women's dilemmas with regard to the conflicting claims of fathers and husbands, brothers and lovers, asked questions about love and loyalty and the place of material advantage and immaterial "honor" in life's choices.

These questions had new meaning in a society dealing for the first time across the board with the social effects of the forces of market capitalism. The fictional formulas balancing self-serving desires with obligations to kin must have fed a new hunger, because novel production steadily increased in England after 1771, with only a brief respite during the American Revolution. Fiction held out a promise that, in a world beset by greed, heroic fidelity to true love above all else was possible. For women, this message had a sexual dimension: to marry without love (or to love without marrying) were variations on the theme of prostitution. A woman could belong to only one man and so she had better choose well the first time. Everything else paled next to the importance of that choice, which was supposed to be made on the intangible ground of feeling rather than for any material advantage. Novels about marriage thus enacted the problematics of bonding and loyalty that faced everyone in one form or another, rehearsing the dilemmas of the larger society in a small compass and giving epic status to individual choices. Battles with dragons and usurpers had been moved inside the psyche; the culture was debating whether the dragons to slay were a person's uncontrollable selfish passions or those old-fashioned authorities, parents and friends, who advised prudence, obedience, and a damping-down of individual impulse. The nature and meaning of sexual feelings were scrutinized as never before, and the novel was a safe space in which to try on these feelings imaginatively in all their permutations and consequences.

7

Farming fiction: Arthur Young and the problem of representation

It has been very justly said that I first excited the agricultural spirit which has since rendered Britain so famous; and I should observe that this is not so great a compliment as at first sight it may seem, since it was nothing more than publishing to the world the exertions of many capital cultivators and . . . common farmers who, with all their merit, were unknown beyond the limits of their immediate district.

Arthur Young, *The Autobiography of Arthur Young*, p. 30.

When a nation abounds in manufactures and mechanic arts, the proprietors of land, as well as the farmers, study agriculture as a science, and redouble their industry and attention. The superfluity, which arises from their labor is not lost . . . In times of peace and tranquillity, this superfluity goes to the maintenance of manufacturers, and the improvers of liberal arts. But it is easy for the public to convert many of these manufacturers into soldiers, and maintain them by that superfluity, which arises from the labour of farmers.

David Hume, "Of Commerce," *Essays* (ed. Eugene Miller), p. 261.

Should a poor man take one of Your sheep from the common, his life would be forfeited by law. But should You take the common from a hundred poor mens sheep, the law gives no redress. The poor man is liable to be hung for taking from You what would not supply You with a meal & You would do nothing illegal by depriving him of his subsistence.

C. Landor to the Marquis of Anglesey, April 26, 1824

Throughout this book I have used literary examples to identify and illustrate historical changes in kin relations – as if that evidence were not the slipperiest of all to interpret. For literature never reflects "reality" in any simple mimetic way. Even "realistic" fiction never records anything that actually happened. Art, like dream, caricatures or exaggerates "reality," projecting hopes, fears, or fixations rather than merely reporting "facts." Fiction can function as magical thinking, wish-fulfillment, catharsis, or theatrical staging. Writers intensify and distort the details of their world according to their imaginative needs. Fiction reflects projections of their world superimposed on an inner landscape of need, desire, and anxiety. Beyond the private purposes they serve for individuals, fictional representations are also ideologically determined, shaping incidents and explaining consequences according to culturally localized understandings of what is important. Finally, representational systems have their own formal rules, their own traditions, their own conventions.

Literary critics, familiar with the formal means used to represent feeling, the iconography of certain themes, the conventions of genres, and/or the effects of certain rhetorical moves or figures of speech, try to distinguish between what is common or traditional and what is personal or idiosyncratic about the treatment of a subject in a particular text. As my reader is all too aware, I have interpreted fictional texts in this book variously – as transparent examples of the historical phenomena I have been describing, as consolatory fantasies about insoluble problems, as nostalgic recreations of persistent myths – but always as indications of tensions and strains in the society. There is no simple formula that tells when a story is functioning in one or another of these ways. The critic must assess the meaning and force of recurrent tropes or themes, usual and unusual narrative moves, the energy and emphasis of special passages – always in their immediate historical context. Only by reading back and forth between literature and history can a critic get a feel for how a text symbolizes, transcends, or comments on its time. Thus, literature can be an invaluable historical source, but it takes literary judgment and historical knowledge to interpret it.

Social historians have been known to use literary texts crudely as evidence, reading them as the unambiguous recording of life as it happened in another era. Literary critics, too often ignorant of the historiography of their period, then adopt these formulations based on naive readings of literary texts that they in fact are better positioned to analyze by virtue of their refined reading skills. Lawrence Klein points out, for example, that literary critics still repeat Lawrence Stone's version of family history (the emotionally cold, tyrannical patriarchy of England in the sixteenth and seventeenth centuries giving way to the cozy, companionate family of the eighteenth century in which parents loved their children and each other), even though most historians rejected Stone's narrative as inconsistent with other historical data.[1] Stone's formulations are in part derived from superficial readings of sentimental fiction, a genre that no literary critic would offer as "realistic" were it not presented as the formulations of a distinguished historian.

In this chapter I want to explore the relation between "fact" and "fiction" in the writings of Arthur Young, a man who wrote novels in his young adulthood and agricultural treatises throughout his life – the man most responsible for encouraging, publicizing, and consolidating the agricultural revolution in England. Making agriculture the point of comparison – juxtaposing fictional accounts of farming with actual agricultural policies and practices – has the additional advantage of adding greater detail to one of the critical economic factors in the cultural shift under examination. Arthur Young's lived reality, the experience of his own life as he recorded it in his autobiography, the data he collected and published on crop rotation, fertilizer, implements, land tenures, size of holdings, rents, prices and wages, livestock, and so on – in comparison with the conventional novels he wrote – offer an ideal *oeuvre* for studying the relation between the realities and representations of rural life in England. An author of fiction and a reporter of material realities, Arthur Young combined in his life and writings the interrelated aspects of the historical period that I am trying to understand.

Young wrote his novels as pot-boilers, to make a little money to exchange in trade with his bookseller for more books. Although his novels contain much of interest to the social historian and the literary critic, Young himself intended posterity to forget these works of fiction.[2] They are no worse than

---

[1] See Lawrence Klein, "The Stories Historians Tell and the Stories Literary Historians Tell about History," unpublished paper delivered at the MLA, Washington, DC, December 27–30, 1996.

[2] Arthur Young's friend and physician, Dr. J. A. Paris, wrote a biographical notice at his death in 1820, stating that Arthur Young wrote four novels while at Lynn, and implying that he wrote them at the suggestion of his bookseller for remuneration in kind, to increase his store of books. See J. A. Paris, "A Biographical Memoir of Arthur Young," *Quarterly Journal of Science, Literature and the Arts* 9 (July 1820), 279–309. This literary activity is not mentioned in the parts of the published *Autobiography* dealing with his years at Lynn or Bradfield, although it should be noted that Young's text was edited in the nineteenth century and the original, complete version has never been recovered. More disturbingly, these novels are only mentioned in a footnote in Gazley's exhaustive biography and not included in his bibliography. In the published *Autobiography*, Young reports that while at Lynn, between 1758 and 1766, "love of reading proved my chief resource" and, when a bookseller gave him ten pounds of books for a pamphlet and urged him to write more, "I wrote three or four more political tracts, each of which procured me an addition to my little library." M. Bentham-Edwards (ed.), *The Autobiography of Arthur Young* (1898; rpt. New York: Augustus M. Kelley, 1967), pp. 29, 24.

The novels, published anonymously, are attributed to Young in the *Dictionary of National Biography* as well as by Frank Gees Black, *The Epistolary Novel in the Late Eighteenth Century* (Eugene: University of Oregon Press, 1940) and James R. Foster, *History of the Pre-Romantic Novel in England* (New York: Modern Language Association, 1949). They are: *The History of Sir Charles Beaufort*, 2 vols. (1766);

most of the novels published at the time – but also no better. He intended his agricultural writings, on the other hand, to change national consciousness about the possibilities of agricultural production, to wake up the nation to the importance of improved agricultural techniques, and to put farming on a par with manufacturing as a source of wealth for the nation.

He did not realize that the commercialization of agriculture, the gospel he preached, was changing the very way of life that he was taking such pains to record. His tireless advocacy of profitable uses for the so-called "waste" lands of England was certainly one of the factors that contributed to the transformation of kinship that I have been describing. Not until 1801, in his famous pamphlet *An Inquiry into the Propriety of Applying Wastes to the Better Maintenance and Support of the Poor*, did Arthur Young publicly recognize the effects of "improvement" on the poor, who lost their kitchen gardens, livestock forage, and woodlots to the capitalizing spirit of parliamentary enclosures.

Arthur Young's work – all his work – is an important link in the chain of events restructuring families in late eighteenth-century England. Unique as an author of romantic fiction as well as of "practical" farming advice and government policy, this writer embodies in his very life the connection between the economic and literary consciousnesses that I am investigating here. The imagination that shines forth in his immensely popular *Tours*, his pamphlets, and his novels, while growing out of the material conditions of his day, became a powerful force to reshape those very material conditions. As the architect of and chief spokesman for enclosure from about 1767 onwards, and as the author of four typical novels which incorporate conventional formulas about fathers and daughters, sisters and brothers, family loyalty and romantic love, Arthur Young demonstrates in his written work two different ways of reacting to the historical moment.

The Adventures of Emmera, or The Fair American, 2 vols. (1767); *The Adventures of Miss Lucy Watson* (1768); and *The History of Julia Benson; or the Sufferings of Innocence*, 2 vols. (1775). The first three were published by W. Nicoll, the bookseller who printed all of Young's agricultural writings in this period. The last, published seven years later, was printed by W. Goldsmith. There is a receipt in the British Library dated August 27, 1765, in the amount of £7 17s 6d made out to William Nicoll from Thomas Lowndes for the purchase of half the copyright in "Sr Charles Beaufort, a novell now in the press – will pay £10 if second edn. to author." Add. MS 38730 ff. 133.

For a complete list of Arthur Young's publications, *excluding* the novels which no one has included in his bibliography since Mr. Paris' bibliographic notice in 1820 and the *DNB* entry, see the bibliography appended to Elizabeth Pinney Hunt's volume of excerpts and summary, *Arthur Young on Industry and Economics* (Philadelphia:Bryn Mawr, 1926), pp. 164–83; John G. Gazley, "Arthur Young, Agriculturalist and Traveller, 1741–1820, Some Bibliographical Sources," *John Rylands Library* 37 (September 1954), 393–428; and, of course, the bibliography in Gazley's excellent biography *The Life of Arthur Young 1741–1820* (Philadelphia: American Philosophical Society, 1973).

MAN'S PLACE IN THE NATURAL WORLD

There was, of course, a literary tradition of pastoral description long before Arthur Young set out to record the farming practices of his day. The
poetry of Marvell, Denham, Pope, and Thomson constitutes the most
significant contemporary strain of this literary tradition. Imitating classical writers such as Horace and Virgil, these and seventeenth-century
poets such as Bacon, Waller, Milton, Cowley, and Vaughan had elaborated the notion that the innocent pleasures of rural life were morally
elevating. Country life was praised as an alternative to the corruptions
of city and court; peaceful contemplation of the calm beauty of the natural world promised greater happiness than any ambition in the world
of men. Nature was the book of God, and the happy man retired from
society in order to read and appreciate it; the Restoration nobleman on
his private estate imitated the classical ideal of Roman philosophers and
poets.

But between the seventeenth and the eighteenth centuries in England,
Maren-Sofie Røstvig tells us, the ideal of the happy man, *beatus vir*, and the
good life in English pastoral and georgic verse underwent a metamorphosis.[3]
A new optimistic rationalism began to transform the earlier conviction
of innate human depravity – from which contemplation of Nature had
been an escape and remedy – and to imagine new possibilities for the
relationship between humans and their physical world. The belief in human
perfectibility, which had begun to generalize to human endeavors in the
natural world, spread to farming. No longer did rural retirement simply
offer an alternative to a sinful world; it now provided an opportunity for
benevolent agency in a world newly conceived of as a model of the world's
variation and harmony. Nature was the experimental field from which
one might deduce God's laws: one did not retire to Nature to leave the
world behind but rather studied Nature the better to understand the world.
Inspired by Nature, the good man might then return to the social world
with renewed energy to act upon it, in imitation of God, to make it a better
place. Thus the happy man, now a friend of mankind rather than a recluse,
might become an agent of sentimental schemes for the improvement of
the poor and distressed as well as improvement of the land. "From this
time on," says Røstvig dryly, "the rural scene will be viewed through a mist

---

[3] Maren-Sofie Røstvig, *The Happy Man: Studies in the Metamorphoses of a Classical Ideal*, vol I: *1600–1700*
(Oslo: Akademisk Forlag, and Oxford: Basil Blackwell, 1954). Donna Landry distinguishes usefully
between pastoral and georgic traditions in *The Invention of the Countryside: Hunting, Walking and
Ecology in English Literature, 1671–1831* (New York: Palgrave, 2001), pp. 57–8.

of thickening tears."[4] Thus the poet's enjoyment of the natural world was understood by the mid-eighteenth century to come from a contemplative interest in the systematic and lawful universe posited by science – together with a desire to successfully manipulate Nature's laws – as well as from the fellow-feeling these interests inspired in him towards the rest of God's creation.[5]

These elements appear in the fiction as well as the poetry of the period, from Fielding's *Joseph Andrews* (1742) to Bage's *Mount Henneth* (1782) with dozens in between. The new, idealized entrepreneurial farmer, in all his energetic and sentimental glory, is an intelligent gentleman who supports himself, his wife, and several rosy-cheeked children with his agricultural labors, usually bringing a ruined estate into harmonious production with good management, hard work, and the latest agricultural techniques. The protagonist of the tale, an eighteenth-century mini-hero, has withdrawn to a small country estate, usually after several misadventures with love, dice, or the bottle, where he lives a happy and useful life, growing exponentially in wisdom and charity. His story tends to be told as an interpolated tale; few novels feature such a protagonist for the entire plot – with the exception of Arthur Young's *The Adventures of Emmera, or the Fair American* (1767). Indeed, in all of Arthur Young's novels, farming tests character: good men and women inevitably appreciate it ("I shall ever consider farming as the most rational, philosophical, and manly employment in the world"[6]), whereas morally flawed characters sneer at it as an occupation for bumpkins. In *The Adventures of Emmera*, farming is the protagonist's chosen way of life – not just an episode he witnesses – and the action revolves around preserving it.

At first, these images of happy, self-sufficient farmers on their small-holdings in mid-eighteenth-century fiction appear to be merely a continuation of the seventeenth-century georgic tradition. But the trope takes on a new emphasis in mid-eighteenth-century fiction. For one thing, the sturdy farmers who till the soil are not always gentlemen who read poetry and philosophy or who are escaping from a dissolute court life. The independence figured in this trope is also an English yeoman's independence from tyrannical landlords, condescending employers, callous debtors, and the alienated commercialism of the city. Farming, in these fictions, becomes

---

[4] Maren-Sofie Røstvig, *The Happy Man: Studies in the Metamorphoses of a Classical Ideal*, vol. II: *1700–1760* (Oslo: Akademisk Forlag, and Oslo University Press; Oxford: Basil Blackwell, 1958), p. 321.

[5] Røstvig notes that Akenside first formulated the connection between moral benevolence (and therefore public virtue) and an innate taste for natural grandeur. "The man who rejoiced in the vaster scenes of nature, so Akenside thought, would also rejoice in the spectacle of moral benevolence – the two innate tastes were actually one and the same." *Ibid.*, vol. II, p. 415.

[6] *The History of Sir Charles Beaufort*, 2 vols. (London, 1767), vol. I, pp. 50–1.

a way to earn a decent living in a hardening world that offers few better opportunities. The sentimental idealization of man's rational labor and Nature's miraculous and lucrative bounty is also new at mid-century insofar as it is linked to the accumulation of wealth. A fascination with the potential productivity of the land underlies and extends the newly rational appreciation of nature and the enlightened belief in God's orderly creation.

THE REALITY OF SMALL-SCALE FARMING

Because the popularity of this theme in fiction from 1742 to the end of the century did not directly reflect "reality," did not reflect an actual increase in the number and success rate of small farmers, we need to ask what this trope signified about the culture that produced and consumed it. Although this era saw the beginning of a serious interest in scientific farming, it was hardly a period in which there was a proliferation of small, self-sufficient farms. On the contrary, historically speaking, this was the period during which small landowners were losing their holdings. Using eighteenth-century land-tax assessments, Arthur H. Johnson concluded long ago that "there was a very remarkable consolidation of estates and a shrinking in the number of the smaller owners" by the end of the century. Tracing land ownership in specific regions, he observed that by 1785, in twenty-four Oxfordshire parishes, there were only 212 owners holding an average of 21 acres, whereas earlier there had been 482 freeholders or copyholders (tenants for life) holding an average of 28 acres. That is, by 1785 half the number of smallholders farmed one-third as much land as had been owned and farmed by smallholders in the previous century.[7] In England as a whole, there was a marked decrease in farms under 100 acres and an increase in those over 300 acres. Between 1740 and 1788, over 40,000 separate small farms disappeared. Studying specific locales, historians have noted as much as a 25 percent to 33 percent decline in the number of small owners and tenant farmers in the course of the century.[8] Even G. E. Mingay, though optimistic about the ultimate economic effects of capitalized agriculture (and at some pains to prove the Hammonds wrong about the harm done to cottagers by parliamentary enclosure), concedes that, whereas a third of the cultivated land of England

---

[7] Arthur H. Johnson, *The Disappearance of the Small Landowner* (Oxford: Clarendon Press, 1909; rpt. with introduction by Joan Thirsk, London: Merlin Press, 1963), p. 132. Johnson also calculates that in ten Gloucestershire parishes in the seventeenth century 229 owners farmed 6,458 acres, but by 1782–5 only 80 smallholders farmed a total of 1,104 acres.

[8] See J. M. Martin, "The Small Landowner and Parliamentary Enclosure in Warwickshire," *Economic History Review* 32, 3 (August 1979), 328–43. See also K. D. M. Snell, *Annals of the Labouring Poor: Social Change and Agrarian England, 1660–1900* (Cambridge: Cambridge University Press, 1985), pp. 190–4.

was worked by owner-occupiers in the late seventeenth century (freeholders of "the better sort" and of "the lesser sort" in Gregory King's taxonomy), only 12 percent of the land was in the hands of owner-occupiers by the end of the eighteenth century.[9] He concurs with A. H. Johnson's conclusion that "the closing years of the seventeenth century and the first fifty years of the eighteenth century were fatal to the small owner."[10]

So it seems that the idealization of the small farmer in fiction accompanied his disappearance in life. These images of happy, rural self-sufficiency – and the sinister, engrossing, property-proud rack-renting landlords who also appear in fiction of this period – while not absolute reflections of the "real" state of agriculture in the late eighteenth century, nonetheless reveal something about cultural attitudes towards farming in the period. They reveal a deep nostalgia for an earlier rural way of life, before the effects of enclosure were felt, in their representations of large and small farmers, alienated and unalienated labor, subsistence and luxury economies, enclosure and common rights, wealth and poverty.

That benevolence for the poor and distressed should have materialized as a virtue integral to this pastoral vision is easier to understand. The enclosure of the wastes and common land that were necessary to rural subsistence and steadily rising prices for food in the course of the century, together with the decreasing need for labor that went with lucrative conversion from arable to pasture, created hardship in the countryside. More and more poor lacked the means to graze their animals or raise their own vegetables after the enclosures, and there was less steady work for agricultural laborers. Their distress provided the heroes and heroines of fiction with many opportunities to prove their moral value with charitable acts. Henry Mackenzie's *Man of Feeling* (1771), for example, is structured as a series of sentimental encounters in which Harley, a gentleman farmer who leaves his small paternal

---

[9] G. E. Mingay, *Enclosure and the Small Farmer in the Age of the Industrial Revolution* (London: Macmillan, 1968), p. 14. The Hammonds are, of course, J. L. Hammond and Barbara Hammond, whose *The Village Labourer 1760–1832: A Study in the Government of England before the Reform Bill* (London: Longmans Green, 1911) gave one of the earliest and most compelling accounts of the disastrous effects of enclosure on the small farmer, the cottager, and the laboring poor in eighteenth-century England as a result of their displacement from the land.

[10] Arthur H. Johnson, *The Disappearance of the Small Landowner*, p. 136. J. M. Neeson notes that Johnson, Davies, Gonner, Clapham, Chambers, Mingay, and W. E. Tate place the disappearance of the small landholder earlier than do the Hammonds, who argued that parliamentary enclosure "in the second half of the eighteenth century was a major cause of the disappearance of the English peasantry." She cites work by W. G. Hoskins, Joan Thirsk, E. P. Thompson, and Alan Everitt to show that landless proletarianized laborers were less common in early eighteenth-century England than Chambers and Mingay suggest, and that England may well have had an eighteenth-century peasantry after all. J. M. Neeson, "An Eighteenth-Century Peasantry," in John Rule and Robert Malcolmson (eds.), *Protest and Survival: Essays for E. P. Thompson* (London: Merlin Press, 1993), pp. 24–59, quotes p. 26 and p. 29.

estate to try to obtain the lease to some adjoining crown lands, demonstrates his rural benevolence towards all those he meets on the road. The recipients of his largesse include, among others, a poor neighbor of his, old Edwards, turned off his farm, victimized by new, commercial methods of land management.

Arthur Young, whose research and writing on behalf of English agriculture was rewarded with the post of the first Secretary for the Board of Agriculture, failed miserably, ironically enough, in his own early attempts to farm his paternal estate at Bradfield. Three times he tried unsuccessfully to wring his fortune from the soil: in Suffolk from 1763 to 1767, at Samford Hall in Essex for six months, and finally on the 100-acre Bradmore Farm in North Mimms, Hertfordshire, between 1768 and 1775. Whether Young's failure demonstrates his ineptitude or is yet another example of the small farmer in this age being undersold by better-funded commercial agriculturalists, these farms never fully supported him. Farming never produced the income he required as a gentleman and he had to supplement his income by writing. He did not possess the capital to fertilize his land, to buy and breed cattle, or to lay down pasture as the commercially minded large landowners had begun to do. Although he was the chief theorist and enthusiast for the movement to enclose the so-called "waste" lands of England and turn them to more "productive" uses, he understood that it was a rich man's game. "The best land is of no avail without a sufficient sum of money to render its fertility of use," he wrote after his northern tour. "Neither skill nor industry will make any amends for want of an ample stock."[11] He spent too much of what money he did have in experiments with seed, sowing, and manuring. He tried drill culture, for example[12]; he built a modern, paved piggery with sheds, troughs, a pond, and "all the adjoining conveniences" for raising hogs. He tried new crops, such as potatoes, cabbages, lucerne, sainfoin, burnet, and Jerusalem artichokes.[13] In 1772, impressed with a letter from Dr. Hunter of York about growing carrots and onions for conversion "by a cheap process into a confection for the use of seamen," he tried it himself.[14] But like his other schemes, this one failed, and his journal memorialized this "new career of industry, ill-exerted, of new hopes and never-failing disappointment, labour and sorrow, folly and infatuation."[15] An entry in

---

[11] Arthur Young, *A Six Months Tour through the North of England*, 4 vols, 2nd edn. (London: W. Strahan and W. Nicoll, 1771), vol. IV, p. 272.

[12] Drill planting means planting seed in rows – rather than "broadcasting" or throwing it out with a sweep of the arm – thus leaving space between the rows for hoeing weeds. Young was a great advocate of drill culture and weeding, both new farming techniques in his time.

[13] John G. Gazley, *The Life of Arthur Young*, pp. 14–15.

[14] *Autobiography of Arthur Young*, p. 62.   [15] *Ibid.*, p. 62.

his diary years later shows what his wife thought of his lifelong compulsion to experiment. She apparently told a German baron visiting at Bradfield that she "detested" all of Young's experiments, for they had ruined him.[16]

THE LITERARY ARTHUR YOUNG

Although Arthur Young had been raised on his family's small estate at Bradfield in western Suffolk, no one in his family expected him to have a professional career in agriculture. His father, the Reverend Arthur Young, the author of several theological tomes, had apprenticed him in 1758 to learn accounting in a mercantile firm in Lynn, Norfolk, which his son found "detestable." His only solace under the circumstances was "surrounding myself with books, and making the acquaintance of Miss Robertson, daughter of my employer's partner." A local bookseller gave him ten pounds' worth of books for a political pamphlet he wrote called "The Theatre of the Present War in North America," which pleased him so well that he wrote several more for the same exchange. He muses in his *Autobiography* that had his father used the £400 apprentice fee to send him instead to the university, he could have been a clergyman and had the living at Bradfield and known nothing of agriculture. "I might have never been of any use to the public," he added, "but my years would have passed in a far more tranquil current, escaping so many storms and vicissitudes which blew me into a tempest of activity and involved me in great errors, great vice, and perpetual anxiety" (22–4).

His older sister, of whom he was very fond, was married and living in London at the time he went to Lynn. Her letters probably supplied some of the details of fashionable London life that found their way into his novels. She described to him the plays, masquerades, and fashionable assemblies she went to, the clothes and equipages she saw, the political battles in Parliament, and all the news of the town. Her presence is also recorded in Young's fiction in his intelligent and well-read heroines and in the affectionate relationships between brothers and sisters depicted in *The History of Sir Charles Beaufort* (1766) and *The Adventures of Emmera* (1767). Young visited her in London in 1758 for the last time, for she died soon after while giving birth. "She was a remarkably clever woman, with

---

[16] *Ibid.*, p. 429. One of Young's enemies, a surveyor named Thomas Stone, reviewing Young's agricultural survey of Lincolnshire, sneered at Young's management of his own family estate, Bradfield Hall Farm in Suffolk, stating that if his neighbors were asked "who was the worst farmer in the country, they would immediately answer, Arthur Young." Quoted in John G. Gazley, *The Life of Arthur Young*, p. 423.

much beauty and vivacity of conversation, combined with much solidity of judgement," he wrote in his *Autobiography* (22).

His father, the Reverend Arthur Young, died in 1759, leaving debts that took his mother two years to pay off. Arthur Young was still without a career, for he hated the business he had been apprenticed to and loved books and writing. While his mother lived, his entire patrimony consisted of a copyhold farm of 20 acres that brought him as many pounds' annual income.[17] In 1762 he launched *The Universal Museum*, a monthly periodical for which he tried to recruit Samuel Johnson among other writers. Johnson advised him that any publication not owned at least in part by booksellers was sure to fail and advised him to get out. After five months, Young saw the wisdom of Johnson's advice and gave over the enterprise to a group of booksellers.[18] Still without a livelihood, he was persuaded by his mother to take over the lease of an 80-acre farm on her estate. For the next three years he farmed for a living, adding a second farm to his holdings.

In 1765 he married Martha Allen, and they boarded with his mother at Bradfield.[19] Still reading voraciously, and now with a new need for income, he wrote three of his four novels in the lean early years of his marriage: *The History of Sir Charles Beaufort* (1766), *The Adventures of Emmera, or the Fair American* (1767), and *The Adventures of Miss Lucy Watson* (1768). (The fourth, *The History of Julia Benson*, was published some years later in 1775). The published autobiography does not mention these productions, and the world seems to have forgotten that he wrote novels, but in his *Autobiography* he records that in 1767 "I worked with incredible avidity both in the agricultural and literary department. I remember once to have written a quire of foolscap in one day!"[20] We will never know if the nineteenth-century editor of his memoirs cut the references to his novels from his autobiography or if Young omitted mention of these productions (which were probably written in exchange for books to supplement his library) because he was ashamed of them or because he thought them unimportant.

Stylistically, there is internal evidence that these novels were written by the same person. They are all epistolary – although the narrative in each novel keeps reverting to dramatic dialogue in moments of crisis. Three of

---

[17] *Autobiography of Arthur Young*, p. 29.   [18] *Autobiography of Arthur Young*, pp. 26–7.

[19] *Autobiography of Arthur Young*, pp. 29–30. Two years later, Martha Allen's older sister Elizabeth, a widow, married Dr. Charles Burney. See *Autobiography of Arthur Young*, p. 32 n. 3; John Gazley, *The Life of Arthur Young*, pp. 24, 37.

[20] *Autobiography of Arthur Young*, p. 45.

the four novels end tragically; only in *The Adventures of Emmera* do the hero and heroine survive their trials to live happily ever after. Ruinous, vindictive lawsuits based on trumped-up charges plague the protagonists in several of the novels. In two of them, *The History of Sir Charles Beaufort* (1766) and *The History of Julia Benson; or the Sufferings of Innocence* (1775), the villain who destroys the good protagonists is a diabolically clever woman, mistress of a thousand disguises, who has been spurned by the hero in favor of the heroine but who has her revenge in the end. Women are powerful in all his novels; Young's heroines, too, are all extremely intelligent, cultivated, and rational although their virtues pale somewhat next to the passionate virulence of his villainesses. The noisy, cursing, macho braggadocio of his male villains is also similar from text to text. Moreover, all four novels display an interest in agriculture that is, in my experience, unique in the fiction of this period. Julia Benson, for example, the eponymous heroine of the last novel, boards with a farmer when down on her luck and walks about his fields with him, learning about nitrogen-fixing grasses and the advantages of weeding. Later, when she marries a man of her own station, she advises his steward and lays out the farm herself, using drill planting, horse-hoeing, alternating corn and lucerne or sainfoin, and the like – all improvements that Young recommended throughout his career.

Other details in these fictions also corroborate Arthur Young's authorship. A serious chess player in his younger days, he creates a protagonist in *The Adventures of Miss Lucy Watson* (1768), Edward Mansel, who is an avid player who teaches chess to his mistress, enthusing: "There is no other game, amusement, or scarce an employment, that fathoms the inmost soul of man more than this of chess."[21] A reference to a *ferme ornée*, an "ornamented farm" laid out in a certain way, from a letter Young received in 1765 finds its way into *The History of Julia Benson* (1775) in a letter the heroine writes to her friend about her new husband: "I have succeeded in bringing him to a relish of farming, by mixing that amusement with his favourite ones of planning and laying out ground," she confides. "The French have a term in their language, ferme ornée."[22] Facts and figures about growing hemp and indigo in America turn up both in *Observations on the Present State of the Waste Lands of Great Britain* (1773) and in *The Adventures of Lucy Watson* (1768). Several of the novels feature heroes who are interested in art and familiar with the works of Titian, Correggio, and Lorraine – paintings

---

[21] *Autobiography of Arthur Young*, p. 28; *The Adventures of Miss Lucy Watson* (London, 1768), p. 17.
[22] *The History of Julia Benson; or the Sufferings of Innocence*, 2 vols. (London, 1775), vol. II, p. 63.

Arthur Young describes in his extensive footnotes to *A Six Months Tour through the North of England* (1771) when enumerating the treasures of the great houses he visited.

Although he wrote about people who farmed successfully during these years when he was trying to make his fortune as a gentleman farmer, Young never did so well in life as the characters in his novels or the novels of his contemporaries, Fielding and Smollett. He did not have the independent fortune of a fictional hero and economies of scale were against him. His income – including what he made from his prolific writing – never averaged more than £300 a year during the decade he practiced farming. His own summary of the period was far from idyllic:

the last four or five years of my life [have] been detestable, my employments degrading, my anxiety endless, every effort unsuccessful, exertion always on the stretch, and always disappointed in the result, uneasy at home, unhappy abroad, existing with difficulty and struggling to live, never out of debt, and never enjoying one shilling that was spent.[23]

THE IDEALIZED SMALL FARMER TROPE

If small, self-sufficient English landowners were failing during the eighteenth century, what explains the proliferation of fictional images at mid-century of contented gentlemen farmers on their small estates? Were these simply wish-fulfillment fantasies of a way of life that was passing – or never had existed? Were they projections of contemporary anxieties about poverty and alienated subsistence? The audience for novels was, for the most part, urban wage-earners, people who no longer lived by tilling the soil. Moreover, in this capitalizing age farming had as much to do with leases and tenancy agreements, keeping accounts and paying taxes, tithes, and rates, as with the actual reaping and sowing of crops. Absentee owners and even farmers in residence with large tracts of land hired land agents to keep track of wages and leases, seed and yields, on a modern cost-accounting management system. Thus, the idea of an intelligent, "hands-on" small landowner was invested with nostalgic yearning probably in inverse proportion to his actual existence. An eighteenth-century version of "back to the land," the images in these novels depicted a less alienated way of life in which one grew the food one ate, provided for the basic needs of one's family without surplus, and dispensed with wasteful spending and the competition for

---

[23] *Autobiography of Arthur Young*, pp. 65–6.

costly commodities. As Mr. Wilson describes it to Parson Adams in *Joseph Andrews* (1742):

whatever you see here is the Work solely of my own Hands. Whilst I am providing Necessaries for my Table, I likewise procure myself an Appetite for them. In fair Seasons I seldom pass less than six Hours of the twenty-four in this Place, where I am not idle, and by these means I have been able to preserve my Health ever since my Arrival here without Assistance from Physic.[24]

Like Milton's Adam, whose labor only served to whet his appetite and sweeten his leisure, Mr. Wilson feels that his farm is a paradise. It rescues him from the profligate, wasteful, unhealthy life he had lived in London and gives him purposeful work. Farming for him, as for other fictional characters in this genre, offered a way to maintain himself honorably in a society increasingly driven by the motives of profit and consumption. His farm boasted "no parterres, no fountains, no statues . . . its only ornament was a short walk, shaded on each side by a filbert hedge" (196). Sentimentalized as a return to subsistence economy rather than cash exchange – filberts rather than fountains – small-scale farming is envisioned as an alternative to the newer system of surplus, luxury, and profit. Small-scale farming – in novels – offered a respite from the wage economy and was generally seen in opposition to it.

Frances Brooke's *The History of Lady Julia Mandeville* (1763), a novel very much concerned with rural social relations, includes another such cameo appearance of a gentleman farmer. Mr. Herbert, having dissipated his patrimony gambling and drinking, retired, with a changed heart, to "a neat house, with a little romantic garden behind it" with his pleasing wife and his son "lovely and playful as a Cupid." He tours his estate with the narrator after a simple but delicious repast, "seventy acres, which he cultivates himself, and has embellished with every thing that can make it lovely."[25] Born to a higher status although down on his luck, Mr. Herbert tells the narrator that he expects better things in the future. Biding his time like royalty in disguise, he shows that no one is too well-born to support himself in this simple and blameless manner.

Frances Burney's *Cecilia* (1782) contains its own indelible image of the happy farmer in the figure of Belfield, educated to be a gentleman but

---

[24] Henry Fielding, *Joseph Andrews*, ed. Douglas Brooks-Davies and Martin C. Battestin (Oxford and New York: Oxford University Press, 1970), p. 196. Subsequent page numbers refer to this edition.

[25] Frances Brooke, *The History of Lady Julia Mandeville*, "By the translator of Lady Catesby's Letters," 2 vols. (London: R. and J. Dodsley, 1763), vol. II, pp. 42–3.

without the means, who enjoys a brief period of happiness during which he is released from the desperate effort of keeping up with his monied friends. He works as a day laborer, and lives in a cottage built on "waste" land. He tells Cecilia that he is truly free at last and that he has discovered the secret of happiness: "Labour with Independence."[26] All of Belfield's enthusiasms prove chimerical, and this one too becomes unsatisfying at last. But while it lasts it seems a better solution than most: honorable, spirited, and free.

There are villains as well as heroes in these fictions, also constructed according to formula. Tucked into these stories of idealized small farmers is frequently an incident of extreme injustice, stemming from the stubborn exercise of property rights. Sometimes the absentee owner manages his estate through a London steward – a man outside the local networks of obligation and custom – who mistreats tenants and squeezes the land for maximum profit. But more often the villains of these episodes are smaller fish, local landowners themselves who get carried away with the idea of their legally exclusive property rights. These villains always pursue a greedy and proprietary policy with regard to land, engrossing smaller tenants' holdings, terminating customary entitlements, raising rents, enclosing common land, or otherwise enforcing the letter of their right of dominion, and punishing the needy men who hunt or fish or forage on the margins of their land. They ignore the earlier sense of land as a right to revenue, conditioned on certain social relations, rather than an absolute right to the material stuff itself – dirt, trees, water, animals. Their mean-spirited selfishness is created to discredit the idea of an alienable and exclusive ownership of a corner of the natural world.

In *Joseph Andrews*, for example, Fanny and Joseph and Parson Adams are listening to Mr. Wilson's tale when his daughter's pet spaniel is shot by the local squire, who apparently has "killed all the dogs, and taken away all the guns in the neighbourhood," implicitly forbidding hunting (199). The squire, whose wealth makes him a dangerous man to oppose, wants to regulate others' use of the land and its creatures. Although he may have been within his legal rights – for the Game Act of 1671 restricted hunting to the lord of the manor or those with an income of £100 or more from

---

[26] Frances Burney, *Cecilia, or, Memoirs of an Heiress*, ed. Peter Sabor and Margaret Anne Doody (Oxford and New York: Oxford University Press, 1988), p. 659. See also Mr. Harrel's suicide note, in which he deplores his fashionable, idle life and writes: "Had I a son, I would bequeath him a plough; I should then leave him happier than my parents left me" (431). These references to the satisfactions of agricultural labor are probably more than a cultural coincidence, for Burney knew Arthur Young well and was quite fond of him. It seems likely that she read his paeans to agriculture and absorbed from him the attitude that to plough and plant was to be supremely useful to society.

freehold property – not all landowners enforced this requirement. Even William Blackstone thought it ridiculous that it took fifty times the property qualification "to kill a partridge, as to vote for a knight of the shire."[27] Within the terms of the novel, the anecdote emphasizes the tyranny of this man who tries to hoard all the living creatures in the neighborhood for himself. To keep anyone else from owning a dog – which is to say, from hunting – and to punish as poachers all those who foraged in the natural world in order to live, was to follow a newly legalistic interpretation of absolute and exclusive property rights rather than the traditional, contingent arrangements by which the bounty of the land belonged to those who lived on it and who needed it.

In Jane Austen's *Sense and Sensibility*, John Dashwood's selfishness is confirmed by the fact that he encloses Norwood common, taking it out of general use and adding it to his private estate – and even complaining about the cost of enclosing! In *Mansfield Park*, Mr. Rushworth, the dim-witted wealthy owner of Sotherton, bores his fiancé, Maria Bertram, by telling her about his hunting and his dogs, "his jealousy of his neighbours, his doubts of their qualifications, and his zeal after poachers."[28] In Henry Mackenzie's *The Man of Feeling* (1771), old Edwards describes to Harley the impersonal management strategy that lost him South-hill, the land farmed by his father, grandfather, and great-grandfather. The new squire, "who had lately got a London attorney for his steward," would not renew his lease "because, he said, he did not chuse to have any farm under £300 a year value on his estate" (96).[29] Renting out land in larger parcels minimized the subsistence extracted from the land and maximized the surplus profit. It also simplified collecting rents. When Edwards' family was turned out of South-hill, their old blind dog refused to leave the place where he had always lived, and followed them no further than the gooseberry bush, where "he gave a short howl, and died!" (97).[30] This pathetic fallacy – animals

---

[27] William Blackstone, *Commentaries on the Laws of England*, 4 vols. (1844; facsimile rpt. Chicago: University of Chicago Press, 1979), vol. IV, p. 175; quoted in Donna Landry, *The Invention of the Countryside*, p. 74. Hare, partridge, pheasant, and moorhen were considered game, while deer and rabbits – because they were raised – were considered private property. After the Game Act of 1671, hunting game required an income of £100 from freehold property or £150 from 99-year leases.

[28] Jane Austen, *Mansfield Park*, ed. Tony Tanner (Harmondsworth and New York: Penguin, 1966), Chapter 12, p. 142.

[29] Page numbers cited come from the combined edition of *The Man of Feeling; and, The Man of the World* (London: Routledge, and New York: E. P. Dutton, 1931).

[30] Beth Fowkes Tobin, in her excellent discussion of this passage in *Superintending the Poor: Charitable Ladies and Paternal Landlords in British Fiction, 1770–1860* (New Haven: Yale University Press, 1993), points out that "The gooseberry bush is associated with wholesomeness, reminding one of homemade (and very English) treats like the gooseberry wine, gooseberry fool, and gooseberry tarts made and

representing the loss felt by their masters – was a common literary tactic in such novels. Animals, because they do not distinguish between one man's property and another's, stand for the principle of use and habit rather than exclusive sovereign ownership in these novels. Their unmediated relation to the natural world shows how absurd, however legal, is the idea that anyone can own a piece of nature.

Later, Edwards tells of starting over again, renting a small farm in the vicinity. True to the fictional formula, the small farm earns an honorable living. Edwards recounts his family's intelligent efforts:

It was a piece of ground which required management to make anything of; but it was nearly within the compass of my son's labour and my own. We exerted all our industry to bring it into some heart. We began to succeed tolerably, and lived contented on its produce, when an unlucky accident brought us under the displeasure of a neighbouring justice of the peace and broke all our family-happiness again. (98)

The organic and reciprocal relation between the land and its cultivator suggested by the idiom of bringing the land "into heart" distinguishes Edwards' attitude towards the land from those for whom it exists merely to extract maximum income. The unlucky accident that interrupts Edwards' "family-happiness" again stems from rigidly defined prerogatives of private property. Old Edwards' son's hunting dog followed some birds from their farm onto their neighbor's land (ironically, a "justice of the peace") where the dog was shot by his gamekeeper. Edwards' son then lost his temper and felled the gamekeeper – for which he was imprisoned. Although Edwards' son was released after paying a fine, the retributive "justice" gave his name to a press gang scouring their county. Chronically shorthanded, the navy relied on local authorities to identify eligible men for service; nor was there any mechanism for protest or redress for victims seized in this manner.[31] In this case, Edwards' son was to be sent to India in the service of the nation, although Edwards persuaded him to stay with his wife and children and went in his stead. When Edwards tells Harley of the consequent hardships and adventures he endured, the sentimental man of feeling sets him up on a small farm in the neighborhood with enough outlay for seed and furniture. Again, the small farm, capable of being worked by a man and his family, is the solution to displacement, poverty, and injustice in the world.

---

served with pride by housewives like Mrs. Primrose in the *Vicar of Wakefield* and Mrs. Wilson in *Joseph Andrews*" (19).

[31] John Brewer, *The Sinews of Power: War, Money and the English State, 1688–1783* (Cambridge, MA: Harvard University Press, 1990), pp. 49–50.

The press gang in this episode is a resonant detail – both because it was a hardship frequently visited upon the poor in fiction, and because the connection between militarism and commercial agriculture suggested by the detail is worth underlining.[32] The escalating military market for agricultural products between 1739 and 1815, during which time England was officially at war 75 percent of the time and unofficially at war for more, was one of the factors that changed agricultural practice. The need for wool (for uniforms) and wheat (to supply what was in fact a standing army and navy through most of the century) was an important factor in changing England's patterns of land use. Rising prices for cloth and foodstuffs encouraged large landowners to acquire more land and lay down pasture, accelerating the process of parliamentary enclosure. The navy, in particular, required huge supplies of beer and beef, butter and biscuits, to feed its more than 40,000 men – a population larger than that of either Norfolk or Bristol.[33] All of this squeezed the small farmer, who could not always afford the costs of enclosing or improving additional land, and the cottager class, who lost their access to commonage and "waste" lands for gardens and forage, while food prices climbed beyond their means. By the end of the century great estate owners and landholding gentry owned more of England and small landowners and yeomen freeholders owned far less.[34]

---

[32] An honest, hardworking farmer is also involuntarily conscripted in Maria Edgeworth's "Simple Susan," a tale of which Sir Walter Scott said, "in that children's story – where the little girl parts with her lamb, and the little boy brings it back again, there's nothing for it but just to put down the book and cry." J. G. Lockhart, *Memoirs of the Life of Sir Walter Scott*, Chapter 82, quoted in the Introduction by Marilyn Butler to the Penguin edition of *Castle Rackrent; and, Ennui* (Harmondsworth and New York: Penguin, 1992), p. 3. The merciless press gang appears with the inevitability of natural disaster in other fictions representing the trials suffered by the poor. In Robert Bage's *Mount Henneth* (1782), several of the poor people recruited as laborers for the utopian community have suffered at the hands of military recruiters. One is a war widow with children whose household goods, including her very bed, have been seized. Another, who began life as a farmer's boy, was impressed and shipped off to America; his leg was shot off in an engagement with a privateer (189–90). In another story, a needleworker's brother tries to support her but is seized for debt and impounded by a press gang. His debt is paid off by the Mt. Henneth philanthropists and he and his sister are relocated in the new community. Mary Wollstonecraft's *Maria; or the Wrongs of Woman* (1798) includes the story of a countrywoman, Peggy, whose husband is impressed and then killed: "the poor are bound to suffer for the good of their country," remarks the narrator (81). She takes in washing until "a recruiting party . . . made free with a large wash" (82) for which she has to make restitution to her clients. When she cannot pay her rent, her goods are seized, including her bed. Citations from Moira Ferguson's edition, New York: Norton, 1975. A later example, from *Romance Readers and Romance Writers: A Satirical Novel*, by the Author of *A Private History of the Court of England & C* [Sarah Green], 3 vols. (London: T. Hookham, Junior, and E. T. Hookham, 1810), tells of a "poor fellow pressed and sent to sea" by a wealthy landholder to remove him from the vicinity of his daughter (vol. III, p. 92).

[33] John Brewer, *Sinews of Power*, pp. 36–7; H. V. Bowen, *War and British Society 1688–1815* (Cambridge: Cambridge University Press, 1998), pp. 78–9.

[34] Mark Overton, *Agricultural Revolution in England: The Transformation of the Agrarian Economy 1500–1850* (Cambridge: Cambridge University Press, 1996), p. 168.

As the value of land rose, rents also rose throughout England. Individual estate records show these rent increases in the eighteenth century. The estate accounts of Sir Mark Stuart Pleydell in Berkshire show substantial increases between 1738 and 1753.[35] The rents of the Duke of Kingston rose 48% from 1750 to 1790 and the rents of Lord Monson rose 44.5% in the same period. The rents on property owned by Guy's Hospital in London rose 30% between 1762 and 1793. The annual value of the Northcote estate in Devon more than tripled in the second half of the eighteenth century.[36] In Northumberland and Durham the rents on the Swinburne estates doubled between 1715 and 1730 and continued rising; rents on the Allgood estates in North Tyndale rose 40% between 1705 and 1730; rents on the Howard estates around Morpeth and Newcastle doubled between 1702 and 1751.[37] A 1997 study of agricultural rent throughout England shows that nominal rents rose twelvefold between 1690 and 1870 and that real rents rose sixfold in that period. Rents rose from "a little over 2 shillings per acre in the 1690s to a little under 8 shillings by the 1770s."[38] Arthur Young's contemporary estimate was that rents more than doubled between 1780 and 1805.[39]

The recruiting Acts of 1745–6, 1757–8, and 1778–9, which gave local officials new powers to conscript able-bodied men for military service,

---

[35] Janie Cottis, "A Country Gentleman and His Estates, c. 1720–68: Sir Mark Stuart Pleydell, Bart., of Coleshill, Berkshire," in C. W. Chalklin and J. R. Wordie (eds.), *Town and Countryside: The English Landowner in the National Economy, 1660–1860* (London and Boston: Unwin Hyman, 1989), pp. 26–51, esp. p. 37.

[36] P. J. Keeley, "A Devon Family and Their Estates: The Northcotes of Upton Pyne, 1660–1851," in Chalklin and Wordie (eds.), *Town and Countryside*, pp. 174–90, esp. p. 177.

[37] Paul Brassley, *The Agricultural Economy of Northumberland and Durham in the Period 1640–1750* (New York: Garland, 1985), pp. 72, 75, 84. Brassley has examined many estate records for this region and gives specific figures for many different estates of rent and fine increases, enclosure of town fields and waste lands, turnover in tenancies, consolidation of farms, etc. (1–134). "By 1750 most of the best land in Northumberland and Durham had been enclosed," he writes. After this date, vast tracts of poorer pasture and waste lands were enclosed: 250,000 acres are estimated to have been enclosed between 1760 and 1810 (182).

[38] M. E. Turner, J. V. Beckett, and B. Afton, *Agricultural Rent in England, 1690–1914* (Cambridge and New York: Cambridge University Press, 1997), p. 228. See also the review of this book by Gregory Clark in *Journal of Economic History* 58, 1 (March 1998), 206–10.

[39] Arthur Young, "An Enquiry into the Progressive Value of Money in England," *Annals of Agriculture* 46, 270 (1812), 104, quoted in B. E. S. Trueman, "The Purchase and Management of Guy's Hospital Estates, 1726–1806," in Chalklin and Wordie (eds.), *Town and Countryside*, pp. 52–82, esp. p. 73.

Housing rents also rose, of course. Gregory Clark's study of properties owned by charities, as recorded by the Charity Commission, shows a 75% rise in housing rents between 1750 and 1820. Gregory Clark, "The Charity Commission as a Source in English Economic History," *Research in Economic History* 18 (1998): 1–52, esp. 37. See also Gregory Clark's unpublished paper, "Housing Rents, Housing Quality, and Living Standards in England and Wales, 1640–1909," October 1999, which shows a steep rise in housing rent between 1770 and 1810. Several of Clark's papers are available at http://www.econ.ucdavis.edu/faculty/gclark/papers/housecost.pdf. I am grateful to Dr. Clark for making this paper available to me.

added to the hardships of the laboring poor, who needed the wages of every member of the family in order to eat. Plucking a husband, brother, father, nephew, or uncle from a family when times were already difficult often made the difference between surviving and not surviving. Thus, the need for troops – to send to India, France, America, or the West Indies – led to the conscription of Edwards' son and simultaneously increased the cash value of land and agricultural products, the return on large capitalized holdings, and the rate of enclosure.

FARMING HEROES AND FARMING VILLAINS IN CHILDREN'S BOOKS

A surprising number of books for children in this period repeat the image of the contented, self-sufficient small farmer on his few acres as a moral lesson to the young, along with villains who profiteer from the land and behave cruelly to those whose lives depend on it. These greedy characters, over whom the good characters inevitably prevail, are tyrannical landowners who squeeze their tenants, enclose the commons and wastes, enforce the game laws, and prosecute those who exercise their customary use rights. *Goody Two-Shoes*, a popular book published anonymously in April 1765 by John Newbery, tells the story of a worthy family dispossessed and destroyed by these new commercial practices. It has been attributed to Oliver Goldsmith because its attitudes remind one of "The Deserted Village," and because Newbery published it just after Goldsmith worked for him (1763–4) while living in Islington lodgings Newbery paid for.[40]

The novel begins when the heroine of *Goody Two-Shoes* falls on hard times because the new landlord, Sir Timothy Gripe, inherits the estate containing her father's farm. This estate had supported twelve different farms in the past, where "tenants lived comfortable, brought up large Families, and carefully supported the poor People who laboured for them." But the new landlord "thought it less Trouble to write one Receipt for his Rent than twelve" (5), and allows Farmer Graspall to buy up all the leases as they expired. The heroine's father tries to resist, but the ensuing lawsuit ruins him and he has to give up his farm when his rent comes due. The family becomes so poor that the heroine has only one shoe. When someone gives her a pair of shoes she is so overjoyed that she goes around showing everyone

[40] Charles Welsh, Introduction to *Goody Two-Shoes* (1765), facsimile edition (London: Griffith & Farran, 1882), p. xvii. Welsh also presents alternative evidence for the authorship of Mr. Giles Jones. I am grateful to Jan Fergus for directing me to this text and even copying it for me!

the delightful symmetry – "See two shoes[!]" – which is how she got her name (21).

The author breaks into his own polemic about the unchecked greed of Sir Timothy Gripe and Farmer Graspall to ask "But what, says the Reader, can occasion all this? Do you intend this for Children, Mr. Newbery?" (11). He replies to his own rhetorical question:

This is not the Book, Sir, mentioned in the Title, but the Introduction to that Book; and it is intended, Sir, not for those Sort of Children, but for Children of six Feet High . . . [T]hese Reflections, Sir, have been rendered necessary, by the unaccountable and diabolical Scheme which many Gentlemen now give into, of laying a Number of Farms into one, and very often of a whole Parish into one Farm; which in the End must reduce the common people to a State of Vassalage, worse than that under the Barons of old, or of the Clans in *Scotland*; and will in Time depopulate the Kingdom. (11–12)

This engrossing of land by the wealthy will leave the poor without the means to survive and will lead to a mass exodus from the countryside, he says. But Goody Two-Shoes is a force for good and reverses the trend. After educating the children in the neighborhood and performing many admirable acts of kindness, she grows up and marries the wealthy Sir Charles Jones. She then buys up the whole manor on which her father had his farm, and "threw it into different Farms, that the Poor might be no longer under the Dominion of two over-grown Men" (137). Thus, she subdivides the land so that it will again support twelve families and their hired laborers, rather than enriching just the owner and one tenant farmer of a single large farm. She encourages her new tenants to go to church, rewards them for getting married and having children, and "gave them such Books as they wanted." And in her will she orders a number of acres "to be planted yearly with Potatoes, for all the Poor of any Parish who would come and fetch them for the Use of their Families; but if any took them to sell they were deprived of that Privilege ever after" (139). The land is restored to supporting those who live on it. All commercial use, all profiteering from the land, is banned. The potato patch is an explicit example of a return to use rights – a corrective to the exploitation of subsistence for exchange and profit – guaranteeing a resource to those without land.

This familiar pattern of the tyrannical insistence on absolute property rights contrasted with idealized small-scale subsistence farming can also be found in several of Mary Wollstonecraft's *Original Stories from Real Life* (1788). Written on the advice of her publisher, Joseph Johnson, in imitation of Mrs. Trimmer's stories for children, the sequence features a wise woman,

Mrs. Mason, and several children who profit from her lessons about distress and charity.[41] In one of the episodes, a harper, living in a poor cottage rudely built on the "waste" in the woods, tells Mrs. Mason that "he had once a very good farm; but he had been so unfortunate as to displease the justice, who never forgave him, nor rested till he had ruined him" (116–17). This tyrant, another ironically designated "justice of the peace," required his tenants to assist him in his harvest before they got in their own, and to give him any fish they caught at whatever price he chose, because they had to cross his land to get to the stream. Like the vindictive "justice of the peace" in Mackenzie's anecdote about old Edwards in *The Man of Feeling* (1771), this cruel man demonstrates the inaccessibility of real justice to the poor. He obliged the harper to leave his farm and threw the harper's son into jail for killing a hare. The harper then built his hut on waste land to shelter his children and supported his little family with his music. Mrs. Mason gets the harper's son released from prison and prevails upon a friend of hers, "a man of consequence in the neighbourhood," to rent the family a small farm on his estate. She also gives them some capital to buy farming tools and stock, the implements of husbandry, and we leave them ready to live happily ever after.

"Simple Susan," a children's story from Maria Edgeworth's *The Parent's Assistant* (1796), details the hardships that arise for farmers not merely from conscription but from absentee landlords and threats of enclosure.[42] Susan's father is in danger of losing his farm because the estate agent to the new lord of the manor, an attorney – never a wholesome profession in sentimental novels – claims that his lease is "flawed." This attorney wants to destroy Farmer Price because he opposes the enclosing and annexing of a bit of land that adjoins his garden. Farmer Price insists that the plot is common land belonging to the parish, land on which the village children play, and that "no man shall enclose it with my good will" (68). The vengeful attorney arranges to have Farmer Price impressed as a sailor; he and his daughter even try to rob "simple" Susan of the guinea hen and lamb she has raised. They are thwarted by a harper, who writes a song about the lamb for a

---

[41] Mrs. Mason is also the name of the heroine of Elizabeth Hamilton's *The Cottagers of Glenburnie* (London, 1808), whose "domestic politics" reform the cottagers and teach them to value cleanliness, economy, and education. See Janice Farrar Thaddeus, "Elizabeth Hamilton's Domestic Politics," *Studies in Eighteenth-Century Culture* 23 (1994), 265–84. The second edition of Wollstonecraft's *Original Stories from Real Life*, published in London in 1791, was illustrated by William Blake. Page numbers are from this edition.

[42] Maria Edgeworth, "Simple Susan," in her *The Parent's Assistant or Stories for Children* (1796; London: Routledge, [1891]): subsequent page references are to this edition. See n. 32 above for Sir Walter Scott's admiration of this tale.

contest, which he wins, thereby exposing the grasping attorney and his daughter and celebrating the generous spirit of simple Susan. The detail of the harper may have been suggested by Wollstonecraft's earlier story.

All of these texts, for adults and children, written between 1742 (*Joseph Andrews*) and 1796 ("Simple Susan") but concentrated in the 1760s and 1770s, with their tyrants and poachers, dogs and hares, and hardworking, deserving farmers, emphasize the same issues: that people have a right to take their living from the land and that whatever interferes with subsistence practices such as fishing or hunting is irrational and unjust. These tales grapple with the ethics – as opposed to the economics – of landownership. They treat the same issues, in rudimentary form, that we face today in sophisticated controversies over patenting genes and plants: the proprietary control for profit of the natural world. The poor, symbolically punished for killing a single hare, evicted from their land, their way of life undermined, are the victims whose suffering illustrates the human loss caused by commodification of the land. The reader's attention is trained on features that promote subsistence rather than profit – Goody Two-Shoes' potato patch and Mr. Wilson's filbert hedge. The tension is between subsistence and capital accumulation, between the livelihood of dozens of people living on smallholdings – as they had been for generations – and the ever greater wealth of one or two large proprietors.

ENLIGHTENMENT AGRICULTURE

Another sign of the times in fiction about farming was a belief that scientific know-how could improve farming yields. Although the land was always generous to those who worked industriously – whether owners, tenant farmers, or laborers – with the latest agricultural knowledge and techniques (so the fiction went) farm production could be made as profitable as manufacturing or trade.[43] These gentlemen on their small estates who practiced scientific agriculture were portrayed as true Enlightenment figures, using their rational capacities to educate themselves about farming, enlivening their leisure and increasing their profit. No world-weary philosophers they, withdrawing from the competitions of court and city life to find peace in the natural world. These fictional gentleman farmers

---

[43] Improvements such as drainage or irrigation, liming or marling, animal breeding, and rotation of crops – which often followed the appropriation of new land by enclosure – *did* raise the profitability of land significantly. It required capital, however, which is why these improvements were not performed on common land; the higher productivity of "improved" land was one of the arguments used in favor of enclosure. See Mark Overton, *Agricultural Revolution in England*, p. 167.

were thoroughly modern men who farmed to make a living, and who turned their hand to this enterprise rather than another because they had inherited the land or thought they understood the business.

Clara Reeve's *The Two Mentors* (1783) includes a gentleman farmer cut to this pattern. He is described by the hero, Edward Saville, in a letter to his college tutor, his good mentor. From his idealistic marriage-for-love to his present prosperity, Franklin is the very model of this independent, enlightened small estate owner.

His name is Franklin, a man of genteel birth and education; he inherited an estate of about five hundred pounds a year; he married, for love, a woman without a shilling. They set out in a style much above their fortunes, and ran out of bounds, till they were involved in debts and difficulties. Just as they were on the brink of ruin, a relation of Mrs. Franklin, who took no notice of her while a poor unportioned girl, hearing she was well married, left her a fortune of five thousand pounds, which restored them to competence and happiness. Mr. Franklin paid off his debts, cleared his estate, took a farm into his own hands, studied agriculture and oeconomy, and was successful in his practice of them: his wife turned her thoughts and attention to the domestic duties and virtues with equal success; in the course of ten years they are become rich, happy, and respectable.[44]

Hard work and intelligent planning always pay off in these novels. A gentleman could always stage a comeback by taking over a farm and making it profitable.

Tobias Smollett's *The Expedition of Humphry Clinker* (1771) contains another such clever gentleman farmer with an inherited estate and enough capital to turn it into a thriving business. This man, like Clara Reeve's Mr. Franklin or Frances Brooke's Mr. Herbert, was not bred to farming but studies its scientific basis and its practicalities. He is Mr. Dennison, whom Matthew Bramble and his entourage meet near the end of the novel, the "best farmer in the country." His entrepreneurial initiative, capital improvement, and knowledgeability show just how lucrative small-scale farming can be.[45] He took over his family estate after it had been run into the ground by his hard-drinking older brother, reasoning (with considerable class prejudice) "that if a person without education, or any great share of natural sagacity, could maintain a large family, and even become opulent upon a farm . . . he himself might hope for some success from his industry, having no rent to pay, but, on the contrary, three or four hundred pounds a year to receive" (363). He tells how he was befriended by a certain Mr. Wilson

[44] Clara Reeve, *The Two Mentors: A Modern Story*, 3rd edn. (London: J. Mawman, 1803), p. 23.
[45] Tobias Smollett, *The Expedition of Humphry Clinker*, ed. Lewis M. Knapp, rev. Paul–Gabriel Boucé (Oxford: Oxford University Press, 1984), p. 357. Subsequent page references are to this edition.

(a tribute to the Wilson of *Joseph Andrews*), who, together with his father-in-law farmer Bland, taught him how to use his capital to fertilize and enclose his domain. So he "drained bogs, burned heath, grubbed up furze and fern" (327–8), enclosed his farms, and tripled his rents. Smollett does not condemn this commercialized relation to the land, although as we have seen (particularly in stories written for children) the man who engrosses more land, capitalizes his estate, and charges higher rents is often seen as the villain.[46] But if Mr. Dennison, a landlord as well as a cultivator, is admirable for his enterprising ways, Matthew Bramble – who, as Judith Frank points out, represents the older reciprocal system of kindly landlords who respect their tenants' common rights – is downright loveable. Bramble does not insist on prompt payment when his tenants are "distressed," overlooks poaching on "what nature seems to have intended for common use" [Bramble's second letter to Dr. Lewis, dated April 17], and makes sure that when her cow dies Morgan's widow receives his good milking Alderney cow as a means of support (14–15).[47] Although in "real life" these two philosophies of landowning – Dennison's and Bramble's – were antithetical, Smollett presents them as sympathetically coexisting, the entrepreneurial farmer who improves his land and triples his rents and the paternalistic landlord who knows his tenants and their families.

The man most responsible for the entrepreneurial attitude towards farming was, of course, Arthur Young. Young, as I have said, was a booster for productive agriculture, beginning with his *The Farmer's Letters to the People of England* (1767), whether arable or pasture, whether geared to luxuries like tobacco or table provisions such as potatoes, onions, or carrots. He was in favor of reclaiming waste lands and commons for private, commercial farming because he believed that increased agricultural production was good for the nation. It disturbed him that so much land in England was being "wasted" and that farmers still used old-fashioned methods which yielded relatively small harvests, such as broadcasting seed rather than drill

---

[46] There is repetition in the detail as well as the themes of these formulaic tales of farming. Men are imprisoned for taking a single hare; dogs are shot. The name Wilson, exemplary in *Joseph Andrews* and *Humphry Clinker*, also figures in *Goody Two-Shoes*. The poor sleep in barns although their families were once the social equals (or betters) of those who now own the land. "His grandfather was cow-boy to mine!" says the harper about the lord of the manor in Mary Wollstonecraft's *Original Stories* (119). A double injustice has thus been done in turning him off the land. Old Edwards in Henry Mackenzie's *Man of Feeling* is the descendant of "a younger brother of that very man's ancestor, who is now lord of the manor" (96). His share in the land has been whittled away over generations. In other words, the newly dispossessed rural poor are descended from the landholders of yesterday.

[47] Judith Frank, *Common Ground: Eighteenth-Century Satiric Fiction and the Poor* (Stanford: Stanford University Press, 1997), pp. 90–100. Frank beautifully describes Smollett's handling of the contradiction between the precapitalist and capitalist visions of agrarian social relations.

planting. He considered the introduction of new methods for fertilizing or irrigating "patriotic" and "visionary," because he believed that the "product of the soil" supplied the wealth of the nation: the sale of produce supported farmers; rent supported landlords; tithes supported clergy; wages supported laborers; and rates, or poor relief, supported the non-laboring poor. These income streams, in turn, sustained industry, for money made from the land was spent on manufactured commodities. A nation's wealth came from agriculture, manufactures, and commerce, he said, and agriculture exceeded the other two and was the foundation of them both.

Anticipating the modern concept of the GNP, he continued that, beyond the capacity of the land to maintain individuals, "[t]here is an aggregate interest which must also be attended to, which consists of two kinds, first, the support of internal government and national works; and secondly, the power of the nation relative to her neighbours."[48] In other words, beyond feeding and clothing the population, the strength and success of a nation depended upon the revenues that supported its administrative bureaucracy and its army and navy. These are what John Brewer has called the "sinews of power" in the "fiscal-military state." To Arthur Young's mind, these too could be traced to the productivity of the land; farmers were the backbone of the nation. As he wrote in 1771: "He, who is the BEST FARMER, is with me the GREATEST MAN."[49]

Young considered it his duty as a citizen to dispel what he thought of as a misguided prejudice against enclosure, to re-glamorize the occupation of farming, and to set the record straight about which innovations and inventions actually worked for farmers large and small around the country. He saw his mission as spreading the word that, for example, Samuel Tucker of Rotheram found that feeding cows on cabbage increased their milk production, but that the butter was not so sweet. Or that the rape-dust left over from the oil mills of Hull, when used as a fertilizer, was of "prodigious benefit" to barley fields there. He praised the example set by the Marquis of Rockingham in hoeing turnips either with hand-held hoes or with the horse-drawn implements that his lordship invented for the purpose, and assured his readers that hoeing fields increased crop yields. Mr. Scroope of Danby ploughed very effectively with a "five-coultered scarifactor" that he designed, recounted Young; but he found that manuring with soap ashes "did not answer."[50] Young traveled the length and breadth of England

[48] Arthur Young, *A Six Months Tour through the North of England*, vol. IV, p. 371.
[49] Arthur Young, *A Six Months Tour through the North of England*, vol. I, p. xiv.
[50] These examples all come from *A Six Months Tour through the North of England*, vol. I, pp. 163, 282–8; vol. II, pp. 110, 381–3.

recording local methods of husbandry, noting acreage planted and crop yields, the price of provisions, wages for rural labor and for manufacturing, and so on. He reported his findings and commented on their meaning in his several volumes of *Tours* through the southern, northern, and eastern counties of England and in his later agricultural reports. He would have been horrified at the laws protecting intellectual property in our own day – although they are a logical extension of his faith in private property and "improvement" – because of the way they inhibit the free sharing of information about ingenious devices and improving techniques that he was at such pains to disseminate.

Young's *Observations on the Present State of the Waste Lands of Great Britain* (1773), one of his dozens of agricultural tracts, is a good example of the tone and attitude animating his writing in this vein. He begins by offering tables and figures to demonstrate the commercial opportunities for agriculture overseas in the new colony on the Ohio river. He spells out the practicalities for those less familiar with the conditions of the new colony: the weather, the terrain, communication by water with the sea. The Mississippi afforded cheap transportation both for staple commodities and for products such as hemp, flax, cotton, and tobacco "in the Ilionois [sic], a country to the north of the Ohio," he explains. The proof of this is that they "employ negroes." Subsistence farmers cannot afford to maintain slaves; "you do not meet with negroes till you meet with tobacco," he adds without moral comment.[51]

But after extolling the possibilities of the new world, he reminds his readers that they might, with less trouble, invest their time and money in a project closer to home and colonize the "wastes" in Northumberland, Cumberland, or Westmoreland (he claimed that "wastes" constituted as much as one-third of the kingdom), rather than going off to Florida or Ohio. He laments the depopulation of England due to emigration; indeed, many were concerned with rebuilding the population after the Seven Years' War. Like many another political arithmetician watching the condition and progress of the nation, he assumed that population was an index of prosperity. He exhorts his countrymen to

at least keep pace at home with those who go abroad; the improvement of our wastes will employ many hands, and therein increase useful population: it will add much to the national wealth and strength; and be attended with all those excellent effects, that increase of people has given to America . . . Sleep, therefore, no more

---

[51] Arthur Young, *Observations on the Present State of the Waste Lands of Great Britain, by the Author of the Tours through England* (London, 1773), pp. 19–20. Subsequent page references are to this edition.

over your moors, your wolds, downs, forests, chaces, and bogs, but exert the same spirit in their improvement, which every other branch of political oeconomy enjoys . . . Would but the owners of our uncultivated lands think of them with the same regret that I do, they would not long remain in their present state. Cultivation should spread through them: farms, villages, and towns, be the successors of foxes and moor game – population would thrive – plenty would be diffused – and while I wished well to *America*, BRITAIN should have my first devoirs. (55–6)

Improvement meant production. Untouched land where animals were free to roam was regrettable. Nothing was more beautiful than thriving, bustling farms and towns filled with purposeful people increasing the output of the nation. The foxes and moor game that signified the hunting privileges of the older landed classes needed to give way to the industry and ambition of newer class formations.[52]

In his Appendix to *Observations on the Present State of the Waste Lands of Great Britain* (1773), Young calculates how much profit could be made from cultivating the English moors. These arithmetical projections were, to his mind, the most irrefutable proof he could offer.[53] In this case, he proposed that 200 "patriotic individuals" give £100 apiece towards this enterprise, and showed that the interest returned on their money would be 4% for the first ten years, 5% for the next ten years, 6% for the ten years after that, and 7% ever after – although he estimated that by that time the project would be showing a surplus in excess of 26% – a profit of £76,602 beyond salaries, interest, implements, and seed. His tone fairly sings with nationalistic fervor and pleasure in accumulation. Making more and more money for "patriotic individuals" and the glory of the nation was an unbeatable combination; his tables and figures proved that it was possible; it only took enterprise and faith.

Young addresses himself in this tract to men like Fielding's Mr. Wilson, Smollett's Mr. Dennison, or Clara Reeve's Mr. Franklin, "country gentlemen of small estates," men of his own class.[54] These were the men hardest

---

[52] Donna Landry discusses the "Englishness" of hunting – or even just gathering – in *The Invention of the Countryside*. Beth Fowkes Tobin argued for its upper-class inflection: "Young and his colleagues constructed this new economic man, the professional estate manager and agricultural expert, in opposition to notions of aristocratic masculinity. While aristocratic males displayed their power and authority by indulging their appetites for blood (hunting, dueling, and cockfighting) and sex, males of the newly emerging middle class sought to demonstrate that 'the pen and the ruler' were mightier than the 'sword and the gun.' " *Superintending the Poor*, p. 35.

[53] For a brilliant treatment of the way numerical proof came to be constructed as the essence of objective knowledge in the eighteenth century, see Mary Poovey, *A History of the Modern Fact: Problems of Knowledge in the Sciences of Wealth and Society* (Chicago: University of Chicago Press, 1998).

[54] Judith Frank argues that the "ethos of improvement" is "powerfully masculinist." *Common Ground*, p. 203 n. 25.

hit by the economic changes of the times, he claimed, men on fixed incomes with respectable positions in society to uphold.

Gentlemen of paternal estates, of from three to six or seven hundred pounds a year, are, in this rich and extravagant age, almost beggars. Thirty years ago they were able to make a genteel appearance; they could bring up their families with some decency, keep a tolerable table, dress, and live like gentlemen. But now! what a change! Let taxes and repairs, rates and tythes, be deducted from their rents, and they have just enough left to support the dignity of their neighbour, My Lord's secretary . . . What sort of figure is made by gentlemen, whose ancestors well supported the credit of their families, upon their patrimony, which is now the object of raillery and contempt? The luxury of the age, though it has contributed to render us a wealthy, potent, and mighty nation, has certainly had the effect of burying whole ranks of the people, useful and valueable ranks, in the dust . . . The antient prospect, which afforded pleasure to twenty generations, is poisoned by the pagodas and temples of some rival neighbour; some oil-man, who builds on the solid foundation of pickles and herrings. At church, the liveries of a tobacconist carry all the admiration of the village; and how can the daughter of the antient, but decayed gentleman, stand the competition at an assembly, with the point, diamonds, and tissues of a haberdasher's nieces! (32–3)

With his novelist's imagination, Arthur Young quickly sketches the contradictions of capitalism. Although luxury was making the nation mighty, buying and selling were sordid occupations, and the lower classes muscling their way to the front ranks of society, with their pagodas and temples, their diamonds and lace, were not worthy of the distinction their money bought. Class mixing was the unpalatable price of trade, the remedy for which was to produce wealth in the old way, using rural laborers to work the land, but enhancing production with new techniques such as feeding turnips to winter livestock or manuring with marle.

And what of the poorer sort of families, whose woods and wolds and bogs with their nut trees and herbs, cresses and berries, fuel and fodder were to be taken to reimburse country gentlemen at the rate of 7 percent return on their money? What would become of those without income if men with £400 and £500 a year were "beggared" by the rising cost of living? Young could hardly ignore the plight of the class that concerned so many contemporary political commentators, at pains to explain and reverse the rising poor rates and to institute national policies to encourage industry on the part of labor. No one understood why poverty was spreading at the same rate as prosperity – why wages did not keep pace with the rising cost of provisions. "Our political writers dwell eternally on the causes of this scarcity [i.e. of bread]," wrote Young. "They talk of posthorses – dogs – commons – inclosures – large farms – jobbers and forestallers – bakers and rascals – but all to little purpose: and their schemes of improvement are as wild as the causes to which they attribute the evil" (38). None of these causes was at the root of the problem, he felt. With a blind faith in the power of the market to correct economic imbalance, Young reasoned that if the poor had not enough bread to eat, all that was necessary was to grow more food. "As you increase the product of a commodity, in proportion will the price fall," he wrote. Put the common lands into production and bread and beef would become cheap and plentiful.

Among the causes wrongly blamed for the scarcity of bread and the visible hunger of the poor, wrote Young, "the engrossing of *farms* makes a capital figure." But any land producing crops for the market was, to his mind, part of the solution and not part of the problem. Rich men's country estates were too often managed by stewards, he said, who were not sufficiently interested in innovative farming techniques. Worse still, the wealthy bought up "waste" lands not to put them into production but only to annex them "for elbow room – for hunting ground (imitating therein the Mohawks and the Cherokees) – for shooting moor-game: – nor have I any doubt, but minds may be found so depraved, as to sigh at the idea of cultivation spreading about their seats," he lamented (43). It was decadent to prefer land left wild and unproductive, to care more about hunting moor game than growing wheat, and to "sigh at the idea of cultivation spreading about their seats." Such resistance to progress was willful primitivism, such as might be expected of the Mohawks or the Cherokees, rather than the patriotic, enterprising men of England. Young's attitude was hardly a leaf from Horace or Virgil: the natural world was not a divine object of contemplation or a resource to sustain the mind and body in a corrupt world. It was an asset to be cultivated for the profit and glory of one's country, and it was a misuse of God's bounty to let it lie unused.

FACT AND FICTION

When Arthur Young wrote *Observations on the Present State of the Waste Lands of Great Britain* (1773), subtitled "Published on the Occasion of the Establishment of a New Colony on the Ohio", he well understood the appeal of America. Six years earlier he had set a novel there, depicting the Ohio territory as a kind of paradise; he had also been thinking seriously of leaving England and going to America to make his fortune.[55] His descriptions of the Ohio territory are idealized in the novel *The Adventures of Emmera, or the Fair American* (1767), as well as in the tract *Observations on the Present State of the Waste Lands* (1773). In the novel, an Englishman rambling in the wilds of America discovers, quite by chance, the small white house of the heroine and her aged father in a beautiful valley "of gently-swelling hills, slopes and lawns, dales, streams and cascades, scattered with all the enchanting negligence of the most picturesque fancy."[56] In *Observations on the Present State of the Waste Lands*, he describes the Ohio territory less as an estate laid out for pleasure and more as a land full of rich natural resources – the "meadows cloathed with verdure, the forests full of the finest timber, the soil capable of the richest productions: one of the noblest rivers in the world flowing though it, smaller streams and brooks plentifully scattered" (24–5). The novel depicts characters who have withdrawn to the American wilderness to enjoy the sweets of life, not to produce more corn or turnips as Young urged in his tracts. *The Adventures of Emmera* is the only one of his novels to end happily; the protagonists in this rural fantasy do not clear more land, hire more labor, or try to produce more profitable surplus. They settle where there is no danger of "cultivation spreading about their seats," nor do they deplore the vast acres of wilderness around them and long for them to be peopled and farmed. The local Indians are their friends and allies, and they are in perfect accord with them about "elbow room" and "hunting ground." Although infatuated with farming like all of Young's fictional characters, Emmera, her father, and Sir Philip Chetwynd (who eventually becomes her husband) are not particularly interested in raising their output, experimenting with nitrogen-fixing grasses, measuring harvests, or inventing new farm machinery. They farm for their subsistence, not for the market. A novel-length version of the gentleman farmer trope that I examined earlier in this chapter, *The Adventures of Emmera* idealizes the small country estate that provides just enough to live on.

Young wrote this novel while he was still hoping to succeed on his own rented farm, and the picture of life he paints is undoubtedly a projection of his hopes at the time for a prosperous, civilized, wholesome existence. The expatriate old gentleman and his lovely daughter – that eighteenth-century idealized pair! – who live on the banks of Lake Erie in perfect amity with

[55] Referring to his never-ending and ill-remunerated labor at farming, Young wrote in his *Autobiography*, "At this time [1772] I was so distressed that I had serious thoughts of quitting the kingdom and going to America." *Autobiography of Arthur Young*, p. 61.
[56] *The Adventures of Emmera, or the Fair American*, 2 vols. (London, 1767) vol. 1, p. 24.

the neighboring Indians, like Prospero and Miranda transposed to America, have everything they need. Until the hero accidentally stumbles upon their free and open life – their house has no front door at all – Emmera has never even seen a European. They provide plentifully for themselves, farming rationally by using drill planting, ploughing between rows to weed, turning over the land for the next year's crop, and fertilizing heavily. Emmera quotes Milton's lines about Adam and Eve doing "no more toil/ Of their sweet gard'ning labour" than enhanced the pleasure of the breeze, leisure, and their supper (1: 98). Sir Philip Chetwynd, a young Englishman exploring the American wilderness, stumbles into their paradise just as the old man is dying. He stays on and, following the young woman's instruction, performs the farm labor her father had done. At length he persuades the young American to return to England with him. They can farm in England on his estate as well as in America, he tells her; and in England they can get married. True to his word, within a few days of their arrival in England they are hard at work ploughing and planting a new garden, for they both enjoy this labor even though their circumstances in England do not require it. But as soon as Emmera is introduced into society, she becomes disillusioned with the waste of time and spirit in so-called civilization; she is disgusted by insincere friends, small talk, and social gambling. She is shocked most of all by cruelty – the way a driver whips his exhausted horses, or the gossip, gleefully reported, of a poor man imprisoned, and his hunting dog confiscated, for killing a hare on someone else's property. She insists on returning to America, where, she says, her eyes, ears, and every sense will not be constantly assaulted by "objects of wretchedness" (11: 187). Giving away all but a fraction of her enormous legacy, she keeps just enough to purchase "some necessaries of life, and transmit them to our old neighbours the Indians, to divide among themselves" (11: 175), and persuades Sir Philip to accompany her back to Lake Erie. They leave the corrupt world of rich and poor behind and return to the simple happy life on their little farm in the wilderness.

The life they embrace in America is one that riches cannot buy. Their relation to the land is regulated by labor and need. There is more land than they can use: they only cultivate what they need for a comfortable existence. As in other tales of happy subsistence that I have mentioned, embedded in this story is the cautionary counterexample of the injustice that comes from trying to own nature and to superintend others' access to it. Like the gamekeeper in Mackenzie's *The Man of Feeling* who killed Edwards' son's pointer for crossing the invisible property line, or the tyrannical lord of the manor in Mr. Wilson's tale who shoots his daughter's pet spaniel, the fox-hunter in this novel who imprisons a man for killing a hare on his property stands as the constitutive antithesis of agrarian idealism.

How is one to account for the difference between these two texts written six years apart, both drawing on the imagined potential of the Ohio territory? Was the meaning of *The Adventures of Emmera* determined by the requirements of the sentimental plot despite the avowed politics of the author? Are the very formulas of fiction antithetical to the instrumentalities of capitalism in the sense that a character who schemes for profit cannot be a hero (although fortunes come to heroes effortlessly)? Or is the discrepancy caused by the difference between the ultimate purposes and audiences of the two genres insofar as the novel projects the conditions for individual happiness whereas agricultural tracts promote the "aggregate good" of the state in relation to other nation states: increasing the national output, fostering industry, increasing population, and so on. These ends – the power of states and the happiness of individuals – may be antithetical; the moral system required for the national good may be at odds with that required for the happiness of private individuals. That is presumably what Arthur Young discovered when he reconsidered his position on the effects of enclosure in *An Inquiry into the Propriety of Applying Wastes to the Better Maintenance and Support of the Poor* (1801). After touring the country in 1800 and seeing the actual effects of his previously abstract policies on the rural poor, he changed his mind.

His position on wages, land use, and policies concerning the poor in the 1801 *Inquiry* is a complete about-face from his earlier position on these matters. In *The Farmer's Letters to the People of England* (1767), he had argued that low wages were beneficial to the nation because they forced laborers to work longer hours. "[I]f four days earnings are sufficient to maintain them six, they will be idle the remaining two," he projected disapprovingly. Their labor was thus "lost to the state" while their relative independence of wages "enable[d] them to treat their masters in a manner not to the service of the business."[57] Many believed that wages had to be lowered so as to make people work harder; Young was hardly alone in this belief.[58] He also thought rising prices were a good thing so that laborers had to work harder for necessities. In his *Six Months Tour through the North of England* (1771) he

---

[57] Arthur Young, *The Farmer's Letters to the People of England* (1767), 3rd edn., corrected and enlarged (Dublin: J. Milliken, 1768), pp. 36–7.

[58] See Peter Mathias, "Leisure and Wages in Theory and Practice," in his *The Transformation of England: Essays in the Economic and Social History of England in the Eighteenth Century* (London: Methuen, 1979), pp. 150–1.

had urged that the higher rents consequent on enclosing and "improving" land created more incentive to labor. "Inclosures raise rents," he wrote, and "high rents make men industrious" (IV: 190). "When men pay dearly for their farms, they learn to value land, and let none of it be lost" (IV: 378). He even went so far as to state that "In no part of *England*, where rents are low, is there good husbandry" (IV: 344). He scoffed at tales of hardship: "It is a common plea that the poor cottagers suffer, but the fact is the direct contrary, for they meet with prodigious additional employment, in return for a mere nominal advantage [i.e. rights of commonage]."[59] Thus, in 1771 he believed that use rights on common land were a negligible advantage when compared to the high wages that he assumed would follow for rural laborers on newly enclosed pasture and field. Moreover, if laboring people had to work harder because of the rising cost of living, and if farmers had to farm more efficiently because rent was high, the resulting productivity was ultimately good for the nation.

WAGES, LAND, AND MARRIAGE

Not everyone believed that enclosure and improvement was good for the nation. Contemporaries feared that enclosure and the highly capitalized agricultural methods that accompanied agricultural consolidation would discourage the poor from marrying, empty the countryside, and reduce the population. Because young people had traditionally postponed getting married until they could inherit or otherwise obtain a habitation – preferably with a few acres and common rights – the shortage of cottages, commons, and small farms would result in the indefinite postponement of marriage. Anxiety over the shortage of cottages and smallholdings began to appear in tracts and treatises in the second half of the eighteenth century.

Commentators feared that when landlords or their stewards pulled down cottages on their estates so as not to harbor any poor families or sustain any claims to common rights,[60] it would interfere with young people's setting up house and marrying. William Cole, a clergyman in Buckinghamshire, thought he saw this trend in his own neighborhood.

The Times are so hard, small Farms so difficult to be met with, the Spirit of Inclosing, & accumulating Farms together, making it very difficult for young

---

[59] Arthur Young, "Agriculture," in his *Political Essays concerning the Present State of the British Empire* (London: W. Strahan and T. Cadell, 1772), pp. 74–171, quote p. 123.

[60] Robert W. Malcolmson, *Life and Labour in England 1700–1780* (London: Hutchinson, 1981), pp. 39–40.

People to marry, as was used; as I know by Experience [in] this Parish, where several Farmers' Sons are forced to live at Home with their Fathers, tho' much wanting to marry & settle for Want of proper Places to settle at.[61]

In a speech against the Hardwicke Marriage Bill on the floor of the House of Commons, Robert Nugent urged that "the humour of preventing the poor from marrying prevails too much of late in all parts of this country: our numerous Bills for inclosing commons have a great tendency this way; and those wise parish politicians called parish-officers, are every where destroying cottages, because they encourage the poor to marry and get children, which may become burdensome to the parish."[62] It was feared that this shortage would prevent the next generation from reproducing.

Goldsmith's *The Deserted Village* (1770) imagines a depopulated countryside because its inhabitants have emigrated to "distant climes" (l. 341) when their farm leases are not renewed. He paints a forlorn image of an empty village with silent paths and overgrown gardens, from which "all the bloomy flush of life is fled" (l. 128), because "One only master grasps the whole domain" (l. 39). Frances Brooke's *The History of Lady Julia Mandeville* (1763) includes another such description of a once-populous village, "reduced to about eight families; a dreary silence reigns over their deserted fields; the farm houses, once the seats of chearful smiling industry, now useless, are falling in ruins" (222). The landlord, we are told, combined his farms and rented them to so few men that the sons of his old tenants had either to become servants to those large tenants or go to another parish to earn their bread. For the sake of a small increase in his rents the landlord was depopulating the country, which in the long run would "lower the

---

[61] *The Blecheley Diary of the Rev. William Cole, 1765–67*, ed. Francis Griffin Stokes introduced by Helen Waddell (London: Constable, 1931), p. 41. A similar complaint can be found in Roger North, *A Discourse of the Poor* (London: Cooper, 1753). "Gentlemen, of late Years, have taken up an Humour of destroying their Tenements and Cottages, whereby they make it impossible that Mankind should inhabit upon their Estates. This is done sometimes bare-faced, because they harbour Poor that are a Charge to the Parish, and sometimes because the Charge of Repairing is great, and if an House be ruinous, they will not be at the Cost of rebuilding and repairing it, and cast their Lands into very great Farms, which are managed with less Housing: And oftimes for Improvement, as it is called; which is done by buying in all Freeholds, Copyholds, and Tenements that have Common, and which harboured very many husbandry and labouring Families; and then enclosing the Commons and Fields"(57–8), quoted in Robert W. Malcolmson, *Life and Labour in England*, p. 139. Malcolmson claims that these words were written in the late seventeenth century although they were not published until 1753. If so, North was describing a phenomenon that only intensified with time: these practices, had become common by the mid-eighteenth century when this still-relevant text was actually published.

[62] William Cobbett, *The Parliamentary History of England from the Earliest Period to the Year 1803*, 36 vols. (London: printed by T. C. Hansard for Longman, Hurst, Orme and Brown, 1806–20), vol. xv, pp. 19–20 (26 George the Second, 1753).

price of all the fruits of the earth, and lessen, in consequence, the value of his estate" (223).

We can now see that enclosure and rising rents did not discourage marriage although it foreclosed that earlier way of life whereby wages were supplemented by hunting, fishing, growing food in kitchen gardens, raising livestock and selling produce in local markets, or engaging in such by-employments as carpentry, spinning or weaving, making ropes or nets, making gloves, knitting stockings, quarrying stone, and the like.[63] Proto-industrial production done at home, piece work in which the whole family helped with different parts of the operation, had often supplemented part-time waged work. These mixed economies had been deplored by political philosophers as "leisure preference" because they made people less dependent on wages and kept the price of labor high. One of Arthur Young's earlier arguments for enclosure was that common lands encouraged "leisure preference." In 1771 he wrote, "Dependence upon a right of commonage is apt to make a poor family more idle than they would otherwise be, which is a publick loss."[64]

But the mixed household economies that supported "leisure preference" began to break down in the second half of the eighteenth century for several reasons. The enclosure of wastes and commons and engrossing small farms created many more landless workers without any use rights in the land. The game laws, as we have seen earlier, were prosecuted much more vigorously, so that it became harder to supplement a family's diet with wild animal food. The customary entitlements from manufacturing processes – "chips" for the shipwright (waste lumber), "thrums" for the weaver (cut ends of cloth), "cabbage" for the tailor (waste cloth)[65] – began to be viewed as

---

[63] R. E. Pahl, *Divisions of Labour*, (Oxford and New York: Basil Blackwell, 1984), pp. 46–50.

[64] Arthur Young, "Agriculture," in *Political Essays*, p. 124. The misleading term "leisure preference" describes a preference not so much for "leisure" as for independence from wages, and hence from surveillance and time discipline. See E. P. Thompson, "Time, Work-Discipline and Industrial Capitalism," first published in *Past and Present* 38 (December 1967), 56–97 and republished in his *Customs in Common: Studies in Traditional Popular Culture* (New York: New Press, 1991), pp. 352–403.

[65] Remuneration earlier in the century often came in kind in addition to cash. Just as the farmers or agricultural workers had the right to glean after a harvest, and servants to expect "vails" or tips from guests, so, too, the manufacturing laborer appropriated some part of the materials of his labor as his due. These time-honored entitlements had always been a legal part of the customary arrangements of labor and pay until the later eighteenth century: see the chapter "Ships and Chips: Technological Repression and the Origin of the Wage," in Peter Linebaugh, *The London Hanged: Crime and Civil Society in the Eighteenth Century* (Cambridge: Cambridge University Press, 1992), pp. 371–401 for a description of the criminalization of traditional entitlements in the eighteenth century. Linebaugh collected this colorful list of workers' perquisites: "Bugging to the hatter, cabbage to the tailor, blue-pigeon flying to the plumbers and glaziers, chippings to the shipwrights, sweepings to the porters, red sailyard docking to navy yard workers, fints and thrums to weavers, vails to servants,

criminal pilfering rather than as a worker's traditional right, and there were
bitter disputes over these perquisites.[66]

The resulting dependence on wages, together with the new scarcity of
land and cottages, rather than discouraging marriage, pushed young people
into earlier marriages. There was no longer any point in waiting for the
family farm, which might well have been drawn into a larger estate, and
the availability of wages in the burgeoning manufacturing sector and for
agricultural labor on large estates meant that young people could marry on
their wages alone and set up house independently from their parents. The
literary images of silent, deserted rural villages may have had some truth
to them, because landless workers were migrating to the swelling cities;
however, contrary to the fears about depopulation, people were marrying
younger and these earlier marriages were causing an unprecedented growth
in population. Mortality was also dropping significantly, possibly because
smallpox had been virtually eliminated, thanks to the inoculation procedure that Lady Mary Wortley Montagu brought back from her travels
in Turkey.[67] With more money in circulation than ever before at mid-
century, it looked as if there were new ways to make a living – although
by the end of the century agricultural real wages had declined to the point
where families could no longer live on them.[68] Wherever they could earn
enough in wages, young people married earlier than ever before. In 1696
the population of England was 4,961,692; by 1796 it had almost doubled

privileges to west country clothiers, bontages to Scottish agricultural workers, scrappings and naxers
to coopers, wastages to framework knitters." Quoted in John Rule, *The Experience of Labour in
Eighteenth-Century Industry* (London: Croom Helm, 1981), p. 125.

[66] In Essex in 1757–8, for example, when the clothiers demanded that the weavers hand over their
thrums, 500 weavers went on strike to support their ancient custom: "The waste is a small perquisite
that hath been granted us for several hundred years past, which we were able to prove by our ancient
Books of Record, which have been no less than 14 or 15 times ratified and confirmed at the General
Quarter Sessions." John Rule, *The Labouring Classes in Early Industrial England 1750–1850* (London
and New York: Longman, 1986), p. 116.

[67] P. E. Razzell, *The Conquest of Smallpox: The Impact of Inoculation on Smallpox Mortality in Eighteenth-
Century Britain* (Firle, Sussex: Caliban Books, 1977), cited in Robert Malcolmson, *Life and Labour
in England 1700–1780*, p. 155. Lady Mary demonstrated the procedure on her own daughter in
front of several witnesses in April, 1721. Isobel Grundy, *Lady Mary Wortley Montagu* (Oxford:
Oxford University Press, 1999), pp. 210–12. It has also been suggested that the decline in overall
mortality in England was due to a decline in childhood mortality in particular, and that the reduction in deaths due to smallpox accounts for the sharp decline in childhood mortality. Tommy
Bengtsson, Osamu Saito, David Reher, and Cameron Campbell, "Population and the Economy:
From Hunger to Modern Economic Growth," in Clara Eugenia Núñez (ed.), *Debates and Controversies in Economic History: Proceedings of the Twelfth International Economic History Congress*
(Madrid: Fundación Ramón Areces, Fundación fomento de la historia económica, 1998), pp. 69–144,
esp. p. 87.

[68] Barry Stapleton, "Inherited Poverty and Life-Cycle Poverty: Odiham, Hampshire, 1650–1850," *Social
History* 18, 3 (October 1993), 339–55, esp. 350–1.

to become 8,198,445.[69] Thus, changed modes of production in agriculture and manufacturing *did* change fertility levels – drastically.

As the population of landless laborers grew, their increasing numbers put pressure on rents – which rose – and depressed wages as new workers flooded the labor market.[70] Poor rates rose precipitously and middle-level farmers and tradesmen who themselves did not hire labor, but who paid poor rates, grumbled.[71] Women and children took waged labor to try to make ends meet, but were paid a pittance because their wages were considered merely supplemental. Nathaniel Kent reports that women and children hired in Yorkshire to pick black canker bugs off turnip plants were paid at the rate of 6d for women and 3d for children per day – roughly a half and a quarter respectively of what a man could earn.[72] Children worked in mines in the north and Shropshire, in the metal trades in Sheffield, and made pins in Gloucester and near Bristol late in the century.[73] They spun wool and picked cotton yarn and mended broken cotton thread in textile factories. When William Hutton was seven, in 1730, he went to work in a silk mill – although at that time he was by far the youngest person employed there. They had to make him a high pair of pattens to stand on for he was not tall enough to reach the machinery without them.[74]

---

[69] E. A. Wrigley and R. S. Schofield, *The Population History of England, 1541–1871: A Reconstruction* (Cambridge, MA: Harvard University Press, 1981), pp. 528–9.

[70] According to J. D. Chambers, "the period of plentiful harvests and cheap living" in Nottinghamshire came to an end around 1765. *Nottinghamshire in the Eighteenth Century: A Study of Life and Labour under the Squirearchy*, 2nd edn. (New York: Augustus Kelley, 1966), p. 288. Robert Malcolmson also places the beginning of the decline of real wages in 1760. See *Life and Labour in England, 1700–1780*, pp. 145–6. For more specific details of the hardships of the poor in this period, see Chapters 2, 3, 5, 9 and 10 in Mick Reed and Roger Wells (eds.), *Class, Conflict and Protest in the English Countryside, 1700–1880* (London: Frank Cass, 1990); or Catharina Lis and Hugo Soly, *Poverty and Capitalism in Pre-Industrial Europe* (Brighton Sussex: Harvester Press, 1979), pp. 131–222. For evidence of malnutrition after about 1750, see Sebastian Coll and John Komlos, "The Biological Standard of Living and Economic Development: Nutrition, Health and Well Being in Historical Perspective," in Clara-Eugenia Núñez (ed.), *Debates and Controversies in Economic History*, pp. 219–82, esp. pp. 224–5; for an account of widespread starvation in the 1790s, see Roger Wells, *Wretched Faces: Famine in Wartime England 1793–1801* (Gloucester: Sutton, 1988), *passim*.

[71] Roger Wells, "Social Protest, Class, Conflict and Consciousness, in the English Countryside 1700–1880," in Mick Reed and Roger Wells (eds.), *Class, Conflict and Protest in the English Countryside, 1700–1880*, pp. 121–214, esp. pp. 132–3. According to R. W. Fogel, poor rates rose 2.3 percent a year – a rate of growth almost three times as much as that for the GNP. R. W. Fogel, "Second Thoughts on the European Escape from Hunger: Famines, Chronic Malnutrition, and Mortality Rates," in S. R. Osmani (ed.), *Nutrition and Poverty* (Oxford: Clarendon Press, 1992), pp. 243–86, esp. p. 271.

[72] Nathaniel Kent, *A General View of the Agriculture of the County of Norfolk* (London, 1796), pp. 19–20. See Chapter 1 above for more information on women's agricultural work.

[73] Hugh Cunningham, "The Employment and Unemployment of Children in England c. 1680–1851," *Past and Present* 126 (February 1990), 115–50, esp. 122.

[74] *The Life of William Hutton* (1816), intro. Carl Chinn (Studley, Warwickshire: Brewin Books, 1998), p. 6.

The effect of these combined conditions on the family was to tighten it as an economic unit and to intensify the economic dependence of women and children on the male wage-earner. Although including women and children in factory production looked like an extension of proto-industrial production carried out collectively by a family in their home, it had one important difference: those who worked in factory production were given individual wages rather than being paid as a family unit for the pieces they produced together. Thus by the late eighteenth century the laboring family was no longer a property-owning unit nor even a collective unit of production but rather a unit of consumption – a collection of individuals pooling their separate wages to pay for food and shelter. Some historians claim that this increased economic interdependence drew the family together and dissolved the basis for patriarchal authority; others argue that the wage structure made women and children dependent as never before on male earnings. I imagine that wage earning caused a psychological disaggregation of the family, an increasing emphasis on individual rather than collective welfare; by the end of the century, most of the population were selling their labor power for individual wages.

Since women made less than half the wages that men earned, and those wages were insufficient to support them, it was difficult for a woman to survive alone. As explained in Chapter 1, this was particularly true in the eastern grain-producing counties such as Berkshire, Bedfordshire, Essex, and Hampshire, where the specialization of farm labor reduced women's participation to low-paying stone-picking or weeding, and less so – at least until the 1780s – in the pastoral western counties, where women continued to participate in dairying and livestock maintenance.[75] Once women began to work in workshops away from home, with a wage assigned to their work, that wage was invariably less than what a man could earn and not enough to live on.[76] William Cobbett tried to invent a new form of cottage industry for women and children in gathering and drying straw to plait bonnets and hats, so that they might be independent of waged labor in textile factories.

---

[75] K. D. M. Snell, "Agricultural Seasonal Unemployment, the Standard of Living, and Women's Work in the South and East, 1690–1860," *Economic History Review* 34, 3 (1981), 407–37. Deborah Valenze describes the way "scientific" dairying by men began to supplant women's practice in the 1780s in "The Art of Women and the Business of Men: Women's Work and the Dairy Industry," in her *The First Industrial Woman* (New York and Oxford: Oxford University Press, 1995), pp. 48–67.

[76] For a full picture of women's industrial opportunities in the early industrial revolution, see Maxine Berg, "Women's Work, Mechanisation, and the Early Phases of Industrialisation in England," in Patrick Joyce (ed.), *The Historical Meanings of Work* (Cambridge: Cambridge University Press, 1987), pp. 64–98; see also Deborah Valenze, *The First Industrial Woman*.

With his usual vivid rhetoric, he wrote

But the Lords of the Loom, the crabbed-voiced, hard-favoured, hard-hearted, puffed-up, insolent, savage and bloody wretches of the North have, assisted by a blind and greedy Government, taken all the employment away from the agricultural women and children. This manufacture of straw will form one little article of employment for these persons. It sets at defiance all the hatching and scheming of all the tyrannical wretches who cause the poor little creatures to die in their factories.[77]

It is pointless to try to rehearse all the particulars of women's waged work in this period, for it is a complicated and by now much-researched subject.[78] I simply wish to assert that by all accounts it became increasingly hard for women to support themselves, with or without children, outside of marriage.

There is no reason to believe that it was easier for women in the literate classes than for those in the working class to support themselves outside of marriage. Margaret Hunt suggests that 11.5 percent of the shopkeepers in England were women and gives examples of independent female traders as well.[79] Many of these, of course, were married and pooled resources with their husbands, or else widows carrying on their husbands' businesses. We know that Charlotte Smith and Frances Burney, among others, supported themselves and their families by writing novels, and that Mary Wollstonecraft supported herself by writing in a variety of genres. But Charlotte Smith was so poor by the end of her life that she had to sell her furniture and her books to pay for food and coal; and Frances Burney had a royal pension to supplement her income from writing. Jan Fergus gives the example of a very distant relation of Jane Austen's, the second daughter of a baronet, advised by her widowed and remarried mother to use her inheritance to purchase an annuity of £80, which would enable her to continue on as a "parlour Boarder" in London where she went to school. Her mother continued that she did not mean that Caroline should continue as a student, but merely proposed "it as a most respectable Asylum for Miss D: . . . as a single young Lady cannot live upon a small income with

77 William Cobbett, *Cottage Economy* (1821; rpt. Oxford: Oxford University Press, 1979), p. 181.

78 An excellent recent anthology on the subject is Pamela Sharpe (ed.), *Women's Work: The English Experience 1650–1914* (London: Arnold, 1998). John Rule asserts that "the participation level of women in productive labour actually fell with the coming of industrialisation." John Rule, *The Labouring Classes in Early Industrial England 1750–1850*, p. 184.

79 Margaret R. Hunt, *The Middling Sort: Commerce, Gender, and the Family in England, 1680–1780* (Berkeley: University of California Press, 1996), pp. 125–46. She also states that "almost all women's work," whether in or outside of the home, "tended to be intermittent and labor rather than capital intensive" (136).

credit or comfort by herself, but would be liable to every inconvenience & probably distress & censure." As Fergus remarks, "Even a baronet's daughter can evidently sink close to the level of Harriet Smith in *Emma*, left to shift for herself as a 'parlour boarder' at Mrs. Goddard's in Highbury."[80]

EFFECTS ON THE RURAL POOR

By the end of the century, Arthur Young was shocked by the wretchedness of the poor, their mean habitations and miserably cultivated patches of ground. As he wrote in the *Annals of Agriculture*, "To hear of a great rise in rents, to see the houses of landlords and farmers improving, and cottages no better than in the last century, is a horrid spectacle."[81] By 1799 he was urging that "the price of labour should be raised, or the weekly allowance to large families should be stated by act of parliament." He even exhorted the wealthy to feed their horses hay so that the poor might have the grain. "Their horses may subsist on hay, but the poor cannot," he wrote.[82]

Although there were a few signs the year before of this concern for the poor, Arthur Young's dramatic change of heart clearly followed the death in 1797 of his most beloved child, his fourteen-year-old daughter Bobbin, of consumption. After her death, he lost interest in encouraging the wealthy to increase the productivity of their holdings and turned his attention instead to the plight of the poor. He began to think seriously about the afterlife, where he hoped to join the spirit of his beloved Bobbin again. He read the New Testament and sermons avidly for solace and strength and prayed "that I may turn this loss to the benefit of my soul."[83] Month after month he gave dinners for poor children in Bobbin's memory. His melancholy intensified his capacity to see and feel compassion for others' suffering. He tried to understand what caused the bad harvests of 1799 and 1800 and sent out questionnaires to farmers about yields and losses. He criticized the corn factors who held back grain in order to manipulate its price. He visited wretched, overcrowded workhouses and the miserable cottages of the ragged poor and urged his fellow citizens to attend to their suffering. No longer did he blame the poor for being lazy or devise strategies to make them work harder. On the contrary, he now felt that the wages paid to

[80] Jan Fergus, "Jane Austen: Tensions between Security and Marginality," in Beth Fowkes Tobin (ed.), *History, Gender & Eighteenth-Century Literature* (Athens: University of Georgia Press, 1994), pp. 258–70, quote p. 261.
[81] *Annals of Agriculture* 29 (1796); quoted in John Gazley, *The Life of Arthur Young*, p. 354.
[82] *Annals of Agriculture* 32 and 33, quoted in John Gazley, *The Life of Arthur Young*, pp. 409 and 413.
[83] *Autobiography of Arthur Young*, p. 284.

laborers were insufficient to feed and clothe them and that without land or livestock there was no way for them to survive. "It is disgraceful to a Christian country to have our poor in the situation I have described," he wrote. "With the commerce and wealth of the world in our hands, our cottagers are miserable; their wives and children half starved and naked, without bedding, without fuel, unless stolen, and in many places inhabiting buildings, or rather ruins, which keep out neither wind nor rain."[84]

In 1800, under the auspices of the Board of Agriculture, Young went on a fact-finding tour to investigate the causes of the food shortages and the rising poor rates. He had noticed that in those parishes where cottagers had managed to preserve a little patch of ground and a pig or a cow, they stoically resisted going on poor relief. His motive for this tour was, in part, to ascertain the actual effect of the enclosures. *An Inquiry into the Propriety of Applying Wastes to the Better Maintenance and Support of the Poor* (London, 1801) was the report of his findings, together with an impassioned appeal for allocating land and cows to poor cottagers unable to feed themselves in times of scarcity. In a remarkable recantation of his earlier position, he now charged that, nineteen times out of twenty, the enclosure bills had injured the poor because they had eliminated the means for subsistence by which the poor had managed to tide themselves over when the price of provisions outstripped their means. He cited the testimonies of several commissioners who had executed the orders.

Mr. Forster, of Norwich, after giving me an account of 20 enclosures in which he had acted as a commissioner, stated his opinion on their general effect on the poor, and lamented that he had been accessory to injuring two thousand poor people, at the rate of 20 families per parish. Numbers in the practice of feeding [on] the commons cannot prove their rights; and many, indeed most who have allotments have not more than an acre, which being insufficient for the man's cow, both cow and land are usually sold to the opulent farmers . . . Mr. Ewen, a commissioner in the same place, observed, that in most of the enclosures he has known the poor man's allotment and cow are sold, five times in six before the award is signed. (20–1)

These men were saying that the pittance that compensated the commoners' rights, when they could legally prove those rights, and the sliver of land allotted to them in the enclosure divisions was usually insufficient to maintain their cows. Sometimes they were also expected to assume the cost of fencing their allotments after the redistribution of common lands, which they could ill afford. In most cases, they were forced to sell out to wealthier

---

[84] *Annals of Agriculture* 34, quoted in John Gazely, *The Life of Arthur Young*, p. 418.

farmers. The poor might say with truth, concluded Young, "*I had a cow, and an act of Parliament has taken it from me*" (43).

If enclosures had actually benefitted the poor, wrote Young, the poor rates would not rise so consistently in parish after parish following each act to enclose common land. Yet the poor rates had doubled in a few years, and the poor were worse off than ever. "Go to an alehouse kitchen of an old enclosed country," wrote Young, remembering or imagining the scene, "and there you will see the origin of poverty and poor rates. For whom are they to be sober? For whom are they to save? (Such are their questions) For the parish? If I am diligent, shall I have leave to build a cottage? If I am sober, shall I have land for a cow? If I am frugal, shall I have half an acre of potatoes? You offer me no motives: you have nothing but a parish officer and a workhouse! – Bring me another pot" (12–13).

Something had to be done to ameliorate the harm done to the cottagers. Believing, as he did, in the motivating power of private property, Young was convinced that the answer was not to bring back the old system of common property but rather to buy every poor family a cow and to give them enough land to feed it through the winter as well as the summer. Wherever commons and wastes still existed, he suggested that some part be permanently appropriated for this purpose. He proposed an amendment to the general enclosure bill that was just then before Parliament, to provide for land allotments and livestock for the poor of every parish. "To pass acts beneficial to every other class in the state, and hurtful to the lowest order only, when the smallest attention would prevent it, is a conduct against which reason, justice, and humanity equally plead," he urged (21). Assuming reason in his readers, he explained that such an outlay would pay off in a very short time, weighed against the rising poor rates; and he did the calculations to prove it.[85]

Not surprisingly, the president and directors of the Board of Agriculture rejected Young's report on the failure of land enclosure to take into account the needs of the poor – and refused to print it. Although he was amazed by the stubborn, irrational resistance he met everywhere to what seemed to him a sensible solution ("Nothing has astonished me more than the . . . strange want of discrimination I have met in the arguments that have been urged

---

[85] Citing work of several economic historians, R. W. Fogel states that poor relief in England in the second half of the eighteenth century "increased at a real rate of 2.3 per cent per annum, which was nearly three times as fast as the growth of either GNP or the pauper class." He claims that the responsiveness of the British authorities to the needs of the "ultra-poor" prevented a revolution of the sort that happened in France. R. W. Fogel, "Second Thoughts on the European Escape from Hunger: Famines, Chronic Malnutrition, and Mortality Rates," in S. R. Osmani (ed.), *Nutrition and Poverty*, pp. 243–86, esp. p. 271.

against the system recommended" [47]), he complied with the Board's insistence that he remove their name from the report. Nevertheless, he published his *Inquiry* piecemeal in the *Annals of Agriculture* and printed it as a pamphlet as well. "I am well persuaded that this is the only possible means of saving the nation from the ruin fast coming on by the misery of the poor and the alarming ruin of rates," he wrote in his diary.[86]

Arthur Young's naiveté is remarkable. He seems to have expected rational arguments alone to convince the establishment to abandon their economic interests and take up his plan for helping the poor. His own change of heart seems more astonishing at the distance of 200 years than their reluctance to agree that livestock and land should be given to the powerless and needy instead of enclosing what was left of the commons and "waste" lands for men of substance to "improve."

There were some issues that Young never changed his mind about, of course. Both in his fiction and in his non-fiction he opposed the laws of settlement. Sometimes called the "old" poor law, this 1662 Act guaranteed parish relief to those who had been born in a parish or who had completed a full year's employment there. Acts passed in 1714 and 1740 further discouraged the mobility of landless laborers looking for work by punishing vagrants. By the middle of the century, the rising poor rates and the growing supply of landless farm labor made local farmers reluctant to "give a settlement" to newcomers and make them the responsibility of the ratepayers in that parish if they lost their jobs. Employers quickly learned to turn off workers just before they had worked a full year to prevent them from going on the rates when out of work, or else required of potential workers a certificate of settlement from their home parish somewhere else before they would hire them.[87] Arthur Young had written against this law as early as 1767, in *The Farmer's Letters to the People of England*, because it interfered with marriage and therefore with population, which he thought essential to the strength of the state. When a young laborer or manufacturer is "an inhabitant, by sufferance, of a parish to which he does not belong," he wrote, "the officers of such parish, the moment they hear of his intention to marry, give him notice to quit their parish, and retire to his own, unless he can

---

[86] *Autobiography of Arthur Young*, p. 351.
[87] The case of Aaron Wall, 1768–1846, illustrates the problem of settlement and the bureaucratic solution. A married man with an injured leg, unable to work, he applied for poor relief. He "was adjudged to have settlement, not in Weare where he and his family had lived for four or five years, not in Wedmore where he was born and his forebears had lived at least since 1561, but in the neighbouring and much smaller parish of Chapel Allerton, where Aaron, as a single man and aged nineteen, had completed a full year's hiring – his last – sixteen years before." William G. Hall, "The Meaning of Poverty – A Somerset Example," *Local Historian* 16 (1984), 15–20., quote 17.

procure a certificate that neither he, nor *his*, shall ever become chargeable to them" (288). Such policies were neither in the public interest, he felt, nor consistent with fairness and justice.

He satirized this law in the novel he wrote the following year, *The Adventures of Miss Lucy Watson* (1768). The worthy heroine, fainting with hunger and exhaustion, with her infant daughter in her arms, is pressed to walk "t'other side the blue post, and then you know she won't be in this parish" (212) by an unfeeling bystander, so that she will not go on the poor rates of the parish in which she has collapsed. No one wants to take responsibility for her or help her. The cruel absurdity of the law is thus displayed, and Lucy Watson dies a few pages later, a victim to the inhumanity of the poor laws.

But it is rather from the contradictions between his fiction and his agricultural tracts that one begins to understand why Arthur Young changed his mind in 1801 about land allotments for the poor. There is an ambiguous character in *The Adventures of Miss Lucy Watson* who, in some respects, is reminiscent of Arthur Young himself. Mr. Cary is always thinking up just the kind of profitable agricultural schemes that appealed to Young and, like him, is always calculating initial outlay and potential profit. Writing to a friend about "our new province in Florida," Mr. Cary confidently asserts in a very Arthur Young-ish tone of voice: "Seven hundred pounds would suffice for a beginning, which I can demonstrate would increase to eight thousand pounds in nine years; by the cultivation of hemp and indigo. A negro yields twenty pounds a year, clear profit; a little multiplication will prove it to you" (123).[88] Arthur Young was never interested in calculating the profits on growing human beings, and Mr. Cary's preoccupation with the cost of slaves is an early warning about his character. The only figure in this novel interested in the agricultural possibilities that fascinated his author, Mr. Cary nevertheless turns out to be a villain. It is noteworthy that Young created this morally ambiguous character to embody his own interests, a darker version of the calculating dreamer that he was himself.

Perhaps Mr. Cary represented Young's residual doubts about commercial agriculture, left unexpressed in his confident polemics on enclosure and

---

[88] In *Observations on the Present State of the Waste Lands of Great Britain* (1773), Young quotes from "Dr. Mitchel's *Present State of North America*" to the effect that the lands on the Ohio and Mississippi "have a natural moisture in them, which is the very soil that both hemp, flax, and indigo delight in; the climate likewise is fit for these commodities . . . Now a crop of indigo, hemp, and flax would be much more profitable than any thing that America produces, whether on the continent or the islands. Every labourer might cultivate two acres or more in hemp, and one or two in indigo, the produce of which would be worth from £30 to £40 a year. This would enable them to purchase negroes, and to enlarge the British plantations beyond what they are otherwise capable of" (21–2n.).

national productivity. For Young never integrated his sense of life's tragedy with his utopian optimism about commerce, but preserved the unambiguous nature of each by writing about them in different genres. Keeping these visions separate permitted him to exaggerate the inevitability of life's reverses on the one hand and the miraculous potential of harnessing natural processes for profit on the other. In neither his fiction nor his treatises did Arthur Young admit complication or paradox – not until Bobbin's death forced his awareness of the suffering around him. He then saw that his best and most rational efforts had consequences that he had not predicted; but he was honest enough to publicize what he saw and to try once more to intervene to correct the situation. His tracts began to have the tragic cast of his novels and he became as pious as any of his heroines. His life in the end conformed to his art.

So "fact" and "fiction" in Arthur Young's *oeuvre* turn out to be opposing interpretations of the same reality, fed by the same fund of experience, infused by the same fascination with farming, one projecting success and one projecting tragedy. Arthur Young's own aspirations at the beginning of his career led him to emphasize the improvements and profits possible for large landowners, while his tragic sense of loss at the end led him to bear witness and plead for the poor. Both aspects of rural life were there all along, available for comment in the thirty-odd years he was observing and writing, but the events of his life predisposed him to see first one and then the other aspect with undivided clarity.

The reversal in Arthur Young's perception, while politically dramatic, was always incipient in his art. Once he gave up all hopes of earthly happiness for himself, he put his rational, problem-solving practicality at the service of subsistence for the poor rather than productivity for the nation. If the pessimism of his fiction had sooner infused his agricultural writings, balancing his approach to national land policies, if he had earlier seen the need for allotments for the poor from existing commons and wastes, then it is possible that the terrible food shortages at the end of the century might have been mitigated for some people.[89] As it was, he played a minor role in

---

[89] Both the real and the relative price of food in England rose steadily in the second half of the eighteenth century and quite sharply after about 1760. The diets of even those whose incomes were increasing moderately began to consist of more carbohydrates and less protein-rich food such as milk or meat. The effects of these changes in nutrition can be seen in the reduced heights of English soldiers twenty to twenty-three years of age between 1770 and 1810. Sebastian Coll and John Komlos, "The Biological Standard of Living and Economic Development: Nutrition, Health and Well Being in Historical Perspective," in Clara Eugenia Núñez (ed.), *Debates and Controversies in Economic History*, pp. 219–82, esp. pp. 224–5.

the grand drama of capitalism, providing the ideological basis for judging national success in terms of commercial productivity. As such, he helped to justify the shift from use rights and customary entitlements to exchange value and absolute property rights, and he did not see what was lost in that trade until it was too late.

His novel *The Adventures of Emmera, or The Fair American* (1767) is at once a manifestation of his own intense interest in the colony on the Ohio river, and at the same time part of a larger literary movement celebrating small, independent farmers – a movement growing out of the increased alienation of the English from rural life. This novel represents at one and the same time Arthur Young's hopes and failures as a farmer, his interest in scientific improvements, and a literary movement which was in itself a compensatory recording of the disappearance of the small landholder from the English countryside. Its setting in America may represent a later stage of pastoral nostalgia – a relocation of innocence from the midlands to the colonies – as capitalism spread globally and the possibilities for subsistence farming in England itself receded.

Thus, this fiction cannot be said to represent "reality" but, rather, one man's reactions to "reality," reactions which cannot be interpreted without knowledge of the historical context. English gentlemen of small means were not decamping for America where they led idyllic lives farming the wilderness in peace with the Indians. But the English countryside was being transformed by new commercial markets for agricultural products, and it led to the impoverishment of the cottagers on the one hand and to fantasies of small-scale self-sufficiency on the other. Literary texts are key to understanding the psychological weight of these changes, for they show in the focus of affect and incident what mattered to the people who lived through these changes and how it affected their imaginative lives.

The effects of these changes on the family in England at the time are enormous. As symbolized in Arthur Young's novel in the way Emmera and her father are superseded by Emmera and her husband, the declining age of marriage in England caused by commercialized land use rooted people more firmly in their conjugal rather than their consanguineal families. Before the widespread use of birth control, this lower age at marriage with its two or three extra years of fertility inevitably meant a rapidly expanding population. The economic pressures on women to marry, apparent in their lower wages and highlighted in the calculation of poor relief initiated at Speenhamland that viewed women and children as supplementary dependents on a male wage-earner,[90] undercut women's independence, directing them towards marriage and motherhood. If I have simplified this story, it is because I am less interested in the complications and contradictions of the historical narrative than in the way literature encapsulates symbolic meanings derived from the life of the time. In the next chapter I look more closely at the roles assigned to mature women in fiction, given this growing emphasis on marriage and maternity for women in eighteenth-century society.

[90] Minutes of the Berkshire Justices' meeting at Speenhamland on May 6, 1795. *Berkshire Sessions Order Book* (1791–5), pp. 434–6. See Sidney and Beatrice Webb, *English Local Government: English Poor Law History*, 3 vols. in 2 (New York: Longmans Green, 1927–9), vol. 1: *The Old Poor Law*, pp. 178–9.

8

The importance of aunts

The sentimental ideal of motherhood is the product of the historical separation of public and private spheres that gave gender polarity its present form as an institutionalized opposition between male rationality and maternal nurturance.

> Jessica Benjamin, *The Bonds of Love: Psychoanalysis, Feminism, and the Problem of Domination*, p. 206.

As late as the seventeenth century there were different words in German for aunt and uncle depending on whether one was referring to the mother's or the father's siblings . . . Not only does it show an awareness of a two-sided kinship, but when one pair of terms was dropped, it was the one for paternal kin (*Vetter* and *Base*). *Oheim* and *Muhme* were transferred to *all* aunts and uncles. The mother's kin must have been extremely important for those terms to have prevailed.

> Beatrice Gottlieb, *The Family in the Western World from the Black Death to the Industrial Age*, pp. 186–7.

But the maternal office was supplied by my aunt, Mrs. Catherine Porten . . . the true mother of my mind as well as of my health.

> Edward Gibbon, *The Memoirs of the Life of Edward Gibbon*, pp. 30, 37.

I have always maintained the importance of Aunts as much as possible.

> Jane Austen to Caroline Austen, October 30, 1815.

Despite the emphasis on marriage and motherhood in late eighteenth-century society, mothers in novels of the period are notoriously absent – dead or otherwise missing. Just when motherhood was becoming central to the definition of femininity, when the modern conception of the all-nurturing, tender, soothing, ministering mother was being consolidated in English culture, she was being represented in fiction as a memory rather than as an active present reality. The orphaned protagonist of fiction usually had to make her (or his) own way through the difficulties of life without a mother to intercede for her, to protect her, to teach her, to guide her, or to alleviate the loneliness which attended individualism, sensibility, and romantic love. Although heroes of these novels as well as heroines had often lost their mothers, maternal absence was more poignant for heroines for they were more vulnerable to the designs of libertine men or the avarice of relatives. Jane Austen's last three novels, for example, feature motherless heroines. In *Mansfield Park*, Fanny Price's mother sends her off to the care of her two aunts (good, if indolent, aunt Bertram and bad aunt Norris) and forgets about her. Emma Woodhouse's mother is dead (*Emma*), as is Anne Elliot's mother (*Persuasion*). But Anne has the love and guidance of Lady Russell, an older woman who was her mother's friend. A substitute for the missing Lady Elliot but not a replacement, Lady Russell is an example of the "aunt" figure examined in this chapter, whose ambiguities of character are a commentary on the meaning of motherhood.

There are many explanations for the striking motherlessness of literary heroines, ranging from reasons of literary expediency to deeper existential necessities. There is to begin with the inevitable trauma of mother-daughter separation, probably universal however culturally defined, which might be said to be behind all these formulaically absent mothers in eighteenth-century fiction. Maternal absence can also signify women's powerlessness. All women "are motherless children in a patriarchal society," wrote Phyllis Chesler, referring to women's inability to protect one another or to pass on wealth and power.[1] The maternal absence in eighteenth-century fiction might be said to represent this essential powerlessness, displaying in high relief the solitary heroine in a field of patriarchal forces.

According to Susan Greenfield, the missing mother in eighteenth-century fiction provides the impetus for the heroine's adventures as she sets about to "resolve the problem of the mother's victimization and reputation" – to extort apologies and recognition from her still-living father (*Evelina*), or to verify the legality of her mother's marriage (*Emmeline*).[2] The heroine must "change the meaning of the mother's finale," writes Greenfield, rewrite the end of her mother's story, to ensure "her own happy ending" (54). As her mother's avenger, setting to rights the injustices of her mother's life, the daughter's personal experience of maternal absence sets in motion her own story.

[1] Quoted by Adrienne Rich in "Jane Eyre: The Temptations of a Motherless Woman," in her *On Lies, Secrets, and Silence: Selected Prose, 1966–1978* (New York: Norton, 1979), p. 91. This discussion of motherlessness is much indebted to Marianne Hirsch, *The Mother/Daughter Plot* (Bloomington: Indiana University Press, 1989), pp. 44–6.

[2] Susan Greenfield, *Mothering Daughters: Novels and the Politics of Family Romance, Frances Burney to Jane Austen* (Detroit: Wayne State University Press, 2002), p. 54.

There is also a logistical literary problem with presenting a powerless woman – a mother – as a protector and role model. Female perfection, into which the heroine is presumably ripening, required a certain submissiveness and resignation – making the best of one's lot. But resignation and submissiveness do not invite confidence in an individual expected to guide and protect a younger person. Motherhood was being defined as a self-effacing role by the late eighteenth century; self and subjectivity may have been expected of a woman before marriage but were increasingly subordinated to the needs of husband and children after marriage. A properly feminine mother, of the sort the heroine was to turn into when she grew up, existed to reflect others rather than to express herself. She could not be expected to exhibit much character or initiative. She might even inhibit – by injunction and example – the heroine's active pursuit of her fate. A young woman might not act autonomously in the world if she identified with her mother's lack of agency. As Marianne Hirsch writes in another context, "It is the mother's absence which creates the space in which the heroine's plot and her activity of plotting can evolve."[3] A young woman would have to defer to her mother were she present, rather than think and act independently.[4]

At a more theoretical level, the absence of the mother – who is the material source of the protagonist and hence of the story – demonstrates the existential lack of grounding for narrative in the world, the disconnection between words and things. The missing mother, who exemplifies the literal, inaugurates according to psychoanalytic theories of creativity a quest for language, art, and culture, which are the inevitably unsatisfying symbolic substitutes for that originary loss.[5]

These explanations for the absence of mothers in the plots of fictional texts were developed, for the most part, in relation to nineteenth-century texts. But the double trajectory for mothers on which they are based – idealization and powerlessness – was a cultural development of eighteenth-century England. As Toni Bowers puts it, there came to be in that period a "dissonance" between "two uneasily reconciled values: unique, coherent

---

[3] Marianne Hirsch, *The Mother/Daughter Plot*, p. 57. Following Freud's essay "Creative Writers and Daydreaming" (1907), in which he differentiates men's dreams of power and ambition from women's dreams of loving a man on whom she can project her own ambition, Hirsch argues that the "female family romance" implied in Freud's essay is founded on the elimination of the mother and the attachment to a husband/father.

[4] Jan Fergus stresses the didactic purpose of this absence: "A good mother, it was felt, would invariably protect the heroine from error and thus from educating herself." *Jane Austen: A Literary Life* (London: Macmillan, and New York: St. Martin's Press, 1991), p. 89.

[5] For a brilliant exploration of these theories in relation to gender, see Margaret Homans, *Bearing the Word: Language and Female Experience in Nineteenth-Century Women's Writing* (Chicago: University of Chicago Press, 1986).

personal identity and sacrificial, self-effacing motherlove."[6] "Motherhood"
and "personhood," she says, began to be seen as mutually exclusive alternatives by mid-century. "For the first time, it became obviously difficult to
reconcile developing norms of self-sacrificing motherlove with increasingly
powerful notions of individual subjectivity."[7] Full-time motherhood was
also becoming an important marker of class, "a central part of middle-class
gentility" according to Leonore Davidoff and Catherine Hall, a development that only intensified in the course of the nineteenth century.[8] But
although the components of virtuous motherhood – "all-engrossing tenderness, long-term maternal breastfeeding, personal supervision and education
of young children, complete physical restriction to domestic space, absence
of sexual desire, withdrawal from productive labor" – began their cultural
life as middle-class expectations, they came before long to be generalized
to all mothers whatever their station.[9]

SENTIMENTALIZED MOTHERHOOD

Before the Augustan period, English culture had not worshiped motherhood, unlike, say, Italian culture. Since the Reformation, there had been no
cult of the Virgin Mary in England. Pregnant women were not idealized in
English literature or painting; nor were women divorced in English society
for barrenness.[10] Marriage rather than childbearing was considered to be
the central event of an Englishwoman's life, although, as explained earlier,
in previous centuries a couple often married when the woman proved with
child. But with the exception of royal or aristocratic women who needed
to produce an heir, it was not assumed in England that a woman's life was
fulfilled primarily by having children. Lady Mary Wortley Montagu was
struck by this difference in the English attitude towards childbearing when
she visited Turkey in 1717. "[I]n this country 'tis more despicable to be
marry'd and not fruitfull," she reported, savoring the cross-cultural ironies,
"than 'tis with us to be fruitfull befor Marriage."[11]

---

[6] Toni Bowers, *The Politics of Motherhood: British Writing and Culture, 1680–1760* (Cambridge: Cambridge University Press, 1996), p. 96.

[7] *Ibid.*

[8] Leonore Davidoff and Catherine Hall, *Family Fortunes: Men and Women of the English Middle Class, 1780–1850* (Chicago: University of Chicago Press, 1987), p. 338.

[9] Quote from Toni Bowers, *Politics of Motherhood*, p. 28.

[10] This insight comes from Alan Macfarlane, *Marriage and Love in England 1300–1840* (Oxford: Basil Blackwell, 1986), pp. 60–1.

[11] *The Complete Letters of Lady Mary Wortley Montagu*, ed. Robert Halsband, 3 vols. (Oxford: Clarendon Press, 1967), vol. I, p. 372. Lady Mary remarks on the difference between the roles women played in English and Turkish society throughout the so-called "Turkish Letters."

Nevertheless, by the middle of the eighteenth century, there was an amendment in this casual English attitude towards motherhood. A discourse about motherhood began to appear (noted above in Chapter 5) that constructed the maternal role as "naturally feminine." Women were expected to nurture their children physically and emotionally without stint – to educate them, to nurse them when ill, to watch over them anxiously at all times. The centrality of mothers to their children's welfare that we take for granted in our post-Freudian world was just beginning to coalesce as an ideology in the eighteenth century. Women who did not breastfeed their own children but who hired wetnurses – as anyone who could afford the extra three or four shillings a week had done at the beginning of the century – were criticized as "unnatural" and "unfeeling."[12] The discourse that emphasized the centrality of the mother-child connection offered extreme examples of motherhood – both positive and negative – focusing public attention on the role. Horrific fictional accounts of unnatural and monstrous motherhood defined by contrast the ideal mother of conduct books and fiction who was entirely selfless and devoted to her child's interests. Women had never before been imagined with more personal significance and less social power.

As maternity was increasingly sentimentalized, maternal feeling was assumed to be powerful and instantaneous. Writers waxed rhapsodic about it. Susan Staves has argued that the contemporary popularity and enduring interest of John Home's *Douglas* (1756) is attributable to the creation of the maternal character of Lady Randolph, a tender mother inconsolable for the loss of her son and overjoyed at his return, dramatizing what was a new perspective in 1756.[13] Courts became more reluctant to convict mothers of infanticide than they had once been, as it became harder and harder for anyone to imagine that a woman, however pressed, might not want her child.[14] One clergyman wrote in 1765 "the great and final Virtue of the Sex is . . . that

---

[12] Jane Sharp, a midwife, wrote in 1671, "There are not many women that want milk to suckle their own children . . . but multitudes pretend weakness when they have no cause for it, because they have not so much love for their own, as dumb creatures have." Quoted in Patricia Crawford and Laura Gowing (eds.), *Women's Worlds in Seventeenth-Century England* (New York and London: Routledge, 2000), p. 196. The *Spectator* 246 (December 12, 1711) charged that "if a Woman does but know that her Husband can spare about three or six Shillings a Week extraordinary . . . she certainly, with the Assistance of her Gossips, will soon persuade the good Man to send the Child to Nurse." For a more extended discussion of the emphasis on breastfeeding as a sign of maternal feeling, see my "Colonizing the Breast: Sexuality and Maternity in Eighteenth-Century England," *Eighteenth-Century Life* 16 n.s. 1 (February 1992), 185–213.

[13] Susan Staves, "Douglas's Mother," in John Hazel Smith (ed.), *Brandeis Essays in Literature* (Department of English and American Literature, Brandeis University, 1983), pp. 51–67.

[14] Peter C. Hoffer and N. E. Hull, *Murdering Mothers: Infanticide in England and New England 1558–1803* (New York: New York University Press, 1981), pp. 68–9, 83–5; referred to in Susan Greenfield's

of a tender and steady Affection for their Husbands and Children." That justified her existence; domestic affection was "the first Duty of her Life, the very Purpose of her Being."[15] By the mid-1780s, the *Lady's Magazine* – arguably the most popular women's magazine by the end of the century – devoted the lion's share of its pages to sentimental stories about mothers and children, together with essays and letters discussing the pleasures and pains of pregnancy, lying-in, childraising, domestic life, and women's duties.[16] Such maternalist writings crowded out the contents of earlier runs of the magazine – sensational stories about separated and reunited lovers, fashion news, reports of masquerades and other events of the beau monde, stories about the travels of the elite, and the like. As Beth Tobin summarizes the change, women were no longer being depicted as "beautiful objects made to please men," as sweethearts and wives, in the pages of the *Lady's Magazine*, but rather increasingly "as mothers and even as benefactresses who nurture their own family and the families of the less fortunate." These representations, she adds, were an important part of the process "by which the ideology of domesticity was created and legitimated."[17]

LEGAL ERASURE OF MATERNITY

Although there may well be a relation between this construction of idealized motherlove that lacks inherent subjectivity and the impossibility of representing living mothers in fiction, it is also possible that both phenomena were manifestations of the dwindling power of mothers in eighteenth-century England. Legally speaking, the mother's *de facto* legal right to be guardian to her children did not exist in eighteenth-century England, having been abolished by statute in 1660 and not reinstated until 1839. According to Cheryl L. Nixon, "the long eighteenth century's legal understanding of maternity is far more restrictive than that of preceding and following centuries."[18] Before 1660, a mother could assert her legal right to the custody of her children on the basis of common-law "guardianship by nature" and "guardianship by nurture." Guardianship "by nature" was a claim based on the mother's intergenerational connection to the child – the fact that

Introduction to Susan C. Greenfield and Carol Barash (eds.), *Inventing Maternity: Politics, Science, and Literature 1650–1865* (Lexington: University of Kentucky Press, 1999), pp. 1–2, 26 n. 3.

[15] John Brown, D. D., *On the Female Character and Education* (London, 1765), pp. 13–14.

[16] Beth Fowkes Tobin, "'The Tender Mother': The Social Construction of Motherhood and the *Lady's Magazine*," *Women's Studies* 18 (1990), 205–21.

[17] *Ibid.*, p. 209.

[18] Cheryl L. Nixon, "Maternal Guardianship by 'Nature' and 'Nurture': Eighteenth-Century Chancery Court Records and *Clarissa*," *Intertexts* 5, 2 (2001), 128–55, esp. 133.

the child would inherit the family's estate; guardianship "by nurture" was a claim based on a recognition that the child needed the bodily nurture that a mother could provide. However "natural" both these claims were thought to be, they were suspended in practice between 1660 and 1839, and the mother's standing before the law evaporated. If a child's father was dead – even if its mother was alive – that child was legally considered to be an orphan whose custody had to be legally assigned by will to a surrogate parent. A mother's right to guardianship of their children had to be specified in her husband's will if she survived him. Testamentary guardianship was a continuation of paternal authority according to Chancery doctrine, and superseded the mother's earlier legal status under common law as guardian by "nurture" or by "nature." As Nixon astutely observes, this legal erasure of motherhood "confounds the assertions of many current historical surveys of the family: while the historian may argue that the mother/child bond gained new emotional and intellectual significance over the course of the eighteenth century, an overview of guardianship law reveals that in an important sense this bond gained new *in*significance."[19] As I have been arguing throughout this book, the sentimentalizing of a relationship is not always a sign of its increased importance.

The contemporary legal case cited by Nixon that tested the maternal claim to guardianship after the 1660 abolition of the Court of Wards (and the transfer of guardianship law to Chancery) was *Eyre v. Countess of Shaftesbury* (1722). In that case, a mother's right to the bodily care and supervision of her twelve-year-old son was contested by the guardian named by the boy's father in his last will and testament. The court decided that Mr. Eyre, the testamentary guardian, had the legal power to determine his ward's education despite the boy's mother's counterclaims. She pointed to her record as a careful mother, ministering to her "tender and sickly" son, as a reason for her legal right to determine his future. Nevertheless, the court found against her and awarded Mr. Eyre the legal power to determine the boy's upbringing. Two years later this contest was renewed when the countess married her still-underage son to the daughter of her friend, the Countess of Gainsborough. The marriage had proceeded without Mr. Eyre's consent, for which he sued her for "ravishment of ward" – a term referring to the economic rather than the sexual abuse of the ward, but whose sensational locution testifies to the conflation of these meanings. In this case "ravishment of ward" referred to the marriage of Mr. Eyre's ward

---

[19] Cheryl Nixon, "Fictional Families: Guardianship in Eighteenth-Century Law and Literature," Ph.D. diss., Harvard University, 1995, p. 298. Nixon explains that the common-law forms of guardianship abolished in 1660 were reintroduced in 1839 with the passage of "Talford's Act."

without his consent. Again, the court found for the testamentary guardian over the mother and, according to Cheryl Nixon, sentenced the countess to "'absolute sequestration,' or imprisonment, for her 'contempt in contriving and effecting this marriage without the consent of the guardian or application to the court.'"[20]

In everyday practice, of course, some women did act as legal guardians for their underage children – possibly because their husbands willed them this testamentary jurisdiction or possibly as a continuation of their common-law rights. Nixon examined 1,945 Chancery court manuscript reports of actual cases concerning underage children in 1735 and found that mothers actively represented the interests of underage children in the courtroom almost as frequently as fathers did. In 15% of the 369 cases involving infants, mothers acted as agents for underage children whereas fathers acted as legal agents for their children in 17% of the cases. In the remaining 68% of cases, male guardians outside the family tended to represent the interests of underage children; less frequently, this role was taken on by a male relative such as an uncle or a brother, and once in a while even by a grandmother. Nixon concludes that legal treatises purporting to summarize case law – Blackstone's *Commentaries*, for example – may have overstated the erasure of maternal guardian rights. There is no way of knowing whether the mother was still living in the 68% of the cases in which neither mother nor father acted as guardian, although it is probable that the fathers were not living. Perhaps the discrepancy between actual case reports in 1735 and the treatment of maternal guardianship in legal treatises represents the difference between customary practice and evolving Chancery law, which was relatively new in this period. That is, practice may have continued the maternal guardianship that obtained earlier, while legal theory increasingly proscribed maternal participation in matters of business and property. Nixon does conjecture that Richardson's equivocal handling of Anna Howe's mother in *Clarissa* – granting her economic power but not emotional power – signifies anxiety concerning the power of maternal guardians at mid-century.[21]

---

[20] Cheryl Nixon, "Fictional Families: Guardianship in Eighteenth-Century Law and Literature," p. 314.

[21] Cheryl Nixon, "Maternal Guardianship by 'Nature' and 'Nurture,'" 146. In trying to make sense of the legal restrictions on maternal guardianship in conjunction with the evolving ideology valorizing motherhood in eighteenth-century England, Nixon suggests that literary representations of mothers contained a critique of restrictive law, showing how necessary mothers were to their children and how single-minded and unselfish mothers were in their desire to protect their children's interests. I would interpret the difference rather as the literary imagination compensating for the constriction of maternal rights.

The case of *R* v. *De Manneville* (1781) offers an example of the legal status of maternal claims later in the century. This case involved a mother who left her husband because of his cruel and abusive treatment, taking with her their nursing infant. When her husband forcibly seized the infant from her breast one night and she tried to obtain legal redress, "the Court remanded the infant to the father, not seeing any ground to impute any motive to him injurious to the health or liberty of the child."[22] The case bears an eerie resemblance to the plot of Mary Wollstonecraft's novel *Maria, or the Wrongs of Woman* (1798), in which Maria's four-month-old infant is "torn from her, even while she was discharging the tenderest maternal office."[23] When Maria pleads her cause in a court of law, the judge dismisses her charges and orders her to "love and obey the man chosen by her parents and relations" (140). She has no rights before the law as a mother or a wife. As she remarks in another context, a husband can rob his wife of everything she owns "with impunity . . . and the laws of her country – if women have a country – afford her no protection or redress" (108). Only the father was the legal parent of a child and he could proscribe the mother's access to her own children if he chose. This poignant fact is illustrated by Sarah Pennington's *An Unfortunate Mother's Advice to Her Absent Daughters* (1761), written by an aristocratic woman whose estranged husband prevented her from seeing her daughters privately or even from corresponding with them. The premise of this conduct book is that it is a caring mother's attempt to communicate with her daughters; she addresses them as part of the reading public because she has no other way to reach them.

Sometimes a distinction was drawn between guardianship by nurture and guardianship by nature – that is, between care of the body of the child and the blood connection which entitled a mother to care for the property and economic interests of the underage child. In the course of the eighteenth century, *pace* Wollstonecraft's *Maria* and Sarah Pennington's *Advice*, the law became somewhat more sympathetic to the mother's right to guardianship by nurture or care of her underage children's bodily needs – perhaps the effect of sentimentalizing motherhood.[24] This was true at the same time as the mother was increasingly barred from taking care of her

---

[22] John David Chambers, *A Practical Treatise on the Jurisdiction of the High Court of Chancery over the Persons and Property of Infants* (London: Saunders and Benning, 1842), pp. 56–7, quoted in Cheryl Nixon, "Legal and Textual Circumscription: The Female Guardian," unpublished seminar paper, pp. 15–16. My understanding of maternal guardianship as an issue comes entirely from Cheryl Nixon's groundbreaking work on the subject.

[23] Mary Wollstonecraft, *Maria, or the Wrongs of Woman*, ed. Moira Ferguson (New York: Norton, 1975), p. 28. Subsequent page numbers are from this edition.

[24] This insight comes from Cheryl Nixon.

children's economic interests and managing their property and assets. A study of Yorkshire wills shows that, in the course of the eighteenth century, men became less and less likely to leave to their surviving widows the sole responsibility for managing the estates of underage children. It had been a more common practice in the seventeenth century for men to designate their widows as sole executors to manage land and money, to raise underage children, and to apportion to them whatever money they needed for their start in life, whether apprenticeship or employment. By the 1730s and 1740s, men (particularly wealthier citizens) began to designate in their wills an outside testator rather than their wives to manage the estate or business – and their children's interests in it – after their death. By the 1770s and 1780s, this trend had become a common practice. John Smail writes that this "shift represents the growing cultural perception that it was not suitable for women to be managing money, let alone running a business."[25]

Even when a woman was granted guardianship of her children upon her husband's death, if she remarried she could forfeit that right. The bonds of marriage were so powerful, it was assumed, that they would obliterate a woman's prior maternal responsibility and submerge it in her duty to a new husband. Furthermore, the legal power that husbands possessed over their wives' lives and property made it difficult for a woman to protect the interests of her children from a former marriage if her new husband chose to plunder their inheritance. Thus the consanguineal relation between children and their mothers was subordinated to the spousal bond and the superseding claims of the conjugal family, however recently established. The practice of appointing a legal guardian for "orphaned" children upon the remarriage of their mother also testifies to the interest of the law in protecting patrilineal property rights at the expense of maternal interests.

Why the repression of maternal rights, with the concurrent idealization and sentimentalization of motherhood, should have happened at this

---

[25] John Smail, *The Origins of Middle-Class Culture: Halifax, Yorkshire, 1660–1780* (Ithaca: Cornell University Press, 1994), p. 170. This cultural perception was at odds with actual practice insofar as women have always worked, managed money, and run businesses.

Richard Grassby also reports that appointing a surviving widow as sole executrix was an "ancient practice" increasingly discontinued in the course of the seventeenth century. By the middle of the eighteenth century, he states, there was a higher percentage of widows appointed as joint executor together with their children or other kin rather than as sole executrix. Grassby also notes that "women rarely served as witnesses of wills" (131). Richard Grassby, *Kinship and Capitalism: Marriage, Family, and Business in the English-Speaking World, 1580–1740* (Cambridge: Cambridge University Press, and Washington, DC: Woodrow Wilson Center Press, 2001), pp. 127–30.

historical time is not entirely clear. Toni Bowers relates it to the broadening base of male leadership in England – to challenges to the monarchy – and states that the "containment of matriarchal authority" was vital "at a time when patriarchal authority was undergoing radical reconception and was therefore particularly vulnerable."[26] As I have argued elsewhere, the democratization of power among men often entails the exclusion of women.[27] Restricting maternal rights and the rights of maternal kin also maximizes the accumulation of family property by focusing and channeling the resources of the larger kin group into the male line. Matrilineality as a system distributes resources more widely among more people. Under a system of patrilineality, relatives such as the father's sisters and the mother's brothers are eliminated from the network of family responsibility.[28]

The assertion of the father's rights to the child together with the suppression of maternal rights to the child, and the limiting of fiscal responsibility accorded to widows and maternal kin, were part of an *ideology* of patrilineality that came to prevail in England in this period. Even though the basic bilateral English kinship system was never legally altered, the provisions that kept women from inheriting family land (primogeniture, entailment, and dowry payments in cash rather than land), in combination with the new interest in establishing family estates associated with a patronymic surname (in imitation of the landed gentry), mimicked patrilineal inheritance patterns and diminished the psychological power of the mother and her consanguineal family.[29] When, for example, Thomas Turner, a Sussex tradesman living in the second half of the eighteenth century, decided to make a genealogical chart of his family, he noted on it the names "of all Turners, dead and living, including his father, both his father's wives and their children, followed by the names of his own wives and children." Naomi Tadmor, who has studied Turner's diary for details of his kin relations, remarks of his stocktaking: "One is also struck by the limited amount of detail about Turner's maternal family and the families of origin of his

---

[26] Toni Bowers, *Politics of Motherhood*, p. 14.

[27] Ruth Perry, "Mary Astell and the Feminist Critique of Possessive Individualism," *Eighteenth-Century Studies* 23, 4 (Summer 1990), 444–57.

[28] There is even some limited evidence that the traditional rights of widows and their children to inherit "reasonable parts" or "thirds" of their husbands' or fathers' moveable goods was being called into question in some parts of England, thus leaving a larger share for the legal heir. According to Amy Louise Erickson, "between 1692 and 1725 the ecclesiastical right of widows and children to reasonable parts in the province of York, Wales, and the city of London was abolished by statute." *Women and Property in Early Modern England* (New York and London: Routledge, 1993), p. 28.

[29] Edmund Leach, "Complementary Filiation and Bilateral Kinship," in Jack Goody (ed.), *The Character of Kinship* (Cambridge: Cambridge University Press, 1973), pp. 53–8.

first and second wives."[30] Psychologically, for this man, maternal lineages did not count.

Absent mothers in fiction may thus literalize a psychological truth: mothers could not always be there for their children; unable to protect them, they were without the most basic power to make and implement decisions about their education and welfare. Ironically, while maternal power was being legally suppressed and socially devalued, the public definition of what constituted good motherhood was becoming ever more formulaic and self-sacrificing.

The effect of telling coming-of-age stories about girls and women who have no mothers is to build up an intense longing for the mother; the absence calls attention to itself. Mary Wollstonecraft's *Maria, or the Wrongs of Woman* (1798), a novel in which the miseries of the main characters stem from their maternal deprivation, is saturated with mother longing. Both Maria and Jemima suffer all their lives for the want of maternal affection and support, for which, briefly, they turn to each other. "I was an egg dropped on the sand," Jemima tells Maria bitterly, as if she were a turtle, vulnerable to predators in an arid world (40).[31] Maria had a mother, but she lavished all her love and attention on her son, Maria's brother. Maria tells Jemima the story of her cruel husband and how, before incarcerating her, he kidnapped their infant daughter – snatched her from Maria's breast while she was nursing – in an attempt to coerce Maria into signing over her inheritance from an uncle. An extreme image of maternal deprivation, the episode echoes her own experience of being unmothered, rendering it more poignant by replicating it in the next generation.

MOTHER SUBSTITUTES

The yearning created by maternal absence in these fictions is sometimes supplied in the text by an older woman who is not the heroine's mother, but who guides and advises her, and stands in the place of a mother to her. As if called into being by a need that could be assuaged no other way, these older women – these symbolic "aunts" – have no narrative purpose except to give their support and appreciation to the poor, motherless heroine. It is as if the mother did not disappear from eighteenth-century novels all at once, but flickered and sputtered for a while first in this liminal figure. Lady Russell, in Austen's *Persuasion*, is an example of the type. Like many of these

---

[30] Naomi Tadmor, *Family and Friends in Eighteenth-Century England: Household, Kinship, and Patronage* (Cambridge: Cambridge University Press, 2001), pp. 81–2, quote p. 82.

[31] Page numbers refer to the Norton edition edited by Moira Ferguson cited above.

surrogate mothers, she had been a friend of the heroine's mother; and she loves and appreciates Anne both for her old friend's sake and for the feeling intelligence of the heroine herself. Widowed, sexually independent (she does not wear rouge) and cultivated, she looks out for Anne's interests and defends her and encourages her, despite several failures of judgment owing to an excessive deference to rank. Like most of these "aunt" figures, she has a highly developed literary sense and delights in verbal acuity. "Lady Russell quite bores one with her new publications," says Elizabeth Elliot, returning unread a book Lady Russell had lent her. "I really cannot be plaguing myself for ever with all the new poems and states of the nation that come out."[32] Like kin but not kin – standing in the place of the mother but not a mother – Lady Russell and others of her type in eighteenth-century fiction are placeholders in the novel for a kind of maternal power in an era before the mother figure definitively disappears from view. For this almost-mother, this strong "aunt," like a ghostly presence, is an eighteenth-century phenomenon, the last trace of an independent woman – on her way to extinction in the nineteenth century.

Her effect on the text is like a bracing tonic. Usually respectable – although often unconventional – learned, wise, and mature, she advises the heroine and helps her through her most difficult times. Doing for the heroine what she cannot do for herself, she adds another kind of female energy to the text, an energy that is not decorous or "feminine" but strong and unafraid of confrontation. Like a fairy godmother with a sharp wit, she seems to exist for the sake of the orphaned young woman whom she protects and advises. She rarely has any other narrative function or any story of her own; if she were removed from the text the story line would not be altered – except that the ingenue heroine would stumble more hesitatingly through the world without this older woman's understanding of life to supplement her inexperience. In a sense, her presence confirms the innocence of the heroine. Sentimental novels are full of examples of this "aunt" figure, and I intend to examine several in this chapter to explore their meaning and demonstrate their variety.

A character of this description, an older woman who is not a mother but who stands in the place of the mother, teaching the heroine what she needs to know to get along in the world, can be found as early as Defoe's *Moll Flanders* (1722). She appears first in the character of the "nurse" in Colchester who takes in the infant Moll and teaches her to read, sew, and to spin worsted; and then again in the figure Moll calls her "governess," the

[32] Jane Austen, *Persuasion*, ed. D. W. Harding (New York and Harmondsworth: Penguin, 1965), Chapter 22, p. 221.

midwife who sends her delicious meals, lodges her, manages her lying-in, and helps to direct her career of crime. Every time Moll gets into trouble, she gets excellent advice from this woman, whom she alternately calls her "governess" and "Mother". It is she who convinces Moll to board her new-born infant and arranges it so that Moll can accept the respectable clerk who wants to marry her. Later she fences Moll's stolen goods, introduces her to those who can teach her the tricks of the thieving trade, and disguises her as a man to escape detection. Most significantly, she is instrumental in getting Moll's death sentence commuted to transportation and furnishing her with supplies for her new life in America. Indeed, Lois Chaber has argued persuasively that the real structure of *Moll Flanders* is matriarchal, with three maternal figures determining Moll's fate: her Colchester "nurse," her "governess," and her mother-in-law – who turns out to be her biological mother. As Chaber says, "All three maternal figures not only exist independent of male relationships but also shelter Moll from the patriarchal authorities constantly impinging on her life: the local magistrates who would put her out to service, the husband who would put her in an institution, the English judiciary who threaten her with the gallows."[33] Highly intelligent, competent, successful in their various endeavors, sexually unattached, all three characters figure female autonomy as well as a kind of social motherhood for Moll.

Like other later examples of this fictional "aunt" character, Moll's "governess" is the most articulate person in the novel – "a Woman of admirable Address," "a Mistress of her Tongue"[34] – able to talk anybody into anything. She talks Moll into giving up her child, into stealing for a living, into becoming the most notorious and successful thief of her day; and with her silver tongue she saves Moll from many close scrapes and manages to arrange a reprieve from execution at the eleventh hour. This woman takes care of Moll materially and psychically, helps her to justify her actions, protects her from reprisals, and gives advice that retrospectively always turns out to have been excellent. Generous, quick-sighted, authoritative, competent, skillful, active, intelligent – except for the fact that hers is not a reputable business nor her charge an innocent, she has all the qualities of the older mentor-women of sentimental fiction later in the century.

Mrs. Evans in *The History of Betty Barnes* (1753) raises and educates the orphaned little girl born in a barn and saved from starvation by a parish

---

[33] Lois A. Chaber, "Matriarchal Mirror: Women and Capital in *Moll Flanders*," *PMLA* 97, 2 (March 1982), 212–26, quote 219.
[34] Daniel Defoe, *Moll Flanders* (1722), ed. and with an Introduction by Juliet Mitchell (Harmondsworth: Penguin, 1978), p. 222

nurse. Mrs. Evans teaches our young heroine "to read, to work, and even to play, mixing all her useful lessons of instruction, with what is most apt to delight the mind of a child; the fox, the ape, and the ass all contributed something towards her education, by opening her mind."[35] Although the years of Betty Barnes' tuition by Mrs. Evans – the ages of five to thirteen – are passed over in little more than a page, the reader is frequently reminded throughout both volumes of Mrs. Evans' abiding influence in the heroine's "delicacy and justness of sentiment" (1: 196) and the unwavering moral sense that the plot keeps calling upon her to display. At the end, when our heroine marries, she faces her last trial, which is to submit to the scrutiny of her new mother-in-law, whose class standing is considerably higher than her own. To everyone's astonishment, this formidable person turns out to be none other than her beloved and long-lost Mrs. Evans. And so, in addition to the reunion with her own biological father which happens in the second volume, our heroine finds her new conjugal family sweetened by the benevolent older woman who took her under her wing as a child. This denouement gives the chosen family of romantic love a consanguineal feel to it, always the most satisfying ending in an eighteenth-century novel as we will see in the next chapter.

Motherless Arabella in Charlotte Lennox's *The Female Quixote* (1752) owes to a wise older woman her dawning realization that real life does not conform to the rules of storybook romance. Her "cure," which is famously effected by the rational discourse of the Doctor who tended her fever during her physical illness, was begun earlier by the Countess of —, an older woman who admires her spirit and intelligence. Having intervened to defend Arabella from the malicious gossip of a group of fashionable young women envious of her beauty, the Countess visits Arabella to see how else she can help her. Charlotte Lennox endows this paragon with every known virtue. Superior in "Wit, Elegance, and Ease" and excelling in the feminine accomplishments of painting, poetry, and music, she also has more "Sense, Learning, and Judgement" than most men.[36] An eighteenth-century pattern of perfection, she dislikes cards, holds no assemblies, and avoids the public entertainments of the beau monde. Her candor, sweetness, modesty, and benevolence place her beyond praise. The Countess, who feels "more than ordinary Affection" for the heroine (329), recognizes that Arabella's

---

[35] [Mary Collyer,] *The History of Betty Barnes*, 2 vols. (1753; rpt. New York: Garland, 1974), vol. 1, p. 15. Subsequent page references are to this edition.

[36] Charlotte Lennox, *The Female Quixote* (1752), ed. Margaret Dalziel, with an Introduction by Margaret Anne Doody (Oxford: Oxford University Press, 1989), p. 322. All subsequent page numbers refer to this edition.

delusions come from "her Studies, her Retirement, her Ignorance of the World and her lively Imagination" (323). She speaks to Arabella in the language of romance, identifying with the young enthusiast, for "she herself had when very young, been deep read in Romances" (323). The Countess informs Arabella that the age of romance is long past. Rather than trying to puncture Arabella's romantic delusions (as the Doctor later does), the Countess tells Arabella that romance morality is outmoded and inappropriate for the contemporary world. "Custom . . . changes the very Nature of Things, and what was honourable a thousand Years ago, may probably be look'd upon as infamous now," she tells her. "The same Actions which made a Man a Hero in those Times, would constitute him a Murderer in These" (328). The Countess thus argues for a moral system that is congruent with the world they live in, rather than simply debunking the moral universe of the romance. Morality is a relative matter, she explains. "[W]hat was Virtue in those Days, is Vice in ours" (329).

Much has been written about the woman-centered romance tradition represented by Arabella, Arabella's mother, and the Countess, as opposed to the masculinist Enlightenment tradition represented by the Doctor, which I am not going to rehearse here. What interests me, rather, is the type embodied by the Countess and her relationship to the heroine. For the Countess, who identifies with Arabella, is another incarnation of the "aunt" figure – the older woman who is not a mother but who stands in the place of the mother to the heroine. Intelligent, articulate, affectionate, interested in the heroine for her own sake, she begins the task of showing Arabella the folly of applying the logic of romances to everyday life without humiliating her, a lesson undone by Sir George's hired actresses and the Doctor's enlightened arguments. The Countess' ministrations are also interrupted by a summons from her own mother, who is indisposed. The summons, in removing the Countess at this juncture, activates a chain of absent mothers (as Debra Malina points out) – Arabella's absent mother, the now absent Countess, as well as the Countess' absent mother – calling attention to the inaugurating problem of the novel, which is Arabella's motherlessness, to which her trouble can be traced. For at the literal level, Arabella has been reading her mother's collection of romances without supervision and has been deprived of maternal guidance in how to understand what she has been reading.[37]

---

[37] See Debra Malina's excellent article, "Rereading the Patriarchal Text: *The Female Quixote, Northanger Abbey,* and the Trace of the Absent Mother," *Eighteenth-Century Fiction* 8, 2 (January 1996), 271–92.

If it is true that Samuel Johnson advised Lennox about the ending of this book, or even partially wrote the sequence in which the Doctor effects Arabella's final cure (368–82), we may conjecture that, left to her own devices, Lennox might have allowed the Countess to succeed in curing Arabella by her method.[38] As it is written, the Countess, who disappears as abruptly as she appears, is like a mirage of free-floating maternal energy that briefly attaches itself to the motherless heroine. Modeling the virtues of female autonomy and educated intelligence as all of these "aunt" figures do, the Countess appears also to be sexually unattached, not integrated into any family, but existing only for the sake of her mother on the one hand and Arabella, her surrogate daughter, on the other. She is thus a link in a chain of mothers that try but never entirely succeed in reclaiming Arabella from the patriarchal world of her father, her lover, and the Doctor.

FICTIONAL "AUNTS" IN NOVELS BY FRANCES BURNEY AND CHARLOTTE SMITH

The helpful older woman who supplies the place of a mother to the heroine in Charlotte Smith's *Emmeline, the Orphan of the Castle* (1788) is Mrs. Stafford: she is the staff afforded Emmeline in that text. Older than Emmeline, with children of her own, she even gives birth to a baby girl a third of the way through the novel, establishing her maternal credentials. Although she is married to a man unworthy of her, he is in France during most of her relationship to Emmeline, so that she acts with an autonomous authority usual for an "aunt." When he does appear, Mrs. Stafford exercises her wifely virtue by attempting to "hide from others what she saw too evidently herself."[39] Highly intelligent, educated, and polished, with "all that ease of manner, which the commerce of fashion can supply," Mrs. Stafford's "mind, originally elegant and refined, was highly cultivated, and embellished with all the knowledge that could be acquired from the best authors" (49). Taking an immediate liking to Emmeline, she instructs

---

[38] Duncan Isles argues that there is no reason to suppose Chapter 11 in Book IX is Johnson's work. See his appendix, especially p. 422, to the Oxford University Press edition referred to above. Patricia Spacks suggests otherwise, citing a number of prior authorities on the subject. Patricia Meyer Spacks, *Desire and Truth: Functions of Plot in Eighteenth-Century English Novels* (Chicago: University of Chicago Press, 1990), pp. 14–15.

[39] Charlotte Smith, *Emmeline, the Orphan of the Castle* (1788; London: Pandora, 1988), p. 192. The description of Mr. Stafford as a man "who having neither perseverance and regularity to fit [him] for business, or taste and genius for more refined pursuits, seek, in every casual occurrence or childish amusement, relief against the tedium of life" (191) – feckless and extravagant, dissipated and irritable – is thought by many to be Charlotte Smith's thinly veiled description of her own husband.

the young rustic in drawing, French, and Italian, and reads with her every day, by which means she transforms the unpolished (but naturally refined) country girl into a cultivated woman fit for polite society.

But Mrs. Stafford's most important function in the novel is to chaperone Emmeline and to protect the orphaned girl from the indelicacies of her situation – which are many. Emmeline is being pursued by the son of her guardian who adores her and wants to marry her. But she has promised his father not to marry the hotheaded Delamere without permission and moreover to keep him – the father – informed of the youth's whereabouts. The combination of Delamere's importunities and her own solemn promise to his father – who is her uncle as well as her guardian – betray Emmeline into many ticklish situations which Mrs. Stafford helps her to resolve.

For example, when Delamere and his friend Fitz-Edward appear unexpectedly, Mrs. Stafford deflates the high-blown romantic rhetoric of the latter and protects Emmeline from the passionate declarations of the former. She also immediately writes, on Emmeline's behalf, to Emmeline's uncle to inform him that his errant son has unexpectedly appeared. To Mrs. Stafford fall all the difficult explanations of the book. Later, when Emmeline's growing affection for Godolphin leads her into further difficulties, Mrs. Stafford continues to explain whatever might damage her young protégée's reputation, to clarify whatever looks ambiguous, and to keep the heroine from embarrassment or indelicate explanations. Because the heroine repeatedly finds herself in double binds (conflicting loyalties; innocent situations that look compromising; others' secrets to be kept; undeclared love), Mrs. Stafford's explanations are essential in this novel, and without them Emmeline's various admirers would have long since given up in disgust, killed each other off, or otherwise resolved the narrative tension that propels the book forward. She is a loyal friend to Emmeline, independent enough to keep her company and to protect her from the worst effects of Delamere's intemperance and able, as a married woman, to refer to sexual improprieties without compromising her own respectability. She hovers over the entire book – involved at every turn, explaining relationships and actions that would cost Emmeline too much delicacy to explain, smoothing over embarrassing moments, protecting Emmeline's reputation with a mother's care but unable to stop the drama by offering her asylum because of her own unsettled circumstances. Like a mother, an older sister, an aunt, she always has Emmeline's interests at heart; she educates her, protects her, intercedes for her, and praises her. An idealized mother with four young children of her own, she acts *in loco maternis* to the motherless heroine, leaving her free enough to call her virtues her own but providing a screen to protect her innocence and delicacy until she is claimed at the altar.

Near the end of the second volume, Delamere's friend Fitz-Edward reads Frances Burney's *Cecilia* (1782) aloud to Mrs. Stafford and Emmeline, with Mrs. Stafford's little boys playing at their feet. Published six years earlier, *Cecilia* proceeds from the same premise as *Emmeline*: the heroine is pursued by the impetuous son of her guardian who forbids her to respond to his disobedient son's proposal of marriage. In both cases, romantic love overwhelms duty for the hot-headed lover as he turns his back on his consanguineal family. For the unprotected, motherless heroine, moral obligation to her consanguineal guardian – an unloving father figure – outweighs the material advantages that would be hers if she married the wealthy young man. Emmeline's resistance to Delamere's importunities – like Cecilia's resistance to Delvile before her – proves her moral worth. Delamere is in any case too ungovernable for her to respect him, although she feels sorry for him and grateful for his love. This scene is Charlotte Smith's tribute to Frances Burney, the younger author acknowledging the older woman's artistic influence, the "aunt" of her imagination. While Fitz-Edward reads to the peaceful family group, Delamere comes in and starts playing with the boys, making so much noise that "Mrs. Stafford laughingly threatened to send all the riotous boys into the nursery together" (205). Then a letter notifies Delamere that his mother is dying and he rushes off. True to his name. Delamere becomes a mother's son again – first in his riotous play with Mrs. Stafford's sons and then in hastening to his mother's side. Mrs. Stafford plays surrogate mother both to Delamere and to Emmeline. Her mere presence makes it respectable for Emmeline to receive Delamere; the plot takes shape under her auspices.

Burney's fiction may have inspired Charlotte Smith's "aunt" figure, Mrs. Stafford, for all three of Frances Burney's earlier novels feature a motherless heroine and a wise older woman who takes her on as a protégée, advises her, and protects her from extravagant and foolish people. The complication in *Cecilia* (1782) is that the older woman whom the heroine admires and wishes to emulate is wife to one of her three guardians and proud mother to Mortimer Delvile, whose suit she is forced to deny for his mother's sake. Although Cecilia longs to be in this woman's family and prefers her company to that of any of her other friends – for Mrs. Delvile is "sensible, well bred, and high spirited, gifted by nature with superior talents, and polished by education and study with all the elegant embellishments of cultivation" (160) – she must pay for her attachment by resisting Mortimer Delvile's all-too-attractive declarations of love.[40] She buys the friendship of the mother by rejecting the son. The surrogate mother thus promotes Cecilia's independence, self-sufficiency, and moral strength – but in a parodic, inverted way, because she does not promote her happiness.

The "aunt" figure Burney created in *Evelina* (1778), Mrs. Selwyn, while truer to type, is paired with a negative inversion in Evelina's violent grandmother, Mme. Duval. Displaying Burney's deep ambivalence towards older women,[41] these two surrogate mothers or "aunts" split the good from the bad, cultivation from vulgarity, self-possession from violent emotional reactions, active from reactive behavior, and upper-class from lower-class manners and style. The contrast between them shows how class interacts with gender ideologically at this historical moment. Remanded first to the custody of Mme. Duval and then to Mrs. Selwyn – a wealthy and independent woman who takes an interest in her welfare – Evelina plays a similarly passive, obedient role in relation to each of these strong-minded women. Each of them takes on the struggle with dangerous and hostile men in the book, leaving to Evelina the luxury of more purely "feminine" behavior. But whereas Mme. Duval falls victim to the men who wish to torment her and is humiliated repeatedly, Mrs. Selwyn stands up to them verbally and bests them without physical violence. Evelina's guardian, the revered Reverend Villars, disapproves of both women – Mme. Duval for the grossness of her connections and tastes, and Mrs. Selwyn for the "masculinity" of her intelligence and her "unmerciful propensity to satire" (269).[42] Neither is "feminine" enough to be a proper female role model, but whereas Mme. Duval is violent and peremptory, drawing Evelina into embarrassing situations that strain her filial obedience, Mrs. Selwyn really does protect and advise her, guiding her through the ordeal of meeting her father, Sir John Belmont. Mme. Duval's vulgarity and violent emotion make Mrs. Selwyn's intelligent protection doubly welcome as she takes Evelina under her wing in the second part of the book and the plot moves into a new phase. In Mme. Duval's custody, Evelina has to exert herself to maintain her composure and cultivation in the trying company of her crude cousins the Branghtons, her

---

40 Page numbers refer to the Oxford World's Classics edition edited by Peter Sabor and Margaret Anne Doody (Oxford and New York: Oxford University Press, 1988).

41 For an account of Burney's dislike for her stepmother Elizabeth Allen and her vexed relationship with Mrs. Thrale, see Margaret Anne Doody, *Frances Burney: The Life in the Works* (New Brunswick, NJ: Rutgers University Press, 1988), pp. 25–30, 36, 66–70, 159–65, 177, 358, 373–5; and Janice Farrar Thaddeus, *Frances Burney: A Literary Life* (London: Macmillan, and New York: St. Martin's Press, 2000), pp. 15, 31, 32, 96–8, 122, 196, 197.

42 All page numbers are taken from the World's Classics edition of *Evelina: or, the History of a Young Lady's Entrance into the World*, ed. Edward and Lillian Bloom (Oxford and New York: Oxford University Press, 1982).

possessive grandmother, and her déclassé lodgings at a hosier's in High Holborn. "For Heaven's sake," asks Sir Clement Willoughby, "who are these people? and how came you so strangely situated?" (212). In the company of Mrs. Selwyn at Bristol Springs and at Clifton, although her external circumstances conform better to her class, her trials are internalized as she wrestles with her own heart to subdue her inclination for Lord Orville.

Mrs. Selwyn is a splendid example of the character type examined in this chapter – an older woman who is not a mother but who stands in the place of a mother. Her power and intelligence partly revenge the grotesque mistreatment of older women in Burney's novel where older women are tricked, thrown down in the mud, hauled down the road, trussed up and left in a ditch, insulted ("I don't know what the devil a woman lives for after thirty: she is only in other folks way" [275]), and raced in public for a gentlemen's bet. Burney, with her love-hate relation to older women, seems to enjoy describing the torment, dishevelment, and fury of Mme. Duval at the hands of the disguised Captain Mirvan. Even gentle Evelina is tempted to laugh at his brutal masculine prank: "Though this narrative almost compelled me to laugh, yet I was really irritated with the Captain, for carrying his love of tormenting, – *sport*, he calls it, – to such barbarous and unjustifiable extremes" (150).

But Mrs. Selwyn is more than a match for men who scorn strength in women. Perceptive and articulate, deracinated from any family grouping and representing independent female intelligence, she is able to take care of herself and to shield the motherless heroine from the threats posed by the patriarchal world. She mocks the fashionable young men who cluster about Evelina, and protects her from their unwanted attentions. She bests them by outwitting them with her repartee and shaming them with her challenge to see who can recite the longest ode of Horace. When they try to dismiss her by remarking that strong minds are unnatural in a woman, she tells them that if they were to be accommodated with women whose sense was inferior to their own, they would have to choose "from Swift's hospital of idiots" (362).[43] Her unassailable position as a rich and independent woman

---

[43] Swift's will left a bequest to establish the first lunatic asylum in Ireland. Hence the last stanza of his poem "Verses on the Death of Dr. Swift":

> He gave the little Wealth he had,
> To build a House for Fools and Mad;
> And shew'd by one satyric Touch,
> No Nation wanted it so much:
> That Kingdom he hath left his Debtor,
> I wish it soon may have a Better.

permits her to speak satirically to these lazy, privileged men and to act on her own perceptions.

Mrs. Selwyn befriends Evelina in full knowledge of her compromised origins; like many of these "aunt" figures, she even knew Evelina's long-dead mother. It is she who explains Evelina's complicated history to Lord Orville when it becomes necessary; it is to her that Lord Orville appeals for Evelina's hand. It is she who brings Evelina into the presence of her father, where he recognizes "her birthright" in her face. And it is she who, by closely questioning the servant who substituted her own daughter for Evelina, discovers the fraud by which Sir John Belmont has recognized an imposter as his daughter rather than Evelina. She is the *deus ex machina*, the fairy godmother who makes everything come out right in the end: Evelina's real name, her inheritance, and her marriage. And then Mrs. Selwyn disappears from the narrative, for once she has steered Evelina safely into marriage she no longer has a role to play. But she is arguably the most entertaining character in the book, the only one whose knowledge of the world makes her scathing honesty compelling and the only one whom the reader trusts to tell the truth. A spokesperson for the author, unrelated by blood to any of the characters in the novel, her autonomous female voice provides the reader with a place to stand in relation to the narrative. One could even argue that this voice of the observant "aunt," somewhat more mannerly but still sharply satiric, becomes the voice of the disembodied narrator in Jane Austen's fiction.

Burney created another such "aunt" figure in *Camilla*, her novel of 1796. The eponymous heroine suffers throughout from lack of proper guidance. Although she has living parents, the novel separates her from them, and catapults her into many adventures from the midst of which she frequently exclaims aloud on her need for someone to advise and direct her. The most visible sign of her excruciating relationship to Edgar Mandlebert turns on this sense of her vulnerability and her need for direction. Whether or not she will ask for his advice, whether he will give it, whether circumstances will then permit her to follow it, and whether he then will see that she does or does not follow his advice – these issues provide the narrative tension in much of the book. Respite from the necessity of fending for herself comes in the person of a woman of fashion, a widow "not young, but still handsome," named Mrs. Arlbery, who invites Camilla to stay with her, and who intervenes on her behalf in a number of situations. Intelligent and idiosyncratic, Mrs. Arlbery is "full of caprice, coquetry, and singularity; yet, though she abused the gift, she possessed an excellent and uncommon understanding."[44] Her epigrammatic wit ("A fop . . . wears no chains but his own" [75]), her cultivation, and her complete self-confidence are striking in this world of misunderstandings and insecurities. Her self-possession is real as well as figurative: she belongs to no one but herself. Like all such "aunt" figures, like Moll Flanders' "governess" or Austen's pamphlet-reading Lady Russell, her verbal facility is exceptional – "wit she possessed at will; and, with exertions which rendered it uncommonly brilliant, she displayed it" (89). Her unconventionality makes priggish Edgar think her an imprudent connection for Camilla, whose conduct and demeanor he is always judging from a distance. But the reader longs for her intervention and protection because, with the exception of Camilla's absent mother, no one else in the book is as competent to help Camilla. When her brother Lionel drags Camilla into a little river, it is Mrs. Arlbery who dries her off, gives her fresh clothes, and sends Lionel off alone in punishment. She dismisses Camilla's visitors when she tires of them, teases men for their egotism, and helps Camilla to see that Edgar still admires her, which gives her the courage to speak to him in a friendly fashion. She also rallies Edgar for his circumspection and over-zealous caution. Although Mrs. Tyrold, Camilla's mother, appears at the last moment for the denouement, Mrs. Arlbery stands in the place of a mother for most of the novel – a strong, independent woman, a figure of autonomy and competence who thinks for herself and talks confidently to male authority. She exists so that the heroine does not have to depend only on men for advice, for, in this book in particular, men counsel self-suppression and passivity. Mrs. Arlbery, on the contrary, active and witty, offers another model for female behavior – not one, to be sure, that the heroine can imitate while retaining her "femininity," but one that opens up this claustrophobic novel and lets in a little fresh air, and reminds us that women need not be subservient and vulnerable and fearful.

VARIATIONS ON A THEME

If this emblematic independent woman who speaks the author's mind and protects the heroine represents an alternative to conventionally confining femininity, Henry Fielding's *Amelia* (1751) offers an interesting variation on the theme. Although the heroine, Amelia, is married, Booth's frequent absences and lapses leave her unprotected from the machinations

---

[44] Fanny Burney, *Camilla; or A Picture of Youth* (1796), ed. Edward A. Bloom and Lillian D. Bloom (Oxford and New York: Oxford University Press, 1983), p. 194. All subsequent page references are to this edition.

of designing men who are drawn to her beauty. From several such plots she is saved by a Mrs. Bennet (who becomes Mrs. Atkinson in the course of volume II), whose experience and wisdom in the ways of the world guide our heroine through many dangers. Mrs. Bennet's own personal story began with the loss of *her* mother and the installation of a duplicitous stepmother who turned her father against her. Forced from her home, she was taken under the protection of a paternal aunt – a spinster vain of her "understanding" – until she married Mr. Bennet, her first husband. Thus Mrs. Bennet/Atkinson, who saves Amelia from seduction and rape, exemplifies the type not only in her successful protection of Amelia but in her own history as a young girl taken in by an aunt. Having had a classical education, Mrs. Atkinson matches wits in Latin with Dr. Harrison on the subject of women's learning, symbolically establishing her ability to move in a "male" world and hence her capacity to inform the naive heroine of how the world really works. Although both "aunt" and "heroine" are married women in Fielding's novel, their relationship nevertheless conforms to the pattern of the protection and guidance of the motherless heroine by an older woman who helps her to preserve her virtue and her reputation.

In the plots of some novels, this relationship between the heroine and her "aunt," while initially promising, does not run smoothly. Sometimes the older woman is too peremptory, too used to having her way, and pushes the heroine too far. The resulting breach then returns the heroine friendless to the world, doubly alone after her brief respite under the protection of the older woman. The plot of Charlotte Lennox's *Henrietta* (1758) works like this. The eponymous heroine, the orphaned granddaughter of an earl, taken in by the wealthy daughter of a soap-boiler who enjoys having "the daughter of a gentleman subjected to her caprice," is discovered and rescued from this "upstart cit" by Lady Meadows, her great-aunt. Although it is family pride rather than compassion for distress that leads Lady Meadows to adopt Henrietta, she provides respectable connections and a safe haven for our familyless heroine, at least temporarily. Strong-minded, sexually unattached, independent, and wealthy, Lady Meadows is a typical "aunt" for a fictional heroine. She is also a committed Catholic, and when she tries to convert Henrietta to her faith and to force her to marry a foolish, but wealthy, superannuated Catholic baronet, Henrietta runs away. She returns to Lady Meadows' protection at the end of the book, after many scrapes during which she longs for this lost refuge.

The interpolated tale of Mrs. Walter in Elizabeth Griffith's *The History of Lady Barton* (1771) tells of another such orphan, consigned to a maiden aunt when her parents die. Too young and impatient to be able to live patiently "sequestered from the world" with this aunt who substituted "the place of instruction, with austerity,"[45] she foolishly elopes with the dangerous Colonel Walter who subsequently deserts her. After giving birth to a daughter, she is visited by Madame de Fribourg, once a friend of her mother's, who undertakes at once to protect her.

The marchioness was about fifty years old, she was uncommonly tall, had been remarkably handsome, her eyes large, black and piercing; but the whole contour of her countenance was rather hard than pleasing . . . [and] inclined you, at first sight, rather to fear than love her. (1: 153–4)

Like other examples of this older female protector, Madame de Fribourg is very masculine: tall, hard, and fear-inspiring. She directs Mrs. Walter to leave behind her infant with a nurse, for she detests children; but after Mrs. Walter's tearful reply she relents and lets Mrs. Walter bring the "brat" to Paris where her hotel is "large enough to prevent her hearing it squall" (1: 255). Like most other characters of this sort, she is intelligent, competent, vain, and overly fond of admiration; but she is not sexually unattached. An immensely wealthy widow, she has recently married a handsome fortune-hunter of whom she is "extravagantly fond and jealous" (1: 260). Predictably, his admiration for Mrs. Walter spells trouble and the marchioness expels the unhappy woman. Once again Mrs. Walter – this time with an infant daughter – is alone in the world, her helplessness accentuated by the abrupt termination of the older woman's support.

Mrs. Walter tells her story to Lady Barton, who immediately undertakes to protect her by removing her to the lodgings of "honest farmer Wilson," one of her tenants. The adventure occasions a disquisition on the need for Protestant nunneries in England in her next letter to her sister, as asylums for "female orphans, young widows, or still more unhappy objects, forsaken, or ill treated wives, to betake themselves to, in such distresses" (II: 56).[46] Afraid that her tyrannical husband will get wind of the affair, Lady Barton sends Mrs. Walter to her unmarried sister, who observes "I have no person to whom I am accountable for my conduct" (II: 43) and then provides handsomely for Mrs. Walter and her daughter. The whole episode emphasizes the vulnerability of poor women outside of families, especially if they become unprotected mothers themselves, and their necessary reliance

---

[45] Elizabeth Griffith, *The History of Lady Barton*, 3 vols. (London: T. Davies and T. Cadell, 1771), vol. 1, p. 203.

[46] Imagining an institution that combined the advantages of today's battered women's shelters with those envisioned by Mary Astell in her *A Serious Proposal to the Ladies* (1694), Lady Barton's sister, Fanny, comments on this scheme of an "English protestant monastery" (II: 71).

on women of wealth. Mrs. Walter is doubly unprotected because of her infant daughter; motherless herself, she doubled her jeopardy by giving birth to a daughter.[47] In a world of predatory men, she needs an "aunt," a woman with the power and capacities of a man who can nevertheless enter into her feelings and appreciate her plight.

REAL AUNTS

Although I have been writing about "aunts" metaphorically, as displacements for strong maternal figures, the real-life aunt who stepped in to care for a motherless child did exist in eighteenth-century England. Aunts beloved by nieces and nephews for their strength of character or their compassion or empathy are memorialized in letters, diaries, and family memoirs. Earlier in this book I mentioned Catherine Perkins, the indefatigable sister who helped William Hutton become a bookseller in Birmingham, and whose extraordinary capacity and independent mind are described by her niece, the novelist Catherine Hutton (see above, Chapter 4, pp. 167–9). James Edward Austen-Leigh wrote a famous account of his aunt Jane Austen, who delighted her many nieces and nephews with her whimsical stories and who advised and directed the literary efforts of some of them. The religious intellectual Mary Leadbeater extolled the virtues of her maternal aunt Carleton in her *Annals of Ballitore*, disclosing a lively woman fourteen years older than her mother whose deeds of kindness and courage saved several lives and endeared her to many others. A healer and a wise woman, she distilled simples which she administered widely throughout the neighborhood, riding out regularly to check on her patients. Less severe than the author's mother, she indulged her niece's love of reading with books of entertainment and even with a collection of ballads that Leadbeater remembers hiding when her mother unexpectedly appeared.

---

[47] In an essay that was unpublished in his lifetime, David Hume recorded an incident that demonstrates the vulnerability of an eighteenth-century mother, however wealthy and intelligent. A letter from a friend in Paris, dated 1737, tells of a woman of birth and fortune who wanted a child but resolved not to marry after hearing the complaints of her friends about the "Tyranny, Inconstancy, Jealousy or Indifference of their Husbands" (542). Accordingly, she fixed upon a man of "engaging Countenance and modest Deportment" to father her child and commenced a friendship with him. When they grew fond of one other, she explained to him her purpose, and at length she became a mother. Finding that his feeling was too passionate to remain within the bounds of friendship, she broke off with him, giving him a large sum of money, upon which he sued her for the child. Hume does not tell the outcome of the suit, merely that the lawyers were puzzled by this extraordinary case. He gives it as an example "not to depart too far from the receiv'd Maxims of Conduct and Behaviour, by a refin'd Search after Happiness or Perfection." David Hume, *Essays*, ed. Eugene F. Miller (Indianapolis: Liberty Classics, 1985), pp. 542–4.

When her nieces stayed with her, she always allowed them one special day to spend playing to their heart's content. When she died in 1778, Mary Leadbeater was inconsolable, mourning "my dearest parent."[48]

Edward Gibbon wrote lovingly about his aunt, Catherine Porten, who raised him, in his autobiography.[49] Maria Edgeworth fictionalizes this relationship in her novella "The Good Aunt," in her creation of Frances Howard, young Charles' aunt, who runs a boarding house in Westminster as Catherine Porten did, housing students so that her nephew might go to school there. In Edgeworth's tale, the aunt teaches her nephew to love and appreciate knowledge and good books. She passes on to him her womanly virtues: protecting the weak, teaching the poor, telling the truth, and standing up to bullies rather than imitating the swaggering, bullying, aristocrataping deportment of his fellows. As Mitzi Myers analyzes it, the good aunt cultivates in her nephew a feminized sensibility that transforms "the masculinist ethos of the public school," like "the authorial good aunt outside the fiction, Maria Edgeworth herself, whose revisionary school story imagines and epitomizes a larger change in a wider world."[50]

The sheer number of fictional orphaned protagonists assigned to aunts when their parents died probably means that some aunts did take in some orphaned children. But as I have been emphasizing, the caretaking aunt was also a literary convention independent of its historical veracity. The orphaned ingenue of eighteenth-century fiction needed the support and direction of an older woman with experience of the world, even when that ingenue was male, as in Smollett's *Roderick Random* (1748). In that novel, the person who takes him in, nurses him back to health, and thereafter advises him on how to proceed with his life is Mrs. Sagely, an older wise woman. As Random describes her, "The whole behaviour of this venerable person, was so primitive, innocent, sensible, and humane, that I contracted a filial respect for her, and begged her advice with regard to my future conduct,

---

[48] Mary Leadbeater, *The Leadbeater Papers: The Annals of Ballitore, Letters from Edmund Burke, The Correspondence of Mrs. R. Trench and Rev. George Crabbe with Mary Leadbeater* (London: Bell and Daldy, 1862), pp. 58–63, 81, 104. Thanks to Phyllis Mack for calling this example to my attention.

[49] See the epigraph to this chapter. Gibbon's other aunt, his father's sister, Hester Gibbon, retired to a small community in King's Cliffe, Northamptonshire, with William Law, the non-juring scholar and mystic, and Mrs. Elizabeth Hutcheson, a wealthy young widow. Hutcheson was, incidentally, Mary Astell's executrix. They lived frugally so as to be able to dispense charity, and spent their days in prayer, study, and cheerful conversation. Law left the house to Hester Gibbon when he died in 1761. Edward Gibbon referred to her as "the Saint."

[50] Mitzi Myers, "Reading Children and Homeopathic Romanticism: Paradigm Lost, Revisionary Gleam, or 'Plus Ça Change Plus C'est la Même Chose'?" in James Holt McGavran (ed.), *Literature and the Child: Romantic Continuations, Postmodern Contestations* (Iowa City: University of Iowa Press, 1999), p. 69.

as soon as I was in a condition to act for myself" (215).[51] Mrs. Sagely is easy and engaging if unconventional. Learned in herbs and simples, she collects, distills, and sells them like a kind of witch-cum-village-apothecary, much as did Mary Leadbeater's aunt in 1766. Deprived of a mother in the first part of his life, Roderick Random gets a second chance at being mothered by this older, worldly-wise Mrs. Sagely, who acts independently of any husband, father, or son. Mrs. Sagely's advice saves Random from several foolhardy actions and helps him to keep in view the lovely Narcissa, whom he eventually claims as his own. He visits Mrs. Sagely from time to time in the course of his adventures and scrapes, and always finds a heartfelt welcome and psychological comfort in her little cottage, as well as sage advice.

THE PERVASIVENESS OF "AUNTS"

To name all the novels in the second half of the eighteenth century with "aunt" figures in them would be almost impossible, and to summarize their plots repetitive and unnecessary. To give some sense of the pervasiveness of the trope, however, let me mention a few of the better-known novels that prominently feature an older woman who stands in the place of a mother – but like a mother cut loose from submissive duty to male relatives, free to direct her charge with the most practical advice even if that advice is unconventional. Harriet Byron, the heroine of Samuel Richardson's *The History of Sir Charles Grandison* (1753–4), feels and thinks and acts with a paternal aunt and a grandmother looking over her shoulder. They comprehend her growing love for the admirable Sir Charles, love that began in gratitude for having saved her from Sir Hargrave Pollexfen, and commiserate with her hopelessness. They sympathize with her desire, under the circumstances, to extricate herself from considering Lady D.'s proposals for her son. Her grandmother, Mrs. Shirley, advises her to cultivate the friendship of Sir Charles' sisters in order to learn the history of their family and the secret of Sir Charles' reserve. When she replies, grateful for their understanding and delicacy – and their tact in replying to Lady D.'s proposals – she signs herself "Harriet Byron-Shirley-Selby" to signal her daughterly relation to them both.[52]

---

[51] Page numbers are from the World's Classics edition edited by Paul-Gabriel Boucé (Oxford and New York: Oxford University Press, 1981).

[52] Vol. ii, letters viii–x, pp. 301–9. Page numbers come from the World's Classics edition edited by Jocelyn Harris (Oxford and New York: Oxford University Press, 1986); all seven volumes of the first edition are marked in the pagination of this single volume.

The heroine of Charlotte Lennox's first novel, *The Life of Harriot Stuart* (1751), leaves her mother in the wilds of America and journeys to England, under the protection first of one and then another "aunt" figure. The first is Mrs. Blandon, a decayed gentlewoman who accompanies our heroine to England where she is to live with her maternal aunt, Lady L. When they arrive, however, they learn that the unfortunate Lady L. has been driven mad by grief over losing her only son. After some adventures our heroine finds herself under the protective wing of Mrs. Dormer, who has her own sad story to tell, but in the end effects the éclaircissement with the hero, Dumont, that leads to marriage.

All of the women who dwell in Sarah Scott's *Millenium Hall* (1762) appear to have lost their mothers at birth; motherlessness was their initiating life experience. Each was raised by a father who subsequently reneged on his responsibility by dying or by being turned against his daughter by a second wife, or both. After these paternal failures, "aunts" supplied the parental need. Miss Mancel, saved from the lascivious designs of her adoptive father, Mr. Hintman, by his convenient death from apoplexy (a symptom of uncontrolled desire), was taken in by several older women. First the much appreciated companion of Lady Lampton (whom she was forced to leave when Lady Lampton's grandson fell in love with her), she then served Mrs. Thoresby, a wealthy widow, only to discover that Mrs. Thoresby was, by extraordinary coincidence, her real mother. Lady Mary Jones, whose father died when she was ten, was adopted by her aunt Lady Sheerness, a wealthy widow with an uncommon vivacity and a penchant for gaming. When Lady Sheerness died, Lady Mary Jones was taken in by another female relative, Lady Brumpton, a wealthy widow vain of her wit and understanding, with a considerable library, who "aimed at making her house a little academy." Lady Brumpton welcomed writers and wits to her house but seemed unable to distinguish between affectation and true learning. Lady Mary nevertheless made the best of her position until Lady Brumpton died, at which time she again had "the melancholy office of closing the eyes of a benefactress and relation whom she sincerely loved" (194).[53] Another tenant of Millenium Hall, Mrs. Trentham, whose father died when she was eight, was raised by her paternal grandmother. Still another, Mrs. Selvyn, educated by her philosophically minded father, was invited when he died by Lady Emilia Reynolds, "a single lady of very large fortune" who lived next door, to retire with her to the country. There they

[53] Page numbers come from the Broadview edition edited by Gary Kelly, *A Description of Millenium Hall* (Peterborough, ON: Broadview Press, 1995).

lived together with "great rational enjoyment" (210), reading, walking, and talking. When Lady Emilia died, she confessed to her beloved Miss Selvyn that she was actually her real mother. Thus two of the women in Millenium Hall are taken in by older women who turn out to be their biological mothers, while several others are taken in by female relatives who protect them and bequeath them fortunes when they die. This adoptive relation to an older, independent, single woman appears to be the essential training – an apprenticeship of sorts – for members of the rational, benevolent, woman-centered community of Millenium Hall.

Betsy Thoughtless, the eponymous heroine of Eliza Haywood's novel (1751), when chastened as the unhappy Mrs. Munden, both seeks and follows the advice of the admirable Lady Loveit. Maria Villiers finds relief and happiness in Frances Brooke's *The Excursion* (1777) under the protection of Lady Sophia Herbert, an elegant and beautiful woman who has devoted her widowhood to educating her grandson, the "open, brave, generous, sincere, well-bred" Col. Herbert (140).[54] Frances Brooke created another aunt to be the presiding narrator of her journal *The Old Maid*, an "amusing, slightly eccentric . . . spinster nearing fifty who has reared her dead sister's child and who is a keen observer of society, manners, and the state of the nation."[55] Sensible, spritely Miss Helen-Maria Stanley in Mrs. Keir's *The History of Miss Greville* (1787), signs herself "your old but not ill-natured aunt," and advises her niece and nephew with humor and sympathy: "As good advice is a diet I never greatly relished myself, even when cooked in the most skillful manner, it goes against my conscience to cram it so unmercifully down poor Harry's throat."[56] Lady Frances Finlay, the utopian social inventor and philanthropist in Lady Mary Walker Hamilton's *Munster Village* (1779), appointed guardian to her niece and nephew when their unfortunate parents die, takes her duties so seriously that she postpones marrying the man she loves until her charges are old enough to be independent of her. Several characters in *The Cry* (1754), by Sarah Fielding and Jane Collier, live with their aunts: Nicanor sends his daughter to his wife's sister when his wife dies (I: 211); and Maria lives with her chiding spinster aunt Brunetta (III: 64).[57] In the lugubrious final volume of *David Simple* (1744), the hero approaches

---

[54] Page numbers come from the edition edited by Paula R. Backscheider and Hope D. Cotton (Lexington: University of Kentucky Press, 1997).

[55] *The Old Maid*, by Mary Singleton [i.e. Frances Brooke], 37 vols. (London: A. Millar, 1755–6). This quotation is taken from the introductory pages bound with the Harvard Library copy of this periodical, p. xiv.

[56] Susanna Harvey Keir, *The History of Miss Greville*, 3 vols. (London: T. Cadell, 1787), vol. III, p. 147.

[57] Sarah Fielding and Jane Collier, *The Cry: A New Dramatic Fable*, 3 vols. (London: J. and R. Dodsley, 1754).

death with the "inexpressible Satisfaction" of knowing that his innocent daughter will be cared for by the faithful Cynthia, another "aunt" figure.[58] Motherless Mathilda Leeson in *The Woodland Cottage* (1796), although exceptionally beautiful and intelligent, depends on the company and advice of Mrs. Mansel, the sensible wife of an absent sea captain. With all "the soft delicacy of her own sex" as well as "the firmness of mind and cool resolution of the other,"[59] Mrs. Mansel takes charge when their carriage breaks down in the middle of the night, and displays admirable *sang-froid* in a ruined castle when they hear wild animals roar, stumble on a bloody dagger, and see some children hanging from a rafter. An androgenous character with the sympathy of a woman and the physical courage of a man, this powerful older woman has the exaggerated agency that comes from wealth and exceptional talents.

THE MEANING OF FICTIONAL AUNTS

The preoccupation in these novels with an older woman who is not the biological mother, but whose love and support is critical to the success of the protagonist, is not easy to interpret. To consider the literal meaning first, the demographic data do not indicate that there was a serious mother shortage in eighteenth-century England, although at least 10 percent of fertile, married (sexually active) women died in childbirth.[60] More symbolically, the trope of a powerful older woman who stands in the place of a mother could be read as a re-imagining of the maternal role at this historical juncture, an alternative to male-dominated social relations. She might stand for the return of what was being repressed in the evolving English sex-gender system – a boiling up of female strength and independence that compensated for the increasing psychological restriction of adult women's lives in the new dispensation emphasizing self-sacrificing maternal love.[61]

---

58 Sarah Fielding, *The Adventures of David Simple*, ed. Malcolm Kelsall (Oxford: Oxford University Press, 1987), p. 432.

59 Anon., *The Woodland Cottage*, 2 vols. (London: Hookham and Carpenter, 1796), vol. I, p. 133.

60 This figure comes from my statistical analysis of the Bills of Mortality in London 1657–1758. See "The Veil of Chastity: Mary Astell's Feminism," *Studies in Eighteenth-Century Culture* 9 (1979), 25–43. For an excellent and thorough account of the dangers of childbearing in relation to Richardson's fiction, see Lois A. Chaber, "'This Affecting Subject': An 'Interested' Reading of Childbearing in Two Novels by Samuel Richardson," *Eighteenth-Century Fiction* 8, 2 (January 1996), 193–250.

61 Amanda Vickery and Margaret Hunt, among others, have demonstrated that a sizeable proportion of women in the late eighteenth century participated in business or politics and escaped the conventionally prescribed social roles for women. "Escape" is the operative word, however, for the public discourse – novels, conduct books, treatises – increasingly *represented* women in restrictive ways. This led, in the nineteenth and twentieth centuries, to the paradox outlined by Carolyn Heilbrun

These "aunts" testify to what was being lost in this cultural shift: power, autonomy, and voice. The ubiquity of this character in the fiction of the second half of the eighteenth century seems to represent some collective need in the culture to retain an image of female strength and competence just when the social construction of femininity was undergoing a change in the opposite direction. Thus, this powerful "aunt" may represent the irreducible residue of female personhood from the evolving social definition of women as soft, pliant, docile, weak, sweet, and hyperemotional.

Imagining such an older woman as a widow, spinster, or wife of an absent husband – outside of a conventional family – kept the fantasy contained and safe, for it meant that her autonomy did not imply insubordination to paternal jurisdiction. Her independence did not constitute a threat to the male-dominated social hierarchy. Yet at the same time, her learning and competence protected the heroine and were usually welcome in the narrative, if sometimes cast as slightly ridiculous. Rather than competing with male authority this "aunt" figure imitated male authority; but she did so outside of the structures of society.[62]

Psychologically, the fact that the heroine must find for herself an older woman to guide her because she has no mother of her own, must negotiate a new intergenerational relationship because the given one has failed, may be a sign of the difficulty, for women, of developing a sense of self without first separating from the mother. This mother who is also a stranger may thus enable the heroine's independent moral existence. All the motherlessness in these novels – and all the play with substitutions and surrogates – may derive from this new necessity in an age of intensifying individualism. The "aunt," being simultaneously both mother and other, solves both the problem of separation and that of identification for the female protagonist. Having already separated from a perfect paragon of a mother, the heroine is

in *Reinventing Womanhood* (New York: Norton, 1979): that women authors – such as Charlotte Brontë, Willa Cather, Mary Renault, and even Simone de Beauvoir – did not grant their fictional female characters as much autonomy as they themselves achieved in their own lives.

[62] In contrast to this respectable older-woman figure, there is also a type of independent younger women who turns up in novels of the period, whose autonomy renders her femininity more equivocal. Miss Stanhope in Arthur Young's *The History of Sir Charles Beaufort* (1767), Harriot Freke in Maria Edgeworth's *Belinda* (1801), and Miss Newenden in Charlotte Smith's *Ethelinde* (1790), all athletic amazons interested in guns and horses, are too manly to be heroines. Amelia Rattle in Hannah More's *Coelebs in Search of a Wife* (1808), Maria Fluart in Robert Bage's *Hermsprong* (1796), and Elinor Joddrel in Burney's *The Wanderer* (1814) are also too strong-minded and intrepid to be treated seriously as heroines.

It is worth noting that this autonomous "aunt," because she is not particularly interested in sex or marriage, circumvents the eighteenth-century satire directed at older women with sexual interests. Lady Wishfort in Congreve's *Way of the World*, Lady Booby or even Mrs. Slipslop in Fielding's *Joseph Andrews*, and Tabitha Bramble in Smollett's *Humphry Clinker* are examples of this latter type.

free to identify with this powerful and independent "aunt" – up to a point. That point, of course, is marriage, when the evolved female self must be subordinated to the new husband and the new conjugal unit.

Literarily, as I have said, the figure of the "aunt" enables the heroine to retain her innocence and delicacy without diminishing her moral independence by having to obey a parental authority. Because Lady Russell is not Anne Elliot's actual mother, the heroine's deference to this older woman is voluntary. It shows at once her judgment in tacitly choosing such a paragon as a guide and her piety in obeying her. The fact that Lady Russell is *not* Anne's mother gives the heroine some degrees of freedom, an extra measure of automony, which allows the reader to see her conscientiousness as her own. Jane Austen uses Lady Russell both ways in *Persuasion*: Anne tells Captain Wentworth that her obedience in giving him up at nineteen was right because "if I had done otherwise, I should have suffered more in continuing the engagement than I did even in giving it up, because I should have suffered in my conscience." But at the same time, she makes it clear that if Lady Russell were to give the same advice to her now, she would follow her own heart and not Lady Russell's counsel.[63]

Not all female intergenerational relationships in these novels are positive, of course. The heroine's conflict with a stepmother – a standard device in fairy tales as well – also registers the disturbance in female intergenerational relations without necessarily resolving it positively. Many a hero and heroine are forced prematurely from their home because their father and protector has married blindly a second time "for love," which is to say without consideration for his children. The villainous stepmother draws in the unsuspecting father with her feminine wiles and turns him against his beloved daughter or son. Ironically, the new emphasis on love-in-marriage disguises the new wife's covetousness and offers an ideological rationale to the remarrying widower for dismissing obligations to his kin. Responsibility for children of earlier marriages might once have been a reason for remarrying; but the new emphasis on conjugal love jeopardized the well-being of children from earlier marriages.

The evil stepmother, however, like the good "aunt," is an example of women's power. Often portrayed in contrast to a true mother's tenderness, she shows what a mother ought *not* to be. Examples of this character abound in fiction and many have already been mentioned – Mrs. Morgan's evil stepmother in *Millenium Hall*, Mrs. Evans' stepmother in her interpolated tale in *The History of Betty Barnes*, or Camilla and Valentine's evil stepmother

---

[63] Jane Austen, *Persuasion*, ed. D. W. Harding, Chapter 23, pp. 246–8.

in Sarah Fielding's *The Adventures of David Simple*. A letter headed "On the Cruel Behaviour of some Step-Mothers" from Eliza Haywood's *The Female Spectator* describes the combination of being unmothered and displaced.

> But how shocking is it for a young Creature, accustomed to Tenderness, and arrived at sufficient Years to know the Value of that Tenderness, to be, all at once, obliged to submit to the insolent and morose Behaviour of a Person, who was an entire Stranger in the Family till Marriage set her at the Head of it![64]

As a plot device, the evil stepmother effectively separates the heroine from her family. The stepmother's cruelty to the heroine is another version of the maternal absence that forces individuation for women in a patriarchally constructed world. Here the figure of the mother is split between the idealized dead mother and the demonized stepmother – a split that ensures that neither mother can be integrated into the heroine's life. Functionally, this stepmother arrangement is the inverse of the plot in which the good "aunt" adopts, guides, and directs the heroine. Both plots can be seen as corrective fantasies to the problem of maternal powerlessness because both include powerful mother figures even though one is evil and one is good. Both fictional formulas begin with the essential ground of interrupted mother-daughter relations, but they work through that lack differently. The evil stepmother plot usually comes full circle when the heroine herself becomes a mother and heals the originating intergenerational breach. The "good aunt" plot, on the other hand, deals with the problem of maternal lack by providing a substitute mother figure who is an honorary male and who helps the heroine to negotiate the world.

Another solution to the mother-seeking of the heroine, and the most sentimentally satisfying, is the plot in which the older woman who loves and supports the heroine turns out to be the mother of the hero – and hence destined to be her mother-in-law. Usually the connection between the heroine and this older woman evolves before the handsome son makes his appearance, but not always. In *The History of Betty Barnes* (1753), the Mrs. Evans who guides and teaches the little orphan girl turns out to be the mother of Mr. Marshall whom she has just married. They explain to the dumbfounded Mr. Marshall that they already know each other. Betty says "I knew no misery till I lost her, and I dread none, if I am blest in her

[64] Eliza Haywood, *The Female Spectator*, 3 vols. (London, 1744–6), vol. III, pp. 190–202. Although the evil stepmother as seen from the point of view of the children of the first marriage is the most prevalent type depicted in the fiction of the period, a more positive portrait of a long-suffering stepmother appears in the *Lady's Magazine*, vols. 16 and 17, in a novella called "The Mother-in-Law," written from the point of view of a saintly stepmother who manages her new husband's difficult children by an earlier marriage with tact and generosity.

protection." Mrs. Evans avers that she is a "happy mother, made doubly so by this instant . . . for next to my dearest Billy, you always lay nearest my heart" (II: 250). That the relation between the two women preceded the love relation by so many years blesses the match anew and confers upon the new conjugal union a longer domestic history. In Frances Burney's *Cecilia* (1788), the orphaned heroine admires Mrs. Delvile and loves her son. From very early in this long book, Cecilia longs to make her home with the Delviles, to settle in Mrs. Delvile's family, to finally come to rest as her daughter as well as Mortimer's wife.

Charlotte Smith's *Ethelinde* (1790) and Susan Ferrier's *Marriage* (1818) also invent prior friendships between the heroine and an admirable widow whose son turns out to be the love interest. In *Ethelinde*, the eponymous heroine feels an "irresistible attraction" for Mrs. Montgomery, whose superior understanding, wide reading, and feeling heart make her the most suitable companion in the neighborhood for Ethelinde.[65] Her handsome son is hardly less suitable, and it turns out by the end of the first volume that their fathers had been close friends. After many separations and misunderstandings, Ethelinde is united to the noble Montgomery and his long-suffering mother in the fifth volume, and they all retire to live happily ever after in the pastoral heartland, Grasmere. In Ferrier's *Marriage*, Mary Douglas finds Mrs. Lennox a welcome relief from her own heartless family. Mrs. Lennox welcomes Mary "with a kindness and simplicity of manner, that reminded Mary of the home she had left, and the maternal tenderness of her beloved aunt."[66] She meets the attractive Colonel Lennox when he visits his mother and, despite the inevitable complications, they plight their troth at Mrs. Lennox's deathbed.

What must have made this plot so appealing to eighteenth-century readers is the symbolic conflation in the sentimental denouement of the consanguineal family and the conjugal family. In this sentimental plot, the respected widow is a figure of motherhood for both members of the new conjugal couple. Both in her bodily experience of childbearing and in her loving allegiance, she combines the consanguineal bond of a biological parent with the affinal obligation of a mother-in-law; she is an affinal relative with the psychological and emotional meaning of a consanguineal relative.

---

[65] Charlotte Smith, *Ethelinde, or The Recluse of the Lake*, 2nd edn., 5 vols. (London: T. Cadell, 1790), quote vol. 1, p. 124.

[66] This novel was written in 1810 although not published until 1818. Mary Douglas, the chief protagonist, rejected by her cold-hearted, spoiled mother when an infant, was raised in Scotland by her intelligent and lovely aunt, Alicia Douglas. She met Mrs. Lennox and her son when she left this home to visit her fashionable mother and sister in England. Susan Ferrier, *Marriage*, ed. and with an Introduction by Herbert Foltinek (Oxford and New York: Oxford University Press, 1986), p. 265.

Thus the new adoptive family of the heroine takes on the emotional tone of her family of origin. As we will see in the final chapter, this fictional solution to the painful shifts in kinship loyalties was a favorite wish-fulfillment fantasy in the fiction of the day. The best ending was one in which the chosen, conjugal family turned out to be the same as the consanguineal family of obligation, after all. Thus the protagonist does not have to choose between these two kinds of relations but can have both, in the best of all fictional worlds.

9

Family feeling

The imprisoning houses of Mr B and Lovelace are metamorphosed into a real medieval castle; tyrannical parents have become feudal princes; family secrets have become real skeletons in the cupboard; arguments in letters materialize into actual duels; contemporary England and the uncivilized barbarities of the Augustan metropolis have become the threatening precincts and tenebral cavities of a late medieval Italian fortress; a Providential universe has been translated into a world of dynastic feuding and historical determination.

> Clive Probyn, *English Fiction of the Eighteenth Century 1700–1789*, p. 171.

If the appearance of Gothic suggests anything, it is some historical factor in this literary development, something which made the family a cultural pressure point.

> Anne Williams, *Art of Darkness: A Poetics of Gothic*, pp. 90–1.

The family, in its contemporary form, must not be understood as a social, economic, and political structure of alliance that excludes or at least restrains sexuality . . . On the contrary, its role is to anchor sexuality and provide it with permanent support . . . [S]ince the eighteenth century the family has become the obligatory locus of affects, feelings, love; that sexuality has its privileged point of development in the family; that for this reason sexuality is "incestuous" from the start.

> Michel Foucault, *The History of Sexuality*, vol. 1, pp. 108–9.

The argument of this book has been that the movement from a consanguineal to a conjugal and affinal basis for kinship in eighteenth-century England can be deduced by examining certain literary formulas and the complex and changing relationships that stand behind them: the excruciating, tearful reunion of a long-separated father and daughter; a brother's care for his sister; parents' pressure on their children to marry for economic reasons rather than for love; missing mothers and the substitution of what I have been calling "aunts." These literary formulas, while not representing

historical reality transparently, foreground vexed issues in familial relationships that were affected by the changing social and economic conditions of
eighteenth-century England.

In this chapter I want to explore some of the ways in which consanguinity itself – the blood relation – was represented in fiction. In the last
chapter I noted that the most satisfying resolution to those novels in which
unrelated "aunts" played an important role was the ending that brought
those "aunts" into an affinal (i.e. mother-in-law) or even rediscovered consanguineal relation to the heroine. Restructuring the social world so that
an unrelated young woman and her beloved older mentor became close
relatives brought together all the threads of the plot in a conclusion that
promised stability and happiness. Bringing the main characters to rest in the
inalterable and "natural" security of blood bonds appealed to eighteenth-
century novel readers. Whether it involved "aunts" or not, the "happily
ever after" of eighteenth-century popular fiction frequently included a triumphal reunion with consanguineal relatives; the loyalty of blood relations
was the conventional permanent antidote to isolation, physical and/or mental suffering and poverty. This preference in fiction, I have been arguing,
reflects the actual erosion of consanguineal relationships by the forces of
modernity and thus represents nostalgia for what was being lost. In constructing fictions in which difficulties and dislocations were resolved in
the arms of one's brother or sister, mother or father, eighteenth-century
writers were projecting a return to a kinship system in which the family
was the bulwark against the insecurities of life, before opportunities for
class mobility and individual advancement altered the terms of success and
security.

As has been made clear in every chapter, changes in kinship were not
symmetrical with respect to gender because the laws governing marriage
and inheritance and the evolving economic structure of households in the
market economy treated men and women differently. The emphasis on the
accumulation of wealth and property in a family to be passed on dynasti-
cally in the male line constructed new consequences for gender difference.[1]
A stricter marriage law (what Catherine Talbot called the "anti-marriage

---

[1] Richard Grassby states that, although partible inheritance had been followed in England in earlier
centuries, legal opposition to it "gathered momentum during the seventeenth century" (344). Partible
inheritance survived in a few counties, but primogeniture became the norm "because it was thought
to safeguard the integrity of landed estates." Nevertheless, the vestiges of the earlier system were visible
in "ecclesiastical law, which had jurisdiction over personalty, [which] favored partible inheritance, as
did the customary law of the towns." Richard Grassby, *Kinship and Capitalism: Marriage, Family,
and Business in the English-Speaking World, 1580–1740* (Cambridge: Cambridge University Press, and
Washington, D.C.: Woodrow Wilson Center Press, 2001), pp. 342–3.

bill"[2]) and stricter property laws had different implications for women than for men insofar as women's property became their husbands' upon marriage and, after 1753, men could no longer be held accountable for the children they fathered without a legally binding marriage. The commodification of women's sexuality intensified as reproduction was increasingly assimilated to production and attitudes towards children changed in the prevailing secular climate. The dispossession of laboring-class families from the land, together with a growing reliance on the wage economy, trimmed back familial responsibility to the conjugal unit in families of this class. The difference in men's and women's earning power changed their balance of power within the working household economy.

Certain cultural values such as "sensibility" and "individualism," too, played out differently in men's and women's lives, because of existing and evolving ideological constructs about gender.[3] Although intense "sensibility" was in vogue for both men and women in the 1740s, 50s, 60s, and 70s, long after the "high period" of sensibility had passed women were still expected to feel deeply about interpersonal relationships. On the other hand, as we saw in Chapters 3 and 4, reciprocity among siblings, and in particular the responsibility brothers felt for their sisters, wilted in the heat of individualism.

THE INCESTUOUS FAMILY

The sexualizing of the family unit itself was another sign and symptom of the new emphasis on a conjugal basis for kinship in eighteenth-century England – and one of the most significant. The older sense of belonging to a network of kin, friends, neighbors, and other close connections where everyone shared responsibility for members' welfare was giving way to a belief in every man's sovereign right to personal satisfaction, including perhaps sexual satisfaction. Families were coming to be seen as the social units that guaranteed an individual's happiness rather than the other way around. No one expected the important members of a family to subordinate their own desires to the needs of the whole; rather, it was expected that the family would serve its important members. In combination with the increased sexualization of the family unit itself – a point to which I will

[2] *A Series of Letters between Mrs. Elizabeth Carter and Miss Catherine Talbot from the Year 1741 to 1770*, ed. Rev. Montagu Pennington, 4 vols. (London: Rivington, 1809), vol. II, p. 123. Letter dated June 5, 1753.

[3] Claudia L. Johnson's *Equivocal Beings: Politics, Gender, and Sentimentality in the 1790s*, (Chicago: University of Chicago Press, 1995) is a brilliant and subtle working out of this point.

return – this attitude may have eventuated in a rise in the actual incidence of incest during this period.

In literature, the difference in the ways in which incest is progressively treated in Defoe's *Moll Flanders* (1722), Burney's *Evelina* (1778), and her later *The Wanderer* (1814) betokens a changed attitude in the culture towards the phenomenon as time went on. Moll, after all, continues to live with her brother as his wife for three years after she becomes aware of their relationship – although she bears him no more children. In *Evelina*, incest is merely a cliché, a plot device, a problem lending drama to the relationship between secondary characters Macartney and Polly Green. Burney handles it with an element of authorial self-mockery, as Glenda Hudson notes, rather than with authentic emotional horror.[4] But by the time Burney wrote *The Wanderer*, begun in the closing years of the century and composed over the next fourteen years, the potential for incest in Lord Melbury's pursuit of Juliet is closer to home and treated with much more serious alarm. Melbury's attentions to the heroine terrify her; when he mentions love, she turns "pale and cold: horrour thrilled through her veins, and almost made her heart cease to beat." She turns from him, knowing him to be her half brother, with "soul-felt repugnance."[5] Incest is not introduced casually here, but is felt as a real threat. Part and parcel of the growing emphasis on conjugality, sensibility, individuality, and the commodification of women's sexuality, incest is the darker side to seeing the family as the "obligatory locus of affects, feelings, love" to quote the epigraph from Foucault for this chapter.[6] The ideology of love-in-marriage was sexualizing family relationships; the seeds of sexuality were planted in the privacy of family life and developed in the hothouse atmosphere of the home.

In concert with this intensification of sexual feeling in conjugal families, the older countervailing sense of duty to support or protect blood relatives was being undermined by the money economy and social mobility. As I have stressed in earlier chapters, fathers' responsibility for their daughters and brothers' responsibility for their sisters waned as consanguineal bonds came to matter less in society at large. John Verney, for example, felt less obligation to support his unmarried female relatives than his father had

---

[4] Glenda Hudson, *Sibling Love & Incest in Jane Austen's Fiction* (New York: St. Martin's Press, 1992), p. 19. Sarah Fielding's *David Simple* (1744) also uses incest as a plot device.

[5] Frances Burney, *The Wanderer; or, Female Difficulties* (1814), ed. Margaret Anne Doody, Robert L. Mack, and Peter Sabor (Oxford and New York: Oxford University Press, 1991), pp. 139–40: all subsequent page references are to this edition. Glenda Hudson makes this point as well.

[6] Michel Foucault, *The History of Sexuality*, trans. Robert Hurley (New York: Random House, 1978), vol. 1, p. 108.

before him. Sir Ralph had given his sisters gifts of money when times were good – although he never paid off their portions. But his son John would not even help his aunt Gardiner's daughters bury their mother or pay their grocer's bills when they were in danger of starving. As Susan Whyman puts it, "The circle within which he [John] felt responsible for favours tightened to include only his nuclear family and those relatives who were not a financial burden . . . John was forsaking the traditional duties of kinship."[7] As the century progressed and fathers and brothers came to feel less and less honorbound by consanguineal bonds, sisters and daughters were increasingly seen as their sexual property rather than as co-carriers of the family blood, female avatars of themselves, and by extension female embodiments of their own family honor. Men began to see their female relatives as sexual prey rather than co-inheritors of family traditions.[8]

In our own day it is well known that stepfathers sexually abuse their stepdaughters far more frequently than do biological fathers, which suggests that the blood tie still counts for something. It restrains at least the acting out of – if not the desire itself for – incestuous contact. The blood tie functioned in a similar way, I think, in England before the eighteenth century.[9] There

---

[7] Susan E. Whyman, *Sociability and Power in Late-Stuart England: The Cultural World of the Verneys 1660–1720* (Oxford and New York: Oxford University Press, 1999), p. 127.

[8] There is an argument currently put forward in as yet largely unpublished papers by David Sabean and Leonore Davidoff that brothers and sisters in the later eighteenth century were drawing closer and conducting their relationships with an incestuous sentimentality. That argument complements my point here: that the responsibility that brothers felt for their sisters and that fathers felt for their daughters was attenuated in this period and that with the erosion of kin bonds came a weakening of the incest taboo. Brothers and fathers came to see their female relatives less as kin with a moral claim to their protection and more as intimate "others" with whom sexual relations were thinkable. David Sabean puts it this way in an article about the relationship between Fanny and Felix Mendelssohn-Bartholdy: "During that period family relations were being reconfigured to emphasize emotional training and self-development. But at the same time the family became the site for practice in fulfilling sharply differentiated gender role expectations. The stress on the feeling was articulated strongly within a sometimes steamy but always eroticized environment" (715). David Sabean, "Fanny and Felix Mendelssohn-Bartholdy and the Question of Incest," *Musical Quarterly* 77, 4 (Winter 1993), 709–17.

[9] Literature from earlier periods would seem to corroborate this hunch. Even in the following passage from *The Revenger's Tragedy* (1606–7), cynical about the near-universality of incest, transgressors stop at the barrier of an actual blood bond. "Any kin now, next to the rim o' th' sister," he says, "is man's meat"; but not sisters and not daughters.

> Some father dreads not (gone to bed in wine)
> To slide from the mother, and cling to the daughter-in-law;
> Some uncles are adulterous with their nieces,
> Brothers with brothers' wives. O hour of incest!
> Any kin now, next to the rim o' th' sister,
> Is man's meat in these days; and in the morning,
> When they are up and dressed and their mask on,
> Who can perceive this, save that eternal eye
> That sees through flesh and all? (1. 3. 59–67)

are even sequences in eighteenth-century novels that remind one that the blood tie could function as a restraint on sexual violence. When vicious Sir Thomas Sindall in Henry Mackenzie's *The Man of the World* (1773) learns that Lucy is his daughter, the offspring of Harriet Annesley whom he has drugged and raped, he stops trying to seduce her and becomes her protector. When Schedoni, in Radcliffe's *The Italian* (1797), sees what he thinks is his own youthful portrait on a miniature worn around the neck of the young woman he is about to stab, he repents instantly and presses her to his bosom, wetting her face with his tears in a much-softened physical assault.

However, as I have been arguing throughout this book, the power of the blood tie began to ebb in the second half of the eighteenth century, its meaning attenuated by transformations in the meaning of family. As daughters were redefined as strangers-in-the-house and commodified as "chickens for other men's tables," fathers took less responsibility for them and mothers began to feel competitive with them. Perhaps that is one meaning of the plots in which stepmothers and even occasionally biological mothers, envious of the heroine's beauty, intelligence, or learning, denigrate or neglect her until she is forced to leave home.[10] Brothers identified increasingly with their fathers rather than their sisters as evolving gender definitions dismantled sibling unity. Thus, both fathers and brothers began to see their female relatives less as extensions of themselves or members of their own clan, and more as possessions in their power and hence possible sexual objects, close at hand and available.

Foucault was referring to this change – albeit from a very different angle – when he stated that in Europe in the eighteenth century the "deployment of alliance" gave way to the "deployment of sexuality" in kin arrangements. Sexuality, he elaborates, had not been foundational in family relationships until the later seventeenth century. Before then, disruptive sexuality belonged to extramarital relationships found outside the kin group. According to Foucault, sexuality first "migrated" to the margins of familial institutions in the seventeenth century – in education, for example – and gradually, by the eighteenth century, came to be central to the family itself.[11] Alliance, in his terminology, was a "system of marriage, of fixation and development

---

The sinners in this passage, with the exception of uncles and nieces, are not related by blood but by marriage. It is not known who wrote this play – possibly Cyril Tourneur or Thomas Middleton. See Brian Gibbons, (ed.), *The Revenger's Tragedy* (New York: Hill and Wang, 1967), p. 20. Thanks to Curtis Perry for this reference.

[10] See, for example, *Memoirs of Mrs. Williams*, contained in *Letters between an English Lady and Her Friend at Paris*, 2 vols. (London: Becket and Dehondt, 1770), the story of Mrs. Mancel in *Millenium Hall*, and the Miss Minifies' *The Histories of Lady Frances S— and Lady Caroline S—* (London: Dodsley, 1763).

[11] Michel Foucault, *The History of Sexuality*, vol. 1, pp. 103–59. Foucault sees this "substitution of sex for blood" – both of which he sees as apparatuses of control – as responsible for many of the

of kinship ties, of transmission of names and possessions" based on status, birth, and blood. "Alliance" maintained the stability of the social body; it was a kinship system based on the practicalities of reproducing society. "Sexuality" on the other hand, although Foucault claims that it grew up on the "ground" of alliance, was located not in laws and hierarchies but rather in the perceptions and sensations of individual bodies. As a system of power, it developed to regulate legitimate and illegitimate sexual congress, to infuse the female body with intense sexual magnetism, and to regulate children's "precocious" sexuality. "Sexuality," by this definition, evolved along with the psychological structures of the modern family.

To this day we believe that sexed individuals are produced in the family and that intrafamilial relations play a central role in constructing sexuality. All of Freud's formulations are based on this conjunction of "sexuality" and "family." The centrality of that intergenerational tension between men that Freud named the Oedipal struggle, its power to shape male desire and construct personality, the way it focuses sexual energy in the family, is another such formulation. Nor is it irrelevant to note that when the Oedipal struggle dominates a family's sexual dynamic – even discursively – it marginalizes the women of the family, whether the mother, sister, or daughter.

Foucault claimed that incest was the linchpin of the parallel evolution of modern sexuality and the modern family. As he wrote about it, the interpenetration of these two systems – alliance (or more generally the rules of kinship) and sexuality (or more particularly heterosexuality) – gave rise to the modern middle-class conjugal family which was incestuous at its inception. The threat – or promise – of incest helped to anchor sexuality in the family and to provide a new energy source for the "deployment of alliance." Incest in the modern family, writes Foucault,

is constantly being solicited and refused; it is an object of obsession and attraction, a dreadful secret and an indispensable pivot. It is manifested as a thing that is continuously demanded in order for the family to be a hotbed of constant sexual incitement. (110)

The possibility of incest keeps the sexual excitement of the family alive and, conversely, the sexual nature of the family with its economies of desire and need keep alive the possibility of incest.

transformations resulting in modernity. He writes, "The new procedures of power that were devised during the classical age and employed in the nineteenth century were what caused our societies to go from *a symbolics of blood to an analytics of sexuality*. Clearly, nothing was more on the side of the law, death, transgression, the symbolic, and sovereignty than blood; just as sexuality was on the side of the norm, knowledge, life, meaning, the disciplines, and regulations" (1: 148).

In our own time of sensationalized stories of incestuous abuse (so long ignored) and extreme counterreaction in the form of the "false memory syndrome," statistical studies on the rate of incest in the USA have shown that between 1 in 3 and 1 in 6 women experience sexual approaches by uncles, fathers, brothers, or grandfathers – with fathers and uncles being the most frequent perpetrators.[12] Furthermore, the modern class distribution suggests that, contrary to stereotype, there is at least an equal if not a greater prevalence of incestuous abuse in white middle-class and upper-class families than in families of other sociological description. This unexpected finding – illustrated by a tremendous outpouring of confessional literature and survival memoirs on the subject – runs directly against the middle-class ideology that *defines* childhood essentially in terms of its innocence in sexual matters. Middle-class analysts and thinkers had previously assumed that incest was "a vice of class and racial others who lack the rationality necessary to control their impulses."[13] Too many people sleeping in the same room, it was assumed, led to flagrant abuse. This vague prejudice is one way that sexuality has been marked in our society in terms of race and class. White middle-class children are not supposed to have sexual experience too early. A protected childhood is important to middle-class mythology and part of the configuration that defines and perpetuates middle-class values.

If one can extrapolate from this contemporary situation to the eighteenth-century English past, it would appear that an increased incidence (or awareness) of incest can be identified with the development of the middle class in the eighteenth century or with the "invention of childhood" that Philippe Ariès associated with the development of that class.[14] Thus the terms "middle-class family," "childhood," and "incest" define one another and their meanings are interdependent. One might even say that incest, as a system of thought and representation, reproduces the sexualized

---

[12] These statistics and their sources, together with an intelligent discussion of the "false memory syndrome," can be found in Elizabeth Wilson, "Not in This House: Incest, Denial, and Doubt in the White Middle Class Family," *Yale Journal of Criticism* 8 (1995), 35–58. The classic discussion of incest, and still the best, is Judith Lewis Herman, *Father-Daughter Incest* (Cambridge, MA: Harvard University Press, 1981).

[13] Elizabeth Wilson, "Not in This House," 38.

[14] Pat Gill, for example, emphasizing the connection between incest and bourgeois domestic life in Restoration drama, argues that while incestuous desire in Restoration plays "still functions as a metaphor for a fundamental disorder in the condition of the state," as it did in Renaissance drama, "it also indicates a developing conception of a bourgeois individual whose primary identity is determined by domestic relations." Thus the plays she discusses "link incest inseparably to the nascent formation of a modern, self-consciously desiring individual." Pat Gill, "Pathetic Passions: Incestuous Desire in Plays by Otway and Lee," *The Eighteenth Century: Theory and Interpretation* 30 (Fall 1998), 192–208, esp. 206, 196.

conjugal family and guarantees its perpetuation and its own fixations with an insistent and repressive mythology of childhood innocence.

Foucault does not speculate as to why the family became the "obligatory locus" of affects, feelings, and love and the privileged origin for the experiences that he sees as central to sexuality. Nor does he comment on why the "deployment of sexuality" began to supplant the "deployment of alliance" in the historical era that it did. But as I have been arguing throughout this book, these changes occurred with the development of agrarian, market, and then industrial capitalism. New sources for the production of wealth and value, along with new legal arrangements for the transmission of wealth between generations, were making the family an accessory to the creation of individual fortunes. The stakes in managing the rules of kinship loomed ever larger with the new potential for accumulating capital and new possibilities for achieving class mobility. Thus the modern family functioned simultaneously to reproduce sexuality and to funnel wealth intergenerationally, hopelessly conflating and imbricating these issues.

These connections suggest why incest was a constitutive element in the modern (middle-class) family form and reinforce my initial surmise that the gradual devaluation of the consanguineal axis of kinship brought with it a rise in the incidence of incest. There is no way to prove or disprove this hunch, of course; empirical data for incest in eighteenth-century England do not exist.[15] But even if the literal incidence of incest did not change in the eighteenth century, the cultural attitude towards it changed drastically and invested it with horror and dread. Whether the actual incidence of incest increased in the eighteenth century, or whether it was simply its social and cultural meaning that changed, incest loomed larger than ever before as an issue and a problem.

There is literary evidence for this heightened awareness of incestuous sexual relations in the immediate success and widespread popularity of the gothic novel, a fictional genre whose *raison d'être* is to create and express forebodings of sexualized violence. That is, when the gothic novel appeared on the literary landscape in the second half of the eighteenth century, it found a permanent place with the English reading public because it registered a change in family relations, one symptom of which may have been a significant rise in the incidence of incest.[16] The quality of fear that

---

[15] Seth Denbo's Ph.D. thesis "Relatively Speaking: Cultural Meanings of Incest in Eighteenth-Century Britain," University of Warwick, 2001, relates more instances of incest than I have seen anywhere else. See below, n. 23 and 24.

[16] I do not want to rehearse the facts about the popular reception of the gothic novel, so well described by E. J. Clery in "The Value of the Supernatural in a Commercial Society," Chapter 5 of her splendid *The Rise of Supernatural Fiction, 1762–1800* (Cambridge: Cambridge University Press,

one associates with the gothic novel, with its references to traumatic secrets and barely suppressed terror, was new to fiction in the period. As many critics have observed, the conventional props and trappings of the gothic novel – the predictable plot devices and even the type of villain derived from Jacobean tragedy – all exist to create a particular kind of apprehensive fear in the reader. Gothic fiction conjures fear of sexualized violence, violence not only to the body but psychologically tormenting violence to the mind. As one scholar puts it, after examining the similarities between gothic and pornographic fiction, "*every* Gothic novel is characterized by undercurrents of 'horror' which are sexual in origin."[17]

INCEST IN THE EIGHTEENTH CENTURY

We know very little about "real life" incest in the eighteenth century; evidence is sparse. Almost no mention of incest appears in court records, because until 1908 there was no criminal statute against incest *per se* and so incestuous attacks could not be prosecuted directly in eighteenth-century courts.[18] Incest therefore appears in court records only incidentally and

1995), pp. 80–91. Suffice it to say that the groundswell for the gothic did not begin until the 1780s. Although Horace Walpole's *The Castle of Otranto*, first published in London in 1764, was an instant success, it was not republished until 1782. Clara Reeve's *The Champion of Virtue* – the next gothic novel after Walpole's – appeared in 1777. This novel was privately printed the first time, and the copyright was sold the following year for £10 and a revised edition brought out under the title of *The Old English Baron*. By 1785, gothicism was sufficiently fashionable for a character in Elizabeth Blower's novel *Maria* to anticipate a visit to Dunslough Castle – like Jane Austen's later Catherine Morland – "impatient to enjoy the delightful horrors of Gothic galleries, winding avenues, gaping chimnies, and dreary vaults." Quoted in E. J. Clery, *The Rise of Supernatural Fiction*, p. 90.

On the prevalence of incest in earlier times, Barbara Hanawalt reports that very few cases of incest were recorded among the many sexual crimes in English court records such as prostitution, fornication, adultery, and rape during the fourteenth and fifteenth centuries. Barbara Hanawalt, *Growing Up in Medieval London: The Experience of Childhood in History* (New York and Oxford: Oxford University Press, 1993). Pat Gill reports that scholars examining Renaissance literary depictions of incest find that "illicit carnal desires operate politically as metaphors for perceived or threatened (catastrophic) social and state conditions" rather than representing personal preoccupations with forbidden individual desires. See Gill, "Pathetic Passions: Incestuous Desire in Plays by Otway and Lee," 194.

[17] Robert Druce, "*Pulex Defixus*, Or, The Spellbound Flea: An Excursion into Porno-Gothic," in Valeria Tinkler-Villani and Peter Davidson, with Jane Stevenson (eds.), *Exhibited by Candlelight: Sources and Developments in the Gothic Tradition* (Amsterdam and Atlanta, GA: Rodopi, 1995), pp. 221–42, quote p. 241.

[18] Antony E. Simpson, "Vulnerability and the Age of Female Consent: Legal Innovation and Its Effect on Prosecutions for Rape in Eighteenth-Century London," in G. S. Rousseau and Roy Porter (eds.), *Sexual Underworlds of the Enlightenment* (Chapel Hill: University of North Carolina Press, 1988), pp. 181–205, esp. p. 199. Simpson explains that there was a high incidence of rape of young girls as a result of a superstitious belief that sex with a virgin could cure venereal disease. The legal response to the frequency of these attacks appears to have been simply to *lower* the age of consent in girls from twelve to ten. Simpson notes that this failure to protect girl children from sexual force contradicts that "opinion which views this period as one in which childhood became defined as a status demanding care and protection" (200).

evidence for it must be gathered indirectly from cases prosecuted for different reasons and from occasional notes in parish and legal records. For example, in a study of 294 cases of rape and 81 cases of attempted rape heard at the Old Bailey in the hundred years between 1730 and 1830, only 189 cases, or about half, specify the relationship between the defendant and victim – of which 10 involved sexual abuse by a member of the victim's own family.[19] When Matthias Brinsden murdered his wife in 1722, it was observed that "'it revived the Story' about his incestuous relationship with one of his daughters (who, it was claimed, had had children by him)."[20] Adam White was brought to trial for raping his eleven-year-old daughter because the woman in whose house the daughter worked insisted on bringing him to trial.[21] Although Elizabeth Jeffryes was "debauched" by the uncle who adopted her, and forced to have an abortion, his incestuous abuse of her was not considered an extenuating circumstance when she was convicted of murdering him.[22] Indeed, it never even came to light until after she was sentenced to hang. A contemporary pamphlet about the case inveighed against Elizabeth Jeffryes' "betrayal" in terms that resonate ironically with our own modern concerns about incest.

What a Shudder must humane Nature receive, when it recollects there is no Place where Security may be depended upon, but at the same Time Persons are baring [sic] Doors from Thieves without, they are inclosing worse Enemies within: Nay, the nearest Ties of Kindred are no Security.[23]

Seth Denbo has uncovered a number of other cases of men who had sexual relations with their daughters in the later eighteenth century, often forcibly, although the criminal charges brought against them were for infanticide or rape and usually did not even mention the fact of their consanguineal relationship to their victims.[24] Denbo also observes that those cases that

---

[19] *Ibid.*, p. 205 n. 75.

[20] Caroline Gonda, *Reading Daughters' Fictions 1709–1834: Novels and Society from Manley to Edgeworth* (Cambridge: Cambridge University Press, 1996), p. 42.

[21] *Ibid.*, p. 244 n. 10.   [22] *Ibid.*, p. 42.

[23] *The Trial at Large of John Swan and Elizabeth Jeffreys*, 2nd edn. (London, 1752), p. 4, quoted in Seth Denbo, "Relatively Speaking," p. 223. The surname of this incest victim is spelled in different ways in different sources: for instance, Denbo has it as "Jeffreys," while Kristina Straub has it as "Jefferies" in her unpublished paper "Feminine Sexuality, Class Identity, and Narrative Form in the Newgate Calendars." In this book I have followed the spelling "Jeffryes," as used by Caroline Gonda in the bibliography of her *Reading Daughters' Fictions*, which is also the spelling used in the Harvard Law School Library and British Library catalogues.

[24] Denbo reports these cases in his Ph.D. thesis, "Relatively Speaking": Job Wells was indicted in 1753 because he, "with force & arms... against the will of the said Maria then & there violently and feloniously did ravish and carnally know" (209); Philip Sherwin was "indicted for a rape upon the body of Mary Sherwin, spinster" in 1779 (209); Thomas Harris assaulted his daughter Ann Harris

mention incest and speculate about its cause often mention the absence of a mother. He illustrates this point with the case of thirteen-year-old Mary Marsland who had been used to sharing a bed with her father and stepmother in between service positions. But one night in 1739 her father's wife was away from home when she got into bed, and her father held a handkerchief over her mouth to stifle her cries and raped her. Denbo gives several other cases of incest in which the mother had recently died or was otherwise absent.[25]

In ecclesiastical courts, illicit sexuality was punished as fornication or adultery without usually distinguishing between incestuous and non-incestuous sex. In canon law, the language of incest was generally used not for sexual violence but for marriages between affinal relatives, people related through marriage such as in-laws or stepsiblings. Polly Morris' study of church court records in Somerset between 1730 and 1835 shows some confusion in the working class about the legality of marriage with a deceased husband's brother or a deceased wife's sister even though these relations had been officially within the prohibited degrees for sexual relations since 1603.[26] Morris suggests that in some cases of marriage between stepsiblings, the connection through a father rather than a mother may have diminished the relatedness of the couple to an acceptable level, a vestigial marker of the earlier significance of maternal lineage. The "incestuous" couples to whom she refers, when called to account, performed penance in their parish church – that is, publicly proclaimed their wrongdoing and separated. They appear not to have been ostracized by the community, however, for public opinion distinguished between incest with consanguineal relatives, which was viewed with horror, and incest with affinal relatives, which although wrong and needing to be stopped, could be atoned for and was a much lesser sin.[27]

Morris also mentions a few known instances of sexual relations between blood relatives, referred to in the Somerset church records when the births of those unions were registered. Most of these recorded cases involved

---

in 1785 (210); Robert Parsivol was tried for assaulting his daughter in Dublin in 1785 (210); Richard Gracemark lived in incest with his daughter for fifteen years and, when she married in 1789, he murdered her (219).

[25] *Ibid.*, pp. 231–4.

[26] See Sybil Wolfram, *In-Laws and Outlaws: Kinship and Marriage in England* (London and Sydney: Croom Helm, 1987), p. 26.

[27] Polly Morris, "Incest or Survival Strategy? Plebian Marriage within the Prohibited Degrees in Somerset, 1730–1835," *Journal of the History of Sexuality* 2 (1991), reprinted in John Fout (ed.), *Forbidden History: The State, Society, and the Regulation of Sexuality in Modern Europe* (Chicago: University of Chicago Press, 1992), pp. 139–69.

father-stepdaughter incest, with some exceptions. John Hobbs married his half sister Margaret in the Bedminster parish church in 1751, by whom he had two children (158). A man performed penance in 1727 for accusing a woman of lying with her father and carrying his child (157). In 1799, a vicar in west Somerset noted in his diary how discomfited he was when a man named Porter "had the impudence to come [to church] . . . His own daughter confesses herself to be with child by him. Oh Abominable Villain. I will punish him if there is any law to be had" (146). But there was no law to be had and Porter went unpunished. The indignant vicar went to visit Porter when he seemed to be dying later that year and charged him to consider the heinousness of his crime. But Porter "shocked me by his insensibility in speaking of the shocking crime he had been guilty of" and remarked belligerently "There are others as bad as me" (147).

Frances Burney's oldest brother James, who sailed as Captain Cook's lieutenant on his last voyage to the South Pacific, scandalized his family and the rest of the world by eloping with his half sister Sarah Harriet in 1798 and living with her for the next five years. Their intimacy had previously alarmed their parents; Sarah's mother, Mrs. Elizabeth Burney, had forbidden her stepson the house while she lived, although Dr. Burney permitted his visits after his wife's death in 1796. Nonetheless, Dr. Burney apparently spoke to his daughter Maria of "his *dreadful* Apprehensions about their uncommon Intimacy" shortly before his two children by different mothers took the "fatal Step."[28] Afterwards, he could not bear to have either Sarah or James mentioned in his presence, and sought to banish them from his mind altogether.

His daughter, Frances Burney, reacted similarly to reading Horace Walpole's play about incest, *The Mysterious Mother* (1768), which she regretted having ever seen. "A story of so much horror, from atrocious and voluntary guilt never did I hear!" she exclaimed in her diary in 1786. "I felt a sort of indignant aversion rise fast and warm in my mind, against the wilful author of a story so horrible . . . which almost made me regard him as the patron of the vices he had been pleased to record." Mrs. Smelt, the friend with whom she had read the wicked tale, "declared she would drive it from her thoughts" and they both "mutually agreed that we felt

---

[28] Margaret Doody discusses this episode in some detail in her groundbreaking *Frances Burney: The Life in the Works* (New Brunswick, NJ: Rutgers University Press, 1988), pp. 277–82. Doody links the elopement psychologically to Elizabeth Burney's death. She also observes that "Sarah Harriet's love for her brother can be traced to her first novel, *Clarentine* (1796), in which the heroine loves a sailor guardian" (278).

　　Claire Harman argues that Sarah and James simply set up house together, without a sexual component, because each needed an escape. *Fanny Burney* (New York: Knopf, 2001), pp. 269–70.

ourselves ill-used in having ever heard of it."[29] The mere idea of incest was so dreadful it had to be driven from one's thoughts.

A few probably spurious stories of incest appear in the print record as well. The *Morning Post* of September 6, 1779 tells of a mother's fatal discovery that her beloved daughter-in-law was actually her own biological daughter, left in a Foundling Hospital years before, and now identified by a mole on her shoulder. A scurrilous pamphlet called *The Modern Atalantis* (1784) tells of a profligate duke, intimate with both of his daughters, one of whom he has married to his valet.[30] A ditty called "The Devonshire Garland," printed in chapbook form, tells of a nobleman who seduces his comely, bright daughter of fifteen, "her tender mother being dead," plying her with wine. When she proves with child, her father sends her away to hide her shame, promising

> And if thy child should chance to live,
> Some twenty pounds a year I'll give,
> To have him nurs'd in Devonshire
> And a thousand pounds I'll give thee there.

She accepts his offer and goes to Devonshire, but the dark deed inevitably comes to light. Her son becomes the living text that discloses their transgression, for on his breast in legible blue letters are the words: "I am your son and brother too." In time, the seduced daughter makes her way to London, apprentices herself to a goldsmith, and when the goldsmith and his wife die, marries the goldsmith's son and inherits the business. At length her own son, unknown to her, comes to London and is apprenticed "Unto that goldsmith and no other/Whose wife happened to be his mother." Inevitably, her husband dies and she marries the comely youth, only to learn what she has done after their wedding night when she sees the legend on his bare breast in the morning.[31]

Thus it ends badly, although the narrative is not played for tragedy or horror but rather for the utter confusion of social roles, the too-dense packing of kin relationships: "Here lies a Woman bereaved of her Life, / Who was my Sister, Mother, and my Wife." Tonally a folk ballad, telling a strange tale, "The Devonshire Garland" is completely without gothic

[29] *The Diary and Letters of Madame D'Arblay*, 7 vols. (London: Henry Colburn, 1842–6), vol. III, p. 235.

[30] *The Modern Atalantis, or, The Devil in an Air Balloon* (London: G. Kearsley, 1784). I owe these references – and much else – to Betty Rizzo. According to Rizzo, this pamphlet is anti-Whig satire and the duke a particular target.

[31] This device – blue letters emblazoned on the body revealing the incestuous truth to unwitting perpetrators – also appears in a broadside called *The Guernsey Garland* and a ballad called *The Leeds Tragedy*. See Seth Denbo, "Relatively Speaking," pp. 110–12 and 153–4.

atmosphere or machinery. Its sense is less of unspeakable horror and more of a grim family secret coming back to trip up its victim despite the attempt to manage it.[32]

Other ballads in the oral tradition as they have come down to us include very few stories of incest, and those are all about sibling incest rather than father-daughter incest. Child Ballads 16, 50, and 51 – "Sheath and Knife," "The Bony Hind," and "Lizie Wan" respectively, with their variants – collected in the late eighteenth and early nineteenth centuries, tell of brothers violating their sisters, sometimes by force, and then killing them when they become pregnant.[33] It is impossible to date the origins of these ballads except to note that they were being sung in the countryside in the eighteenth century.[34]

An extraordinary account of father-daughter incest, the only detailed record that I have found for the eighteenth century, appears in the memoirs of a pioneer woman in New Hampshire in the 1780s and 90s, Abigail Abbot Bailey. She was the mother in this case, and when her husband Asa began to force their sixteen-year-old daughter Phebe to have sex with him, Abigail felt helpless to protect the girl for she "belonged" to her father until she reached her majority. Abigail vigilantly intercepted his designs and prevented his isolation with Phebe as best she could. Living on her own homestead, in relative isolation, she did not appeal to her neighbors or her husband's relatives, a number of whom lived nearby. (Her own consanguineal relatives lived at some distance.) But the minute Phebe turned eighteen, Abigail helped her escape to one of her own relatives. Hardly impervious to her husband's incestuous desire – it haunted her and darkened her existence for several years – Abigail Abbot seems to have taken his incestuous acting out as a burden to be lived through until remedy was possible. It was not so catastrophic as to warrant leaving him, calling in legal or familial intervention, or trying more desperate measures. As for the daughter, Abigail was well aware that Phebe did not want her father's attentions, but she had no twentieth-century fear that the experience would cause her permanent psychic damage. She was envious, in a complicated way, of her daughter's attractions for her husband, which she experienced as

---

[32] To be sung to the tune of "The Bleeding Heart," this chapbook is no. 25276.33 in the Harvard collection. I am grateful to the late Janice Thaddeus for the reference.

[33] Francis James Child (ed.), *The English and Scottish Popular Ballads*, 5 vols. (1882–98; rpt. New York: Dover Books, 1965), vol. I, pp. 185, 444, 447.

[34] These ballads in particular were collected from William Motherwell's *Minstrelsy: Ancient and Modern* (Glasgow: John Wylie, 1827), Cromek's *Select Scotish Songs* (London: Cadell and Davies, 1810), and Herd's MSS I, 151 and 224 – the latter with a note added that it was copied from the singing of a milkmaid in 1771.

a kind of sexual rejection of herself. But beyond that, she wanted to protect her young daughter from a kind of assault and pressure that was clearly to her mind wrong, perverted, and unnatural.[35]

INCEST IN FICTION

Such is the scanty and fragmentary evidence of actual incest in eighteenth-century England (and America). The literary record is a good deal fuller – whether because it reflects actual incestuous practices in the society or a general cultural interest in the problem or both. As a number of critics have observed, incest is fairly common in eighteenth-century fiction.[36] In her thought-provoking book on incest in the English novel, Ellen Pollak claims that the discursive use of incest in narratives about transgressing the boundaries of the self and of society was central to the construction of modernity. The prevalence of narratives of incest in English prose fiction of this period formed a "discursive matrix within which 'truths' about culture, gender, and desire" were being produced, she explains.[37] Even novels not literally about incest, according to Margot Backus, have an incestuous tinge in the obsessive way male family members appropriate and dominate the bodies of their female relatives insofar as they control their marriages. She also remarks suggestively that while the incest taboo had once ensured the forging of bonds between different kin groups, the dissolution of this system of mutually balancing multiple kin groups in the eighteenth century meant that "within the privacy of the nuclear family,

---

[35] *Religion and Domestic Violence in Early New England: The Memoirs of Abigail Abbot Bailey*, ed. Ann Taves (Bloomington and Indianapolis: Indiana University Press, 1989).

[36] Glenda A. Hudson, in her fine book *Sibling Love & Incest in Jane Austen's Fiction*, remarks that "incest becomes almost a *sine qua non* in eighteenth-century fiction" (12). Margaret Doody refers to "the incest-fixated eighteenth century" in her biography *Frances Burney*, p. 161.

J. M. S. Tompkins also noted the pervasiveness of the incest theme in late eighteenth-century fiction in her classic, *The Popular Novel in English 1770–1800* (1932; rpt. Lincoln: University of Nebraska Press, 1961), pp. 62–6. She mentions Ann Radcliffe's *The Romance of the Forest* (1791), John Chater's *The History of Tom Rigby* (1773), Henry Brooke's *Juliet Grenville* (1771), and *The Adventures of Jonathan Corncob, Loyal American Refugee, Written by Himself* (1787). She notes that incest is "suspected or avoided" in the following novels: *Indiana Danby* (1765), *The Adventures of a Jesuit* (1771), *The Modern Fine Gentleman* (1774), Sophia Lee's *The Recess* (1783–5), Dr. John Moore's *Helena Zeluco* (1789), *Gabrielle de Vergy* (1790), Charlotte Smith's *Celestina* (1791), and Mary Robinson's *Vancenza* (1792). Other examples of the sustained threat of incest, ultimately deflected, can be found in Agnes Musgrave's *The Solemn Injunction* (1798). See Eugenia C. DeLamotte, *Perils of the Night: A Feminist Study of Nineteenth-Century Gothic* (New York and Oxford: Oxford University Press, 1990), pp. 53–4. Professor DeLamotte reports that Musgrave's novel has this suggestive epigraph: "In a solitary chamber, and midnight hour / How many strange events may arise."

[37] Ellen Pollak, *Incest and the English Novel 1684–1814* (Baltimore: Johns Hopkins University Press, 2003), p. 5.

the sexual appropriation of female family members no longer imperiled the process of circulation that the incest taboo once ensured."[38]

These are some of the current explanations for the emergence of incest themes in the English novel in the later eighteenth century. In the terms elaborated in this book, incest may also have represented a kind of experiment with the meaning of blood relations, a testing of limits, in a society in which consanguineal connections were under pressure. Sometimes, as in Frances Burney's *The Wanderer; or, Female Difficulties* (1814), incest threatened because the principals were ignorant of their true blood relationship. Mistaken identities led characters perilously close to incestuous violations. Uncles were mixed up with fathers, aunts with mothers, and siblings with cousins. Confusions about their parents led the lovers in *Joseph Andrews* (1742) and in *Evelina* (1778) to imagine for a brief horrified moment that they were siblings. Sometimes, as in Agnes Maria Bennett's *Agnes De-Courci* (1789), the confusion was fatal. In that novel, the newly wed couple discover that they are actually brother and sister, whereupon he kills himself and she takes leave of her senses. Father-daughter incest has a more sinister cast in Charles Johnstone's *Chrysal, or the Adventures of a Guinea* (1760) in the grim story of a "large athletic" man who embezzles his ward's fortune and then tries to force his natural daughter to have sexual relations with him. She, "in the utmost agony of distress," begs protection of a lady of her acquaintance from her father's "impious passion . . . which had been the motive of all his care and expense in her education."[39] Shunned by his acquaintances, he then turns to charity work, the only place where he will be received by "persons of character and fortune" (130). But even in this enterprise his character asserts itself; stealing money from a relief project, he again preys on those who rely on him.

INCEST AS THE MEANING OF THE GOTHIC

In some novels incest is incidental to the main action of a novel; in *Chrysal* – as in *Moll Flanders* – incest is just another episode. But incest was at the heart of the newly invented gothic novel, testifying to a new fear and a new fixation in English society. The point of the gothic novel was never to portray everyday life realistically, but to offer a set of conventions (untamed landscapes, wild winds, ruined abbeys, dark castles, locked rooms, footsteps

[38] Margot Gayle Backus, *The Gothic Family Romance: Heterosexuality, Child Sacrifice, and the Anglo-Irish Colonial Order* (Durham, NC: Duke University Press, 1999), p. 43.
[39] Charles Johnstone, *Chrysal, or the Adventures of a Guinea*, ed. and with an Introduction by E. A. Baker (London: Routledge, 1907), p. 130.

in the dark, subterranean passages, and the like) to evoke a nameless, foreboding dread of sexual danger. Plots feature the predatory desire of an older man determined to possess a beautiful virgin young enough to be his daughter or niece, and the cast of characters usually includes a missing mother or aunt. There is always a dark secret at the center of the mystery that the hero or heroine has to solve. The action is usually set in a time and space sufficiently far from contemporary reality so that there is "no intrusion of everyday standards of factual probability and morality."[40] Old buildings with secret passages into every room, inexplicable rustlings and groans in the night, mysterious personal histories and suppressed consanguineal relations – these elements suggest the incest motif.

A number of critics have pointed out that the confusion of good and evil projected by the attractive male villain produces in its readers a perverse attraction to threatening force, a hankering after unnatural domination, what one critic has called the "paradox of cruelty," a fascination with power in reader and victim alike.[41] Pamela Kaufman has summarized the aesthetic of the gothic as "a deliberate masochistic revelling in terror."[42] These critical assessments suggest the discursive construction of a sensibility associated with the subjective experience of incest, as if the ambivalence and complicated feelings of an incestuous exchange are built into the conventions of the standard gothic novel.

Architecture and landscape, essential elements of gothic settings, externalize aspects of the scenario of incest. That the danger is indoors, on home ground so to speak, where the heroine sleeps, signifies domestic transgression. Doors and gates lock only from the outside; there is no security in one's own room. The horrors happen in old mansions and castles that have fallen into disrepair – domestic spaces not maintained, homes that have become places of feudal oppression. As Eugenia DeLamotte points out, frightening things happen in secret places that have never been fathomed before: "labyrinthine passageways, unsuspected doors, secret staircases, sliding panels, forgotten rooms." Skeletons lie beneath the floorboards or locked away in closets; live prisoners are secreted in underground dungeons; dusty manuscripts waiting to be discovered are half-hidden in the

[40] Robert Hume, "Gothic versus Romantic: A Revaluation of the Gothic Novel," *PMLA* 84 (March 1969), 282–90, quotation 286.
[41] Philip Hallie's *The Paradox of Cruelty* (Middleton, CT: Wesleyan University Press, 1969) explores the paradoxical way victims in gothic novels admire their oppressors. Robert Hume argues that the reader experiences "a non-Christian or anticlerical feeling" ("Gothic versus Romantic," 287).
[42] Pamela Kaufman, "Burke, Freud and the Gothic," *Studies in Burke and His Time* 13, 3 (Spring 1972), 2179–92, quote 2179.

backs of cupboards.[43] Whatever is horrifying is right there on the premises, lying in wait, ready to spring.

The attached abbeys, chapels, and monasteries, with their nuns and monks, signify celibacy, austerity, and repressed sexuality; but they are redolent always in these fictions of broken vows, limits transgressed, and orgiastic pleasures. Heavy creaking doors; small, hard-to-find openings in basement vaults and grates; massy keys; dark, narrow, and uncomfortable passages and staircases; extinguished lamps; footsteps in the dark – all these physical features have expressive meaning when associated with the scenario of a girl singled out, against her will, in her own domestic space, for the sexual attentions of a father, an uncle, or a brother. These gothic structures with their labyrinthine internal passages also stand metonymically for the body of the heroine, a body under siege in which she is hopelessly and desperately trapped.[44]

Outside, the settings for these terrifying places always feature howling storms, thick dark forests, deep chasms, hidden caverns, and jagged mountains. These elements establish an environment that is both hostile and exciting, an eroticized landscape which is also impenetrable. Ann Ronald argues that the images used to describe the buildings or their environs in the gothic novel "invite the reader to think about sex." Such features as high round towers, jutting turrets, and dark thickets suggest "a variety of sexual organs and actions, both female and male." Thus, when the ancient servant draws the bolts from Udolpho's gate, "forcing back the huge folds of the portal, to admit his lord," it is hard not to think of rape.[45]

Transplanted to southern France or Italy, Catholic countries coded in the literature of the day as superstitious, irrational, hierarchical (as opposed to Protestant, rational, *scientific*), the heroine is cut off from all that is familiar and comforting. Castles and dungeons, monasteries and abbeys – those sometimes violated sanctuaries where the action in most gothic novels takes place – are symbols of domination and subjection, holdovers from a more overtly despotic era. Catholicism, in this genre, figures tyranny in all its forms: political, intellectual, and sexual. It symbolizes "a ruined order,

---

[43] Eugenia C. DeLamotte, *Perils of the Night*, p. 15. In defining the genre, DeLamotte explains that these elements are "an objective correlative for the terrors of 'the spirit engaged with the forces of violence'" (15).

[44] See Claire Kahane, "The Gothic Mirror," in Shirley Nelson Garner, Claire Kahane, and Madelon Sprengnether (eds.), *The (M)other Tongue: Essays in Feminist Psychoanalytic Interpretation* (Ithaca, NY: Cornell University Press, 1985), pp. 334–51.

[45] Ann Ronald, "Terror-Gothic: Nightmare and Dream in Ann Radcliffe and Charlotte Bronte," in Juliann E. Fleenor (ed.), *The Female Gothic* (Montreal and London: Eden Press, 1983), pp. 176–86, quote p. 179.

the vestiges of a feudal system distinguished by hierarchical power, inherited property rights, and ancient gender patterns."[46] As Kate Ellis has written, the church in gothic fiction stands in "not only for the gender domination that the Malcolms, Mazzinis, de Montalts and Montois who own the castle exercise over the women who are their prisoners, but for all superstitiously grounded, arbitrary, or irrational control of one individual or group by another."[47] Even in Jane Austen's parody of the genre, *Northanger Abbey*, General Tilney's tyrannical hold over domestic arrangements conforms to the expectation that women in gothic novels are prisoners rather than managers in their own homes.[48]

All English gothic novels since Walpole's *Castle of Otranto* include some of these details, from Clara Reeve's *The Old English Baron* (1778) to Ann Radcliffe's *A Sicilian Romance* (1791), *The Romance of the Forest* (1791), *The Mysteries of Udolpho* (1794), and *The Italian* (1797) or Matthew G. Lewis' *The Monk* (1796). These elements are part of an elaborate code representing family curses and repressed secrets, horrible deeds played out in the seclusion of isolated mansions, but rising to the surface at last, often by supernatural means, bursting their bonds and coming to light. Even the fragmentary nature of unexplained mystery is part of the formula, for the gothic atmosphere of ominous foreboding is often in excess of any explicit occasion, a feeling of dread seeking its reason for being, fear whose ultimate explanation always seems anti-climactic and beside the real point. I believe that these literary conventions express the fascination and horror of incest, an ancient crime that took on a new life in the eighteenth century, fueled by the reconfigured affect of domestic life in families.[49]

---

[46] This language is from Robert Miles' Introduction to a special issue he edited on female gothic writing. *Women's Writing* 1, 2 (1994), 131–42, quote 137.

[47] This excellent article by Kate Ellis in the special issue of *Women's Writing* edited by Robert Miles discusses the meaning of the pervasive Catholicism in these novels. "Ann Radcliffe and the Perils of Catholicism," *Women's Writing* 1, 2 (1994), 161–9, esp. 167. Ellis argues that because Catholicism was no longer a political threat in the second half of the eighteenth century, because of the decisive defeat of the Jacobites and the successive Whig regimes, it was "freed up for other metonymic uses" (167).

[48] See Claire Lamont, "Jane Austen's Gothic Architecture," in Valeria Tinkler-Villani and Peter David-son with Jane Stevenson (eds.), *Exhibited by Candlelight*, pp. 107–15, especially p. 109.

[49] Feminist critics have read the threat of danger and imprisonment in gothic fiction as a comment on the lives of contemporary women – although they have stopped short of imagining that it reveals the threat of incest. In her groundbreaking book on the subject, *The Contested Castle: Gothic Novels and the Subversion of Domestic Ideology* (Urbana: University of Illinois Press, 1989), Kate Ellis argued that the genre reveals the essentially gothic meaning of the home. The confinement of women indoors in gothic fiction, she wrote, linked "the 'safe' space of the home inseparably to its dark opposite, the Gothic castle" (x). My assertion that the gothic represents the terror of incest is an extension of her argument.

Maggie Kilgour, on the other hand, contends that women's everyday daylight domestic lives were "ratified" by their difference from their gothic "nightmare counterpart" and that the relief

HISTORY IN THE GOTHIC

Gothic fiction's historicity is part of its represention of dangerous families. Locating the action in the remains of a gothic past uses a narrative vocabulary that expresses, among other things, the importance of the past to the meaning of the present, an essential aspect of incestuous threats and incestuous longings. Gothic remains invoke – and telescope – the history of a society to figure the history of an individual. The medieval past functions in these tales as a golden age in which good and evil could not long be dissembled, when justice was proved by supernatural forces, the righteous rewarded and usurpers punished. All of nature participates in this moral alignment: the wind howls at hidden wrongs and storms rage against unnatural succession. Thus gothic fiction recreates a time of lost organicity, before mechanism usurped explanatory power, a world organized by analogy and correspondences rather than by cause and effect, a world in which all relations mirror and reflect one another.[50] The violent weather, the beating of a terrified heart, the winding half-ruined staircases, and flickering candles that go out at a crucial moment all fit together in an organic whole, each element an extension of the others.

The taste for gothicism and medieval history in the late eighteenth century was also fed by a growing nationalistic sentiment. The past was a link in a continuous national tradition from which the modern, powerful, imperial Britain could be said to have come. Eighteenth-century antiquarians were enthusiastic about collecting folk tales and ballads and examples of Saxon architecture and carvings. A revived linguistic interest in Anglo-Saxon produced several grammars and dictionaries – an interest spurred, in part, by a desire to demonstrate a continuous religious tradition in England independent of continental Catholicism. So great was the appetite for English antiquities that several inventive poets produced plausible forgeries, among them Thomas Chatterton's "Rowley" poems and James Macpherson's works of "Ossian."

Class mobility, facilitated by the new fortunes made in the East and West Indies, also contributed to the renewed interest in the historic structures,

---

at normalcy reinforced the bourgeois ideal of a woman safe alone in her home. In both readings, however, women continue to be incarcerated "in the home that is always the man's castle." Maggie Kilgour, *The Rise of the Gothic Novel* (New York: Routledge, 1995), pp. 38–9.

For other excellent feminist treatments of the gothic, see the special issue of *Women's Writing* edited by Robert Miles on female gothic writing, and Eugenia C. DeLamotte, *Perils of the Night*.

[50] Maggie Kilgour makes this point about an emerging modern world-view replacing an organic medieval model, citing Timothy J. Reiss, *The Discourse of Modernism* (Ithaca, NY: Cornell University Press, 1982). Kilgour, *The Rise of the Gothic Novel*, p. 39.

intact and in ruins, visible throughout England. The newly landed gentry wanted country estates and bought up the old buildings, the traditional signs of inherited wealth, to legitimate their new moral authority in society. These icons of continuous and stable power became the indispensable sites on which social authority was to be detached from earlier aristocratic lineages and hierarchical institutions and reattached to their new owners.[51]

These historical resonances undoubtedly contributed to the popularity of gothic fiction. But for the purposes of this chapter, I want to emphasize the psycho-sexual meaning of the historicity which is an essential feature of the genre. Incest implies the violation of genealogical principles and hence the attempt to short-circuit true succession and disrupt history. But the past is always with us, it cannot be willed away, falsified, or ignored. Family secrets will be revealed. Whatever is in the locked trunk, the locked room, the locked castle will come to light, and true identities will be revealed at last. All those women imprisoned in secret rooms, haunting the corridors at night, are immured in their histories, trapped in their families' problems, paying with their freedom for someone else's refusal to accept his present reality. The gothic suggests that no one can create himself *sui generis*, ignore genealogy, or create a new line.[52] No one can pervert the rightful succession, usurping another man's place or another generation's place. The meaning of the present can only be made out in terms of the past; the crimes of the past will see the light of day.

Nor is actual incest ever far from the plots of these novels. *The Castle of Otranto* is saturated with incest, beginning with Manfred's marriage to Hippolita, a woman whom he claims is related to him "within the forbidden degrees."[53] The circulation in these novels of the name of Hippolytus (also the name of Julia Mazzini's lover in Ann Radcliffe's *A Sicilian Romance*), the

---

[51] In another context, Jenny Sharpe argues that "the European fear of interracial rape" occurs when "colonial structures of power" are threatened. In other words, the dominant culture figures a threat to itself as sexual assault on "its" women. Following this line of reasoning, the sexual threat in the gothic, usually to well-born women, could be seen as a manifestation of class conflict. Jenny Sharpe, *Allegories of Empire: The Figure of the Woman in the Colonial Text* (Minneapolis: University of Minnesota Press, 1993), p. 3.

[52] Chris Baldick has written about this theme in shorter gothic fiction: "the decline and extinction of the old family line," in which the "centre of interest is less the claustrophobia of incarceration within the old house as building than the claustrophobia of heredity with the old house as dynasty" (149). Chris Baldick, "The End of the Line: The Family Curse in Shorter British Fiction," in Valeria Tinkler-Villani and Peter Davidson, with Jane Stevenson (eds.), *Exhibited by Candlelight*, pp. 147–57.

[53] Horace Walpole, *The Castle of Otranto*, with Sir Walter Scott's Introduction of 1821 and a new Introduction by Marvin Mudrick (New York and London: Macmillan, 1963), pp. 57, 72.

classical victim of incestuous lust, signals the theme. When Manfred's son, Conrad, is killed before he marries Isabella of Vicenza, Manfred pursues her, proposing a trade to her father, Frederic, the Marquis of Vicenza, "who listened but too eagerly to the offer," whereby each older man would take to wife the other's virgin daughter without interference.[54] The gigantism too – the giant who interrupts the wedding in Lorenzo's dream in *The Monk*, the enormous helmet that crushes Conrad to death on his wedding day in the opening pages of *Otranto*, the gigantic leg and foot stretched out in the gallery, the swelling up of Alfonzo (the real owner of Otranto) to such a size that the walls of the castle are burst open – suggests children's primitive perceptions of frighteningly large grown-ups and/or the shock of seeing an adult male erection.

But the plot convention that argues most powerfully for the troping of incest is the scenario in novel after gothic novel of a nubile heroine locked in an old building at the mercy of an older man who has sexual designs on her – or who she thinks has sexual designs on her. Sooner or later in these novels, a terrified woman is chased blindly through underground passages she did not know existed, as if trapped in the unconscious of everyday life: "beautiful, weak, sublime, helpless females crouching on floors, hiding behind doors, dominated by brutal lascivious males, kidnapped, murdered or worse, their virtue always at stake, their beauty their great misfortune."[55] The lack of a protective maternal figure or of an age-appropriate mate (he is either dead, incarcerated, or otherwise rendered ineffectual by the lusting, powerful father figure) completes the picture. The catalogue of imprisoned nubile women in gothic novels is long, from Isabella in *The Castle of Otranto*, chased through the secret passages of the castle of Otranto by her (almost) father-in-law while his wife is co-opted by her misdirected piety, to the beautiful Laura in Ann Radcliffe's first novel, *The Castles of Athlin and Dunbayne* (1789), locked up in Dunbayne Castle with her baroness mother for eighteen years by the evil Malcolm. Julia Mazzini is locked up by her father as sexual swag for his age-mate and psychological double, the Duke de Luovo, in *A Sicilian Romance* (1790), and later imprisoned again as a sexual prize for banditti. Adeline is pursued mercilessly in a decaying abbey by the Marquis de Montalt in *The Romance of the Forest* (1791). Her protector, M. La Motte, explicitly a father figure, is blackmailed into delivering her into the hands of the Marquis de Montalt, whom Adeline takes to be her

[54] *Ibid.*, p. 95. The daughter swap in *Otranto* is like the sister swap in Otway's *The Orphan*. See Pat Gill, "Pathetic Passions: Incestuous Desire in Plays by Otway and Lee," 199–200.

[55] Manuel Aguirre, "The Roots of the Symbolic Role of Woman in Gothic Literature," in Tinkler-Villani and Davidson (eds.), *Exhibited by Candlelight*, pp. 57–63, quote p. 57.

father, beholding him "with an emotion entirely new to her, and which was strongly tinctured with horror."[56]

In Matthew Lewis' *The Monk* (1796), Antonia is attacked by Ambrosio, who is actually her brother although he is twice her age, and whom she calls "father," because he is her confessor. Left alone with her, he cannot resist handling her, fastening "his lips greedily upon hers," violating "with his bold hand the treasures of her bosom," while she cries out "Father! . . . release me, for God's sake."[57] Further perverse and necrophiliac adventures follow as Ambrosio tries to evade public exposure.

In *The Italian* (1797), Ellena is locked up by Schedoni, who steals in upon her at night to stab her with his dagger. Although one might have supposed that a dagger sharp enough to kill could also cut through fabric, his murderous design appears to be hindered by cloth, which suggests rape rather than murder. First his clothes get in the way ("it was some time before his trembling hand could disengage [his weapon] from the folds of his garments") and then "her dress perplexed him; it would interrupt the blow."[58] When he stoops to turn her robe aside he discovers the miniature around her neck which looks like his younger self and convinces him that he is her biological father.

These indoor sexual terrors are unmistakable in Charlotte Smith's pseudo-gothic sentimental novels, where they are all the clearer for being dished up with realistic rather than melodramatic detail. Emmeline Mowbray, left unprotected by the death of the respectable housekeeper Mrs. Carey (the first of several mother figures in *Emmeline*), is repeatedly disturbed by the sexual importunities of men on the premises. Mr. Maloney and then Delamere keep trying to get into her room, knocking on her door, disturbing her rest and solitude, reminding her that her space and her person are not at her own disposal. In *The Old Manor House*, too, Monimia is locked up in a turret with a secret door, through which orifice Orlando comes at her in the dead of night – Orlando who speaks of Monimia as a sister although he loves her with sexual desire. Monimia's gothic descriptions of her experience during his long absence, locked up every night in a

---

[56] Ann Radcliffe, *The Romance of the Forest*, ed. Chloe Chard (Oxford and New York: Oxford University Press, 1991), p. 340. The marquis turns out not to be her father but her uncle, who has murdered her father who was his half brother.

[57] Matthew G. Lewis, *The Monk*, original text, variant readings, and "A Note on the Text" by Louis G. Peck, with an Introduction by John Berryman (New York: Grove Press, 1952), p. 260. Subsequent page references are to this edition.

[58] Ann Radcliffe, *The Italian; or the Confessional of the Black Penitents*, ed. Frederick Garber (Oxford and New York: Oxford University Press, 1968), p. 234. All subsequent page numbers refer to this edition.

melancholy room at the end of the north gallery, listening to the howling wind, terrified "at the visions my fancy raised" when stimulated by rustling damask hangings or the portrait on the wall, accompany her experience of being harassed, chased, and sexually pressured by a womanizing baronet, Sir John Belgrave, who also tries to force his way through her secret turret door. Dreading violation, frightened night after night by the family portrait of the Rayland ancestor in armor brandishing his sword, Monimia's experience of home, family, and history is suffused with sexual fear.

GENRE-LICENSED SEXUAL EXPRESSION

It is an odd fact of the authorship of gothic fiction that it was written in the closing decades of the eighteenth century by women and homosexual men. Allen Grove has suggested that this is so because the highly erotic terms of the gothic – the given conventions of the genre and hence not "chosen" or invented by the author – offered women and gay men a chance to write about sexual matters without seeming to have decided to do so. The conventions provided protective camouflage that allowed these writers to write about erotic impulses, their attractions, their danger, and their power.[59]

George Haggerty has argued that the novels of Walpole, Beckford, and Lewis – all homosexual authors – display unresolved conflicts over sexual urgency and sexual fear. That is, the suggestion of incest in these fictions, the combination of sexual compulsion and perverse desire, saturated with a "dark and brooding sensuality," is a screen for another sort of forbidden desire. He writes:

the fear of sexuality on the one hand and the struggle for sexual expression on the other . . . was nurtured and given its ghoulish strength in the crenellated castles and subterranean vaults which the Gothic novel popularized. Sexuality in the Gothic novel is harrowing in its "aberrant" nature and in its association with the perversion of power.[60]

Haggerty's language is suggestive for my argument in connecting "aberrant" sexuality with "the perversion of power." The gothic genre, in addition to representing an "aberrant" sexuality, offered the terms to critique a kinship system that invested a sinister degree of power in individual men over their immediate conjugal families by displaying hyperbolically the dangers of

---

[59] See the final chapter of Allen Grove's "Coming Out of the Castle: Renegotiating Gender and Sexuality in Eighteenth-Century Gothic Fiction", Ph.D. diss., University of Pennsylvania, 1996. The chapter's title is "Sexual Chaos: Genre and the Politics of Complexity," pp. 151–99.

[60] George E. Haggerty, "Literature and Homosexuality in the Late Eighteenth Century: Walpole, Beckford, and Lewis," *Studies in the Novel* 18, 4 (Winter 1986), 341–52, especially 343.

that power. For women and for men who revolted against the prospect of a male-dominated heterosexual empire, the gothic offered a ready-made set of literary conventions to show the evil potential in this new ideal of male individualism.[61]

Outside of the gothic genre, incest is figured in eighteenth-century novels, but with less predictable frequency. It occasionally appears as an instantaneous and inexplicable repugnance to sexual contact with a man who turns out to be blood kin. Instinctual disgust warned the sister and brother, although ignorant of their consanguineal connection, that their mating was somehow beyond the pale. Scenes of this sort occur in *Maria Brown* (1766), a narrative about a prostitute sometimes attributed to John Cleland,[62] and *Miss Melmoth; or, The New Clarissa* (1771) by Sophia Briscoe. In both cases the heroines have presentiments about otherwise appropriate men that prevent their sexual contact with those men. Maria Brown, usually without scruples about her sexual partners, cannot bear to bed a man who is subsequently discovered to be her brother Charles.[63] And the extremely delicate Caroline Melmoth, cast out by her friends and reduced to poverty by the diabolical slander of her envious rival, shrinks nonetheless from marrying the wealthy Sir John Evelin, who believes in her, adores her, and wants to save her. She believes that her hesitation grows from an inability to love a second time, after having been betrayed the first time. But she finds herself unable to make even an expedient marriage with this worthy man. "I know not how," she writes her best friend, "I felt a kind of repugnance – no, it was not a repugnance neither, – I cannot find a name for it. – I think

---

[61] Betty Rizzo sees the genre as defined by this excessive and unjust male power: "The single most important identifying feature of the gothic . . . is that it accomplishes, though usually in symbolic terms, the exposure of the usurping patriarch, an imposter who is willing to use his power in the most brutal ways in order to perpetuate it." See her "Renegotiating the Gothic," in Paula R. Backscheider (ed.), *Revising Women: Eighteenth-Century "Women's Fiction" and Social Engagement* (Baltimore: Johns Hopkins University Press, 2000), pp. 58–103, quote p. 61.

Howard Anderson's "Gothic Heroes," in Robert Folkenflik (ed.), *The English Hero, 1660–1800* (Newark: University of Delaware Press, 1982), pp. 205–21, makes the point that the hero/villains of gothic novels test the relation between freedom and morality, the extent to which the "ecstatic possibilities of individual fulfillment through sexual experience" are at odds with social responsibility, in particular to the family (214). Gothic hero/villains, Anderson argues, try to free themselves from their past and present obligations to assume absolute individual freedom. Yet "each character is related to that haunting past in his own way" (220).

[62] Although William H. Epstein, in his biography of Cleland, doubts the attribution "for various stylistic and chronological reasons," Maurice Renfrew edited and reissued the British Library's first edition in 1981 without demur as "by the author of *Fanny Hill*." William H. Epstein, *John Cleland: Images of a Life* (New York: Columbia University Press, 1974), pp. 144 and 233 n. 108.

[63] *Genuine Memoirs of the Celebrated Miss Maria Brown, Exhibiting the Life of a Courtezan in the most Fashionable Scenes of Dissipation by the Author of* A Woman of Pleasure, edited and with an introduction by Maurice Renfrew (London: Hamlyn Paperbacks, 1981), pp. 110–11.

of him with pleasure in every other relation . . . How is it I cannot forbear shuddering when I think of being his wife?"[64]

Caroline's response, like that of many a gothic heroine, delineates a sexual consciousness that is shuddering, nervous, overheated – not frank, open, earthy, bawdy and celebratory but rather voluptuous, close, fervid, intense, forbidden – even horrific – and fascinated. It is above all mental, rather than physical, as in *The Monk* when Ambrosio fantasizes in front of the portrait of the beautiful blonde Madonna, stares "with insatiable avidity" upon Mathilda's naked breast (87), dreams lustful wet dreams, and finally – after a long chapter that functions as foreplay – drunk with desire, collapses on the bosom of his seducer. In these fictions, family ties are loosened by abductions, murders, imprisonment, sea voyages, abandonment, and adoption – with the result that uncles attack their nieces, men rape their sisters-in-law or marry their brothers' widows, and brothers lust after, rape, or marry their own blood sisters. Sex and blood ties are confused by ignorance and criminal lust and in the process sex becomes unholy, dirty, fascinating, and repugnant. Gothic sex has a fetishistic quality that sends tremors, shudders, and shivers through the sensitive frame of a novel's heroine – not to mention its readers. The sexuality is terrifyingly omnipresent. When Ambrosio is bitten by a serpent so that his hand swells "to an extraordinary size" (92), we know what is swelling. Sex infuses everything, even if it is not always acted out in these novels.

The conventions of the genre thus treated explicit incestuous threat with a new fascinated horror. Playing out themes of incest in a highly sensationalized atmosphere, associating them with a claustrophobic fear of danger, the gothic novel invested the incest motif with a new kind of foreboding. The cultural work of the gothic was to testify to the terrific power of sex and to its dangerous and omnipresent potential in the family. If, as Foucault argues, sexuality was being constituted and reproduced in the home with the energy of contained incestuous impulse, the gothic novel bears witness to this new function for the family. It took the Romantic era, with its famously transgressive brother-sister matings, to cash in on the promise of the gothic, and take advantage of the forbidden excitement promised on the pages of these novels.

BLOOD WILL OUT

If the loosening of consanguineal ties brought with it the sexualizing of the family, represented in the sexual fear and horror of blood relations gone

---

[64] Sophia Briscoe, *Miss Melmoth; or, The New Clarissa*, 3 vols. (London, 1771), vol. III, pp. 71–2. Just as one guessed, John Evelin does turn out to be the brother of Caroline Melmoth.

wrong in the gothic novel, this spotlight on incest was only the most sensational sign of the focus on kinship in fiction. The assertion of genealogical
inevitability in eighteenth-century novels, gothic and sentimental novels
alike – the way usurpers are punished and rightful heirs reinstated, the way
lineage always triumphs, the way noble characters feel their rightful place
in the social order despite the lowly status in which they were bred – must
be read in part as a literary wish-fulfillment response to fragmenting kin
ties and the pulling apart of consanguineal bonds due to accelerating geographical and class mobility. That characters in novels always find their way
in the end to the right social level, the right class, the right castle, the right
family, reveals some anxiety about the displacements and disruptions in society caused by modernity. It was comforting to imagine that, whatever the
odds, "blood" would triumph in inherited mental and moral superiority,
and re-establish families and lineages.

Although in "reality" people may have felt less economic and social
responsibility for their relatives than in earlier periods, the emotional power
of consanguinity in eighteenth-century fiction invariably compensates for
the emotional repressions required by relations predicated on property. The
trope of the *cri du sang* discussed earlier – the cry of blood, the special feelings
of connectedness experienced by persons who were related but unaware
of it – was revived enthusiastically in sentimental fiction.[65] Even when
separated at birth, growing up without ever seeing one another, fictional
brothers and sisters, mothers and daughters, fathers and sons immediately
sensed their special bonds with one another when they came into the
presence of these perfect strangers. Antonia feels a "fluttering in her bosom"
when she first hears Ambrosio preach in Matthew Lewis' *The Monk* (1796);
"the sound of his voice seemed to penetrate into her very soul" (45). Roderick
Random "is struck with a profound veneration" for a stranger who is his
biological father; Evelina feels drawn at first sight to a young Scots poet
Macartney who turns out to be her half brother; Betty Barnes finds herself "strangely influenced in [a] poor woman's favour, without being able to
account for the cause" – a few pages later she discovers her to be a paternal
aunt.[66]

So common in fiction were these extraordinary feelings and the relations they presaged that Jane Austen parodied them in her 1790 send-
up of sentimental fiction, *Love and Freindship*. The sentimental heroine

---

[65] For a fuller discussion of this phenomenon, see Ruth Perry, "De-Familiarizing the Family; or, Writing
Family History from Literary Sources," *Modern Language Quarterly* 55, 4 (December 1994), 415–27.
[66] Tobias Smollett, *The Adventures of Roderick Random* (1748), ed. Paul-Gabriel Boucé (Oxford and
New York: Oxford University Press, 1981), p. 411; [Mary Collyer,] *The History of Betty Barnes*, 2 vols.
(1753; rpt. New York: Garland, 1974), vol. II, p. 91.

of this youthful satire, Laura, who sees everything through the lens of fiction, feels "wonderfully affected" at the sight of an older gentleman descending from a coroneted coach at an inn. "[A]n instinctive Sympathy whispered to my Heart, that he was my Grandfather," she continues, and she follows the "Venerable Stranger" and throws herself on her knees beseeching him

to acknowlege me as his Grand-Child. – He started, and after having attentively examined my features, raised me from the Ground and throwing his Grand-fatherly arms around my Neck, exclaimed "Acknowledge thee! Yes dear resemblance of my Laurina and my Laurina's Daughter, sweet image of my Claudia and my Claudia's Mother, I do acknowledge thee as the Daughter of the one and the Grandaughter of the other." [67]

The visible proof in her countenance, the details of successive generations – these improbable conventions are hardly alluded to when another young woman and two young men come forth to be claimed as the offspring of Laurina's other daughters. "But tell me," asks the old gentleman after acknowledging them, "looking fearfully towards the Door," "have I other Grand-children in the House [?]" Assured that no more relatives are lurking about, he quickly doles out £50 banknotes to his newly discovered relations and escapes, announcing that he has "done the Duty of a Grandfather" (92). Austen, an avid reader of this fiction and deeply familiar with its formulas, is, of course, satirizing the improbabilities of the *cri du sang*. But these highly sentimental reunions of consanguineal relatives that Austen found so comic abound in eighteenth-century fiction and apparently had great power to move eighteenth-century readers.

Chapter 2, "Fathers and Daughters," examined scenes in which fathers and daughters rediscover one another after having been separated for a long time. At that stage in the argument I explained these scenes as part of a cultural pattern that sentimentalized father-daughter relationships because new economic pressures were putting a strain on fathers' responsibilities to their daughters. I now want to argue that these father-daughter reunions are only a special case of a much larger phenomenon in eighteenth-century fiction to which the *cri du sang* also belongs, a category of episodes and conclusions representing the triumph of consanguinity. The standard fictional plot of the second half of the eighteenth century is structured as a quest for family, whatever else the orphaned heroes and heroines seek. Plots build to scenes in which long-lost blood relatives find one another after many trials

---

[67] *The Collected Works of Jane Austen*, ed. Robert W. Chapman, 6 vols. (Oxford: Oxford University Press, 1954), vol. VI, p. 91. All non-standard spellings in this quotation are sic in the original.

and feel an immediate and unconditional love for one another. Characters express their unequivocal joy at belonging to one another and immediately give preference to their newly rediscovered relatives in whatever terms the novel has set. The hostile world instantly assumes a benign and welcoming aspect with the reconstruction of the consanguineal unit because the hero or heroine no longer faces it alone; the ending comes quickly after the discovery of family identity.

Reunions between heroines and their fathers, as I have said, have a special narrative energy because they usually result in restoring the orphaned heroine to her name and fortune. Rediscovered mothers do not usually have the same power to protect, raise up, or enrich their worthy daughters. Nonetheless, their joy in recovering their sons or daughters has great sentimental force. When Julia Mazzini in Ann Radcliffe's *A Sicilian Romance* (1790) finds her mother in a small, womblike room at the end of a winding underground passage, their reunion offers no material advantage to Julia, but it leads to several tearful scenes in which her mistreated mother thanks God for allowing her to see her children once again and declares that for one such glorious moment she is recompensed for a life of misery. When Ellena Rosalba, in Ann Radcliffe's *The Italian* (1797), learns that the beautiful nun Olivia, who helped her escape from the convent, is actually her biological mother, she feels "a degree of happiness, such as she had perhaps never experienced" (378). Ellena and Olivia already love each other; indeed, before the reader learns of their biological tie their relationship has the erotic feel of a love affair between an older and a younger woman. Ellena is first drawn to Olivia by the quality of her voice singing in the choir – just as the hero, Vivaldi, is first attracted to Ellena herself by "the sweetness and fine expression" of *her* singing voice in church (5). Like mother, like daughter, their spiritual quality announces itself in their devotional singing to those capable of hearing it even before their physical beauty is seen. After anticipating for some pages the discovery of their consanguineal relationship, the reader is treated to a climactic scene in which Olivia presses Ellena to her bosom, "weeping, trembling, and almost fainting" (178).

Nothing in sentimental fiction, apparently, was more fulfilling than being reunited with one's biological family. Fathers, mothers, brothers, and sisters all find one another in the pages of these novels as their authors ring the changes on loss and reconstruction. Reflecting well on everyone concerned, reconstituted consanguineal relationships seemed to have a higher moral status than other relationships because they were more disinterested and more selfless than those pursued for romance or friendship. In loving and supporting one another, members of a consanguineal unit were obeying the dictates of conscience as well as blood, re-knitting the fabric of society in conformity to the needs of culture as well as those of nature.

Although mothers did not repair the fortunes of their disinherited daughters as predictably as fathers and brothers did, they did sometimes establish a higher-class origin for their long-suffering daughters than they had been thought to have. Indeed, characters' discovering their lost families always improved their social status, revising upwards in the social scale their adopted identities. As if scripted from Sigmund Freud's "Family Romances" – in which he explains the common childhood fantasy of having been adopted or otherwise abducted from a far richer or nobler family – rediscovered relatives in eighteenth-century fiction confirm their characters in a more exalted lineage.[68] Freud's explanation for this fantasy was the disillusionment children always feel when they begin to comprehend that their parents are not perfect and all-powerful after all; imagining superior parents was, to him, "an expression of the child's longing for the happy, vanished days when his father seemed to him the noblest and strongest of men and his mother the dearest and loveliest of women" (IX: 241).[69] He also speculated that this fantasy followed from a sexual interest in siblings – it permitted "the young phantasy-builder" to "get rid of his forbidden degree of kinship with one of his sisters" for example, "if he finds himself sexually attracted by her" (IX: 240). Similarly, imagining a different father and an unfaithful mother was a safe way to project sexual thoughts about his parents without acknowledging an incestuous interest in them. Thus, for Freud, imagining a prior, lost family created a safe psychic space in which to revel in otherwise repressed incestuous thoughts and longings about them. That Freud's essay reads like a gloss on eighteenth-century sentimental fiction is hardly surprising, for these fictional formulas were an early popular manifestation of the reorganization of kinship and gendered identity whose more advanced consolidations Freud spent his career

---

[68] In Sarah Scott's *A Description of Millenium Hall* (1762), Miss Mancel learns that Mrs. Thoresby, the kind and wealthy woman she serves, is her biological mother (148). Mrs. Selvyn learns, when her beloved Lady Emilia is on her deathbed, that this cultivated lady is her biological mother (211–18). Page numbers are from Gary Kelly's 1995 Broadview edition of this text. In Sarah Fielding's *The History of the Countess of Dellwyn*, 2 vols. (London, 1759), Mrs. Bilson's beautiful stepdaughter is rediscovered and claimed by "a Lady of considerable Fashion" in Bristol, who turns out to be her biological mother (I: 211–14). The eponymous hero Tom Jones, in Henry Fielding's novel, and Humphry Clinker in Smollett's novel are two more examples of this phenomenon.

[69] "Der Familienroman der Neurotiker" was first published in 1908, although Freud uses the term in letters to Fleiss of January 24 and May 25, 1897 and June 20, 1898. The essay was translated by Otto Rank in 1913 and by James Strachey in 1950. Quotations are from the frequently reprinted Strachey translation, *The Standard Edition of the Complete Works of Sigmund Freud*, 24 vols. (London: Hogarth Press, 1953–74).

analyzing. As Ellen Pollak observes, "modern theory reproduces so many of the early novel's structuring presuppositions about human nature and society" because the eighteenth-century novel was the first literary proving ground of those presuppositions.[70]

THE TRIUMPH OF CONSANGUINITY

The celebration of consanguinity takes many forms in eighteenth-century fiction and can be found in most of the best-known works. A few examples will have to suffice to make the point. In Frances Sheridan's *Memoirs of Miss Sidney Bidulph* (1761), a male kinsman who has struck it rich in the West Indies – that common fictional *deus ex machina* for providing fortunes to worthy young men – tests first Sidney's brother's spirit of kinship and then her own.[71] Unrecognized Mr. Warner, a first cousin – their father's sister's son – appeals to each in turn as if he were a needy man. Sir George Bidulph turns away the supplicant without giving him anything. He almost relents several times – he even puts his hand in his pocket once – but his wife quashes his compassionate impulses. Generous Sidney, on the other hand, although impoverished herself, offers to pay for his lodging and to feed him until he gets on his feet again. Mr. Warner, moved to tears, reveals to her his true condition and gives her a banknote for £1,000, demonstrating both that virtue will be rewarded and that family feeling will be remunerated. At the end of this sequence, Sidney and her brother Sir George have a conversation which clarifies the extent of Sidney's poverty. Sir George's wife, it seems, has misrepresented Sidney's situation to him to prevent him visiting or assisting her. Like Mrs. John Dashwood in Austen's *Sense and Sensibility*, she has stood between her husband and his sister(s), trying to stem the tide of his generous brotherly impulses. The conjugal relation has once again interfered with consanguineal duty.

Evelina's discovery of her brother in Frances Burney's novel is also mutually redemptive. She wants to save his life – for which he adores her. When she tells him "we are not merely bound by the ties of friendship, but by those of blood" we see that this paragon is capable of positive moral commitment and warm attachment. When she declares "I feel for you, already, all the affection of a sister; I felt it, indeed, before I knew I was one," we know, despite the muting effect of the adverbs, that her emotional

---

[70] Ellen Pollak, *Incest and the English Novel 1684–1814*, p. 4.

[71] When Jane Austen has Captain Wentworth make his fortune in *Persuasion* by capturing French frigates in skirmishes in the West Indies, she is making use of this formula.

responses are morally aligned: she feels as she ought to feel.[72] This is the only relationship fully sanctioned by her guardian; she can let down her inhibiting watchfulness with this young man. Because she loves this poor desperate poet when she learns that he is her brother, the novel grants her a father, a name, riches, and a worthy husband. Her consanguineal loyalty to her brother and her newly secured identity in relationship to her father crown the novel's action, testifying to the primacy of blood connections.

In Smollett's *Humphry Clinker* (1771), the reader feels the power of consanguineal relations from the outset. The family traveling together through England and Scotland is not a nuclear family although it looks like one, with a father, mother, and two children. But Matthew and Tabitha Bramble are brother and sister rather than a married couple, and the children who travel with them are the offspring of their deceased sister. So the family that focuses all the action of the novel is, in fact, a consanguineal rather than a conjugal family.

The surprises that befall this little social unit tend to emphasize consanguineal rather than conjugal connections as well. The worthy and loyal Humphry Clinker, who has twice saved Matthew Bramble's life, turns out to be his natural (i.e. illegitimate) son. Like many an eighteenth-century foundling, he can even produce the documentation to prove his lineage – he carries it on his person in an old wooden snuffbox. His real name, we learn, is Matthew Loyd, the name of his father's maternal family, the name that Bramble carried at the time he sired Humphry Clinker. Humphry Clinker was simply the name given to him by the farrier to whom he was apprenticed, although he always knew that his real name was Matthew Loyd, after his biological father. The boy and his mother lost track of Bramble when the latter sold his mother's lands in Glamorganshire in order to clear his paternal estate and dropped his maternal cognomen, Loyd, in favor of his father's name, Bramble. The suppression of his maternal inheritance thus effectively covered Matthew's tracks so that the boy and his mother could not find him again.

Thus, in fiction's explanation, the consanguineal connection is associated with the maternal line and is reinstated with the rediscovery of the maternal name. Bramble's overvaluing of his patrilineage – selling his maternal estate to clear the paternal one and dropping his mother's name in favor of his father's name – is what led to his disconnection from his biological

[72] Frances Burney, *Evelina or the History of a Young Lady's Entrance into the World* (1778), ed. Edward and Lillian Bloom (Oxford and New York: Oxford University Press, 1982), p. 363.

offspring. But the reinscription of that maternal name leads to the discovery of an unexpected relation – a flesh-and-blood son; acknowledging
his connection to his mother leads Bramble back to his dead wife and his
live son.

The second significant surprise in this novel involves the identity of the
incognito Mr. Wilson, who has been following Lydia through most of the
novel, showing up in various disguises and vowing eternal love for her.
Wilson turns out to be the son and heir of the admirable Mr. Dennison, an
old friend of Matthew Bramble's. It is Mr. Dennison who first calls Bramble
by the name of Loyd – the name by which he had known him in college –
and so identifies him to Humphry Clinker as his long-lost progenitor. Thus,
these two discoveries are linked, each in its own way attesting to the power
of consanguineal relationships. The two young lovers are reunited with the
full concurrence of their two families. What had looked like a match in
opposition to parental wishes turns out instead to be the choice of relatives
on both sides, as the generous marriage settlements attest.

Henry Brooke's *The Fool of Quality* (1765–7) celebrates the consanguinity of brothers. Generous little Harry becomes the instrument of many
heart-warming charitable projects, including several family reconciliations.
The story of Ned, a boy whom Harry takes in, is also an example of miraculously reconstituted consanguinity. It seems that Ned was stolen from
his parents as an infant (with the disclaimer that this only happens in romances) but is recognized by them by means of a burn scar. His father,
Mr. Fielding, who drives up in a coach and six, presses Ned to his bosom
crying "my first and my last, the only offspring of my bowels! thou shalt
no more be a wanderer, no more be a beggar my babe!"[73]

The reunions of mothers and daughters in *Millenium Hall*, mentioned
in the last chapter, further exemplify the sentimental power of consanguinity in eighteenth-century fiction. Tom Jones' discovery of his parent-
age at the end of Fielding's novel makes possible the comedic ending.
Sophia Melcomb is reunited with her longed-for sister and brother, not to
mention her father, in the happy denouement of Clara Reeve's *The Two
Mentors* (1783). Louisa Villars finds a mother in Mrs. Rivers (to whose cottage Providence directs her at the beginning of the tale) and a father in
Mr. Belmont in Elizabeth Helme's *Louisa; or, the Cottage on the Moor*
(1787). All tear-jerking sequences, these scenes of reunited families are the
sentimental climaxes of their respective novels. And Juliet, the mysterious

---

[73] Henry Brooke, *The Fool of Quality* (1765–7), ed. Charles Kingsley (London: Routledge, 1906),
pp. 247–8.

Incognita of Frances Burney's *The Wanderer* (1814), after 800 pages, acquires in rapid succession a half sister, a half brother, a maternal uncle (Admiral Powel), a stepuncle (Lord Denmeath), an esteemed guardian (the bishop, her "more than father"), a husband, and even a son. In the last fifty pages of the novel she is given the choice between conjugality and consanguinity, wifehood or siblinghood, as she is repeatedly whiplashed between the threat of a brutal, mercenary, and loathed French husband and the consolations of her loving and cultivated sister and brother. Every time she is about to be dragged off by the man who calls himself her husband, she is given another chance to be reconciled with her adored siblings, Lady Aurora Granville and Lord Melbury. As the dialectic alternation repeats, the emotional level escalates. "I have coveted this precious moment," cries Juliet as she embraces, caresses, and weeps with Lady Aurora, "almost beyond light or life" (818), only to explain to her newly found sister a short while later why she must sacrifice herself and return to France to a loathed marriage to save the bishop's life. As usual, Burney presents a wild dreamscape of female consciousness: you can sacrifice yourself to conjugality to save a life or you can assert your consanguineal rights and assure yourself of a life surrounded by loved ones. Meanwhile, the radical feminist Elinor Joddrel delivers her longest harangue in an argument with Harleigh on the question of religion and faith. She wants to know whether this life is all there is or whether the soul lives after death. While Juliet is choosing between her guardian's life and her own ease, Elinor is implicitly commenting on her choice by asking whether one acts for oneself alone or as part of a larger design. Selfish and individualistic, Elinor's speeches are a foil for Juliet's overdeveloped sense of duty to her guardian, her readiness to sacrifice herself to save him. No sooner does she decide to give herself up, to be true to the man who raised her, than the novel rewards her with a full circle of consanguineal relatives from her own family of origin and the beginnings of a new consanguineal family in some children of her own.

These fictional attempts to celebrate a revived moral responsibility to consanguineal families were, of course, doomed; the forces of history were against them, however much fiction sentimentalized these obligations. One can see that inexorable historical movement in the last of Jane Austen's novels, *Persuasion* (1818), where the claustrophobia of the consanguineal family contrasts with the opening vistas promised by the new sort of marriage. Sir Walter Eliot and Elizabeth, with their disdain for any but their own consanguineal relatives – including the pallid Lady Dalrymple and plain and awkward Miss Carteret – must give way to Anne and Wentworth, the new couple who make their way alone, independent of any relations, loyal to the disembodied State rather than to any particular kin. Conjugality trumps consanguinity in this last novel. The admiral and Mrs. Croft, as Glenda Hudson reminds us, that ideal couple who have shipped out together in all kinds of weather, "have no permanent abode and no offspring."[74] Families are in upheaval in this novel. There is a generation gap in the Musgrove family: "The father and mother were in the old English style, and the young people in the new." Their modern daughters, like "thousands" of other young ladies, live "to be fashionable, happy, and merry," which Austen acerbicly remarks is alteration but not necessarily improvement.[75] Mary Musgrove and her husband, neither of whom has the patience for family life, evade their parental responsibility when it interferes with their own pleasure. Even their grandmother complains that the children are "spoilt" and "troublesome" because her daughter-in-law does not know how to manage them (71). One feels that Anne and Wentworth will be away from their relatives a good deal.

This weighting of marriage and family relationships is new in *Persuasion*; it hardly describes any of Austen's earlier novels. Sisters settle within a stone's throw of one another in *Sense and Sensibility* and only thirty miles apart in *Pride and Prejudice*, where they can tend their consanguineal bonds happily ever after. In *Mansfield Park*, the first-cousin marriage consolidates the maternal connection between the Prices and the Bertrams rather than straining it. Fanny also never quite forsakes her aunt's service, but provides a second self, her sister Susan, to remain at Mansfield as "the stationary niece."[76] In doubling herself, she thus retains an interest in her consanguineal family even after she marries. Similarly, Emma Woodhouse notoriously arranges never to leave her father, but to keep one foot in her family of origin, to live in the house she grew up in, even as she begins a conjugal alliance. The conjugal family never entirely supersedes the consanguineal family in these novels; marriage never cancels those earlier obligations and loves. But the balance shifts in *Persuasion*, as if some irremediable point had been passed and even the moral appeal of the consanguineal family had become, at last, a thing of the past. Thus Austen's psychological realism leaves us a record of the historical moment, just as those shelves of eighteenth-century novels testify to an earlier psychological reality, in which the obligations of consanguinity had the highest moral claim of all.

---

[74] Glenda A. Hudson, *Sibling Love & Incest in Jane Austen's Fiction*, p. 94.
[75] Jane Austen, *Persuasion*, ed. D.W. Harding (Harmondsworth: Penguin, 1965), p. 67.
[76] Jane Austen, *Mansfield Park*, ed. Tony Tanner (Harmondsworth and New York: Penguin, 1966), p. 456.

AFTERWORD

One writes a book because one wants to read such a book and none exists. Once I had begun this project, I meant to document all the main kin relationships depicted in fiction that seemed to me symptomatic of the gradual replacement of a consanguineal kin formation by a conjugal kin formation in eighteenth-century English society. I have not completed that task here. The chapter about enclosure grew out of my desire to understand some of the reasons *why* this kin shift took place when it did, and what its economic and legal corollaries were. Ending it here, without examining more of the eighteenth-century fiction that still exists unread in great quantities to fill out the picture I have sketched in this book, leaves plenty of work to be done. It is my fondest hope that this effort will encourage other scholars to read for the kin relations in eighteenth-century fiction and that in time a sharper picture of the relationships among siblings, aunts and uncles, nieces and nephews, parents and children, maternal and paternal relatives, and unrelated friends of the family, made up by this collective vision, will emerge.

Bibliography

PRIMARY SOURCES

Addison, Joseph, and Sir Richard Steele, *The Spectator*, London: 1711–15.

[Anon.], *The Adventures of George Maitland, Esq.*, 3 vols., London: 1786.

Alleyne, John, *The Legal Degrees of Marriage Stated and Considered, in a Series of Letters to a Friend* (1775), The Marriage Prohibitions Controversy (facsimile series), ed. Randolph Trumbach, New York: Garland, 1985.

[Anon.], *Anecdotes of a Convent, by the Author of Memoirs of Mrs. Williams*, 3 vols., London: 1771.

Astell, Mary, *Some Reflections upon Marriage*, 3rd edn., London: 1706.

Austen, Jane, *The Collected Works of Jane Austen*, ed. Robert W. Chapman, 6 vols., Oxford: Oxford University Press, 1954.

    Emma (1816); ed. Ronald Blythe, Harmondsworth: Penguin, 1966.

    "Love and Freindship" (sic, written 1790); in *Catharine and Other Writings*, by Jane Austen, ed. Margaret Anne Doody and Douglas Murray, intro. Doody, Oxford World's Classics, Oxford: Oxford University Press, 1993, 75–106.

    Mansfield Park (1814); ed. Tony Tanner, Harmondsworth and New York: Penguin, 1966.

    Northanger Abbey (1818).

    Persuasion (1818); ed. D. W. Harding, Harmondsworth: Penguin, 1965.

    Pride and Prejudice (1813).

    Sense and Sensibility (1811); ed. Ros Ballaster, London: Penguin, 1995.

Bage, Robert, *Barham Downs* (1784), Ballantyne's Novelist's Library, vol. 9, pp. 241–375, London: Hurst Robinson, 1824.

    Hermsprong, or Man as He Is Not, London: 1796.

    James Wallace (1788), Ballantyne's Novelist's Library, vol. 9, pp. 377–508, London: Hurst Robinson, 1824.

    Mount Henneth (1782), Ballantyne's Novelist's Library, vol. 9, pp. 111–239, London: Hurst Robinson, 1824.

Bailey, Abigail Abbot, *Religion and Domestic Violence in Early New England: The Memoirs of Abigail Abbot Bailey*, ed. Ann Taves, Bloomington and Indianapolis: Indiana University Press, 1989.

Ballard, George, *Memoirs of Several Ladies of Great Britain Who Have Been Celebrated for Their Writings or Skill in the Learned Languages, Arts and Sciences* (1752), ed. Ruth Perry, Detroit: Wayne State University Press, 1985.

Barker, Jane, *Exilius: or, the Banish'd Roman*, London: 1715.

Barwell, Richard, "The Letters of Mr. Richard Barwell," *Bengal Past and Present: Journal of the Calcutta Historical Society* 8–13 (1914–16).

Battestin, Martin C., and Clive T. Probyn, eds., *The Correspondence of Henry and Sarah Fielding*, Oxford: Clarendon Press, 1993.

Beale, Mrs. C. H., *Reminiscences of a Gentlewoman of the Last Century*, Birmingham: 1891.

Behn, Aphra, *Love-Letters between a Nobleman and His Sister*, London: 1684–7.

Benger, E. O., *Memoirs of the Late Mrs. Elizabeth Hamilton*, 2 vols., London: Longman, 1818.

Bennett, Agnes Maria, *Agnes De-Courci*, London: 1789.
　The Beggar Girl and Her Benefactors, London: 1797.

Bennett, John, *Letters to a Young Lady, on a Variety of Useful and Interesting Subjects*, 2 vols., London: 1789.

Berkshire Justices, Minutes of the Berkshire Justices Meeting at Speenhamland on May 6, 1795, *Berkshire Sessions Order Book* (1791–5), 434–6.

Blackstone, William, *Commentaries on the Laws of England* (1844), 4 vols., facsimile reprint, Chicago: University of Chicago Press, 1979.

Blandy, Mary, *Miss Mary Blandy's Own Account of the Affair between Her and Mr. Cranstoun. From the Commencement of Their Acquaintance, in the Year, 1746. To the Death of Her Father, in August 1751, with All the Circumstances Leading to That Unhappy Event*, London: A. Millar, 1752.

Bonhote, Elizabeth, *Darnley Vale; or, Emelia Fitzroy*, London: 1789.
　Ellen Woodley, London: 1790.

Boswell, James, *The Life of Samuel Johnson*, 2 vols., London: Dent, and New York: Dutton, 1973.

Briscoe, Sophia, *The Fine Lady. A Novel by the Author of* Miss Melmoth, 2 vols., London: 1772.
　Miss Melmoth; or, The New Clarissa, 3 vols., London: 1771.

The British Novelists; with an Essay and Prefaces Biographical and Critical by Mrs. Barbauld, 50 vols., London: F. C. and J. Rivington, 1810.

Brooke, Frances, *The Excursion* (1777), ed. Paula R. Backscheider and Hope D. Cotton, Lexington: University of Kentucky Press, 1997.
　The History of Emily Montague, 4 vols., London: 1769.
　The History of Lady Julia Mandeville, 2 vols., London: 1763.
　The Old Maid, by Mary Singleton [i.e. Frances Brooke], 37 vols., London: A. Millar, 1755–6 (periodical).

Brooke, Henry, *The Fool of Quality, or, The History of Henry Earl of Moreland* (1765–7), ed. Charles Kingsley, London: Routledge, 1906.

Brown, John, D. D., *On the Female Character and Education*, London: 1765.

Burney, Frances, *Camilla, or A Picture of Youth* (1796), ed. Edward A. Bloom and Lillian D. Bloom, Oxford and New York: Oxford University Press, 1983.

Cecilia, or, Memoirs of an Heiress (1782), ed. Peter Sabor and Margaret Anne Doody, Oxford and New York: Oxford University Press, 1988.

The Diary and Letters of Madame D'Arblay, Edited by Her Niece, 7 vols., London: Henry Colburn, 1842–6.

Evelina or the History of a Young Lady's Entrance into the World (1778), ed. Edward and Lillian Bloom, Oxford and New York: Oxford University Press, 1968; paperback 1982.

Memoirs of Doctor Burney Arranged from His Own Manuscripts, from Family Papers, and from Personal Recollections. By His Daughter, Madame D'Arblay, 3 vols., London: Edward Moxon, 1832.

The Wanderer; or, Female Difficulties (1814), ed. Margaret Anne Doody, Robert L. Mack, and Peter Sabor, Oxford and New York: Oxford University Press, 1991.

Carter, Elizabeth, and Catherine Talbot, *A Series of Letters between Mrs. Elizabeth Carter and Miss Catherine Talbot from the Year 1741 to 1770*, ed. Rev. Montagu Pennington, 4 vols, London: F. C. and J. Rivington, 1809.

Chambers, John David, *A Practical Treatise on the Jurisdiction of the High Court of Chancery over the Persons and Property of Infants*, London: Saunders and Benning, 1842.

Chapone, Hester Mulso, *Letters on the Improvement of the Mind*, London: 1773.

The Posthumous Works of Mrs. Chapone, 4 vols., London: 1807.

[Chapone, Sarah], *The Hardships of the English Laws in Relation to Wives*, London: Bowyer, 1735.

Charke, Charlotte, *A Narrative of the Life of Mrs. Charlotte Charke*, London: W. Reeve, 1755.

Chudleigh, Lady Mary, *The Ladies Defence: or, The Bride-Woman's Counsellor Answer'd*, London: 1701.

The Poems and Prose of Mary, Lady Chudleigh, ed. Margaret J. M. Ezell, New York: Oxford University Press, 1993.

Clare, John, *John Clare by Himself*, ed. Eric Robinson and David Powell, Ashington: Mid-Northumberland Arts Group, and Manchester: Carcanet Press, 1996.

Cleland, John, *Genuine Memoirs of the Celebrated Miss Maria Brown, Exhibiting the Life of a Courtezan in the most Fashionable Scenes of Dissipation, by the Author of* A Woman of Pleasure (1766), ed. Maurice Renfrew, London: Hamlyn Paperbacks, 1981.

Memoirs of a Woman of Pleasure [*Fanny Hill*], London: 1748–9.

[Anon.], *Cleora: or, the Fair Inconstant*, London: 1752.

Cobbett, William, *Cottage Economy*, London: 1821; rpt. Oxford: Oxford University Press, 1979.

Cobbett, William, *The Parliamentary History of England from the Earliest Period to the Year 1803*, 36 vols., London: T. C. Hansard for Longman, Hurst, Orme and Brown, 1806–20.

Cole, William, *The Blecheley Diary of Rev. William Cole*, ed. Francis Griffin Stokes, with an introduction by Helen Waddell, London: Constable, 1931.

Collier, Mary, *The Woman's Labour: An Epistle to Mr. Stephen Duck; In Answer to His Late Poem, Called The Threasher's Labour*, London: 1739.

Collyer, Mary, *Felicia to Charlotte: being Letters from a Young Lady in the Country to Her Friend in the Town*, London: Jacob Robinson, 1744.

The History of Betty Barnes, 2 vols., London: 1753; rpt. New York: Garland, 1974.

[Anon.], *Considerations on the Causes of the Present Stagnation of Matrimony*, London: 1772.

[Anon.], *Constantia; or, A True Picture of Human Life*, 2 vols., London: 1751.

Cowley, Hannah, *The Belle's Stratagem*, London: 1780.

Cromek, R. H., ed., *Select Scotish Songs, Ancient and Modern; with Critical Observations and Biographical Notices*, by Robert Burns, London: T. Cadell and W. Davies, 1810.

Dawe, Anne, *The Younger Sister: or, The History of Miss Somerset*, London: 1770.

de la Barre, François Poullain, *The Woman as Good as the Man*, ed. Gerald MacLean, Detroit: Wayne State University Press, 1988.

Defoe, Daniel, *Conjugal Lewdness or, Matrimonial Whoredom: A Treatise concerning the Use and Abuse of the Marriage Bed* (1727), ed. Maximillian Novak, Gainesville, FL: Scholars' Facsimiles & Reprints, 1967.

The Family Instructor, London: 1715.

Moll Flanders, London: 1722; ed. and intro. Juliet Mitchell, Harmondsworth: Penguin, 1978.

Roxana: The Fortunate Mistress (1724), ed. David Blewett, Harmondsworth: Penguin, 1982.

Delany, Mary, *The Autobiography and Correspondence of Mrs. Delany*, ed. Lady Llanover, 1st series, 3 vols., London: Richard Bentley, 1861.

"Devonshire Garland" (chapbook), Harvard University collection, no. 25276.33. Variant "The Guernsey Garland," London: ca. 1760, Harvard University collection.

Dodd, William, *An Account of the Rise, Progress, and Present State of the Magdalen Hospital . . . Together with Dr. Dodd's Sermons*, London: 1776.

The Sisters, London: 1754.

Douglas, Francis, *Reflections on Celibacy and Marriage in Four Letters to a Friend*, London: 1771.

Dugard, Simon, *The Marriages of Cousin Germans, Vindicated from the Censures of Unlawfullnesse, and Inexpediency* (1673), The Marriage Prohibitions Controversy (facsimile series), ed. Randolph Trumbach, New York: Garland, 1985.

Edgeworth, Maria, *Belinda*, London: 1801.

Castle Rackrent [1800]; and, Ennui [1809], ed. Marilyn Butler, Harmondsworth: Penguin, 1992.

Harrington, London: 1817.

Helen, London: 1834.

Memoirs of Richard Lovell Edgeworth, Esq. Begun by Himself and Concluded by His Daughter, Maria Edgeworth, 2 vols., Boston: Wells and Lily, 1820.

The Parent's Assistant, London: 1796.

Patronage, London: 1814.

Elstob, Elizabeth, trans., *An English-Saxon Homily on the Birthday of St. Gregory* (by Aelfric), London: 1709.

[Erskine, Thomas], *Reflections on Gaming*, 2nd edn., London: 1777.

[Anon.], *Family Pictures*, 2 vols., Dublin: 1764.

Farington, Joseph, *The Diary of Joseph Farington*, ed. Kenneth Garlick, Angus Macintyre, and Kathryn Cave, 16 vols. [as of 1996], New Haven and London: Yale University Press for the Paul Mellon Centre for Studies in British Act, 1978–.

[Anon.], *The Fashionable Friend*, 2 vols., London: 1773.

[Anon.], *The Female American*, London: 1767.

[Anon.], *Female Friendship: or the Innnocent Sufferer*, 2 vols., London: 1770.

Ferrier, Susan, *Marriage* (1818), ed. and intro. Herbert Foltinek, Oxford and New York: Oxford University Press, 1986.

Fielding, Henry, *Amelia* (1751), rpt. in 2 vols., London: Dent, 1930.

    The Complete Works of Henry, Fielding, Esq., ed. William Ernest Henley, 16 vols., London: Heinemann, 1903.

    The Covent-Garden Journal and A Plan of the University Register-Office (1752), ed. Bertrand A. Goldgar, Oxford: Clarendon Press, 1988.

    The Covent Garden Tragedy, London: 1732.

    Joseph Andrews (1742), ed. Douglas Brooks-Davies and Martin C. Battestin, Oxford and New York: Oxford University Press, 1970.

    The Modern Husband, London: 1731.

    Tom Jones, London: 1749.

    A True State of the Case of Bosavern Penlez, London: 1749.

Fielding, Sarah, *The Adventures of David Simple* (1744), ed. Malcolm Kelsall, Oxford: Oxford University Press, 1987.

    The Governess or, Little Female Academy (1749), facsimile rpt. Oxford: Oxford University Press, 1968.

    The History of the Countess of Dellwyn, 2 vols., London: 1759.

    The Histories of Some of the Penitents in the Magdalen House, as Supposed to be Related by Themselves, 2nd edn., 2 vols., Dublin: 1760.

    The Lives of Octavia and Cleopatra, London: 1757.

    Remarks on Clarissa (1749), ed. and intro. Peter Sabor, Augustan Reprint Society nos. 231–2, Los Angeles: William Andrews Clark Memorial Library, 1985.

Fielding, Sarah, trans., *Memoirs of Socrates* (by Xenophon), London: 1762.

Fielding, Sarah, and Jane Collier, *The Cry: A New Dramatic Fable*, 3 vols., London: 1754.

Fleetwood, Willam, *The Relative Duties of Parents and Children, Husbands and Wives, Masters and Servants* (1705), facsimile rpt. New York: Garland, 1985.

[Anon.], *The Fruitless Repentance; or the History of Miss Kitty LeFever*, 2 vols., London: 1769.

Fry, John, *The Case of Marriages between Near Kindred Particularly Considered, with Respect to the Doctrine of Scripture, the Law of Nature, and the Laws of England* (1756), The Marriage Prohibitions Controversy (facsimile series), ed. Randolph Trumbach, New York: Garland, 1985.

Garfield, John, *The Wandring Whore* (1660), rpt. New York: Garland, 1986.

Gibbes, Phoebe, *The History of Lady Louisa Stroud and the Honourable Misses Stretton*, 2 vols., London: 1764.

Gibbon, Edward, *The Memoirs of the Life of Edward Gibbon*, ed. George Birkbeck Hill, London: Methuen, 1900.

Gisborne, Thomas, *An Enquiry into the Duties of the Female Sex*, London: 1797.

Goldsmith, Oliver, *The Deserted Village*, London: 1770.

   The Vicar of Wakefield, London: 1766.

[Goldsmith, Oliver?], *Goody Two-Shoes* (1765), facsimile ed., intro. Charles Welsh, London: Griffith and Farran, 1882.

Graves, Richard, *The Spiritual Quixote*, 3 vols., London: 1773.

[Green, Sarah], *Romance Readers and Romance Writers: A Satirical Novel*, 3 vols., London: T. Hookham, Junior, and E. T. Hookham, 1810.

Gregory, John, *A Father's Legacy to His Daughter*, London: 1774.

Griffith, Elizabeth, *The Delicate Distress*, 2 vols., London: 1769.

   The History of Lady Barton, 3 vols., London: 1771.

   The Story of Lady Juliana Harley, 2 vols., London: 1776.

Gunning, John, *An Apology for the Life of Major General G—*, London: 1792.

[Anon.], *Half an Hour after Supper*, London: 1789.

Hamilton, Elizabeth, *Cottagers of Glenburnie*, London: 1808.

   Memoirs of Modern Philosophers, 3 vols., London: 1800.

   Translation of the Letters of a Hindoo Rajah, 2 vols., London: 1796.

Hamilton, Lady Mary, *Memoirs of the Marchioness de Louvoi*, 3 vols., London: 1777.

   Munster Village, London: 1779.

Hanway, Jonas, *A Plan for Establishing a Charity-House, or Charity-Houses, for the Reception of Repenting Prostitutes to be Called the Magdalen Charity*, London: 1758.

Hastings-Wheler family, *Hastings Wheler Family Letters 1693–1704: Lady Betty Hastings and Her Brother*, Part I, London: privately printed at the Chiswick Press, 1929.

Hayley, William, *A Philosophical, Historical, and Moral Essay on Old Maids, by a Friend to the Sisterhood*, 3 vols., London: T. Cadell, 1785.

Hays, Mary, *The Victim of Prejudice*, London: 1799.

Haywood, Eliza, *The Fatal Secret*, London: 1724.

   The Female Spectator, 4 vols., London: 1744–6.

   The Fortunate Foundlings, London: 1744.

   The History of Betsy Thoughtless, London: 1751; rpt. London: Pandora Press, 1986.

   The History of Jemmy and Jenny Jessamy, London: 1753.

   The Husband, London: 1756.

   Love in Excess, London: 1719.

   The Mercenary Lover, London: 1726.

   A Present for a Servant-Maid, London: 1743.

Helme, Elizabeth, *Clara and Emmeline; or, The Maternal Benediction*, London: 1788.

   Louisa, or the Cottage on the Moor, London: 1787.

Herd, David, *Songs from David Herd's Manuscripts*, ed. Hans Hecht, Edinburgh: W. J. Hay, 1904.

[Anon.], *The History of Charlotte Summers, the Fortunate Parish Girl*, London: 1750.

[Anon.], *The History of the Human Heart*, London: Freeman, 1749.

[Anon.], *The History of Indiana Danby*, London: 1765.

[Anon.], *The History of Miss Pamela Howard, by the Author of* Indiana Danby, 2 vols., Dublin: 1773.

[Anon.], *The History of Sophia Shakespear*, London: 1753.

Holcroft, Thomas, *The Family Picture; or, Domestic Dialogues on Amiable or Interesting Subjects*, London: 1783.

Home, John, *Douglas*, London: 1756.

Hume, David, *Essays*, ed. Eugene F. Miller, Indianapolis: Liberty Classics, 1985.

Hutton, Catherine, Hutton MS 4/2, Birmingham Public Library.

Hutton, William, *The Life of William Hutton* (1816), intro. Carl Chinn, London and Birmingham: Brewin Books, 1998.

Inchbald, Elizabeth, *Nature and Art*, London: 1796.

A Simple Story (1791), rpt. Oxford and New York: Oxford University Press, 1988.

[Anon.], *Jessy; or, the Bridal Day*, 2 vols., London: 1771.

Johnson, J., *The Laws Respecting Women* (1777), rpt. Dobbs Ferry, NY: Oceana, 1974, with foreword by Shirley Raissi Bysiewicz.

Johnson, Samuel, *Johnsonian Miscellanies*, ed. George Birkbeck Hill, 2 vols., New York: Harper, 1897.

Letters of Samuel Johnson, ed. George Birkbeck Hill, New York: Harper, 1892.

Johnstone, Charles, *Chrysal, or the Adventures of a Guinea* (1760), ed. and intro. E. A. Baker, London: Routledge, 1907.

Johnstoun, James, *A Juridical Dissertation concerning the Scripture Doctrine of Marriage Contracts, and the Marriages of Cousin-Germans* (1734), The Marriage Prohibitions Controversy (facsimile series), ed. Randolph Trumbach, New York: Garland, 1985.

Josselin, Ralph, *The Diary of the Rev. Ralph Josselin*, ed. E. Hockliffe, London: Offices of the Royal Historical Society, 1908.

[Justice, Elizabeth], *Amelia: or, the Distress'd Wife: A History Founded on Real Circumstances*, London: 1751.

Kelly, Hugh, *Memoirs of a Magdalen: or, The History of Louisa Mildmay*, 2 vols., London: 1767.

Keir, Mrs., *The History of Miss Greville*, London: 1787.

Kent, Nathaniel, *A General View of the Agriculture of the County of Norfolk*, London: 1796.

Knight, Ellis Cornelia, *The Autobiography of Miss Knight, Lady Companion to Princess Charlotte*, ed. Roger Fulford, London: W. Kimber, 1960.

Lackington, James, *Memoirs of the Forty-Five First Years of the Life of James Lackington*, 13th edn., London: 1794.

[Anon.], *The Lady's Drawing Room*, London: 1744.

The Lady's Magazine: or Entertaining Companion for the Fair Sex (periodical), London: 1770–1820.

Leadbeater, Mary, *The Leadbeater Papers: The Annals of Ballitore, Letters from Edmund Burke, The Correspondence of Mrs. R. Trench and Rev. George Crabbe with Mary Leadbeater*, London: Bell and Daldy, 1862.

Lee, Sophia, *The Recess; or, A Tale of Other Times, by the Author of* The Chapter of Accidents, 3 vols., London: T. Cadell, 1785.

Leeson, Margaret, *The Memoirs of Mrs Leeson* (1795–7), ed. Mary Lyons, Dublin: The Lilliput Press, 1995.

Lennox, Charlotte, *Euphemia*, London: 1790.

　The Female Quixote, or, The Adventures of Arabella (1752), ed. Margaret Dalziel, intro. Margaret Anne Doody, with Duncan Isles, Oxford: Oxford University Press, 1989.

　Henrietta, 2 vols. London: A. Millar, 1758.

　The History of Harriot and Sophia, London: 1761; as *Sophia*, 2 vols., London: 1762.

　The Life of Harriot Stuart, London: 1751.

　The Sister, London: 1769.

[Anon.], *Leonora: or, Characters Drawn from Real Life*, 2 vols., London: Thomas Davies, 1745.

[Anon.], *A Letter from a Bystander Containing Remarks on and Objections to the Bill Now Depending in Parliament, for the Better Preventing Clandestine Marriages*, London: M. Sheepey, 1753.

[Anon.], *A Letter to the Public Containing the Substance of What Hath Been Offered in the Late Debates upon the Subject of the Act of Parliament, for the Better Preventing of Clandestine Marriages* (1753), rpt. New York: Garland, 1985.

[Anon.], *Letters on Love, Marriage, and Adultery; Addressed to the Right Honorable the Earl of Exeter*, London: J. Ridgway, 1789; rpt. New York: Garland, 1984.

Lewis, Matthew, *The Monk*, London: 1796; original text, variant readings, and "A Note on the Text" by Louis G. Peck, intro. John Berryman, New York: Grove Press, 1952.

[Anon.], *The Life of Patty Saunders*, London: 1752.

Lockhart, J. G., *Memoirs of the Life of Sir Walter Scott, Bart*, 7 vols., Edinburgh: R. Cadell, and Boston: Otis, Broaders, 1837–8.

Mackenzie, Henry, *Julia de Roubigné*, London: 1777.

　The Man of Feeling [1771]; *and, The Man of the World* [1773], London: Routledge, and New York: E. P. Duton, 1931.

Mangin, Edward, *George the Third*, 3 vols., London: 1807.

Manley, Delarivier, *The Adventures of Rivella* (1714), ed. Katherine Zelinsky, Peterborough, ON: Broadview Press, 1999.

　Secret Memoirs and Manners . . . from The New Atalantis (1709); as *New Atalantis*, ed. Ros Ballaster, London: Pickering and Chatto, 1991.

Meades, Anna, *The History of Sir William Harrington*, 4 vols. (1771); rpt. New York: Garland, 1974.

Middleton, Thomas [?] [or Cyril Tourneur?], *The Revenger's Tragedy* (1606–7), ed. Brian Gibbons, New York: Hill and Wang, 1967.

Minifie, Susannah [Mrs. Gunning], and Margaret Minifie, *The Histories of Lady Frances S— and Lady Caroline S—*, London: R. and J. Dodsley, 1763.

Misson, Henri, *M. Misson's Memoirs and Observations in His Travels over England*, trans. John Ozell, London: D. Browne, 1719.

[Anon.], *The Modern Atalantis, or, The Devil in an Air Balloon*, London: G. Kearsley, 1784.

Montagu, Lady Mary Wortley, *The Complete Letters of Lady Mary Wortley Montagu*, 3 vols., ed. Robert Halsband, Oxford: Clarendon Press, 1967.

More, Hannah, *Coelebs in Search of a Wife*, London: T. Cadell and W. Davies, 1808.

Motherwell, William, *Minstrelsy: Ancient and Modern*, Glasgow: J. Wylie, 1827.

The Mysteries of Conjugal Love Reveal'd, London: 1712.

A New and Complete Collection of Trials for Adultery: or A General History of Gallantry and Divorces, London: J. Gill, 1796.

North, Roger, *A Discourse of the Poor*, London: M. Cooper, 1753.

Northcote, James, *The Life of Sir Joshua Reynolds*, 2 vols., London: Henry Colbourn, 1818.

Opie, Amelia, *Adeline Mowbray, or the Mother and Daughter*, 3 vols., London: 1805.

Paris, J. A., "A Biographical Memoir of Arthur Young," *Quarterly Journal of Science, Literature and the Arts* 9 (July 1820), 279–309.

Pennington, Sarah, *An Unfortunate Mother's Advice to her Absent Daughters*, London: 1761.

"Philogamus," *The Present State of Matrimony: or, The Real Causes of Conjugal Infidelity and Unhappy Marriages*, London: 1739.

Pierce, Eliza, *The Letters of Eliza Pierce, 1751–1775*, ed. Violet M. Macdonald, London: Frederick Etchells and Hugh Macdonald, 1927.

Pinckney, Elise, ed., *The Letterbook of Eliza Lucas Pinckney, 1739–1762*, Columbia: University of South Carolina Press, 1997.

Pratt, Samuel, *Shenstone-Green; or the New Paradise Lost*, London: 1780.

Prior, Matthew, *Poems on Several Occasions*, 5th edn., 2 vols., London: H. Lintot, 1741.

Quick, John, *A Serious Inquiry into That Weighty Case of Conscience, Whether a Man May Lawfully Marry His Deceased Wife's Sister* (1703), The Marriage Prohibitions Controversy (facsimile series), ed. Randolph Trumbach, New York: Garland, 1985.

Radcliffe, Ann, *The Castles of Athlin and Dunbayne: A Highland Story*, London: 1789.

The Italian; or the Confessional of the Black Penitents (1797), ed. Frederick Garber, Oxford and New York: Oxford University Press, 1968.

The Mysteries of Udolpho, London: 1794.

The Romance of the Forest (1791), ed. Chloe Chard, Oxford and New York: Oxford University Press, 1991.

A Sicilian Romance, London: 1790.

Radcliffe, Mary Ann, *The Female Advocate*, Edinburgh: 1810.

Reeve, Clara, *Destination; or, Memoirs of a Private Family*, 3 vols., London: 1799.
  Fatherless Fanny, London: 1819.
  The Old English Baron, London: 1778 (originally published as *The Champion of Virtue*, Colchester: 1777).
  Plans of Education, London: 1792.
  The Progress of Romance, London: 1785.
  The Two Mentors: A Modern Story, London: 1783.
Repton, Humphrey, *Observations on the Theory and Practice of Landscape Gardening*, London: 1803.
Reynolds, Frances, *An Enquiry concerning the Principles of Taste, and of the Origin of Our Ideas of Beauty*, London: J. Smeeton, 1789; ed. James Clifford, Los Angeles: William Andrews Clark Memorial Library, University of California, 1951.
  A Melancholy Tale, London: 1790.
Richardson, Samuel, *Clarissa* (1747–8), ed. Angus Ross, London: Penguin, 1985.
  Pamela, 4 vols., London: 1741; ed. Peter Sabor and intro. Margaret A. Doody, Harmondsworth: Penguin, 1980. (The Penguin edition contains only vols. I and II of the first edition; vols. I–IV are included in *Pamela or Virtue Rewarded*, intro. William Lyon Phelps, 4 vols., New York: Croscup & Sterling, 1901.)
  The History of Sir Charles Grandison (1753–4), ed. Jocelyn Harris, Oxford and New York: Oxford University Press, 1986.
Robinson, Mary, *The Natural Daughter*, London: 1799.
  Vancenza, or, The Dangers of Credulity, 3rd edn., 2 vols., London: 1792.
  Walsingham, London: 1797.
Roche, Regina Maria, *Children of the Abbey*, 2 vols., London: 1796.
Rousseau, Jean-Jacques, *Julie, ou La Nouvelle Héloïse*, Paris: 1761.
Ryder, Dudley, *The Diary of Dudley Ryder*, ed. William Matthews, London: Methuen, 1939.
Salmon, Thomas, *A Critical Essay concerning Marriage* (1724), rpt. New York: Garland, 1985.
Savile, George, Marquis of Halifax, *The Lady's New-Year's Gift; or, Advice to a Daughter*, London: 1688.
Schimmelpenninck, Mary Anne, *The Life of Mary Anne Schimmelpenninck, Author of "Select Memoirs of Port Royal" and Other Works*, 2nd edn., ed. Christiana C. Hankin, 2 vols., London: Longman, Brown, Green, Longmans, and Roberts, 1858; Philadelphia: Henry Longstreth, 1859.
Scott, Sarah, *Agreeable Ugliness*, London: 1754.
  A Description of Millenium Hall (1762), ed. Gary Kelly, Peterborough, ON: Broadview Press, 1995.
  The History of Cornelia, London: A. Millar, 1750.
  The History of Sir George Ellison (1766), ed. Betty Rizzo, Lexington: University of Kentucky Press, 1996.
  Journey through Every Stage of Life, London: 1754.
  The Test of Filial Duty, London: 1772.

Seward, Anna, *The Letters of Anna Seward: Written between the Years 1784 and 1807*, 7 vols., Edinburgh: Constable, 1811.

Shebbeare, John, *The Marriage Act*, London: 1754.

Sheridan, Frances, *Eugenia and Adelaide*, 2 vols., London: 1791.

The Memoirs of Miss Sidney Bidulph, London: 1761.

Skinn, Mrs., *The Old Maid*, 3 vols. London: 1771.

Smith, Adam, *The Wealth of Nations* (1776), ed. Andrew Skinner, Harmondsworth and New York: Penguin, 1973.

Smith, Charlotte, *Celestina*, London: 1791.

Desmond, London: 1792.

Emmeline: The Orphan of the Castle (1788), London: Pandora, 1988.

Ethelinde, or The Recluse of the Lake, 5 vols., London: 1790.

Letters of a Solitary Wanderer: Containing Narratives of Various Description, London: 1800.

Rambles Farther: A Continuation of Rural Walks: in Dialogues Intended for the Use of Young Persons, 2 vols., London: 1796.

Rural Walks: in dialogues: Intended for the Use of Young Persons, 2 vols., London: 1795.

The Young Philosopher, 4 vols., London: 1798.

Smollett, Tobias, *The Adventures of Peregrine Pickle*, Landon: 1751.

The Adventures of Roderick Random (1748), ed. Paul-Gabriel Boucé, Oxford and New York: Oxford University Press, 1981.

The Adventures of Sir Launcelot Greaves, London: 1760–2.

The Expedition of Humphry Clinker, London: 1771.

Travels through France and Italy, London: 1766.

Works of Tobias Smollett, New York: Routledge, 188?.

[Anon.], *Sophronia; or, Letters to the Ladies*, London: William Johnston, 1761.

Spence, Joseph, *Anecdotes*, ed. James M. Osborn, Oxford: Clarendon Press, 1966.

Spencer, Georgiana, *Emma: or, the Unfortunate Attachment*, London: 1773.

Steele, Sir Richard, *The Tatler*, ed. Donald F. Bond, 3 vols., Oxford: Oxford University Press, 1987.

Sterne, Laurence, *A Sentimental Journey through France and Italy, by Mr. Yorick*, London: 1768; ed. Graham Petrie, intro. A. Alvarez, Harmondsworth: Penguin, 1767.

Tristram Shandy, London: 1760–5.

Stout, William, *The Autobiography of William Stout of Lancaster 1665–1752*, ed. J. D. Marshall, Manchester: Manchester University Press, and New York: Barnes and Noble, 1967.

Stuart, Lady Lousia, *Lady Lousia Stuart: Selections from Her Manuscripts*, ed. James Home, New York and London: Harper, 1899.

Swinburne, Henry, *A Treatise of Spousals, or Matrimonial Contracts* (1686), rpt. New York: Garland, 1985.

Temple, William, *The Works of Sir William Temple*, 4 vols., London: J. Clarke et al., 1757.

Thrale, Hester, "The Imposter," Rylands MS 650, Rylands Library, University of Manchester, England.

Thraliana, the Diary of Mrs. Hester Lynch Thrale, 1776–1809, ed. Katherine C. Balderston, 2 vols., Oxford: Clarendon Press, 1951.

Todd, Elizabeth, *The History of Lady Caroline Rivers*, London: 1788.

The Town and Country Magazine, or Universal Repository of Knowledge, Instruction, and Entertainment (1769–96).

[Anon.], The Trial at Large of John Swan and Elizabeth Jeffreys, 2nd edn., London: 1752.

[Anon.], *The True History of Henrietta de Belgrave, a Woman Born to Great Calamities*, London: 1750.

[Anon.], *The Unnatural Mother and Ungrateful Wife*, London: 1730.

Voltaire [François Marie Arouet], *Letters on the English Nation* (1733), trans. Leonard Tancock, Harmondsworth: Penguin, 1980.

Wakefield, Priscilla, *Reflections on the Present Condition of the Female Sex, with Suggestions for Its Improvement*, London: Joseph Johnson, 1798.

Walpole, Horace, *The Castle of Otranto*, London: 1764.

The Mysterious Mother, London: 1768.

Weeton, Ellen, *Miss Weeton 1807–1811: Journal of a Governess*, ed. Edward Hall, Landon: Oxford University Press, 1936.

Welch, Saunders, *A Proposal to Render Effectual a Plan, to Remove the Nuisance of Common Prostitutes from the Streets of this Metropolis*, London: 1758; facsimile rpt. in *Prostitution Reform: Four Documents*, New York: Garland, 1985.

West, Jane, *The Gossip's Story*, London: 1796.

Williams, Charlotte, *Letters between an English Lady and Her Friend at Paris, in Which Are Contained The Memoirs of Mrs. Williams*, 2 vols., London: T. Becket and P. A. DeHondt, 1770.

Wollstonecraft, Mary, *Letters Written during a Short Residence in Sweden, Norway, and Denmark*, London: 1796.

Maria, or the Wrongs of Woman (1798), ed. Moira Ferguson, New York: Norton, 1975.

Original Stories from Real Life (1788), 2nd edn., London: 1791.

The Works of Mary Wollstonecraft, ed. Marilyn Butler and Janet Todd, 7 vols., New York: New York University Press, 1989.

Woodfin, Mrs. A., *The Auction*, London: 1770.

[Anon.], *The Woodland Cottage*, 2 vols., London: Hookham and Carpenter, 1796.

Young, Arthur, *The Adventures of Emmera, or the Fair American*, 2 vols., London: 1767.

The Adventures of Miss Lucy Watson, London: 1768.

Annals of Agriculture and Other Useful Arts, 46 vols., London: Arthur Young, 1784–1815 (periodical).

The Autobiography of Arthur Young, ed. M. Bentham-Edwards, London: 1898; rpt. New York: Augustus M. Kelley, 1967.

"An Enquiry into the Progressive Value of Money in England," *Annals of Agriculture* 46.270 (1812).

The Farmer's Letters to the People of England (1767), 3rd edn., corrected and enlarged, Dublin: J. Milliken, 1768.

The History of Julia Benson; or the Sufferings of Innocence, 2 vols., London: 1775.

The History of Sir Charles Beaufort, 2 vols., London: 1766.

An Inquiry into the Propriety of Applying Wastes to the Better Maintenance and Support of the Poor, London: 1801.

Letters concerning the Present State of the French Nation, London: 1768.

Observations on the Present State of the Waste Lands of Great Britain, by the Author of the Tours through England, London: 1773.

Political Essays concerning the Present State of the British Empire, London: W. Strahan and T. Cadell, 1772.

A Six Months Tour through the North of England, 4 vols., 2nd edn., London: W. Strahan and W. Nicoll, 1771.

Travels during the Years 1787, 1788, and 1789, Undertaken More Particularly with a View of Ascertaining the Cultivation, Wealth, Resources, and National Prosperity of the Kingdom of France, 2 vols., Dublin: 1793.

SELECTED SECONDARY SOURCES

Abelove, Henry, "Some Speculations on the History of Sexual Intercourse during the Long Eighteenth Century in England," *Genders* 6 (November 1989), 125–30.

Aguirre, Manuel, "The Roots of the Symbolic Role of Woman in Gothic Literature," in *Exhibited by Candlelight: Sources and Developments in the Gothic Tradition*, ed. Valeria Tinkler-Villani and Peter Davidson, with Jane Stevenson, Amsterdam and Atlanta, GA: Rodopi, 1995, 57–63.

Anderson, Howard, "Gothic Heroes," in *The English Hero, 1660–1800*, ed. Robert Folkenflik, Newark: University of Delaware Press, 1982, 205–21.

Anderson, Michael, *Approaches to the History of the Western Family 1500–1914*, London and Basingstoke: Macmillan, 1980.

Andrew, Donna T., *Philanthropy and Police: London Charity in the Eighteenth Century*, Princeton, NJ: Princeton University Press, 1989.

Ariès, Philippe, *Centuries of Childhood: A Social History of Family Life*, trans. Robert Baldick, New York: Random House, 1962.

Armstrong, Nancy, *Desire and Domestic Fiction: A Political History of the Novel*, New York and Oxford: Oxford University Press, 1987.

Armstrong, Nancy, and Leonard Tennenhouse, *The Imaginary Puritan: Literature, Intellectual Labor, and the Origins of Personal Life*, Berkeley: University of California Press, 1992.

Ashby, M. K., *The Changing English Village: A History of Bledington, Gloucestershire, 1066–1914*, Kineton: Roundwood Press, 1974.

Ashmore, Helen, "Do Not, My Love, Burn Your Papers," in *Frances Reynolds and Samuel Johnson: A Keepsake to Mark the 286th Birthday of Samuel Johnson and the 49th Annual Dinner of The Johnsonians*, Cambridge, MA: Houghton Library, Harvard University, 1995, 1–19.

Backscheider, Paula, ed., *Revising Women: Eighteenth-Century "Women's Fiction" and Social Engagement*, Baltimore and London: Johns Hopkins University Press, 2000.

Backus, Margot Gayle, *The Gothic Family Romance: Heterosexuality, Child Sacrifice, and the Anglo-Irish Colonial Order*, Durham, NC: Duke University Press, 1999.

Baldick, Chris, "The End of the Line: The Family Curse in Shorter British Fiction," in *Exhibited by Candlelight: Sources and Developments in the Gothic Tradition*, ed. Valeria Tinkler-Villani and Peter Davidson, with Jane Stevenson, Amsterdam and Atlanta, GA: Rodopi, 1995, 147–57.

Ballaster, Ros, *Seductive Forms: Women's Amatory Fiction from 1684 to 1740*, Oxford: Clarendon Press, 1992.

Bank, Stephen, and Michael Kahn, "Intense Sibling Loyalties," in *Sibling Relationships: Their Nature and Significance across the Life Span*, ed. Michael E. Lamb and Brian Sutton-Smith, Hillsdale, NJ: Lawrence Erlbaum Associates, 1982, 251–66.

The Sibling Bond, New York: Basic Books, 1982.

Barker, Gerard A., *Grandison's Heirs: The Paragon's Progress in the Late Eighteenth-Century English Novel*, Newark: University of Delaware Press, 1985.

Barrell, John, *The Dark Side of the Landscape: The Rural Poor in English Painting, 1730–1840*, Cambridge: Cambridge University Press, 1980.

Baruth, Philip, E., "Who Is Charlotte Charke?" in *Introducing Charlotte Charke*, ed. Philip E. Baruth, Urbana and Chicago: University of Illinois Press, 1998, 9–62.

Battestin, Martin C., and Ruthe R. Battestin, *Henry Fielding: A Life*, London and New York: Routledge, 1989.

Beattie, J. M., *Crime and the Courts in England, 1660–1662*, Princeton: Princeton University Press, 1986.

Bengtsson, Tommy, Osamu Saito, David Reher, and Cameron Campbell, "Population and the Economy: From Hunger to Modern Economic Growth," in *Debates and Controversies in Economic History: Proceedings of the Twelfth International Economic History Congress*, ed. Clara Eugenia Núñez, Madrid: Fundación Ramón Areces, Fundación fomento de la historia económica, 1998, 69–144.

Benjamin, Jessica, *The Bonds of Love: Psychoanalysis, Feminism, and the Problem of Domination*, New York: Pantheon Books, 1988.

Bennett, Lynn, *Dangerous Wives and Sacred Sisters: Social and Symbolic Roles of High-Caste Women in Nepal*, New York: Columbia University Press, 1983.

Berg, Maxine, "Commerce and Creativity in Eighteenth-Century Birmingham," in *Markets and Manufacture in Early Industrial Europe*, ed. Maxine Berg, London: Routledge, 1991, 173–201.

"Women's Property and the Industrial Revolution," *Journal of Interdisciplinary History* 24.2 (Autumn 1993), 233–50.

"Women's Work, Mechanisation, and the Early Phases of Industrialisation in England," in *The Historical Meanings of Work*, ed. Patrick Joyce, Cambridge: Cambridge University Press, 1987, 64–98.

Berg, Maxine, ed., *The Age of Manufactures, 1700–1830*, New York: Oxford University Press, 1985.

Markets and Manufacture in Early Industrial Europe, London: Routledge, 1991.

Berg, Maxine, and Pat Hudson, "Rehabilitating the Industrial Revolution," *Economic History Review* 45.1 (1992), 24–50.

Berkner, Lutz K., "The Stem Family and the Development Cycle of the Peasant Household: An Eighteenth-Century Austrian Example," *American Historical Review* 77 (April 1972), 398–418.

"The Use and Misuse of Census Data for the Historical Analysis of Family Structure," *Journal of Interdisciplinary History* 5.4 (Spring 1975), 721–38.

Black, Frank Gees, *The Epistolary Novel in the Late Eighteenth Century*, Eugene: University of Oregon Press, 1940.

Blewett, David, "Changing Attitudes toward Marriage in the Time of Defoe: The Case of Moll Flanders," *Huntington Library Quarterly* 44.2 (Spring 1981), 77–88.

Blum, Carol, Introduction to "Demographic Thought and Reproductive Realities, from Montesquieu to Malthus," *Eighteenth-Century Studies* 32.4 (Summer 1999), 535–69.

Bonfield, Lloyd, "Affective Families, Open Elites, and Strict Family Settlements in Early Modern England," *Economic History Review* 2nd ser., 39 (1986), 341–54.

"Marriage Settlements and the 'Rise of Great Estates': The Demographic Aspect," *Economic History Review* 2nd ser., 32.4 (1979), 483–93.

"Normative Rules and Property Transmission: Reflections on the Link between Marriage and Inheritance in Early Modern England," *The World We Have Gained: Histories of Population and Social Structure*, ed. Lloyd Bonfield, Richard M. Smith, and Keith Wrightson, Oxford: Basil Blackwell, 1986, 155–76.

Boose, Lynda E., "The Father's House and the Daughter in It: The Structures of Western Culture's Daughter-Father Relationship," in *Daughters and Fathers*, ed. Lynda E. Boose and Betty S. Flowers, Baltimore: Johns Hopkins University Press, 1989, 19–74.

Boulton, Jeremy, "Clandestine Marriages in London: An Examination of a Neglected Urban Variable," *Urban History* 20.2 (October 1993), 191–210.

"Itching after Private Marryings? Marriage Customs in Seventeenth-Century London," *London Journal* 16 (1991), 15–34.

Bowen, H. V., *War and British Society 1688–1815*, Cambridge: Cambridge University Press, 1988.

Bowers, Toni, "'A Point of Conscience': Breastfeeding and Maternal Authority in *Pamela 2*," *Eighteenth-Century Fiction* 7.3 (April 1995), 259–78.

The Politics of Motherhood: British Writing and Culture, 1680–1760, Cambridge: Cambridge University Press, 1996.

Brant, Clare, "Speaking of Women: Scandal and Law in the Mid-Eighteenth Century," in *Women, Texts and Histories 1575–1760*, ed. Clare Brant and Diane Purkis, London and New York: Routledge, 1992, 242–70.

Brassley, Paul, *The Agricultural Economy of Northumberland and Durham in the Period 1640–1750*, New York: Garland, 1985.

Brewer, John, *The Sinews of Power: War, Money and the English State, 1688–1783*, Cambridge, MA: Harvard University Press, 1990.

Brink, J. R., ed., *Female Scholars: A Tradition of Learned Women before 1800*, Montreal: Eden Press, 1980.

Brown, E. H. Phelps, and Sheila V. Hopkins, "Seven Centuries of the Price of Consumables Compared with Builders' Wage-Rates," in *Essays in Economic History*, ed. E. M. Carus-Wilson, London: E. Arnold, 1962, 179–96 and in Brown and Hopkins, *A Perspective of Wages and Prices*, London and New York: Methuen, 1981, 13–59.

Brown, Richard, *Society and Economy in Modern Britain 1700–1850*, London: Routledge, 1991.

Bushaway, Bob, *By Rite: Custom, Ceremony and Community in Eighteenth-Century England, 1700–1800*, London: Junction, 1982.

Butler, Marilyn, *Jane Austen and the War of Ideas*, Oxford: Clarendon Press, 1975.

Carlton, Charles, *The Court of Orphans*, Leicester: Leicester University Press, 1974.

Carus-Wilson, E. M., ed., *Essays in Economic History*, 3 vols., London: Arnold, 1954.

Castle, Terry, Review of *Jane Austen's Letters*, ed. Deirdre Le Faye, *London Review of Books*, August 3, 1995.

Chaber, Lois A, "Matriarchal Mirror: Women and Capital in *Moll Flanders*," *PMLA* 97.2 (March 1982), 212–26.

"'This Affecting Subject': An 'Interested' 'Reading of Childbearing in Two Novels by Samuel Richardson," *Eighteenth-Century Fiction* 8.2 (January 1996), 193–250.

Chambers, J. D., "Enclosure and Labour Supply in the Industrial Revolution," *Economic History Review* 2nd ser., 5.3 (1953), 319–43.

Nottinghamshire in the Eighteenth Century: A Study of Life and Labour under the Squirearchy, 2nd edn., New York: Augustus Kelley, 1966.

Chaytor, Miranda, "Household and Kinship: Ryton in the Late 16th and Early 17th Centuries," *History Workshop Journal* 10 (Autumn 1980), 25–60.

Child, Francis James, ed., *The English and Scottish Popular Ballads*, 5 vols., New York: Houghton Mifflin, 1882–98; rpt. New York: Dover Books, 1965.

Chinn, Carl, Introduction to *The Life of William Hutton*, Studley, Warwickshire: Brewin Books, 1998.

Chowdhry, Prem, *The Veiled Women: Shifting Gender Equations in Rural Haryana 1880–1990*, Delhi: Oxford University Press, 1994.

Clark, Alice, *The Working Life of Women in the Seventeenth Century* (1919); rpt. New York: Augustus M. Kelley, 1968.

Clark, Anna, *The Struggle for the Breeches: Gender and the Making of the British Working Class*, Berkeley: University of California Press, 1995.

Women's Silence, Men's Violence: Sexual Assault in England 1770–1845, New York and London: Pandora, 1987.

Clark, Gregory, Review of M. E. Turner, J. V. Beckett, and B. Afton, *Agricultural Rent in England, Journal of Economic History*, 2nd ser., 58 (March 1998), 206–10.

"The Charity Commission as a Source in English Economic History," *Research in Economic History* 18 (1998), 1–52.

"Housing Rents, Housing Quality, and Living Standards in England and Wales, 1640–1909," unpublished paper, October 1999.

Clay, C., "Property Settlements, Financial Provisions for the Family, and Sale of Land by the Great Landowners, 1660–1790," *Journal of British Studies* 21 (1981), 18–38.

Clayton, Ellen, *English Female Artists*, 2 vols., London: Tinsley Brothers, 1876.

Clery, E. J., *The Rise of Supernatural Fiction, 1762–1800*, Cambridge: Cambridge University Press, 1995.

Cohen, Paula Marantz, *The Daughter's Dilemma: Family Process and the Nineteenth-Century Domestic Novel*, Ann Arbor: University of Michigan Press, 1991.

"Stabilizing the Family System at Mansfield Park," *ELH* 54.3 (1987), 669–93.

Coll, Sebastian, and John Komlos, "The Biological Standard of Living and Economic Development: Nutrition, Health and Well Being in Historical Perspective," in *Debates and Controversies in Economic History: Proceedings of the Twelfth International Economic History Congress*, ed. Clara Eugenia Núñez, Madrid: Fundación Ramón Areces, Fundación fomento de la historia económica, 1998, 219–82.

Collier, Jane Fishburne, *Marriage and Inequality in Classless Societies*, Stanford: Stanford University Press, 1988.

Collier, Jane Fishburne, and Sylvia Junko Yanagisako, eds., *Gender and Kinship: Essays towards a Unified Analysis*, Stanford: Stanford University Press, 1987.

Cooper, J. P., "Patterns of Inheritance and Settlement by Great Landowners from the Fifteenth to the Eighteenth Centuries," in *Family and Inheritance*, ed. Jack Goody, Joan Thirsk, and E. P. Thompson, Cambridge: Cambridge University Press, 1976.

Cooper, Sheila M. "Intergenerational Social Mobility in Late-Seventeenth- and Early-Eighteenth-Century England, *Continuity and Change* 7.3 (1992), 283–301.

Copeland, Edward, "The Burden of *Grandison*: Jane Austen and Her Contemporaries," *Women and Literature* 3 (1983), 98–106.

Women Writing about Money, Cambridge: Cambridge University Press, 1995.

Cott, Nancy, "Eighteenth-Century Family and Social Life Revealed in Massachusetts Divorce Records," *Journal of Social History* 10 (1976), 20–43.

Public Vows: A History of Marriage and the Nation, Cambridge, MA: Harvard University Press, 2000.

Cottis, Janie, "A Country Gentleman and His Estates, c. 1720–68: Sir Mark Stuart Pleydell, Bart., of Coleshill, Berkshire," in *Town and Countryside: The English Landowner in the National Economy, 1660–1860*, ed. C. W. Chalklin and J. R. Wordie, London and Boston: Unwin Hyman, 1989, 26–51.

Crawford, Patricia, and Laura Gowing, eds., *Women's Worlds in Seventeenth-Century England*, New York and London: Routledge, 2000.

Crawford, Patricia, and Sara Mendelson, "Sexual Identities in Early Modern England: The Marriage of Two Women in 1680," *Gender & History* 7.3 (November 1995), 362–77.

Cressy, David, *Birth, Marriage and Death: Ritual, Religion and the Life Cycle in Tudor and Stuart England*, Oxford: Oxford University Press, 1997.

"Kinship and Kin Interaction in Early Modern England," *Past and Present* 113 (1986), 47–73.

Literacy and the Social Order: Reading and Writing in Tudor and Stuart England, Cambridge: Cambridge University Press, 1980.

Cunningham, Hugh, "The Employment and Unemployment of Children in England c. 1680–1851," *Past and Present* 126 (February 1990), 115–50.

Cunningham, Kiran, "Let's Go to My Place: Residence, Gender and Power in a Mende Community," in *Gender, Kinship, Power: A Comparative and Interdisciplinary History*, ed. Mary Jo Maynes, Ann Waltner, Birgitte Soland, and Ulrike Strasser, New York: Routledge, 1996, 335–49.

Daunton, M. J., "Towns and Economic Growth in Eighteenth-Century England," in *Towns in Societies: Essays in Economic History and Historical Sociology*, ed. Philip Abrams and E. A. Wrigley, London and New York: Cambridge University Press, 1978, 245–77.

Davidoff, Leonore, *Worlds Between: Historical Perspectives on Gender and Class*, Cambridge: Polity Press, 1995.

Davidoff, Leonore, and Catherine Hall, *Family Fortunes: Men and Women of the English Middle Class, 1780–1850*, Chicago: University of Chicago Press, 1987.

Davis, Lennard J., *Factual Fictions: The Origins of the English Novel*, New York: Columbia University Press, 1983.

DeLamotte, Eugenia C., *Perils of the Night: A Feminist Study of Nineteenth-Century Gothic*, Oxford and New York: Oxford University Press, 1990.

Denbo, Seth, "Relatively Speaking: Cultural Meanings of Incest in Eighteenth-Century Britain," Ph.D. diss., University of Warwick, 2001.

DeRitter, Jones, "'Not the Person She Conceived Me': The Public Identities of Charlotte Charke," *Genders* 19 (1994), 3–25.

Derry, Stephen, "Sources of Chapter Two of *Sense and Sensibility*," *Persuasions* 16 (December 1994), 5–27.

Donoghue, Emma, *Passions between Women: British Lesbian Culture 1668–1801*, London: Scarlet Press, 1993.

Doody, Margaret Anne, *Frances Burney: The Life in the Works*, New Brunswick, NJ: Rutgers University Press, 1988.

Druce, Robert, "*Pulex Defixus*, Or, The Spellbound Flea: An Excursion into Porno-Gothic," in *Exhibited by Candlelight: Sources and Developments in the Gothic Tradition*, ed. Valeria Tinkler-Villani and Peter Davidson, with Jane Stevenson, Amsterdam and Atlanta, GA: Rodopi, 1995, 221–42.

Duckworth, Alistair, *The Improvement of the Estate: A Study of Jane Austen's Novels*, Baltimore: Johns Hopkins University Press, 1971.

Earle, Peter, "The Female Labour Market in London in the Late Seventeenth and Early Eighteenth Centuries," *Economic History Review* 2nd ser., 42.3 (1989), 328–53.

The Making of the English Middle Class: Business, Society and Family Life in London, 1660–1730, Berkeley: University of California Press, 1989.

Eaves, T. C. Duncan, and Ben D. Kimpel, *Samuel Richardson: A Biography*, Oxford: Clarendon Press, 1971.

Ellis, Kate, "Ann Radcliffe and the Perils of Catholicism," *Women's Writing* 1.2 (1994), 161–9.

The Contested Castle: Gothic Novels and the Subversion of Domestic Ideology, Urbana: University of Illinois Press, 1989.

Elshtain, Jean Bethke, *The Family in Political Thought*, Amherst: University of Massachusetts Press, 1982.

Engels, Frederick, *The Origins of the Family, Private Property, and the State*, 1884; rpt. Harmondsworth: Penguin, 1985.

Epstein, William H., *John Cleland: Images of a Life*, New York: Columbia University Press, 1974.

Erickson, Amy Louise, "Common Law versus Common Practice: The Use of Marriage Settlements in Early Modern England," *Economic History Review* 2nd ser., 43.1 (1990), 21–39.

Women and Property in Early Modern England, New York and London: Routledge, 1993.

Fabricant, Carole, "Binding and Dressing Nature's Loose Tresses: The Ideology of Augustan Landscape Design," *Studies in Eighteenth-Century Culture* 8 (1979), 109–35.

Farb, Peter, and G. Armelagos, *Consuming Passions: The Anthropology of Eating*, Boston: Houghton Mifflin, 1980.

Feinstein, Charles H., "Pessimism Perpetuated: Real Wages and the Standard of Living in Britain during and after the Industrial Revolution," *Journal of Economic History* 58.3 (September 1998), 625–58.

Fergus, Jan, *Jane Austen: A Literary Life*, London: Macmillan, and New York: St. Martin's Press, 1991.

"Jane Austen: Tensions between Security and Marginality," in *History, Gender & Eighteenth-Century Literature*, ed. Beth Fowkes Tobin, Athens: University of Georgia Press, 1994, 258–70.

"Provincial Servants' Reading in the Late Eighteenth Century," in *The Practice and Representation of Reading in England*, ed. James Raven, Helen Small, and Naomi Tadmor, Cambridge: Cambridge University Press, 1996, 202–25.

Fildes, Valerie A., *Breasts, Bottles, and Babies: A History of Infant Feeding*, Edinburgh: Edinburgh University Press, 1986.

Fildes, Valerie A., ed., *Women as Mothers in Pre-Industrial England: Essays in Memory of Dorothy McLaren*, London and New York: Routledge, 1989.

Flandrin, J. L., *Families in Former Times: Kinship, Household and Sexuality*, trans R. Southern, Cambridge: Cambridge University Press, 1979.

Fletcher, Anthony, *Gender, Sex, and Subordination in England 1500–1800*, New Haven and London: Yale University Press, 1995.

Fletcher, Loraine, *Charlotte Smith: A Critical Biography*, Basingstoke, Hampshire: Palgrave, 1998.

Flinn, M. W., "Trends in Real Wages, 1750–1850," *Economic History Review* 2nd ser., 27.3 (August 1974), 395–413.

Flint, Christopher, *Family Fictions: Narrative and Domestic Relations in Britain 1688–1798*, Stanford: Stanford University Press, 1998.

"The Family Piece: Oliver Goldsmith and the Politics of the Everyday in Eighteenth-Century Domestic Portraiture," *Eighteenth-Century Studies* 29.2 (Winter 1995–6), 127–52.

Fogel, R. W., "Second Thoughts on the European Escape from Hunger: Famines, Chronic Malnutrition, and Mortality Rates," in *Nutrition and Poverty*, ed. S. R. Osmani, Oxford: Clarendon Press, 1992, 243–86.

Foster, James R., *History of the Pre-Romantic Novel in England*, New York: Modern Language Association, 1949.

Foucault, Michel, *The History of Sexuality*, trans. Robert Hurley, vol. 1: *An Introduction*, New York: Random House, 1978.

Fout, John, ed., *Forbidden History: The State, Society, and the Regulation of Sexuality in Modern Europe*, Chicago: University of Chicago Press, 1992.

Foxon, David, *Libertine Literature in England 1660–1745*, New Hyde Park, NY: University Books, 1965.

Frank, Judith, *Common Ground: Eighteenth-Century Satiric Fiction and the Poor*, Stanford: Stanford University Press, 1997.

Freud, Sigmund, *The Standard Edition of the Complete Works of Sigmund Freud*, 24 vols., ed. and trans. James Strachey, London: The Hogarth Press, 1953–74.

"The Taboo of Virginity" (1918), in *Collected Papers*, trans. Joan Rivière, 5 vols., New York: Basic Books, 1959, IV: 217–35.

Friedl, Ernestine, *Women and Men: An Anthropologist's View*, New York: Holt, Rinehart and Winston, 1975.

Froide, Amy M., "Marital Status as a Category of Difference: Singlewomen and Widows in Early Modern England," in *Singlewomen in the European Past, 1250–1800*, ed. Judith M. Bennett and Amy M. Froide, Philadelphia: University of Pennsylvania Press, 1999, 236–69.

Gailey, Christine Ward, "Evolutionary Perspectives on Gender Hierarchy," in *Analyzing Gender*, ed. Beth Hess and Myra Ferree, Newbury Park, CA: Sage, 1988, 32–67.

From Kinship to Kingship: Gender Hierarchy and State Formation in the Tongan Islands, Austin: University of Texas Press, 1987.

Gallagher, Catherine, *Nobody's Story: The Vanishing Acts of Women Writers in the Marketplace 1670–1820*, Berkeley: University of California Press, 1994.

Gautier, Gary, "Fanny Hill's Mapping of Sexuality, Female Identity, and Maternity," *Studies in English Literature* 35.3 (Summer 1995), 473–91.

Landed Patriarchy in Fielding's Novels: Fictional Landscapes, Fictional Genders, Studies in British Literature 35, Lewiston, NY: Edwin Mellen Press, 1998.

"Marriage and Family in Fielding's Fiction," *Studies in the Novel* 27 (Summer 1995), 111–28.

Gazley, John G., "Arthur Young, Agriculturalist and Traveller, 1741–1820, Some Bibliographical Sources," *John Rylands Library* 37 (September 1954), 393–428.

The Life of Arthur Young 1741–1820, Philadelphia: American Philosophical Society, 1973.

George, Margaret, *Women in the First Capitalist Society*, Urbana: University of Illinois Press, 1988.

Gilbert, Sandra M., "Life's Empty Pack: Notes toward a Literary Daughteronomy," *Critical Inquiry* 11 (1985), 355–84.

Gilboy, E. W., "The Cost of Living and Real Wages in Eighteenth-Century England," *Review of Economic Statistics* 18 (1936), 134–43.

Gill, Pat, "Pathetic Passions: Incestuous Desire in Plays by Otway and Lee," *The Eighteenth Century: Theory and Interpretation* 30 (Fall 1998), 192–208.

Gillis, John R., *For Better, for Worse: British Marriages, 1600 to the Present*, New York: Oxford University Press, 1985.

"Peasant, Plebian, and Proletarian Marriage in Britain, 1600–1900," in *Proletarianization and Family History*, ed. David Levine, New York: Academic Press, 1984, 129–62.

Glass, D. V., *Numbering the People: The Eighteenth-Century Population Controversy and the Development of Census and Vital Statistics in Britain*, Farnborough, Hants: Saxon House, 1973.

Glass, D. V., and D. E. C. Eversley, eds., *Population in History: Essays in Historical Demography*, London: Edward Arnold, 1965.

Glover, Lorri, *All Our Relations: Blood Ties and Emotional Bonds among the Early South Carolina Gentry*, Baltimore: Johns Hopkins University Press, 2000.

Gonda, Caroline, *Reading Daughters' Fictions 1709–1834, Novels and Society from Marley to Edgeworth*, Cambridge: Cambridge University Press, 1996.

Goode, William J., *World Revolution and Family Patterns*, New York: Free Press, 1963; rpt. 1970.

Goody, Jack, ed., *The Character of Kinship*, Cambridge: Cambridge University Press, 1973.

Goody, Jack, "A Comparative Approach to Incest and Adultery," *British Journal of Sociology* 7 (December 1956), 286–305.

The Development of the Family and Marriage in Europe, Cambridge: Cambridge University Press, 1983.

Production and Reproduction: A Comparative Study of the Domestic Domain, Cambridge and New York: Cambridge University Press, 1976.

Goody, Jack, and S. J. Tambiah, *Bridewealth and Dowry*, Cambridge: Cambridge University Press, 1973.

Goody, Jack, Joan Thirsk, and E. P. Thompson, eds., *Family and Inheritance: Rural Society in Western Europe, 1200–1800*, Cambridge: Cambridge University Press, 1976.

Gottlieb, Beatrice, *The Family in the Western World from the Black Death to the Industrial Age*, Oxford and New York: Oxford University Press, 1993.

Gough, Richard, *The History of Myddle*, ed. David Hey, Harmondsworth: Penguin, 1981.

Gourvish, T. R., "Flinn and Real Wage Trends in Britain, 1750–1850: A Comment," *Economic History Review* 2nd series, 29.1 (February 1976), 136–42.

Gowing, Laura, *Domestic Dangers: Women, Words, and Sex in Early Modern London*, Oxford: Oxford University Press, 1996.

Grassby, Richard, *Kinship and Capitalism: Marriage, Family and Business in the English-Speaking World, 1580–1740*, Cambridge: Cambridge University Press, and Washington, DC: Woodrow Wilson Center Press, 2001.

Green, Mary Elizabeth, "Elizabeth Elstob: The Saxon Nymph (English, 1683–1765)," in *Female Scholars: A Tradition of Learned Women before 1800*, ed. J. R. Brink, Montreal: Eden Press, 1980, 137–60.

Greenfield, Susan, Introduction to *Inventing Maternity: Politics, Science, and Literature 1650–1865*, ed. Susan C. Greenfield and Carol Barash, Lexington: University of Kentucky Press, 1999, 1–33.

   Mothering Daughters: Novels and the Politics of Family Romance Frances Burney to Jane Austen, Detroit: Wayne State University Press, 2002.

Gretton, M. Sturge, *Three Centuries in North Oxford*, Oxford: Oxford University Press, 1902.

Grossman, Joyce, "Social Protest and the Mid-Century Novel: Mary Collyer's *The History of Betty Barnes*," *Eighteenth-Century Women* 1 (2000), 165–84.

Grove, Allen, "Coming Out of the Castle: Renegotiating Gender and Sexuality in Eighteenth-Century Gothic Fiction," Ph.D. diss., University of Pennsylvania, 1996.

Grundy, Isobel, *Lady Mary Wortley Montagu*, Oxford: Oxford University Press, 1999.

   "Samuel Johnson as Patron of Women," *The Age of Johnson: A Scholarly Annual* 1 (1987), 59–77.

Guest, Harriet, *Small Change: Women, Learning, Patriotism 1750–1810*, Chicago: University of Chicago Press, 2000.

Gullickson, Gay L., "Love and Power in the Proto-Industrial Family," in *Markets and Manufacture in Early Industrial Europe*, ed. Maxine Berg, London: Routledge, 1991, 205–26.

Gwilliam, Tassie, "Female Fraud: Counterfeit Maidenheads in the Eighteenth Century," *Journal of the History of Sexuality* 6.4 (April 1996), 518–48.

Haagen, Paul H., "Eighteenth-Century English Society and the Debt Law," in *Social Control and the State: Historical and Comparative Essays*, ed. Stanley Cohen and Andrew Scull, Oxford: Basil Blackwell, 1985.

Habakkuk, Hrothgar John, *Marriage, Debt, and the Estates System: English Landownership 1650–1950*, Oxford: Clarendon Press, 1994.

   "Marriage Settlements in the Eighteenth Century," *Transactions of the Royal Historical Society* 4th ser., 32 (1950), 15–30.

Haggerty, George E., "Literature and Homosexuality in the Late Eighteenth Century: Walpole, Beckford, and Lewis," *Studies in the Novel* 18.4 (Winter 1986), 341–52.

Unnatural Affections: Women and Fiction in the Later Eighteenth Century, Bloomington and Indianapolis: Indiana University Press, 1998.

Hainsworth, D. R., *Stewards, Lords and People: The Estate Steward and His World in Later Stuart England*, Cambridge: Cambridge University Press, 1992.

Hajnal, John, "European Marriage Patterns in Perspective," in *Population in History: Essays in Historical Demography*, ed. D. V. Glass and D. E. C. Eversley, London: Edward Arnold, 1965, 101–43.

"Two Kinds of Pre-Industrial Household Systems," *Population and Development Review* 8.3 (1982), 449–94.

Hall, William G., "The Meaning of Poverty – A Somerset Example," *Local Historian* 16 (1984), 15–20.

Hallie, Philip, *The Paradox of Cruelty*, Middleton, CT: Wesleyan University Press, 1969.

Halsband, Robert, *The Life of Lady Mary Wortley Montagu*, Oxford: Clarendon Press, 1956.

Hammond, Brean, "Swift's Censorship, Corinna's Dream," unpublished paper.

Hammond, J. L., and Barbara Hammond, *The Skilled Labourer 1760–1832*, London: Longmans, 1919.

The Village Labourer 1760–1832: A Study in the Government of England before the Reform Bill, London: Longmans Green, 1911.

Hanawalt, Barbara, *Growing Up in Medieval London: The Experience of Childhood in History*, Oxford and New York: Oxford University Press, 1993.

Haney-Peritz, Janice, "Engendering the Exemplary Daughter: The Deployment of Sexuality in Richardson's *Clarissa*," in *Daughters and Fathers*, ed. Lynda E. Boose and Betty S. Flowers, Baltimore: Johns Hopkins University Press, 1989, 181–207.

Hanley, Sarah, "Engendering the State: Family Formation and State Building in Early Modern France," *French Historical Studies* 16.1 (Spring 1989), 4–27.

Hareven, Tamara K., "The History of the Family and the Complexity of Social Change," *American Historical Review* 96 (February 1991), 95–124.

Harman, Claire, *Fanny Burney*, New York: Knopf, 2001.

Harris, C. C., *The Family and Industrial Society*, London: Allen & Unwin, 1983.

Harris, Olivia, "Households and Their Boundaries," *History Workshop Journal* 13 (1982), 143–52.

Harth, Erica, "The Virtue of Love: Lord Hardwicke's Marriage Act," *Cultural Critique* 9 (Spring 1988), 123–54.

Hasbach, W., *A History of the English Agricultural Labourer*, trans. Ruth Kenyon, London: P. S. King, 1908.

Hay, Douglas, Peter Linebaugh, John G. Rule, E. P. Thompson, and Cal Winslow, eds., *Albion's Fatal Tree: Crime and Society in Eighteenth Century England*, New York: Pantheon Books, 1975.

Hecht, J. Jean, *The Domestic Servant in Eighteenth-Century England*, London: Routledge and Kegan Paul, 1956.

Heilbrun, Carolyn, *Reinventing Womanhood*, New York: Norton, 1979.

Herman, Judith Lewis, *Father-Daughter Incest*, Cambridge, MA: Harvard University Press, 1981.

Hertier, Françoise, "The Symbolics of Incest and Its Prohibition," in *Between Belief and Transgression: Structuralist Essays in Religion, History, and Myth*, ed. Michel Izard and Pierre Smith, trans. John Leavitt, Chicago: University of Chicago Press, 1982, 152–79.

Hill, Bridget, *Women, Work, and Sexual Politics in Eighteenth-Century England*, Oxford: Basil Blackwell, 1989.

Hill, Christopher, *Liberty against the Law*, London: Allen Lane, 1996.

    Review of Lawrence Stone's *Family, Sex, and Marriage* (1977) and Peter Laslett's *Family Life and Illicit Love in Earlier Generations* (1977), *Economic History Review* 2nd ser., 31.3 (August 1978), 452–4.

Hirsch, Marianne, *The Mother/Daughter Plot*, Bloomington: Indiana University Press, 1989.

Hitchcock, Tim, "Redefining Sex in Eighteenth-Century England," *History Workshop Journal* 41 (1996), 73–90.

Hobsbawm, E. J., *The Age of Revolution, 1789–1848*, New York: New American Library, 1964.

Hobsbawm, E. J., and George Rude, *Captain Swing*, London: Lawrence and Wishart, 1970.

Hoffer, Peter C., and N. E. Hull, *Murdering Mothers: Infanticide in England and New England 1558–1803*, New York: New York University Press, 1981.

Holderness, B. A., and Michael Turner, eds., *Land, Labour, and Agriculture, 1700–1920: Essays for Gordon Mingay*, London and Rio Grande: Hambledon Press, 1991.

Hollingsworth, T. H., "A Demographic Study of the British Ducal Families," in *Population in History: Essays in Historical Demography*, ed. D. V. Glass and D. E. C. Eversley, London: Edward Arnold, 1965, 354–78.

Holmes, Geoffrey, and Daniel Szechi, *The Age of Oligarchy: Pre-Industrial Britain, 1722–1783*, London: Longman, 1993.

Homans, Margaret, *Bearing the Word: Language and Female Experience in Nineteenth-Century Women's Writing*, Chicago: University of Chicago Press, 1986.

Houlbrooke, Ralph, *English Family Life 1576–1716*, Oxford: Basil Blackwell, 1988.

Houston, Rab, and K. D. M. Snell, "Proto-Industrialization? Cottage Industry, Social Change, and Industrial Revolution," *Historical Journal* 27.1–2 (1984), 473–92.

Howell, Cicely, "Peasant Inheritance Customs in the Midlands, 1280–1700," in *Family and Inheritance: Rural Society in Western Europe, 1200–1800*, ed. Jack Goody, Joan Thirsk, and E. P. Thompson, Cambridge and London: Cambridge University Press, 1976.

Hudson, Glenda, "Mansfield Revisited: Incestuous Relationships in Jane Austen's *Mansfield Park*," *Eighteenth-Century Fiction* 4.1 (October 1991), 53–68.

    "'Precious Remains of the Earliest Attachment': Sibling Love in Jane Austen's *Pride and Prejudice*," *Persuasions* 11 (December 1989), 125–31.

Sibling Love & Incest in Jane Austen's Fiction, New York: St. Martin's Press, 1992; rpt. 1999.

Hudson, Pat, "Landholding and the Organization of Textile Manufacture in Yorkshire Rural Townships c. 1660–1810," in *Markets and Manufacture in Early Industrial Europe*, ed. Maxine Berg, London: Routledge, 1991, 261–91.

Hufton, Olwyn, "Women and the Family Economy in Eighteenth Century France," *French Historical Studies* 9.1 (Spring 1975), 1–22.

Hughes, Diana Owen, "From Brideprice to Dowry," *Journal of Family History* 3 (Fall 1978), 262–96.

Hughes, Helen Sard, "An Early Romantic Novel," *Journal of English and Germanic Philology* 15 (1916), 564–98.

Hughes, Mary Joe, "Child-Rearing and Social Expectations in Eighteenth-Century England: The Case of the Colliers of Hastings," *Studies in Eighteenth-Century Culture* 13 (1984), 79–100.

Hume, Robert D., "Gothic versus Romantic: A Revaluation of the Gothic Novel," *PMLA* 84 (March 1969), 282–90.

"Marital Discord in English Comedy from Dryden to Fielding," *Modern Philology* 74 (February 1977), 248–72.

"Texts within Texts: Notes towards a Historical Method," *Philological Quarterly* 71 (1992), 69–99.

Humphries, Jane, "Enclosures, Common Rights, and Women: The Proletarianization of Families in the Late Eighteenth and Early Nineteenth Centuries," *Journal of Economic History* 50.1 (March 1990), 17–42.

Hunt, Elizabeth Pinney, *Arthur Young on Industry and Economics*, Philadelphia: Bryn Mawr, 1926.

Hunt, Lynn, *The Family Romance of the French Revolution*, Berkeley: University of California Press, 1992.

Hunt, Margaret, R., *The Middling Sort: Commerce, Gender, and the Family in England, 1680–1780*, Berkeley: University of California Press, 1996.

"Time Management, Writing, and Accounting in the Eighteenth-Century English Trading Family: A Bourgeois Enlightenment," *Business and Economic History*, 2nd ser., 18 (1989), 150–9.

"Wife Beating, Domesticity and Women's Independence in Eighteenth-Century London," *Gender & History* 4.1 (Spring 1992), 10–33.

Hunter, Paul, *Before Novels: The Cultural Contexts of Eighteenth-Century English Fiction*, New York: Norton, 1990.

Jehlen, Myra, "Archimedes and the Paradox of Feminist Criticism," *Signs* 6 (Summer 1981), 575–601.

Johnson, Arthur H., *The Disappearance of the Small Landowner*, Oxford: Clarendon Press, 1909; rpt. with an introduction by Joan Thirsk, London: Augustus M. Kelley at the Merlin Press, 1963.

Johnson, Claudia L., *Equivocal Beings: Politics, Gender, and Sentimentality in the 1790s*, Chicago: University of Chicago Press, 1995.

Jane Austen: Women, Politics and the Novel, Chicago: University of Chicago Press, 1988.

Jones, Robert, *Gender and the Formation of Taste in Eighteenth-Century Britain: The Analysis of Beauty*, Cambridge: Cambridge University Press, 1998.

Jones, Vivien, "Scandalous Femininity: Prostitution and Eighteenth-Century Narrative," in *Shifting the Boundaries: Transformation of the Languages of Public and Private in the Eighteenth Century*, ed. Dario Castiglione and Lesley Sharpe, Exeter: University of Exeter Press, 1995, 54–70.

Jones, Wendy, "The Dialectic of Love in *Sir Charles Grandison*," *Eighteenth-Century Fiction* 8.1 (October 1995), 15–34.

Joseph, Suad, "Brother/Sister Relationships: Connectivity, Love, and Power in the Reproduction of Patriarchy in Lebanon," *American Ethnologist* 21.1 (February 1994), 50–73.

Kahane, Claire, "The Gothic Mirror," in *The (M)other Tongue: Essays in Feminist Psychoanalytic Interpretation*, ed. Shirley Nelson Garner, Claire Kahane, and Madelon Sprengnether, Ithaca, NY: Cornell University Press, 1985, 334–51.

Kaufman, Pamela, "Burke, Freud and the Gothic," *Studies in Burke and His Time* 13.3 (Spring 1972), 2179–92.

Keeley, P. J., "A Devon Family and Their Estates: The Northcotes of Upton Pyne, 1660–1851," in *Town and Countryside: The English Landowner in the National Economy 1660–1860*, ed. C. W. Chalklin and J. R. Wordie, London and Boston: Unwin Hyman, 1989, 174–90.

Kelly, Gary, *English Fiction of the Romantic Period 1789–1830*, London and New York: Longman, 1989.

The English Jacobin Novel 1780–1805, Oxford: Clarendon Press, 1976.

Kertzer, David, and Marzio Barbagli, eds., *Family Life in Early Modern Times, 1500–1789*, New Haven: Yale University Press, 2001.

Kibbie, Ann Louise, "Sentimental Properties: *Pamela* and *Memoirs of a Woman of Pleasure*," *ELH* 58.3 (Fall 1991), 561–77.

Kilgour, Maggie, *The Rise of the Gothic Novel*, New York: Routledge, 1995.

Klein, Lawrence, "The Stories Historians Tell and the Stories Literary Historians Tell about History," Paper delivered at the annual meeting of the Modern Language Association, Washington, DC, December 27–30, 1996.

Kowaleski-Wallace, Elizabeth, *Their Father's Daughters: Hannah More, Maria Edgeworth, and Patriarchal Complicity*, New York: Oxford University Press, 1991.

Kussmaul, Ann, *A General View of the Rural Economy of England 1538–1840*, Cambridge: Cambridge University Press, 1990.

Servants in Husbandry in Early Modern England, Cambridge: Cambridge University Press, 1981.

Lamb, Michael, and Brian Sutton-Smith, eds., *Sibling Relationships: Their Nature and Significance across the Life Span*, Hillsdale, NJ: Lawrence Erlbaum Associates, 1982.

Lamont, Claire, "Jane Austen's Gothic Architecture," in *Exhibited by Candlelight: Sources and Developments in the Gothic Tradition*, ed. Valeria Tinkler-Villani and Peter Davidson, with Jane Stevenson, Amsterdam and Atlanta, GA: Rodopi, 1995, 107–15.

Landry, Donna, *The Invention of the Countryside: Hunting, Walking and Ecology in English Literature, 1671–1831*, New York: Palgrave, 2001.

Lang-Peralta, Linda, ed., *Women, Revolution, and the Novels of the 1790s*, East Lansing: Michigan State University Press, 1999.

Langford, Paul, *A Polite and Commercial People: England 1727–1783*, Oxford: Clarendon Press, 1989.

Lanser, Susan, "Singular Politics: The Rise of the British Nation and the Production of the Old Maid," in *Singlewomen in the European Past, 1250–1800*, ed. Judith M. Bennett and Amy M. Froide, Philadelphia: University of Pennsylvania Press, 1999, 297–323.

Larson, Edith Sedgwick, "A Measure of Power: The Personal Charity of Elizabeth Montagu," *Studies in Eighteenth-Century Culture* 16 (1986), 197–210.

Laslett, Peter, "Introduction: The History of the Family" and "Mean Household Size in England since the Sixteenth Century," in *Household and Family in Past Time*, ed. Peter Laslett and Richard Wall, Cambridge: Cambridge University Press, 1972, 1–89 and 125–58.

The World We Have Lost: England before the Industrial Age, New York: Charles Scribner and Sons, 1965.

Laslett, Peter, and Richard Wall (eds.), *Household and Family in Past Time: Comparative Studies in the Size and Structure of the Domestic Group over the Last Three Centuries in England, France, Serbia, Japan, and Colonial North America*, Cambridge: Cambridge University Press, 1972.

Leach, Edmund, "Complementary Filiation and Bilateral Kinship," in *The Character of Kinship*, ed. Jack Goody, Cambridge: Cambridge University Press, 1973, 53–8.

Leacock, Eleanor, "Interpreting the Origins of Gender Inequality: Conceptual and Historical Problems," *Dialectical Anthropology* 7.4 (February 1983), 263–84.

Leacock, Eleanor, and Helen I. Safa, eds., *Women's Work: Development and the Division of Labor by Gender*, South Hadley, MA: Bergin and Garvey, 1986.

LeFaye, Deirdre, *Jane Austen: A Family Record*, Boston: G. K. Hall, 1989.

Leneman, Leah, *Alienated Affections: The Scottish Experience of Divorce and Separation, 1684–1830*, Edinburgh: Edinburgh University Press, 1998.

Levine, David, *Family Formation in an Age of Nascent Capitalism*, New York: Academic Press, 1977.

Reproducing Families: A Political Economy of English Population History, Cambridge: Cambridge University Press, 1987.

Levine, David, and Keith Wrightson, *The Making of an Industrial Society: Whickham 1560–1765*, Oxford: Clarendon Press, 1991.

Lewis, Judith Schneid, *In the Family Way: Childbearing in the British Aristocracy, 1760–1860*, New Brunswick: Rutgers University Press, 1986.

Lindert, Peter H., and Jeffrey G. Williamson, "English Workers' Living Standards during the Industrial Revolution: A New Look," *Economic History Review* 2nd ser., 36.1 (February 1983), 1–25.

Linebaugh, Peter, *The London Hanged: Crime and Civil Society in the Eighteenth Century*, Cambridge: Cambridge University Press, 1992.

Lis, Catharina, and Hugo Soly, *Poverty and Capitalism in Pre-Industrial Europe*, Brighton, Sussex: Harvester Press, 1979.

Lonsdale, Roger, *Dr. Charles Burney: A Literary Biography*, Oxford: Clarendon Press, 1965.

Lovell, Terry, *Consuming Fiction*, London: Verso, 1987.

MacCannell, Juliet Flower, *The Regime of the Brother: After the Patriarchy*, London and New York: Routledge, 1991.

Macfarlane, Alan, *The Family Life of Ralph Josselin: A Seventeenth-Century Clergyman*, Cambridge: Cambridge University Press, 1970.

Marriage and Love in England 1300–1840, Oxford: Basil Blackwell, 1986.

"The Myth of the Peasantry: Family and Economy in a Northern Parish," in *Land, Kinship and Life Cycle*, ed. Richard M. Smith, Cambridge: Cambridge University Press, 1984, 333–49.

"Review Essay: *The Family, Sex, and Marriage in England 1500–1800*, by Lawrence Stone," *History and Theory* 18 (1979), 103–26.

Macherey, Pierre, *A Theory of Literary Production*, trans. Geoffrey Wall, London: Routledge and Kegan Paul, 1978; rpt. 1989.

Malcolmson, Robert W., *Life and Labour in England 1700–1780*, London: Hutchinson, 1981.

Malina, Debra, "Rereading the Patriarchal Text: *The Female Quixote, Northanger Abbey*, and the Trace of the Absent Mother," *Eighteenth-Century Fiction* 8.2 (January 1996), 271–92.

Markley, Robert, "Sentimentality as Performance: Shaftesbury, Sterne, and the Theatrics of Virtue," in *The New Eighteenth Century: Theory, Politics, English Literature*, ed. Felicity Nussbaum and Laura Brown, New York and London: Methuen, 1987, 210–30.

Martin, J. M., "The Small Landowner and Parliamentary Enclosure in Warwickshire," *Economic History Review* 32.3 (August 1979), 328–43.

Mathias, Peter, *The Transformation of England: Essays in the Economic and Social History of England in the Eighteenth Century*, London: Methuen, 1979.

Maurer, Shawn Lisa, *Proposing Men: Dialectics of Gender and Class in the Eighteenth-Century English Periodical*, Stanford: Stanford University Press, 1998.

Maynes, Mary Jo, Ann Waltner, Birgitte Soland, and Ulrike Strasser, eds., *Gender, Kinship, Power: A Comparative and Interdisciplinary History*, New York: Routledge, 1996.

Mayo, Robert, *The English Novel in the Magazines 1740–1815*, Evanston: Northwestern University Press, 1962.

McCloskey, Donald, "The Economics of Enclosure: A Market Analysis," in *European Peasants and Their Markets*, ed. William N. Parker and Eric L. Jones, Princeton: Princeton University Press, 1975, 123–60.

McClure, Ruth, *Coram's Children: The London Foundling Hospital in the Eighteenth Century*, New Haven and London: Yale University Press, 1981.

McCrea, Brian, *Impotent Fathers: Patriarchy and Demographic Crisis in the Eighteenth-Century Novel*, Newark: University of Delaware Press, and London: Associated University Presses, 1998.

McDowell, Paula, *The Women of Grub Street: Press, Politics, and Gender in the Literary Marketplace, 1678–1730*, Oxford: Clarendon Press, 1998.

McKendrick, Neil, John Brewer, and J. H. Plumb, eds., *The Birth of a Consumer Society: The Commercialization of Eighteenth-Century England*, London: Europa, 1982.

McKeon, Michael, *The Origins of the English Novel 1600–1740*, Baltimore: Johns Hopkins University Press, 1987.

McMullan, Lorraine, *An Odd Attempt in a Woman: The Literary Life of Frances Brooke*, Vancouver: University of British Columbia, 1983.

Medick, Hans, "The Proto-Industrial Family Economy," in *Industrialization before Industrialization*, ed. Peter Kriedte, Hans Medick, and Jurgen Schlumbohm, Cambridge: Cambridge University Press, 1981, 38–73.

"The Proto-Industrial Family Economy: The Structural Function of Household and Family during the Transition from Peasant Society to Industrial Capitalism," *Social History* 1.3 (October 1976), 291–315.

Medick, Hans, and David W. Sabean, eds., *Interest and Emotion: Essays on the Study of Family and Kinship*, Cambridge: Cambridge University Press, 1984.

Merrell, Susan Scarf, *The Accidental Bond: The Power of Sibling Relationships*, New York: Random House, 1995.

Middleton, Chris, "Women's Labour and the Transition to Pre-Industrial Capitalism," in *Women and Work in Pre-Industrial England*, ed. L. Charles and L. Duffin, London: Croom Helm Ltd., 1985, 181–206.

Miles, Robert, Introduction to *Women's Writing* 1.2 (1994), 131–42.

Miller, Nancy K., *Subject to Change: Reading Feminist Writing*, New York: Columbia University Press, 1988.

Mingay, G. E., *Enclosure and the Small Farmer in the Age of the Industrial Revolution*, London: Macmillan, 1968.

Moffit, Louis W., *England on the Eve of the Industrial Revolution*, London: Frank Cass, 1963.

Morgan, Fidelis, with Charlotte Charke, *The Well-Known Trouble Maker: A Life of Charlotte Charke*, London and Boston: Faber and Faber, 1988.

Morris, Polly, "Incest or Survival Strategy? Plebian Marriage within the Prohibited Degrees in Somerset, 1730–1835," in *Forbidden History: The State, Society, and the Regulation of Sexuality in Modern Europe*, ed. John C. Fout, Chicago: University of Chicago Press, 1992, 139–69.

Morton, A. L., *A People's History of England*, New York: Random House, 1938.

Muldrew, Craig, *The Economy of Obligation: The Culture of Credit and Social Relations in Early Modern England*, Basingstoke and London: Macmillan, 1998.

Mullan, John, *Sentiment and Sociability: The Language of Feelings in the Eighteenth Century*, Oxford: Clarendon Press, 1988.

Muller, Viana, "Kin Reproduction and Elite Accumulation in the Archaic States of Northwest Europe," in *Power Relations and State Formation*, ed. Thomas C. Patterson and Christine W. Gailey, Washington, DC: American Anthropological Association, 1987, 81–97.

Myers, Mitzi, "Impeccable Governesses, Rational Dames, and Moral Mothers: Mary Wollstonecraft and the Female Tradition in Georgian Children's Books," *Children's Literature* 14 (1986), 31–59.

"Reading Children and Homeopathic Romanticism: Paradigm Lost, Revisionary Gleam, or 'Plus Ça Change Plus C'est la Même Chose'?" in *Literature and the Child: Romantic Continuations, Postmodern Contestations*, ed. James Holt McGavran, Iowa City: University of Iowa Press, 1999, 44–84.

"'Reform or Ruin': A Revolution in Female Manners," *Studies in Eighteenth-Century Culture* 11 (1982), 199–216.

"Sensibility and the 'Walk of Reason': Mary Wollstonecraft's Literary Reviews as Cultural Critique," in *Sensibility in Transformation: Creative Resistance to Sentiment from the Augustans to the Romantics*, ed. Syndy McMillan Conger, London and Toronto: Associated University Presses, and Rutherford, NJ: Fairleigh Dickinson University Press, 1990, 120–44.

"Shot from Canons; or, Maria Edgeworth and the Cultural Production and Consumption of the Later Eighteenth-Century Woman Writer," in *The Consumption of Culture 1600–1800*, ed. Ann Bermingham and John Brewer, New York: Routledge, 1995, 193–214.

Nash, Stanley, "Prostitution and Charity: The Magdalen Hospital, a Case Study," *Journal of Social History* 17 (Summer 1984), 617–28.

Neale, R. S., *Writing Marxist History: British Society, Economy, and Culture since 1700*, Oxford: Basil Blackwell, 1985.

Neeson, J. M., *Commoners: Common Right, Enclosure and Social Change in England, 1700–1820*, Cambridge: Cambridge University Press, 1993.

"An Eighteenth-Century Peasantry," in *Protest and Survival: Essays for E. P. Thompson*, ed. John Rule and Robert Malcolmson, London: Merlin Press, 1993, 24–59.

Nelson, T. G. A., *Children, Parents, and the Rise of the Novel*, Newark: University of Delaware Press, 1995.

"Women of Pleasure," *Eighteenth-Century Life* 11 (1987), 181–98.

Newby, Howard, *Country Life: A Social History of Rural England*, London: Weidenfeld and Nicolson, 1987.

Nichols, R. H., and F. A. Wray, *The History of the Foundling Hospital*, London: Oxford University Press, 1935.

Nicholson, Linda J., *Gender and History: The Limits of Social Theory in the Age of the Family*, New York: Columbia University Press, 1986.

Nixon, Cheryl, "Fictional Families: Guardianship in Eighteenth-Century Law and Literature," Ph.D. diss., Harvard University, 1995.

"Legal and Textual Circumscription: The Female Guardian," unpublished seminar paper.

"Maternal Guardianship by 'Nature' and 'Nurture': Eighteenth-Century Chancery Court Records and *Clarissa*," *Intertexts* 5.2 (2001), 128–55.

Nussbaum, Felicity, and Laura Brown, eds., *The New Eighteenth Century: Theory, Politics, English Literature*, New York and London: Methuen, 1987.

O'Day, Rosemary. *The Family and Family Relationships, 1500–1900: England, France, and the United States of America*, Basingstoke: Macmillan, 1994.

Outhwaite, R. B., *Clandestine Marriage in England*, Rio Grande, OH: Hambledon Press, 1995.

Marriage and Society: Studies in the Social History of Marriage, London: Europa, 1981.

Overton, Mark, *Agricultural Revolution in England: The Transformation of the Agrarian Economy 1500–1850*, Cambridge: Cambridge University Press, 1996.

Pahl, R. E., *Divisions of Labour*, Oxford and New York: Basil Blackwell, 1984.

Parker, Stephen, *Informal Marriage, Cohabitation and the Law, 1750–1989*, London: Macmillan, 1990.

Pateman, Carol, *The Sexual Contract*, Stanford: Stanford University Press, 1989.

Patterson, Thomas C., and Christine W. Gailey, eds., *Power Relations and State Formation*, Salem, WI: Sheffield Publishing Company, 1992.

Paulson, Ronald, *Satire and the Novel in Eighteenth-Century England*, New Haven: Yale University Press, 1967.

Perkin, Harold, *The Origins of Modern English Society 1780–1880*, London: Routledge and Kegan Paul, 1969.

Perry, Ruth, *The Celebrated Mary Astell: An Early English Feminist*, Chicago: University of Chicago Press, 1986.

"Clarissa's Daughters, or the History of Innocence Betrayed: How Women Writers Rewrote Richardson," *Women's Writing* 1.1 (1994), 5–24; also published in *Clarissa and Her Readers: New Essays for the Clarissa Project*, ed. Carol Houlihan Flynn and Edward Copeland, New York: AMS Press, 1999, 119–41.

"Colonizing the Breast: Sexuality and Maternity in Eighteenth-Century England," *Eighteenth-Century Life* 16, n.s. 1 (February 1992), 185–213.

"De-Familiarizing the Family; or, Writing Family History from Literary Sources," *Modern Language Quarterly* 55.4 (December 1994), 415–27.

"Interrupted Friendships in Jane Austen's *Emma*," *Tulsa Studies in Women's Literature* 5.2 (Fall 1986), 185–202.

Introduction to George Ballard's *Memoirs of Several Ladies of Great Britain* (1752), ed. Ruth Perry, Detroit: Wayne State University Press, 1984.

"Mary Astell and the Feminist Critique of Possessive Individualism," *Eighteenth-Century Studies* 23.4 (Summer 1990), 444–57.

"The Veil of Chastity: Mary Astell's Feminism," *Studies in Eighteenth-Century Culture* 9 (1979), 25–43.

Women, Letters, and the Novel, New York: AMS Press, 1980.

Phillips, Roderick, *Putting Asunder: A History of Divorce in Western Society*, Cambridge: Cambridge University Press, 1988.

Pinchbeck, Ivy, *Women Workers and the Industrial Revolution 1750–1850*, London: Routledge, 1930; rpt. London: Virago Press, 1981.

Plumb, J. H., "The New World of Children in Eighteenth-Century England," in *The Birth of a Consumer Society: The Commercialization of Eighteenth-Century*

England, ed. Neil McKendrick, John Brewer, and J. H. Plumb, London: Europa, 1982, 286–315.

Polanyi, Karl, *The Great Transformation* (1944), rpt. Boston: Beacon Press, 1957.

Pollak, Ellen, *Incest and the English Novel 1684–1814*, Baltimore: Johns Hopkins University Press, 2003.

"Moll Flanders, Incest, and the Structure of Exchange," *The Eighteenth Century: Theory and Interpretation* 30.1 (1989), 3–21.

Pollock, Linda, "'An Action like a Stratagem': Courtship and Marriage from the Middle Ages to the Twentieth Century," *Historical Journal* 30 (1987), 488–98.

Forgotten Children: Parent-Child Relations from 1500 to 1900, Cambridge and New York: Cambridge University Press, 1983.

A Lasting Relationship: Parents and Children over Three Centuries, Hanover and London: University Press of New England, 1987.

"'Teach Her to Live under Obedience': The Making of Women in the Upper Ranks of Early Modern England," *Continuity and Change* 4.2 (1989), 231–58.

Pomata, Gianna, "Blood Ties and Semen Ties: Consanguinity and Agnation in Roman Law," in *Gender, Kinship, Power: A Comparative and Interdisciplinary History*, ed. Mary Jo Maynes, Ann Waltner, Birgitte Soland, and Ulrike Strasser, New York: Routledge, 1996, 42–64.

Poovey, Mary, "Fathers and Daughters: The Trauma of Growing up Female," in *Men by Women*, ed. Janet Todd, New York: Holmes and Meier, 1982, 39–58.

A History of the Modern Fact: Problems of Knowledge in the Sciences of Wealth and Society, Chicago: University of Chicago Press, 1998.

Porter, Roy, "'The Secrets of Generation Display'd': *Aristotle's Master-piece* in Eighteenth-Century England," in *'Tis Nature's Fault: Unauthorized Sexuality during the Enlightenment*, ed. Robert Purks Maccubbin, Cambridge: Cambridge University Press, 1987, 1–21.

Porter, Roy, and Lesley Hall, *The Facts of Life: The Creation of Sexual Knowledge in Britain 1650–1950*, New Haven: Yale University Press, 1995.

Price, Leah, "*Sir Charles Grandison* and the Executor's Hand," *Eighteenth-Century Fiction* 8.3 (April 1996), 329–42.

Probyn, Clive T., *English Fiction of the Eighteenth Century 1700–1789*, London and New York: Longman, 1987.

Raven, James, *British Fiction, 1750–1770: A Chronological Check-List of Prose Fiction Printed in Britain and Ireland*, London: Associated University Presses, and Newark: University of Delaware Press, 1987.

Introduction to James Raven and Antonia Forster, *The English Novel 1770–1829: A Bibliographical Survey of Prose Fiction Published in the British Isles*, 2 vols., Oxford and New York: Oxford University Press, 2000, vol. 1: 15–123.

Judging New Wealth: Popular Publishing and Responses to Commerce in England 1750–1800, Oxford: Clarendon Press, 1992.

Rawson, Claude, "The Phrase 'Legal Prostitution' in Fielding, Defoe and Others," *Notes and Queries* (August 1964), 298.

"Review of *Tom Jones*, ed. Martin Battestin (1974)," *Notes and Queries* (January–February 1977), 49–52.

Razzell, P. E., *The Conquest of Smallpox: The Impact of Inoculation on Smallpox Mortality in Eighteenth-Century Britain*, Firle, Sussex: Caliban Books, 1977.

Reeves, John K., "The Mother of *Fatherless Fanny*," *ELH* 9 (December 1942), 224–33.

Reiss, Timothy J., *The Discourse of Modernism*, Ithaca, NY: Cornell University Press, 1982.

Reynolds, Myra, *The Learned Lady in England 1650–1750*, Boston: Houghton Mifflin, 1920.

Rich, Adrienne, *On Lies, Secrets, and Silence: Selected Prose, 1966–1978*, New York: Norton, 1979.

Richards, Eric, "Women in the British Economy since about 1700: An Interpretation," *History* 59.147 (October 1974), 337–57.

Richardson, T. L., "Agricultural Laborers' Wages and the Cost of Living in Essex, 1790–1840: A Contribution to the Standard of Living Debate," in *Land, Labour, and Agriculture, 1700–1920: Essays for Gordon Mingay*, ed. B. A. Holderness and Michael Turner, London and Rio Grande: Hambledon Press, 1991, 69–90.

Rizzo, Betty, *Companions without Vows: Relationships among Eighteenth-Century British Women*, Athens: University of Georgia Press, 1994.

    Introduction to Sarah Scott, *The History of Sir George Ellison* (1766), Lexington: University of Kentucky Press, 1996.

    "Renegotiating the Gothic," in *Revising Women: Eighteenth-Century "Women's Fiction" and Social Engagement*, ed. Paula R. Backscheider, Baltimore: Johns Hopkins University Press, 2000, 58–103.

Roberts, M., "Sickles and Scythes: Women's Work and Men's Work at Harvest Time," *History Workshop Journal* 7 (1979), 3–28.

Rogers, James E. Thorold, *Six Centuries of Work and Wages: The History of English Labour*, London: Swan Sonnenschein, 1894.

Ronald, Ann, "Terror-Gothic: Nightmare and Dream in Ann Radcliffe and Charlotte Bronte," in *The Female Gothic*, ed. Juliann E. Fleenor, Montreal and London: Eden Press, 1983, 176–86.

Rosenthal, Laura, *Infamous Commerce: Prostitution in Eighteenth-Century British Literature and Culture*, Ithaca: Cornell University Press, 2006.

Ross, Deborah, *The Excellence of Falsehood: Romance, Realism, and Women's Contributions to the Novel*, Lexington: University of Kentucky Press, 1991.

Røstvig, Maren-Sofie, *The Happy Man: Studies in the Metamorphoses of a Classical Ideal*, 2 vols., I: *1600–1700*, Oslo: Akademisk Forlag, and Oxford: Basil Blackwell, 1954; II: *1700–1760*, Oslo: Akademisk Forlag, and Oxford: Basil Blackwell, 1958.

Rousseau, G. S., and Roy Porter, eds., *Sexual Underworlds of the Enlightenment*, Chapel Hill: University of North Carolina Press, 1988.

Rubin, Gayle, "The Traffic in Women: Notes on the 'Political Economy of Sex,'" in *Towards an Anthropology of Women*, ed. Rayna R. Reiter, New York: Monthly Review Press, 1975, 157–210.

Rule, John, *The Experience of Labour in Eighteenth-Century Industry*, London: Croom Helm, 1981.

The Labouring Classes in Early Industrial England 1750–1850, London and New York: Longman, 1986.

Rule, John, and Robert Malcolmson, *Protest and Survival: Essays for E. P. Thompson*, London: Merlin Press, 1993.

Sabean, David, "Fanny and Felix Mendelssohn-Bartholdy and the Question of Incest," *Musical Quarterly* 77.4 (Winter 1993), 709–17.

Kinship in Neckarhausen, 1700–1870, Cambridge: Cambridge University Press, 1998.

Sacks, Karen, *Sisters and Wives*, Urbana and Chicago: University of Illinois Press, 1982.

Sanders, Valerie, *The Brother-Sister Culture in Nineteenth-Century Literature: From Austen to Woolf*, Houndmills: Palgrave, 2002.

Schneider, David M., Introduction to *Matrilineal Kinship*, ed. David M. Schneider and Kathleen Gough, Berkeley and Los Angeles: University of California Press, 1961, 1–33.

Schnorrenberg, Barbara Brandon, "Is Childbirth Any Place for a Woman? The Decline of Midwifery in Eighteenth-Century England," *Studies in Eighteenth-Century Culture* 10 (1981), 393–408.

Schofield, R., "Age-Specific Mobility in an Eighteenth-Century Rural English Parish," *Annales de Demographie Historique* (1970), 261–74.

Schwoerer, Lois, "Seventeenth-Century English Women Engraved in Stone?" *Albion* 16 (1984), 389–403.

Seccombe, Wally, *A Millennium of Family Change: Feudalism to Capitalism in Northwestern Europe*, London and New York: Verso, 1992.

"The Western European Marriage Pattern in Historical Perspective: A Response to David Levine," *Journal of Historical Sociology* 3 (March 1990), 50–74.

Segalen, Martine, *Historical Anthropology of the Family*, trans. J. C. Whitehouse and S. Matthews, Cambridge: Cambridge University Press, 1986.

Shamas, Carole, "The Eighteenth-Century Diet and Economic Change," *Explorations in Economic History* 21 (1984), 254–69.

Shanley, Mary Lyndon, and Uma Narayan, *Reconstructing Political Theory*, University Park, PA: Penn State University Press, 1997.

Shannon, H. A., "The Coming of General Limited Liability," in *Essays in Economic History*, ed. E. M. Carus-Wilson, 3 vols., London: Arnold, 1954, I: 358–79.

Sharpe, J. A., "Plebeian Marriage in Stuart England: Some Evidence from Popular Literature," *Transactions of the Royal Historical Society* 36 (1986), 69–90.

Sharpe, Jenny, *Allegories of Empire: The Figure of the Woman in the Colonial Text*, Minneapolis: University of Minnesota Press, 1993.

Sharpe, Pamela, "Literally Spinsters: A New Interpretation of Local Economy and Demography in Colyton in the Seventeenth and Eighteenth Centuries," *Economic History Review* 2nd ser., 44.1 (1991), 46–65.

Sharpe, Pamela, ed., *Women's Work: The English Experience 1650–1914*, London: Arnold, 1998.

Shell, Marc, *The End of Kinship: "Measure for Measure," Incest and the Ideal of Universal Siblinghood*, Stanford: Stanford University Press, 1988.

Shorter, Edward, *The Making of the Modern Family*, New York: Basic Books, 1975.

Simpson, Antony E., "Vulnerability and the Age of Female Consent: Legal Innovation and Its Effect on Prosecutions for Rape in Eighteenth-Century London," in *Sexual Underworlds of the Enlightenment*, ed. G. S. Rousseau and Roy Porter, Chapel Hill: University of North Carolina Press, 1988, 181–205.

Slater, Miriam, *Family Life in the Seventeenth Century: The Verneys of Claydon House*, London: Routledge and Kegan Paul, 1984.

Smail, John, *The Origins of Middle-Class Culture: Halifax, Yorkshire, 1660–1780*, Ithaca, NY: Cornell University Press, 1994.

Smallwood, Angela, *Fielding and the Woman Question*, Hemel Hempstead, Hertfordshire: Harvester Wheatsheaf, 1989.

"L'Education feminine à la scène: les femmes dramaturges dans le Londres georgien," ["Staging Female Education: Women Playwrights in Georgian London"] in *L'Education des femmes en Europe et en Amérique du Nord de la Renaissance à 1848*, ed. Guyonne Leduc, Paris: L'Harmattan, 1997, 337–49.

Smelser, Neil J., *Social Change in the Industrial Revolution*, Chicago: University of Chicago Press, 1959.

Smith, Raymond T., *The Matrifocal Family: Power, Pluralism, and Politics*, London: Routledge, 1996.

Smith, Richard M., "Fertility, Economy, and Household Formation in England over Three Centuries," *Population and Development Review* 7.4 (December 1981), 595–622.

"Some Issues concerning Families and Their Property in Rural England 1250–1800," in *Land, Kinship and Life-Cycle*, ed. Richard M. Smith, Cambridge and New York: Cambridge University Press, 1984, 1–86.

Smith, Sidonie, "The Transgressive Daughter and the Masquerade of Self-Representation," in *Introducing Charlotte Charke*, ed. Philip E. Baruth, Urbana and Chicago: University of Illinois Press, 1998, 83–106.

Snell, K. D. M., "Agricultural Seasonal Unemployment, the Standard of Living, and Women's Work in the South and East, 1690–1860," *Economic History Review* 2nd ser., 34.3 (1981), 407–37.

Annals of the Labouring Poor: Social Change and Agrarian England, 1660–1900, Cambridge: Cambridge University Press, 1985; rpt. 1995.

Spacks, Patricia Meyer, *Desire and Truth: Functions of Plot in Eighteenth-Century English Novels*, Chicago: University of Chicago Press, 1990.

Speck, W. A., "The Harlot's Progress in Eighteenth-Century England," *British Journal for Eighteenth-Century Studies* 3.2 (Summer 1980), 127–39.

Spencer, Jane, *The Rise of the Woman Novelist: From Aphra Behn to Jane Austen*, Oxford: Basil Blackwell, 1986.

Spring, Eileen, "The Family, Strict Settlement, and Historians," *Canadian Journal of History / Annales Canadiennes d'Histoire* 18 (December 1983), 379–98.

"Law and the Theory of the Affective Family," *Albion* 16 (Spring 1984), 1–20.

Law, Land, and Family: Aristocratic Inheritance in England, 1300 to 1800, Chapel Hill: University of North Carolina Press, 1993.

Spufford, Margaret, "Peasant Inheritance Customs and Land Distribution in Cambridgeshire from the Sixteenth to the Eighteenth Centuries," in *Family and Inheritance: Rural Society in Western Europe, 1200–1800*, ed. Jack Goody, Joan Thirsk, and E. P. Thompson, Cambridge and London: Cambridge University Press, 1976.

Stapleton, Barry, "Inherited Poverty and Life-Cycle Poverty: Odiham, Hampshire, 1650–1850," *Social History* 18.3 (October 1993), 339–55.

Staves, Susan, "British Seduced Maidens," *Eighteenth-Century Studies* 14.2 (Winter 1980–1), 109–34.

"Douglas's Mother," in *Brandeis Essays in Literature*, ed. John Hazel Smith, Department of English and American Literature, Brandeis University, 1983, 51–67.

"Fielding and the Comedy of Attempted Rape," in *History, Gender & Eighteenth-Century Literature*, ed. Beth Fowkes Tobin, Athens: University of Georgia Press, 1994, 86–112.

Married Women's Separate Property in England, 1660–1833, Cambridge, MA: Harvard University Press, 1990.

"Money for Honor: Damages for Criminal Conversation," *Studies in Eighteenth-Century Culture* 11 (1982), 279–97.

"Resentment or Resignation? Dividing the Spoils among Daughters and Younger Sons," in *Early Modern Conceptions of Property*, ed. John Brewer and Susan Staves, London and New York: Routledge, 1996, 194–218.

Stephens, W. B., "Literacy in England, Scotland, and Wales, 1500–1900," *History of Education Quarterly* 30.4 (Winter 1990), 545–71.

Stewart, Douglas J., "Pornography, Obscenity, and Capitalism," *Antioch Review* 35.4 (Fall 1977), 389–98.

Stewart, Maaja, *Domestic Realities and Imperial Fictions*, Athens: University of Georgia Press, 1993.

Stone, Lawrence, *Broken Lives: Separation and Divorce in England 1660–1857*, Oxford: Oxford University Press, 1993.

The Crisis of the Aristocracy, 1558–1601, Oxford: Clarendon Press, 1965.

"Family History in the 1980s: Past Achievements and Future Trends," *Journal of Interdisciplinary History* 12.1 (Summer 1981), 51–87.

The Family, Sex, and Marriage in England 1500–1800, New York: Harper and Row, 1977.

Road to Divorce: England 1530–1987, Oxford: Oxford University Press, 1992.

Stone, Lawrence, and Jeanne C. Fawtier Stone, *An Open Elite? England 1540–1880*, Oxford: Clarendon Press, 1984.

Straub, Kristina, "Feminine Sexuality, Class Identity, and Narrative Form in the Newgate Calendars," in *Eighteenth-Century Genre and Culture: Serious Reflections on Occasional Forms*, eds. Dennis Todd and Cynthia Wall, Newark: University of Delaware Press, 2001, 218–35.

Sexual Suspects: Eighteenth Century Players and Sexual Ideology, Princeton: Princeton University Press, 1992.

Sussman, Charlotte, *Consuming Anxieties: Consumer Protest, Gender, and British Slavery, 1713–1833*, Stanford: Stanford University Press, 2000.

Tadmor, Naomi, "The Concept of the Household-Family in Eighteenth-Century England," *Past and Present* 151 (1995), 111–40.

"Dimensions of Inequality among Siblings in Eighteenth-Century English Novels: The Cases of *Clarissa* and *The History of Miss Betsy Thoughtless*," *Continuity and Change* 7.3 (1992), 303–33.

"'Family' and 'Friend' in *Pamela*: A Case-Study in the History of the Family in Eighteenth-Century England," *Social History* 14 (1989), 289–306.

Family and Friends in Eighteenth-Century England: Household, Kinship, and Patronage, Cambridge: Cambridge University Press, 2001.

Tanner, Tony, "Julie and 'La Maison Paternelle': Another Look at Rousseau's *La Nouvelle Héloïse*," in *The Family in Political Thought*, ed. Jean Bethke Elshtain, Amherst: University of Massachusetts Press, 1982, 96–124.

Taylor, A. J., ed., *The Standard of Living in Britain in the Industrial Revolution*, London: Methuen, 1975.

Taylor, John Tinnon, *Early Opposition to the English Novel: The Popular Reaction from 1760 to 1830*, New York: Kings Crown Press, 1943.

Thaddeus, Janice Farrar, "Elizabeth Hamilton's Domestic Politics," *Studies in Eighteenth-Century Culture* 23 (1994), 265–84.

Frances Burney: A Literary Life, London: Macmillan, and New York: St. Martin's Press, 2000.

Thomas, Keith, "The Double Standard," *Journal of the History of Ideas* 20.2 (1959), 195–216.

Thompson, E. P., *Customs in Common: Studies in Traditional Popular Culture*, New York: New Press, 1991.

Review of Lawrence Stone's *The Family, Sex, and Marriage in England 1500–1800* (1977), *New Society* Sept. 8, 1977: 499–501.

"Time, Work-Discipline and Industrial Capitalism," *Past and Present* 38 (December 1967), 56–97.

Whigs and Hunters: The Origin of the Black Act, New York: Pantheon, 1975.

Thompson, James, *Models of Value: Eighteenth-Century Political Economy and the Novel*, Durham, NC: Duke University Press, 1996.

"Patterns of Property and Possession in Fielding's Fiction," *Eighteenth-Century Fiction* 3.1 (October 1990), 21–42.

Thompson, Roger, *Unfit for Modest Ears: A Study of Pornographic, Obscene, and Bawdy Works Written or Published in England in the Second Half of the Seventeenth Century*, Totowa, NJ: Rowman and Littlefield, 1979.

Tilly, Louise A., and Joan W. Scott, *Women, Work, and Family*, New York and London: Methuen, 1987.

Tinkler-Villani, Valeria, and Peter Davidson, with Jane Stevenson, eds., *Exhibited by Candlelight: Sources and Developments in the Gothic Tradition*, Amsterdam: Rodopi, 1995.

Tobin, Beth Fowkes, "The Moral and Political Economy of Property in Estate Portraiture," unpublished paper, 1992.

Superintending the Poor: Charitable Ladies and Paternal Landlords in British Fiction, 1770–1860, New Haven: Yale University Press, 1993.

"'The Tender Mother': The Social Construction of Motherhood and *The Lady's Magazine*," *Women's Studies* 18 (1990), 205–21.

Todd, Janet, *Mary Wollstonecraft: A Revolutionary Life*, New York: Columbia University Press, 2000.

Sensibility: An Introduction, London: Methuen, 1986.

The Sign of Angellica: Women, Writing and Fiction: 1660–1800, London: Virago, 1989.

Tompkins, J. M. S., *The Popular Novel in English 1770–1800*, London: Constable, 1932; rpt. Lincoln: University of Nebraska Press, 1961.

Trueman, B. E. S., "The Purchase and Management of Guy's Hospital Estates, 1726–1806," in *Town and Countryside: The English Landowner in the National Economy, 1660–1860*, ed. C. W. Chalklin and J. R. Wordie, London and Boston: Unwin Hyman, 1989, 52–82.

Trumbach, Randolph, "Modern Prostitution and Gender in *Fanny Hill*: Libertine and Domesticated Fantasy," in *Sexual Underworlds of the Enlightenment*, ed. G. S. Rousseau and Roy Porter, Manchester: Manchester University Press, 1987, 69–85.

The Rise of the Egalitarian Family: Aristocratic Kinship and Domestic Relations in Eighteenth-Century England, New York and London: Academic Press, 1978.

Sex and the Gender Revolution: Heterosexuality and the Third Gender in Enlightenment London, Chicago: University of Chicago Press, 1998.

Tucker, R. S., "Real Wages of Artisans in London, 1729–1935," *Journal of the American Statistical Association* 31 (1936), 73–84.

Turner, M. E., J. V. Beckett, and B. Afton, *Agricultural Rent in England, 1690–1914*, Cambridge and New York: Cambridge University Press, 1997.

Turner, Mary, "Two Entries from the Marriage Register of Taxal, Cheshire," *Local Population Studies* 21 (Autumn 1978), 64.

Turner, Michael, *Enclosures in Britain 1750–1830*, London: Macmillan, 1984.

English Parliamentary Enclosure: Its Historical Geography and Economic History, Folkestone, Kent: Dawson and Sons, 1980.

Turner, Rufus, "Charlotte Smith (1749–1806): New Light on Her Life and Literary Career," Ph.D. diss., University of Southern California, 1966.

Valenze, Deborah, *The First Industrial Woman*, New York and Oxford: Oxford University Press, 1995.

Van Baal, J., *Reciprocity and the Position of Women*, Amsterdam: Van Gorcum, Assen, 1975.

Vickery, Amanda J., *The Gentleman's Daughter: Women's Lives in Georgian England*, New Haven and London: Yale University Press, 1998.

"Golden Age to Separate Spheres? A Review of the Categories and Chronology of English Women's History," *Historical Journal* 36 (1993), 383–414.

Von Tunzelmann, G. N., "Trends in Real Wages, 1750–1859, Revisited," *Economic Review* 2nd ser., 32.1 (February 1979), 33–49.

Wall, Richard, "Mean Household-Size in England from Printed Sources," in *Household and Family in Past Time*, ed. Peter Laslett and Richard Wall, Cambridge: Cambridge University Press, 1972, 159–203.

Watson, Nicola, *Revolution and the Form of the British Novel, 1790–1825: Intercepted Letters, Interrupted Seductions*, Oxford: Clarendon Press, 1994.

Watt, Ian, *The Rise of the Novel*, Berkeley and Los Angeles: University of California Press, 1957.

Weatherill, Lorna, *Consumer Behavior and Material Culture in Britain 1660–1760*, New York: Routledge, 1988.

Webb, R. K., *The British Working-Class Reader 1790–1848: Literacy and Social Tension*, London: Allen and Unwin, 1955.

Webb, Sidney, and Beatrice Webb, *English Local Government: English Poor Law History*, 3 vols. in 2, New York: Longmans Green, 1927–9.

Weiner, Annette B., *Inalienable Possessions: The Paradox of Keeping-While-Giving*, Berkeley: University of California Press, 1992.

   "Reassessing Reproduction in Social Theory," in *Conceiving the New World Order: The Global Politics of Reproduction*, ed. Faye D. Ginsburg and Rayna Rapp, Berkeley: University of California Press, 1995, 407–24.

Wells, Roger, "Social Protest, Class, Conflict and Consciousness, in the English Countryside 1700–1880," in *Class, Conflict and Protest in the English Countryside, 1700–1880*, ed. Mick Reed and Roger Wells, London: Frank Cass, 1990, 121–214.

   Wretched Faces: Famine in Wartime England 1793–1801, Gloucester: Sutton, 1988.

Welsh, Alexander, *Strong Representations: Narrative and Circumstantial Evidence in England*, Baltimore: Johns Hopkins University Press, 1992.

Welsh, Charles, Introduction to *Goody Two-Shoes* (1766), facsimile edn., London: Griffith and Farran, 1882.

Wendorf, Richard, *Sir Joshua Reynolds: The Painter in Society*, Cambridge, MA: Harvard University Press, 1996.

Wendorf, Richard, and Charles Ryskamp, "A Blue-Stocking Friendship: The Letters of Elizabeth Montagu and Frances Reynolds in the Princeton Collection," *Princeton University Library Chronicle* 41.3 (Spring 1980), 173–207.

Wheaton, Robert, "Family and Kinship in Western Europe: The Problem of the Joint Family Household," *Journal of Interdisciplinary History* 5.4 (Spring 1975), 601–28.

Wheaton, Robert, and Tamara K. Hareven, *Family and Sexuality in French History*, Philadelphia, PA: University of Pennsylvania Press, 1980.

Whyman, Susan E., *Sociability and Power in Late-Stuart England: The Cultural World of the Verneys 1660–1720*, Oxford and New York: Oxford University Press, 1999.

Williams, Anne, *Art of Darkness: A Poetics of Gothic*, Chicago: University of Chicago Press, 1995.

Williams, Raymond, *The Country and the City*, New York: Oxford University Press, 1973.

   Marxism and Literature, Oxford: Oxford University Press, 1977.

Wilson, Elizabeth, "Not in This House: Incest, Denial, and Doubt in the White Middle Class Family," *Yale Journal of Criticism* 8 (1995), 35–58.

Wolf, Margery, "The Self of Others, the Others of Self: Gender in Chinese Society," Paper presented at the conference "Perceptions of the Self: China, Japan, India," East-West Center, University of Hawaii, August 1989.

Wolfram, Sybil, *In-Laws and Outlaws: Kinship and Marriage in England*, London and Sydney: Croom Helm, 1987.

Wood, Elizabeth, "Prostitution Unbound," in *Sexuality and the Body in Russian Culture*, ed. Jane T. Costlow, Stephanie Sandler, and Judith Vowles, Stanford: Stanford University Press, 1993, 124–35.

Woodbridge, Homer E., *Sir William Temple, the Man and His Work*, New York and London: Oxford University Press, 1940.

Woolf, Virginia, *Three Guineas*, London: The Hogarth Press, 1938.

Wrightson, Keith, "Critique: Household and Kinship in Sixteenth-Century England," *History Workshop Journal* 12 (1981), 151–8.

   Earthly Necessities: Economic Lives in Early Modern Britain, New Haven and London: Yale University Press, 2000.

   "Kinship in an English Village: Terling, Essex 1550–1700," in *Land, Kinship and Life-Cycle*, ed. Richard M. Smith, Cambridge: Cambridge University Press, 1984, 313–32.

   "The Social Order of Early Modern England: Three Approaches," in *The World We Have Gained: Histories of Population and Social Structures*, ed. Lloyd Bonfield, Richard M. Smith, and Keith Wrightson, Oxford: Basil Blackwell, 1986, 177–202.

Wrightson, Keith, and David Levine, *Poverty and Piety in an English Village: Terling, 1525–1799*, Oxford: Oxford University Press, 1979.

Wrigley, E. A., "Fertility Strategy for the Individual and the Group," in *Historical Studies in Changing Fertility*, ed. Charles Tilly, Princeton: Princeton University Press, 1978, 135–54.

   "Marriage, Fertility and Population Growth in Eighteenth-Century England," in *Marriage and Society: Studies in the Social History of Marriage*, ed. R. B. Outhwaite, London: Europa, 1981.

   People, Cities and Wealth: The Transformation of a Traditional Society, Oxford: Basil Blackwell, 1987.

Wrigley, E. A., and R. S. Schofield, *The Population History of England, 1541–1871: A Reconstruction*, Cambridge, MA: Harvard University Press, 1981.

Yaeger, Patricia, and Beth Kowaleski-Wallace, eds., *Refiguring the Father: New Feminist Readings of Patriarchy*, Carbondale, IL: Southern Illinois University Press, 1989.

Zomchick, John P., *Family and the Law in Eighteenth-Century Fiction*, Cambridge: Cambridge University Press, 1993.

Zonitch, Barbara, *Familiar Violence: Gender and Social Upheaval in the Novels of Frances Burney*, Newark: University of Delaware Press, and London: Associated University Presses, 1997.

Zukow, Patricia Goldring, *Sibling Interaction across Cultures: Theoretical and Methodological Issues*, New York: Springer-Verlag, 1989.

Zwinger, Lynda Marie, *Daughters, Fathers, and the Novel: The Sentimental Romance of Heterosexuality*, Madison: University of Wisconsin Press, 1991.

Index

449